Kodály Today

Kodály Today Handbook Series

Micheál Houlahan and Philip Tacka

Kodály Today: A Cognitive Approach to Elementary Music Education, second edition
Kodály in the Kindergarten Classroom: Developing the Creative Brain in the 21st Century
Kodály in the First Grade Classroom: Developing the Creative Brain in the 21st Century
Kodály in the Second Grade Classroom: Developing the Creative Brain in the 21st Century
Kodály in the Third Grade Classroom: Developing the Creative Brain in the 21st Century
Kodály in the Fourth Grade Classroom: Developing the Creative Brain in the 21st Century
Kodály in the Fifth Grade Classroom: Developing the Creative Brain in the 21st Century

Kodály Today

A Cognitive Approach to Elementary Music Education

Second Edition

Micheál Houlahan
Philip Tacka

OXFORD
UNIVERSITY PRESS

Oxford University Press is a department of the University of
Oxford. It furthers the University's objective of excellence in research,
scholarship, and education by publishing worldwide.

Oxford   New York
Auckland   Cape Town   Dar es Salaam   Hong Kong   Karachi
Kuala Lumpur   Madrid   Melbourne   Mexico City   Nairobi
New Delhi   Shanghai   Taipei   Toronto

With offices in
Argentina   Austria   Brazil   Chile   Czech Republic   France   Greece
Guatemala   Hungary   Italy   Japan   Poland   Portugal   Singapore
South Korea   Switzerland   Thailand   Turkey   Ukraine   Vietnam

Oxford is a registered trademark of Oxford University Press
in the UK and certain other countries.

Published in the United States of America by
Oxford University Press
198 Madison Avenue, New York, NY 10016

© Oxford University Press 2015

All rights reserved. No part of this publication may be reproduced, stored in
a retrieval system, or transmitted, in any form or by any means, without the prior
permission in writing of Oxford University Press, or as expressly permitted by law,
by license, or under terms agreed with the appropriate reproduction rights organization.
Inquiries concerning reproduction outside the scope of the above should be sent to the
Rights Department, Oxford University Press, at the address above.

You must not circulate this work in any other form
and you must impose this same condition on any acquirer.

Library of Congress Cataloging-in-Publication Data
Houlahan, Micheál, author.
Kodály today: a cognitive approach to elementary music education/by Micheál Houlahan and
Philip Tacka.—2nd edition.
   pages cm
Includes bibliographical references and index.
ISBN 978–0–19–025501–5 (hardback)—ISBN 978–0–19–023577–2 (paperback)
1. School music—Instruction and study.   2. Cognitive learning.   3. Kodály, Zoltán, 1882-1967.
I. Tacka, Philip, author.   II. Title.
MT1.H838 2015
372.87′dc23
2014032953

We are the music-makers,
And we are the dreamers of dreams,
Wandering by lone sea-breakers,
And sitting by desolate streams;
World-losers and world-forsakers,
On whom the pale moon gleams:
Yet we are the movers and shakers
Of the world for ever, it seems.

Ode, by Arthur O'Shaughnessy

[. . .] eratque tam turpe Musicam nescire quam litteras

from *De Musica,* by Isidoris Hispalensis

"Legyen A Zene Mindenkié" [Music should belong to everyone]

Zoltán Kodály

Contents

Acknowledgments • xiii

About the Companion Website • xv

Introduction • 1

1 Building the Framework of a Music Curriculum Based on the Kodály Concept • 14
Zoltán Kodály: A Biographical Outline • 15
A Brief Examination of Zoltán Kodály's Philosophy of Music Education • 18
The Kodály Method or Concept of Music Education • 27
Building the Framework of a Curriculum Based on the Multiple Dimensions of Music • 28
Music Philosophy Prompt Questions • 35
Linking a Music Curriculum Based on the Kodály Concept to the National Content Standards for Music Education • 37
The Kodály Concept and the Common Core Standards • 39
Lesson Planning • 40
Key Components of Lesson Plan Designs • 42
Discussion Questions • 47
Ongoing Assignment • 48
Connections to Grade Handbooks • 48
Bibliography • 48

2 Developing a Music Repertoire of Songs for the Elementary Music Classroom • 53
Folk Music in the Classroom • 54
Selecting Music for Classroom Use • 57
Creating an Alphabetized Song Repertoire List for Each Grade • 59
Analyzing Song Repertoire • 59
Performance and Notation of Folk Songs • 73
Lesson Planning • 73
Connections to Grade Handbooks • 87
Discussion Questions • 87
Ongoing Assignment • 87
Bibliography • 87

Contents

3 **Developing Creative Expression in the Elementary Classroom Through Singing, Movement, and Playing Instruments** • 99
Singing • 100
Singing in Tune with Relative Solmization • 110
Teaching Songs • 112
Introducing Songs Within a Lesson • 118
Singing Games and Movement Activities • 120
Developing Creative Movement and Improvisations in the Classroom • 131
Body Warm-ups and Creative Movement • 132
Instruments • 134
Lesson Planning • 138
Connections to Grade Handbooks • 145
Discussion Questions • 145
Ongoing Assignment • 146
Bibliography • 146

4 **Teaching Tools and Techniques for Developing Audiation and Music Literacy Skills** • 153
Teaching Tools for Developing Music Literacy Skills • 154
A Rhythmic and Melodic Sequence for Developing Music Literacy Skills • 162
The Relationship Between Musical Concepts and Elements • 164
Preparation, Presentation, and Practice of Musical Elements for Grades 1 Through 5 • 170
The Connection Between Teaching Basic Rhythmic and Melodic Patterns and Common Stylistic Characteristics of Folk Songs • 175
Lesson Planning • 176
Connections to Grade Handbooks • 184
Discussion Questions • 185
Ongoing Assignment • 185
Bibliography • 185

5 **From Sound to Symbol: A Model of Learning and Instruction for Teaching Music Concepts, Elements, and Skills** • 191
A New Learning Theory Model • 193
A Comparison of the Houlahan and Tacka Model of Learning with Current Teaching Approaches Adopted by Kodály Instructors • 204
Summary • 208
Connections to Grade Handbooks • 208
Discussion Questions • 208
Ongoing Assignment • 209
Bibliography • 209

6 Grades 1 Through 5 Teaching Strategies for Rhythmic and Melodic Concepts and Elements • 216
  Strategies for Teaching Music Elements • 217
  Grade 1 Teaching Strategies • 218
  Grade 1, Teaching Strategy 1, for Quarter and Eighth Notes • 218
  Grade 1, Teaching Strategy 2, for a Two-Note Child's Chant • 223
  Focus Songs for Grade 1 • 230
  Grade 2 Teaching Strategies • 231
  Grade 2, Teaching Strategy 1, for Introducing the Tonic • 231
  Grade 2, Teaching Strategy 2, for Half Note • 239
  Focus Songs for Grade 2 • 246
  Grade 3 Teaching Strategies • 248
  Grade 3, Teaching Strategy 1, for an Eighth Note Followed by Two Sixteenth Notes • 249
  Grade 3, Teaching Strategy 2, for low la • 256
  Focus Songs for Grade 3 • 265
  Grade 4 Teaching Strategies • 267
  Grade 1, Teaching Strategy 1, for Syncopation • 267
  Grade 4, Teaching Strategy 2, for la Pentatonic Scale • 273
  Focus Songs for Grade 4 • 283
  Grade 5 Teaching Strategies • 286
  Grade 5, Teaching Strategy 1, for Major Scale • 286
  Grade 5, Teaching Strategy 2, for an Eighth Note Followed by a Dotted Quarter Note • 294
  Focus Songs for Grade 5 • 304
  Developing a Lesson Plan Design Based on the Teaching Strategies • 306
  Connections to Grade Handbooks • 324
  Discussion Questions • 325
  Ongoing Assignment • 325
  Bibliography • 325

7 Developing Musicianship Skills in the Classroom • 329
  Musical Skills Practiced in the Classroom • 329
  Musical Skills: Sample Curriculum • 332
  Expanding Your Students' Musical Skills • 337
  Practicing Form, Improvisation, and Composition • 358
  Integrating Listening into a Music Lesson • 375
  Developing the Three Primary Musical Skill Areas • 395
  Developing Music Skills in a Music Lesson Plan • 396
  Creating Lesson Plans That Develop Students' Musical Skills • 397
  Connections to Grade Handbooks • 401
  Bibliography • 401

Contents

8   **Technology in the Kodály Classroom** • 405
    How to Choose and Assess Music Technology for the Kodály Classroom • 406
    Technology Resources for the Kodály Classroom • 408
    Technology Resources for the Kodály Student • 412
    Kodály-Based Lessons for the Interactive White Board • 414
    Sample Kodály Lesson Plan Incorporating Technology • 431
    Discussion Questions • 438
    Ongoing Assignment • 438
    Bibliography • 438

9   **Applying the Kodály Concept to the Elementary Choir** • 440
    Auditioning Students for an Elementary Choir • 441
    Choral Rehearsal Activities • 444
    Repertoire for Developing Part Work and Music Literacy • 459
    How to Teach Simple Two-Part Song Arrangements • 466
    Selecting Repertoire for Children's Choir • 476
    Score Preparation and Teaching a Choral Composition • 478
    Discussion Questions • 482
    Ongoing Assignment • 482
    Bibliography • 482

10   **Sequencing and Lesson Planning** • 485
    Lesson Plans and Learning Outcomes • 489
    Transitions in Lesson Plans • 520
    General Considerations for Planning Lessons • 529
    Adapting Lesson Plans for the Inclusive Classroom • 532
    Connections to Grade Handbooks • 538
    Discussion Questions • 538
    Ongoing Assignment • 538
    Bibliography • 539

11   **Teaching Musicianship Skills Starting in the Upper Grades** • 540
    Curriculum Summary • 541
    Curriculum Guide • 542
    Getting Started • 546
    Selecting Song Repertoire for Older Beginners • 547
    Considerations, Techniques, and Procedures for Developing Older Students' Singing Skills • 549
    Teaching Songs • 562
    Lesson Design • 564
    Developing Music Skills • 568
    A Few Final Considerations for Teaching Older Beginners • 572
    Discussion Questions • 574

Ongoing Assignment • 574
Bibliography • 574

12 Evaluation and Assessment • 576
Assessing the Effectiveness of Music Teaching • 577
Developing a Class Profile Summarizing the Child's Achievement • 586
Assessment and Evaluation of Students: Student Profiles • 588
Connections to Grade Handbooks • 597
Discussion Questions • 597
Ongoing Activities • 597
Bibliography • 598

13 Organizing Your Teaching Resources for the Elementary Classroom • 600
What Are the Components of a Teaching Resource Folder? • 601
Discussion Questions • 604
Ongoing Assignment • 604
Bibliography • 605

Notes • 607

Song Index • 615

Subject Index • 625

Acknowledgments

A debt of gratitude is due to the many individuals who inspired, encouraged, and helped us with our research for this publication. We were both fortunate enough to study at the Franz Liszt Academy/Kodály Pedagogical Institute in Hungary and at the Kodály Center of America with world-renowned Kodály experts, many of whom were his pupils and colleagues, who shared their knowledge with us over many years. Among them were László Eősze, Peter Erdei, Katalin Forrai, Lilla Gábor, Erzsébet Hegyi, Ildiko Herboly-Kocsár, Mihály Ittzés, Katalin Kiss, Klára Kokas, Katalin Komlos, Klára Nemes, Helga Szabo, and Eva Vendrai. We are indebted to Lauren Bain, elementary music specialist in the Northeast School District of San Antonio, Texas, for her willingness to pilot lesson plans and document her teaching through videos. We also thank Rebecca Morgan of the Montessori School of San Antonio, Texas, for her willingness to field-test materials and lessons. This was a tremendous labor of love.

Special thanks are due to these individuals for critically reading portions of the manuscript and for their insightful suggestions regarding this approach to instruction and learning: Lauren Bain; Nick Holland, lower school music teacher at St. Paul's School in Baltimore, Maryland; Georgia Katsourides, music specialist in the Lancaster City School District, Pennsylvania; Vivian Ferchill, retired music specialist from Round Rock, Texas; Meredith Riggs, music specialist in the Austin Independent School District, Austin, Texas. We would also like to thank Holly Kofod and Lisa Roebuck for their comments, which helped us bring this book to completion. Special thanks go to Nick Holland for his contributions to the lesson plans and for providing videos that incorporate the use of smart board technology.

We are grateful to Patty Moreno, instructional coordinator of fine arts for the Austin Independent School District, Texas, and director of the Kodály Certification Program at Texas State University, San Marcos, Texas, for her support and continued encouragement of this project. For more than a decade she has facilitated our research and field testing with teachers in the Austin Independent School District as well as the Houston Independent School District and the Sicorro Independent School District in El Paso, Texas.

Many of our students in Kodály Certification Programs at Texas State University, Belmont University in Nashville, Tennessee, and the Eastman School of Music in Rochester, New York, have helped us shape the approach to instruction and learning that is presented herein. Our many years of work with our students have not only contributed to the information we present but also served as a continuing source of inspiration with the pedagogical processes we have shaped.

Acknowledgments

We would like to thank our students at Millersville University of Pennsylvania for helping us with technical and practical matters related to the manuscript. Special thanks are owed to Jamie Duca, Emma Noble, Lillian Noble, Honorah Harvey, Andrea Kurnat, and Demetrius Archer for their hands-on assistance.

This book would not be as complete as it is in terms of pedagogy and educational content were it not for readings and comments from Blaithín Burns, math teacher and Kodály instructor at the Blue Coat School in England. She provided invaluable assistance in the initial design of the book and field-tested many teaching strategies. Richard Schellhas deserves thanks for his personal patience and understanding as well as words of encouragement and advice throughout the writing of this manuscript.

Research for this publication was supported by a grant from Millersville University, and the State System for Higher Education in Pennsylvania. The university's library assistance; technical, administrative, and financial support; and overall encouragement for this project have allowed us to bring this volume to completion. We would like to express our gratitude to Gabriela Montoya-Stier and Faith Knowles for their permission to include songs from their collections *El Patio de Mi Casa: Traditional Rhymes, Games and Folk Songs from Mexico* and *Vamos a Cantar.*

We wish to thank Suzanne Ryan, Editor-in-Chief of Humanities and Executive Editor of Music at Oxford University Press for her encouragement and critical guidance. We thank Lisbeth Redfield, assistant editor at Oxford University Press, and Molly Morrison of Newgen, who oversaw editing and production. Very special thanks are due our editor, Thomas Finnegan, for his impeccable scrutiny and thoughtful editorial assistance with our manuscript.

About the Companion Website

www.oup.com/us/kodalytoday2e

The primary purpose of this web resource is to give music teachers realistic demonstrations of how to provide a musical education for elementary children based on the Kodály concept of music education that is cognitively and developmentally appropriate. The videos and activities are aligned to national content standards for music education as well as Core Curriculum Content that will enhance creativity and reinforce aural skills, visual literacy and numeracy skills in children.

The website contains samples of music teachers teaching concepts and skills by using the processes outlined in the book. In addition, each website chapter includes a "teacher's perspective" on the content of that chapter. All teaching video activities are aligned with information contained in *Kodály Today*. The foundational aspects of these videos constitute a detailed guide for teaching children to sing, move, and play instruments; develop music literacy skills; enhance music listening; and promote creativity skills. The hallmark of this teaching pedagogy is integration of the development of problem solving, critical thinking, and collaboration skills into the teaching and learning of music. The web material is indicated in the text with this symbol ▶.

All of the videos for this website have been videotaped by teachers in their own classrooms. Videos have not been edited.

Kodály Today

Introduction

I learned, amazed, how much there is for a Bard to know, outside and beyond his music, and I began to realize the power that lies in the harper's hands; power greater than a king's reaching beyond a man's own death-day, into the tomorrow of the world. Like all mysteries, one cannot speak of it, except to a fellow craftsman, for it has to do with hidden things, that must not be profaned. Like all mysteries, its core is the truth in man, and in his relationship to the world he knows, and the universe beyond it. At its deepest level it is concerned with the harmony, the measure, the rhythm out of which all things were created, and by which they must be governed, consciously or unconsciously. It is the life thread that holds us suspended safely above ultimate chaos, and the navel cord that joins life to eternity.[1]

Like the Bard, Diarmed, from *The Pendragon*, music instructors must exemplify excellent musicianship in order to transmit to their students "strict meticulous discipline" that will afford them the secret control of their voices so that "the truth can sing" through them "and touch the spirit of those who listen."[2] This is no small task. David Elliott reminds us, "To teach music effectively, we must know our subject—music. We must embody and exemplify musicianship. This is how children develop musicianship themselves: through actions, transactions, and interactions with musically proficient teachers."[3] Elsewhere, Elliott writes: "Teachers with insufficient musicianship or educatorship are highly prone to philosophical and practical misunderstandings. Thus many school choral and instrumental programs squander the opportunity to educate students musically because the teachers involved are not concerned with authentic musical performing and artistic music listening, only with simplistic 'sound producing.'"[4] We hope that *Kodály Today* will enable music instructors to initiate their students into the many aspects of music, including performing, critical thinking, listening, creativity, and becoming stewards of their cultural heritage.

Since its introduction to the United States in the early 1970s, the Kodály philosophy of music education has gained significant importance in undergraduate and graduate music methods courses as well as elementary, middle, and high school choral curriculums. The reasons for the renewed interest in the Kodály philosophy in the United States are many. In a music curriculum shaped by the Kodály philosophy and taught by an artist teacher, children are first

> actively involved in a combination of music making, singing, creating rhythmic and vocal accompaniments to songs, and active listening. Second, the Kodály approach offers a rich array of tools and concepts for the development of musical literacy. Third, Kodály specialists have been at the forefront of the movement to include world folk music in the curriculum. Fourth, Kodály teaching techniques provide excellent ways of approaching what Elliott calls "musical problem solving" and "problem reduction" in music education. Fifth, children who study music in a Kodály-based program tend to develop lifelong skills and excellent musical ears.[5]

Another significant reason for the impact of Kodály-inspired music instruction is its effect on student behavior outside the music classroom. The broad effects of this type of teaching and learning have also been documented by Dr. Martin F. Gardiner of the Center for the Study of Human Development at Brown University:

> The specific methods of arts training common to these studies is Kodály music training. The Kodály training is a methodology for building skills in individual and group singing that, along with specific musical skills, gives the children an opportunity to practice and build individual attitudes of attention, learning and sensitivity to the group, and capabilities for working together. It is possible to hypothesize that attitudes and behaviors towards learning in this arts training helped to build the more general improvements in classroom attitudes and behaviors that were documented by the teachers … and were in turn closely related to improvements in reading. Teacher reports support this viewpoint, as does recent data showing greater improvements in classroom behavior in those students receiving more extensive Kodály training.[6]

The motivating force for writing this book was our work with teachers over the last twenty years. We conducted focus discussions and surveys to learn and understand the pedagogical needs and concerns of music specialists. These teachers voiced their concern about the lack of specificity concerning issues relating to the teaching of music according to the Kodály philosophy. Of particular concern are issues dealing with

- How to teach traditional notation in tandem with rhythmic and melodic solfège syllables
- How to understand the rhythm syllable systems in current use
- How to teach compound meter
- How to teach music to older beginners
- How to design lesson plans that develop critical-thinking skills
- How to develop strategies for musical skills and keep track of these skills throughout the year
- How to develop harmonic hearing in the elementary classroom
- How to teach improvisation and composition
- How to develop evaluation and assessment tools for use in the classroom

This text provides viable answers to the concerns and questions raised by music teachers working in the field. All of the ideas and lesson plans in the text have been field-tested over a period of six years with music teachers.

We spell out teaching procedures and lesson preparation examples in considerable detail. The suggestions given should be used as a point of departure for each teacher's own creativity and personality and need not be taken too literally. It is expected that teachers will apply these suggestions in a way that is responsive to the needs, backgrounds, and interests of their own students. The sample lesson plans and sample curriculums we provide are not meant to be comprehensive. We expect that music instructors will infuse these ideas with their own national and regional benchmarks for teaching. *Kodály Today* offers a pathway as to how children may develop as performers, listeners, critical thinkers, composers and improvisers, and stewards of their cultural heritage. We appreciate that teachers must develop their own philosophy for teaching music and their own repertoire of songs, procedures, and processes for teaching musical skills, as well as consider such factors as the frequency of music instruction, the size of the class, the length of the class, and current music abilities of students.

In the Preface to the *Kodály Concept of Music Education*, by Helga Szabá, Madame Sarolta Kodály suggests: "A good teacher does not need ready-made prescriptions; in fact, she should not be given any, for this would only hamper the unfolding of her talent and clip the wings of her independent creative work. The number of techniques and devices used in teaching can be increased indefinitely, but they must not be mistaken for the totality of the method, nor for the basic concept from which they sprang."[7] For music teachers who do not have the possibility of studying in Hungary, we think that it is important to spell out the processes and techniques of teaching according to the Kodály concept. What seems natural and intuitive to Hungarian music teachers is often very difficult for music teachers who have not been exposed to intensive musicianship training based on the Kodály concept. We have furnished a pedagogical framework for teachers to develop their knowledge of the Kodály concept. But of course we must never forget the true essence of the concept, and that is singing. The techniques of teaching can never be the focus of a lesson. Techniques that are skillfully employed by a well-trained music teacher will lead to artistry in the classroom. Otherwise music techniques will lead to dull mechanical lessons.

Through our experiences working with teachers in the field, we have developed and modified aspects of processes and procedures commonly associated with the Kodály philosophy that are congruent with national and state standards. Some readers may note that we have strayed from what they recognize as the Kodály concept of music education. We believe that the findings and procedures we present in this book are in keeping with the composer's philosophy. Kodály asserts: "It is the fate of science that each successive age produces new results and usually modifies or completely refutes the results obtained by the preceding age."[8] In his lecture *Ancient Traditions—Today's Musical Life*, Kodály said, "But this is part and parcel of the development of science. Science keeps on changing and fluctuating . . . ."[9]

In the early 1970s Dr. Klára Kokas, a psychologist and graduate of the Franz Liszt Academy of Music in Budapest and a pupil of Kodály, began to experiment with the philosophy of Kodály. She has long been a proponent of adaptation and modification of the Kodály philosophy, the "musical compass" through which she researches and develops her own approach to teaching. She offers an insightful glimpse into why the Kodály concept needs to be adapted and modified.

> In Hungary, Kodály's principles were applied and developed within the traditional framework of centralized education. The central control exercised by the Ministry of Education, its lower representative organs, and the centralized form of assessment of teaching standards left little room for teacher initiative. Our personal visions were strongly circumscribed by the Marxist-Leninist philosophy and the aesthetics introduced by the establishment as a compulsory component at each level of education. Thus the frameworks in kindergartens—and even more so in school education—were strictly limited. In the given political set-up, Kodály's method had little scope for further refinement and development.[10]

We have written this book with the continuous input of teachers in the field. Over the past twenty years we have been engaged in a dialogue with music instructors who teach in Title I schools, urban schools, private schools, and other public schools; with teachers who see their students three and four times a week, and teachers who see their students three times a month; with teachers who have a strong background in teaching pedagogies and with beginning music instructors. Instead of constantly pushing our pedagogical procedures on them, we worked with them to address their needs and concerns both musical and practical.

The goal of *Kodály Today* is to give music instructors a practical guide on adapting the Kodály philosophy for today's classroom. For those teachers who do not have the time to devote many years of study to learning about the Kodály philosophy of music education, we have written this book as an essential introduction. We have tried to give elementary music instructors a reference of information and materials about adopting a teaching approach inspired by the Kodály philosophy of music education. We hope that *Kodály Today* will enable music instructors to initiate their students into the dimensions of musicianship that are common in the aural/oral and written music traditions. Some of these dimensions are performing, critical thinking, listening, improvising, composing, and becoming stewards of a cultural heritage that includes knowledge of aural/oral (folk music) and written musical traditions (classical music). Teaching procedures and sample lesson examples are presented in considerable detail. They may be used as a point of departure for each teacher's own creativity and personality. We hope that teachers will apply these suggestions in a way that is responsive to the needs, backgrounds, and interests of their own students. The sample lesson plans and sample curriculum we present are not meant to be comprehensive. Music instructors should infuse our suggestions with their own national and regional benchmarks for teaching.

Kodály Today offers teachers a practical way to help children develop as performers (singing, playing instruments, and movement), stewards of their cultural heritage, critical thinkers (reading and writing), composers, and informed audience members. We appreciate that teachers must develop their own philosophy for teaching music, their repertoire of songs reflecting the musical needs of their communities, the procedures, and the processes for teaching music skills while considering such factors as the frequency of music instruction, the size of the class, the length of the class, and current music abilities of students.

Outline

The second edition of *Kodály Today* is divided into thirteen chapters. Each chapter ends with updated key sources and a bibliography. Since the publication of the first edition of *Kodály Today*, we have modified our model of teaching and learning, which creates a number of changes to teaching strategies and lesson plan designs.

Introduction

This Introduction presents an overview of the text.

Chapter 1: Building the Framework of a Music Curriculum Based on the Kodály Concept

This chapter is a brief introduction to the Kodály philosophy and allows teachers to understand how this information can create a framework for developing a music curriculum. The information in this chapter is aligned with Chapter 1 in the accompanying Kodály Today grade handbooks.

Chapter 2: Developing a Music Repertoire of Songs for the Elementary Music Classroom

This chapter lays out a rationale for the selection and analysis of music repertoire for teaching music. It addresses how such selection and analysis affects lesson planning. It also includes websites, references, and sample lessons. The information in the chapter is aligned with Chapter 2 in the accompanying Kodály Today grade handbooks.

Chapter 3: Developing Creative Expression in the Elementary Classroom Through Singing, Movement, and Playing Instruments

The focus of this chapter is to show teachers how to develop in-tune singing, creative movement, and instrumental performance skills. There is an accompanying website that includes videos on how to teach singing in the elementary classroom. The chapter has updated key sources and bibliography, and it features a new unit on lesson planning related to developing creative expression. There are websites, references, and sample lessons. The information in the chapter is aligned with Chapter 3 in the accompanying Kodály Today grade handbooks.

Chapter 4: Teaching Tools and Techniques for Developing Audiation and Music Literacy Skills

This chapter discusses how to develop a sequence for teaching music literacy based on the frequency of music elements in music repertoire used for each grade level. Included is a discussion of the use of several types of rhythmic syllables, and it presents a sequence for teaching rhythmic and melodic elements. The chapter includes references and sample lessons. The information here is aligned with Chapter 4 in the accompanying Kodály Today grade handbooks.

Chapter 5: From Sound to Symbol: A Model of Learning and Instruction for Teaching Music Concepts, Elements, and Skills

This chapter discusses a model of learning and instruction for developing music knowledge and skills in the elementary music classroom. The hallmark of this teaching and learning model is integration of the development of problem-solving, critical-thinking, and collaboration skills into the teaching and learning of music. There is also a discussion of how this model promotes deeper learning in young children. The chapter includes websites, references, and sample lessons.

Chapter 6: Grades 1 Through 5 Teaching Strategies for Rhythmic and Melodic Concepts and Elements

This chapter presents examples of teaching strategies for each grade level based on the model of learning presented in Chapter 5. The chapter includes references and sample lessons. The information in it is aligned with Chapters 3 and 4 in the accompanying Kodály Today grade handbooks.

Chapter 7: Developing Musicianship Skills in the Classroom

This chapter describes how various music skills such as reading, writing, listening, improvisation, and composition can be developed in the elementary classroom. The chapter includes references and sample lessons, and the information is aligned with Chapter 3 in the accompanying Kodály Today grade handbooks.

Chapter 8: Technology in the Kodály Classroom

This chapter presents on overview of some technologies that can be used by the music teacher and the students in the Kodály music classroom. It addresses the use of the Smart Board and how it can be successfully introduced into the music classroom. The chapter includes references and sample lessons.

Chapter 9: Applying the Kodály Concept to the Elementary Choir

This chapter presents an overview as to how to train an elementary music choir on the basis of the principles of Kodály. Particular attention will be paid to vocal exercises, warm-up exercises, the role of solfège in intonation, and developing music skills such as part singing in the choral rehearsal. The chapter includes references and sample lessons.

Chapter 10: Sequencing and Lesson Planning

This chapter describes the lesson plan structures that are revised for this edition. There is a new section included in this chapter on how to adapt lesson plans for the inclusive classroom. The chapter features references and sample lessons. The information here is aligned with Chapter 5 in the accompanying Kodály Today grade handbooks.

Chapter 11: Teaching Musicianship Skills Starting in the Upper Grades

This chapter describes how to teach music to older beginners. It includes websites, references, and sample lessons and presents a discussion on how to design a lesson plan suitable for older beginners.

Chapter 12: Evaluation and Assessment

This chapter describes how to assess and evaluate students' learning as well as how to evaluate a successful lesson plan. Sample rubrics are furnished to assess singing, reading, writing, and improvisation. The chapter includes websites, references, and sample lessons. The information is aligned with Chapter 6 in the accompanying Kodály Today grade handbooks.

Chapter 13: Organizing Your Teaching Resources for the Elementary Classroom

This chapter presents some general considerations for organizing resources for teaching music in the elementary school. Organizing binders will include a philosophy statement, repertoire list, sequence for teaching music literacy, strategy plans for teaching concepts, lesson plans, activities for developing music skills, listening examples, evaluation and assessment forms, and internet resources.

Distinctive Features

Timely Publication

In July 2012 the National Research Council challenged teachers to cultivate approaches to teaching that develop "deeper learning." The second edition of *Kodály Today* and the accompanying handbooks will supply music teachers with resources that promote twenty-first-century skills.

Transcending All Methods of Teaching Music

The researchers have used the Kodály philosophy as a pedagogical compass for these handbooks. The foundation for the second edition and the accompanying handbooks is the development of students' performance (singing, moving, playing instruments), repertoire, reading and writing of music, and listening and music creative skills—key components of any music curriculum. Teachers certified in Kodály, Orff, and Dalcroze training piloted these handbooks. Any teacher, regardless of personal philosophy and particular pedagogy, can use the handbooks.

Writing Style

The writing style of this text is accessible and instantly engages the reader. The text is filled with examples of activities as well as detailed lesson plans that translate a theoretical model of learning and instruction into a practical guide for teaching music in the K–5 music classroom.

Organic Pedagogy

The authors use an organic approach to teaching music that begins with the careful selection of repertoire. This repertoire is then used to build students' singing, movement,

Introduction

instrumental playing, reading, writing, listening, and creative music skills through an "immersion" approach to teaching.

Sequential Pedagogy

The research outlines the process for presenting musical concepts and developing music skills. Although several works describing Kodály-based techniques and curriculums exist, few spell out detailed teaching procedures for presenting musical concepts and integrating them with musical skill development. Some educators familiar with Kodály-inspired teaching may already know the teaching ideas presented in this text. However, we have combined these ideas with current research findings in the field of music perception and cognition to develop a model of music instruction and learning that offers teachers a map to follow that will develop their students' musical understandings and metacognition skills. We have worked to present a clear picture of how one develops a K–5 music curriculum based on the philosophy of Kodály, the teaching and learning processes needed to execute this curriculum, as well as the development of assessment tools.

Vertical Alignment of Music Classes

Because of the pedagogy used in this publication, it offers a compelling example of how to achieve vertical alignment in the elementary music curriculum. Like all other subject areas in the elementary curriculum, the second edition of *Kodály Today* and the handbooks develop routines and procedures that are common to music lessons regardless of grade level and teaching philosophy. We have delineated the teaching process by including more than forty lesson plans for each grade for teaching music according to the Kodály philosophy and based on the *Kodály Today* text. These handbooks present a clear picture of how the teaching and learning processes go hand-in-hand during the music lesson.

New Cognitive Model for Teaching Music

Kodály Today and the handbook series present detailed instructions on how to present music concepts, elements, and skills based on a model of learning developed in *Kodály Today*. This model builds on the accepted process of teaching music: prepare, make conscious, reinforce, and assess. Although the researchers have adopted these phases of learning, each one of these phases is further broken down into stages that allow sequential teaching of music concepts and elements as well as the means for their assessment. This model of learning inspires the music curriculum, lesson plans, and assessment rubrics for each handbook.

Second Edition

The aim of a second edition of *Kodály Today* is to present an updated practical guide on how to impart a Kodály-based musical education to students in the elementary school that is aligned with current research in the fields of music pedagogy, music perception and cognition, and Kodály studies. Since the publication of *Kodály Today* in 2008, there has been a tremendous growth in music education research related to Kodály studies, music education, and music perception and cognition.[11] Professional organizations are requesting that teachers become proficient in practical applications of research to improve teaching techniques that are germane for teaching music in the twenty-first century. A clarion call has been sounded: create teaching resources that focus on the techniques of music teaching and make available concrete roadmaps as to how to teach music in the twenty-first century that develops "deeper learning."[12]

New to the Second Edition

- All chapters include updated sources and bibliographies.
- Chapters include actual lesson plans in addition to lesson outlines.
- A new chapter on music technology has been included to help teachers adopt more interactive approaches in the classroom.
- A new chapter on the application of the Kodály concept to children's choir has been included.
- All lesson plan designs have been updated and organized systematically for all grades.
- More-user-friendly language is included in the lesson plans.
- Chapter 10, "Sequencing and Lesson Planning," contains a new unit on how to adapt lesson plans for the inclusive classroom.
- A companion website offers instructors extensive additional resources, including sample videos of students as well as music teachers demonstrating techniques and lesson plans. The site also includes worksheets for each grade.
- There is a handbook series accompanying this book. Many practical applications for classroom use contained in these handbooks are cross-referenced to the second edition of this book.

Who Should Read This Book?

This book will appeal to methods instructors, pre-service music teachers, beginning music teachers, and practicing/veteran music teachers for a number of reasons. This is a book with a distinctive methodological foundation that focuses on creatively enhancing the learning environment of children. Therefore, it appeals to methods instructors who will use the book over the course of a semester to show the necessary elements of a comprehensive music education. Effective methods instruction includes what to teach, how to teach, and why to teach, and this book addresses all of these areas. Second, pre-service music teachers will gravitate toward the sequencing and lesson planning included in the book, as well as the specific resources (songs, books), when practice-teaching during methods courses, field experiences, and student teaching. Third, beginning teachers are often most concerned with long-term planning for each grade level. The unit and lesson plans within *Kodály Today* will appeal to these teachers. Finally, this book will appeal to practicing/veteran music teachers because it can be used to refresh knowledge of teaching music in the early childhood classroom while presenting it in ways that advocate for music education (e.g., connections to literacy). This book updates traditional Kodály ideas and makes them relevant for today's classrooms.

Bibliography

Ádám, J. "A Message to My Colleagues, the Music Pedagogues of the U.S.A." *Bulletin of the International Kodály Society*, 1996, *21*(2): 40–41.

Altenmüller, E., W. Gruhn, D. Parlitz, and G. Liebert. "The Impact of Music Education on Brain Networks: Evidence from EEG-Studies." *International Journal of Music Education*, 2000, *35*: 47–53.

Altenmüller, E., M. Wiesendanger, and J. Kesselring. *Music, Motor Control and the Brain.* Oxford: Oxford University Press, 2006.

Bacon, D. "No One Can Be a Real Artist Who Is Not a True Man—Zoltán Kodály." *Bulletin of the International Kodály Society*, 2010, *35*(1), 3–10.

Bacon, D. "Quality Teacher Training for Music Teachers Through the Kodály Approach." *Bulletin of the International Kodály Society*, 1977, *2*(1–2): 36–39.

Barrett, M. S. "Sounding Lives in and Through Music: A Narrative Inquiry of the 'Everyday' Musical Engagement of a Young Child." *Journal of Early Childhood Research*, 2009, *7*(2): 115–134.

Blackford, L., and R. Stainthorp. "The Interpretation of Kodály's Philosophy of Music Education by Teachers Working in England and Scotland." *Bulletin of the International Kodály Society*, 2007, *32*(1): 30–38.

Borthwick, S. J., and J. W. Davidson. "Developing a Child's Identity as a Musician: A Family 'Script' Perspective." In *Musical Identities*, ed. R. A. MacDonald, D. J. Hargreaves, and D. E. Miell, pp. 60–78. Oxford: Oxford University Press, 2002.

Boynton, S., and R. Kok (eds.). *Musical Childhoods & the Cultures of Youth.* Middletown, CT: Wesleyan University Press, 2006.

Burton, S. L., and C. C. Taggart. *Learning from Young Children: Research in Early Childhood Music Education.* Lanham, MD: Rowman & Littlefield, 2011.

Caylor, F. "Music for Our Children's Children." *Bulletin of the International Kodály Society*, 1979, *4*(2): 10–26.

Choksy, L. "Toward a Musical Culture." *Bulletin of the International Kodály Society*, 2007, *32*(2): 4–10.

Christian, C. *The Pendragon.* New York: Warner Books, 1980.

Costa-Giomi, E. "Music Instruction and Children's Intellectual Development: The Education Context of Musical Participation." In *Music, Health, and Wellbeing*, ed. R.A.R. MacDonald, G. Kreutz, and L. Mitchell, pp. 339–356. Oxford: Oxford University Press 2012.

Custodero, L., and L. C. Hafteck. "Harmonizing Research, Practice, and Policy in Early Childhood Music: A Chorus of International Voices." Special issues. *Arts Education Policy Review*, 2007/2008, *109*(2–3): 3–6 (issue 2), 3–8 (issue 3).

De Greeve, G. "The Worth of Kodály's Philosophy in One's Personality Development." *Bulletin of the International Kodály Society*, 1987, *12*(1): 16–18.

De Greeve, G. "Zoltán Kodály's Inspiration and the Challenges of the 21st Century." *Bulletin of the International Kodály Society*, 2005, *30*(2): 5–9.

DeNora, T. *Music in Everyday Life*. Cambridge: Cambridge University Press, 2000.

Dissanayake, E. *Art and Intimacy: How the Arts Began*. Seattle: University of Washington Press, 2000.

Dolloff, Lori-Anne. "Elementary Music Education: Building Cultures and Practices." In *Praxial Music Education. Reflections and Dialogues*, ed. David J. Elliott, pp. 281–296. New York: Oxford University Press, 2009.

"Education for Life and Work: Developing Transferable Knowledge and Skills in the 21st Century." Report Brief. National Research Council, July 12, 2012.

Elliott, D. J. *Music Matters: A New Philosophy of Music Education*. New York: Oxford University Press, 1995.

Elliott, D. J. *Praxial Music Education: Reflections and Dialogues*. New York: Oxford University Press, 2005.

Flohr, J. "Best Practices for Young Children's Music Education: Guidance from Brain Research." *General Music Today,* 2010, *23*(2): 13–19.

Flohr, J., and C. Trevarthen. "Music Learning in Childhood: Early Developments of a Musical Brain and Body." In *Neurosciences in Music Pedagogy*, ed. W. Gruhn and F. Rauscher, pp. 53–100. New York: Nova Biomedical Books, 2008.

Gardiner, M. F. "Arts Training in Education." *The Teaching Exchange*, January 1999.

Gardiner, M. F., A. Fox, F. Knowles, and D. Jeffrey. "Learning Improved by Arts Training." *Nature*, May 23, 1996, *381*(6580): 284.

Hargreaves, D. J., R. A. MacDonald, and D. E. Miell. "What Are Musical Identities, and Why Are They Important?" In *Musical Identities*, ed. R. A. MacDonald, D. J. Hargreaves, and D. E. Miell, pp. 60–78. Oxford: Oxford University Press, 2002.

Ittzés, M. "Kodály, the Methodologist." *Bulletin of the International Kodály Society*, 2010, *35*(2): 8–15.

Kodaly, Zoltán. "Ancient Traditions—Today's Musical Life." In *The Selected Writings of Zoltán Kodály*, ed. Ferenc Bánis, trans. Halápy and Macnicol, pp. 165–184. Budapest: Zeneműkiadá Vállalat, 1964; London: Boosey & Hawkes, 1974.

Kodaly, Zoltán. "Bartók the Folklorist." In *The Selected Writings of Zoltán Kodály*, ed. Ferenc Bánis, trans. Halápy and Macnicol, pp. 102–108. Budapest: Zeneműkiadá Vállalat, 1964; London: Boosey & Hawkes, 1974.

Kokas, Klára. *Joy Through the Magic of Music*. Budapest, Hungary: Akkord Zenei Kiadá, 1999.

Lancy, D. *The Anthropology of Childhood: Cherubs, Chattel, Changelings*. Cambridge: Cambridge University Press, 2008.

McPherson, G. E., ed. *The Child as Musician: A Handbook of Musical Development.* New York: Oxford University Press, 2006.

McPherson, G. E., and G. F. Welch, eds. *The Oxford Handbook of Music Education.* Vols. 1 and 2. New York: Oxford University Press, 2012.

Mills, J. *Music in the Primary School* (3rd ed.). Oxford: Oxford University Press, 2009.

Mithen, S. *The Singing Neanderthals: The Origins of Music, Language, Mind and Body.* London: Weidenfeld & Nicholson, 2005.

Papoušek, H. "Musicality in Infancy Research: Biological and Cultural Origins of Early Musicality." In *Musical Beginnings: Origins and Development of Musical Competence,* ed. I. Deliège and J. Sloboda, pp. 37–55. Oxford: Oxford University Press, 1996.

Qvortrup, J., W. Corsaro, and M. S. Honig (eds.). *The Palgrave Handbook of Childhood Studies.* Basingstoke, UK: Palgrave, 2009.

Rogoff, B. *The Cultural Nature of Human Development.* Oxford: Oxford University Press, 2003.

Sanders, P. D. "Historical Precedents of the Kodály Approach." *Bulletin of the International Kodály Society*, 1994, *19*(1): 44–49.

Sanders, P. D. "Historical Research on the Kodály Approach in the United Sates." *Bulletin of the International Kodály Society*, 2002, *27*(1): 16–22.

Schellenberg, E. G. "Examining the Association Between Music Lessons and Intelligence." *British Journal of Psychology*, 2011, *102*(3): 283-302.

Seidel, S., S. Tishman, E. Winner, L. Hetland, and P. Palmer. *The Qualities of Quality: Understanding Excellence in Arts Education.* Cambridge, MA: Harvard Graduate School of Education, 2009.

Smithrim, K., and R. Upitis (eds.). *Listen to Their Voices: Research and Practice in Early Childhood Music.* Vol. 3, Research to Practice: A Biennial Series. Lee Bartel (ed.). Canadian Music Educators Association, 2007.

Szabá, Helga, and Geoffry Russell-Smith. *The Kodály Concept of Music Education.* New York: Boosey & Hawkes, 1969.

Tudge, J. *The Everyday Lives of Young Children: Culture, Class, and Child Rearing in Diverse Societies.* Cambridge: Cambridge University Press, 2008.

Turine, T. *Music as Social Life: The Politics of Participation.* Chicago University of Chicago Press, 2008.

Welch, G. F. "The Musical Development and Education of Young Children." In *Handbook of Research on the Education of Young Children*, B. Spodek and O. Saracho (eds.), pp. 251–267. Mahwah, NJ: Erlbaum, 2006.

Website

meNet: Music Education Network. http://menet.mdw.ac.at/menetsite/english/index.html (accessed Oct. 27, 2010).

Chapter 1

Building the Framework of a Music Curriculum Based on the Kodály Concept

> Philosophy works to render the implicit explicit, with the ultimate intent of enriching both understanding and perception. Among its greatest allies is a persistent curiosity. Its enemies are the habitual, the stereotypical, the unexamined, the acritical, the "common sense" assumption or assertion. The philosophical mind critically challenges and explores received doctrine, renounces the security and comfort of dogma, exposes inconsistencies, weighs and evaluates alternatives. It explores, probes, and questions, taking very little for granted.
>
> Wayne Bowman, "Philosophy, Criticism, and Music Education," p. 4

Key Questions

- What are the major tenets of the Kodály philosophy of music education?
- How can the Kodály philosophy of music education serve as a model for developing a personal philosophy of music education?
- What are the multiple dimensions of musicianship training?
- How do the multiple dimensions of musicianship training connect to the Kodály philosophy of music education?
- How can we develop a music curriculum based on the Kodály philosophy of music education?

- How can we develop a lesson plan framework based on a music curriculum inspired by the Kodály philosophy of music education?
- How is the Kodály philosophy connected to the national content standards for music education?

What you teach and how you teach will be determined by your own personal philosophy of music education. Exploring Zoltán Kodály's philosophy of music education can provide a helpful model for developing your own personal philosophy of music education. This allows you to examine your goals and purpose in the classroom as well as to become an advocate for the inclusion of music in the school curriculum. The goal of this chapter is to offer a short introduction to Kodály's philosophy of music education as a basis for understanding the components to consider in designing a successful music curriculum. To give a context for understanding Kodály's philosophy, we are furnishing a brief biographical outline of the composer. Although Kodály never wrote any systematic methodology, his philosophy of music education inspired his colleagues and pupils to develop a methodology of teaching. It is important not to confuse Kodály's philosophy of music education with the Kodály Method, an approach to teaching guided by Kodály's philosophy of music education. The composer's philosophy of music education can be briefly summarized as follows: excellent musicians using quality repertoire to teach the joy of music to students during daily music lessons. The tools normally associated with the Kodály Method are discussed in Chapter 4; our focus in this chapter is to convey the Kodály philosophy of music. There are many challenges to implementing a curriculum based on this philosophy of music education, but we believe that it is worth the effort.

Zoltán Kodály: A Biographical Outline
The Early Years: 1882–1905

Zoltán Kodály (1882–1967)[1] was a Hungarian composer, ethnomusicologist, and music educator who along with Béla Bartók is recognized for creating a new style of Hungarian art music based on the folk music heritage of Hungary. Through his efforts in music education, Kodály sought to cultivate a far-reaching, musically literate Hungarian society. His philosophical and pedagogical contributions to the field of music education have become known as the Kodály concept or Kodály Method of music education now in worldwide use.[2]

Zoltán Kodály was born in Kecskemét, Hungary, on December 16, 1882. His early musical experiences and education prepared him for a career as an artist and a scholar. His father, an amateur violinist, and his mother, an amateur pianist and singer, filled the Kodály house with chamber music of the European masters. He studied language and literature at university, where he was a member of the Eötvös Collegium and composition at the Ferenc Liszt National Academy of Music in Budapest. He earned degrees in composition and teaching in 1904 and 1905, respectively. In April 1906 he was awarded the

Ph.D. for his thesis *A Magyar népdal stráfaszerkezete* [The Stanzaic Structure of Hungarian Folk Song]. Kodály compiled research material from existing Hungarian folk music collections, music that he had gathered in Galánta, and Béla Vikár's phonograph cylinder recordings. The work reflects his interests and scholarship in the interdisciplinary aspects of music and language. After receiving his doctorate, Kodály settled in Buda and began an ambitious investigation of Hungarian folk tradition.

The Young Composer: 1905–1922

Kodály met Béla Bartók in 1905 when they began to further investigate Hungarian folk music together. In 1906, Kodály took part in a study tour in Berlin and Paris and then began his teaching career as a music theory instructor at the Budapest Ferenc Liszt Academy of Music. At the same time, Kodály continued collecting folk songs, composing, and offering musical criticism. His folk song collection grew to more than three thousand songs. His compositional efforts included piano, chamber, and choral works. Kodály's writings on related aspects of musicology, ethnomusicology, composition, and music performance appeared in literary journals and newspapers.

Kodály became a faculty member at the Liszt Academy (then known as the Budapest Hungarian Royal Academy of Music until 1925) in 1907; there he taught music theory, composition ethnomusicology, and solfège until the mid-1950s. He officially retired from the academy in 1942. His association with Bartók led to a joint concert of their works in 1910. Kodály's use of folk tunes and unfamiliar harmonies earned for him the title "deliberate heretic." He was accused of holding "both thought and melody in contempt."

The Creative Period: 1923–1939

The years 1923–1939 were Kodály's most prolific as both a composer and an author. His most noted compositions of the period were written for the opera and chorus. Kodály wrote *Psalmus Hungaricus*, for choir and orchestra, to mark the fiftieth anniversary of the united city of Budapest. The period saw the premiere, first in Hungary and then abroad, of the singspiel *Háry János, Dances of Galanta,* and the *Concerto for Orchestra*. Kodály made his conducting debut with the Concertgebouw Orchestra in 1927.

His scholarly works of the period included a number of articles that sought to define the nature of Hungarian folk music. He contributed a historical survey of Hungarian folk music to the *Zenei lexikon* [Dictionary of Music]. He then published his own work on the topic entitled *Folk Music of Hungary*.

Kodály stated that 1925 was the year in which he turned his attention to the musical education of children. Beginning in 1927, Kodály's former students started the Youth Choral Movement in Hungary. The most famous were Jenő Ádám, Lajos Bárdos, György Kerényi, Zoltán Vásárhelyi, Endre Borus, and Adrienne Sztojanovits. The first choral collection, *Little Pieces for Children's Choir*, was published in 1928 and edited by Kerényi. In 1929 Kodály recognized that music education would need to become more systematic, and that only music materials of the highest quality and that singing should form the foundation. In 1937 Kodály wrote the first volume of *Bicinia Hungarica*, in which he discusses the benefits of using relative solmization.[3] *The ABC of Singing* [*Énekes Ábécé*], a music textbook containing folk music materials and the first real effort to use relative solmization in Hungary, was compiled by Kerényi and Benjamin Rajeczky in 1938 and published by Magyar Kárus, Budapest. Based on relative solmization, it contained about three hundred folk songs, classical music, and fundamentals of music. A teacher's manual, *Éneklő iskola* [Singing School], was published two years later in 1940 by Irma Bors and Győrgy Gulyás.

The Educator: 1940–1967

In his later years, Kodály pursued with even greater zeal the improvement of musical education in Hungarian schools. *Let Us Sing Correctly* was published in 1941 and presented a pathway to achieving acoustically correct vocal intonation. During this time he wrote other collections of two-part music, including *15 Two-Part Singing Exercises*. In 1954 he wrote *33 Two-Part Singing Exercises* as well as *Tricinia*, and in 1965 he wrote *22 Two-Part Singing Exercises*. He wrote *77 Two-Part Singing Exercises* in 1967 and 1968; they were based on Ainu melodies from Japan. He edited numerous songbooks tailored specifically for children and set forth principles for early musical education in works such as "Zene az ovodában" [Music in the Kindergarten]. In 1943–44, Magyar Kárus published Kodály and Kerényi's two-volume school song collection *Iskolai Énekgyüjtemény I–II* [Collected Songs for Schools]. This was a collection of 630 melodies, including Hungarian and European folk songs and canons arranged according to a methodological sequence. In this collection, folk song material was classified using a musically sequenced order. In 1943 Kodály's 333 reading exercises were published and four booklets of *Pentatonic Music*.[4] The *Szá-mi* I–VIII books were written with Ádám and published in 1944 and 1946. This was a selection of materials from the *Collected Songs for Schools* for grades one through eight. During 1944 a handbook to Kodály's school song collection and to the *Szá-mi* songbook by Kodály and Ádám was published by Ádám, called *Módszeres énektanítás a relatív szolmizáció alapján* [Methodical Music Teaching Based on Relative Solmization]. In these books Kodály began melodic training with the minor third interval. In 1945 and 1947 he published *Pentatonic Music*,[5] and in 1945 he gave a lecture in Pécs on November 19 titled "Hungarian Musical Education." He discussed the importance of basing Hungarian musical education on Hungarian folk music. The composer defended the notion of teaching Hungarian music as a prerequisite to the music of other nations. He also addressed the value of teaching singing before giving an instrument.[6]

In 1946, a specialized primary school was established consistent with Kodály's principles. His article "100 Éves terv" [A Hundred Year Plan] was published in *Énekszá*. The ambitious goal of the composer's plan was to restore Hungarian musical culture by making reading and writing music a part of general education throughout the Hungarian school system. Kodály's plan is perhaps best summarized in his own words: "The aim: Hungarian musical culture. The means: making the reading and writing of music general, through the schools.

At the same time the awakening of a Hungarian public taste in music and continual progress towards what is better and more Hungarian. To make masterpieces of world music literature public property, to convey them to people of every kind and rank."[7] The Hungarian minister of education recognized his efforts and awarded Kodály the Grand Cross of the Order of the Republic in 1948. He was a member, and then president, of the Hungarian Academy of Sciences (1946–1949), where he established the folk music research group.

Kodály lobbied Hungarian leaders for better education in singing in the schools. In 1950 the first music primary school started in Kecskemét, led by Márta Nemesszeghy. His ideas on the importance of developing musicianship were reflected in a speech, "Who Is a Good Musician?" given at the end of the 1953–54 academic year at the Liszt Academy. He summarized the characteristics of a good musician as someone who had (1) a well-trained ear, (2) a well-trained intelligence, (3) a well-trained heart, and (4) a well-trained hand. In a preface to Erzsébet Szőnyi's *Musical Reading and Writing*,[8] Kodály provides a brief overview of music education focusing on the German model and commenting on the curriculum of the Paris Conservatory. He praises Szőnyi's *Musical Reading and Writing* for constructing an outline for a music education but cautions that it is the artistry of the teacher that will set the musical example for the students, not books.[9] In the Foreword to *Let Us Sing Correctly*[10] published in 1964, Kodály explains that proper intonation in singing matches the acoustic, not the tempered, intervals and that the singing teacher or choral director should not depend on the piano for pitch. He examines the use of part singing and solfège for developing good intonation. Musical examples are presented and analyzed.

The 1964 Budapest Conference of the International Society for Music Education drew international attention to the phenomenon of musical education taking place in Hungarian music education; this was called "the Kodály Method."[11] Accordingly, Kodály was recognized as a prominent figure in twentieth-century music education.

Further accolades were bestowed on Kodály in his final years; he was presented with three Kossuth prizes as well as honorary degrees from Oxford, Humboldt, and Toronto universities. Kodály became a citizen of the world; he was invited to conduct in Great Britain, the Soviet Union, and the United States; he was selected to chair conferences held by the International Folk Music Council and the International Society for Music Education; and he was an honorary president of the latter. As a final tribute from his own people, Kodály received the title of Eminent Artist from the Hungarian People's Republic.

A Brief Examination of Zoltán Kodály's Philosophy of Music Education

To understand Kodály's philosophy of music education, it is best to examine his musical compositions, writings, and speeches. Here we consider some of his most famous statements concerning the justification for including music in the school curriculum and the importance of a well-trained music teacher, as well as his views on the essential components of a music education. The majority of these statements were originally written in Hungarian and translated into English. We do not attempt to correct grammatical errors (or use of gendered pronouns) or English translations. The quotes appear as they have originally been translated. Although some statements are awkward, the essence of Kodály's thoughts is evident.

We have chosen quotes from Kodály's writings that permit insights into (1) justifying music in the school curriculum, (2) the importance of excellent musicianship training for music instructors, and (3) offering a comprehensive music education that includes performance, stewardship of culture, critical thinking, creativity, and listening. We refer to these various components as the multiple dimensions of musicianship.

Justifying Music in the School Curriculum

Kodály believed that music should belong to everyone and not just to a musical elite: "It is the right of every citizen to be taught the basic elements of music, to be handed the key with which he can enter the locked world of music. To open the ear and heart of the millions to serious music is a great thing."[12]

He states that "with a few years' technical preparation children can achieve results measurable by the most exacting of absolute artistic standards."[13] He observed, "With music, one's whole future life is brightened. This is such a treasure in life that it helps us over many troubles and difficulties. Music is nourishment, a comforting elixir. Music multiplies all that is beautiful and of value in life."[14] Other observations:

> Taken separately, too, the elements of music are precious instruments in education. Rhythm develops attention, concentration, determination and the ability to condition oneself. Melody opens up the world of emotions. Dynamic variation and tone colour sharpen our hearing. Singing, finally, is such a many-sided physical activity that its effect in physical education is immeasurable—if there is perhaps anyone to whom the education of the spirit does not matter. Its beneficial effect in health is well known; special books have been written on this.[15]

> With us it is scarcely every twentieth person who uses his speech and breathing organs correctly. This, too, should be learned during the singing lesson. The discipline of rhythm, the training of the throat and lungs set singing right beside gymnastics. Both of them, no less than food, are needed daily.[16]

> Our age of mechanization leads along a road ending with man himself as a machine; only the spirit of singing can save us from this fate.[17]

The Importance of Excellent Artist-Teachers

We believe that students should be taught music on the basis of an apprenticeship model of instruction that closely mirrors a teaching model used by exceptional studio instructors. Simply stated, students learn the craft of music from individuals who themselves are excellent musicians. In Kodály's words: "There is a need for better musicians, and only those will become good musicians who work at it every day. The better a musician is the easier it is for him to draw others into the happy, magic circle of music. Thus will he serve the great cause of helping music to belong to everyone."[18]

These additional quotes verify Kodály's conviction that only excellent music instructors should teach.

> It is more important who the singing master at Kisvárda is than who the director of the Opera House is, because a poor director will fail. [Often even a good one.] But a bad teacher may kill the love of music for thirty years in thirty classes of pupils.[19]

> Teach music and singing at school in such a way that it is not a torture but a joy for the pupil; instill a thirst for finer music in him, a thirst which will last for a lifetime. Music must not be approached from its intellectual, rational side, nor should it be conveyed to the child as a system of algebraic symbols, or as the secret writing of a language with which he has no connection. The way should be paved for direct intuition. If the child is not filled at least once by the life-giving stream of music during the most susceptible period—between his sixth and sixteenth years—it will hardly be any use to him later on. Often a single experience will open the young soul to music for a whole lifetime. This experience cannot be left to chance; it is the duty of the school to provide it.[20]

> Music instructors should develop students' inherent musical abilities in the classroom through performance, musical literacy skills, creativity, and listening, as well as enabling their students to become stewards of their musical and cultural heritage. The goal of music instruction is to create a community of learners that experience and explore all of the various facets of music and begin to share this knowledge as a service to the community.

> But professional music education in music itself is still not sufficiently inspired by the idea that music-making is not an end in itself but that it must stand at the service of the whole people.[21]

> It is the bounden duty of the talented to cultivate their talent to the highest degree, to be of as much use as possible to their fellow men. For every person's worth is measured by how much he can help his fellow men and serve his country. Real art is one of the most powerful forces in the rise of mankind and he who renders it accessible to as many people as possible is a benefactor of humanity.[22]

Comprehensive Music Education: The Multiple Dimensions of Musicianship

In addition to addressing the value of music in the school curriculum, Kodály spoke about the need to give children a comprehensive music education. For us the multiple dimensions of musicianship include performance, musical literacy, and critical thinking skills, creativity, listening, as well as stewardship of a community's musical and cultural heritage. It is clear that when developing children's musicianship skills we need to address the several facets of what it means to be a musical human being. If we are to develop children's self-knowledge, self-awareness, and emotions, we need to educate them to be

- Stewards of their musical and cultural heritage
- Performers
- Critical thinkers
- Creative human beings
- Informed audience members

Children as Stewards of Their Cultural Heritage: Music Repertoire

Although some music educators[23] have alleged that the music education of children is more important than transmission of a musical and cultural heritage, Kodály argued otherwise.

> Not even the most excellent individual creation can be a substitute for traditions. To write a folksong is as much beyond the bounds of possibility as to write a proverb. Just as proverbs condense centuries of popular wisdom and observation, so, in the traditional songs, the emotions of centuries are immortalized in a form polished to perfection. No masterpiece can replace traditions.[24]

Kodály believed that material suited to the physical, developmental, and psychological needs of the young could be best found in folk songs. Kodály valued folk songs for their simplicity, beauty, and heritage, but he emphatically stressed the importance of using only authentic folk songs, linking them to the finest art songs and art music.

Through their tradition of oral transmission, folk songs have long been considered ideal for developing ear training and musical memory. This renders them well suited to fostering musical literacy. Using folk songs and singing games in the school allows the teacher to work with appropriate material that is already part of the child's cultural experience. Ruth Crawford Seeger believed also that it is "one of the aims of education to induct the child into the realities of the culture in which he will live, may we not say that this traditional music and language and ideology, which has not only grown out of but has in turn influenced that culture—and is still influencing and being used by it—should occupy a familiar place in the child's daily life, even though it may not be current in the particular neighborhood in which he happens to be living."[25]

As students' skills develop, folk songs of other cultures are gradually introduced along with art music of the great composers. Kodály: "There are strictly speaking only two kinds of music: good and bad. . . . Bad foreign and bad native music are equally damaging, like the plague."[26]

It was Kodály's belief that communication of inferior music inhibits the growth of maximum musical understanding. Therefore he maintained that the type of material used and the manner of presentation have a lasting effect on the development of a child's musical taste.

> Bad taste spreads by leaps and bounds. In art this is not so innocent a thing as in, say, clothes. Someone who dresses in bad taste does not endanger his health, but bad taste in art is a veritable sickness of the soul. It seals the soul off from contact with masterpieces and from the life giving nourishment emanating from them without which the soul wastes away or becomes stunted, and the whole character of the man is branded with a peculiar mark.[27]
>
> The pure soul of the child must be considered sacred; what we implant there must stand every test, and if we plant anything bad, we poison his soul for life.[28]

The use of contrived or diluted music is not suitable for instruction.

> Let us stop the teachers' superstition according to which only some diluted art-substitute is suitable for teaching purposes. A child is the most susceptible and the most enthusiastic audience for pure art; for in every great artist the child is alive—and this is something felt by youth's congenial spirit. Conversely, only art of intrinsic value is suitable for children! Everything else is harmful. After all, food is more carefully chosen for an infant than for an adult. Musical nourishment which is 'rich in vitamins' is essential for children.[29]

Quality music literature for each grade will expand students' knowledge of folk songs, music of the masters, and recently composed music. We need to consider the cultural backgrounds of our students and then determine the songs that should be included in a curriculum. From that point we can determine which materials may be taught through music reading, or through a rote approach to instruction.

Children as Performers: Singing, Instruments, and Movement

Music performance is at the core of a music program. Through performance students engage in singing, movement, playing instruments, and conducting.

Singing

Kodály was convinced that singing is the most direct means to a musical education. Singing requires rapid internalization of sound and provides immediate participation in the musical experience. Kodály's intent was to lead students to a deep appreciation of art music. Since the human voice is the most intimate of all instruments and the inner ear is more easily developed through this personal medium, the voice is the most logical starting point.

> If one were to attempt to express the essence of this education in one word, it could only be—singing. The most frequent word to be heard on Toscannini's [sic] lips during his orchestral rehearsals was "Cantare!" expressed in a thousand and one shades of meaning.[30]

Fortunate indeed is the child who creates with his own voice the first association linking it with the picture of the notes. If he starts singing based on the concepts of instrumental techniques, then our endeavors to make the singing and aural concepts primary can hardly succeed. And if he does not sing at all, it will be nearly impossible for him to achieve free and intimate "singing" on any instrument. Even the most talented artist can never overcome the disadvantages of an education without singing.[31]

There is a well-known saying of Bulows: He who cannot sing, be his voice good or bad, should not play the piano either. What did Bulow mean by this? He did not mean that every movement and part of a Beethoven sonata should be sung before it is played. But that nobody can play it well if he does not feel and know where the essence of the melody is, and if he cannot bring it to life with his voice whatever his voice may be like.[32]

Most singing teachers and chorus masters believe in controlling the pitch of the voice by the piano. But singing depends on the acoustically correct "natural" intervals, and not on the tempered system. Even a perfectly tuned piano can never be a criterion of singing, not to speak of the ever "out-of-tune" pianos available at schools and rehearsal rooms. Yet how often have I found chorus masters attempting to restore the shaky intonation of their choirs with the help of a mistuned piano![33]

We must look forward to the time when all people in all lands are brought together through singing, and when there is a universal harmony.[34]

Instruments

The composer also alleged that instrumental instruction should incorporate the use of singing.

Understand once and for all what this is all about: the psychological procedure of our whole music making is faulty—it must be inverted. So far it is the fingers that have run ahead, with the head and heart hobbling after them. The way for the true musician is the opposite: he starts with the head and the heart and from there directs the fingers, the larynx, or whatever instrument. It is because they do not go about it in this way that so many of our pianists play mechanically. When someone is twenty or thirty they announce that he has no talent. But perhaps if he had tried to make music with his voice when he was six years old, he might have come closer to the soul of the music and his piano playing might have been more musical as a result.[35]

We should not allow anyone even to go near an instrument until he or she can read and sing correctly. It is our only hope that one day our musicians will be able also to "sing" on their instruments.[36]

Kodály Today

> To teach a child an instrument without first giving him preparatory training and without developing singing, reading and dictating to the highest level along with the playing is to build upon sand.[37]

> I heard the finest singing in the world by the world's worst voice—Toscannini [sic], when at rehearsal he demonstrated a phrase in his blunt hoarse voice for his players and singers. And this is why they could sing so beautifully under his baton. His most frequent comment to the orchestra was "Cantare! Cantare!"[38]

Kodály did acknowledge appropriate and tasteful song accompaniments: "But it is an even greater 'pleasure and amusement' for children if they accompany themselves on their instruments. . . . The xylophone is not so bad either. I shall never forget the charming sight and sound in Nagyvárad in 1942 of forty children playing the xylophone simultaneously."[39] Kodály believed that students should perform simple melodies on instruments: "However, these pieces can be played on any other instrument or can be sung unaccompanied, wordlessly or with a text if a suitable one can be invented."[40]

Movement
Additionally, the composer was convinced that movement through singing games and folk dancing is critical for the music development of children.

> Children's singing games allow a more profound insight than anything else into the primeval age of folk music. Singing connected with movement and action is a much more ancient and, at the same time, more complex phenomenon than is a simple song. It offers much more hitherto untouched material to science for all kinds of investigation than any other branch of folk music, on which its thorough examination can also throw new light.[41]

Children as Critical Thinkers: Music Literacy
Kodály believed that all students should become musically literate, that is, they should be able to read and write music with ease, comparable to the ease with which they read and write their own language: "I was always amazed how an intelligent adult was willing without the slightest protest to let himself be treated like a parrot. A choir which has even half an idea of reading will in a given period of time learn ten times as many works and its perspectives will become ten times as broad as one which repeats like a parrot by ear."[42]

Kodály inspired many musicians and teachers to work with folk materials and to analyze them from a musicological and pedagogical perspective. Together they determined melodic intervals, rhythms, meters, and forms that are common in Hungarian music. After careful analysis, a pedagogical sequence was established that introduced the most common musical elements first; through performance these elements would be familiar to students. This approach differed from the older subject-logic approach to music learning in which the material was taught in a manner that is logical in terms of content but did not take into account how children learn. For example, rhythm was often taught by explaining note values—"a whole note receives four beats"—and then dividing the whole into half notes, quarter notes, and so on. The Kodály concept advocates beginning the study of rhythm with rhythmic and melodic patterns most common to children's singing games and chants. Thus, patterns of quarter and eighth notes are taught in the context of music that the child has already experienced in many ways.

As Kodály's ideas were developed, Hungarian teachers began using teaching techniques that have sometimes been thought to constitute a "Kodály method." These techniques include use of the moveable *do* system of solmization, use of hand signs to indicate the notes of the scale, rhythmic syllables, and a form of musical shorthand derived from the solfège and rhythmic systems. These devices were adapted by Kodály's colleagues and found useful in teaching music to children. However, they did not originate with Kodály-based teaching.

The moveable *do* or tonic-solfa system can be traced to the eleventh century, when Guido d'Arezzo used it for musical instruction. An Englishman, John Curwen, developed the hand signs used to represent the notes of the scale in 1862. Hand signs offer physical and visual reinforcement of the musical sound. Musical shorthand, or stick notation, was developed in Hungary and is simply a rapid way of writing music without the use of the staff.

It is the use of these teaching techniques in combination with the folk song, art music, and recently composed music in a child-centered curriculum where children develop their critical-thinking skills through discovery-based learning that makes the Kodály concept of music education unique.

> For the roots of science and of art are the same. Each, in its own way, reflects the world. The basic conditions: sharp powers of observation, precise expression of the life observed, and raising it to a higher synthesis. And the foundation of scientific and artistic greatness is also the same: just man, vir Justus.[43]

> On the basis of what has been said, the characteristics of a good musician can be summarized as follows: a well trained ear, a well trained intelligence, a well trained heart, and a well trained hand. All four must develop together, in a constant equilibrium. As one lags behind or rushes ahead, there is something wrong.[44]

The aspect of literacy is addressed as children develop critical-thinking skills. Music literacy goals may include teaching specific rhythmic and melodic elements as well as developing students' reading and writing skills. Music tools such as rhythmic and solfège syllables and numbers should be used to develop music reading and writing skills. When teaching according to the Kodály concept, we derive all rhythmic and melodic elements from song material. Activities for the development of inner hearing (audiation), music memory skills, form and analysis skills, and harmonic skills should also be included in the curriculum.

Children as Creative Human Beings: Music Composition and Improvisation

Music improvisation, the art of composing extemporaneously, and composition, the art of formulating and writing music, are indispensable components of a music education. Kodály believed that students should possess a well-trained ear to engage in music improvisation and composition: "How often has it happened that pupils studying composition without a trained ear write down something quite different from what they have imagined?. . . . Here, too, we have seen often enough what a struggle the study of composition, and even of simple harmony, is for one who failed to learn the reading and writing of music early enough."[45]

Two types of improvisation and composition activities are used in the music classroom: one is where students improvise a rhythm or melody without identifying the pitches or sounds being used, and the other is where students consciously use specific rhythmic or melodic elements. The instructor who teaches music inspired by the Kodály concept uses improvisation and composition so students will develop the ability to engage in the creative process as well as understand the stylistic elements of a piece of music. Students who are able to improvise and compose music based on the typical forms and melodic and rhythmic patterns of folk songs and art music have developed a greater feeling and understanding for a musical style.

Activities for developing students' improvisation and composition skills should be included in a music curriculum. These activities need to be correlated to the repertoire being studied and presented sequentially.

Children as Informed Audience Members and Listeners

Music listening is an important component of the Kodály concept. No matter what the activity in the music classroom, children are constantly encouraged to listen when they perform or create, or while they are developing their critical thinking skills. Of course the music teacher also needs to give students guided listening activities, which enables them to form connections between the song repertoire they are singing and art music.

Kodály believed that there was a significant connection between folk music and art music: "For instance, Haydn, the best to begin with, has manifest connection with folksong, but even in many works of Mozart it is easy to recognize the sublimated Austrian folk songs. Beethoven's many themes are also folk-songlike."[46]

He stressed the importance of listening for the music student.

> It is not enough to listen once, fleetingly, to great works; one has to prepare for them and to follow the notes through the pages before and after hearing them in order to implant them abidingly in one's mind.[47]

> It is the richness of both the musical experiences themselves and the memory of them that makes a good musician. Individual singing plus listening to music (by means of active and passive well-arranged experiences) develops the ear to such an extent that one understands music one has heard with as much clarity as though one were looking at a score; if necessary—and if time permits—one should be able

to reproduce such a score. This, and certainly no less, is what we expect from the student of a language; and music is a manifestation of the human spirit similar to a language. Its great men have conveyed to mankind things unutterable in any other language. If we do not want such things to remain dead treasures, we must do our utmost to make the greatest possible number of people understand their secrets.[48]

Activities for developing students' listening skills should be included in the curriculum. These activities should be closely correlated to the students' knowledge of rhythmic and melodic elements and used in practicing melodic or rhythmic elements. Listening activities may include songs sung or performed by the music teacher or other students, as well as performance of repertoire by professional musicians. The curriculum should include specific listening repertoire that incorporates or reinforces musical elements and concepts at each grade level. Provide children with additional information about the piece of music. Consider talking about the form, instrumentation, and a brief biographical sketch of the composer.

The Kodály Method or Concept of Music Education

Zoltán Kodály's philosophy of music education inspired the Kodály Method or the Kodály concept of music education. Kodaly's students and colleagues helped develop the approach to teaching. The method is a comprehensive approach to developing music skills.

Here are the hallmarks of the Kodály method, shaped by Kodály's philosophy of music education.

Caliber of Music Teachers

Teachers need to possess excellent musicianship and conducting skills and have considerable knowledge of music repertoire to successfully develop a Kodály-inspired music program.

Singing

Singing is the essence of the Kodály concept, and tuneful singing is the foundation of this approach to music education. Everyone possesses a voice and can be taught to sing tunefully; therefore learning music through this approach has no restrictions. Aspects of singing should be taught before formal instrumental lessons. Singing allows children to develop the skill of audiation.

Repertoire

A child should be empowered to see his or her background with pride and respect. Respect comes from knowledge. A key component of anyone's cultural heritage is folk music; this music includes children's songs and games. Such repertoire includes the basic rhythmic and melodic building blocks of music, and these building blocks can be used to make connections to all styles of music. A music curriculum should include certain materials:

- Folk songs and games of the American culture and backgrounds of the students in your school
- Traditional children's songs and games
- Folk songs of other cultures
- Art music (music of the masters)
- Pedagogical exercises written by composers
- Recently composed music written by excellent composers

Reading and Writing

Teaching children how to read and write music is another essential component of the Kodály approach. Practitioners of the Kodály method use a variety of tools to develop a child's fluency in reading and writing music. (These tools are discussed in more detail in Chapter 4 of this book.) The teaching tools used include

- Relative solmization, moveable *do*, where the tonic note is *do* in major and *la* in minor
- Hand signs
- Rhythm syllables

Sequencing

A vital feature of the Kodály concept is the teacher's ability to sequence materials and present musical concepts and elements to children derived from the students' musical repertoire. This is an experience-based approach to learning.

Building the Framework of a Curriculum Based on the Multiple Dimensions of Music

When designing a curriculum based on the Kodály philosophy of music education, include:

- Children as stewards of their cultural heritage: Develop children's knowledge of music repertoire, to include
    - Folk songs and games of the American culture
    - Traditional children's songs and games
    - Folk songs of other cultures
    - Art music (music of the masters)

Pedagogical exercises written by composers
Recently composed music written by excellent composers

- Children as performers: Develop children's performance skills through singing, playing instruments, and movement.
- Children as critical thinkers: Develop children's knowledge and critical thinking skills about music by expanding reading and writing skills. To do this successfully, we need to develop children's ability to use musical tools such as solfège syllables, hand signs, and rhythm syllables. These tools enable them to deconstruct the repertoire they are singing and advance reading and writing skills.
- Children as creative human beings: Develop children's ability to improvise music. This is often a natural skill for children, and as they learn to read and write music and understand the forms of the repertoire they are singing, it gives them a model to imitate in their own compositions.
- Children as informed audience members: Active listening skills need to be developed in the music classroom. There is a distinction between entertainment and listening. Often children are not used to actively listening to music; many feel more comfortable being entertained. Teachers need to help students cross this divide.

Music education, to quote the author Daniel H. Pink, is "fundamental, not ornamental."[49] Learning music gives children many opportunities to perform music, to become stewards of their cultural heritage, to develop critical thinking skills (reading and writing music), to have opportunities to be creative human beings, and to be informed listeners and audience members. Through these multiple dimensions of their music education, children develop skills that not only will make them more accomplished musicians but will also prepare them for life as citizens of the twenty-first century.

Sample of a Grade 1 Music Curriculum Shaped by the Kodály Concept of Music Education

The following is a sample grade 1 curriculum that is shaped by our understanding of the philosophy of Zoltán Kodály. Each section of the curriculum will be discussed in greater detail in subsequent chapters. We have suggested a music curriculum as the teaching demands placed on music teachers differ from one school district to another. The goal of this curriculum is to furnish a model for constructing your own curriculum based on the Kodály philosophy of music education and on current successful models of the Kodály teaching. Once you gain an understanding of the Kodály philosophy and the approach to teaching, you will be able to make modifications to suit your own particular teaching situations. Our goal is to show how the major tenants of the Kodály philosophy and current practices in teaching music using techniques associated with the Kodály method can shape a music curriculum.

Kodály Today

Outline List

I. Children as Stewards of Their Cultural and Musical Heritage: Repertoire

Children experience singing a repertoire of music that includes folk music from a variety of cultures, art music, patriotic music, recently composed music, and seasonal music. This exposure deepens children's understanding of the various styles of music, giving them tools to understand diverse music cultures and styles. Strive to offer an historical context for all repertoire being studied.

Children will grow to recognize how different types of music share the same "building blocks" as well as what makes each music composition unique. Understanding a particular music style helps students develop their own creative style. This is an invaluable and unique aspect of music education as it develops children's cultural knowledge and understanding.

Expand song repertoire to add to students' knowledge of songs and games, folk music of the children's culture, art music, and recently composed music.

II. Children as Performers: Performance

A child's music education should begin with singing appropriate music repertoire that is developmentally appropriate for students. Children sing while performing singing games and singing part music, and they develop their knowledge of music literacy through singing as well as using the voice to create their own music. Singing is the glue that connects all of the music skills and knowledge taught in the music classroom. Singing develops the most significant and essential skill in music: the ability to think in sound. This ability leads to significant gains in a child's ability to perform musically on an instrument. When children have the ability to think in sound, they are able to play an instrument with musical understanding. Playing a music instrument is more than the technical aspects of learning the instrument; it involves learning how to translate an aural image of a piece into acoustic sound. Learning the technique required for playing an instrument is only one part of the process necessary for translating notation into sound. A child's aural image of the piece of music will dictate how to perform the piece of music. Children also begin to develop their movement and conducting skills in this grade. It is essential that there be an organic connection between singing, instrumental, movement, and conducting skills.

1. Singing tunefully
   A. Sing songs independently and tunefully in a six-note range.
   B. Be familiar with a varied repertoire of at least thirty folk songs and singing games, classical music, and recently composed music (a few songs will be sufficient here).
   C. Know by memory ten to fifteen songs and be able to sing them with solfège and rhythm syllables.
   D. Perform all songs with accurate intonation, clear diction, clear head tone, musical phrasing/breathing, appropriate dynamics, and tempi.
   E. Perform songs using appropriate tempo, including allegro and largo, and dynamics, including forte and piano.

2. Movement
    A. Explore music making with body percussion.
    B. Perform acting-out games
    C. Perform chasing games.
    D. Perform winding games.
    E. Perform simple line games.
    F. Perform circle games.
    G. Improvise words and movement to known songs.
    H. Explore games, activities, and movement in personal space or general space.
3. Instruments
    A. Play instruments independently or in a group.
    B. Play ethnic music with unpitched instruments and body percussion.
    C. Students demonstrate first grade melodic and rhythmic concepts on classroom instruments.
    D. Students accompany classroom singing on classroom instruments.
4. Part work (activities may be combined with instruments)
    A. Sing songs antiphonally.
    B. Practice singing intervals simultaneously with solfège syllables and hand signs. Note: the intervals are not named, but simply performed (*so, mi, la*), and intervals are formed by them from known songs (*so-mi, mi-so, so-la, la-so, mi-la, la-mi*).
    C. Accompany a song with a rhythmic ostinato using quarter and eighth notes and quarter note rests.
    D. Accompany a song with a melodic ostinato using *la, so,* and *mi*.
    E. Chant simple rhythmic canons derived from the rhythms of familiar songs.
    F. Sing simple melodic canons derived from the melodic motifs of familiar songs.
    G. Perform two-part rhythmic exercises based on rhythmic motifs of known songs.
    H. Perform two-part melodic exercises based on the rhythmic and melodic motifs of known songs.
    I. Perform simple folksongs in canon.
5. Conducting
    A. Students conduct in duple meter.

III. Children as Critical Thinkers and Problem Solvers: Music Literacy

Learning how to read and write music is closely connected to understanding stylistic features. In order to develop children's music literacy skills, it is important that they study a core repertoire of songs that share similar rhythmic and melodic characteristics. Each piece of music studied is an opportunity for the teacher to share with students the commonalities between the works, and it also introduces students to new music elements. This can be accomplished through developing children's reading and writing of music.

Kodály Today

As critical thinkers, children will use an inquiry-based approach to learn how to read and write music.

We approach the teaching of every new music concept and element as a problem to be solved. In our approach to learning and instruction, the teacher is guided to ask questions about a new concept or element being studied. What are the characteristics of the new concept or element? For children, how can you create a representation of the new music concept or element? Analyze your representation with the help of a friend and draw conclusions about your representations. Share your findings with the class about what you discovered. How do we notate a new rhythmic or melodic element? Children will gather kinesthetic, aural, and visual information about a new music concept or element before they learn the process of how to notate this new element. Part of the problem-solving activities for children is to engage them in a process where they create their own notations for a new element and try to capture the characteristics of the new element through their own notations. The act of taking music apart, studying those parts, and then putting it all back together again to perform repertoire more musically teaches children how to understand music more thoughtfully, but it can be applied to other subjects as well.

Critical thinking is applied through reading and writing music to develop music literacy skills. First grade students will gain fluency using rhythm syllables for quarter and two eighth notes, quarter rest and solfège syllables for *so, mi,* and *la*. They will learn how to read and write known rhythms and melodies, sight-read new melodies, and write new songs using stick notation, traditional notation, and staff notation. At the same time they will also develop their inner hearing, knowledge of form, and memory skills while enhancing their music literacy skills.

1. Rhythm elements (duple meter, quarter, eighth notes, and quarter note rest)
    A. Identify steady beat in musical performances, and faster or slower.
    B. Perform songs with rhythm syllables.
    C. Perform rhythmic ostinati.
    D. Perform rhythmic canons.
    E. Perform two-part rhythmic exercises.
    F. Recognize tunes from clapped rhythm patterns.
    G. Identify a skipping song and a marching song.
2. Melodic elements (*so mi la*)
    A. Perform songs with solfège syllables and hand signs.
    B. Perform melodic ostinato.
    C. Perform canons.
    D. Perform two-part melodic exercises from a teacher's hand signs.
    E. Recognize tunes hummed by a teacher.
    F. Recognize a tune by reading a teacher's hand signs.
3. Reading and writing of rhythmic elements
    A. Know names and written symbols for quarter notes, eighth notes, quarter note rest, accented beat, and bar lines. Conduct in duple meter. (This should

Building the Framework of a Music Curriculum

be the final step of learning rhythms. We suggest that students be guided to sing repertoire fluently with rhythm syllables before being taught the technical names of notes.)
  B. Read well-known rhythmic patterns with stick notation and traditional rhythmic notation.
  C. Read a two-part rhythmic exercise.
  D. Write well-known rhythmic patterns with stick notation and traditional rhythmic notation.
  E. Write rhythmic patterns from memory or when dictated by the teacher in stick notation and traditional rhythmic notation.
4. Reading and writing of melodic elements
  A. Know the names and written syllables for the solfège syllables *so, mi,* and *la.*
  B. Read well-known melodic patterns with traditional rhythmic notation and solfège syllables as well on staff notation.
  C. Read a two-part melodic exercise from notation.
  D. Write well-known melodic patterns with traditional rhythmic notation and solfège syllables as well on staff notation.
  E. Write melodic patterns found in focus songs from memory or when dictated by the teacher using stick and solfège syllables, traditional notation, and solfège syllables or staff notation.
5. Inner hearing
  A. Silently sing melodic motifs or melody from the teacher's hand signs.
  B. Silently sing known songs with rhythmic syllables.
  C. Silently sing known songs with melodic syllables.
  D. Silently read full or partial rhythms or melodies written in traditional notation with solfège syllables or staff notation.
  E. Sing back short known melodic or rhythmic motives from memory using text (if the student recognizes the song it is abstracted from), rhythm syllables, or solfège syllables.
6. Form
  A. Recognize same, similar, or different phrases in a song either aurally or through music reading.
  B. Recognize repeated musical motifs that are the same and the ones that are different.
  C. Use letters to label repetition and contract in simple songs: ab, aaba, or abac patterns.
  D. Use repeat signs correctly in reading and writing.
7. Musical memory
  A. Echo four- and eight-beat rhythm patterns clapped by the instructor with rhythm syllables.
  B. Echo four- and eight-beat solfège patterns sung by the instructor with solfège and hand signs.

Kodály Today

   C. Memorize short melodies through hand signs.
   D. Memorize rhythm patterns of four or eight beats from known songs from traditional rhythmic notation.
   E. Memorize melodic patterns of four or eight beats from known songs from traditional rhythmic notation with solfège syllables or from staff notation.

IV. Children as Creative Human Beings: Improvisation and Composition

When children learn how to express themselves through improvisation and composition, they learn more about who they are and what they are capable of accomplishing. The act of improvising and composing music gives a child the opportunity to engage creative abilities. We believe that it is important for children to develop their own creative skills by manipulating known rhythmic or melodic elements before they begin to create their own composition. This curriculum guides children to be creative in a musical context. They should be provided with various rhythmic and melodic improvisation exercises, including individual and class improvisation or composition of movement, singing, and playing on classroom instruments. Students are guided to improvise with short rhythmic and melodic patterns derived from known repertoire to create new versions of repertoire studied.

1. Rhythmic improvisation based on the rhythmic building blocks of song repertoire
   A. Improvise rhythm patterns, of four or eight beats, by clapping and saying rhythm syllables.
   B. Improvise rhythm patterns of four or eight beats using rhythm instruments.
   C. Improvise a new rhythm to one measure or more of a well-known song written in traditional notation by either clapping or playing a classroom instrument.
   D. Improvise question-and-answer motives using known rhythm patterns.
   E. Improvise to a given form.
2. Melodic improvisation (based on the melodic building blocks of song repertoire)
   A. Improvise melodic patterns of four or eight beats by singing with solfège and hand signs.
   B. Improvise melodic patterns of four or eight beats using barred instruments.
   C. Improvise short musical motives (*la-so-mi*) using hand signs, hand staff, or body signs.
   D. Improvise pentatonic bichord and trichord (*so-mi-la*) melodies to simple four- or eight-beat rhythms using the voice or a barred instrument.
   E. Improvise a melody to one measure or more of a well-known song.
   F. Improvise question-and-answer motives using known melodic patterns.

V. Children as Informed Audience Members: Listening

Children are surrounded every day with music from a variety of media sources. Our responsibility as music educators is to help students become critical listeners so that they

Building the Framework of a Music Curriculum

can identify and distinguish the various meanings and purposes of music. Children need to appreciate that the music they listen to with their friends (social music) can differ in purpose from music repertoire studied in music classes. Of course, students must eventually understand that all music can fall into two categories: good music or bad music. It is our job as educators to help children differentiate between good and bad music and allow them to make their own listening choices. We need to develop their ability to listen actively to a variety of styles of music and understand the stylistic elements of this repertoire. However, we strongly believe that the music repertoire we choose to use in our music curriculum should reflect the same type of processes that literature teachers use when they select book to be read in a literature class. Although there can certainly be disagreement as to what constitutes quality repertoire, there is a general consensus as to what makes great literature.

1. Expand listening repertoire and revisit kindergarten musical concepts.
   A. Distinguish among singing, inner, whispering, calling, and speaking voices.
   B. Recognize phrase forms (same or different) in classroom song repertoire, folk music, and masterworks.
   C. Recognize known rhythmic features in classroom song repertoire, folk music, and masterworks, including quarter, eighth notes, and quarter note rest.
   D. Recognize known melodic features in classroom song repertoire, folk music, and masterworks.
   E. Develop awareness of expressive controls—that is, dynamics, tempo, timbre—and their distinctive characteristics in masterworks of various historical periods. Use basic music terminology in describing changes in tempo, including allegro and largo, and dynamics, including forte and piano; students should be able to recognize comparatives, fast-slow, loud-soft.
   F. Distinguish same/different between beat/rhythm, higher/lower, louder/softer, faster/slower in musical performances
   G. Recognize and identify aurally the instrument families.
   H. Recognize and identify aurally one instrument from the instrument families
   I. Practice appropriate audience behavior during live performances.

Music Philosophy Prompt Questions

Here are prompt questions to help you tailor the curriculum above to your own specific needs. It is important that your curriculum reflect your teaching philosophy, your personality, and your own content knowledge or expertise. Remember also to reinforce the vision and mission of the school with your music programs, and review your state standards for music education.

- Where are you coming from?
    What is your philosophy of music education?
    What role does the Kodály concept of music play in the development of your curriculum?

What are the mission and vision of your school?
How do you reinforce the mission of your school in your music curriculum?
How do you and your music students become advocates for music?
How do you develop the teaching of music in your school so that music is treated as a core subject area?
- What repertoire do you use in the classroom?
  How do you select music repertoire for your curriculum?
  Do you use this repertoire to develop all the children's music skills in performance, playing instruments, music literacy, improvisation, and composition as well preparing them to become critical consumers of music?
  How will you encourage students to use the known rhythmic and melodic building blocks to create and build musical compositions, bolstering critical-thinking skills and creativity?
  How will music benefit students' overall academic achievement?
  How does your classroom reinforce the core curriculum and the vision of the campus?
  How do you assess student growth in musicianship skills and music literacy throughout the year?
  How does your classroom embrace cultural diversity though songs?
  What is the role of foreign folk, art, and popular music being brought in by children of various cultures, and how do you use it to draw parallels with other genres in your class?
- What music skills and content will you develop in each grade?
  How will you find a balance among the skills of singing, creative movement, playing instruments, reading and writing music, composing and improvising, and listening to music?
  How do you create music lesson plans that will develop all of a child's music skills?
- How do you tailor your teaching to various student populations with specific learning needs?
  What are some ways in which you meet the various needs of bilingual and transitioning students to strengthen their primary language and promote acquisition of the English language through repertoire?
  How do you use a broad range of music genres and styles to reach various populations of your campus and promote a lasting love and respect for all music?
  How do you use a broad range of learning styles to reach various populations of your campus?
  What is the place of technology in the music classroom?
  How do you ensure a safe environment that encourages learning?
- How do you keep your teaching relevant to modern music styles and genres?
  How do you incorporate modern styles and genres of music in the music classroom?
- What is needed to encourage children, faculty, staff, and the larger community to embrace music learning at your campus?

How do you encourage your faculty, staff, and administration to support your music program?

What steps will you take to ensure your philosophy of music learning is supported by your campus?

How do you foster relationships on your campus?

Linking a Music Curriculum Based on the Kodály Concept to the National Content Standards for Music Education

A music curriculum built on the Kodály concept of music education aligns with the national content standards for music education.[50] Here is a brief summation of how a curriculum built on the philosophy of Kodály is reflective of the national content standards. Each standard is cited along with a brief overview of how it relates to a Kodály curriculum.

Content Standard One: Singing, Alone and with Others, a Varied Repertoire of Music

Singing is the foundation of all learning in the Kodály classroom. Through singing students are guided to discover and subsequently internalize the elements of music. Students learn a varied repertoire of multicultural music, classical music, and recently composed music through singing. The curriculum engages students in group and solo singing, call and response songs, melodic ostinati, rounds, canons, partner songs, and art music.

Content Standard Two: Performing on Instruments, Alone and with Others, a Varied Repertoire of Music

Kodály teachers use a variety of rhythm instruments as reinforcement of beat and rhythmic concepts. Melody instruments such as barred instruments and step bells are used to perform borduns and ostinati and may be used to practice melodic concepts. Recorders, guitar, and auto harp may be introduced into classroom activities once students have reached a level of maturation that enables them to perform on the instruments. In keeping with the main tenets of the Kodály concept, students should first sing the patterns they perform on instruments.

Content Standard Three: Improvising Melodies, Variations, and Accompaniments

Students use their knowledge of rhythmic and melodic elements as well as their stylistic knowledge of folk music as the basis for their improvisation activities and compositions in the classroom. Instructors engage students in myriad improvisation activities such as improvising rhythmic or melodic answers to questions, improvising within a given form, and creating melodic and rhythmic ostinati. These activities also permit assessment of student understanding of musical elements and musical styles as well as their skill of performance.

Content Standard Four: Composing and Arranging Music Within Specific Guidelines

Students in a Kodály classroom learn to inner-hear music (audiation, the skill of thinking music) before they write it down rather than using a computer or instruments to first create the sounds they write. Activities may include learning to create melodies to a given text, learning to arrange a folk song for two voices, and composing a new song within given compositional parameters.

Content Standard Five: Reading and Writing Music

Kodály-trained students learn to read and write music using stick or staff notation, solfège and rhythm syllables, and hand signs. Beginning reading and writing exercises and examples include simple pentatonic, pentachord, and hexachord melodies and progress to diatonic major, minor, and modal melodies as well as two- and three-part compositions.

Content Standard Six: Listening to, Analyzing, and Describing Music

Kodály-trained students are guided to listen, analyze, and describe music using their knowledge of music elements. Young students are taught how to listen for elements in a piece of music and how to describe these elements. Instructors may focus on analysis when they sight-sing additional pieces of music that include the same elements in listening examples. Both rhythmic and melodic dictation strategies include identifying the forms and compositional elements of musical examples.

Content Standard Seven: Evaluating Music and Music Performance

Because singing and performance are at the heart of the Kodály classroom, instructors and students continuously evaluate their performance. Knowledge of musical elements improves the stylistic knowledge of the repertoire studied. The instructor may supply assessment rubrics for performance that can be used by students for evaluation.

Content Standard Eight: Understanding Relationships Between Music, the Other Arts, and Disciplines Outside the Arts

Kodály-inspired music education develops students' kinesthetic abilities as well as spatial, mathematic, and reading aptitudes in the music classroom, skills that are readily transferred to other areas of the curriculum.

Content Standard Nine: Understanding Music in Relation to History and Culture

Kodály-trained students study the folk music and art music of numerous cultures and eras. Children learn the text of folk songs in their original language—something that permits the music instructor as well as classroom teachers to discuss historical information and make connections to related disciplines and art forms. The study of art music includes history and an understanding of the various style periods common to other art forms: visual arts, architecture, and dance.

The Kodály Concept and the Common Core Standards

Many school districts are now adopting the Common Core Standards. These standards "provide a consistent, clear understanding of what students are expected to learn, so teachers and parents know what they need to do to help them. The standards are designed to be robust and relevant to the real world, reflecting the knowledge and skills that our young people need for success in college and careers. With American students fully prepared for the future, our communities will be best positioned to compete successfully in the global economy."[51]

At the time of publication of this book, there are no published common core guidelines for music; but we can begin to intuit what these new standards will look like for music. So how do the common goals relate to music education? Some of the main trends in common core conversations are seen in the emerging guidelines discussed here.

Children should engage "in deep, sustained study of a limited number of works of art (paralleling the ELA [English Language Arts] Standards' recommendation of studying fewer texts in greater depth), and to utilize the arts as powerful tools to develop and refine skills of observation and interpretation that are a cornerstone of the Common Core."[52] What is interesting about these observations is the fact that music teachers, especially those following a Kodály curriculum, should be aware that they are in compliance with Common Core Standards. Therefore we should articulate that we are already following the standards, as the activities in teaching music according to the Kodály concept are directed toward developing students'

- Knowledge of music repertoire
- Performance abilities
- Knowledge of music literacy
- Ability to improvise music
- Ability to listen to music in an informed manner

Each of these Common Core Standards can be translated into knowledge and skills that are taught in each grade. The work of Wiggins and McTighe (2011, 2012) presents a framework as to how standards can be used for developing curriculum in the classroom.[53] They suggest in their work that teachers unpack Common Core Standards into (1) long-term transfer goals, (2) overarching understandings, (3) overarching essential questions, and (4) a set of recurring cornerstone tasks.

According to Wiggins and McTighe, transfer goals refer to what students should be able to do with the information they acquire in their learning. Overarching understandings are what learners will need to transfer their knowledge to new situations; overarching essential questions allow students to make meaning and develop learning skills. Cornerstone tasks are intended to engage students in applying their knowledge and skills in an authentic and relevant context.

New knowledge acquired in the music classroom is used to understand the music repertoire being performed in the classroom. Since the repertoire used throughout the curriculum becomes more complex in each grade, student's knowledge of performance, music literacy, improvisation, and listening skills also develop. This direction in teaching also allows students to transfer the knowledge gained in the music class and participate in a musical life after graduation as performers, composers, and informed audience members. And perhaps this should be the point of developing a music curriculum: it should be relevant for the musical future of our children.

For example, teachers following a curriculum based on the Kodály concept have always adhered to the principle that children need to be exposed to artistic repertoire beginning with folk music; the skills and knowledge they develop as performers, improvisers, and listeners enable them to understand other types of musical repertoire. In this book we advocate that teachers use an organic orientation to teaching. We begin with artistic materials and work with children to understand how the materials are constructed. In doing so, children learn the foundations of music literacy, understanding how to read and write music. When students understand how repertoire is constructed, it provides a model for creating their own improvisations and compositions. Knowledge of how pieces of music are constructed develops the ability to become more informed audience members and to appreciate diverse styles of music.

Teachers will also learn that the model of learning and instruction in this book develops a child's ability to observe and interpret; these are key components of any learning process. Students also learn to become independent learners because of the scaffolding furnished by the music teacher. The models for developing lessons include stated music learning outcomes. The outcomes promote sequential learning and music skills. All music outcomes are performance-based. Students are guided to demonstrate the essential knowledge and skills of the curriculum with their own singing voice. This becomes the foundation for assessment in the music classroom. But knowledge of music is always developed as a communal activity, beginning with singing and students working collaboratively together to solve music problems and strengthen their own music skills and abilities.

Lesson Planning

Now that we have created a sample curriculum, we can develop lesson plan outcomes and lessons for teaching music. We advise that your lesson focus on

Building the Framework of a Music Curriculum

- Developing students' knowledge of repertoire: teach a new song.
- Developing students' performance skills: learning to sing, play instruments, and move to music.
- Developing students' critical-thinking skills: teach music concepts and elements to children according to their frequency of occurrence in the song material they are singing.
- Developing students' creative skills: teach students how to improvise and compose.
- Developing students' listening skills: teach students how to actively listen to music.

We address all of these goals in detail throughout the book. Here we begin the process of lesson planning. A primary task for music instructors is to teach basic rhythmic and melodic elements. To accomplish this successfully, students need to be guided through a variety of experiential activities (preparation activities) before learning how to identify sounds and labeling them with rhythmic or melodic syllables, or learning the notation of these sounds (practice activities). Once learned, students can apply this information (practice) to expand their musical skills through reading, writing, and improvisation.

Lesson planning and acquiring music literacy skills are closely intertwined. Teaching a musical element takes eight steps.

Preparation
1. Prepare the learning through kinesthetic activities.
2. Prepare the learning through aural activities.
3. Prepare the learning through visual activities.

Presentation
4. Present the solfège syllable or rhythm label for the new sound.
5. Present the notation for the new sound.

Practice
6. Incorporate the new element (now identified as a familiar element) into the practices of reading.
7. Incorporate the new element (now identified as a familiar element) into the practices of writing.
8. Incorporate the new element (now identified as a familiar element) into the practices of improvisation.

To undertake these steps, there are two basic lesson plan designs: preparation/practice lessons and presentation lessons.

In a preparation/practice lesson, we prepare one musical element and practice another. For example, when preparing a new element B (steps 1, 2, and 3) we also practice a familiar element A (steps 6, 7, and 8). Once we have taught steps 1, 2, and 3 for element B in a preparation/practice lesson, we address steps 4 and 5 for element B in presentation lessons.

Key Components of Lesson Plan Designs

Here, in Table 1.1, is the Basic Preparation/Practice Lesson Plan Design we use throughout the book. In each chapter we will add to this basic lesson plan design to incorporate and reflect the information in the chapter. We use a lesson plan structure that divides all lessons into three sections: *introduction, core activities,* and *closure.* This design can be modified to accommodate the learning objectives for developing children's skills as performers, critical thinkers, improvisers, composers, listeners, and stewards of their cultural and musical heritage.

Table 1.2 is an explanation of the segments of a basic preparation/practice lesson plan design.

Table 1.1   Components of the Basic Preparation/Practice Lesson Plan Design

INTRODUCTION	
Performance and demonstration of known musical concepts and elements	
CORE ACTIVITIES	
Acquisition of repertoire	
Preparation of a rhythmic or melodic element	Element B: this is section of the lesson is used for steps 1–3 of preparing a new element
Creative movement	
Practice and performance of musical skills	Element B: this section of the lesson is used for step 6
CLOSURE	
Review and summation	

Table 1.2   Explanation of the Preparation/Practice Lesson Plan

LESSON SECTION 1: THE INTRODUCTION	
Demonstration of known musical concepts and elements	This segment of the lesson includes vocal warm-up exercises, singing known songs, developing tuneful singing, and singing known songs with rhythmic or melodic syllables. During this section of the lesson, we address music learning outlined in the music curriculum under the title of "Children as Stewards of Their Cultural Heritage: Repertoire" and "Children as Performers: Performance."

Table 1.2 Continued

LESSON SECTION 2: CORE ACTIVITIES	
This section involves acquisition of repertoire and performance of new concepts or elements.	
Acquisition of repertoire	Teaching a new song serves two purposes. First, it expands students' repertoire, and second, the new song should also include rhythmic or melodic concepts or elements that will be addressed in upcoming lessons. We present new repertoire for a variety of reasons. Sometimes we wish to teach a song simply to develop students' singing ability. Sometimes a song may be taught because we need to provide a musical context for teaching future musical concepts. The teacher may need to teach repertoire for a future performance or concert. During this section of the lesson, we address music learning outlined in the music curriculum under the title "Children as Stewards of Their Cultural Heritage: Repertoire."
Preparation of a new concept or element	Here activities focus on leading students to discover the attributes of a new musical concept or element. The instruction focuses on guiding students through kinaesthetic (step 1), aural (step 2), and visual (step 3) learning activities. During this section of the lesson, we address music learning outlined in the music curriculum under the title "Children as Critical Thinkers." Critical thinking is associated with literacy. Through discovery-based learning children acquire music literacy skills. In this section of the lesson, students are guided to understand the basic rhythmic or melodic building blocks of the song material as well as the formal music structures.
This first period of concentration is followed by a period of relaxation.	
Creative movement	Students learn singing games and folk songs. Activities focus on the sequential development of age-appropriate movement skills through songs and folk games. A sequence for age-appropriate movement skill development is provided in Chapter 3 and in the curriculum under "Movement," in "Children as Performers." These games are used as the foundation for developing creative activities.
This period of relaxation is followed by a second period of concentration.	

(continued)

Table 1.2 Continued

Practice and musical skill development	In this section, the instructor practices the music skills outlined in the music curriculum under the title "Children as Critical Thinkers." This section reinforces known musical elements while focusing on a particular music skill such as reading(step 6), writing (step 7), or improvisation and composition (step 8). Of course we use these skills as anchors for practicing all other music skills such as inner hearing, form, memory, part work, and listening.
LESSON SECTION 3: CLOSURE	
Review and summation	Review the lesson outcomes. Review the new song. Review the lesson content. Review the new song. Students may review known songs or play a game. The instructor may also perform the next new song that will be taught in a subsequent lesson.

Tables 1.3 and 1.4 are the two Basic Presentation Lesson Plan Designs we use throughout the book; we use the first to label sounds with syllables and the second to present the notation (see also Tables 1.5 and 1.6).

Table 1.3 Components of the Basic Presentation Lesson Plan Design for Labeling Sounds with Syllables

INTRODUCTION	
Performance and demonstration of known musical concepts and elements	
CORE ACTIVITIES	
Acquisition of repertoire	
Presentation of a new concept or element	Element B This segment of the lesson is used for step 4
Creative movement	
Presentation of a new concept or element	Element B This segment of the lesson is used for step 4
CLOSURE	
Review and summation	

Table 1.4 Explanation of Presentation Lesson Plan for Labeling Sounds with Syllables

LESSON SECTION 1: THE INTRODUCTION	
Demonstration of known musical concepts and elements	
LESSON SECTION 2: CORE ACTIVITIES	
This section involves acquisition of repertoire and performance of new concepts or elements.	
Acquisition of repertoire	
Presentation of a new concept or element	Using a known song, the instructor presents the label for the new sound with either rhythmic or melodic syllables. Here the instructor will be presenting elements that are outlined in the music curriculum under the title "Children as Critical Thinkers." Students are guided to first label the sound of the new musical element and second to learn the notation of the musical element. They label the sound of the basic rhythmic or melodic building blocks of the song material and subsequently learn the notation.
This first period of concentration is followed by a period of relaxation.	
Movement development Creative movement	
This period of relaxation is followed by a second period of concentration.	
Presentation of a new concept or element	Using another known song, the instructor presents the label for the new sound with either rhythmic or melodic syllables. Here the instructor will be presenting elements that are outlined in the music curriculum under the title "Children as Critical Thinkers." They label the sound of the basic rhythmic or melodic building blocks of the song material.
LESSON SECTION 3: CLOSURE	
Review and summation	Review the lesson outcomes. Review the new song. Review the lesson content. Review the new song. Students may review known songs or play a game. The instructor may also perform the next new song that will be taught in a subsequent lesson.

Kodály Today

Table 1.5 Components of the Basic Presentation Lesson Plan Design for Notating a New Element

INTRODUCTION	
Performance and demonstration of known musical concepts and elements	
CORE ACTIVITIES	
Acquisition of repertoire	
Presentation of a new concept or element	Element B This segment of the lesson is used for step 5
Creative movement	
Presentation of a new concept or element	Element B This segment of the lesson is used for step 5
CLOSURE	
Review and summation	

Table 1.6 Explanation of the Presentation Lesson Plan Design for Notating New Element

LESSON SECTION 1: THE INTRODUCTION	
Demonstration of known musical concepts and elements	
LESSON SECTION 2: CORE ACTIVITIES	
This section involves acquisition of repertoire and performance of new concepts or elements.	
Acquisition of repertoire	
Presentation of a new concept or element	Element B Using a known song, the instructor presents the notation for the new element. Here the instructor will be presenting concepts that are outlined in the music curriculum under the title "Children as Critical Thinkers."
This first period of concentration is followed by a period of relaxation.	
Movement development Creative movement	
This period of relaxation is followed by a second period of concentration.	

(continued)

Table 1.6 Continued

Presentation of a new concept or element	Element B Using another known song, the instructor presents notation for the new element. Here the instructor will be presenting concepts that are outlined in the music curriculum under the title "Children as Critical Thinkers."
LESSON SECTION 3: CLOSURE	
Review and summation	Review the lesson outcomes Review the new song Review the lesson content. Review the new song. Students may review known songs or play a game. The instructor may also perform the next new song that will be taught in a subsequent lesson.

It is important to note that in this process, once we have presented the label and the notation for element, this element now becomes a known element. When we are practicing a known element, we will also be incorporating knowledge of all other known elements in practice activities.

Discussion Questions
1. Explain the value of a music education and the place of music in the school curriculum.
2. As a teacher, do you really need to be guided by a philosophy of music?
3. What is the difference between the Kodály philosophy of music education and the Kodály Method?
4. How would you describe the Kodály concept of music education?
5. Compare and contrast the Kodály concept of music education with other music teaching approaches.
6. Collect four research articles that document the effects of music on cognitive development of students. Discuss your findings with your peers.
7. What are the characteristics of a well-trained music instructor?
8. What are the multiple dimensions of musicianship training?
9. How does Kodály's concept of musicianship training align with the national content standards for music education?
10. Check websites for three school districts. Locate their philosophy statements, and write a summary statement for each district. Do they connect to Kodály's philosophy of music education?

Ongoing Assignment

1. Write a statement of your personal philosophy of music education. How will your philosophy statement change for each grade level you teach?
2. Review the curriculum goals for grades 1 through 5. Compare these curriculum goals with those of another music instructor. Add curriculum goals into section two of your curriculum folder.
3. Using the template of a lesson plan provided in this chapter, determine some teaching activities for each section of the lesson for grades 1 and 3. You may use repertoire that is age-appropriate.

Connections to Grade Handbooks

The information in this chapter is aligned with Chapter 1 in our Kodály grade-level handbooks.

Bibliography

Abernethy, L. A. "Multi-Ethnic Teaching: Some Curricular and Sociomusicological Implications." *Bulletin of the International Kodály Society,* 1982, *7*(1): 10–15.

Ádám, Jenö. "The Influence of Folk Music on Public Musical Education in Hungary." *Studia Musicologica,* 1965, *7*(1–4): 11–18.

Àdàm, J. *Growing in Music with Moveable Do: A Manual of Systematic Vocal Instruction, Grades 1 to 4.* New York: Pannonius Central Service, 1971.

Àdàm, J. *Mòdszeres Ènektanìtàs a Relativ Szolmizàciò Alapjàn (Systematic Vocal Instruction on the Basis of Relative Solmization).* Budapest: Turul, 1944.

Alperson, P. "Music as Philosophy." In *What Is Music? An Introduction to the Philosophy of Music.* University Park: Pennsylvania State University Press, 1994.

Alperson, P., ed. *What Is Music? An Introduction to the Philosophy of Music.* New York: Haven, 1987.

Alperson, P. "What Should One Expect from a Philosophy of Music Education." *Journal of Aesthetic Education,* 1991, *25*(3): 215–229.

Bacon, D. *Hold Fast to Dreams: Writings Inspired by Zoltán Kodály.* Wellesley, MA: Kodály Center of America, 1993.

Bacon, D., Katinka Daniel, Mary Alice Hein, and Lorna Zemke. "Realizing Zoltan Kodaly's Vision in America: Challenges for the 21st Century." From lecture at OAKE National Conference of Cultural and Conference Centre of Kecskemét, San Francisco, Mar. 25, 2004.

Barkòczi, I., and Csaba Pléh. *Psychological Effects of Kodály Conception of Music Education.* Kecskemét, Hungary: Zoltán Kodály Pedagogical Institute of Music, 1978.

Barrett, J. R. "Currents of Change in the Music Curriculum." In *International Handbook of Research in Arts Education,* ed. L. Bresler. Dordrecht: Springer, 2007, pp. 147–161.

Barrett, J. R., C. W. McCoy, and K. K. Veblen. *Sound Ways of Knowing: Music in the Interdisciplinary Curriculum.* New York: Schirmer, 1997.

Barrett, J., and K. Veblen. "Meaningful Connections in a Comprehensive Approach to the Music Curriculum." In *The Oxford Handbook of Music Education,* ed. G. McPherson and G. F. Welch, vol. 1, pp. 361–380. New York: Oxford University Press, 2012.

Bartolome, S. J. "The Virtual Field Experience: An Immersive Approach Toward Multicultural Music Education." *Kodaly Envoy,* 2013, *39*(2): 14–18. Education Research Complete. Web, Mar. 4, 2013.

Battersby, S., and D. Snyder. "Best Practices for Preservice Preparation: Getting a Jump Start on Implementing a Kodály-Based Music Classroom." *Kodály Envoy,* 2011 *38*(1): 4–10.

Bowman, W. "Philosophy, Criticism, and Music Education: Some Tentative Steps Down a Less-Travelled Road." *Bulletin of the Council for Research in Music Education,* 1992, *114*: 1–19.

Carmody, P. B. "Early Childhood Music Curriculum and Techniques." *Kodály Envoy,* 1985, *12*(2).

Choksy, L. *The Kodaly Method,* 2nd ed. Upper Saddle River, NJ: Prentice-Hall, 1999.

Choksy, L., R. M. Abramson, A. E. Gillespie, D. Woods, and F. York. *Teaching Music in the Twenty-First Century,* 2nd ed. Upper Saddle River, NJ: Prentice-Hall, 2001.

Coleman, D. "Guiding Principles for the Arts: Grades K–12." 2011. http://usny.nysed.gov/rttt/docs/guidingprinciples-arts.pdf. Retrieved June 15, 2012.

Consortium of National Arts Education Associations. *National Standards for Arts Education.* Reston, VA: Music Educators National Conference, 1994.

Drake, S. M. "Planning Integrated Curriculum: The Call to Adventure." Alexandria, VA: Association for Supervision and Curriculum Development, 1993.

Edelstein, S., L. Choksy, P. Lehman, N. Sigurdsson, and D. Woods. *Creating Curriculum in Music.* Menlo Park, CA: Addison-Wesley, 1980.

Eisner, E. "Educating the Whole Person: Arts in the Curriculum." *Music Educators Journal,* 1987, *73*(2): 37–41.

Eősze, L., M. Houlahan, and P. Tacka. "Zoltán Kodály (1882–1967)." *The New Grove Dictionary of Music and Musicians,* ed. S. Sadie, vol. 13, pp. 716–726. London: Macmillan, 2002.

Forrai, K. *Music in Preschool.* Trans. and adapted by J. Sinor, 1974. Reprint, Budapest: Zeneműkiadò, 1988.

Gardner, H. *Frames of Mind: The Theory of Multiple Intelligences.* New York: Basic Books, 1983.

Gordon, E. E., et al. *Jump Right In! The Music Curriculum.* Chicago: GIA, 2003.

Green, L. *Music, Informal Learning and the School: A New Classroom Pedagogy.* Aldershot, UK: Ashgate, 2008.

Hanley, B., and J. Montgomery. "Contemporary Curriculum Practices and Their Theoretical Bases." In *The New Handbook of Research on Music Teaching and Learning,* ed. Richard Colwell and Carol Richardson, pp. 113–143. New York: Oxford University Press, 2002.

Herboly-Kocsár, I. "Do We Need a Method in Music Education?" *Kodaly Envoy,* 1988, *14*(4): 5–9.

Herboly-Kocsár, I. "Is the 'Hundred Year Plan' Still Timely in the 21st Century?" *Bulletin of the International Kodaly Society,* 2007, *31*(1): 3–8.

Hope, S. "Response to J. Terry Gates 'Why Study Music?' " In *Vision 2020.* Reston, VA: Music Educators National Conference, 2000.

Horowitz, F. D., L. Darling-Hammond, and J. Bransford., et al. "Educating Teachers for Developmentally Appropriate Practice." In *Preparing Teachers for a Changing World: What Teachers Should Learn and be Able to Do,* ed. L. Darling-Hammond and J. Bransford, pp. 88–125. San Francisco: Jossey-Bass, 2005.

Houlahan, M., and Philip Tacka. *From Sound to Symbol: Fundamentals of Music Theory.* New York: Oxford University Press 2009, 2011. Newly revised 2nd ed. including an audio CD and interactive skill development DVD and web-based supplementary materials for eleven chapters.

Houlahan, M., and P. Tacka. *Kodály in the Kindergarten: Developing the Creative Brain in the 21st Century.* New York: Oxford University, 2015.

Houlahan, M., and P. Tacka. *Sound Thinking: Developing Musical Literacy, Vol. I and Vol. II.* New York, London: Boosey & Hawkes, 1995.

Houlahan, M., and P. Tacka. *Sound Thinking: Music for Sight-Singing and Ear Training, Vol. I and Vol. II.* New York, London: Boosey & Hawkes, 1990.

Houlahan, M., and P. Tacka. *Zoltán Kodály: A Guide to Research.* New York: Routledge, 1998.

Hundoegger, A. *Lehrweise Nach Tonika Do (The Way of Teaching According to Tonic-Do),* Vol. 9. Lippstadt, Ger.: Tonika Do Verlag/Kistner Siegel, 1897.

Hyson, M. *Enthusiastic and Engaged Learners: Approaches to Learning in the Early Childhood Classroom.* New York: Teachers College Press, 2008.

Ittzés, M. "Kodaly, the Methodologist." *Bulletin of the International Kodaly Society,* 2010, *35*(2): 8–15.

Ittzés, M. "Zoltan Kodaly." *International Journal of Music Education,* 2004, *22*(2): 131–147.

Ittzés, M. *Zoltán Kodály, In Retrospect: A Hungarian National Composer in the 20th Century on the Border of East and West.* Kecskemét, Hung.: Zoltán Kodály Pedagogical Institute of Music, 2002.

Ittzés, M. *Zoltán Kodály's Singing Exercises.* Kecskemét, Hung.: Petőfi Nyomda, 1972.

Jaccard, J. "Intonation Begins in Kindergarten: The Art and Science of Teaching Music Acoustically." *Kodály Envoy,* 2004, *30*(4); repr. Spring 2014, *40*(3).

Jacobs, H. H. *Interdisciplinary Curriculum: Design and Implementation.* Alexandria, VA: Association for Supervision and Curriculum Development, 1989.

Johnson, J. "Art Music in the Music Curriculum." *Kodaly Envoy,* 2006, *32*(2).

Jorgensen, E. *In Search of Music Education.* Urbana: University of Illinois Press, 1997.

Jorgensen, E. "On Philosophical Method." In *Handbook of Research on Music Teaching and Learning,* ed. R. Colwell, pp. 91–101. New York: Schirmer, 1992.

Kecskemeti, I. *Kodály the Composer: Brief Studies on the First Half of Kodaly's Oeuvre.* Kecskemét, Hung.: Zoltán Kodály Pedagogical Institute of Music, 1986.

Kester, N. "Laying the Foundation: Music at the Pre-School Level." *Kodály Envoy,* 1987, *14*(1): 6–12.

Kodály, Z. "Inauguration of the New Building of the Kecskemét Music Primary School." *Bulletin of the International Kodály Society,* 1985, *10*(1): 8–10.

Kodály, Z. *Mein Weg Zur Musik—Fünf Gespräche mit Lutz Besch (My Path to Music—Five Conversations with Lutz Besch).* Zürich: Peter Schiefferli Verlags "Die Arche," 1966.

Kodály, Z. "The Role of Authentic Folksong in Music Education." [Lecture presented at Interlochen, 1966.] *Bulletin of the International Kodály Society,* 1985, *10*(1):15–19.

Kodály, Z. *The Selected Writings of Zoltán Kodály*, ed. F. Bonis, trans. L. Halapy and F. Macnicol. London: Boosey & Hawkes, 1974.

Lange, D. M. "An Introduction to Organizing and Assessing Concepts and Skills in an Elementary Music Curriculum." *General Music Today,* 2006, *19*(3): 6–12. Apr. 7, 2013.

Lehman, P. "Curriculum and Program Evaluation." In *Handbook of Research on Music Teaching and Learning* (chap. 18), ed. R. Colwell. New York: Schirmer, 1992.

Marosi, E. "The Challenges in Implementing a Kodály-based Curriculum in Northeastern Italy." *Bulletin of the International Kodály Society,* 2006, *31*(2): 19–27.

McCarthy, M., and J. S. Goble. "The Praxial Philosophy in Historical Perspective." In *Praxial Music Education: Reflections and Dialogues,* ed. D. J. Elliott, pp. 19–51. New York: Oxford University Press, 2009.

Mills, J. *Music in the Primary School.* Cambridge: Cambridge University Press, 1991.

Mithen, S. "The Music Instinct: The Evolutionary Basis of Musicality." *Annals of the New York Academy of Sciences,* 2009, *1169*: 3–12.

Pantev, C. "Musical Training and Induced Cortical Plasticity." *Annals of the New York Academy of Sciences,* 2009, *1169*: 131–132.

Pink, Daniel H. *A Whole New Mind: Why Right-Brainers Will Rule the Future.* New York: River Head Trade, 2006.

Promonti, E. "Kodaly's Epigrammes." *Bulletin of the International Kodaly Society,* 1993, *18*(1): 16–22.

Regelski, T. "Curriculum Reform: Reclaiming 'Music' as Social Praxis." *Action, Criticism, and Theory for Music Education,* 2009, *8*(1). http://act.maydaygroup.org/articles/Regelski8_1.pdf (accessed June 22, 2010).

Ruksenas, J. "The Benefits of Music Classes for Preschoolers: The ABC of Do Re Mi." 20th International Kodaly Symposium. Kodaly Institute. Lecture at Griffith University, Brisbane, Australia. July 5, 2011. Also printed in the *Bulletin of the International Kodály Society,* 2012, *37*(1): 19–26.

Seeger, Ruth Crawford. *American Folk Songs for Christmas.* Garden City, NY: Doubleday, 1953.

Sennyey, C. P. "The Kodaly Method in Post-Communist Hungary: A Decade of Change." *Kodaly Envoy,* 2001, *27*(2): 15–16.

Shehan Campbell, P. *Songs in Their Heads: Music and Its Meaning in Children's Lives.* New York: Oxford University Press, 1998.

Sloboda, J. A., and J. W. Davidson. "The Young Performing Musician." In *Musical Beginnings: Origins and Development of Musical Competence*, ed. I. Deliège and J. Sloboda, pp. 171–190. New York: Oxford University Press, 1996.

Small, C . *Musicking: The Meanings of Performing and Listening.* Hanover, NH: Wesleyan University Press, 1998.

Szabá, H., and Geoffrey Russell-Smith. *The Kodály Concept of Music Education.* New York: Boosey & Hawkes, 1969.

Szőnyi, Erzsèbet. *Kodály Zoltán Nevelèsi Eszmèi a Harmadik Èvezred Küszökbèn* (Zoltán Kodály's Ideals on the Threshold of the Third Millennium). Kecskemét: Zoltán Kodály Pedagogical Institute of Music, 1999. (Originally published 1974.)

Szőnyi, Erzsèbet. *Musical Reading and Writing*, trans. I. Halapy. London: Boosey & Hawkes, 1954. English ed., 1974.

Welch, G. F. "Addressing the Multi-faceted Nature of Music Education: An Activity Theory Research Perspective." *Research Studies in Music Education,* 2007, *28*: 23–37.

What Every Young American Should Know and Be Able to Do in the Arts: National Standards for Arts Education. Reston, VA: Music Educators National Conference, 1994.

Wiggins, G., and J. McTighe. *The Understanding by Design Guide to Advanced Concepts in Creating and Reviewing Units.* Alexandria, VA: ASCD, 2011.

Wiggins, G., and J. McTighe. *Unpacking the Common Core Standards Using the Ubé Framework.* (DVD.) Alexandria, VA: ASCD, 2012.

Wittgenstein, L. *Philosophical Investigations.* Oxford: Blackwell, 1953.

Chapter 2

Developing a Music Repertoire of Songs for the Elementary Music Classroom

Children are not simply musical embryos waiting to become musical adults but have a musical culture of their own, with its own musical and social rules, and with functions such as integration of person and expression of ethnicity.

Bruno Nettl, "Foreword," *Songs in Their Heads*

By giving status to children's own musical cultures in the formal music education environment, and by using their spontaneous music making as a springboard for adult-directed learning programs, we can provide contexts that offer children security and respect.

David J. Elliott, *Praxial Music Education*, p. 255

It is through the indigenous musics of their cultures that children receive the stories of their people, those that ancestors pass down from generation to generation and others that are contemporary and reflect new customs. Folk music is the treasure trove of children's values, beliefs, cultures, knowledge, games and stores. The music of children's own cultures must be given respect and status in the classroom, indirectly giving children a sense of their own values and status. Receptivity toward the music of other cultures can be developed from this point of reference, thereby fostering cultural awareness, tolerance and respect.

David J. Elliott, *Praxial Music Education*, p. 258

Kodály Today

> By building the multicultural musical experiences of the young, we are nurturing the familiar cultures of the children and facilitating their musical development within and across cultures. The musical experiences the children have now are those from which they create the music of their future.
>
> David J. Elliott, *Praxial Music Education*, p. 258

Key Questions

- What songs should we select for teaching music?
- What criteria do we use to select songs for teaching?
- Why are pentatonic songs important to teach to students?
- How can we construct a repertoire list of songs for each grade?
- How do we analyze song repertoire for teaching?
- What are some song resources for classroom use?

In Chapter 1 we presented a brief survey of Kodály's philosophy of music education, explained how this philosophy formed the basis of developing a methodology for teaching, and described how it can be used to build the basic framework for a music curriculum. We also offered a basic lesson plan design that begins to address the structure of individual Kodály-based lessons. A principal component of Kodály's philosophy is selection of a repertoire of quality music for teaching. The purpose of this chapter is to furnish information on how to select and analyze musical repertoire for teaching. Songs have been primarily selected from four publications—Peter Erdei and Katalin Komlás, *150 American Folk Songs to Sing, Read and Play*; Eleanor G. Locke, *Sail Away: 155 American Folk Songs to Sing, Read and Play*; Ida Erdei, Faith Knowles, and Denise Bacon, *My Singing*; and Faith Knowles, ed., *230 Folk Songs of Spanish-Speaking People to Sing, Read, and Play*—as well as Gabriela Montoya-Stier's publication *El Patio de Mi Casa: Traditional Rhymes, Games and Folk Songs from Mexico*. At the end of this chapter you will find a selected folk music bibliography as well as discography for your consultation.

Folk Music in the Classroom

As stated in the previous chapter, Kodály was convinced that a child's music education should begin with the folk music of his or her own culture. He believed that folk music is the "musical mother tongue" of all peoples in all nations; music instruction ought to begin with folk music and children's singing games.[1]

> Children's singing games allow a more profound insight than anything else into the primeval age of folk music. Singing connected with movement and action is a much more ancient and at the same time, more complex phenomenon than a simple song.[2]

> Each nation has a rich variety of folk songs, very suitable for teaching purposes. Selected gradually, they furnish the best material to introduce musical elements and make the children conscious of them. Singing first by ear, then writing, dictation, all methods combined make surprisingly quick results. It is essential that the materials used should be musically attractive.[3]

Kodály believed that children should be taught folk music and that folk music should lead to the introduction of art music and recently composed music: "The final purpose of all this must be to introduce pupils to the understanding and love of great classics of past, present and future."[4]

Once the connections to folk music are established, students may be guided to understand the association between folk music and classical music.

> For instance Haydn, the best to begin with, has manifest connection with folk song, but even in many works of Mozart it is easy to recognize the sublimated Austrian folk song. Beethoven's many themes are also folk-songlike. And all the national schools originated already in the nineteenth century are based on the foundations of their own folk music.[5]

Kodály on the Subject of Authenticity in Folk Music

The subject of authenticity arises in most discussions of folk music.

> That is a difficult question, I confess that even with us in Hungary, in the years around the turn of the century it was not at all clarified. Hungary was resounding with hundreds of popular songs known by everybody, regarded generally as folk songs. It is mostly this material which in foreign countries was regarded as Hungarian folk music. But closer research [revealed] that many of those songs were relatively very new, composed by still living or recently dead composers. Some decades of field-work were necessary to probe that there is another folk song the authors of which will never be found. And this is the layer of the old tradition and it has taken much time to understand the difference.[6]

Sometimes folk song texts are not appropriate for school use, and in fact the instructor can and should modify folk song texts. For example, it may not be appropriate to talk about "sword and pistol by his side" in some communities where violence is an unfortunate part of daily life. Instead of using words such as "boyfriend" or "girlfriend," use "new friend." Kodály reminds us, "The folksong entitles us to exchange the text for another one, if it is less suitable for one reason or other. Such an intervention is quite justified, even desirable, if we want to save a melody that has a poor text, by finding a good one for it."[7]

Kodály Today

In 1966 Kodály spoke about some of the difficulties American music educators face in selecting American folk song repertoire for music programs. In an address at the International Society for Music Education Conference held at Interlochen, Michigan, he stated:

> Now, I know, for Americans it is a difficult question, what is American folk song? I have just read some redlections [*sic,* reflections] about it by Bernstein. Bernstein talking about the multifarious ancestry of Americans asks, what, is it that we have in common, what we could call our folk music? He points out that America is a very young country, has not had very much time to develop a folk music, and since the Americans are descendants of all nations on the earth, its folk music is probably the richest in the world. . . . I think, since America is such a very big country, uniform American music will hardly ever exist. If little Hungary produced as many Hungarian styles as there are composers that may apply all the more to America.[8]

Clearly, he admonishes us to begin developing a curriculum based on songs of the cultural heritage of the children's community. Ideally, music specialists should explore and research to find the most authentic folk music for their music curriculum. The ultimate task for the music specialist is to select quality materials.

Selecting the best teaching material from the vast folk repertoire involves selecting songs that are suitable for specific age levels. The text as well as the music should be interesting and comprehensible to the students. In the best folk songs, there is a unity between the rhythm and melody; word and musical accents fall together logically. The body of songs selected for classroom use must include not only songs that incorporate musical elements for teaching but also songs for pleasure, seasonal songs, and songs that give students opportunities for artistic expression. We have included many examples of carefully selected and appropriate repertoire in the accompanying grade handbooks for this book.

Folk Music of Closely Related Cultures

Music teachers in the United States may include a selection of Anglo-American, African American, Hispanic, Asian American, and Hebrew materials. Music of England, Ireland, Scotland, Wales, France, and Germany may be included because of its close connection with Anglo-American folk music. Working with a predominantly Latino population, we may use the music of Latin America and Spain to form the basis of the curriculum.

The Role of Pentatonic Music

Pentatonic melodies are composed of five notes: the first, second, third, fifth, and sixth degrees of the major scale. These notes create a major second or a minor third from each other. When considering solfège syllables, a pentatonic scale uses the notes *do, re, mi, so,* and *la*. Although Kodály-inspired teaching appears to overemphasize pentatonic music in the primary grades, it is important to consider Kodály's rationale for including pentatonic music in the music curriculum.

Developing a Music Repertoire of Songs

Nowadays it is no longer necessary to explain why it is better to start teaching music to small children through the pentatonic tunes: first, it is easier to sing in tune without having to use semitones (half-steps), second, the musical thinking and the ability to sound the notes can develop better using tunes which employ leaps rather than stepwise tunes based on the diatonic scale often used by the teacher.[9]

Kodály's ethnographic research and musicological investigations made it possible for him to determine the connection between art music and folk music.

Finally, pentatony is an introduction to world literature: it is the key to many foreign world literatures, from the ancient Gregorian chant, through China to Debussy.[10]

Nobody wants to stop at pentatony. But indeed, the beginning must be made there; on the one hand, in this way the child's biogenetical development is natural and, on the other, this is what is demanded by rational pedagogical sequence. Only in this way are we able to create in the child an impression of it which will last for a lifetime.[11]

Selecting Music for Classroom Use

The aforementioned considerations supply six guiding principles concerning the types of musical materials we select for classroom use.

1. Select quality musical materials.
2. Songs must have a musical appeal.
3. The text of the song and the music should complement each other; the rhythmic accent and melodic inflection should match the structure of the language.
4. Songs should be developmentally appropriate; songs should be relevant for specific age groups.
5. Selected songs should reflect the cultural backgrounds of students in your classroom.
6. Some songs should be selected for their pedagogical function.

Music materials are critical to the success of a music curriculum. Both the instructor and students should enjoy the songs, games, and activities. Selected repertoire should include

- Songs for singing, movement, and playing on instruments
- Songs for listening
- Songs for pedagogical use

Songs for Singing, Movement, and Playing on Instruments

Music curricula may include songs with no specific pedagogical purpose other than the enjoyment of singing. These songs may have little merit in terms of musical elements or concepts; they are simply fun to sing. Such songs are often an opportunity for solo singing as well as improvisation. In some songs, the students will be able to sing all verses, while in others it might be appropriate for students to sing selected verses. When considering song materials for primary grades, instructors may also select repertoire for students appropriate for performing on music instruments.

Songs for classroom use should include

- Children's games
  Nursery rhymes and songs
  Jump-rope games
  Counting-out rhymes
  Lullabies
  Acting-out games
  Wind-up games
  Circle games
  Choosing games
  Chase games or double-chase games
  Partner games
  Double circle
  Line
  Double-line games
- Folk music
  Folk songs
  Play parties
  Ballads
  Folk dances
- Composed music

Believing that composers should dedicate a portion of their creative efforts to composing music for children, Kodály himself wrote numerous song arrangements, piano compositions, and singing exercises for children and adults, many of which are based on Hungarian folk music: "Original works are to be written, compositions starting from the child's soul, from the child's voice in text, tune and colour alike."[12]

> We have very few pentatonic folksongs of sufficiently limited compass and rhythm. For this reason smaller children need tunes written in the spirit of folksongs but without their difficulties. In such pieces, by making them into games, we can prepare the ground for the genuine folksongs. With much the same object in view I wrote 333 Elementary Exercises, where most of the pieces can be used as tunes for marching and so on.[13]

Songs for Listening

Songs selected for listening activities function as an important part of the music curriculum. Songs used for listening in primary grades may be reintroduced in the upper elementary grades for teaching musical concepts. Although intended for listening, and depending on the example, it may be appropriate to accompany some of these songs with simple rhythm instruments or with a dulcimer, guitar, or piano.

Songs for Pedagogical Use

This category of songs is included in the curriculum not just because they are beautiful examples of music; additionally they can be used to teach rhythmic or melodic elements.

Creating an Alphabetized Song Repertoire List for Each Grade

From the criteria given above, we can compile a list of repertoire suitable for each grade, arrange the songs in alphabetical order, and include a rationale for selection of the song. For example, we might have chosen a particular song not just because students will enjoy singing it but also because it can be used to reinforce a particular melodic or rhythmic concept or element. Include the source for the song and the type of game or movement activity associated with the song. This information may be organized in chart form as shown in Table 2.1.

Table 2.1

Song Alphabetical Listing	Date Taught	Tone Set	Game/ Movement	Source

The repertoire list should include songs that

- Reflect the cultural diversity of the student population
- Are appropriate for developing beautiful singing
- Develop music literacy skills
- Develop listening skills
- Are suitable for creative activities such as improvisation and composition
- Are appropriate for holidays and special events

Analyzing Song Repertoire

Analysis (the examination of a song's phrase structure, rhythmic and melodic content, and so on) helps determine how a song may be used in a curriculum. Analysis enables us to establish pedagogical implications within a body of song repertoire.

Kodály Today

Here is a sample of a simplified analysis sheet that may be used for analyzing songs. After analyzing your repertoire, you may construct a database or retrieval system using the information from the analysis of your songs to help you plan. You are encouraged to view the database of folk songs made available by the Kodály Program at Holy Names University in Oakland, California (see http://kodaly.hnu.edu/).

Name: "Who's That Tapping at the Window?"
Origin: African American
Comfortable Starting Pitch (CSP): F
Metronome Marking: 110   <110> (This song can also be sung with a duple meter time signature.)

Fig. 2.1 "Who's That Tapping at the Window?" Copy

Who's that tap-ping at the win-dow? Who's that knock-ing at the door?
Mom-my's tap-ping at the win-dow, Dad-dy's knock-ing at the door.

Fig. 2.2 "Who's That Tapping at the Window?" Stick Notation

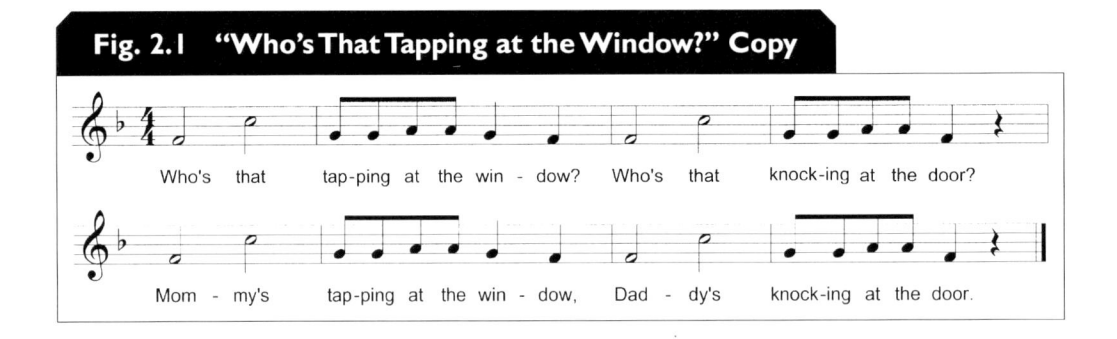

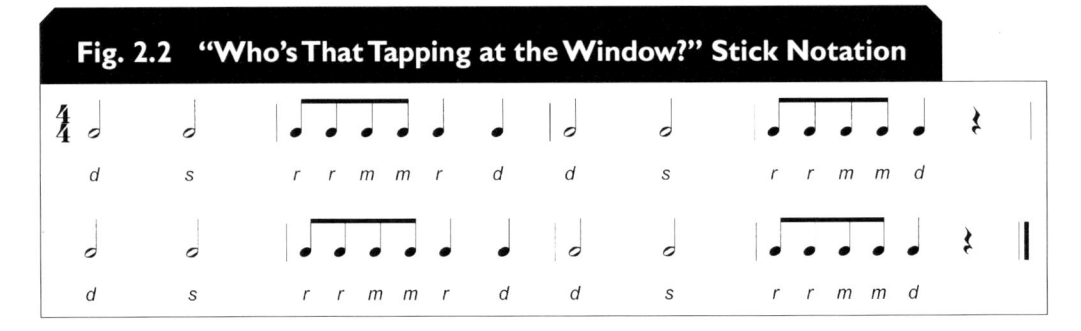

d s r r m m r d d s r r m m d
d s r r m m r d d s r r m m d

Table 2.2

Analysis	Pedagogical Use
Tone set: **do** re mi so	Rationale: four-four meter
Rhythm: ♪, ♩, ‡	Half note
	do, re, mi, so
Form: A A	Connections to books/literacy:
Game: Guessing	
Other:	Other:

Source: Erdei, Peter. *150 American Folk Songs to Sing, Read and Play* (Boosey & Hawkes, p. 7).

Song Analysis Definitions

Song Title
Write the title of your song for inclusion in your database. It is usually best not to include the definite or indefinite articles "The," "A," and "An" when putting this into your alphabetical listing or retrieval system.

Origin
This category is for listing the ethnic origin of the song, geographic location, or any historical connections, for example, Hispanic folk song, Jamaican folk song, Civil War era, and so on.

Comfortable Starting Pitch
Some song collections are written so that all the songs end on G. Ethnomusicologists adopt this approach to notating songs so that it is easier to compare variations of the same song. In this case, it is necessary to indicate a comfortable starting pitch (CSP) to put the song in the best singing range for your students. If the song is written in a comfortable range for your students, then you do not need to indicate a comfortable starting pitch.

Metronome Marking
Indicate an appropriate metronome marking for performing the piece of music. Tempos can determine the feel for a meter. If a song is sung with a slow tempo it may be in quadruple meter but performed with a fast tempo, it will be in duple meter.

Staff Notation
Write the song in staff notation. In most cases, it is preferable to write the song phrase by phrase, as this allows you to see the structural similarities.

Stick Notation or Rhythmic Notation
Write the song in stick notation (traditional rhythmic notation without note heads) or tradition rhythmic notation with solfège syllables included below the notation. For analysis purposes, some musicians believe it is sometimes easier to analyze songs written in stick notation in that it helps to more clearly see both rhythmic and melodic motives. Whichever system you adopt, it is preferable to write the notation in phrases.

Analysis and Pedagogical Use

You will notice that at the end of the analysis sheet for each song there are two sections: analysis and pedagogical use.

Analysis
On our analysis sheet these categories appear: tone set, rhythm, melodic form, game, rationale, connections to books/literacy, other, and source.

Tone Set
This is sometimes referred to as pitch class set or scale. We use solfège syllables to indicate the notes of the tone set. Tone sets are written in ascending order. Write solfège syllables

Kodály Today

in lower case and italicized. When identifying notes below *do* use a subscript mark (*so,* also called *low so*); notes above *ti* are marked with a superscript (*do'*, also called *high do*). Underline or circle the final note to indicate the tonic of the song.

In a major key the notes of the scale are *do-re-mi-fa-so-la-ti-do'*
The minor natural scale is *la,-ti,-do-re-mi-fa-so-la*
Harmonic minor is notated *la,-ti,-do-re-mi-fa-si-la*
Melodic minor is notated *la,-ti,-do-re-mi-fi-si-la-so-fa-mi-re-do-ti,-la,*

This category may also include the type of scale that results from this combination of tone sets. There are three: pentatonic, diatonic, and nontraditional. We restrict our discussion to pentatonic and diatonic scale types.

Pentatonic Scales

There are two types of pentatonic scales: hemitonic and anhemitonic. The former includes half steps and the latter does not. The notes of the anhemitonic pentatonic system are *do-re-mi-so-la*. For songs to be truly pentatonic they must emphasize intervals of a major second, perfect fourth, and minor third. Notes of the pentatonic scale can also be rearranged to fit a circle-of-fifths order: *do-so-re-la-mi*. Notes may appear in any octave. The solfège syllable *la* is the fifth step of the pentatonic scale. When identifying the range of a melody, we need to compare it to the diatonic scale. Therefore, the range of a melody from *do* to *la* is one to six even though *la* is the fifth step of the pentatonic scale.

Songs that contain all the notes of the pentatonic scale and end on *do* are called *do* pentatonic or major pentatonic. Songs that contain all the notes of the pentatonic scale and end on *la* are called *la* pentatonic or minor pentatonic. Accordingly, if a song ends on *re* it is called *re* pentatonic, and so on.

"Rocky Mountain" is in the major pentatonic scale (*do* pentatonic; Fig. 2.3).

Fig. 2.3 "Rocky Mountain"

Developing a Music Repertoire of Songs

"Sioux Indian Lullaby" is in the minor pentatonic scale (*la* pentatonic; Fig. 2.4).

Fig. 2.4 "Sioux Indian Lullaby"

Lul - la - by, lit - tle pa - poose. *Fine*
Moth - er is near you, noth - ing can harm you. *D.C. al Fine*

Method One for Describing Subsets of the Pentatonic Scale In this method,[14] we use the word *chord* to describe a tone set where all the pitches are adjacent; we use the word *tonic* when there is a gap in the tone set. For example, a melody containing *mi-so* can be referred to as a pentatonic bichord or a child's chant. "Seesaw" is an example of a pentatonic bichord (Fig. 2.5).

Fig. 2.5 "Seesaw"

See - saw, up and down, in the sky and on the ground.

A melody containing *do-re* can be described as a bichordal melody.

A melody containing *mi-so-la* can be described as a pentatonic trichord. The traditional children's chant "Lucy Locket" is an example of a pentatonic trichord (Fig. 2.6).

Fig. 2.6 "Lucy Locket"

Lu - cy Lock - et lost her pock - et, Kit - ty Fish - er found it.
Not a pen - ny was there in it, on - ly rib - bon round it.

A melody containing *do-re-mi* is an example of a trichord. "Hot Cross Buns" is an example (Fig. 2.7).

Fig. 2.7 "Hot Cross Buns"

Hot cross buns, hot cross buns, one a pen - ny, two a pen - ny, hot cross buns.

Kodály Today

A melody containing *do-re-mi-so* can be described as a *do* pentatonic tetrachord. "Dinah" is an example (Fig. 2.8).

Fig. 2.8 "Dinah"

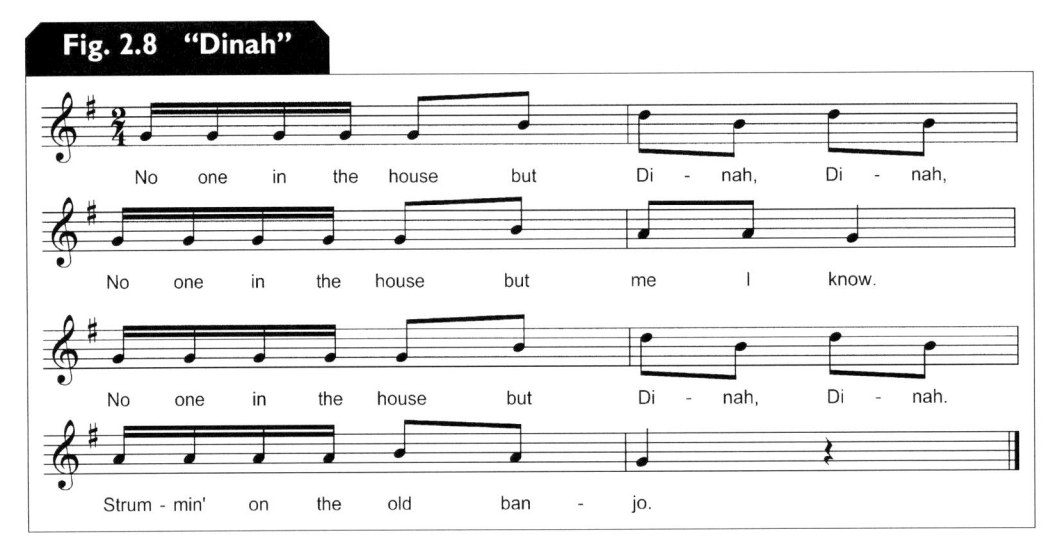

No one in the house but Di-nah, Di-nah,
No one in the house but me I know.
No one in the house but Di-nah, Di-nah.
Strum-min' on the old ban-jo.

A melody containing *la,-do-re-mi* (*low la–do-re-mi*) and ending on *la,* is a *la* pentatonic tetrachord. "Skin and Bones" is an example (Fig. 2.9).

Fig. 2.9 "Skin and Bones"

There was an old wom-an all skin and bones, oo-oo-oo-oooo.
She o-pened the door and BOO!

Method Two for Describing Subsets of the Pentatonic Scale   Songs[15] containing *so-mi* and *la-so-mi* are commonly referred to as a child's chant.

Songs that are composed of two notes following each other in the circle-of-fifths order of the pentatonic system are called *bitonic so,-do; do* bitonic plagal range (we use the word *plagal* to indicate notes a fourth below the tonic). "La patita" (Fig. 2.10) and "A don chin chino" (Fig. 2.11) are examples of bitonic melodies.

Fig. 2.10 "La Patita"

Mue - va la pa - ta, pe - rro vie - jo
Mue - ve la pa - ta de co - ne - jo
Mue - ve la pa - ta, pe - rro gan - so
Mue - ve la pa - ta de gar - ba - zo

Fig. 2.11 "A Don Chin Chino"

A - llá en Fran - cia se cas - sa un chi - no con u - na Chi - na y.al o - tro dí - a co - mien - zan a bai - lar un bal - le muy bo - ni - to que di - ce.a - sí a don chin chi - no a don chin chi - no.

Songs that are composed of three notes that follow one another in the circle-of-fifths order of the pentatonic system are called *tritonic do-so-re; so,-do-re*; "Santo Domingo" is a *do* tritonic plagal range (Fig. 2.12).

Fig. 2.12 "Santo Domingo"

San - to Do - min - go de la bue - na, bue - na bue - na vi - da
ha - cen a - sí, a - sí, a - sí, los car - pin - te - ros
" " " " " " " los pa - na - de - ros
" " " " " " " los he - rra - do - res
" " " " " " " los le - ña - do - res
" " " " " " " los za - pa - te - ros

Note that the tone set for this melody is *so,-do-re*, and *do* is the tonic note.

Songs that are composed of four notes that follow one another in the circle-of-fifths order of the pentatonic system are called *tetratonic*.

When the notes of a tone set do not follow the circle-of-fifths order, other names may be used. Notice that the lowest note in the tone set should be the tonal center of the folk song. Songs that are composed of two notes within the pentatonic system are called *pentatonic bichords*, as with the *so-mi* pentatonic bichord "Seesaw" (Fig. 2.13).

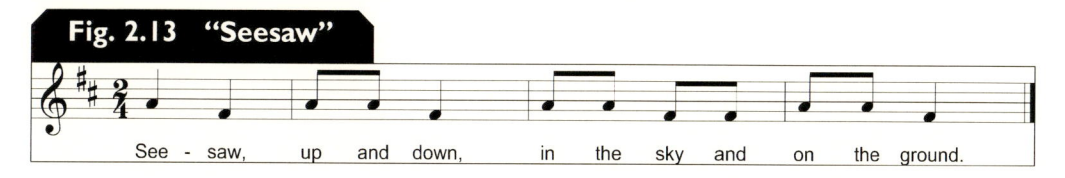

Fig. 2.13 "Seesaw"

See - saw, up and down, in the sky and on the ground.

Kodály Today

Songs that are composed of three notes within the pentatonic system are called *pentatonic trichords*, as with the *la so mi* pentatonic trichord "Bounce High" (Fig. 2.14).

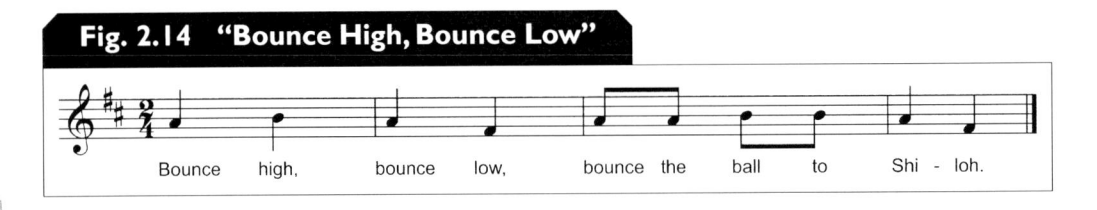

Fig. 2.14 "Bounce High, Bounce Low"

Bounce high, bounce low, bounce the ball to Shi - loh.

Songs that are composed of four notes within the pentatonic system are called *pentatonic tetrachords*. "Dinah" is an example of a *do* pentatonic tetrachord (Fig. 2.15).

Fig. 2.15 "Dinah"

No one in the house but Di - nah, Di - nah,
No one in the house but me I know.
No one in the house but Di - nah, Di - nah.
Strum - min' on the old ban - jo.

"Draw a Bucket of Water" is an example of a *do* pentatonic tetrachord, plagal range. "Skin and Bones" is a *la* pentatonic tetrachord (Fig. 2.16).

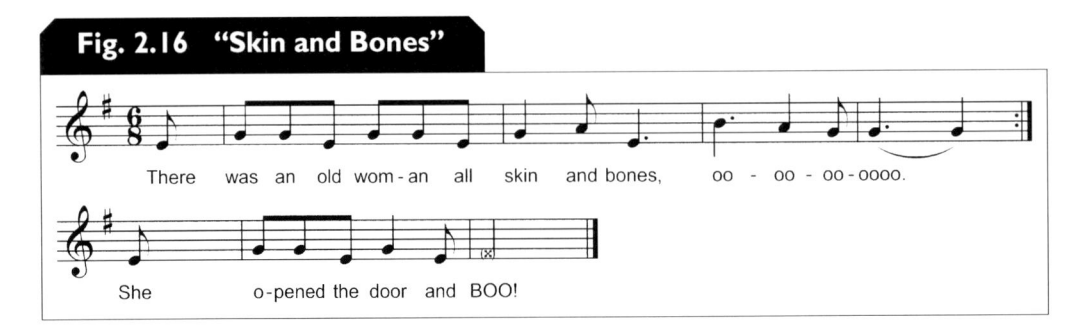

Fig. 2.16 "Skin and Bones"

There was an old wom - an all skin and bones, oo - oo - oo - oooo.
She o - pened the door and BOO!

If songs having notes of the pentatonic scale do not fit these criteria, then we can label them as *incomplete pentatonic scales*. "Lonesome Road" is an incomplete *do* pentatonic scale (Fig. 2.17).

Developing a Music Repertoire of Songs

Fig. 2.17 "Lonesome Road"

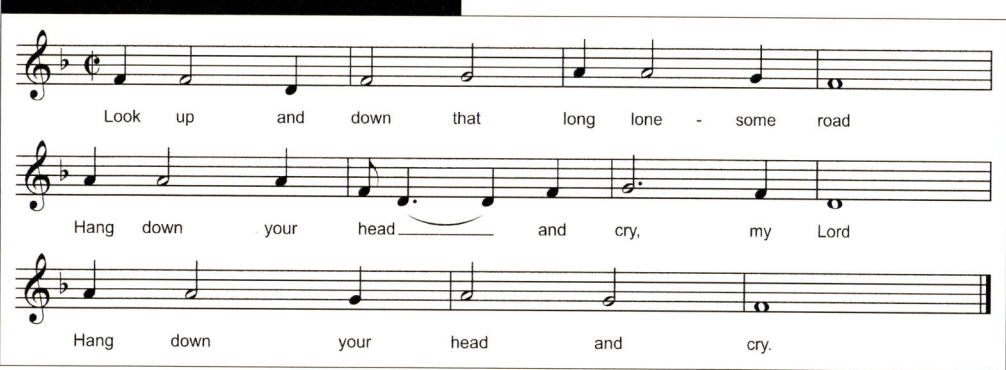

Look up and down that long lone - some road
Hang down your head and cry, my Lord
Hang down your head and cry.

Diatonic Scales

Major Scale The notes of a major diatonic scale include *do-re-mi-fa-so-la-ti-do'*. An example is "Alleluia," a major diatonic scale (Fig. 2.18).

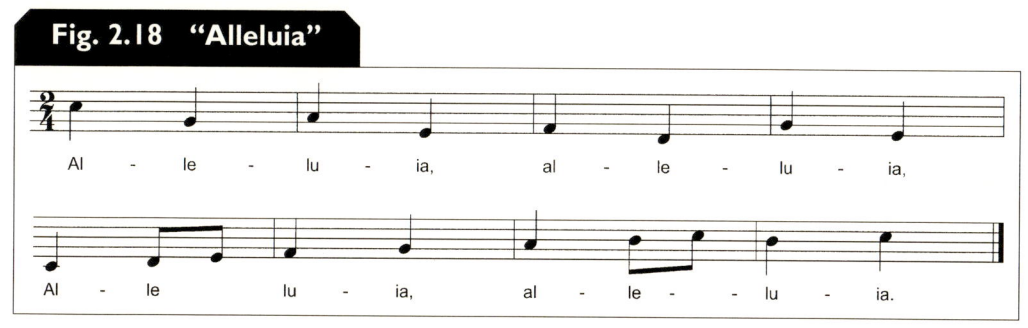

Fig. 2.18 "Alleluia"

Al - le - lu - ia, al - le - lu - ia,
Al - le - lu - ia, al - le - lu - ia.

Minor The notes of a minor diatonic scale are *la,-ti,-do-re-mi-fa-so-la*. This is referred to as the *natural* minor scale, as with "Hushabye" (Fig. 2.19).

Fig. 2.19 "Hushabye"

Hush - a - bye, don't you cry, go to sleep - y lit - tle ba - by.
When you wake, you shall have all the pret - ty lit - tle hors - es.
Blacks and bays, dap - ples and grays, coach and six a lit - tle hors - es
Hush - a - bye, don't you cry, go to sleep - y lit - tle ba - by.

Kodály Today

In minor, when the seventh degree of the scale (*so*) is raised to a *si*, it is called a *harmonic* minor; if the sixth and seventh degrees of the natural minor are raised (*fi si*) and lowered coming down (*so, fa*), the scale is referred to as the *melodic* form of the minor scale.

The following are subsets of the diatonic scale. When there are three adjacent notes within a diatonic scale, we call it a trichord. In a major scale, *do re mi* is a *do* trichord; *la ti do'* is a *la* trichord. Four adjacent notes are labeled a tetrachord. In a major scale, *do re mi fa* is a *do* tetrachord; *la ti do re* is a *la* tetrachord. Five adjacent notes are labeled a pentachord. In a major scale, *do re mi fa so* is a *do* pentachord; *la ti do re mi* is a *la* pentachord. Six adjacent notes are a hexachord. In a major scale, *do re mi fa so la* is a *do* hexachord; *la ti do re mi fa* is a *la* hexachord.

do trichord *do re mi*	*la* trichord *la ti do,*
do tetrachord *do re mi fa*	*la* tetrachord *la ti do re*
do pentachord *do re mi fa so*	*la* pentachord *la ti do re mi*
do hexachord *do re mi fa so la*	*la* hexachord *la ti do re mi fa*

"Aunt Rhody" is an example of a *do* pentachord (Fig. 2.20).

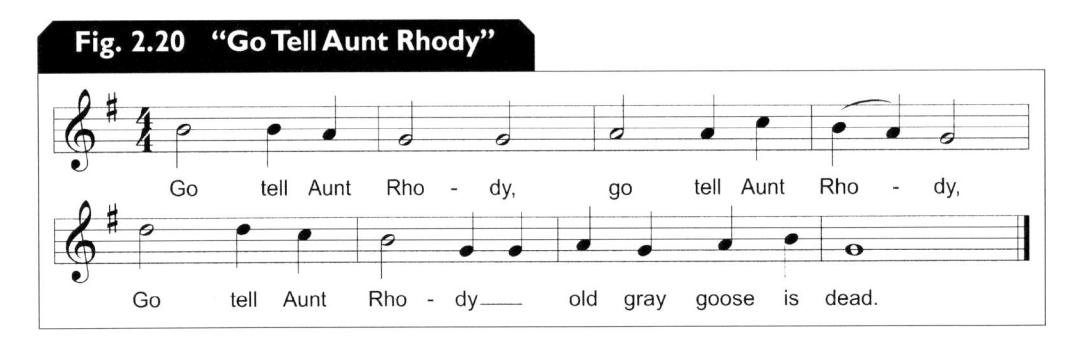

Fig. 2.20 "Go Tell Aunt Rhody"

"Twinkle, Twinkle Little Star" is an example of a *do* hexachord (Fig. 2.21).

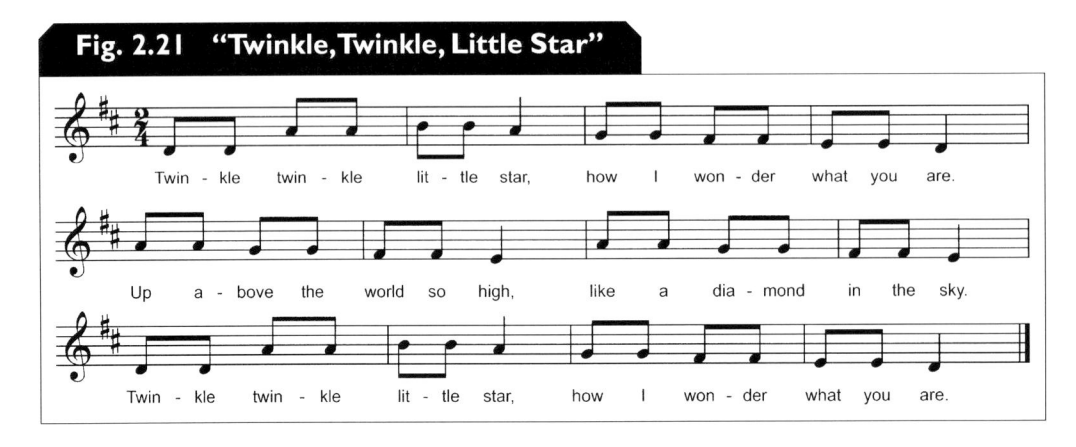

Fig. 2.21 "Twinkle, Twinkle, Little Star"

Modal Scales

Modal scales are composed of the tone set *do re mi fa so la ti* but have different ending notes. This chart indicates the connection between the ending note and the modal scale name.

Ending Note	Modal Scale Name
do	Ionian/major
re	Dorian (also sung with *la* plus *fi*)
mi	Phrygian (also *la* and *ta*)
fa	Lydian (*do* plus *fi*)
so	Mixolydian (*do* plus *ta*)
la	Aeolian/minor
ti	Locrian

The Difference Between a Major Scale and the Ionian Mode   When a song ends on *do* and notes of the melody outline triads, we usually refer to the song as being related to the major scale. When a song ends on *do* and the melody moves in steps, we may refer to the melody as being related to the Ionian mode.

The Difference Between a Minor Scale and the Aeolian Mode   When a song ends on *la*, and notes of the melody outline triads, we usually refer to the song as being related to the minor scale. When a song ends on *la*, and the melody moves in steps, we can refer to the song as being related to the Aeolian mode.

Modes and Their Comparative Scale Names   When we sing Dorian, Ionian, Aeolian, Mixolydian, or Lydian modal scales from the same pitch, we can classify each mode as either major-like or minor-like. This classification is dependent on the interval between the root and the third of the mode.

For example, Mixolydian mode begins *so-la-ti*. The distance between *so* and *ti* is a major third. Because the Mixolydian mode has a major third between the root (*so*) and the third (*ti*), we designate Mixolydian mode as a major mode.

The Dorian mode begins *re-mi-fa*. The distance between *re* and *fa* is a minor third. Because the Dorian mode has a minor third between the root (*re*) and the third (*fa*), we designate Dorian mode as a minor mode.

Major Modal Scales   Ionian mode is clearly a major mode because it begins and ends on *do* and the half steps occur between *mi-fa* and *ti-do'*. The Lydian mode is another major-sounding mode. There are two ways to use solfège syllables to sing the Lydian mode (Fig. 2.22). It may be sung without altering solfège syllables when sung from *fa* to *fa*. Because the first three notes on the Lydian mode are major seconds, it may also be sung beginning on *do* and ending on *do'* if we raise the fourth degree a half step (fa becomes fi).

Kodály Today

Fig. 2.22 Lydian mode

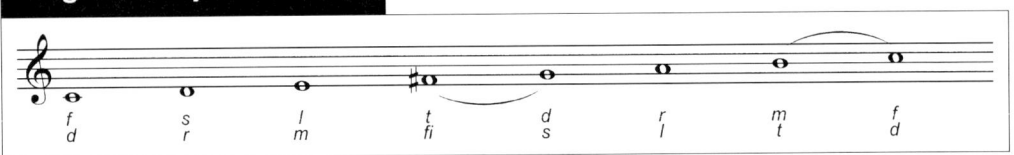

[Musical notation showing the Lydian mode scale with solfège syllables below each note:]
f/d, s/r, l/m, t/fi, d/s, r/l, m/t, f/d

Mixolydian mode (Fig. 2.23) is another major-sounding scale because the first six notes match the major scale structure; in Mixolydian mode the seventh degree is lowered. For this reason, it may be sung from *so* to *so* using solfège syllables or from *do* to *do* using the lowered seventh degree (*ti* becomes *ta*).

In the example of "Old Joe Clark" (Fig. 2.24), we can sing this melody with two solfège possibilities: in the key of F major with the altered tone *ta*, or in B flat major with a beginning *so* solfège note.

Fig. 2.23 Mixolydian mode

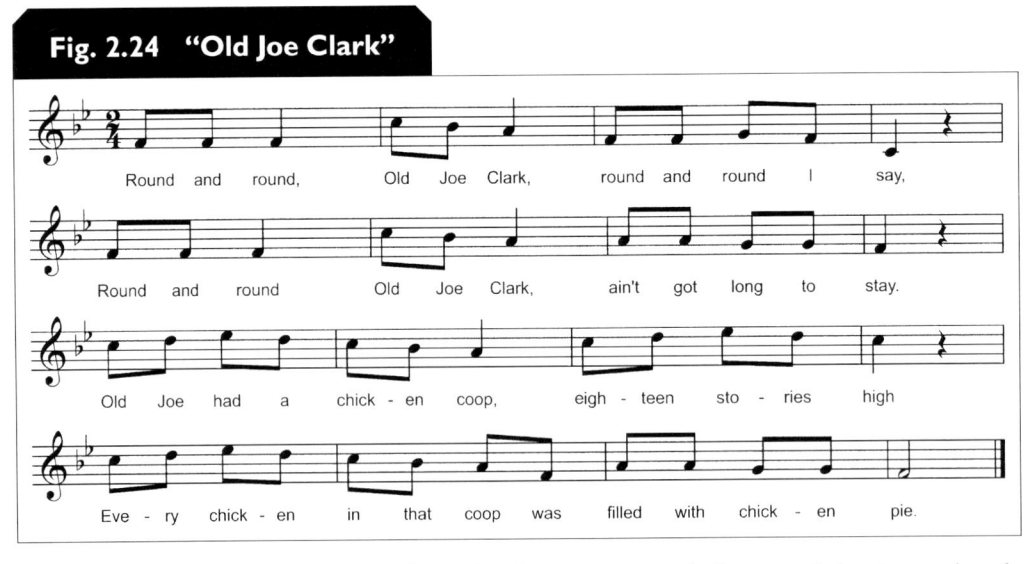

[Musical notation showing the Mixolydian mode scale with solfège syllables:]
s/d, l/r, t/m, d/f, r/s, m/l, f/ta, s/d

Fig. 2.24 "Old Joe Clark"

[Musical notation with lyrics:]
Round and round, Old Joe Clark, round and round I say,
Round and round Old Joe Clark, ain't got long to stay.
Old Joe had a chick-en coop, eigh-teen sto-ries high
Eve-ry chick-en in that coop was filled with chick-en pie.

Minor Modal Scales   Aeolian mode is clearly a minor mode because it begins and ends on *la* and the half steps occur between *ti* and *do* and *mi* and *fa*. The Dorian mode is another minor-sounding mode. There are two ways to use solfège syllables to sing the Dorian mode (Fig. 2.25). It may be sung without altering solfège syllables when sung from *re* to *re*. Because the first three notes on the Dorian mode consist of a major second followed by a minor second, it may also be sung beginning on *la* and ending on *la* if we raise the sixth degree a half step (*fa* becomes *fi*).

Developing a Music Repertoire of Songs

Here is an example of the tonic note being sung as *re* or with *la* and the accidental note *fi* ("Scarborough Fair," major diatonic scale; Fig. 2.26).

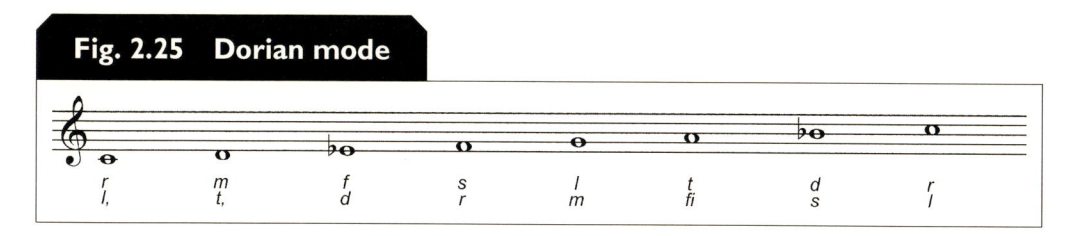

Fig. 2.25   Dorian mode

Fig. 2.26   "Scarborough Fair"

Phrygian Mode   The Phrygian mode (Fig. 2.27) may be sung as a minor scale by lowering the second degree of the minor scale a half step.

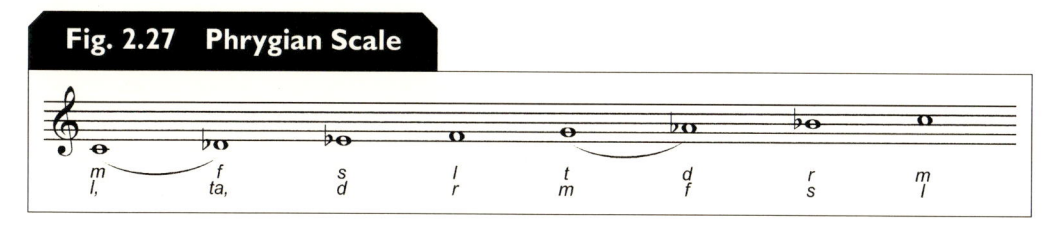

Fig. 2.27   Phrygian Scale

We can also have incomplete forms of these scales.

Tone Set (Range of Notes)

You may wish to indicate the range of the notes of a composition. The final note is indicated with 1. Notes above the final are written using Arabic numbers and notes below the final are written using Roman numerals. For the sake of simplicity and comparing variations of the same folk songs, we use the diatonic scale system for describing the range of notes in the pentatonic system. For example, in a major pentatonic melody where the tone set is *do re mi so la* the range of the notes is 1–6 even though there are only five notes.

Kodály Today

Rhythm

This section is for listing the specific note values and rests (such as quarter notes, half notes, and so on) from the smallest to largest note values. You may also include the meter of the song as well as whether the song has upbeats. Target rhythmic motives (usually found in four-beat patterns) may also be included in this category.

The rhythmic form of a song may differ from the melodic form. *Isorhythmic* refers to phrases having the same rhythm. *Heterorhythmic* refers to phrases of a song that are different.

Podia refers to the number of rhythmic stresses within a phrase. We use the terms *bipodic* to describe two stresses within a phrase, *tripodic* to describe three stresses within a phrase, and *tetrapodic* to describe four stresses within a phrase. When a song consistently has the same number of stresses in every phrase we refer to it as *isopodic;* when a song has a differing number of stresses in the phrases we refer to it as *heteropodic*. Normally the number of stresses in a phrase equates to the number of measures in a phrase.

Melodic Form

Indicate the form of phrases using capital letters. When a phrase is four beats in length, use capital letters. For phrases or motifs that are less than four beats, use lowercase letters. Variants of phrases may be indicated with a subscript "v," for example, A A_v. Use a superscript with a number to indicate sequences occurring in a folk song or songs containing transpositions of phrases: A A^5 A^5_v A. You can also use an A' to indicate a variation if you do not want to use V. We believe that students can identify more readily with using a V for variation.

Game

Describe the type of game (circle, double circle, partner, double line, and so on). You might also describe the category of song, such as a holiday song or work song.

Analysis: Other

This will allow you to note anything interesting about the song. For example, does it have a sequence or repeated phrase where a repeat sign might be used?

Rationale

This is where we indicate the pedagogical purpose for using the song. A song can be used for many reasons, among them singing, teaching a game, performing on an instrument, acting as the basis of an improvisation exercise, noting a specific form, listening, or teaching a rhythmic or melodic element. When we teach a melodic or rhythmic element we use three phases of learning: preparation, presentation, and practice. During the preparation stage, we teach a variety of songs that include the rhythmic or melodic element to be taught. For teaching music literacy skills, we isolate the new rhythmic or melodic element, usually in a four-beat motif, noting the placement of the new element within the four-beat motif. The most common occurrence of the new element on a particular beat is referred to as the target pattern. The song containing the target pattern is referred to as the focus song.

Connections to Curriculum Areas
This category is useful for integrating music into additional areas of the school curriculum. Indicate connections to literacy or other subject areas; for example, "work songs" or "Civil War songs" may be linked to particular eras in a social studies curriculum.

Pedagogical Use: Other
You might want to indicate other uses for the song in addition to these headings.

Source
Source refers to the resource where the song was found. Generally speaking, it is important to list whether the source is primary or secondary. (In general, a primary source indicates the original source for the song as well as a transcription of the song from a field recording. Recordings can also be considered as a primary source. A secondary source indicates when the song was first published but does not provide the original source of the folksong.) It is also helpful to include references to additional variations of the folk song.

Performance and Notation of Folk Songs

We learn to sing folk songs in a stylistically appropriate manner by listening to authentic performances and noting rhythmic and melodic ornamentations. It's helpful to become familiar with the authentic performance practice of folk songs so we can pass it along to our students. Students, particularly in the early elementary grades, have an impressive ability to imitate a style of singing that uses vocal ornamentations and stylistic elements. Become acquainted with such traditional singers as Jean Ritchie, Almeda Riddle, Bessie Jones, Peter Seeger, and Woody Guthrie as well as the field recordings from the Library of Congress.

Folk songs are often written in a simplified version for teaching purposes. The actual notation of an authentic performance of a song would, in fact, be quite complex. It is for this reason that field recordings of songs lend important insight regarding performance practice. Consideration of this on a simple level would include being mindful when singing a folk song to determine if it can be sung more musically in duple meter than in quadruple.

Use songs found in primary sources. Many of these sources include performance directions and are important roadmaps for the performance practice. Try to include all verses of a folk song. Singing one verse may not give students the full emotional experience associated with the song.

Teachers should also review Jill Trinka's four-volume set *Folk Songs, Singing Games, and Play Parties*, published by GIA in 2006.

My Little Rooster, vol. 1 GIA, Chicago, 2006
Bought Me a Cat, vol. 2, 2006
John, the Rabbit, vol. 3, 2006
The Little Black Bull, vol. 4, 2006

These books and CD collections feature

- Song transcriptions of all songs
- Directions for all games and play parties
- Both simple and more advanced directions
- Song history and comparative source information
- Suggestions for use in music curricula
- Music reading examples based on the folk songs
- Complete indices of subject matter, instrumentation, song type, grade level, meter and time signatures, tone sets, melodic elements and patterns, and rhythmic elements and patterns

Teachers will enjoy learning songs directly from a CD sung by a knowledgeable folksinger who understands folksong performance practice. Students will also enjoy listening to these songs as part of their listening curriculum.

Lesson Planning

At the conclusion of each chapter, we will apply the information from the chapter to lesson planning. We will present lesson plan designs that reflect a number of techniques you will learn in each chapter. We will also include abbreviated lesson plans to show how a basic lesson plan can be modified. Sometimes lesson plans will include information that is not discussed in detail in the chapter, but try to gain an understanding of the bigger picture and become fluent with terminology being used. In this section we will discuss how to

1. Create a lesson plan design that is based on incorporating material from the alphabetized list
2. Create a preparation/practice lesson plan
3. Create a presentation lesson plan

In the accompanying handbooks for each grade we have included an alphabetized repertoire list with examples of materials that can be used for teaching singing, music literacy, practicing music skills, and listening. The lesson plans in this chapter and subsequent chapters of this volume emphasize the sections that can be expanded as a result of information presented in the chapter. Table 2.3 shows how information from the alphabetized list can be incorporated into a basic lesson plan template. Our purpose here is to emphasize that everything we do in a music lesson is always related to song material sung by students.

Table 2.3 Basic Preparation/Practice Lesson

INTRODUCTION	
Performance and demonstration of known musical concepts and elements	Ss demonstrate their prior knowledge of known repertoire and musical elements through performance of songs selected from the alphabetized repertoire list
CORE ACTIVITIES	
Acquisition of repertoire	New song selected from the alphabetized repertoire list that expands Ss' repertoire and prepares for the learning of a music rhythmic or melodic concept or element
Preparation and presentation of a rhythmic or melodic element	Learning activities in which a new musical concept or element is prepared through known songs found in the alphabetized repertoire list
Movement development	Focus on the sequential development of age-appropriate movement skills through songs and folk games found in the alphabetized repertoire list
Practice and performance of musical skills	Ss reinforce their knowledge of musical concepts and elements working on the skill areas of form, memory, inner hearing, ensemble work, improvisation and composition, and listening through known songs found in the alphabetized repertoire list
CLOSURE	
Review and summation	Review of lesson content; T may perform the next new song to be learned in a subsequent lesson found in the alphabetized repertoire list

Creating a Preparation/Practice Lesson Plan

Before we label any element in a music lesson, we give students practical experiences that guide them to make a connection with the new element through kinesthetic, aural, and visual activities. This is always done in the context of performance. We call these preparation activities. Once we label an element, we practice it. In other words we are developing lessons that focus on preparing a new concept as well as practice known concepts.

Generally speaking, we try to address both rhythmic and melodic skills in each lesson. When we are preparing a rhythmic element in the first part of a lesson, we practice a melodic element in the second part of a lesson. Conversely, if we prepare a melodic element in the first part of a lesson, we practice a rhythmic element in the second part of a lesson.

Table 2.4 is an example of a basic Preparation/Practice Lesson Plan Template. Note that in the template lesson we used the wording "Performance and Demonstration of Known Musical Concepts and Elements" as a generic term for all activities in the introduction.

Table 2.4 Basic Preparation/Practice Lesson Plan Template Explained

INTRODUCTION	
Performance and demonstration of known musical concepts and elements	Ss demonstrate their prior knowledge of repertoire and musical elements through performance of known songs selected from the alphabetized repertoire list
CORE ACTIVITIES	
Acquisition of repertoire	New song selected from the alphabetized repertoire list that expands Ss' repertoire and prepares for the learning of a music rhythmic or melodic concept or element. Instructional context: When we are preparing a rhythmic element, the new song should be selected to prepare the next melodic element, and when we are preparing a melodic element, the new song should be selected to prepare the next rhythmic element.
Preparation and presentation of a rhythmic or melodic element	Learning activities in which Ss are taught a new musical concept through known songs found in the alphabetized repertoire list. When preparing a rhythmic element, the second part of the lesson practices a melodic element; when preparing a melodic element, the second part of the lesson practices a rhythmic element.
Movement development Creative movement	Known song or game found in the alphabetized repertoire list or singing game list Focus on the sequential development of age-appropriate movement skills through songs and folks games.

(*continued*)

Table 2.4 Continued

Practice and performance of musical skills	Ss reinforce their knowledge of musical elements working on the skill areas of reading, writing, form, memory, inner hearing, ensemble work, improvisation and composition, and listening through known songs found in the alphabetized repertoire list. When practicing a rhythmic element, the first part of the lesson prepares a melodic element; when practicing a melodic element the first part of the lesson prepares a rhythmic element.
CLOSURE	
Review and summation Review the lesson outcomes Review the new song	Review of lesson content; T may perform the next new song to be learned in a subsequent lesson found in the alphabetized repertoire list

We will continue to use this wording in lesson plan templates so that the reader can focus on the core activities of the lesson.

In the first section (Preparation of a New Concept) of a lesson, we guide students in discovering the concept behind a new element. For example, if we want to teach the musical elements of quarter and eighth notes, students need to be guided to understand the concept of one or two sounds on a beat.

In the second section (Practice) of the lesson the instructor reinforces and further develops students' understanding of preceding known musical elements through a variety of musical skills. Of course, musical skills may also be practiced during any section of the lesson. This section of the lesson may also include assessment activities to help the instructor identify students who may require extra help.

Each preparation/practice lesson has an instructional context (preparation) and a reinforcement (practice) context. In this type of lesson we continue to develop singing abilities and teach new repertoire and further develop movement and listening skills of students. During the preparation/practice lesson, we do not name the new concept or element but create opportunities for music students to discover the attributes of the new concept or element being studied. This dual structure of the preparation/practice lesson gives students time to process their understandings of the new concept, while permitting opportunities to further develop their musical skills with the previously learned musical element. This is crucial for positive self-esteem and enjoyment needed for learning to take place.

Table 2.5 is an example of this type of a lesson plan, where the teacher prepares the concept of four sounds on a beat through aural analysis and guides students to practice writing a *mi-re-do* pattern.

Kodály Today

Table 2.5 Preparation Lesson Plan, Preparing Sixteenth Notes and Practicing *mi re do*

GRADE 2: UNIT 5, FOUR SIXTEENTH NOTES, LESSON 2	
Outcome	Preparation: analyzing repertoire that contains four sounds on a beat
	Practice: writing melodies that contain *re*
INTRODUCTORY ACTIVITIES	
Warm-up	• Body warm-up
	• Beat activity
	Rondo alla Turca, W. A. Mozart (1756–1791)
	• Breathing: Ss practice blowing a balloon and watch how air is released when deflating the balloon.
	• Resonance: explore a cow sound using low and high voice. Make sure Ss are inhaling and exhaling correctly with the support muscles.
	• Posture: remind Ss of the correct posture for singing.
Sing known songs	"Are You Sleeping?"
	CSP: F
	• Ss sing the song as a two-part canon.
Developing tuneful singing	"Cumberland Gap"
Tone production	CSP: F#
Diction	• Ss sing song.
Expression	• Sirens. Imitate the sound of a siren with the voice. Challenge Ss to make soft and loud, high and low, long and short sirens, sirens that go up and come down or do both.
	• Falling off a cliff. Pretend you're falling of a cliff and say "aaaahhhhhhhhhh!"
	• Ball. Throw a ball from one S to another; Ss have to follow the movement of the ball with their voices.
	• Ss sing the song with the ostinato.
Review known songs and rhythmic elements	"Sea Shell"
	CSP: D
	• Ss sing song.
	• Ss sing song with rhythm syllables and conduct.
	• T sings phrases from "All Around the Buttercup," "Bow Wow Wow," "Here Comes a Bluebird," and other known songs that use known rhythms; Ss echo-sing using rhythm syllables as they tap the beat.
CORE ACTIVITIES	
Teach a new song	"Hush Little Minnie"
	CSP: D
	• T sings song while Ss keep the beat.

(continued)

Developing a Music Repertoire of Songs

Table 2.5 Continued

	• T echo-sings each phrase with Ss. • Ss sing the song. • T selects significant words in the song to be replaced with motions, so that Ss must inner-hear pieces of the song. ➤ Ss continue the beat into the next song.
Develop knowledge of music literacy concepts Describe what you hear	"Paw Paw Patch" CSP: F • Ss sing the song. • Review kinesthetic activities. • T and Ss sing phrase 1 on "loo" and keep the beat. Ss must sing the phrase before T asks each of these questions: • T: "Andy, how many beats did we tap?" (four) • T: "Andy, which beat had the most sounds?" (three) • T: "Andy, how many sounds did we sing on beat 3?" (four) • T: "Andy, if beat 3 has four sounds, how many sounds are on each of the other beats?" (two) • T: "Let's sing phrases 1, 2, and 3 with rhythm syllables, and sing 'loo' on beat 3. It will sound like this: 'tadi tadi loolooloo tadi'. Tap the beat as we sing."
Creative movement	"Great Big House in New Orleans" CSP: A • Ss sing the song while continuing the ostinato. • Ss sing and play the game.
Practice of music, performance, and literacy skills Writing	"Hot Cross Buns" CSP: A • Ss sing "Hot Cross Buns." • Ss sing the song with solfège syllables and hand signs. • T shows Ss the traditional rhythmic notation and solfège syllables (or the melody written on the staff) for "Hot Cross Buns," with incomplete measures. • Ss complete the missing measures. • Ss play the *mi re do* motive on xylophones as an accompaniment to songs that they know.
SUMMARY ACTIVITIES	
Review lesson outcomes Review the new song	"Hush Little Minnie" CSP: D

Kodály Today

The outcomes for this lesson are

- Preparation: analyzing repertoire that contains four sounds on a beat
- Practice: writing melodies that contain *re*
- Preparation: analyzing or describing repertoire in duple meter
- Practice: writing melodies that contain a *so-mi-la* pattern.

Creating a Presentation Lesson

There are two presentation lessons. In the first we associate solfège or rhythm syllables with the new element, and in the second we present the notation for the new lesson plan. Throughout this book, we identify specific songs for teaching specific elements. We refer to these songs as focus songs. They contain core building blocks that we want students to master. Sometimes we target a specific phrase in a focus song; we refer to this phrase as the target phrase for the song.

As mentioned above, in the first presentation lesson we simply name or label the concept or element studied during the preparation/practice lesson and continue developing singing abilities, movement, and listening skills and teaching new repertoire. In the second presentation lesson we show students how to notate target patterns.

Table 2.6 shows a basic presentation lesson plan template for labeling the sound.

Table 2.6 Basic Lesson Plan Template for Presenting Rhythmic or Solfège Syllables

	INTRODUCTION
Performance and demonstration of known musical concepts and elements	Students demonstrate their prior knowledge of repertoire and musical elements, including the new musical element to be presented through performance of songs selected from the alphabetized repertoire list.
	CORE ACTIVITIES
Acquisition of repertoire	New song selected from the alphabetized repertoire list that expands Ss' repertoire and prepares for the learning of a music rhythmic or melodic concept or element. Instructional context: when we are preparing a rhythmic element, the new song should be selected to prepare the next melodic element; when we are preparing a melodic element, the new song should be selected to prepare the new rhythmic element.
Presentation of a rhythmic or melodic element	T labels the name of the new musical element with rhythm or solfège syllables for the focus pattern.

(continued)

Table 2.6 Continued

Creative movement	Known song or game found in the alphabetized repertoire list. Focus on the sequential development of age-appropriate movement skills through songs and folk games.
Presentation of a rhythmic or melodic element	T labels the name of the new musical element with rhythm or solfège syllables in a related pattern.
CLOSURE	
Review and summation	Review of lesson content; T may perform the next new song to be learned in a subsequent lesson found in the alphabetized repertoire list.

Table 2.7 offers a sample presentation where four sounds on a beat are labeled with rhythmic syllables.

Table 2.7 Sample Presentation lesson for Labeling Four Sounds on a Beat with Rhythm Syllables

GRADE 2: UNIT 5, FOUR SIXTEENTH NOTES, LESSON 4	
Outcome	Presentation: label four sounds on a beat with the rhythm syllables *takadimi*.
INTRODUCTORY ACTIVITIES	
Warm-up	• Body warm-up • Beat activity *Rondo alla Turca*, W. A. Mozart (1756–1791) • Breathing: Ss practice blowing a balloon and watch how air is released when deflating the balloon. • Resonance: explore a cow sound using low and high voice. Make sure Ss are inhaling and exhaling correctly with the support muscles. • Posture: remind Ss of the correct posture for singing.
Sing known songs	"Sea Shell" CSP: F • Ss sing the song and keep the beat. • Ss sing the song in canon after four beats. "Mama Buy Me a Chiney Doll" CSP: A • Ss sing song. • Ss perform the song with an ostinato.

(continued)

Kodály Today

Table 2.7 Continued

Develop tuneful singing Tone production Diction Expression	"Dance Josey" CSP: F • Ss sing the song with the ostinato. • Sing song with the word "yip" to develop tone production. • Sing known songs with the word "koo" to develop tone production. • Ss sing the song in canon after two beats.
Review known songs and rhythmic elements	"Hot Cross Buns" CSP: A • Ss sing the song with an ostinato. Ss may play the ostinato on an instrument as accompaniment. • Ss sing song with rhythm syllables. • T sings phrases from "All Around the Buttercup," "Bow Wow Wow," "Here Comes a Bluebird," and other known songs; Ss echo-sing using rhythm syllables as they tap the beat.
CORE ACTIVITIES	
Teach a new song	"Who Killed Cocky Robin?" CSP: C • T sings the song while Ss play a simple rhythmic ostinato. • T sings and Ss quietly clap the ostinato written on the board. • Ss join the T and sing the song.
Presentation of music literacy concepts Describe what you hear with rhythm syllables	"Paw Paw Patch" CSP: F • Ss sing the song. • Briefly review kinesthetic, aural, and visual awareness. • T labels the sound (T: "When we hear four sounds on a beat we call it 'takadimi.'") • T and Ss sing the whole song with rhythm syllables and clap the rhythm. • T echo-sings individual phrases from the song with four to eight individuals; Ss echo-sing using rhythm syllables.
Creative movement	"Ida Red" CSP: F • Ss sing the song while performing a rhythmic ostinato. • Ss compose additional ostinati with which to accompany the song.

(*continued*)

Table 2.7 Continued

Presentation of music literacy concepts
 	
Describe what you hear with rhythm syllables
	"Dinah"
	CSP: D
	• Ss sing the song.
	• T reviews the new rhythm syllables.
	• Ss sing with rhythm syllables and keep the beat.
	• T repeats the process with these songs:
	  ◦ "Tideo"
	  ◦ "Cumberland Gap"
	  ◦ "Dance Josey"
	  Ss create ostinati that use sixteenth notes on xylophones to accompany their songs.

Summary Activities	
Review lesson outcomes Review the new song	"Who Killed Cocky Robin?" CSP: C

Table 2.8 is a basic lesson plan template for notation rhythmic or melodic elements.

Table 2.8 Basic Lesson Plan Design for Notating Rhythmic or Melodic Elements

	INTRODUCTION
Performance and demonstration of known musical concepts and elements	Students demonstrate their prior knowledge of repertoire and musical elements, including the new musical element to be presented through performance of songs selected from the alphabetized repertoire list.
	CORE ACTIVITIES
Acquisition of repertoire	New song selected from the alphabetized repertoire list that expands Ss' repertoire and prepares for the learning of a music rhythmic or melodic concept or element. Instructional context: when we are preparing a rhythmic element, the new song should be selected to prepare the next melodic element; when we are preparing a melodic element, the new song should be selected to prepare the next rhythmic element.
Presentation of a rhythmic or melodic element	T presents the notation in the focus pattern.

(continued)

Table 2.8 Continued

Creative movement	Known song or game found in the alphabetized repertoire list. Focus on the sequential development of age-appropriate movement skills through songs and folk games.
Presentation of a rhythmic or melodic element	T presents the notation in related patterns.
CLOSURE	
Review and summation	Review of lesson content; T may perform the next new song to be learned in a subsequent lesson found in the alphabetized repertoire list.

Table 2.9 is an example of a presentation lesson where we notate four sounds on a beat with sixteenth notes. Note that the lesson still includes many additional musical skills and other learning.

Table 2.9 Sample Presentation Lesson for Notating Four Sounds on a Beat with Four Sixteenth Notes

GRADE 2 UNIT 5, FOUR SIXTEENTH NOTES, LESSON 5	
Outcome	Presentation: notate melodies with four sixteenths using standard rhythmic notation.
INTRODUCTORY ACTIVITIES	
Warm-up	• Body warm-up • Beat activity "Surprise" Symphony, Allegretto, Franz Joseph Haydn (1732–1809) • Breathing: Ss practice blowing a balloon and watch how air is released when deflating the balloon. • Resonance: explore a cow sound using low and high voice. Make sure Ss are inhaling and exhaling correctly with the support muscles. • Posture: remind Ss of the correct posture for singing.
Sing known songs	"Here Comes a Bluebird" CSP: A • Ss sing and step the beat. • Ss sing the song in canon after eight beats.

(continued)

Table 2.9   Continued

Develop tuneful singing Tone production Diction Expression	"Tideo" CSP: F# • Ss sing the song with the ostinato. • Ss sing with a "koo" sound. • Ss sing with a "yip" sound. • Ss sing the song with the syllables "Mi-oh."
Songs to review known elements	"Bye Bye Baby" CSP: D • Ss sing the song. • Ss sing song with rhythm names and conduct. • Ss sing song in canon. • T sings phrases from "All Around the Buttercup," "Bow Wow Wow," "Here Comes a Bluebird," and finally "Paw Paw Patch"; Ss echo-sing using rhythm syllables as they tap the beat.
CORE ACTIVITIES	
Teach a new song	"Green Gravel" CSP: D • T sings the song while Ss show the phrases. • Ss sing the song. • Ss sing the song and T demonstrates how to play the game. • Ss sing and play the game.
Presentation of music literacy concepts Notate what you hear	"Paw Paw Patch" CSP: F • Ss sing the song. • T briefly reviews kinesthetic, aural, and visual awareness activities. • T reviews aural presentation. • T: "When the beat is a quarter note, we can use four sixteenth notes to represent four sounds on a beat. A sixteenth note has a note head, a stem, and two flags. Four sixteenth notes have a double beam." • T: "This is how the first phrase of 'Paw Paw Patch' looks with standard rhythmic notation." $\frac{2}{4}$ ♫ ♫ | ♬ ♫ ‖ • T: "We can read this rhythm pattern using our rhythm syllables." • T sings rhythm syllables while pointing to the rhythm on the board. Ss echo T using rhythm syllables while pointing to the rhythm.

(continued)

Kodály Today

Table 2.9 Continued

Notate what you hear	• T repeats the previous three steps but writes using stick notation.
	  $\frac{2}{4}$ ♩♩ | ♫♩ ‖
	• T shows the remaining phrases with standard rhythmic notation and Ss read and sing.
	  $\frac{2}{4}$ ♫♫ | ♬♫ |
	  ♫♫ | ♬♫ |
	  ♫♫ | ♬♫ |
	  ♫♬ | ♫♩ ‖

Creative movement	"Clap Your Hands Together (Cut the Cake)" CSP: C • T sings the song while Ss clap a rhythmic ostinato. • Ss may choose an instrument on which to perform the rhythm. • T will also choose a S to play the beat on a drum. • Ss sing and play the game.

Presentation of music literacy concepts
 	
Notate what you hear
	"Dinah"
	CSP: F
	• Ss sing the song.
	• Ss sing with rhythm syllables.
	• T reviews visual presentation (T: "We can use four sixteenth notes to represent four sounds on a beat. A sixteenth note has a note head, a stem, and two flags. Four sixteenth notes have a double beam.")
	• Ss read the rhythm of "Dinah" written in traditional rhythmic notation on the board with rhythm syllables, and they keep the beat.
	• T shows Ss how to count with numbers.
	• T transforms the song into other known songs containing four sixteenth notes.
	  ◦ "Dance Josie"
	  ◦ "Tideo"

Summary Activities	
Review lesson outcomes Review the new song	"Green Gravel" CSP: D

Connections to Grade Handbooks

The second chapter of each of the handbooks presents teachers with an overview of basic repertoire used for developing singing, playing instruments, creative movement, improvisation, and listening. Included in this section is an alphabetized list of songs with sources, as well as a pedagogical list of songs. The pedagogical list of songs gives teachers suggestions on the best songs for teaching rhythmic and melodic elements in a grade. Chapter 2 of the handbook also includes game directions for singing games in each grade.

Discussion Questions
1. How is an alphabetized repertoire list useful for teaching?
2. What kinds of repertoire should be included in an alphabetized repertoire list?
3. What criteria do we use for selecting repertoire for an elementary music curriculum?
4. Talk to a reading specialist or kindergarten or prekindergarten teacher, and ask him or her to explain how books are selected to read to the students. Make a list of all of the suggestions and try to draw a parallel between selecting books for use in the classroom and selecting musical repertoire.
5. What does analysis of a folk song entail?
6. How important is it to think about the quality of the song material you use when teaching?
7. How can we further develop a lesson plan framework based on the selection of musical repertoire?
8. Discuss each section of a preparation/practice lesson plan.
9. Discuss each section of a presentation lesson plan.

Ongoing Assignment

1. Sing through a selection of the songs suggested in the chapter. Do a sample analysis of several songs.
2. Interview a Kodály music teacher and ask him or her to share with you how song material is chosen for the classroom. Begin to compile your own lists of songs for each grade level that you teach, according to the selection criteria outlined in this chapter.
3. Using the lesson plan formats given in this chapter, create a lesson plan where you prepare a rhythmic element and practice a melodic element for grade 1 and grade 3.

Bibliography
Addo, A. O. "Children's Idiomatic Expressions of Music Cultural Knowledge." *International Journal of Music Education*, 1997, *30*: 15–25.
Alperson, P. A. "Introduction." In *What Is Music? An Introduction to the Philosophy of Music*, ed. P. A. Alperson, pp. 3–30. University Park: Pennsylvania State University Press, 1994.

Anderson, William M., and Patricia Shehan Campbell, eds. *Multicultural Perspectives in Music Education*. Reston, VA: Music Educators National Conference, 1996.

Barrett, J. R. "Currents of Change in the Music Curriculum." In *International Handbook of Research in Arts Education,* ed. L. Bresler, pp.147–161. Parts I and II. Dordrecht, Netherlands: Springer, 2007.

Bartolome, Sarah J. "The Virtual Field Experience: An Immersive Approach Toward Multicultural Music Education." *Kodaly Envoy*, 2013, *39*(2): 14–18.

Bass, Randall V., and J. W. Good. "Educare and educere: Is a Balance Possible in the Educational System?" *Educational Forum*, 2004, *68*(Winter): 161–168.

Blacking, J. *Venda Children's Songs: A Study in Ethnomusicological Analysis.* Chicago: University of Chicago Press, 1995. (Original work published 1967.)

Bliss, H. "Folksong Classification and Retrieval." *Kodály Envoy*, 1983, *10*(2): 2–7.

Bowman, W. *Philosophical Perspectives on Music.* New York: Oxford University Press, 1998.

Brumfield, S. "Folk Music in the Classroom: Performance Practice and the Music Teacher." *Kodály Envoy*, 1998, *24*(2): 8–11.

Burton, B. "Weaving the Tapestry of World Musics." In *World Musics and Music Education: Facing the Issues,* ed. B. Reimer, pp. 161–185. Reston, VA: MENC, 2002.

Campbell, P. S. "Global Practices." In *The Child as Musician: A Handbook of Musical Development,* ed. G. E. McPherson, pp. 415–437. New York: Oxford University Press, 2006.

Campbell, P. S. *Teaching Music Globally: Experiencing Music, Expressing Culture.* Oxford: Oxford University Press, 2004.

Choksy, L. "American Folksongs and Music Education." *Kodály Envoy*, 1977, *4*(2).

Choksy, L. "On Using Native Music in Teaching." *Bulletin of the International Kodály Society*, 1990, *15*(1): 3–6.

Choksy, L., and D. Brummitt. "120 Singing Games and Dances for Elementary Schools." Englewood Cliffs, NJ: Prentice-Hall, 1987.

Cowan, D. "Folk Music of the South Carolina Sea Islands." *Kodály Envoy*, 1991, *17*(4): 25–31.

Cuskelly, J. "The Importance of Folk Materials: The 'Little Story' and the 'Big Story.'" *Bulletin of the International Kodály Society*, 2011, *36*(2): 3–7.

Downey, J. "Informal Learning in Music in the Irish Secondary School Context." *Action, Criticism and Theory for Music Education*, 2009, *8*(2): 47–59.

El Sistema. (July 1, 2010). Retrieved from http://www.el-sistemafilm.com/el_Sistema_The_Story.html. Accessed Oct. 29, 2010.

Elliott, David J. *Praxial Music Education: Reflections and Dialogues.* New York: Oxford University Press, 2005.

Epstein, Mary, and Jonathan C. Rappaport. *The Kodály Teaching Weave. Vol. 2: Song Analysis Forms and Definitions.* Westborough, MA: Pro Canto Press 2000.

Eshelman, D. "The Upper Elementary General Music Class: Song Literature with Characteristics for Success." *Bulletin of the International Kodály Society*, 1994, *19*(2), 50–57.

Farkas, M. "Folk Song as a Living Force in the Lives of Hungarian Children." *Kodály Envoy*, 1977, *4*(1).

Fitzpatrick, Kate R. "Cultural Diversity and the Formation of Identity: Our Role as Music Teachers." *Music Educators Journal*, 2012, *98*(4): 53–59. Education Research Complete. Web. March 4, 2013.

Fox, Donna Brink, et al. "Looking Back, Looking Forward: A Report on Early Childhood Music Education in Accredited American Preschools." *Journal of Research in Music Education*, 2006, *54*(4): 278–292.

Garrett, D. "Ruth Crawford Seeger's 'American Folk Songs for Children' at Fifty Years." *Kodály Envoy*, 1998, *24*(3): 7–8.

Harwood, E. *The Memorized Song Repertoire of Children in Grades Four and Five in Champaign, Illinois.* Unpublished doctoral diss., University of Illinois, 1987.

Hegyi, Erzsébet. "Masterpieces in the Highlight of the World of Folk Songs." *Bulletin of the International Kodaly Society*, 1987, *12*(2): 3–15.

Herboly-Kocsár, Ildikó. "The Place, Role and Importance of Art Music in School." *Bulletin of the International Kodály Society* 1993, *18*(1): 41–44.

Hickerson, J. "The Archive of Folk Song in the Library of Congress." *Kodály Envoy*, 1977, *3*(4).

Higgins, K. M. *The Music of Our Lives.* Philadelphia: Temple University Press, 1991.

Ittzés, Mihály. "Zoltán Kodály's Singing Exercises: A Summary." *International Kodály Society Journal*, 1995, *20*(1): 50–53.

Jorgensen, E. "Philosophical Issues in Curriculum." In *The New Handbook of Research on Music Teaching and Learning*, ed. R. Colwell and C. Richardson, pp. 48–62. New York: Oxford University Press, 2002.

Kania, A. "The Philosophy of Music." *The Stanford Encyclopedia of Philosophy*, 2007. http://plato.stanford.edu/entries/music/. Accessed June 22, 2010.

Kirk, C. "Black Song." *Kodály Envoy*, 1978, *5*(2).

Klinger, R. *Matters of Compromise: An Ethnographic Study of Culture-Bearers in Elementary Music Education.* Unpublished Ph.D. diss., University of Washington, 1996.

Kodály, Zoltán. "Ancient Traditions—Today's Musical Life." In *Selected Writings of Zoltán Kodály*, 1974, 165–184.

Kodály, Zoltán. "Children's Choirs." In *Selected Writings of Zoltán Kodály*, 1974, pp. 119–126.

Kodály, Zoltán. "A Hundred Year Plan." In *Selected Writings of Zoltán Kodály*, 1974, pp. 160–162.

Kodály, Zoltán. "Music in the Kindergarten." In *Selected Writings of Zoltán Kodály*, 1974, pp. 127–151.

Kodály, Zoltán. "Pentatonic Music." In *Selected Writings of Zoltán Kodály*, 1974, pp. 221–228.

Kodály, Zoltán. "The Role of the Authentic Folksong in Music Education." *Bulletin of the International Kodály Society*, 1985, *10*(1): 15–19.

Kodály, Zoltán. *The Selected Writings of Zoltán Kodály*, ed. F. Bonis, trans. L. Halapy and F. Macnicol. London: Boosey & Hawkes, 1974.

Lineburgh, N. E., and L. Chet-Yeng. "Early Childhood Repertoire: Inherently Musical/Positively Enchanting." *Kodály Envoy*, 2006, *33*(1): 5–8.

Lum, C. H. *Musical Networks of Children: An Ethnography of Elementary School Children in Singapore.* Unpublished doctoral diss., University of Washington, Seattle, 2007.

Lund, Floice R. *Research and Retrieval: Music Teacher's Guide to Material Selection and Collection*, pp. 4–10. Westborough, MA: Pro Canto Press, 1981.

Marsh, K. "Music in the Lives of Refugee and Newly Arrived Immigrant Children in Sydney, Australia." In *Oxford Handbook of Children's Musical Cultures,* ed. P. S. Campbell and T. Wiggins. New York: Oxford University Press, 2013.

Marsh, K., and S. Young. "Musical Play." In *The Child as Musician: A Handbook of Musical Development,* ed. G. McPherson, pp. 289–310. Oxford, UK: Oxford University Press, 2006.

McCarthy, M., and J. S. Goble. "The Praxial Philosophy in Historical Perspective." In *Praxial Music Education: Reflections and Dialogues,* ed. D. J. Elliott, pp. 19–51. New York: Oxford University Press, 2009.

McIntosh, J. A. *Moving Through Tradition: Children's Practice and Performance of Dance, Music and Song in South-Central Bali.* Unpublished doctoral diss., Queen's University, Belfast, 2008.

Nettl, Bruno. *Folk and Traditional Music of the Western Continents.* 2nd ed. Englewood Cliffs, NJ: Prentice-Hall, 1991.

Nettl, Bruno. "Foreword." In *Songs in Their Heads: Music and Its Meaning in Children's Lives*, ed. Patricia Shehan Campbell. New York: Oxford University Press, 1998.

Nettl, Bruno, Charles Capwell, Philip V. Bohlman, Isabel K. F. Wong, and Thomas Turino. *Excursions in World Music.* 3rd ed. Englewood Cliffs, NJ: Prentice-Hall, 2000.

Novak, Ruth M. "Camp Kodály: Using Camp Songs in a Kodály Curriculum." *Missouri Journal of Research in Music Education*, 2005, *42*: 81.

O'Flynn, J. "Re-appraising Ideas of Musicality in Intercultural Contexts of Music Education." *International Journal of Music Education*, 2005, *23*(3): 191–203.

Parnell, C. "Children's Songs in the Archive of Folk Song." *Kodály Envoy*, 1978, *4*(3): 10–12.

Regelski, T. "Curriculum Reform: Reclaiming 'Music' as Social Praxis." *Action, Criticism, and Theory for Music Education*, 2009, 8(1): 66–84. http://act.maydaygroup.org/articles/Regelski8_1.pdf. Accessed June 22, 2010.

Regelski, T. "On 'Methodolatry' and Music Teaching as Critical and Reflective Praxis." *Philosophy of Music Education Review*, 2002, *10*(2): 102–123.

Renwick, J. M., and G. E. McPherson. "Interest and Choice: Student-selected Repertoire and Its Effect on Practising Behaviour." *British Journal of Music Education,* 2002, *19*: 173–188.

Reimer, B. *A Philosophy of Music Education: Advancing the Vision*, 3rd ed. Upper Saddle River, NJ: Prentice-Hall, 2003.

Roberts, C. "Children's Music in the Smithsonian Folkways Collection." *Kodály Envoy*, 2010, *37*(1): 4–7.

Robinson, J. (ed.). *Music Meaning.* Ithaca: Cornell University Press, 1997.

Schön, D., M. Boyer, S. Moreno, M. Besson, I. Peretz, and R. Kolinsky. "Songs as an Aid for Language Acquisition." *Cognition,* 2008, *106*(2) 975–983.

Shehan Campbell, Patricia, Sue Williamson, and Pierre Perron. Traditional *Songs of Singing Cultures: A World Sampler.* Miami: Warner Bros. Publications, 1996.

Szabá, Helga. "Medieval Monody—Its Relevance for Classroom Teaching." *Bulletin of the International Kodaly Society,* 1979, 4(2): 26–36.

Vogt, J. "Philosophy—Music Education—Curriculum: Some Casual Remarks on Some Basic Concepts." *Action, Criticism, and Theory for Music Education,* 2003, *2*(1): 2–25. http://act.maydaygroup.org/articles/Vogt2_1.pdf. Accessed June 22, 2010.

Taggart, G., K. Whitby, and C. Sharp. *International Review of Curriculum and Assessment Frameworks Curriculum and Progression in the Arts: An International Study.* UK: Qualifications and Curriculum Authority (QCA) and National Foundation for Educational Research, 2004.

Taylor, Donald M. "Refining Learned Repertoire for Percussion Instruments in an Elementary Setting." *Journal of Research in Music Education,* 2006, *54*(3): 231–243.

Tsang, C., and N. J. Conrad. "Does the Message Matter? The Effect of Song Type on Infants' Pitch Preference for Lullabies and Playsongs." *Infant Behavior and Development,* 2010, *33*: 96–100.

Vikár, L. "Folk Music in Music Education." *Kodály Envoy,* 1982, 9(2). Reprinted 2014 40(3): 21–23.

Welch, Graham F. "Singing and Vocal Development." In *The Child as Musician: A Handbook of Musical Development,* ed. Gary McPherson, pp. 311–330. New York: Oxford University Press, 2006.

Catalogues

The Whole Folkways Catalog (a catalog of historic folkways recordings). Smithsonian/Folkways, Center for Folklife Programs and Cultural Studies, 955 L'Enfant Plaza, Suite 2600, Smithsonian Institution, Washington, DC 20560; (202) 287-3262.

Collections

World Music Press, P.O. Bow 2565, Danbury, CT 06813. Catalog: www.worldmusicpress.com/.

Selected Folk Music Bibliography

Abrahams, Roger, and George Foss. *A Singer and Her Songs: Almeda Riddle's Book of Ballads.* Baton Rouge: Louisiana State University Press, 1970.

Ames, L. D. "Missouri Play Party." *Journal of American Folklore,* 1911, *24*(93): 295–318.

Armitage, Theresa. *Our First Music.* Boston: C. C. Birchard, 1941.

Arnold, Byron. *Folksongs of Alabama.* Birmingham: University of Alabama Press, 1950.

Asch, Moses. *104 Folk Songs.* New York: Robbins Music, 1964.

Baez, Joan. *The Joan Baez Songbook,* ed. Elie Siegmeister. New York: Ryerson Music, 1964.

Beckwith, Martha W. *Folk Songs of Jamaica.* Poughkeepsie, NY: Folklore Publications, Vassar College, 1922.

Bierhorst, John. *A Cry from the Earth: Music of the North American Indians.* New York: Four Winds Press, 1979.

Bierhorst, John. *Songs of the Chippewa.* New York: Farrar Strauss & Giroux, 1974.

Botkin, Benjamin A. *The American Play Party.* New York: Frederick Ungar, 1963; 1st ed. University of Nebraska Press, 1937.

Botsford, Florence H. *Songs of the Americas.* New York: Schirmer, 1930.

Boyer, Walter E., et al. *Songs Along the Mahantongo: Pennsylvania Dutch Folk Songs.* Lancaster: Pennsylvania Folklore Center, 1951.

Broadwood, Lucy E. *English County Songs.* London: Boosey, 1893.

Bronson, B. H. *The Singing Tradition of Child's Popular Ballads.* Princeton: Princeton University Press, 1976.

Brown, Florence W., and Neva L Boyd. *Old English and American Games for School and Playground.* Chicago: Soul Brothers, 1915.

Brown, Frank C. *Collection of North American Folklore.* Durham, NC: Duke University Press, 1962.

Brown, Frank C. *North Carolina Folklore.* Durham, NC: Duke University Press, 1962.

Burlin, Natalie C. *Negro Folk-Songs.* New York: Schirmer, 1918.

Burton, Thomas G., and Ambrose N. Manning. *East Tennessee State University Collection of Folklore: Folksongs.* Institute of Regional Studies, Monograph no. 4. Johnson: East Tennessee State University Press, 1967.

Chappell, Louis W. *Folk Songs of Roanoke and the Albemarle.* Morgantown, WV: Ballard Press, 1939.

Chase, Richard. *American Folk Tales and Songs.* New York: Dover, 1971.

Choksy, Lois. *The Kodaly Context.* Upper Saddle River, NJ: Prentice-Hall, 1981.

Colcord, Joanna. *Roll and Go: Songs of American Sailormen.* Indianapolis: Bobbs-Merrill, 1924.

Colcord, Joanna. *Songs of American Sailormen.* New York: Oak, 1964.

Coleman, Satis N. *Songs of American Folks.* New York: John Day, 1942.

Courlander, Harold. *Negro Folk Music USA.* New York: Columbia University Press, 1963.

Courlander, Harold. *Negro Songs from Alabama.* New York: Oak, 1963.

Cox, John Harrington. *Traditional Ballads, Mainly from West Virginia.* New York: National Service Bureau, 1939.

Creighton, Helen. *Songs and Ballads from Nova Scotia.* New York: Dover, 1972.

Dallin, Leon, and Lynn Dallin. *Heritage Songster.* Dubuque, IA: W. C. Brown, 1966.

Dykema, Peter. *Twice 55 Games with Music.* Boston: Birchard, 1924.

Eddy, Mary O. *Ballads and Songs from Ohio.* Hatboro, PA: Folklore Associates, 1964.

Elder, Jacob D. *Song Games from Trinidad and Tobago.* Columbus, OH: Publication of the American Folklore Society, 1965.

Erdei, Ida, Faith Knowles, and Denise Bacon. *My Singing Bird,* vol. 2 of *150 American Folk Songs from the Anglo-American, African-American, English, Scottish and Irish Traditions.* Columbus, OH: Kodály Center of America, 2002.

Erdei, Peter, and Katalin Komlos. *150 American Folk Songs for Children to Sing and Play.* New York: Boosey & Hawkes, 1974.

Farnsworth, Charles H., and Cecil J. Sharp. *Folk-Songs, Chanteys and Singing Games.* New York: H. W. Gray, 1909.

Fenner, T. P. *Religious Folk Songs of the Negro.* Hampton, VA: Hampton Institute Press, 1909.

Fife, Austin E., and S. Alta. *Cowboy and Western Songs.* New York: Clarkson N. Potter, 1969.

Fife, Austin E., and S. Alta. *The Songs of the Cowboys.* Thorp Collection. New York: Clarkson N. Potter, 1966.

Fowke, Edith. *Sally Go Round the Sun: 300 Children's Songs, Rhymes, and Games.* Garden City, NY: Doubleday, 1969.

Fowke, Edith, and Norman Cazden. *Lumbering Songs from the Northern Woods.* Austin: University of Texas Press, for the American Folklore Society, 1970.

Gillington, Alice E. *Old Surrey Singing Games and Skipping Rope Rhymes.* London: J. Curwen & Sons, 1909.

Glass, Paul, and Herman B. Vestal. *Songs and Stories of the North American Indians.* New York: Grosset and Dunlop, 1968.

Gomme, Alice B., and Cecil J. Sharp. *Children's Singing Games.* London: Novello and Co., 1912.

Gomme, Alice B., and Cecil J. Sharp. *The Traditional Games of England, Scotland, and Ireland,* 2 vols. New York: Dover, 1964, 1st ed. 1894–1898.

Gordon, Dorothy. *Sing It Yourself: Folk Songs of All Nations.* New York: Dutton, 1928.

Greig, Duncan. *The Greig Duncan Folk Song Collection I.* Aberdeen, Scotland: Aberdeen University Press, 1981.

Greenleaf, Elisabeth B., and Grace Yarrow Mansfield. *Ballads and Songs of Newfoundland.* Cambridge, MA: Harvard University Press, 1933.

Hall, Doreen, and Arnold Walter. *Orff Schulwerk, Vol. I: Pentatonic.* Mainz/London: B Schott Sohne, 1956.

Harlow, Frederick Pease. *Chanteying Aboard American Ships.* Barre, MA: Barre Gazette, 1962.

Henry, Millinger E. "Still More Ballads and Folk-Songs from the Southern Highlands." *Journal of American Folklore,* 1932, 45(175): 1–176.

High Road of Song: Then and Now, Music for Young Americans. Chicago: Scott Foresman, 1971.

Hofman, Charles. *American Indians Sing.* New York: John B. Day, 1967.

Hopekirk, Helen. *Seventy Scottish Folk Songs.* Boston: Oliver Ditson, 1905.

Hudson, Florence. *Songs of the Americas.* New York: Schirmer, 1922.

Hugill, Stan. *Shanties and Sailor's Songs.* New York: Praeger, 1969.
Ives, Burl. *The Burl Ives Song Book.* New York: Ballantine Books (p.b.), 1953.
Jackson, Bruce. *Wake up, Dead Man: Afro-American Worksongs from Texas Prisons.* Cambridge, MA: Harvard University Press, 1972.
Jackson, George Pullen. *Spiritual Folksongs of Early America.* New York: Augustin, 1937.
Johnson, Guy B. *Folk Culture on St. Helena Island, South Carolina.* Hatboro, PA: Folklore Associates, 1968.
Johnson, James Weldon, and J. Rosamund. *The Books of Negro Spirituals.* New York: Viking Compass, 1969; 1st ed. Viking Press, 1925.
Jones, Bessie, and Bess Lomax Hawes. *Step It Down.* New York: Harper and Row, 1972.
Karpeles, M. *Folk Songs from Newfoundland.* London: Faber and Faber, 1971.
Katz, Bernard. *The Social Implications of Early Negro Music in the US.* New York: Arno Press, 1963.
Knowles, Faith, ed., Vamos a Cantar: *230 Latino and Hispanic Folk Songs to Sing, Read, and Play.* Columbus, Ohio: Kodály Institute at Capital University, 2006.
Kwami, Robert Mawuena. *African Songs for School and Community: A Selection from Ghana.* New York: Schott, 1998.
Kennedy, Robert E. *Black Cameos.* New York: Albert & C. Boni, 1924.
Kenney, Maureen. *Circle Round the Zero: Play Chants and Singing Game of City Children.* St. Louis: Magnamusic-Baton, 1974.
Kersey, Robert E. *Just Five—A Collection of Pentatonic Songs.* Westminster, MD: Westminster Press, 1970.
Kolb, Sylvia, and John Kolb. *A Treasury of Folk Songs.* New York: Bantam Books, 1948.
Korson, George. *Pennsylvania Songs and Legends.* Philadelphia: University of Pennsylvania Press, 1949.
Landeck, Beatrice. *Songs to Grow On: A Collection of American Folk Songs for Children.* New York: Edward B. Marks, 1950.
Langstaff, John. *Hi! Ho! the Rattlin' Bog, and Other Folk Songs for Group Singing.* New York: Harcourt Brace and World, 1969.
Langstaff, John, P. Swanson, and G. Emlen. *Celebrate the Spring: Spring & Mayday Celebrations for Schools and Communities.* Watertown, MA: Revels, 1998.
Larkin, Margaret. *The Singing Cowboy.* New York: Knopf, 1931.
Leisy, James. *The Folk Song Abecedary.* New York: Bonanza Books, 1966.
Linscott, Eloise Hubbard. *Folk Songs of Old New England.* Hamden, CT: Archon Books, 1962.
Lloyd, A. L., et al. *Folk Songs of the Americas.* New York: Oak (for UNESCO), 1966.
Locke, Eleanor G. *Sail Away: 155 American Folk Songs to Sing, Read and Play.* New York: Boosey & Hawkes, 2004.
Lomax, Alan. *The Folk Songs of North America.* New York: Doubleday, 1960.
Lomax, John, and Alan Lomax. *Our Singing Country: A Second Volume of American Ballads and Folk Songs.* New York: Macmillan, 1941.

Lomax, John, and Alan Lomax, with Charles Seeger and Ruth Crawford Seeger. *Folk Song USA: The 111 Best American Ballads.* New York: Signet New American Library, 1966.

Matteson, Maurice. *American Folk-Songs for Young Singers.* New York: Schirmer, 1947.

McIntosh, David. *Singing Games and Dances.* New York: Association Press, 1957.

McIntosh, David, and Dale R. Whiteside. *Folk Songs and Singing Games of the Illinois Ozarks.* Carbondale and Edwardsville: Southern Illinois University Press, 1974.

Mendoza, Vicente T. *Lírica Infantil de México.* Mexico D. F.: El Colegio de Mexico, 1980.

Morse, Jim, et al. *Folk Songs of the Caribbean.* New York: Bantam Books, 1958.

Moses, Irene E. P. *Rhythmic Action, Plays and Dances.* Springfield, MA: Milton Bradley, 1915.

Newell, William Wells. *Games and Songs of American Children.* New York: Dover, 1963; 1st ed. 1882.

Niles, John Jacob. *Seven Kentucky Mountain Songs.* New York: Schirmer, 1929.

Okun, Milton. *Something to Sing About.* New York: Macmillan, 1958.

Owens, Bess A. "Songs of the Cumberlands." *Journal of American Folklore*, 1936, 49(193): 215–242.

Owens, William A. *Swing and Turn: Texas Play and Party Games.* Dallas: Tardy, 1936.

Pietroforte, Alfred. *Songs of the Yokuts and Paiutes.* Healdsburg, CA: Naturegraph, 1965.

Porter, Grace Cleveland. *Negro Folk Singing Games and Folk Games of the Habitants.* London: J. Curwin and Sons, 1914.

Randolph, Vance. *Ozark Folksongs.* Columbia: State Historical Society of Missouri, 1949.

Richardson, Ethel Park. *American Mountain Songs.* New York: Greenburg, 1927.

Ritchie, Jean. *Golden City: Scottish Children's Street Games & Songs.* Edinburgh-London: Oliver A. Boyd, 1965.

Ritchie, Jean. *Singing Family of the Cumberlands.* New York: Oxford University Press, 1955.

Rosenbaum. *Folk Visions and Voices: Traditional Music and Song in North Georgia.* Athens: University of Georgia Press, 1983.

Sandburg, Carl. *The American Songbag.* New York: Harcourt Brace, 1927.

Scarborough, Dorothy. *On the Trail of Negro Folksongs.* Hatboro, PA: Folklore Association, 1963.

Seeger, Pete. *American Favorite Ballads.* New York: Oak, 1961.

Seeger, Ruth Crawford. *American Folk Songs for Children.* Garden City, NY: Doubleday, 1948.

Seeger, Ruth Crawford. *American Folk Songs for Christmas.* Garden City, NY: Doubleday, 1953.

Seeger, Ruth Crawford. *Animal Folk Songs for Children.* Garden City, NY: Doubleday, 1950.

Sharp, Cecil J. *Twelve Folksongs from the Appalachian Mountains.* London: Oxford University Press, 1945.

Sharp, Cecil J., and Maud Karpeles. *English Folk Songs from the Southern Appalachians.* Vols. I and II. London: Oxford University Press, 1932.

Siegmeister, Ellie. *Work and Sing.* New York: William R. Scott, 1944.

"Sing Out." *The Folk Song Magazine.* 505 Eighth Ave., New York, NY 10018.

Sturgis, Edith, and Robert Hughes. *Songs from the Hills of Vermont.* Boston: Schirmer, 1919.

Thomas, Jean, and Joseph A. Leeder. *The Singing' Gatherin': Tunes from the Southern Appalachians.* Upper Saddle River, NJ: Silver Burdett, 1939.

Tobitt, Janet Evelyn. *A Book of Negro Songs.* Pleasantville, NY: published by author, 1950.

Trent-Johns, Altona and Annie O. Warburton. *Play Songs of the Deep South.* Washington, DC: Associated, 1944.

Walter, Lavinia Edna. *Old English Singing Games.* London: A. & C. Black, 1926.

Warner, Anne, and Frank Warner. *Collection of Traditional American Folksongs.* New York: Syracuse University Press, 1984.

The Weavers' Songbook. New York: Harper & Brothers, 1960.

White, Newman Ivey. *American Negro Folk Songs.* Hatboro, PA: Folklore Associates, 1965.

White, Newman Ivey, with Jan Schinhan, music ed. *The Frank C. Brown Collection of North Carolina Folklore.* Durham, NC: Duke University Press, 1952.

Barrett, Margaret, and Johannella Tafuri. "Creative Meaning-Making in Infants' and Young Children's Musical Cultures." In *The Oxford Handbook of Music Education,* vol. 1, Gary E. McPherson and Graham F. Welch, pp. 296–313. New York: Oxford University Press, 2012.

Discography

Afro-American Blues and Game Songs. Library of Congress, Recording Laboratory, AAFS L4.

American Favorite Ballads, Vol. I. Pete Seeger, Folkways Records.

American Folk Songs Sung by the Seegers. The Seegers, Folkways Records, FA 2005.

American Folk Songs for Children. Mike and Peggy Seeger, Rounder Records, 8001, 8002, 8003.

American Folk Songs for Children. Pete Seeger, Folkways Records, FP 701.

American Folksongs for Children. Southern Folk Heritage Series, Atlantic, SD 1350.

American Play Parties. Pete Seeger, Folkways Records, 1959, FC 7604.

American Sea Songs and Chanties. Library of Congress, Recording Laboratory, AAFS L26.

Anglo-American Songs and Ballads. Library of Congress, Recording Laboratory, AAFS L12 and AAFS L14.

Animal Folk Songs for Children. Peggy Seeger, Scholastic Records, 1957, SC 7551.

Anthology of American Folk Music. Harry Smith, Folkway Records, 2951, 2952, 2953.

Asch Recordings. Compiled by Moses Asch and Charles E. Smith, Folkways Records, ASCH AA 3/4.

Birds, Beasts, Bugs, and Bigger Fishes. Pete Seeger, Folkways Records.
Birds, Beasts, Bugs, and Little Fishes. Pete Seeger, Folkways Records.
Brave Boys. Sandy Paton, Recorded Anthology of American Music, NWR 239.
Children's Jamaican Songs and Games. Folkways Records, FC 7250.
Children's Songs and Games, from the Southern Mountains. Sung by Jean Ritchie, Folkways Records, FC 7059.
The Cool of the Day: The Music of Jean Ritchie. The Dusing Singers (Jean Ritchie), Greenhays Recordings, 1991.
Cowboy Songs, Ballads and Cattle Calls from Texas. Compiled by John Lomax, Library of Congress, Recording Laboratory. AAFS L28.
A Cry from the Earth. John Bierhorst, Folkways Records, 3777.
Edna Ritchie of Viper Kentucky. Folk-Legacy Records, FSA-3; Sharon, CT.
Folk Music from Wisconsin. Library of Congress, Recording Laboratory, AAFS L9.
Folk Music USA. Folkways Records, FE 4530.
Folk Song and Minstrelsy. Vanguard Recordings, RL 7624.
Georgia Sea Island Songs. Alan Lomax, Recorded Anthology of American Music, NWR 278.
Instrumental Music of the Southern Appalachians. Diane Hamilton, Tradition Records, TLP 1007.
I've Got a Song. Sandy and Caroline Paton, Folk-Legacy Records, FSK 52.
Jean Ritchie Sings Children's Songs and Games. Folkways Records, FC 7054.
Latin American Children's Game Songs. Henrietta Yurchenco, Folkways Records, FC 7851.
The Negro People in America. Heirloom Records, 1964.
Negro Work Songs and Calls. Library of Congress, Recording Laboratory, AAFS L8.
Old Mother Hippletoe. Kate Rinzler, Recorded Anthology of American Music, NWR 291.
Old Times & Hard Times. Hedy West, Folk-Legacy Records, 1967, FSA 32.
1,2,3, and a Zing, Zing, Zing. Tony Schwartz, Folkways Records, FC 7003 A.
Play and Dance Songs and Tunes. Library of Congress, Recording Laboratory, AAFS L55.
Ring Games. Harold Courlander and Ruby Pickens Tartt, Folkways Records, FC 7004.
Ring Games, Line Games, and Play Party Songs of Alabama. Folkways Records, FC 7004.
So Early in the Morning. Diane Hamilton, Tradition Records, TLP 1034.
Songs and Ballads of the Anthracite Miners. Library of Congress, Recording Laboratory, AAFS L16.
Songs of Love, Luck, Animals, and Magic. Charlotte Heth, Recorded Anthology of American Music, NWR 297.
Songs of the Michigan Lumberjacks. Library of Congress, Recording Laboratory, AAFS L56.
Songs Traditionally Sung in North Carolina. Folk-Legacy Records, FSA 53.

Sounds of the South. Alan Lomax, Atlantic Recording Corporation, Southern Folk Heritage, 1993.
Spanish-American Children's Songs. Jenny Wells Vincent, Cantemos Records.
Spiritual with Dock Reed and Vera Hall Ward. Folkways Records, FA 2038.
Step It Down. Bessie Jones, Rounder Records, 8004.
Versions and Variants of "Barbara Allen." Library of Congress, Recording Laboratory, AAFS L54.

Chapter 3

Developing Creative Expression in the Elementary Classroom Through Singing, Movement, and Playing Instruments

Key Questions

- How do I develop students' singing voices?
- What types of vocal warm-up exercises are appropriate for elementary age children?
- What are the best approaches to teaching a song?
- How can I develop a sequence for teaching movement activities in the elementary school?
- How can I integrate instruments into a music lesson?
- How can I develop a lesson plan framework that includes techniques for developing a student's performance skills?
- What are the differences between a preparation/practice lesson plan, a presentation lesson plan, and an initial practice lesson plan?

In the previous chapter, we discussed the criteria necessary for selecting songs for classroom use. This chapter includes an overview of how to teach the basics of singing[1] movement and playing instruments, and how this information will affect the planning and design of a music lesson. The chapter also includes a section on some approaches to teaching a song material.

Singing

Listen to children as they are playing on a playground. Many games are often accompanied by a song or chant. Regardless of social background, race, or musical ability, the voice is the one instrument that is available to all children. Singing has a significant impact on a child's intellectual development because it facilitates language development through performance of beat and rhythm in music. Singing helps children learn and articulate the text of a song; it facilitates memory, as well as development of vocabulary. Every child has the ability to sing; the voice is the most accessible musical instrument of all. Children love to sing.[2]

In the classroom we can encourage singing for enjoyment while at the same time promoting correct intonation and a proper singing tone. The instructor's vocal example can significantly improve students' singing and the development of good vocal intonation. Young voices have less volume, less endurance, and naturally higher ranges than adult voices. Consider modifying your voice to accommodate this. Male instructors might consider singing in a falsetto range until young students are able to match pitch. *A capella* singing allows students to hear their own voices and enjoy active music making. Kodály addressed the importance of *a capella* singing:

> Most singing teachers and chorus masters believe in controlling the pitch of the voice by the piano. But singing depends on the acoustically correct "natural" intervals, and not on the tempered system. Even a perfectly tuned piano can never be a criterion of singing, not to speak of the ever "out-of-tune" pianos available at schools and rehearsal rooms. Yet how often have I found chorus masters attempting to restore the shaky intonation of their choirs with the help of a mistuned piano![3]

Singing Posture

Here are suggestions to help students find their correct posture for singing. The body needs to be balanced for students to project a beautiful singing tone.

1. Balance the head. To accomplish this, the face should look straight ahead. Try several exercises, such as moving the head up and down and sideways to relax the head and neck muscles. Stand with your back against a wall and make sure that your head and the heels of your feet are touching the wall. The head should feel suspended as if you are a puppet or a balloon. Keep the spine straight.
2. Correct seated position:
   Shoulders should be relaxed and rotated toward the back.
   Neck muscles should be relaxed.
   Tongue should be relaxed in the bottom of the mouth.
   Spine should be extended.

Rib cage is lifted.
Students should sit at the edge of their chairs when singing.
Feet are on the floor.
Hands are on the legs.
Eyes are on the conductor.
3. Correct standing position:
Shoulders should be relaxed and rotated toward the back.
Neck muscles should be relaxed.
Tongue should be relaxed in the bottom of the mouth.
Spine should be extended.
Rib cage is lifted.
Feet are on the floor.
Arms should dangle freely at the sides. Hands should be relaxed at the sides.
Knees should be relaxed and very slightly bent.
Feet should be firmly placed on the ground and roughly 10 to 12 inches apart. The distance should be smaller than the width of the shoulder. Make sure the body is resting on the balls of the feet.
Eyes are on the conductor.

Body Warm-up Exercises

Begin the class by allowing students to stretch and bend to relax their bodies. We suggest playing a piece of classical music with good pulsation, and creating expressive movements to reflect the form of the music. Eliminate tension by performing several of these stretching exercises with your students:

1. Body stretches. Keep shoulders down and reach for the stars; each hand should alternate with the other.
2. Shaking arms. Extend arms and shake each arm separately.
3. Shoulder roll. Roll each shoulder separately, making a circle.
4. Shrugging shoulders. Shrug shoulders, hold position for several counts, and then release.
5. Head rolls. Drop head to left shoulder and trace a half circle, moving chin toward chest and right shoulder.
6. Neck stretch. Drop the right ear to the right shoulder and the left hear to the left shoulder. Move the neck making yes-and-no motions.
7. Facial stretch. Ask students to act surprised.
8. Try to drop your jaw and say "mah, mah, mah" several times.
9. Knee flex. Arms should be extended forward and hands should be relaxed; bounce the body by flexing the knees.
10. Wiggle toes. Wiggle toes inside your shoes.

Some of these techniques can also be done while listening to music.

Breathing Exercises

Breathing exercises teach students to inhale and exhale correctly. Exercises that concentrate on exhaling are particularly valuable in that they generate control.

1. Correct breathing posture. Students lie on the floor with a book placed on the abdominal muscles. When inhaling the book rises, and when exhaling the book lowers. Then have students stand and place a hand on the abdominal muscles. Exhale and inhale, paying attention to abdominal muscle and not raising their shoulders. Students need to be encouraged to take in a deep breath, not a shallow one, through their nose and mouth. Sometimes it is helpful for students to exhale air against the palm of their hand.
2. Awareness of the diaphragm and other abdominal muscles for breathing. These exercises will help students with understanding use of the abdominal muscles for breathing:
   Show students how to sip through a straw correctly and expand their waist.
   Show students how to release air using a "sss" or hissing sound.
   Show students how to release air using the words "ha."
   Guide the students to yawn, as this opens up the back of the throat and relaxes the voice.
3. Sighing helps access a higher voice than a typical speaking voice. Try sighing few times, starting each sigh a little higher than the last.
4. Practice breathing. Breathe in through the nose for four counts, hold for four counts, and exhale through the mouth for four counts. As students gain greater control, extend the length of time they inhale and exhale.

Resonance, Tone Production, and Tuneful Singing

Here are examples of exercises and vocalizations to help develop beautiful singing. Encourage students to vocalize high and low sounds, as well as soft and loud sounds.

1. Sirens. Imitate the sound of a siren with the voice. Challenge the students to make soft and loud, high and low, long and short sirens, and sirens that go up, come down, or both. *Imitating a siren* is something young students delight in. It also engages the voice in such a way that the extremes of one's vocal range can be explored without straining the voice.
2. Falling off a cliff. Pretend you're falling off a cliff and sigh "aaaahhhhhhhhhh!"
3. Use a ball. Throw it from one student to another; students have to follow the movement of the ball with their voices.

Tone Production

1. Songs that contain the "oo" sound are particularly good for developing in-tune singing, as with "Cuckoo" (Fig. 3.1). Consider adding a high-pitched "toot" to the end of "Engine, Engine, Number Nine" (Fig. 3.2) as the students are marching while chanting.

Fig. 3.1 "Cuckoo"

Cuck-oo, what are you? I'm a bird. Do you sing? Yes, I do. Sing, then! Cuck-oo!

Fig. 3.2 "Engine, Engine, Number Nine"

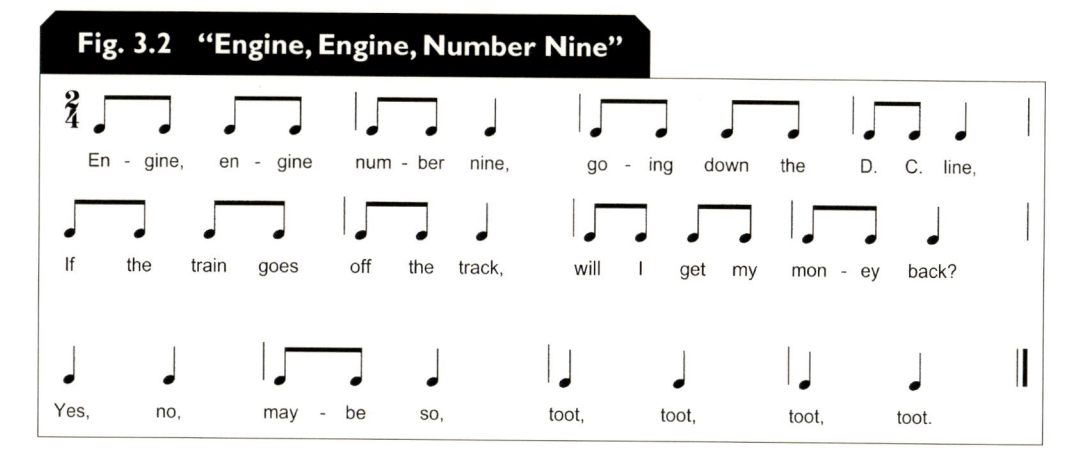

En-gine, en-gine num-ber nine, go-ing down the D. C. line,
If the train goes off the track, will I get my mon-ey back?
Yes, no, may-be so, toot, toot, toot, toot.

2. Many ordinary vocal sounds are actually excellent warm-up exercises. Sing known songs with neutral syllables such as "noo," "moo," "la," and so on.
3. Humming is a gentle (and quiet) way of using the singing voice. Humming a favorite song before singing it is also an opportunity to focus on the song's melody.
4. Copying animal sounds, such as barking like a dog, roaring like a lion, and meowing like a cat, also engages the extremes of a child's vocal range.
5. Singing a phrase of a pentatonic melody with the *nn* placement sound or the vowel sound in "noo."
6. Singing known songs with the syllable "yip." Students sing a known song with a yip sound.
7. Speaking using the syllable "koo," or repeating the "koo" sound to known rhythm patterns.
8. Singing with a "koo" sound. Students sing known melodies using the syllable "koo."
9. Lip trills. Use lip trills to sing a known song.
10. Pure vowel sounds, singing with known solfège syllables and hand signs.
11. Vowel scales. Vowel sounds can be unified by singing descending pentatonic and pentachord scales on "mee," "meh," "mah," "moh," and "moo."
12. Combination vowels. Students sing the sequence of "oh-oo-ah" on notes of the pentatonic scale. For example, sing the three vowel sounds on *mi* and then *re* and finally *do*. Pay attention to their jaw on each of the vowel sounds. Have them keep repeating, but singing a minor second higher each time.

13. Extending vocal range. Students practice singing a phrase of a song and repeating it a minor second higher. They use a pure vowel sound. Each time they repeat, they can sing another on another vowel sound.
14. Students sing vowel sounds while pointing to a vowel sound chart or using a motion associated with vowels.
15. Singing a known song and pointing to the vowel sounds on a chart.

Diction

1. Tongue twisters. Students gain flexibility by saying tongue twisters on one pitch and repeating at intervals of a minor second.
2. Tongue twisters sung in two voice parts. Students gain flexibility by singing tongue twisters at the interval of a fourth or fifth.
3. Unvoiced consonants. Speaking unvoiced consonants—*p, t, k*—using rhythm patterns of songs.
4. Voiced consonants. Singing songs using voiced consonants—*b, d, g,* and *j*—using rhythm patterns from songs.
5. Singing melodic patterns with an inner smile. Ask students to keep their lips closed and do an inner smile. Using this position, ask them to echo-sing melodic patterns with this "inner smile."
6. Practice in singing diphthongs. (Dominant vowel sound and a lesser vowel sound.) For example, they can practice saying and singing on a pitch "How now brown cow" and "The rain in Spain stays mainly in the plain."
7. Singing using a sustained "m" or "n." Ask students to sing the sequences "Moo moh mah meh mee" and "noo noh nah neh nee" on a sustained note or using notes of the pentatonic scale.

Vocal Ranges

When teaching music to students consider the vocal ranges described in Table 3.1. These are only suggestions but can help teachers select appropriate repertoire for their students' vocal skills and prepare them for singing.

Table 3.1   Guide to Children's Vocal Skills and Ranges

Grade	Vocal Skills	Vocal Range
Pre-Kindergarten	Perform children's chants and say nursery rhymes with voice inflection	
Kindergarten	S understands the concept of singing and speaking voice	Sing in tune from D (above middle C) to B This range could be lower or higher for some Ss

(continued)

Table 3.1 Continued

Grade	Vocal Skills	Vocal Range
Grade 1	Develop head voice Greater control of pitch	
Grade 2	More control of head voice; Ss perform simple canons or melodic ostinati in tune	Sing in tune from middle C to high D
Grades 3 and 4	Greater expressive control of voice; Ss can sing simple canons and two-part songs in tune	Can sing up to high E flat
Grade 5	More resonance in voice; Ss can begin to perform three-part songs	Can sing up to high E

Tuneful Singing

1. Singing phrases of songs on "oh" sound. Students sing phrases of songs on "oh"; make sure that the tone is very light and relaxed.
2. Singing with dynamic markings. Students should sing known melodies using the correct dynamic names and terms:
   pp pianissimo
   p piano
   mp mezzo piano
   mf mezzo forte
   f forte
   ff fortissimo
   It is best to sing songs using two very different dynamics: *f* and *p*.
3. Divide class into two groups and have students sing in two parts from your hand signs. Show a two-part exercise with hand signs and have students read.
4. Singing longer phrases. Students sing known songs but combine two phrases into one phrase.
5. Tempo markings. Students should be taught the Italian terms and English meanings:
   Largo: very slow
   Adagio: slow
   Andante: moderately slow
   Moderato: moderate
   Allegretto: moderately fast
   Allegro: fast
   Presto: very fast
   Students should begin singing known songs using two types of tempi.

6. Practicing stagger breathing with children. Students sing on one pitch using the word "loo." They must learn to breath quietly and enter softly after each breath to maintain the sound and vowel color.
7. Staccato and legato. Students practice singing songs legato and staccato.
8. Crescendo and decrescendo. Students should sing songs using crescendo and decrescendo.

Head Voice and Chest Voice

The technical difference between "head voice" and "chest voice" has to do with how vocal cords vibrate when singing. We use the terms *head* and *chest* to designate where vibrations are most strongly felt when singing. When singing in head voice, the vibrations are felt behind the nose and cheeks. When singing in chest voice vibrations are felt in the throat and chest. Students most often sing in their chest voice, so they need help finding their head voice.

Finding Your Head Voice

There are a number of initial vocal exercises you can do to find your head voice:

1. Pretend you are talking to a baby. Notice how your speaking voice is much higher in pitch. You may also pretend to talk like Mickey Mouse. For those students who know the character, this exercise often inspires them to change the focus of their voices quickly.
2. Pretend to be an owl and make a high-pitched "whoooo" sound. Repeat this several times; each time try to make the "whoooo" a little higher than the last.
3. Pretend to be a child on a playground, taunting another child: "Nyah-nyah-nyah-nyah-nyah."
4. Pretend you're falling off a cliff: "aaaahhhhhhhhhh!"
5. Say "Cock-a-doodle-doo" or "Qui-quiri-qui" (Spanish for "Cock-a-doodle-doo").

The head voice vibrates and radiates more in your head. The head voice is helpful for leading students in singing because they are still trying to make the distinction between singing and speaking. We are not saying that they should not sing at all in the chest voice; for example, some songs in the African American tradition might sound better in the chest voice. However, as music educators we need to make students aware of the different energy and aspects of head and chest voices. Often they have a tendency to shout rather than sing in an effort to sing loudly. Model appropriate singing for your students whether singing in head or chest voice.

Steps to Finding the Singing Voice

Here are suggestions for developing students' singing voices using their head and chest voice. These activities will help students sing in tune. We also believe that it is important to tell students if they are out of tune. Gentle and specific corrections are completely acceptable. A simple "a little higher" and then lavish praise when they perform the task

Developing Creative Expression with Movement and Instruments

correctly will not damage self-esteem. The entire class will begin to listen and ask themselves whether they sing in tune or not.

1. Pitch exploration exercises (these can also be used as vocal warm-ups). Pitch exploration exercises allow students to activate the vocal muscles that are used when singing in the head voice. When using these exercises, it is best to begin with descending and then ascending sliding sounds. Begin these exercises as a class activity. Ask students to imitate the sliding sounds of a slide whistle with their voice. Once the class is comfortable with the exercises, encourage individual students to perform the exercises on their own. These are examples of pitch exploration exercises.
    A. When telling stories in class, modulate your voice to include a high, medium, and low voice for characters in the story or high, low, and medium sounds for events in the story. Repeat the story and ask students to make the sounds.
    B. As you move a flashlight beam projected onto the blackboard in a room, ask students to follow the contour of the moving beam of light.
    C. Imitate the sound of a siren whistle with the voice.
2. Develop awareness of the kind of voice. Music instructors can help students discover the difference between their speaking voice and singing voice. Young children need to become aware of the several sounds their voices can produce, and you can guide students to discover them:
Talking voice
Whispering voice
Loud voice
Soft voice
Singing voice
Internal voice
3. Voice modulation. Select songs and rhymes that can be used to develop a child's singing voice. As young children say chants, they may be guided to speak using a "baby bird voice" (high) or a "grandfather's voice" (low). Chanting using these voice types will teach a young learner how to modulate their voice. Guide young students to perform the chant "Bee, Bee, Bumble Bee" (Fig. 3.3) using a high voice; then perform the chant using a low voice. Also perform "Engine, Engine, Number Nine" (Fig. 3.4) using a grandfather's voice or a baby's voice.

"Fig. 3.3" "Bee, Bee, Bumble Bee"

Bee, bee, bum - ble bee, stung a man up - on his knee,
stung a pig up - on his snout, I de - clare that you are out!

Kodály Today

Fig. 3.4 "Engine, Engine, Number Nine"

En - gine, en - gine num - ber nine, go - ing down the D. C. line,
If the train goes off the track, will I get my mon - ey back?
Yes, no, may - be so, toot, toot, toot, toot.

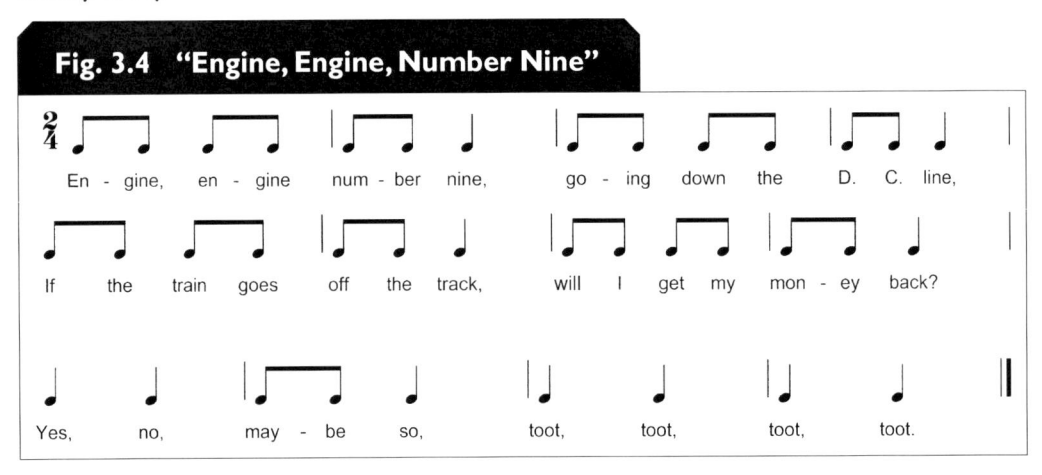

4. Song with narrow range. Sing songs that use two or three pitches, such as "Bounce High, Bounce Low" (Fig. 3.5).

Fig. 3.5 "Bounce High, Bounce Low"

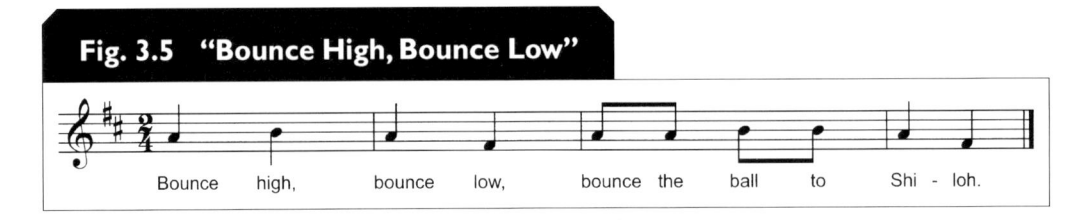

Bounce high, bounce low, bounce the ball to Shi - loh.

5. Descending melodic patterns. Generally, songs that begin with a descending melodic pattern are easier for young students to hear and sing; this type of song offers a greater opportunity for the young learner to hear accurately, and subsequently a better chance to sing in tune. The song "Lemonade" (Fig. 3.6) has simple descending melodic patterns.

Fig. 3.6 "Lemonade"

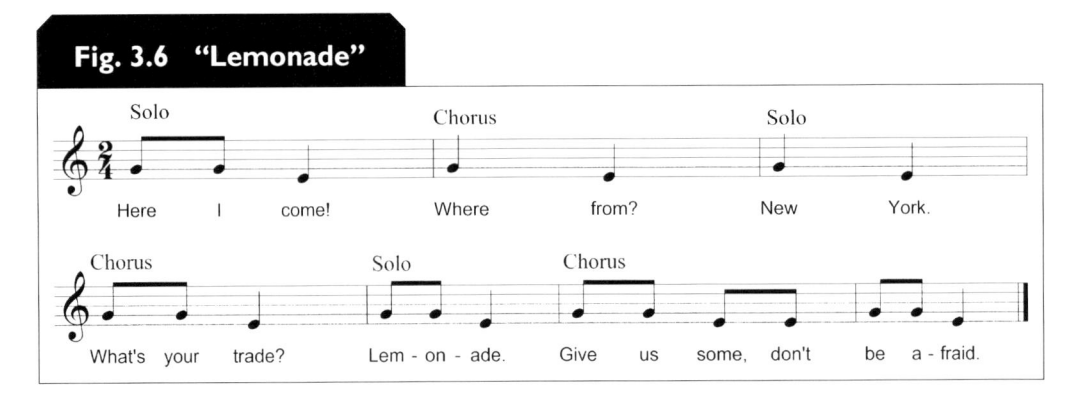

Solo: Here I come!
Chorus: Where from?
Solo: New York.
Chorus: What's your trade?
Solo: Lem - on - ade.
Chorus: Give us some, don't be a - fraid.

6. Call-and-response singing. Call-and-response songs are ideal for developing children's singing voices as they simply sing a repeated melodic pattern. "Pizza Pizza" (Fig. 3.7) is an example of a call-and-response song. When teaching a call-and-response song, this procedure may be used:

Developing Creative Expression with Movement and Instruments

Fig. 3.7 "Pizza Pizza"

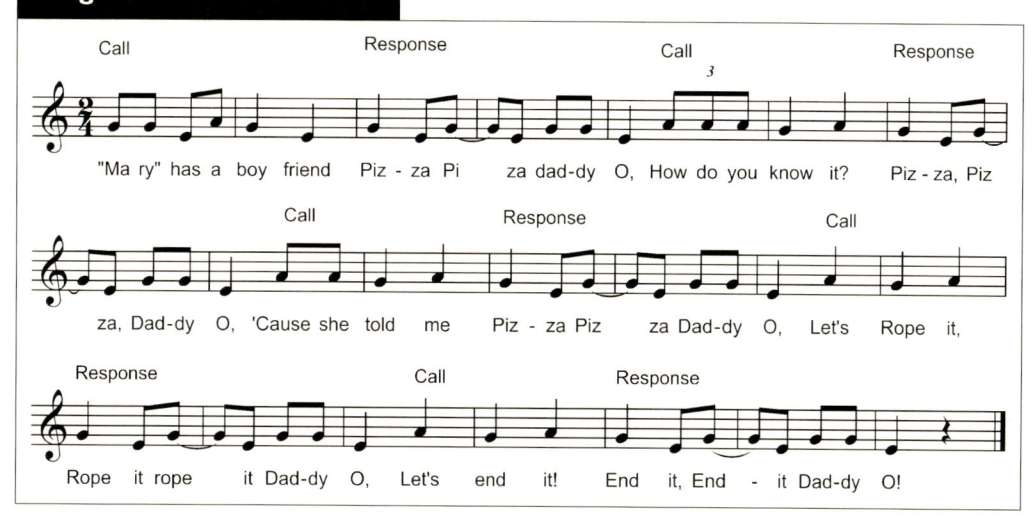

[Musical notation with call-and-response structure]

Call: "Ma ry" has a boy friend Piz - za Pi
Response: za dad-dy O, How do you know it?
Call: Piz - za, Piz za, Dad-dy O, 'Cause she told me
Response: Piz - za Piz za Dad-dy O,
Call: Let's Rope it,
Response: Rope it rope it Dad-dy O, Let's end it!
Call: End it, End - it Dad-dy O!

- Sing the call-and-response song for the students as a listening activity. Consider using two hand puppets to distinguish the part of the song that is the call from the response.
- Sing the call and guide students to sing the response; use a pretend microphone to help young students understand the alternation.
- Have a group of students take the part of the instructor and perform the call.
- Later, ask individual students to take the role of the instructor; they can sing the call and the class can perform the response.

7. Providing a model for singing. Before students sing a song, they need to hear it performed by the instructor a number of times. Model the song correctly; sing with good intonation, use clear pronunciation, and model the song's character. Begin each song on a comfortable starting pitch for your students. Indicate the starting pitch of the song clearly; consider singing the first phrase of the song to establish the beginning pitch. You should sing using an appropriate tempo for the song. If the tempo is too fast, then students could sing out of tune.

8. Singing softly. Students should be encouraged to sing songs softly as a means for developing good intonation.

9. Movement. Singing in combination with a movement not only can help reinforce the concept of beat but also helps with intonation.

10. Individual singing. Encourage and allow students to sing on their own. This helps the young learner develop greater vocal independence. Some students can sing in tune with a group but do not sing in tune when singing on their own. One way to help a student having trouble singing on her own is to sit in front of her and have her observe the movement of your mouth. Allowing students to sing individually develops independence and gives you an opportunity to evaluate the progress of the class. Once they know a song well

Kodály Today

and can sing it fluently, you should not sing with the class. Singing alone and in small groups will encourage vocal independence.

11. Singing names to simple melodic motifs. Encourage young students to sing their names or short motifs based on patterns found in song material. While seated in a circle, roll a ball or toss a bean bag to a student and ask him to sing his name.
12. Recognizing different timbres. Guide the young learner to recognize timbres—environmental sounds, as well as the sounds of instruments and voices.
13. Piano accompaniment. Avoid using piano accompaniment when teaching a new song. Young students need to hear the voice of the instructor, as well as their own voice. Playing an accompaniment to a new song may decrease students' ability to hear their own singing voices. The piano may be used for accompaniment once students have learned a new song or know a song from memory.
14. Vowels and consonants. The correct pronunciation of vowels is critical to development of good intonation. Practice singing vowel exercises using the syllables *no*, *nu*, *naw*, *ni*, and *nah*, and using descending pentachord scales. Consonants help define the rhythmic character of singing. Using vocalizations that include *n* and *m* consonants encourages good singing, as well as proper pronunciation.
15. Singing a greeting to students. Begin the music class by greeting the students (Fig. 3.8 and 3.9). You may sing the greeting or use a puppet for younger children. The puppet then leads the class in singing the greeting "Good Morning Boys and Girls." Sing a greeting to each student individually by name. Sing using a beat motion such as waving.

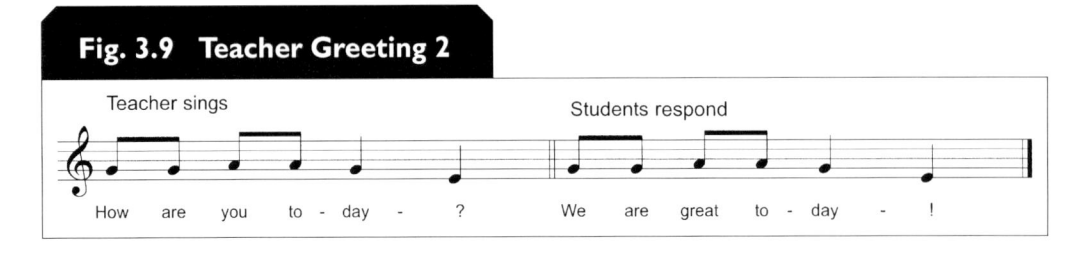

Fig. 3.8 Teacher Greeting 1

Teacher sings: Hel-lo boys and girls!
Students respond: Hel-lo teach-er!

Fig. 3.9 Teacher Greeting 2

Teacher sings: How are you to-day?
Students respond: We are great to-day!

Singing in Tune with Relative Solmization

Relative solmization helps develop pure intonation.[4] Teachers are attracted to singing with solfège syllables because of the successes they observe in their students' overall intonation and learning; but singing with solfège syllables is significantly more than only using syllables. When performed correctly, singing with solfège syllables engages students' vocal singing mechanism, cognitive thinking, and emotional well-being. Singing in tune involves complex teaching skills. Sing solfège syllables with Latin pronunciation; this encourages singing using pure vowels. (This is one reason we use the word *syllable: so* instead of *sol* or *re* instead of *ray*.) Teaching students to sing the *re* with a Latin pronunciation with flipped *r* will help with intonation of the syllable *re*; it is then less likely to be sung out of tune.

An in-tune vocal model is essential for student performance. Solo singing in the classroom allows students to hear their own voice as well as their peers. It also permits the teacher to become aware of each student's vocal characteristics so she can provide the proper vocal modifications.

Beginning in the second grade, consider using some of Kodály's intonation exercises found in *Let Us Sing Correctly*.[5] Professor Zsuzsanna Kontra's book *Let Us Try to Sing Correctly* is a practical guide for using Kodály's work and has additional insights for singing the Kodály exercises in tune.[6]

During classroom teaching and choral rehearsals, music teachers need to find time for training the voice and also considering development of students' listening skills. Warming up the voice and the ear are integral components to singing in tune. The sound of music should always be shaped by a student's ability to critically listen. The development of training the voice and coordinating this with development of the student's ear begins in the pre-Kindergarten classroom.

Consider the intervals we teach; there's a noteworthy difference between sung intervals and tempered intervals. The *so-mi* interval is an important one in the pentatonic scale and can be difficult to sing in tune. It is much wider than the tempered minor third. The *so-la-so-mi* pattern is an opportunity for you to explore the "small major" second, *so-la*, compared to the tempered second or larger major second, *la-ti*, presented in later grades. When *high do* is presented in the third grade, practice both the *do'- la-so* and the *la-so-mi* patterns. Consciously practice the *m-l* interval as well as the *mi-so-la* interval common to a child's chant. With the introduction of *do* in the second grade, children can now explore singing the *do-so* interval both harmonically and melodically and internalize the sound of the perfect fifth interval. The note *re* is often sung out of tune. To remediate this concern find song repertoire that emphasizes *so*. Remember that the syllable *re* in a major tonality is closely linked to *low so*. The major second between *do* and *re* will need to be sung as a wider interval; think of the *re* tuning up to the *so* rather than down to the *do*.

By the end of the second grade or in the third grade, students will become familiar with singing melodies with *low la*. Low la forms a perfect fourth interval with *re*. Singing *re* linked to a *low la* will force the *re* to be sung closer to the *do*, and this creates a small major second interval, compared to the *do-re* interval in a major melody, where it is a wider major second interval.

With the introduction of *fa* and *ti* in grades four and five, the minor second intervals take on greater significance. Singing canons and simple two-part works helps overall intonation at this stage of vocal development. Here is a helpful summary that distinguishes the large and small, or narrow and wide, intervals in major and minor tonalities.

Major
do-re large major second
re-mi small major second
fa-so large major second
so-la small major second
la-ti large major second

Minor scale
la-ti large major second
do-re small major second
re-mi large major second
fa-so large major second
so-la large major second

Teaching Songs

The quality of music teaching is governed by (1) the choice of musical materials and (2) the methods of presenting that material. The Kodály concept of music education incorporates folk songs and art songs to encourage music appreciation, as well as develop music literacy skills. Folk songs are particularly appropriate for classroom use. In general, there are two methods for teaching songs: by rote or by note. When teaching a song by note, the students learn the song or part of it through reading the rhythms or the melody of the song.

Technique One: Teaching Songs by Rote

When teaching songs by rote, you make the initial presentation of the song. Remember that it might take several lessons to teach one song. As the teacher, you serve as a model for the best performance of the song. For this reason, music must be presented in a stylistically correct manner. The mood for the presentation of the song may be set through a story or another well-known song. Consider talking about the phrasing, mood, style, and form of the song. Students may quietly pat the beat the second time you sing the new song. Next, determine the phrasing and form of a new song. Once the initial presentation is made, these techniques may be used for teaching a song.

1. *Questioning Techniques*
Ask questions relating to specific musical elements or to the text of the song. Asking questions can (1) direct students' attention, (2) help strengthen their analytical skills, and (3) aid in remembering the song.

Guidelines for Asking Questions

Use the fewest number of words possible. By asking specific questions, you give the students listening tasks that help them focus their attention on a particular musical element or an aspect of the text.

Sing the song before asking each question. In this way the students will become familiar with the melody and text before they are eventually asked to sing the song. Sing "Star Light, Star Bright" (Fig. 3.10) and ask any or all of these questions before allowing the students to sing the phrase.

Fig. 3.10   "Star Light, Star Bright"

Star - light, star bright, first star I see ton - night,
Wish I may, wish I might, have the wish I wish to - night.

1. "How many phrases do you hear?"
2. "What word did I sing that rhymes with light?"
3. "How many times did I say the word 'star'?"
4. "How many times did I say the word 'I'?"
5. "How many times did I say the word 'wish'?"

When asking questions, be certain to sing the phrase or the entire song before asking a second question. Remember that in order to answer the questions, students have to draw on their memory of what was sung. It is important to ask questions concerning the music. If you ask about a word, it should relate to the music in some way. A questioning procedure for presenting the song "Rocky Mountain" (Fig. 3.11) might be as follows:

1. After performing the entire song several times, perform the first phrase.
2. Ask "How many times did I sing 'Rocky Mountain'?" (three times)
3. Ask "Did I sing 'Rocky Mountain' in every phrase of the song?" (no)
4. Ask "Which phrases of the song had the words 'Rocky Mountain'?" (phrases 1 and 2)
5. Ask "How many times did I say the word 'do' in the whole song?" (ten times)
6. Perform the entire song.

Kodály Today

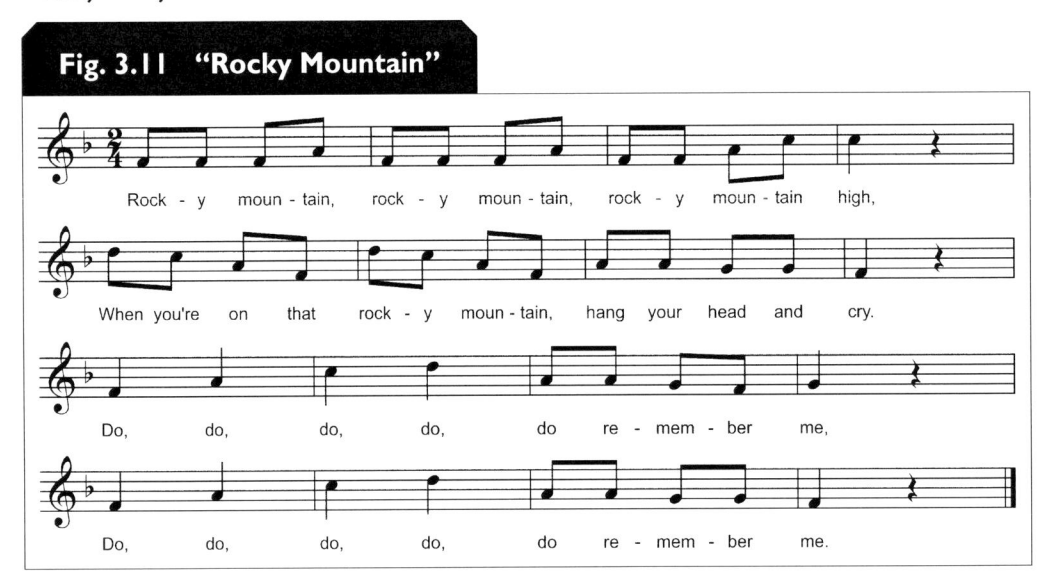

Fig. 3.11 "Rocky Mountain"

[Musical notation for "Rocky Mountain" with lyrics:]

Rock-y moun-tain, rock-y moun-tain, rock-y moun-tain high,

When you're on that rock-y moun-tain, hang your head and cry.

Do, do, do, do, do re-mem-ber me,

Do, do, do, do, do re-mem-ber me.

2. Phrase-by-Phrase Song Presentation

On first hearing, the song should be presented in its entirety. After that, a phrase-by-phrase presentation is helpful when presenting longer and more complex songs by rote. This approach is more appropriate when working with older students. Younger students should hear the song repeated many times in its entirety. Reserve the use of phrase-by-phrase presentation of songs for upper-grade students. The phrase-by-phrase presentation is exactly that, presenting each phrase of a song and having students repeat the phrase. This type of song presentation can be used to focus students' attention on a particular rhythmic or melodic pattern. It should be avoided with younger children because they need to grasp the context of the entire song before focusing on specific features.

1. Sing the song in its entirety.
2. Focus on one phrase at a time. If a song is particularly difficult, you may ask the students to perform it with a simple rhythmic activity, for example, keeping the beat when listening. This keeps the students occupied and focused while you perform the entire song again.

The unique or salient features in the song will suggest the best means for presentation and memorization. The song's text, rhythmic, and melodic elements will enable you to make decisions as to the best teaching approach.

3. Presenting a Song by Acting Out the Text

Performing motions or acting out a story line helps students memorize songs and rhymes. The teacher creates movements or a game to accompany a song. For example, consider "Bee, Bee, Bumble Bee" (Fig. 3.12):

Developing Creative Expression with Movement and Instruments

Fig. 3.12 "Bee, Bee, Bumble Bee"

Bee, bee, bum-ble bee, stung a man up-on his knee,
stung a pig up-on his snout, I de-clare that you are out!

1. Phrase 1: students flap their arms to the beat.
2. Phrase 2: students point to their knee to the beat.
3. Phrase 3: students point to their nose to the beat.
4. Phrase 4: students point to other children in the circle to the beat.

For "Engine, Engine, Number Nine" (a traditional children's chant; Fig. 3.2 and 3.4), the students move their arms, imitating the motion of the wheels of the engine, and march around the classroom while chanting:

Engine, engine number nine,
Going down Chicago line,
If the train should jump the track,
Would you want your money back?
Yes, no, maybe so,
Toot, toot, toot, toot!

For the song "Cobbler, Cobbler" (Fig. 3.13), students can pantomime hammering their shoes to the beat of the rhyme. Movement activities help students learn and memorize songs quickly and easily. The teacher and students may create their own games and motions to accompany songs. For example, high-and-low or up-and-down motions may be used with the song "Seesaw" (seen in Chapter 2) to convey the concept of high and low. Later the simple motion of bending knees may be used to reflect the solfège syllables *so-mi*. Motions that are initiated by the instructor or students may reflect the beat or recurring rhythmic patterns. The teacher encourages students to use their imagination and create motions to accompany songs.

Fig. 3.13 "Cobbler, Cobbler"

Cob-bler, Cob-bler mend my shoe, Get it done by half past two.
Half past two is at the door, Get it done by half past four.

Kodály Today

4. Call-and-Response Songs
Songs containing repeated patterns can be practiced in call-and-response style. Initially, young children should sing only the response; the instructor sings the *call*. After many repetitions, students may sing either or both the *call* and the *response*.

5. Teach a Song Using Visuals
Pictures associated with the text of a song can be a combination of visuals that remind the students of the text coupled with visuals that remind them of the form or melodic contour.

6. Teaching a Song Using Manipulatives
An example of teaching using manipulatives is, with "Old Mr. Rabbit," having children select a fruit or a vegetable to help them remember the sequence of vegetables.

7. Teaching Songs Using a Traditional Game
The teacher teaches the song as well as the traditional game or movement to accompany the song.

8. Teaching Song by Creating a Story
The teacher creates a story about her friend Oliver Twist (Fig. 3.14), who does the strangest motions but then always manages to touch his knees, touch his toes, clap his hands, and spin around!

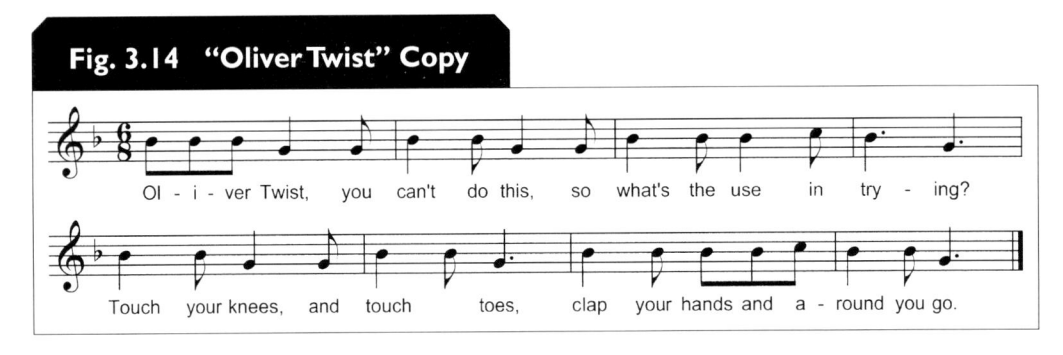

Fig. 3.14 "Oliver Twist" Copy

Technique Two: Teaching Songs by Note

This method of teaching songs can be used to teach either a whole song or phrases of a song. The teacher presents the notation of the song to the students and sequentially guides them to read the song from notation. Here is a procedure to use as a possible guide for teaching songs by note. There are many ways to teach songs by rote, but the most important are

1. Reading a song from the teacher's hand signs
2. Reading a song from a tone ladder or from a scale written on the board

3. Reading the rhythmic notation of songs
4. Reading the rhythmic notation of songs with solfège syllables
5. Reading a melody from the staff

These teaching techniques may be adapted for all types of reading exercises:

1. Make students aware of the meter. The meter of the song may be prepared by having students sing and conduct a known song that has the same meter as the new songs.
2. Practice each rhythm pattern found in the song with the students. They may either echo-clap or read these rhythm patterns from notation. Difficult rhythms abstracted from the song can be practiced with a rhythmic ostinato that can include subdivision of the beat to help students develop a more precise sense of the rhythm.
3. Clap the rhythm of the song and sing the rhythm syllables.
4. Conduct and sing the rhythm syllables.
5. When preparing to teach a new song, have students read a known song from the staff in the key of the new song. Once absolute pitch names have been introduced and students have an understanding of key signatures, guide them to determine the tonic and dominant notes and where they occur throughout the song.
6. Practice melodic patterns abstracted from the song by having students read the melodic patterns with solfège syllables from your hand signs before presenting the notation of the song.
7. Guide students to think through the melody of the entire song. Students may conduct or use hand signs while thinking through the melody.
8. Sing the song with solfège syllables and hand signs.
9. Sing the song with neutral syllables.
10. Sing the song with words as students follow the score.
11. Students sing the song with words.

Assessing the Presentation of a Song

Certain questions will help you assess and evaluate your teaching of songs to your students.

- Did I introduce the song in an interesting manner?
- Have I memorized the song correctly?
- Did I determine the best method of presentation for introducing this song?
- Did I sing the song in a stylistically appropriate way?
- Did I begin singing the song on a pitch that is appropriate for the students I am teaching?
- Did I engage my students with eye contact and facial expressions as I performed the song?

- Did I use clear mouth movements?
- Did I stay in tune as I sang the song?
- Was the tempo appropriate for learning? Was my pronunciation clear? Could the text be easily understood?
- Did I conduct?
- Did I keep a steady beat and tempo as the children were singing phrase by phrase?
- Was the teaching pace appropriate for students to understand and learn the song?
- Did I correct students' mistakes and intonation problems?

The Lifecycle of a Song: The Many Uses of a Folk Song

The same song may be sung many times throughout the year and even revisited in different grade levels. Selecting good-quality repertoire allows you to repeat the song many times without students becoming bored. Generally speaking, if the song is a good song, students enjoy performing it. Here are suggestions for using the same song for a variety of activities.

- Songs may be presented as listening activities.
- They may be learned for their formal structure (AABA and so on).
- Perform songs with a repeated rhythmic pattern (ostinato).
- Sing the song with text and then with rhythm syllables.
- Sing it with text and then with solfège syllables.
- Perform pentatonic songs in canon.
- Use the song to make particular rhythm or melodic elements known to the students.

Introducing Songs Within a Lesson

In this section we provide suggestions for introducing songs in a lesson.

Movement

Associate a motion or game with a known song. You may perform one motion associated with the performance of a song; students join in singing when they recognize the song. Once the students recognize the song, sing the starting pitch so all students can join.

Visuals

Create pictures or assemble visuals associated with a particular song; the students sing the song once they recognize the visual clue.

Introducing Songs to Students Using a Rhythmic Focus

- Ask students to sing the song.
- Recognize the song from rhythmic clapping.
- Have students read the rhythm of a song written on the board; as soon as they recognize it, they may begin to sing it with text as they clap the rhythm.
- Write the rhythm of a song, but mix up the order of the phrases. Students read the phrases and try to identify the song.
- Have them recognize a song hearing it performed on a percussion instrument.
- Sing a song on a neutral syllable as you perform a rhythm ostinato on a percussion instrument.
- Students recognize a song by hearing an internal phrase (not the first phrase) clapped by the teacher.
- Clap the rhythm of a song and have the students perform in canon, after two beats.

Introducing Songs to Students Using a Melodic Focus

- Ask students to sing a song.
- Have them recognize the song by hearing you sing using a neutral syllable.
- Students read from hand signs with solfège syllables once they recognize the song.
- They read an internal phrase of music from your hand signs with solfège syllables to recognize a song.
- Students read your hand signs using inner hearing and recognize a song.
- Students read an internal phrase of the song from your hand signs (or those of another student) using inner hearing and recognize a song.
- Students read in canon from your hand signs and recognize a song.
- Read from the tone ladder using solfège syllables and hand signs and have them recognize the song.
- Read an internal phrase of the song from the tone ladder using solfège syllables and hand signs and recognize a song.
- Read from the tone ladder, using inner hearing with solfège syllables and hand signs, and have them recognize a song.
- Read an internal phrase of the song from the tone ladder, using inner hearing with solfège syllables and hand signs to recognize a song.
- Read from traditional rhythmic notation with solfège syllables beneath, thus using solfège syllables and hand signs to recognize a song.
- Read an internal phrase from a song written in traditional rhythmic notation with solfège syllables beneath, thus using solfège syllables and hand signs to recognize a song.
- Read from traditional notation with solfège syllables beneath, using inner hearing to recognize a song.

Singing Games and Movement Activities

Singing games are a fun way to reinforce musical concepts and skills, as well as develop students' social, emotional, and kinesthetic skills and abilities. Singing games should be age-appropriate; the game or movement activity should correspond to the students' developmental abilities. Movement and motions in the games should be simple enough for them to perform as they sing.

The instructor's role is essential in presenting singing games and movement activities; you must be able to sequence the presentation of movements and motions logically as well as perform the song at the same time. Large beat motions and moving to the beat is usually best presented before more complicated movements at specific points in the performance. You may determine it best to present the song to the students before introducing the game, movements, or motions. There are situations when it is appropriate for students to learn the motions as they sing the song. When presenting the song along with a game, have students listen (and not sing) to focus the learning on motions or movement activities. Table 3.2 shows a sequence of movement activities appropriate for the young learner.

Sequential Progression for Teaching Games

Here is a suggested sequence for teaching folk games.

Acting Out
Long-Legged Sailor
Wishy Washy

Wind up
Snail, Snail

Circle
Circle Round the Zero
Old Mister Rabbit
Wishy Washy
Wallflowers
Down in the Valley

Choosing
Wishy Washy
Down in the Valley

Chase
Charlie over the Ocean

(continued on p. 122)

Table 3.2

Pre-Kindergarten	Kindergarten	Grades 1 and 2	Grade 3	Grades 4 and 5
Free movement in place (sitting)	Begins to develop greater control of small muscles	Marching and skipping to the beat	Can perform beat on a drum or triangle as well as clap the rhythm of an uncomplicated song in simple and compound meter	Can perform beat on a drum or triangle as well as clap the rhythm of more rhythmically complicated songs in simple and compound meter
Free movement in space	Changing directions	Chasing games, jumping games		
Movement to a beat while sitting	Acting-out games	Line games, partner games	Can perform hand-clapping games	Can conduct in duple, triple, and quadruple meter
Movement to a beat while walking	Choosing games	Double-circle games	Can conduct in duple meter	Can perform simple ostinati on xylophones
Standing in a circle	Follow the leader	Develop the ability to clap the rhythm of a rhyme or melody	Can perform sustained bourdons on xylophone	Can show muscle coordination for playing recorder, keyboard
T plays with S as a partner	Chase games			Can respond quickly and accurately through movement to tempo, rhythmic patterns, texture)
Movements with a partner	Line games		Chasing games, jumping games, line games, partner games, and double circle games	Can perform more complex folk dances in circles, lines, squares, and with partners
Starting and stopping with music	Winding games			
	Moving circle game			Line games, winding games, moving circle game

Cut the Cake
Mouse Mousie

Partner
Quaker Quaker
Bow Wow Wow
Long-Legged Sailor
Wishy Washy
Fed My Horse (starts out as a partner game)
Miss Mary Mack (starts out as a partner game)
Down in the Valley

Double Circle
Tideo
Dance Josey
Fed My Horse
Miss Mary Mack
Great Big House
Turn the Glasses Over
I've Been to Haarlem

Double-Line Reel
Alabama Gal
Amassee
Billy, Billy
Zudio
Over the River to Feed My Sheep
Paw Paw Patch
I Wonder Where Maria Has Gone?
Bow Belinda

Single Line
Twenty-four Robbers
Debka Hora
Hashivenu

Square Games
Weevily Wheat
Draw a Bucket
Four White Horses

Square Dances
Old Brass Wagon
Red River Valley
Knock the Cymbals
Golden Ring Around the Susan Girl
I's the Bye
Older Betty Larkin
O Susanna
Going Down the Cairo

Developing a Movement Sequence

Here is a suggested movement sequence that you can follow.

1. Performing the Beat

Students copy the instructor's beat movement while singing known songs. It is important to remember that younger students must begin to find their own "internal beat" before they can imitate a beat given by the teacher. At the beginning of each lesson, we suggest that you open with a body movement activity that can be performed to a piece of music. The goal is for the students to prepare their bodies for singing as well as prepare the class to move together to the beat. This beat activity should be closely related to the beat and character of the first song the students will sing in the lesson.

2. Students Create Their Own Beat Movement

Students may create their own beat movement. For example, when singing "Rain, Rain" (Fig. 3.15), they may tap the beat on different parts of their bodies or point to imaginary drops of rain on the window.

Fig. 3.15 "Rain, Rain" Copy

Rain, rain, go a-way, come a-gain some oth-er day.
Lit-tle Sus-ie wants to play, rain, rain, go a-way.

Kodály Today

Students may sing and create their own movement in a space. Ask them to consider all the ways a squirrel can move; they can sing and hop, skip, walk, jump, or climb to the beat as they sing "Hop, Old Squirrel" (Fig. 3.16).

Fig. 3.16 "Hop, Old Squirrel"

[Musical notation: Hop old squirrel, ei-dle-dum, ei-dle-dum. Hop old squirrel, ei-dle-dum dee. Hop old squirrel, ei-dle-dum, ei-dle-dum. Hop old squirrel, ei-dle-dum dee.]

Generally speaking, students may perform specific beat movements suggested by the song. They remain in one position, sitting or standing, and perform a motion to accompany a song. These beat motions often help illustrate the mood as well as text of a song. An appropriate beat motion for any lullaby might be to hold a doll and rock it in your arms.

"Let Us Chase the Squirrel" (Fig. 3.17) has a specific game associated with it; however, students may also hop, skip, march, or walk to the beat while singing this song.

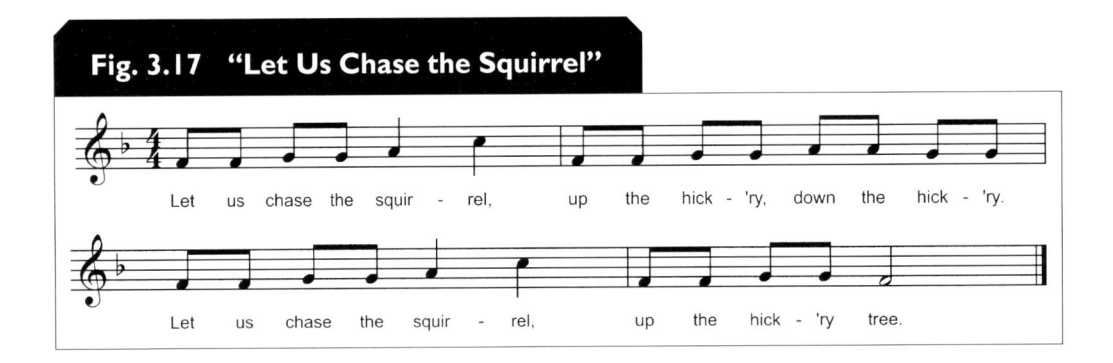

Fig. 3.17 "Let Us Chase the Squirrel"

[Musical notation: Let us chase the squir-rel, up the hick-'ry, down the hick-'ry. Let us chase the squir-rel, up the hick-'ry tree.]

3. Moving to Music

Students may create their own movement to a beat while listening to a composed composition. Consider using these musical compositions:

"March" from the *Nutcracker Suite,* Tchaikovsky
"Hornpipe" from *Water Music,* Handel
"Spring" from *The Seasons,* Vivaldi

4. Acting-Out Games

Children may sing a song and act out motions suggested by the text.

Fig. 3.18 "Hot Cross Buns"

Hot cross buns, Hot cross buns, One a pen-ny, Two a pen-ny, Hot cross buns.

Guide students in making a cake while they sing "Hot Cross Buns" (Fig. 3.18). Using motions that follow the beat, they can mix the batter, spoon the batter into the cake pan, and place the hot cross buns on a tray.

5. Winding Games

In "Snail, Snail" (Fig. 3.19), you lead the circle of students to sing and make a circle that winds inward to form the shell of a snail.

Fig. 3.19 "Snail, Snail"

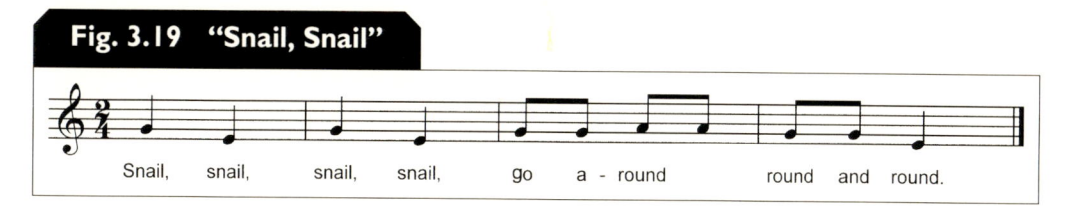

Snail, snail, snail, snail, go a-round round and round.

6. Circle Games

Games may involve circles, as with "Ring Around the Rosy" (Fig. 3.20), "Bow Wow Wow" (Fig. 3.21), and "Wall Flowers" (Fig. 3.22).

Fig. 3.20 "Ring Around the Rosy"

Ring a-round the ro-sy, pock-et full of po-sy, Ash-es, ash-es, we all fall down.

In "Bow Wow Wow," students join hands, walk in a circle, and "fall down" at the end.

Fig. 3.21 "Bow Wow Wow"

Bow, wow, wow, whose dog art thou? Lit-tle Tom-my Tuck-er's dog bow, wow, wow.

Kodály Today

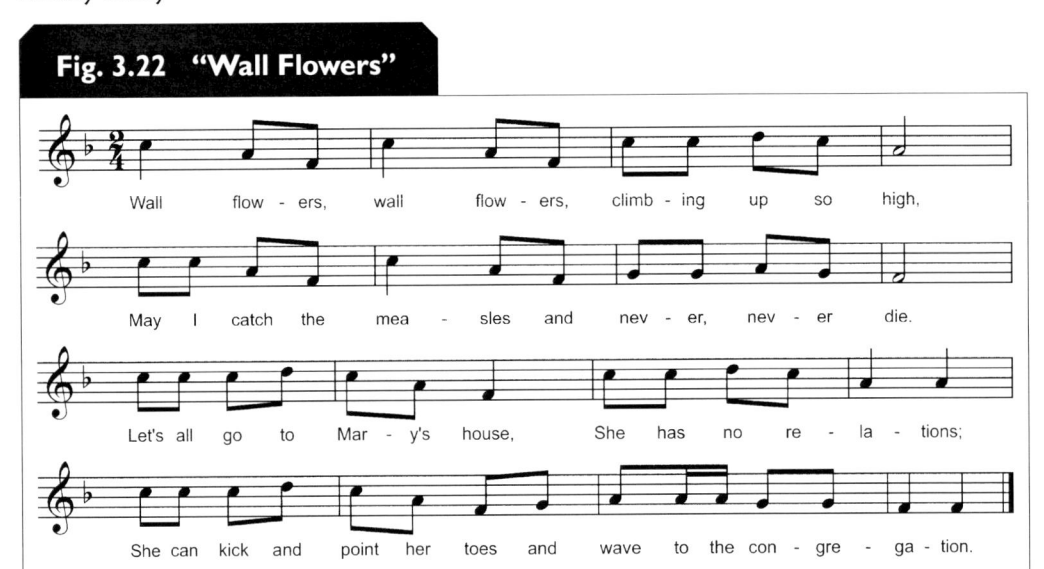

Fig. 3.22 "Wall Flowers"

Wall flow - ers, wall flow - ers, climb - ing up so high,
May I catch the mea - sles and nev - er, nev - er die.
Let's all go to Mar - y's house, She has no re - la - tions;
She can kick and point her toes and wave to the con - gre - ga - tion.

1. Students form a circle and stand facing a partner.
2. You say, "Bow wow wow" and stamp your feet three times (right, left, right).
3. "Whose dog art thou?" Tell one student in each pair to point to the partner three times, shaking a finger.
4. At "Little Tommy Tucker's Dog," partners join hands and circle in place.
5. "Bow wow wow"; tell them to stamp their feet three times, then jump in the air, and turn their back to the partner, at which point they will all see a new partner.

With "Wall Flowers," students join hands and walk in a circle. One student stands in the center of the circle. In phrase 3, the student in the center points to a friend during "Let's all go to Mary's house." (Substitute the child's name for Mary.) That student stays in the circle but turns around and faces the outside. The game continues until all students are facing out.

Another type of circle game involves moving around the circle with improvised motions, as in "Walk Daniel" or "Jim Along Josie" (Fig. 3.23). Students improvise actions while walking in a circle; for example, "skip Jim along" or "jump Jim along."

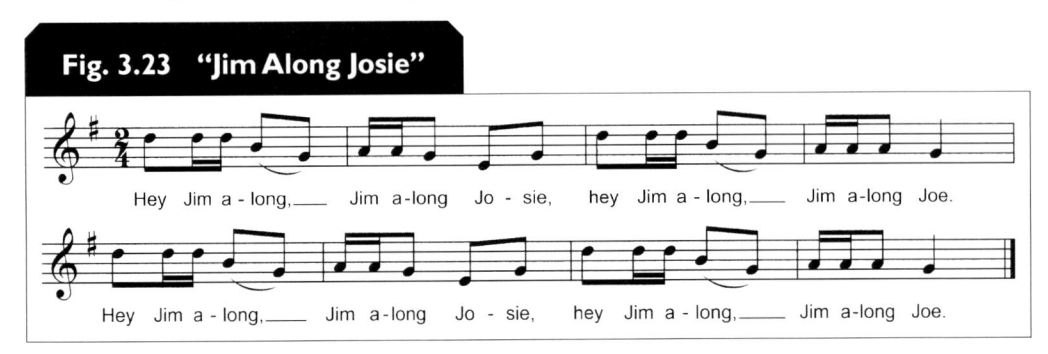

Fig. 3.23 "Jim Along Josie"

Hey Jim a - long,___ Jim a-long Jo - sie, hey Jim a - long,___ Jim a-long Joe.
Hey Jim a - long,___ Jim a-long Jo - sie, hey Jim a - long,___ Jim a-long Joe.

7. Choosing Games

Fig. 3.24 "Little Sally Water"

Lit - tle Sal - ly Wa - ters, sit - ting in a sau - cer,
Rise, Sal - ly, rise, Sal - ly, wipe a - way your tears, Sal - ly.
Turn to the east, Sal - ly, turn to the west, Sal - ly,
Turn to the one that you love the best, Sal - ly.

"Little Sally Water" (Fig. 3.24) is both an acting-out singing game and a choosing game. Sing it with students standing, holding hands, and walking in a circle. The student in the center of the circle performs the motions suggested in the text: *sit, rise, wipe your tears, turn to the east, turn to the west,* and *turn to the one that you love the best.* At the end of the game, a new student is chosen to take the position in the center of the circle.

For "Here Comes a Bluebird" (Fig. 3.25), students sing holding hands and walking in a circle. A student in the center chooses one in the circle and *hops in the garden.* That student becomes the new "bluebird" and will subsequently choose another one.

Fig. 3.25 "Here Comes a Bluebird"

Here comes a blue - bird through the _ win - dow, Hey, did - dle - dum a day day day.
Take a lit - tle part - ner hop in the gar - den Hey, did - dle - dum a day day day.

8. Chase Game with a Stationary Circle

Both "Charlie over the Ocean" (Fig. 3.26) and "A Tisket, a Tasket" (Fig. 3.27) can be played in the same way. The students sit in a circle, sing the song, and keep the beat. A student walks around the outside of the circle, successively tapping the beat on the head of each student in the circle. The person who is tapped at the end of the song chases the "tapper" around the circle. That one becomes the new tapper.

Kodály Today

Fig. 3.26 "Charlie over the Ocean"

Char - lie o - ver the o - cean, Char - lie o - ver the sea —
Char - lie caught a black - bird, Can't catch me.

Fig. 3.27 "A Tisket, a Tasket" Copy

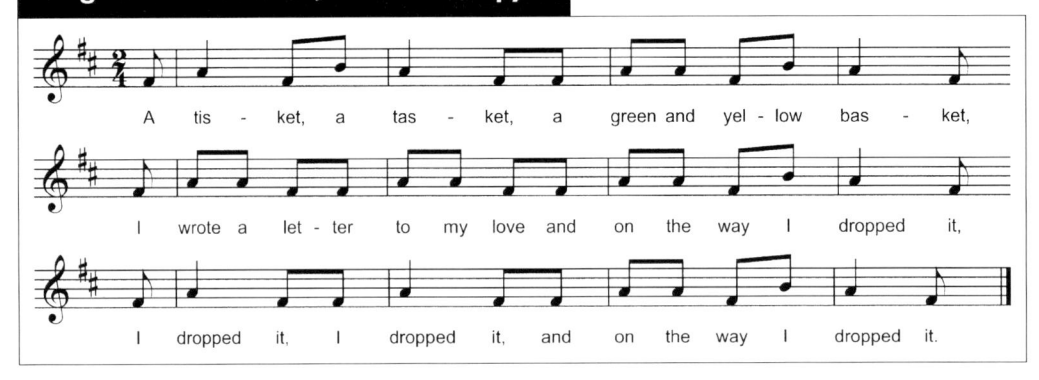

A tis - ket, a tas - ket, a green and yel - low bas - ket,
I wrote a let - ter to my love and on the way I dropped it,
I dropped it, I dropped it, and on the way I dropped it.

9. Partner Games

Partner games are those in which two students act out or interact with each other performing a motion, as with "Bow Wow Wow" (Fig. 3.28).

Fig. 3.28 "Bow Wow Wow"

Bow, wow, wow, whose dog art thou? Lit - tle Tom - my Tuck - er's dog bow, wow, wow.

10. Line Games

The most common way for students to play this kind of game is to have two players make an arch while the other players pass through in single file. In "London Bridge" (Fig. 3.29), on the word *lady* the arch is lowered to "catch" a player.

Fig. 3.29 "London Bridge"

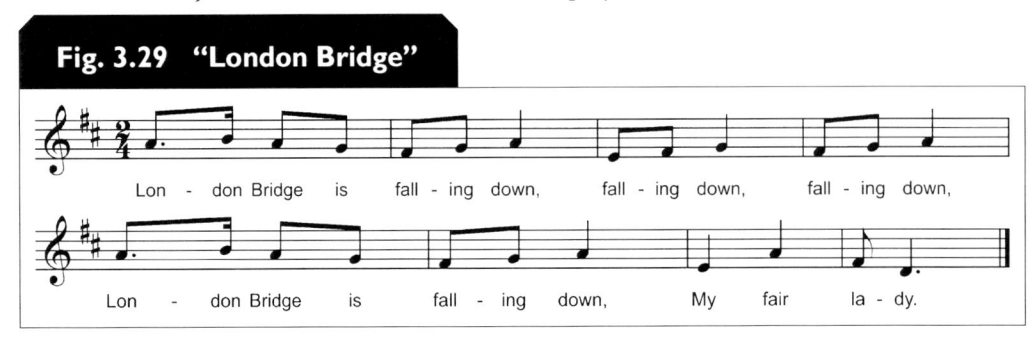

Lon - don Bridge is fall - ing down, fall - ing down, fall - ing down,
Lon - don Bridge is fall - ing down, My fair la - dy.

11. Double-Circle Games

Students form two circles that will interact together. An example of this game is "Great Big House in New Orleans" (Fig. 3.30). More complicated forms of the double-circle game involve changing partners during the game, as with "I've Been to Haarlem" (Fig. 3.31).

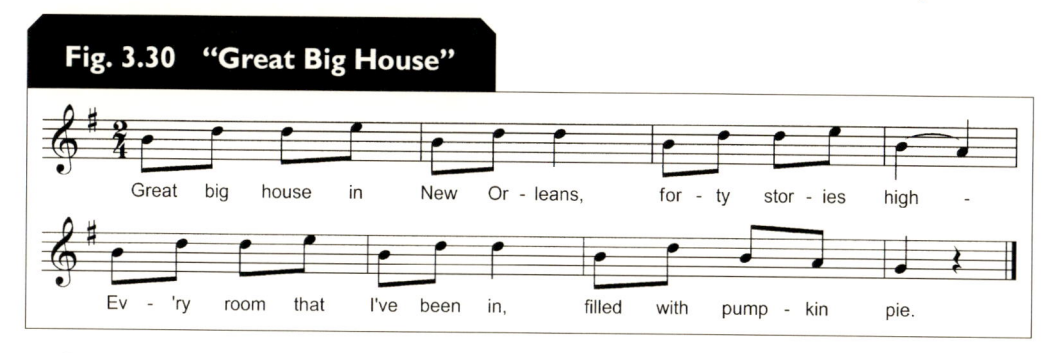

Fig. 3.30 "Great Big House"

Great big house in New Or-leans, for-ty stor-ies high
Ev-'ry room that I've been in, filled with pump-kin pie.

In dance formation there is a single circle of partners, girls on the right.

1. With a strutting step, and swinging arms, the circle sings and moves in a clockwise direction while singing "Great Big House in New Orleans."
2. On "went down to the old mill stream," ladies take four small steps toward the center of the circle and join hands.
3. On "fetch a pail of water," the men move toward the center and reach both arms across between two ladies, and down toward the floor as if to pick up a pail of water.
4. Men join hands at the end of the "picking up" gesture and swing arms (on "put one arm") over the heads of the ladies, making a circle behind their backs, at waist level.
5. On "the other round my daughter," the ladies raise their joined hands back over the men's heads, freeing the dancers, and on the fourth phrase, "with the golden slippers," the men move along one position to be ready to start the next round with a new partner.

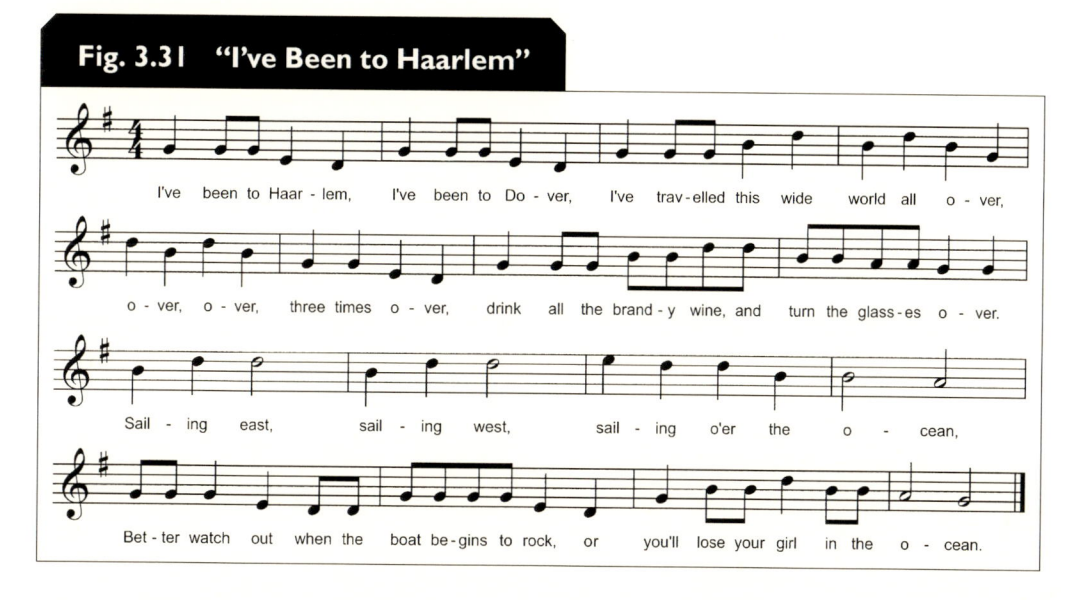

Fig. 3.31 "I've Been to Haarlem"

I've been to Haar-lem, I've been to Do-ver, I've trav-elled this wide world all o-ver,
o-ver, o-ver, three times o-ver, drink all the brand-y wine, and turn the glass-es o-ver.
Sail-ing east, sail-ing west, sail-ing o'er the o-cean,
Bet-ter watch out when the boat be-gins to rock, or you'll lose your girl in the o-cean.

Kodály Today

With "I've Been to Haarlem":

1. Students take partners, boys on girls' left, cross hands as in a skating position and walk around in a circle while singing the first part of this song.
2. When they reach the phrase "And turn the glasses over," partners "wring the dish rag," that is, raise their crossed hands while each student turns completely around without dropping his or her partner's hands.
3. On "sailing east" and so forth, hands are dropped and the boys make a circle inside the girls' circle. The boys move around in a clockwise direction while the girls continue counterclockwise. In other words, the circles are moving in opposite directions.
4. At the end of the song, boys choose the girls they are nearest and the dance begins again.

13. Double-Line Games

This category involves the reel dancing type. Sometimes these games are easier because the students can observe the lead couple. An example of this is "Come Thru 'Na Hurry" (Fig. 3.32).

Fig. 3.32 "Come Thru 'Na Hurry"

14. Square Games

These include such games as "Four White Horses" and "Draw Me a Bucket of Water."

15. Square Dances

Movement activities can progress to more complicated dance forms, such as square dancing. The familiar song "Old Brass Wagon" can be performed with several verses and more complex dance formations.

General Guidelines for Teaching More Advanced Singing Games

Before introducing students to a new singing game, it may be a good idea to use the song as a listening activity at the close of a music lesson to introduce the song to the students.

Consider teaching the singing game as a new song in a lesson without the movements. Individual phrases from the game song might be used to teach or reinforce known rhythmic or melodic elements.

If the singing game has easy-to-follow movements, they may be taught to the students when teaching the song. Once the song is familiar to them, the game may be taught. Of course, many games may be taught at the same time the song is introduced because the actions for the game are dictated by the text of the song. First demonstrate the motion of the song and then select another student to perform with you before asking all of the students to join.

Developing Creative Movement and Improvisations in the Classroom

Provide time for students to improvise creatively in the classroom. On learning a variety of singing games, they absorb a number of basic movement activities in songs; they can then borrow these activities and create their own games and movement variations. Once your students have mastered a song's game or movement activities, encourage them to create their own movements, hand clapping sequences, or dance patterns. These activities can encourage students to create their own actions and movement sequences.

1. Play the game.
2. Create an improvisation as a game.
    A. Improvise movements to reflect the form of the singing game. Discuss the form of the song and ask students to create a new movement that reflects the form:
        i. Create groups of students in the classroom.
        ii. Allow the groups to come up with new game that reflects the form.
        iii. Have the class sing while individual groups show the game. Switch.
        iv. If appropriate, perform the improvised game in canon with two groups from the class.
    B. Create a rhythmic ostinato to accompany a game.
        i. Divide the class into groups of students.
        ii. Have individual groups create a rhythmic ostinato for each phrase of their song to reflect the form.
        iii. Allow each student to perform the ostinato for one phrase before passing it along to another student.
        iv. Each group can perform its game song accompanied by the ostinato of another group.
    C. Create a melodic ostinato to accompany a game.
        i. Divide the class into groups of students.
        ii. Have individual groups create a melodic ostinato for each phrase of their song to reflect the form.
        iii. Allow each student to perform the ostinato for one phrase before passing it along to another students.
        iv. Each group can perform their game song accompanied by the ostinato of another group.

D. Create new words and motions to a song.
   i. Challenge students to create their own words to a known game song using the traditional game motions from other singing games. Students can then make up their own movements for a singing game.
E. Create new music to a known game song.
   i. Challenge students to create their own music and text to accompany a known game. They can also create their own game rules and motions.

Body Warm-ups and Creative Movement

In Table 3.3 we offer movement examples that can be used as an introductory activity for each lesson and be part of the body "warm-up" for students. We recommend choosing a movement piece that connects to the next singing activity in the lesson. Look for examples that are in the same meter, tempo, tonality, key, and dynamics as the next song in the lesson. Recorded examples for movement may also include some of the listening repertoire that students will later read and listen to in the music lesson. The examples in the table were developed by teachers in the Kodály Certification Program at Texas State University in 2014.

Table 3.3

MOVEMENT LIST		
Song Title	Composer	Features
Classical		
"Ballet of the Unhatched Chicks" from *Pictures at an Exhibition*	Modest Mussorgsky (1839–1928)	Presto, staccato, orchestra
"Alla Turca" from Piano Sonata, No. 11 in A	Wolfgang Amadeus Mozart (1756–1791)	Allegro, piano solo, 2/4, ♫♫
"March of the Toy Soldiers" from *Nutcracker Suite*	Pyotr Tchaikovsky (1840–1893)	Vivace, fanfare, orchestra
"Fossils" from *Carnival of the Animals*	Camille Saint-Saëns (1835–1921)	Allegro, orchestra, xylophone, ♫♫
"In the Hall of the Mountain King" from *Peer Gynt, Suite No. 1*	Edvard Grieg (1843–1907)	Moderato, accelerando, orchestra, dynamic contrast
"Moderato" from Minuet in G, No. 2	Ludwig van Beethoven (1770–1827)	Moderato, triple meter, strings
"Les Toreadors" from *Carmen*	Georges Bizet (1838–1875)	Allegro, march, orchestra

(continued)

Table 3.3 Continued

Funeral March of a Marionette	Charles Gounod (1818–1893)	Allegro, compound meter, orchestra
Hungarian Dance No. 5	Johannes Brahms (1833–1897)	Contrasting tempi, orchestra
Turkish March, Op. 113	Ludwig van Beethoven (1770–1827)	Allegro, march, accents
"Overture" from *William Tell*	Gioachino Rossini (1792–1868)	Allegro vivace, fanfare, finale, orchestra
"Trepak" from *Nutcracker Suite*	Pyotr Tchaikovsky (1840–1893)	Molto vivace, orchestra
Eine kleine Nachtmusik (Serenade No. 13 for strings), I	Wolfgang Amadeus Mozart (1756–1791)	Allegro, strings only
Fur Elise (Bagatelle No. 25)	Ludwig van Beethoven (1770–1827)	Allegro, triple meter, piano solo
Organ Concerto in G minor, Op. 4, IV	George Frideric Handel (1685–1759)	Andante, compound meter, organ and strings
Military March No. 1	Franz Schubert (1797–1828)	Allegro vivace, orchestra
An Evening in the Village	Béla Bartók (1881–1945)	Lento, rubato, form, *la pentatonic*
A Doll's Funeral Procession, Op. 39, No. 7	Pyotr Tchaikovsky (1840–1893)	Grave, form, ♫, piano solo
Playing Soldiers, Op. 31, No. 4	Vladimir Rebikov (1866–1920)	Allegro, march, piano solo, ♫
Minuet in G, BMV Anh 114	Johann Sebastian Bach (1685–1750)	Moderato, triple meter, keyboard solo
Contemporary Classical		
Palladio	Karl Jenkins (1944–)	Moderato, strings only
Jamaican Rumba	Arthur Benjamin (1893–1960)	Lively, piano duet, syncopation over one beat
Classical Opera		
"Non so più" from *The Marriage of Figaro*	Wolfgang Amadeus Mozart (1756–1791)	Allegro vivace, staccato vs. legato
Jazz		
Maple Leaf Rag	Scott Joplin (c. 1867–1917)	Lively, ragtime, piano solo

(continued)

Table 3.3   Continued

Crazy Race	Roy Hargrove (1969–)	Moderato, hip-hop influence
It Don't Mean a Thing	Duke Ellington (1899–1974)	Presto, big band, vocals
Groovin' Hard	Don Menza (1936–)	Moderato, big band
Take the A Train	Duke Ellington (1899–1974)	Allegro, big band
Concert Band		
Stars and Stripes Forever	John Philip Sousa (1854–1932)	Allegro, march
Short Ride in a Fast Machine	John Adams (1947–)	Fast, minimalism, woodblock throughout
Contemporary		
Montezuma	Cusco (ca. 1979)	Presto, South American flutes
Chariots of Fire	Vangelis (1943–)	Andante, electronic
Popular		
ABC	Berry Gordy, Alphonzo Mizell, Freddie Perren, Deke Richards (performed by the Jackson 5)	Andante, dance, Motown
Blame It on the Boogie	Mick Jackson (performed by the Jacksons)	Allegro, dance, Motown
YMCA	Jacques Morali (performed by the Village People)	Allegro, dance
Sir Duke	Stevie Wonder	Allegro, funk
Folk		
Wassail Wassail	Anonymous (performed by Mannheim Steamroller)	Adagio, compound meter, Renaissance

Instruments

Kodály believed that music education should begin with singing but be enhanced by introducing musical instruments.

> An instrumental culture can never become a culture of the masses.... Why, is it only through tormenting the violin, through strumming on the piano that the path

leads to the holy mountain of music? Indeed it often rather leads away from it. . . . What is the violin or piano to you? You have an instrument in your throat, with a more beautiful tone than any violin in the world, if you will only use it. With this instrument you will come invigoratingly near to the greatest geniuses of music—if there is only somebody to lead you on![7]

How valuable are "brilliant" pianists if they cannot sing simple folksongs without making errors? There must be a strenuous attempt to replace music that comes from the fingers and the mechanical playing of instruments with music from the soul and based on singing. We should not allow anyone even to go near an instrument until he or she can read and sing correctly. It is our only hope that one day our musicians will be able also to "sing" on their instruments.[8]

Table 3.4 presents a possible sequence for introducing instruments to children.

Table 3.4   A Sequence for Introducing Instruments

Grade 1	Grades 2 and 3	Grades 4 and 5
Tambour Tambourine Claves Chime bars Finger cymbals Bongo drums Mallet Triangle	Finger cymbals, bongo drums Mallet Triangle Congo drum Tone bells Orff instruments Xylophones; for simple drones, bourdons and ostinatos Recorder, limited range Autoharp Keyboard	Xylophone; for playing a moving drone, ostinato, and melodies by two mallets striking Recorder, more extended range Autoharp Guitar, for playing chords Keyboard Orchestral winds and brass Hand chimes Congo drums

Singing and Playing Music instruments

Singing is a more direct means to developing and solving music problems in the music classroom. Singing allows students to perform a piece musically, as opposed to first mastering the technical difficulties of playing a music instrument. Therefore if we are going to use music instruments in the classroom, it is important to develop students' musicianship skills before introducing instruments that will not allow students to develop their musicality.

It is also important to remind ourselves that solfège is a wonderful tool to develop such music activities as reading, writing, and inner hearing. All of these skills are prerequisites for instrumental playing, and therefore solfège can be considered an important skill to develop before teaching a music instrument.

Playing a musical instrument takes patience, and it can be very time-consuming in the general music education classroom. It is important that students apply their knowledge of solfège, inner hearing, and theoretical knowledge to ensure that performance on a music instrument will be musical.

Using Instruments in the Classroom

Before the beginning of each lesson, have your instruments available so you do not have to spend time taking them out during the music lesson.

Remember to consider the age and size of the students and their motor skill ability when choosing instruments.

Encourage students to experiment with the sound of the instruments before using them as part of an accompaniment.

Incorporating Instruments into the Music Curriculum

1. Beat
Use simple percussion instruments to keep the beat of a rhyme or folk song.

2. Beat and rhythm
Use simple rhythm instruments to perform the beat with a folk song and the rhythm to a folk song; then use them to perform the beat and rhythm of a folk song simultaneously.

3. Rhythmic ostinati
Use simple rhythmic instruments to perform a rhythmic ostinato (a repeated rhythmic pattern) to a folk song. Then use them to perform two simultaneous sounding ostinati to a folk song.

4. Melodic ostinati
Use glockenspiels, xylophone, metalophones, and melody bells to perform a melodic ostinato to a folk song.

5. Recorder
The music instructor can begin teaching the recorder in the third or fourth grade. Students should be able to sing all music before it is performed on the recorder. No matter what sequence is being used, the students should always be able to sing the song material they are performing with text as well as with rhythm and solfège syllables. There are some

Developing Creative Expression with Movement and Instruments

instances when children will not have covered the solfège syllables needed to sing the material, but they should know how to sing the example. At the beginning stages, it is important for the teacher to associate the fingering for the recorder with solfège syllables before students read from their recorder music from the staff.

Here is a recorder sequence you can use. It is important for students to be able to sing all of the material.

Absolute Letter Names and Corresponding Solfège Syllables: GAB (*mi re do*)
   Songs
   "Hot Cross Buns," "Frog in the Meadow," "Closet Key"
   Call and response: "Grandma Grunts," "Amasee," "Bluebird"

Absolute Letter Names: E GAB (*la so mi* and *mi re do low la*)
   la so mi **Repertoire**
   "We Are Dancing in the Forest" ("Lucy Locket"), "Hush Little Baby," "Yangtze Boatman's Chantey," "Skin and Bones" ("The Birch Tree")

   mi re do low la **Repertoire**
   "Poor Little Kitty Puss," "C-Line Woman" ("Sea-Lion"), "Canoe Song" "Rosie Darling Rosie"

Absolute Letter Names: DE GAB (*la so mi*) (*mi re do la,*) (*mi re do la, so,*)
   "Old McDonald," "Chatter with the Angels," "Cotton Eye Joe," "Old Grey Mare," "Sioux Indian Lullaby"

Absolute Letter Names: DE F# GAB (*do re mi so la*) (*do re mi fa so*)
   "Twinkle Twinkle," "Old Woman," "Who's That Tapping at the Window?" "Dinah," "Wall Flowers," "Ida Red," "Firefly," "Let Us Chase the Squirrel"

Absolute Letter Names: D E F# A B D (*do re mi so la do'*)
   "Hogs in the Cornfield"

Absolute Letter Names A and C' (*so mi*)
   "Seesaw"
   Call and Response: "Teddy Bear," "Pizza Pizza"

Absolute Letter Names A and C' D' (*la so mi*)
   "We Are Dancing in the Forest" ("Lucy Locket"), "Bye Baby Bunting"

Harmonic Instruments

Students learn to play harmonic instruments, such as autoharps and guitars.

Use this teaching progression when playing percussion:

1. Beginning music examples should be derived from known singing material. Sing the song with text.
2. Perform the music with rhythm syllables and conduct.
3. Read the music with rhythm syllables and conduct.
4. Inner-hear with rhythmic syllables while performing on a rhythm instrument.

Use this teaching progression when playing a melodic instrument:

1. Beginning music examples should be derived from known singing material. Sing the song with text.
2. Perform the music with rhythm syllables and conduct.
3. Perform the music with solfège syllables and hand signs.
4. Connect the fingering to solfège syllables and perform.
5. Read the music with rhythm syllables and conduct.
6. Read the music solfège syllables and hand signs.
7. Sing the music with letter names and hand signs.
8. Perform the example, but inner-hear the solfège syllables.

Lesson Planning

Designing a Preparation/Practice Lesson Plan Design That Includes Music Skills

In this chapter we have presented activities for developing a student's singing voice, movement skills, and instrumental skills, as well as how the instructor can develop music literacy skills. As a result of the information contained in this chapter, certain modifications to our basic preparation/practice lesson plan can be considered:

Developing a student's voice through vocal warm-up exercises
Establishing a comfortable starting pitch (CSP) for each song
Selecting appropriate techniques for teaching a new song by rote
Developing appropriate creative movement activities for students
Developing appropriate instrumental activities for students

Designing a Preparation/Practice Lesson Plan Template That Includes Music Skills

Table 3.5 presents a Preparation/Practice Lesson Plan Template that shows how the information for this chapter can now be used to modify a lesson plan design. We have bolded the sections of the lesson plan that can be modified to incorporate material from Chapter 4.

Table 3.5 Preparation/Practice Lesson Plan Design Template

INTRODUCTION	
Performance and demonstration of known musical concepts and elements	Body warm-ups and breathing exercises. Ss demonstrate their prior knowledge of repertoire and musical elements through performance of songs selected from the alphabetized repertoire list. These songs may be accompanied by rhythmic or melodic instruments.
CORE ACTIVITIES	
Acquisition of repertoire	Teach a new song by rote using an appropriate technique.
Preparation of a new concept	Learning activities in which Ss are taught a new musical concept through known songs found in the alphabetized repertoire list.
Creative movement	Focus on the sequential development of age-appropriate movement skills through songs and folk games.
Practice and musical skill development	Ss reinforce their knowledge of musical concepts and elements, working on the skill areas of reading and writing, form, memory, inner hearing, ensemble work, instrumental work, improvisation and composition, and listening, through known songs found in the alphabetized repertoire list.
CLOSURE	
Review and summation	Review of lesson content; T may perform the next new song to be learned in a subsequent lesson found in the alphabetized repertoire list.

Preparation/Practice Lesson Plan Design Template

When repertoire and selected activities are applied to the preparation/practice lesson framework, the lesson itself becomes more visible. The lesson plan in Table 3.6 includes repertoire and several activities; some procedural portions of this lesson have been removed.

Designing a Presentation Lesson Plan Template That Includes Music Skills

Table 3.7 offers a Presentation Lesson Plan Template. We want to show how the information in this chapter can be incorporated into this lesson.

Kodály Today

Table 3.6

GRADE 3: *LOW LA*, LESSON 2	
Outcome	Preparation: analyzing repertoire that contains a pitch a skip below *do* Practice: writing musical phrases that contain an eighth note followed by two sixteenth notes
INTRODUCTORY ACTIVITIES	
Warm-up	• Body warm-up • Beat activity • Breathing: Ss practice blowing a balloon and watch how air is released when deflating the balloon. • Resonance: explore a cow sound using low and high voice. Make sure Ss are inhaling and exhaling correctly with the support muscles. • Posture: remind Ss of the correct posture for singing.
Sing known songs	"Hunt the Cows" CSP: C • Ss sing the song. • Ss perform the rhythm of the last four beats of phrase 2 as a rhythmic ostinato into the next song ($\frac{4}{4}$ ♫ ♫ ♩ 𝄽 :‖). "Over the River" CSP: C • Ss sing the song and perform a beat motion or ostinato.
Develop tuneful singing Tone production Diction Expression	"Old Mr. Rabbit" CSP: F • Ss sing the song. • Imitate the sound of a siren with the voice. Challenge Ss to make soft and loud, high and low, long and short sirens, and sirens that just go up, just come down, or do both. • Falling off a cliff. Pretend you're falling off a cliff and say "aaaahhhhhhhhhh!" • Use a ball. Throw it from one S to another; Ss have to follow the movement of the ball with their voices. Kodály Choral Library, *Let Us Sing Correctly*, no. 38
Review known songs and melodic elements	"Let Us Chase the Squirrel" CSP: F • T and Ss sing song. • T has the incomplete rhythm of the song on the board.

(continued)

Table 3.6 Continued

Review known songs and melodic elements	• Ss sing the song while pointing to the beats. • Ss identify the missing solfège syllables and write them in. • Ss sing the solfège syllables of the whole song. • T sings the text of phrases of "Let Us Chase the Squirrel," "Rocky Mountain," "Bow Wow Wow," "Here Comes a Bluebird," and other known songs that use the solfège syllables *l s m r* and *d*; S echo-sing using solfège syllables and hand signs.
CORE ACTIVITIES	
Teach a new song	"Hogs in the Cornfield" CSP: D • T sings again and Ss identify the number of phrases in the song. (two) • T sings again, pausing after each phrase for Ss to identify and label the form of the song. (AB) • T and Ss sing and play the game.
Develop knowledge of music literacy concepts Describe what you hear	"Phoebe in Her Petticoat" CSP: A • T directs half the class to continue the ostinato while the remaining sing the song; switch. • Review kinesthetic awareness activities. • T and Ss tap the beat and sing the first phrase on "loo" before asking each question: • T: "Andy, how many beats did we tap?" (four) • T: "Andy, which beat has the lowest pitch?" (four) • T: "Let's sing the phrase on 'loo' but sing 'low' for the lowest note." • T sings the first four pitches on "loo." • T: "Andy, what hand signs do we use to sing those pitches?" (*mi re do do*) • T: "Let's sing our phrase with solfège syllables and hand signs but sing 'low' for our lowest pitch." (*mi re do do re do low*) • Ss sing and point down for the low pitch. • T: "Andy, is our lowest pitch a step or a skip from *do*?" (skip) • Ss sing as a whole group; then T may select individuals to sing the target phrase. (*mi re do do re do low*) ○ Ss sing "Phoebe in Her Petticoat" while T sings "Over the River" as a partner song.

(continued)

Table 3.6 Continued

Creative movement	"Over the River" CSP: C • T and S play game
Practice music, performance, and literacy skills Writing	"Fed My Horse" CSP: A • Ss sing the song. • Ss sing phrase 1 with rhythm syllables. • Ss sing the rhythm syllables and point to the four blank beats that T has placed on the board. • Ss identify the rhythms for each beat and fill in the blanks. • T erases the board and distributes writing materials. • Ss sing the first phrase of "Fed My Horse" with rhythm syllables while touching the beats on their paper. • Ss fill in the rhythm with stick notation. • T repeats the process with the first phrase of "Fire in the Mountain." • Ss use one of the rhythms to create a rhythmic accompaniment on a xylophone to accompany the song above or other known songs.
SUMMARY ACTIVITIES	
Review lesson outcomes Review the new song	"Hogs in the Cornfield"

Table 3.7   Presentation Lesson Plan Design Template

INTRODUCTION	
Performance and demonstration of known musical concepts and elements	Body warm-ups and breathing exercises. Ss demonstrate their prior knowledge of repertoire and musical elements through performance of songs selected from the alphabetized repertoire list. These songs may be accompanied by rhythmic or melodic instruments.
CORE ACTIVITIES	
Acquisition of repertoire	Teach a new song by rote using an appropriate technique.
Presentation of new element	Ss are presented with the syllables for the new element or how to notate the new element.

(continued)

Table 3.7 Continued

Creative movement	Focus on sequential development of age-appropriate movement skills through songs and folk games.
Presentation of new element	Ss are presented with the syllables for the new element or how to notate the new element.
CLOSURE	
Review and summation	Review of lesson content; T may perform the next new song to be learned in a subsequent lesson found in the alphabetized repertoire list.

Again, when repertoire and selected activities are applied to a lesson, the lesson planning process itself becomes more evident. Table 3.8 is a lesson plan that includes activities appropriate to a presentation lesson.

Table 3.8

GRADE 3: *LOW LA*, LESSON 4	
Outcome	Presentation: label the pitch a skip below *do* as *low la*,
INTRODUCTORY ACTIVITIES	
Warm-up	• Body warm-up • Beat activity • Breathing: Ss practice blowing a balloon and watch how air is released when deflating the balloon. • Resonance: explore a cow sound using low and high voice. Make sure Ss are inhaling and exhaling correctly with the support muscles. • Posture: remind Ss of the correct posture for singing.
Sing known songs	"Firefly" CSP: A • Ss sing the song with an ostinato (2/4 ♫♫♩ | ♫♩ :|). "Do, Do Pity My Case" CSP: F# • Ss sing song with the ostinato. • S sing the song in canon after four beats.
Develop tuneful singing Tone production	"Old Mr. Rabbit" CSP: F • Ss sing the song and continue the ostinato. • Ss sing the song with lip trills.

(continued)

Table 3.8 Continued

Diction Expression	• Ss sing the song on a hum. • Ss sing the song on "ng." • Ss hiss the rhythm of the song. • Kodály Choral Library, *Let Us Sing Correctly*, no. 39
Review known songs and melodic elements	"Let Us Chase the Squirrel" CSP: F then "Fire in the Mountain" CSP: A • Ss sing the song while T claps the rhythm. • Ss sing entire song with solfège syllables and hand signs. • Divide the class into two groups. Sing the songs phrase by phrase; group A sings the text, and group B echoes the phrase with solfège syllables and hand signs. • T sings the text of phrases of "Let Us Chase the Squirrel," "Rocky Mountain," "Bow Wow Wow," "Here Comes a Bluebird," or other known songs that use the solfège syllables *la so mi re* and *do*; Ss echo-sing using solfège syllables and hand signs.
CORE ACTIVITIES	
Teaching a new song	"Hop, Old Squirrel" CSP: A • T and Ss sing and keep beat, and then play game.
Presentation of music literacy concepts Describe what you hear with rhythm or solfège syllables	"Phoebe in Her Petticoat" CSP: A • Ss sing the song. • Review kinesthetic, aural, and visual awareness activities. • T: "When we hear a pitch a skip below *do*, we call it *low la*." (show sign) • T sings phrase 1 with solfège syllables and hand signs. • Class sings the target phrase with solfège syllables and hand signs. • Approximately six to eight individual Ss sing the target phrase with solfège syllables and hand signs. • Ss perform the rhythm of phrase 1 as a rhythmic ostinato into the next song ($\frac{2}{4}$ ♫ ♫ | ♫ ♩ :|).
Creative movement	"Hogs in the Cornfield" CSP: D • Ss continue the ostinato while T sings the song; Ss play game. • Ss choose instruments and create ostinati with which to accompany the song.

(continued)

Table 3.8 Continued

Presentation of music literacy concepts
 	
Describe what you hear with rhythm or solfège syllables
	"Jim Along Josie"
	CSP: A
	• Ss continue the ostinato while T sings the song.
	• T directs part of the class to continue the ostinato while the remaining sing the song; switch.
	• Ss sing the target phrase with solfège syllables and hand signs.
	• Ss identify the solfège syllables of the remaining phrases.
	• Ss sing the song with solfège syllables and hand signs.
	• T connects *low la* to other known songs; T and Ss sing these songs with solfège syllables and hand signs:
	   ◦ "Rosie, Darling Rosie"
	   ◦ "Big Fat Biscuit"
	   ◦ "Jim Along Josie"
	   ◦ "Old Mr. Rabbit"

SUMMARY ACTIVITIES	
Review lesson outcomes Review the new song	"Old Betty Larkin"

Connections to Grade Handbooks

The content of this chapter is closely aligned to Chapter 4 of each handbook. Teachers will find there more guidance on how to teach singing, playing instruments, and developing creative movement as well as how to integrate music instruments successfully into the music lesson.

Discussion Questions

1. What kinds of songs should we include in our repertoire list that will promote singing in tune?
2. Discuss the types of vocal warm-up exercises that you can use in your music lessons.
3. Discuss the various techniques you would use with your students to discover their head voice.
4. What kinds of instruments should you have in your music classroom?
5. Discuss how your music program can connect to the physical education curriculum.
6. Discuss the principal ways of teaching a song by rote to students.

Kodály Today

7. What are some of the key questions you need to answer in order to evaluate your effectiveness in teaching a new song to your students?
8. What do we mean by the use of the word *performance* in the school curriculum?
9. How can we further develop a preparation/practice lesson plan framework that includes singing, movement, and instrumental activities?
10. How can we further develop a presentation lesson plan framework that includes singing, movement, and instrumental activities?

Ongoing Assignment

1. Familiarize yourself with the performance outcomes for all the music curriculums for each grade.
2. Select a song from each grade you are going to teach next year, and write a teaching strategy as to how you are going to teach this song.
3. Select a game from each grade you are going to teach next year, and write a teaching strategy for how you are going to present the game.
4. Using the lesson plan formats given in this chapter, create a lesson plan where you prepare a rhythmic element and practice a melodic element.

Bibliography

Abramson, R. *Feel It! Rhythm Games for All* (Books/CDs). Miami: Warner Bros., 2003.

Abramson, R. *Rhythm Games for Perception and Cognition.* New York: Music and Movement Press, 1973.

Adzenyah, Abraham K., Dumisani Maraire, and Judith Cook Tucker. *Let Your Voice Be Heard!: Songs from Ghana and Zimbabwe.* Danbury, CT: World Music Press, 1997.

Allsup, R. E., and C. Benedict. "The Problems of Band: An Inquiry into the Future of Instrumental Music Education." *Philosophy of Music Education Review*, 2008, 16(2): 156–173.

Ansdell, Gary. "Musical Companionship, Musical Community: Music Therapy and the Process and Value of Musical Communication." In *Musical Communication,* ed. Dorothy Miell, Raymond Macdonald, and David J. Hargreaves. New York: Oxford University Press. 2005.

Anvari, S. H., L. J. Trainor, J. Woodside, and B. A. Levy. "Relations Among Musical Skills, Phonological Processing, and Early Reading Ability in Preschool Children." *Journal of Experimental Child Psychology*, 2002, 83(2): 111–130.

Bachmann, Marie-Laure. *Dalcroze Today: An Education Through and Into Music,* trans. David Parlett. New York: Oxford University Press, 1993.

Bacon, D. "The Importance of Kodály Training for Performers." *Bulletin of the International Kodály Society*, 1988, 13(2): 14–19.

Barrett, Margaret, and Johannella Tafuri. "Creative Meaning-Making in Infants' and Young Children's Musical Cultures." In *The Oxford Handbook of Music Education,* vol. 1., ed. Gary E. McPherson and Graham F. Welch, pp. 296–313. New York: Oxford University Press, 2012.

Barter, B. "The Relevance of Dance in Music Education." *Bulletin of the International Kodály Society*, 1991, *16*(2): 41–48.

Bennett, P. *Rhymeplay: Playing with Children and Mother Goose.* Van Nuys, CA: Alfred Music, 2010.

Bishop, J. C., and M. Curtis. *Play Today in the Primary School Playground: Life, Learning, and Creativity.* Ballmoor, Buckingham, UK: Open University Press, 2001.

Blacking, J. *How Musical Is Man?* London: Faber & Faber, 1976.

Boston, L. *Sing! Play! Create!: Hands-on Learning for 3- to 7-Year-Olds.* Charlotte, VT: Williamson Books, 2006.

Burakoff, Gerald. *How to Play the Recorder.* Ft. Worth, TX: Sweet Pipes, 1997.

Campbell, P. "The Child-Song Genre: A Comparison of Songs by and for Children." *International Journal of Music Education*, 1991, *17*: 14–23.

Campbell, P. *Lessons from the World: A Cross-Cultural Guide to Music Teaching and Learning.* New York: Schirmer, 1991.

Campbell, P. "Of Garage Bands and Song-Getting: The Musical Development of Young Rock Musicians." *Research Studies in Music Education*, 1995, *4(1)*: 12–20.

Campbell, P. S. *Teaching Music Globally: Experiencing Music, Expressing Culture.* Oxford: Oxford University Press, 2004.

Campbell, P. S., J. Drummond, P. Dunbar-Hall, K. Howard, H. Schippers, and T. Wiggins, eds. *Cultural Diversity in Music Education: Directions and Challenges for the 21st Century.* Brisbane: Australian Academic Press, 2005.

Carroll, A. "Katalin Forrai's Inspiring Influence on Early Childhood Music Education in Australia." *Bulletin of the International Kodály Society*, 2007, *32*(2): 18–25.

Chen-Hafteck, L. "Music and Language Development in Early Childhood: Integrating Past Research in the Two Domains." *Early Child Development and Care*, 1997, *130(1)*: 85–97.

Choksy, Lois, and David Brummitt. *120 Singing Games and Dances for Elementary Schools.* Englewood Cliffs, NJ: Prentice-Hall, 1987.

Collins, M., and C. Wilkinson. *Music and Circle Time: Using Music, Rhythm, Rhyme and Song.* Thousand Oaks, CA: Sage, 2006.

Cope, P. "Informal Learning of Musical Instruments: The Importance of Social Context." *Music Education Research*, 2002, *4*(1): 93–104.

Cox, Heather, and Garth Rickard. *Sing, Clap, and Play the Recorder*, vols. 1–2. St. Louis: Magnamusic-Baton, 1985.

Creech, A., and S. Hallam. "Parent-Teacher-Pupil Interactions in Instrumental Music Tuition: A Literature Review." *British Journal of Music Education*, 2003, *20*(1): 29–44.

Davidson, Jane. "Bodily Communication in Musical Performance." In *Musical Communication,* ed. Dorothy Miell, Raymond Macdonald, and David J. Hargreaves, pp. 215–238. New York: Oxford University Press, 2005.

Davis, S. G. *Fostering a Musical Say: Enabling Meaning Making and Investment in a Band Class by Connecting to Students' Informal Music Learning Processes.* Unpublished doctoral diss., Oakland University, Rochester, MI, 2008.

Douglas, S., and P. Willatts. "The Relationship Between Musical Ability and Literacy Skills." *Journal of Research in Reading*, 1994, *17*(2): 99–107.

Dowling, W. J. "Tonal Structure and Children's Early Learning of Music." In *Generative Processes in Music: The Psychology of Performance, Improvisation, and Composition*, ed. J. Sloboda, pp. 113–128. Oxford: Oxford University Press, 1998.

Fernald, A. "Intonation and Communicative Intent in Mothers' Speech to Infants: Is the Melody the Message?" *Child Development*, 1989, *60*(6): 1497–1510.

Fenton, W. C. "Improving Choral Tone Through Solfège." *Bulletin of the International Kodály Society*, 1993, *18*(1): 33–36.

Findlay, Elsa. *Rhythm and Movement: Applications of Dalcroze Eurhythmics.* Evanston, IL: Summy-Birchard, 1999.

Forrai, K. "The Influence of Music on the Development of Three-Year-Old Children." *Kodály Envoy*, 1976, *3*(3).

Fowke, E. "*Ring Around the Moon.*" Englewood Cliffs, NJ: Prentice-Hall, 1977.

Frego, R. J., D. Nawrocki, and T. L. Nawrocki. "Movement in the Elementary Music Class." *Kodály Envoy*, 1999, *25*(3): 5–8.

Froseth, J. *Do It! Play in Band.* Chicago: GIA, 2000.

Gault, B. "Developing Preschool Children's Preference for Classical Music Through the Use of Movement Experiences." *Kodály Envoy*, 1998, *24*(2): 14–16.

Gaunt, K. D. *The Games Black Girls Play: Learning the Ropes from Double-Dutch to Hip-Hop.* New York: New York University Press, 2006.

Goetze, Mary. "Children's Singing Voices." *Kodaly Envoy* 1981, *7*(4): 23–27.

Goetze, Mary. "Time, Technology, and Demographics." *Kodaly Envoy* 2010, *36*(4): 20–22.

Green Gilbert, Anne. *Creative Dance for All Ages.* Reston, VA: National Dance Association/American Alliance for Health, Physical Education, Recreation and Dance, 1992.

Green Gilbert, Anne. "BrainDance" (video). Reston, VA: NDA/AAHPERD, 2003.

Green Gilbert, Anne. *Brain-Compatible Dance Education.* Reston, VA: NDA/AAHPERD, 2006.

Gratier, M., and C. Trevarthen. "Musical Narrative and Motives for Culture in Mother-Infant Vocal Interaction." *Journal of Consciousness Studies*, 2008, *15*(10–11): 122–158.

Hargreaves, D. J., A. C. North, and M. Tarrant. "Musical Preference and Taste in Childhood and Adolescence." In *The Child as Musician: Musical Development from Conception to Adolescence*, ed. G. E. McPherson, pp. 135–154. Oxford: Oxford University Press, 2006.

Harwood, E. "Music Learning in Context: A Playground Tale." *Research Studies in Music Education*, 1998, *11*(1): 52–60.

Humphreys, J. T. "Instrumental Music in American Education: In Service of Many Masters." *Journal of Band Research,* 1995, *30(2):* 39–70.

Ittzés, M. "Pedagogical Consequences of Research in Ethnomusicology and Linguistics in Kodály's Oeuvre." *Bulletin of the International Kodály Society,* 2004, *29*(1): 3–14.

Jaccard, Jerry. "Intonation Begins in Kindergarten: The Art and Science of Teaching Music Acoustically." *Kodály Envoy* 2004, *30*(4): 5–27; republished 2014, *40*(3): 60–67.

Jentschke, S., S. Koelsch, and A. D. Friederici. "Investigating the Relationship of Music and Language in Children: Influences of Musical Training and Language Impairment." *Annals of the New York Academy of Sciences,* 2005, *1060*(1): 231–242.

Jones, P. M. "Music Education for Society's Sake: Music Education in an Era of Global Neo-Imperial/Neo-Medieval Market-Driven Paradigms and Structures." *Action, Criticism and Theory Music Education,* 2007, *6*(1): 2–28.

Jones, S. "Singing Games Sequence—Via Kodály Principles." *Kodály Envoy,* 1983, *10*(1).

Kardos, Pál. *The Foundations of Education Towards Pure Intonation.* Kecskemét, Hungary: Zoltán Kodály Pedagogical Institute of Music, 1972.

Kendall, M. J. "A Review of Selected Research in Elementary Instrumental Music Education with Implications for Teaching." *Journal of Band Research,* 1990, *25*(2): 64–82.

Kodály, Zoltán. "Children's Choirs." In *The Selected Writings of Zoltán Kodály,* 1974.

Kodály, Zoltán. *Énekeljünk Tisztán.* Budapest, Hungary: Editio Musica, 1941.

Kodály, Zoltán. "Fifty-Five Two-Part Exercises: Preface to the Hungarian Edition." In *The Selected Writings of Zoltán Kodály,* 1974.

Kodály, Zoltán. "Let Us Sing Correctly." In *The Selected Writings of Zoltán Kodály,* 1974.

Kontra, Zsuzsanna. *Let Us Try to Sing Correctly—Training for Singing in Parts.* Kecsemét, Hungary: Zoltán Kodály Pedagogical Institute of Music, 1995.

Lamont, A., D. Hargreaves, N. A. Marshall, and M. Tarrant. "Young People's Music in and out of School." *British Journal of Music Education,* 2003, *20*(3): 229–241.

Lum, C.-H., and P. Shehan Campbell. "The Sonic Surrounds of an Elementary School." *Journal of Research in Music Education,* 2007, *55*(1): 31–47.

Marsh, K. "Cycles of Appropriation in Children's Musical Play: Orality in the Age of Reproduction." *World of Music,* 2006, *48*(1): 9–32.

Marsh, K. *The Musical Playground: Global Tradition and Change in Children's Songs and Games.* New York: Oxford University Press, 2008.

Marsh, K., and S. Young. "Musical Play." In *The Child as Musician: A Handbook of Musical Development,* ed. Gary McPherson, pp. 289–310. New York: Oxford University Press, 2006.

Mazokopaki, K., and G. Kugiumutzakis. "Infant Rhythms: Expressions of Musical Companionship." In *Communicative Musicality: Exploring the Basis of Human Companionship,* ed. S. Malloch and C. Trevarthen, pp. 545–564. Oxford: Oxford University Press, 2009.

McLucas, A. Dhu. *The Musical Ear: Oral Tradition in the USA.* Farnham, Surrey, UK: Ashgate, 2010.

McPherson, G. E. "From Child to Musician: Skill Development During the Beginning Stages of Learning an Instrument." *Psychology of Music*, 2005, *33*(1): 5–35.

McPherson, G. E., and J. W. Davidson. "Playing an Instrument." In *The Child as Musician: A Handbook of Musical Development,* ed. G. E. McPherson, pp. 331–352. Oxford: Oxford University Press, 2006.

Merrill-Mirsky, C. *Eeny Meeny Pepsadeeny: Ethnicity and Gender in Children's Musical Play*. Unpublished doctoral diss., University of California, Los Angeles, 1988.

National Standards for Arts Education: What Every Young American Should Know and Be Able to Do in the Arts. Reston, VA: MENC, 1994.

Minks, A. *Interculturality in Play and Performance: Miskitu Children's Expressive Practices on the Caribbean Cost of Nicaragua*. Unpublished doctoral diss., Columbia University, New York, 2006.

Minks, A. "Performing Gender in Song Games Among Nicaraguan Miskitu Children." *Language and Communication*, 2008, *28*(1): 36–56.

Nielsen, S. G. "Learning Strategies in Instrumental Music Practice." *British Journal of Music Education*, 1999, *16*(3), 275–291.

Nelson, J. "The Baroque Recorder: Fifteen Activities for 'B-A-G'!" *Kodály Envoy*, 1994, *20*(4): 11–13.

Nettl, B. *The Study of Ethnomusicology: 31 Issues and Concepts*. Urbana: University of Illinois Press, 2005.

Papoušek, M. "Intuitive Parenting: A Hidden Source of Musical Stimulation in Infancy." In *Musical Beginnings: Origins and Development of Musical Competence,* ed. I. Deliège and J. Sloboda, pp. 88–112. Oxford: Oxford University Press, 1996.

Parsons, M. "Art and Integrated Curriculum." In *Handbook of Research and Policy of Art Education,* ed. E. W. Eisner and M. D. Day, pp. 775–794. Mahwah, NJ: Erlbaum, 2004.

Pearce, Gordon, and Carole Lindsay-Douglas. S*ound Singing: Ideas for Improving the Quality of Singing in Class & Choir*. Bedfordshire, UK: Lindsay Music, 2000.

Phillips-Silver, J., and Trainor, L. J. "Feeling the Beat: Movement Influences Infant Rhythm Perception." *Science*, 2005, *308*(5727): 1430.

Phillips, Kenneth H. *Directing the Choral Music Program*. New York: Oxford University Press, 2004.

Phillips, Kenneth H. *Teaching Kids to Sing (with Supporting Materials)*. New York: Schirmer, 1993.

Rao, Doreen. *We Will Sing!: Choral Music Experience for Classroom Choirs*. New York: Boosey and Hawkes, 1993.

Rice, T. "Traditional and Modern Methods of Learning and Teaching Music in Bulgaria." *Research Studies in Music Education*, 1996, *7(1)*: 1–12.

Riddell, C. *Traditional Singing Games of Elementary School Children in Los Angeles*. Unpublished doctoral diss., University of California, Los Angeles, 1990.

Roberts, D., and P. Christenson. "Popular Music in Childhood and Adolescence." In *Handbook of Children and the Media,* ed. D. Singer and J. Singer, pp. 395–413. Thousand Oaks, CA: Sage, 2001.

Rodrigues, H. M., P. M. Rodrigues, and J. S. Correia. "Communicative Musicality as Creative Participation: From Early Childhood to Advanced Performance." In *Communicative Musicality: Exploring the Basis of Human Companionship*, ed. S. Malloch and C. Trevarthen, pp. 585–610. Oxford: Oxford University Press, 2009.

Rosacker, M. "Training the Child's Singing Voice in the Kodály Classroom." *Kodály Envoy*, 1983, *10*(2).

Schippers, H. *Facing the Music: Shaping Music Education from a Global Perspective*. New York: Oxford University Press, 2010.

Schmid, Will. *World Music Drumming: A Cross-Cultural Curriculum*. Milwaukee: Hal Leonard, 1998.

Schmidt, Oscar. *The Many Ways to Play Autoharp*. Jersey City, NJ: Oscar Schmidt-International, 1966.

Schön, D., M. Boyer, S. Moreno, M. Besson, I. Peretz, and R. Kolinsky. "Songs as an Aid for Language Acquisition." *Cognition*, 2008, *106*(2): 975–983.

Seeger, A. "Catching up with the Rest of the World: Music Education and Musical Experience." In *World Musics and Music Education: Facing the Issues*, ed. B. Reimer, pp. 103–116. Reston, VA: MENC, 2002.

Seeman, E. *Implementation of Music Activities to Increase Language Skills in the At-Risk Early Childhood Population*. Unpublished M.A. thesis, Saint Xavier University, Chicago, 2008.

Shehan Campbell, Patricia. *Songs in Their Heads: Music and Its Meaning in Children's Lives*. New York: Oxford University Press, 1998.

Shehan Campbell, Patricia, and Bonnie C. Wade. "Performance as Enactive Listening." In *Teaching Music Globally: Experiencing Music, Expressing Culture* and *Thinking Musically: Experiencing Music, Expressing Culture* (two books). New York: Oxford University Press, 2004.

Sloboda, J. "Talent and Skill Development: The Acquisition of Music Performance Expertise." *Exploring the Musical Mind: Cognition, Emotion, Ability, Function*, ed. J. Sloboda, pp. 274–296. New York: Oxford University Press, 2005.

Sloboda, J. A., J. W. Davidson, M.J.A. Howe, and D. G. Moore. "The Role of Practice in the Development of Performing Musicians." *British Journal of Psychology*, 1996, *87(2)*: 287–309.

Taylor-Howell, S. "Recorder in the Kodály Classroom. An Integrated Methodology." *Bulletin of the International Kodály Society*, 1995, *20*(1): 34–37.

Thaut, Michael H. "Rhythm, Human Temporality and Brain Function." In *Musical Communication*, ed. Dorothy Miell, Raymond Macdonald, and David J. Hargreaves, pp. 171–192. New York: Oxford University Press, 2005.

Torff, Bruce. "Making Music and Making Sense Through Music: Expressive Performance and Communication." In *MENC Handbook of Musical Cognition and Development*, ed. Richard Colwell, pp. 189–224. New York: Oxford University Press, 2006.

Trehub, S. E., and L. J. Trainor. "Singing to Infants: Lullabies and Play Songs." *Advances in Infancy Research*, 1998, *12*: 43–77.

Trehub, S. E., L. J. Trainor, and A. M. Unyk. "Music and Speech Processing in the First Year of Life." *Advances in Child Development and Behavior*, 1993, *24*: 1–35.

Trevarthen, C. "Origins of Musical Identity: Evidence from Infancy for Musical Social Awareness." In *Musical Identities,* ed. R.A.R. MacDonald, D. J. Hargreaves, and D. Miell, pp. 21–38. Oxford: Oxford University Press, 2009.

Tsang, C., and N. J. Conrad. "Does the Message Matter? The Effect of Song Type on Infants' Pitch Preference for Lullabies and Playsongs." *Infant Behavior and Development*, 2010, *33*: 96–100.

Warner, Brigitte. *Orff-Schulwerk: Applications for the Classroom.* Englewood Cliffs, NJ: Prentice-Hall, 1997.

Weikart, P. S. *Teaching Movement and Dance: A Sequential Approach to Rhythmic Movement* (2 vols.). Ypsilanti, MI: High/Scope, 2003.

Welch, Graham F. "Singing and Vocal Development." In *The Child as Musician: A Handbook of Musical Development,* ed. Gary McPherson, pp. 311–330. New York: Oxford University Press, 2006.

Welch, Graham F. "Singing as Communication." In *Musical Communication,* ed. Dorothy Miell, Raymond Macdonald, and David J. Hargreaves, pp. 239–260. New York: Oxford University Press, 2005.

Whitcomb, R. "Improvisation in Elementary General Music: A Survey Study." *Kodály Envoy*, 2007, *34*(1): 5–10.

Whitehead, A. N. *Process and Reality: An Essay in Cosmology.* (The Gifford Lectures 1927–28, corrected edition, ed. D. R. Griffin and D. W. Sherburne.) New York: Free Press, 1978.

Wicks, D. "Modern Vocal Pedagogy: Implications for Educators Who Employ the Kodály Concept." *Bulletin of the International Kodály Society*, 2007, *32*(1): 43–51.

Wong, P. C., E. Sloe, N. M. Russo, T. Dees, , and N. Kraus. "Musical Experience Shapes Human Brainstem Encoding of Linguistic Pitch Patterns." *Nature Neuroscience*, 2007, *10(4)*: 420–422.

Websites

Informal Learning: http://www.infed.org
Musical Futures Projects: http://www.musicalfutures.org
Simán Bolívar Musical Foundation: http://www.fundamusical.org.ve
Smithsonian Folkways: http://www.smithsonianglobalsound.org.
Wider Opportunities: http://ks2music.org.uk

Chapter 4

Teaching Tools and Techniques for Developing Audiation and Music Literacy Skills

Among other things, we are still living in a musical culture that exists without writing. And yet it is indeed a real culture: one which includes instrumental music after the oral tradition—playing by ear.... But the time for a culture of handed-down oral tradition is over, and outside Hungary the world has long since entered into the era of a written culture. In our own country, there is no more urgent task than the hastening of this transition if we do not want to be left behind for good. Without literacy today there can no more be a musical culture than there can be a literary one. Thus the promotion of musical literacy is as pressing now as was the promotion of linguistic literacy between one and two hundred years ago.

Zoltán Kodály, "Preface to *Musical Reading and Writing*"

Part of the musicianship of many (but not all) musical practices worldwide is knowledge about notation and knowledge of how to decode and encode musical sound patterns in staff notation, graphic notation, hand signs, or rhythmic syllables. But "music literacy," or the ability to decode and encode a system of musical notation, is not equivalent to musicianship. It is only part of the formal and procedural dimensions of musicianship. Moreover, literacy should be taught and learned parenthetically and contextually—as a coding problem to be gradually reduced within the larger process of musical problem solving through active music making.

D. J. Elliott, *Music Matters*, p. 61

Key Questions

- How do pedagogical tools affect our teaching of music literacy skills?
- How do we develop a sequence for teaching rhythmic and melodic elements for elementary music students that is based on repertoire?

The previous chapter addressed the development of students' performance skills in the classroom through singing, movement, and playing instruments. The goal of this chapter is to learn how teaching tools can develop their audiation skills and expand music literacy skills using their classroom repertoire. The most common recurring rhythmic and melodic elements within the students' repertoire become the basis for teaching musical reading and writing. Included in this chapter is a discussion and comparison of different types of rhythmic syllable systems. Our goal is to demonstrate the importance of teaching traditional notation to students and to explain how rhythmic and melodic syllables are successful tools to accomplish this outcome. This chapter also addresses how the goal of music literacy affects lesson planning.

Teaching Tools for Developing Music Literacy Skills

To accommodate the teaching of rhythmic and melodic elements, Hungarian music teachers gradually began adapting certain teaching tools that are sometimes mistakenly thought to be the "Kodály method." These *tools* facilitate instruction and learning, but they also enhance students' musical skill development as well as their musicality. They include use of the moveable *do* system of solmization, use of hand signs to indicate the pitches of the scale, rhythmic syllables, and musical shorthand derived from solfège and rhythmic syllables (stick notation). These teaching tools or techniques were adapted by Kodály's colleagues and are seen as a feature of this type of classroom teaching.

Solfège Syllables and Relative Solmization

> From the example of the Paris Conservatoire it will be seen that the time is approaching when it is acknowledged that, just as writing cannot be learned unless reading has been learned first, singing or playing an instrument cannot be mastered unless solfège has itself been mastered first.[1]

> Finally: relative solmization can be of great help and should not be dismissed. Successions of syllables are easier and more reliably memorized than letters; in addition, the syllables indicate at the same time the tonal function and, by memorizing the interval, we develop our sense of the tonal function.[2]

Kodály was convinced that students would gain greater command of their voices through systematic solfège instruction and that relative solmization was valuable for developing both ear training and sight-singing abilities. Relative solmization is used to describe an approach to teaching melodic elements beginning with *so-mi*. In this system, students read from the staff, employing a *do* clef that can represent any key. In grades one and two students are

Teaching Tools and Techniques

not encumbered with theoretical information about sharps and flats to read from the staff. Music theory is kept at a minimum until students develop fluency in reading from all staff positions, indicated by a moveable *do* clef. In grade three or four students will learn about the flat and sharp signs and understand how a tonic note is related to the placement of a sharp or flat in the key signature. Moveable *do* (*do* is the tonic in major and *la* the tonic in minor) is used to describe an approach to teaching melodic elements beginning with the complete major scale. The moveable *do* or tonic-solfa system can be traced to the eleventh century, when Guido d'Arezzo used a form of it for musical instruction. This system was later adapted by Sarah Glover (1785–1867), an English music teacher; her system was later adopted and improved by John Curwen (1816–1880), an English Congregational minister. Relative solmization links sounds to tonal images in one's hearing and may be used with any tonal system: major, minor, modal, or pentatonic.

Figure 4.1 shows the solfège syllables for the natural, raised, and lowered steps of the major scale. Solfège syllables are always written in lowercase italicized letters. The major scale tonic is *do* (d) and *la* (l) is the minor scale tonic.

Fig. 4.1

do is the major scale tonic and *la* is the minor scale tonic											
raised scale steps		*di*		*ri*		*		*fi*		*si*		*li*		*	
natural scale steps	d		r		m		f		s		l		t		d
lowered scale steps	*	*ra*		*ma*		*		*		*lo*		*ta*			
* = not used											

The upper octave is sometimes indicated by a superscript prime placed on the syllable, for example, *high do* or *do'*. The lower octave is sometimes indicated by a subscript prime on the syllable, for example, *low so* or *so,*.

Letter Names

In the pedagogy associated with the Kodály concept, students learn solfège syllables prior to letter names. Solfège helps students understand the relationships between letter names. The German letter names are used for singing because they may be sung with one syllable and therefore singing with letter names will not compromise the rhythmic integrity of the musical example. For example, instead of singing F sharp (two syllables) students sing "fis." Letter names are always written with upper case. The German system of letter names is as follows.

German Letter Names

Sharps	ais ("ice")	bis	cis	dis	eis	fis	gis
Natural	A	B	C	D	E	F	G
Flats	ass ("ace")	bes	ces	des	ees	fes	ges

Hand Signs

The hand signs used to illustrate the notes of the scale (solfège syllables) were developed by Curwen in 1862. They were later adopted and adapted in Hungary. Hand signs physically and visually help orient students to intervallic relationships as well as develop audiation skills. They should be made with the whole arm and be spatially placed to give an indication of position in the scale (Fig. 4.2).

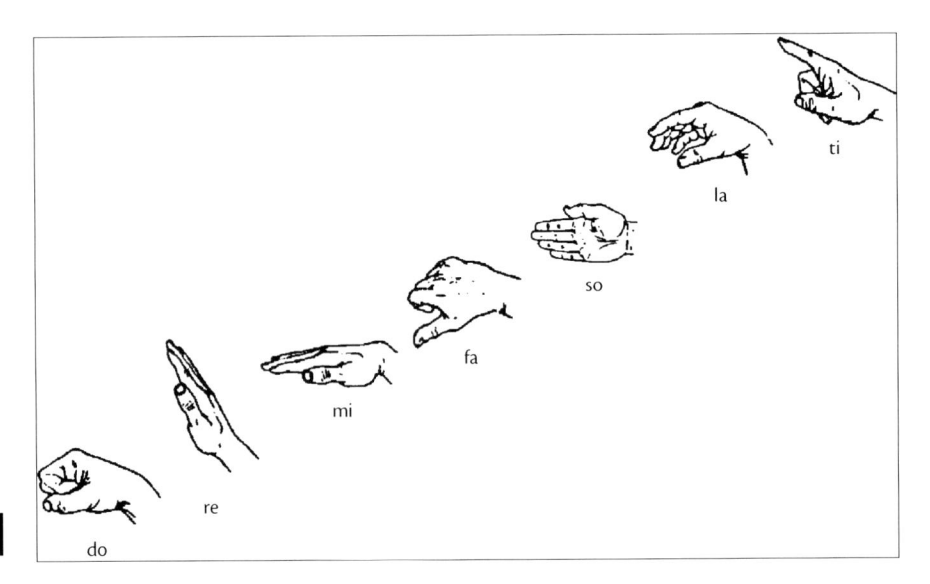

FIG. 4.2

Singing using hand signs is an important tool; the kinesthetic movement of the hand associates a pattern of music with a pattern of movement. By associating a kinesthetic motion with a melodic pattern, we enhance cognition by connecting a pattern of movement with a melodic pattern. A student's repertoire of songs should contain many same and similar melodic patterns; therefore it's possible to connect a pattern found in one song to a pattern in another song. Singing songs and patterns with hand signs helps develop intonation and inner-hearing skills.

Simple forms also create an important connection between songs in a repertoire. Many children's songs are two or four phrases in length and usually have four-beat phrases. Form can therefore create a simple but significant connection between songs.

Random drilling of notes from hand signs will not be as effective as making some of the aforementioned connections. Prior to reading a piece of music, ask students to read from hand signs to give them a framework for their reading. Furnishing a context or framework will help students audiate a melodic turn with greater accuracy; rhythmic notation will be less likely to distract them.

Tone Steps

Tone steps can be used to show the steps of the scale. The *do* pentatonic scale is shown in Figure 4.3.

Once the tone steps are placed on the board, you may point to the solfège syllables of a song; students sing the syllables and show the melodic contour with hand signs. Tone steps help students visualize the position of solfège syllables.

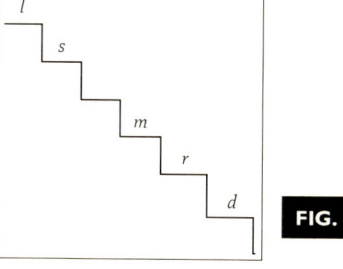

FIG. 4.3

Finger Staff

If you spread your fingers and hold your hand parallel to your body, your hand creates a representation of the music staff, the four fingers and thumb serving as the five lines of the staff. Use a finger from your other hand to point to the notes. This provides another means of helping students visualize solfège syllables or letter names on a staff.

Child's Piano

Position students standing, kneeling, or sitting to represent a particular tone set. The tallest student may be the lowest sound if you are showing a barred instrument or piano string, but this may be confusing, since the longer student is also taller or higher. A half-step may be represented by positioning students so their shoulders touch.

Notes on Staff

Write the tone set of a melody on the stave and point to notes that create a new or familiar melody.

Rhythm Syllables

Rhythm syllables help the learner associate a "syllable" with the number of sounds heard on particular beats. The French music theorist and pedagogue Émile Chevé (1804–1864) developed rhythm syllables in the nineteenth century. Hungarian teachers adopted and adapted this system of rhythm syllables to suit the Hungarian language.

Hungarian music educators use rhythm syllables to represent the duration of the sounds on a beat. For example, students sing songs, substitute the text of the songs with play words, and then replace these words with rhythm syllables. Szabò states that

> The foregoing methods, using movements and play-words, are designed to be a preparation for the separation of the rhythm from the pitch of the notes from a

Kodály Today

tune. Once this has been achieved without difficulty by the children, the play words which are peculiar to each particular song must be replaced by syllables which are applicable to all tunes, i.e., *ta* and *ti* representing notes of longer and shorter values respectively.... Similarly the rhythm of No. 9 from Pentatonic Music II, formerly practiced to the words "clip, clop, clippy clop," is now practiced to "ta ta ti-ti ta...."

Therefore in the original Hungarian method for teaching rhythms, the teacher used word substitutions that were replaced by rhythm syllables.

As noted by Klinger, "There are several perfectly acceptable sets of rhythm syllables one can use to facilitate rhythm reading or singing. A sampling of the simple meter rhythm syllables most frequently used by Kodály educators is listed below. If you are currently using different syllables successfully, please continue! It is not what is used, but the logic and consistency as well as the success that counts."[3]

We believe that teaching rhythm becomes more challenging in classroom situations where students do not have music classes four or five times a week; it is important that we reevaluate our process of teaching and use approaches that are inherently musical and will help students connect their aural and visual understandings. To this end we recommend the use *takadimi* syllables.[4]

Table 4.1 indicates two rhythm syllable systems that can be used for reading rhythms. The first is the *takadimi* syllables, and the second is the traditional Kodály rhythm syllables. We use the *takadimi* system with slight modifications. We recommend it because the rhythm syllables are not related to notation but rather to location of sounds on a beat.

Table 4.1

Rhythmic Element Duple Meter	*Takadimi* Rhythm Syllables	Kodály Rhythm Syllables	Counting with Numbers
♩	ta	ta	1
♫	ta di	ti-ti	1 &
♩	ta ah	ta ah	1 2
o	ta ah ahah	ta ah ahah	1 2 3 4
♬♬	taka di mi	ti-ri-ti-ri	1 e & ah
♩♫	ta di mi	ti---ti-ri	1 & ah
♫♩	taka di	ti-ri--ti	1 e &
♩.♪	ta mi	timri	1 ah

(continued)

Table 4.1 Continued

Rhythmic Element Duple Meter	*Takadimi* Rhythm Syllables	Kodály Rhythm Syllables	Counting with Numbers
♪ ♩.	taka	ri-tim---	1 e
♩. ♪	ta----------di	tie------ti	1 &
♪ ♩ ♪	ta-di--------di	syn---co--pa	1 &&
♪♪♪ (3)	taki da	tri-o-la	1 la le
Compound Meter			
♪♪♪ (3)	taki da	ti---ti--ti	1 2 3 or 1 la le
♩.	ta	ta	1
♩ ♪	ta da	tati	1 3 or 1 le
♪ ♩	taki	ti--ta	1 2 or 1 la

Linking Common Rhythmic Elements to Rhythm Syllables

Rhythm syllables, now associated with the Kodály concept, have become popular in many countries. A shortcoming of several rhythm syllable systems is that the syllables themselves do not enable the learner to distinguish where a sound falls on a beat. Consider the rhythm system that uses *ta* for a quarter note and *ti-ti* for two eighth notes. The rhythm syllable for the eighth note *ti* is used in both simple and compound meter. This system is used in common simple meter where the beat is equal to a quarter note or for compound meters where the beat is equivalent to a dotted quarter note. Although the Kodály rhythm syllables have been effective with elementary classroom music teachers, they have not been widely adopted by instrumental, middle school, high school teachers, or college instructors. Finding a system of rhythm syllables that can be used by music specialists at all levels of instruction and can be easily correlated to counting using numbers is necessary for consistency. The *takadimi* system of rhythm pedagogy provides this link. We have put this system in use with very slight alterations.

Kodály Today

The *takadimi* system emphasizes the "location of sounds within a beat." Here is a simple illustration. Any attack on the beat is called *ta*; an attack on the second half of the beat is called *di*. In Figures 4.4 and 4.5, there are two examples of the song "Rocky Mountain," one written in 2/4 and the other written in 2/2. Both versions of "Rocky Mountain" can be sung with the same rhythm syllables. This illustrates that the rhythm syllables are associated with where sounds fall on a beat rather than with note values. Another way to say this is that the *takadimi* rhythm syllables are associated with the concept behind the note values. For example, one sound on a beat will always be *ta* and two sounds on a beat will always be *ta-di* in simple meter, regardless of the value of the beat.

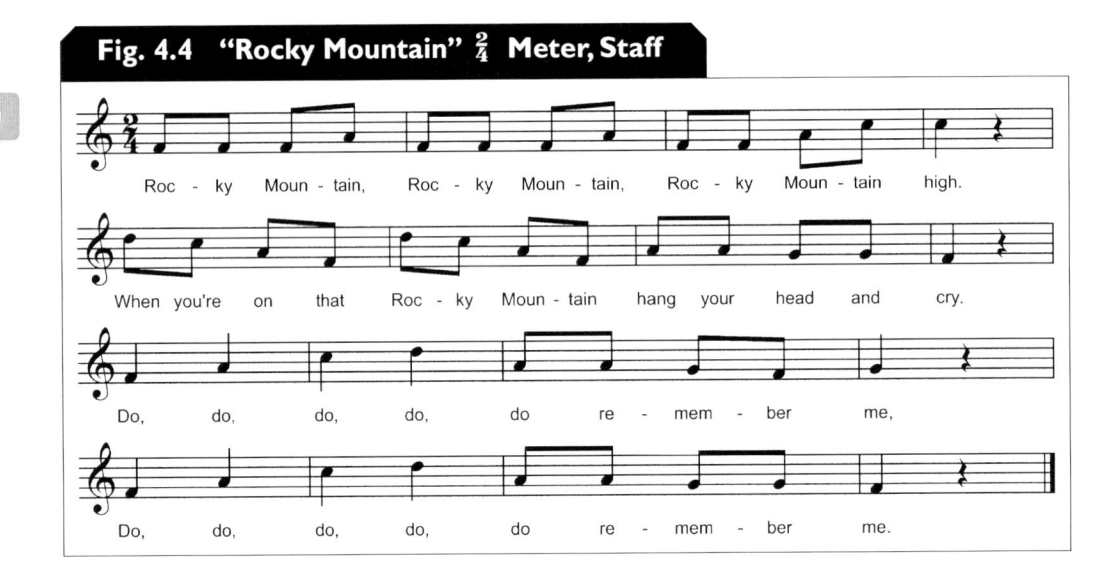

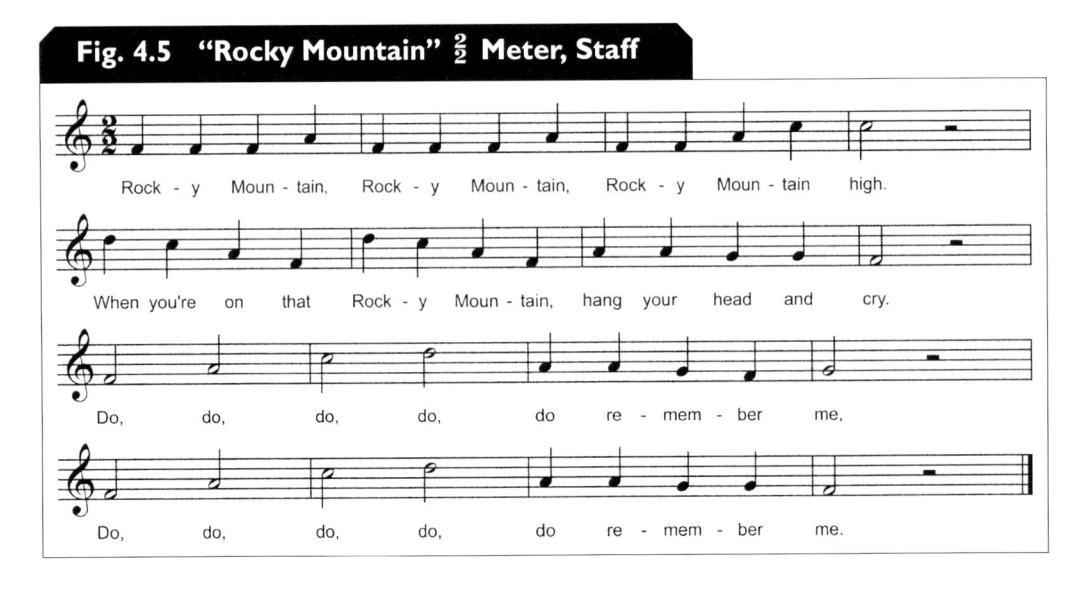

Fig. 4.4 "Rocky Mountain" 2/4 Meter, Staff

Fig. 4.5 "Rocky Mountain" 2/2 Meter, Staff

Example of Rhythm Syllables

The song "Paw Paw Patch" (Fig. 4.6) can be sung with rhythm syllables. The same syllables can be used if the piece is written in 2/2 or 2/8.

Fig. 4.6 "Paw Paw Patch"

Where, oh where is pret-ty lit-tle Su-sie?
Where, oh where is pre-ty lit-tle Su-sie?
Where, oh where is pret-ty lit-tle Su-sie?
Way down yon-der in the paw paw patch.

"Paw Paw Patch" may be sung using the *takadimi* system for reading (Fig. 4.7).

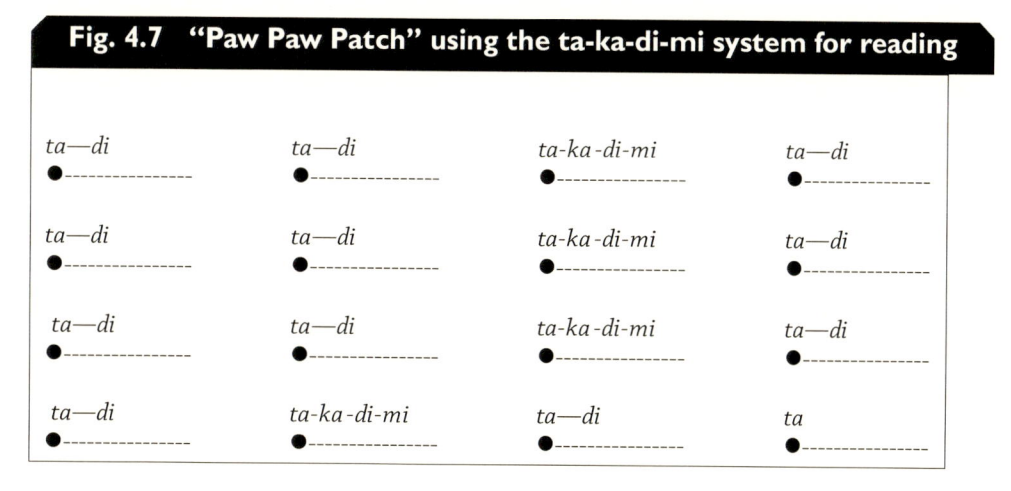

Fig. 4.7 "Paw Paw Patch" using the ta-ka-di-mi system for reading

ta—di	*ta—di*	*ta-ka-di-mi*	*ta—di*
ta—di	*ta—di*	*ta-ka-di-mi*	*ta—di*
ta—di	*ta—di*	*ta-ka-di-mi*	*ta—di*
ta—di	*ta-ka-di-mi*	*ta—di*	*ta*

The *takadimi* system easily transfers to counting with numbers. Because *ta* is the unit of beat, *ta* relates to the number used as a beat; the syllable *di* relates to the sound falling on the second half of the beat, or when counting with numbers, the "&." Remember, rhythm syllables should be used to aurally access sound and not used primarily to read music. We are convinced of two things regarding the *takadimi* system: (1) it has a much closer correlation to counting with numbers than traditional Kodály rhythm syllables, and (2) the *takadimi* rhythm syllables are more flexible than other rhythm syllable systems.

Traditional Rhythm and Stick Notation

A musical shorthand or stick notation was developed in Hungary and is simply a rapid way of writing music without using staff notation. The example below demonstrates how traditional notation can be written in stick notation. In stick notation rhythms are written without note heads (except for the half notes and whole notes); solfège syllables may be written below both traditional rhythm notation and stick notation.

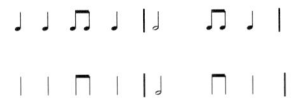

♩ ♩ ♫ ♩ | ♩ ♫ ♩ |

| | ⊓ | | ⊓ | |

A Rhythmic and Melodic Sequence for Developing Music Literacy Skills

A primary goal of music education is to guide students in their love of the art of music and music making. Love and respect for the art form increases when students discover the many meanings of the repertoire they sing. Performance with understanding is one of the goals of all music teaching. We are convinced that understanding comes, in large measure, from the ability to listen, sing, memorize, describe, and analyze what you hear and perform. This implies that learning takes place in the context of performance and listening; the ability to describe and analyze the performance is enhanced by knowledge of the elements of music.

As previously stated, teaching music according to the Kodály concept begins with collecting and selecting a body of musical repertoire appropriate to the age and experience of the student population. The parameters and suggestions for song material have been outlined in Chapter 3. Once repertoire and materials are selected, they need to be analyzed to determine song type, frequency of rhythmic and melodic patterns, tone sets, and scale and tonality, among additional classifications as outlined in Chapter 2.

The order of rhythmic and melodic elements set out in the next two tables offers a suggested sequence of musical elements that may be presented on the basis of the song materials found in this book. This sequence may depend on the repertoire you use with your own students. Our progression of rhythmic and melodic elements is based on the frequency of musical elements as they usually appear in typical four-beat patterns in the repertoire selected for this book. We determine the rhythmic and melodic sequence from the frequency of occurrence in the repertoire. Our rationale was to first select the most common four-beat pattern for teaching a new musical element.

We approach the teaching of music literacy skills through discovery-based learning activities. In other words, children are guided to understand the concept behind the sounds before a symbol is presented. Traditional approaches to teaching music literacy begin with the symbol associated with the sound of music; for example, "this is a whole note 𝅝; it gets four beats. This is a half note 𝅗𝅥; it gets two beats."

Here is a teaching sequence for the beginning rhythmic elements:

Teaching Quarter and Eighth Notes
Quarter note rest
2/4 meter
Half note and half note rest
Tie

Teaching Sixteenth Notes
4/4 meter
Whole note and whole note rest

Teaching Sixteenth Note Combinations
(Those made up of one eighth note or two sixteenth notes or two sixteenth notes and one eighth note)
Internal upbeats
External upbeats
Syncopation
Dotted quarter note followed by an eighth note
3/4 meter
Dotted eighth followed by sixteenth note
Sixteenth note followed by a dotted eighth note
Eighth note followed by a dotted quarter note
Eighth note rest
6/8 meter with even division
6/8 meter with uneven divisions
Triplet
Duplet
2/2 meter
Ties across the barline
Changing meter
Asymmetric meter

Note: prior to teaching any rhythmic elements, you must teach the concept of beat in the kindergarten classroom and review it in grade one.

Here is a teaching sequence for beginning melodic elements:

1. Introducing Notes of the Pentatonic Scale
so-mi
la-so-mi

la-so-mi-do
la-so-mi-re-do

2. Introducing Notes of the Extended Pentatonic Scale
low la
low so
high do

3. The Diatonic Scales
Notes of the major pentachord scale
Notes of the major hexachord scale
Notes of the minor pentachord scale
Notes of the minor hexachord scale
Notes of the major scale
Notes of the natural minor scale
Notes of the harmonic minor scale
Notes of the melodic minor scale

4. Modal Scales
Dorian mode
Mixolydian mode

Note: prior to teaching any melodic elements, teach speaking voice and singing voice and the concept of high and low in the kindergarten classroom and review them in grade one.

The Relationship Between Musical Concepts and Elements

We are interested in teaching three aspects of each musical element: (1) the *concept* behind the element, (2) the *solfège* or *rhythm syllables* of the new element that can be used for aural identification and reading purposes, and (3) the *traditional notation* used to represent the sound or pitch of the new element. Once students sing and learn a song that contains the new element, you can isolate the phrase or motif containing this element. Through questioning, you enable students to discover the concept behind the element. For example, with rhythmic concepts students must identify the number of sounds on a beat; for melodic concepts they must determine the position of the new pitch in relation to known pitches. Once these determinations are made, we associate the rhythm or solfège syllables to the aural sound of the new element in the four-beat pattern. After the sound is labeled, we present the traditional notation. Tables 4.2 and 4.3 present an initial list of rhythmic and melodic elements and the concept associated with each element.

Teaching Tools and Techniques

Table 4.2 A Teaching Sequence for Beginning Rhythmic Elements

Element	Concept	Rhythm Solfège	Related Elements, Music Theory
Quarter and eighth notes	One and two sounds on a beat	*ta* and *ta di*	
Quarter note rest	A beat with no sound		
Simple meter	Pattern of strong and weak beats within a measure; the beat is divisible by 2		Time signature, bar lines, measures, double bar lines
Half note	One sound that lasts for two beats	*ta-ah*	
Half note rest	Two beats with no sound		Rhythms can be written in 2/4 meter. Ss may rewrite melodies containing one, two, or no sounds on the beat. In 2/2 meter, one sound on the beat is a half note, two sounds on the beat make two quarter notes, and no sound on the beat is a half note rest.
Tie	A curved line that connects two notes together		
Sixteenth notes	Four even sounds within one beat	*taka di mi*	Rhythms can be written in $\frac{2}{2}$ meter (introduction of the single eighth note)
Single eighth note			
Eighth note rest			Rhythms can be written in $\frac{2}{8}$ meter (single eighth note)
Meter 4/4	A group of four beats, one strong and three weak beats within a measure		Rhythm can be written in $\frac{4}{4}$, $\frac{4}{2}$, or $\frac{4}{8}$ meter
Whole note	One sound that lasts four beats	*ta-ah-ah-ah*	Songs written in C may be written in $\frac{4}{2}$

(continued)

Table 4.2 Continued

Element	Concept	Rhythm Solfège	Related Elements, Music Theory
Whole note rest	Four beats with no sound		
Sixteenth note combinations made up of one eighth note and two sixteenth notes or two sixteenth notes and one eighth note	Three sounds on a beat that are not even; the first sound is longer than the last two sounds, long sound followed by two short sounds	*ta--di-mi*	
	Three uneven sounds on a beat; the last sound is held longer than the first two sounds, two short sounds followed by a long sound	*ta-ka--di*	
Internal upbeats	Internal phrases begin with unstressed beats		
External upbeats	External phrase begins with unstressed beats		
Syncopation	Three uneven sounds, one short, one long, and one short	*ta-di-----di*	
	Three uneven sounds on one beat	*taka--mi*	
Dotted quarter followed by an eighth note	Two uneven sounds over two beats where the first sound lasts a beat and a half	*ta--------di*	Dot placed after a note
$\frac{3}{4}$ meter	A pattern of one strong and two weak beats within a measure		

(continued)

Table 4.2 Continued

Element	Concept	Rhythm Solfège	Related Elements, Music Theory
Dotted eighth followed by a sixteenth note	Two uneven sounds on one beat; the first sound is three times longer than the second	*ta--mi*	
Sixteenth note followed by a dotted eighth	Two uneven sounds on one beat; the first sound is shorter than the second	*ta-ka---*	
Eighth note followed by a dotted quarter note	Two uneven sounds over two beats where the first sound lasts half a beat and the second sound lasts a beat and a half	*ta-di----*	
$\frac{6}{8}$ meter	A pattern of strong and weak beats where the beat is divisible by 3		
Compound meter			
Dotted quarter note	One sound on the beat	*ta*	
Three eighth notes	Three even sounds on the beat	*taki da*	
Quarter note followed by eighth note	Two sounds on the beat, one long followed by one short	*ta--da*	
Eighth note followed by a quarter note	Two sounds on the beat, one short followed by one long	*taki--*	
Six sixteenth notes	Six even sounds on a beat	*tavaki di da ma*	
6/8 meter with uneven divisions			

(*continued*)

Table 4.2 Continued

Element	Concept	Rhythm Solfège	Related Elements, Music Theory
Dotted eighth note followed by sixteenth note and eighth note	Three uneven sounds on a beat	*ta-di-da*	
Triplet	Three sounds on one beat in simple meter	*ta-ki-da*	
Duplet	Two sounds on one beat in compound meter	*ta-di*	
Meter			
Changing meter			
Asymmetric meter			

Table 4.3 A Teaching Sequence for Beginning Melodic Elements

Element/Solfège	Concept	Related Elements, Music Theory
so-mi	Two pitches, one higher and one lower, a skip apart (minor third)	Bichord of the pentatonic scale
la	A note a step (major second) above *so*	Trichord of the pentatonic scale
do	A skip (major third) down from *mi*	Tetrachord of the pentatonic scale
re	A note between *do* and *mi*; a step above *do* (major second), a step below *mi* (major second)	Major pentatonic scale
low *la*	*la,* is a note a (minor third) skip down from *do*	Major extended pentatonic scales; minor pentatonic scale
low *so*	*so,* is a note a (perfect fourth) skip down from *do* or a step (major second) from *la,*	Major extended pentatonic scales; minor pentatonic scale

(*continued*)

Table 4.3 Continued

Element/Solfège	Concept	Related Elements, Music Theory
high do	*do'* is a note a skip (minor third) above *la*	Major extended pentatonic scale
	A composition that uses the notes *do re mi so la* where the final note is *re*	*re* pentatonic
	A composition that uses the notes *do re mi so la* where the final note is *so*	*so* pentatonic
fa do re me fa so	*fa* a note between *mi* and *so*; a step down from *so* (major second); a step up from *mi* (minor second)	Major pentachord scale; flat; intervals minor second, major second, major third, perfect fourth, perfect fifth
do re me fa so la		Major hexachord scale; major sixth
low t la, ti, do re mi	*ti*, a note a step (major second) above *la*, and a step (minor second) below *do*	Minor pentachord scale; sharp Minor third intervals
la, ti, do re mi fa		Minor hexachord scale; minor sixth intervals
ti	A note a step above *low la*, and a step below *high d'*	
do re mi fa so la ti do'		Major scale; intervals major sixth, major seventh
la, ti, do re mi fa so la		Minor scale; minor sixth, minor seventh
si	*si* is a note a half step below *la*	Harmonic minor scale; augmented second
fi la, ti, do re mi fi si la so fa mi re do ti, la,	*fi* is note a whole step above *mi*	Melodic minor scale
re mi fa so la ti do re' Or la, ti, do re mi fa so la		Dorian mode
so, la, ti, do re mi fa so Or do re mi fa so la ta do		Mixolydian mode

(continued)

Table 4.3 Continued

Element/Solfège	Concept	Related Elements, Music Theory
mi fa so la ti do re mi Or *la ta do re mi fa so la*		Phrygian mode
fa so la ti do re mi fa Or *do re mi fa so la ti do*		Lydian mode

Preparation, Presentation, and Practice of Musical Elements for Grades 1 Through 5

Most teachers would agree that there are three phases of instruction and learning involved in teaching: preparation, presentation, and practice. Teaching musical concepts depends on several factors, notably the age of the students, their physical and emotional maturity, and the frequency of their music instruction. Older students and those with prior musical experience generally tend to require less preparation for rhythmic elements but may need more practice with melody. If the music instructor is fortunate enough to see the students several times a week, the lessons may include considerable variety and practice. Students who have music lessons once or twice a week require more review, so fewer elements will be covered during each school year. Melodic elements and concepts should not be taught until students can sing in tune.

We have created a preparation/practice teaching progression for rhythmic and melodic elements. We suggestion which musical concepts and elements should be addressed in each grade. Tables 4.4 through 4.8 are presented as teaching units, with each unit having two sections: preparation of a new music concept, and practice of known musical elements.

Table 4.4 Grade 1 Preparation/Practice Chart

GRADE 1		
Unit	Prepare	Practice
Unit 1		Review Kindergarten concepts: loud and soft, beat, high and low speaking voice, fast and slow, high and low singing voice, rhythm
Unit 2	Concept: one and two sounds on a beat Element: quarter and two beamed eighth notes	Melodic contour

(continued)

Table 4.4 Continued

Unit 3	Concept: two pitches, one higher and one lower, a skip apart Element: bichord of the pentatonic scale, *so-mi*	Quarter and two beamed eighth notes
Unit 4	Concept: a beat with no sound Element: quarter rest	*so-mi*
Unit 5	Concept: three pitches, with a skip between one pair of the pitches Element: trichord of the pentatonic scale, *la*	Quarter rest
Unit 6	Concept: organization of strong and weak beats; duple meter Element: duple meter time signature	*la*

Table 4.5 Grade 2 Preparation/Practice Chart

GRADE 2		
Unit	Prepare	Practice
Unit 1		Review first grade concepts: one and two sounds on a beat, *so-mi*, a beat with no sound, *la*, and duple meter
Unit 2	Concept: a pitch that is a skip lower than *mi* Element: *do*	Duple meter
Unit 3	Concept: one sound that lasts for two beats Element: half note	*do*
Unit 4	Concept: a pitch between *mi* and *do* Element: *re*	Half note
Unit 5	Concept: scale that is made up of steps and a skip between *m* and *s* Element: major pentatonic scale	*re*
Unit 6	Concept: four sounds on a beat Element: sixteenth notes	Major pentatonic scale
Unit 7	Concept: a pattern of four beats: one strong and three weak beats within a measure Element: quadruple meter	Sixteenth notes

Table 4.6 Grade 3 Preparation/Practice Chart

GRADE 3		
Unit	Prepare	Practice
Unit 1		Review second grade concepts: *do*, one sound that lasts for two beats, *re*, major pentatonic scale, and sixteenth notes
Unit 2	Concept: three uneven sounds on a beat; the first sound is longer than the last two sounds Element: eighth note followed by two sixteenth notes	Quadruple meter
Unit 3	Concept: a note that is a skip lower than *do* Element: a skip below *do*; *la* pentatonic scale	Eighth note followed by two sixteenth notes
Unit 4	Concept: three uneven sounds on a beat, the last sound held longer than the first two sounds Element: two sixteenth notes followed by an eighth note	*low la*
Unit 5	Concept: a note that is a stop lower than *low la* Element: *low so*	Two sixteenth notes followed by an eighth note
Unit 6	Concept: a phrase that begins before the strong beat Element: single eighth note as an internal upbeat	*low so*
Unit 7	Concept: a note that is a skip higher than *la* Element: *high do*	Single eighth note as an internal upbeat
Unit 8	Concept: phrases beginning with unstressed upbeats Element: external upbeat; represented as an eighth note or a quarter note	*high do*

Table 4.7 Grade 4 Preparation/Practice Chart

GRADE 4		
Unit	Prepare	Practice
Unit 1		Review third grade concepts: eighth note followed by two sixteenth notes, *low la*, two sixteenth notes followed by an eighth note, *low so*, single eighth note as an internal upbeat, *high do*, external upbeat
Unit 2	Concept: three uneven sounds (short-long-short) occurring over two beats Element: syncopation	External upbeat
Unit 3	Concept: scale that is made up of steps and skips Element: *l*, pentatonic scale	Syncopation
Unit 4	Concept: two uneven sounds over two beats where the first sound lasts a beat and a half Element: dotted quarter note followed by an eighth note	*l*, pentatonic scale
Unit 5	Concept: a note between *m* and *s*, the new pitch *fa* closer to *m* Element: major pentachord and hexachord scale; half step, intervals major and minor seconds, perfect fourth and fifth, and major sixth	Dotted note quarter note followed by an eighth note
Unit 6	Concept: three-beat meter, a pattern of one strong and two weak beats within a measure Element: triple meter	*fa* and major pentachord and hexachord scale
Unit 7	Concept: a pitch a half step below *d* Element: *low ti*	Triple meter
Unit 8	Concept: two uneven sounds on a beat, a short sound followed by a long sound Element: a dotted eighth note followed by a sixteenth note	Low *ti*

Kodály Today

Table 4.8 Grade 5 Preparation/Practice Chart

\multicolumn{3}{c}{GRADE 5}
Unit	Prepare	Practice
Unit 1		Review fourth grade concepts: syncopation, *low la* pentatonic scale, dotted note, *fa* and major pentachord and hexachord scale, triple meter
Unit 2	Concept: a pitch between *la* and *high do*; a note that is a half step below *do* and a whole step above *la*; major diatonic scale Element: *high ti*	Triple meter
Unit 3	Concept: two uneven sounds on two beats; the first sound is short and the second sound is long Element: eighth note followed by a dotted quarter note	*high ti*
Unit 4	Concept: natural minor scale; a scale with half steps between the second and third degree and fifth and sixth degrees Element: minor scale	Eighth note followed by a dotted quarter note
Unit 5	Concept: compound meter 1; the subdivision of the beat into three even sounds on a beat Element: three beamed eighth notes on a beat; a quarter note followed by an eighth note on a beat; a dotted quarter note on a beat	Natural minor scale
Unit 6	Concept: harmonic minor scale; a scale with half steps between the second and third degrees, fifth and sixth degrees, and seventh and eighth degrees Element: *si*	Compound meter 1 Subdivision of beat into three even sounds

(*continued*)

Table 4.8 Continued

Unit 7	Concept: compound meter 2; subdivision of the beat into six even sounds Element: six sixteenth notes on a beat	Harmonic minor scale
Unit 8	Concept: sound that is a half step above *fa*; raised sixth of a minor scale leading to the harmonic minor scale; Dorian mode Element: *fi*	Compound meter 2 Subdivision of beat into six even sounds
Unit 9	Concept: compound meter 3; uneven divisions of the beat in compound meter Element: an dotted eighth note followed by a sixteenth note followed by an eighth note on one beat	*fi*
Unit 10	Concept: a pitch a half step below *ti*; lowered seventh degree of the major scale Element: *ta*	Compound meter 3 Uneven subdivision of beat

The Connection Between Teaching Basic Rhythmic and Melodic Patterns and Common Stylistic Characteristics of Folk Songs

Teaching in the primary grades focuses on singing and developing inner hearing skills. Additionally we believe that it is important to introduce students to the form as well as the basic rhythmic and melodic building blocks of the repertoire they are singing. To accomplish this, we need to teach students repertoire that shares similar stylistic elements. If students have three or more lessons of music per week, then the teacher can immerse students in the study of stylistic elements rather quickly. If a teacher has only one or two lessons a week of music, then they will need to move very sequentially and follow a two-step process.

Step 1: initially it is important to focus on the form of a song as well as specific rhythmic and melodic elements typically found in four-beat patterns. Students should be singing repertoire that contains recurring melodic and rhythmic patterns.

Step 2: as students' knowledge of rhythmic and melodic elements and patterns develops, we can promote their understanding of stylistic elements by referencing aspects of form, cadence structure, typical rhythms, melodic patterns and turns, and meters and tonalities associated with a particular repertoire of songs.

Kodály Today

In selecting repertoire to be sung in a particular grade, we need to be aware of the common stylistic characteristics shared by this repertoire so the focus of our teaching can be more than simply preparing, presenting, and practicing specific rhythmic and melodic elements. Some of the music repertoire that we currently use in our teaching, such as "Rocky Mountain" and "Liza Jane," contains the five notes of the pentatonic scale. In step one of our process we teach students about notes of the pentatonic scale.[5] In step two of the process, students begin to sing pentatonic melodies and analyze the form as well as typical rhythmic motifs, melodic turns, and cadential endings.

This means that we have to deconstruct the music material for students and enable them to both aurally and visually identify such stylistic traits as form and common rhythmic and melodic building blocks or rhythmic/melodic turns. Students' discovering these building blocks gives teachers a possible sequence for presenting form, rhythmic, and melodic elements as well as meter and tonalities. Understanding these stylistic elements enables students to feel comfortable with a particular musical style; they can readily transfer their knowledge about one piece of music to another. For example if students are studying African American spirituals then they should be able to perform this music accompanied with clapping hands and stamping feet, reflect the verse and refrain forms of these songs though performance, identify common syncopation patterns, and identify the lowered third, fifth, or seventh notes of the scale ("blue" notes). A true understanding of style emerges when students can improvise/compose melodies reflecting these stylistic traits.

Lesson Planning

Incorporating Music Literacy Activities into Your Preparation/Practice and Presentation Lessons

The goal of this section is to incorporate information for developing musical literacy into the preparation/practice and presentation lesson plan formats. Our lesson plan formats now include:

- Singing and performing known songs with rhythmic and solfège syllables
- Selecting specific melodic and rhythmic concepts to be taught for each lesson on the basis of preparation, presentation, and practice of musical elements for grades one through five
- Introducing the rhythm syllables, traditional names, and traditional notation during the presentation lesson for a rhythmic element
- Introducing the solfège syllables, hand signs, and tone steps during the presentation lesson for a melodic element
- Introducing traditional rhythmic notation with solfège syllables written underneath as well as the staff

The Preparation/Practice Lesson

In a preparation/practice lesson, we prepare a new musical concept and practice a familiar musical element. During this lesson, we continue to develop singing abilities, teach new repertoire, develop movement skills, and enhance the listening skills of students. To formulate this lesson plan, we need

- Curriculum goals to determine objectives (see grade handbooks for each grade)
- Alphabetized list of songs to determine songs for singing (see grade handbooks for each grade)
- Pedagogical list of songs to determine the best songs for preparing each new musical element and the corresponding connection to musical literacy (see grade handbooks for each grade)

Table 4.9 presents a sample preparation/practice lesson plan format for preparing *high do* and practicing internal upbeat. Remember that this is just a sketch; we are not attempting to create smooth transitions between one section of the lesson and another. Review this lesson plan to see how music concepts and elements are being prepared and practiced. Note the importance attached to active music making and how students gain an understanding of rhythm and melody through use of rhythm and solfège syllables.

Table 4.9 Example of a Grade 3 Preparation/Practice Lesson Plan

	GRADE 3, UNIT 7, *HIGH DO*, LESSON 3
Outcome	Preparation: create a visual representation of a note that is a skip higher than *la*
	Practice: improvisation of internal upbeat
	INTRODUCTORY ACTIVITIES
Warm-up	• Body warm-up
	• Beat activity
	New Mexico March, John Philip Sousa (1854–1932)
	• Breathing: Ss practice blowing a balloon and watch how air is released when deflating the balloon
	• Resonance: explore a cow sound using low and high voice; make sure Ss are inhaling and exhaling correctly with the support muscles.
	• Posture: remind Ss of the correct posture for singing
Sing known songs	"Old Brass Wagon"
	CSP: C
	• Ss sing song.
	• Ss perform a motion to the beat that can carry into the next song.
	"Mr. Rabbit"
	CSP: C
	• Ss sing the song.
	• Ss sing the song with an ostinato.
	• Ss continue the ostinato into the next song.

(continued)

Kodály Today

Table 4.9   Continued

Develop tuneful singing Tone production Diction Expression	"John Kanaka" CSP: A • Ss sing song. • T isolates phrase 5 and Ss sing on a pure vowel ([i] [ɛ] [a] [o] [u]). • Kodály Choral Library, *Let Us Sing Correctly*, no. 46
Review known songs and melodic elements	"Dance Josey" CSP: F • Ss sing song with text and keep the beat. • Ss sing song with solfège syllables and hand signs. • T hums motifs and Ss sing back with solfège syllables and hand signs.
	• T sings phrases of "Jim Along Josie," "Phoebe in Her Petticoat," "Old Mr. Rabbit," or other known songs that use the solfège syllables *la so mi re do low la* and *low so*; Ss echo-sing using solfège syllables and hand signs.
CORE ACTIVITIES	
Teach a new song	"Above the Plain" CSP: A • T sings the song while Ss keep the beat and show the phrases with their body. • Ss identify the form (ABCC). • Ss sing C; T sings A and B. • Ss sing A and B; T sings C. • T and Ss sing song.
Develop knowledge of music literacy concepts Create a visual representation of what you hear	"Hogs in the Cornfield" CSP: D • Ss sing the song. • Review kinesthetic and aural awareness activities. • T hums target phrase and asks Ss to create a visual representation of the melody of the target phrase; Ss use manipulatives. • T: "Pick up what you need to recreate what you heard" or "Draw what you heard"; T assesses understanding. • Ss share representations with each other. • T picks one S to share his or her representation with the class; make necessary corrections by reviewing aural awareness. • Ss sing focus phrase and point to their representation. • Ss sing the rhythm of the song with rhythm syllables. • Ss sing the song while putting away their supplies and moving into position for the next song.

(continued)

Table 4.9 Continued

Creative movement	"Jolly Miller" CSP: D • Ss sing the song. • Ss sing the song and play the game. • Ss create simple rhythmic ostinati with which to accompany the song.
Practice music performance and literacy skills	"Old Mr. Rabbit" • Ss sing song and play game. • Ss identify from the phrase marks the internal and read the rhythm of the song from the board.
Improvisation	• Ss improvise a new text to the rhythm but keep the upbeats. • Ss create a four-beat ostinato that uses known rhythm patterns and perform it on xylophones as an accompaniment to any of their known songs.
SUMMARY ACTIVITIES	
Review lesson outcomes Review the new song	"Above the Plain"

Table 4.10 and Table 4.11 are two presentation lessons focusing on syncopation.

Table 4.10 Example of Presentation Lesson for Labeling the Sounds

GRADE 4, UNIT 2, ♪♩ ♪ , LESSON 4	
Outcome	Presentation: label three sounds unevenly distributed over two beats with rhythm syllables as ta di---di
INTRODUCTORY ACTIVITIES	
Warm-up	"Hoedown," from *Rodeo* by Aaron Copland (1900–1990) • Body warm-up • Breathing exercise • Beat/movement activity
Sing known songs	"Riding in the Buggy" CSP: D • Ss sing the song with an ostinato.

(continued)

Kodály Today

Table 4.10 Continued

Develop tuneful singing Tone production Diction Expression	"Weevily Wheat" CSP: A - Ss sing and conduct. - Ss sing with a "koo" sound. - Lip trills: T directs Ss to then use lip trills to sing the song. - Kodály Choral Library, *Let Us Sing Correctly*, no. 11
Review known songs and rhythmic elements	"Shoes of John" CSP: C - Ss perform song and conduct. - Ss identify known rhythm elements. - T sings each of the phrases of "Old Mr. Rabbit," "Tideo," "Ida Red," or "Chickalalelo"; Ss echo-sing each phrase, singing with rhythm syllables while tapping the beat.
CORE ACTIVITIES	
Teach a new song	"Who Killed Cocky Robin?" CSP: A - T expressively sings the song, with all verses, and accompanies on an instrument - Ss show the phrases; Ss identify the number of phrases. (four) - Ss identify the form. (AAvBC) - Ss sing "Who Killed Cocky Robin?"
Presentation of music literacy concepts Describe what you hear with rhythm syllables	"Canoe Song" CSP: A - T and Ss sing "Canoe Song" and T plays melodic ostinato on pitched instrument. - Ss sing in canon. - One group walks the beat while they sing, the other claps the rhythm. - T sings the target phrase while tapping the beat. - Ss echo-sing on "loo." - T repeats; Ss echo (*short-long-short tadi ta*). - T invites one S to come to board to draw a representation of the target phrase. - Ss sing and point to the representation. - T: "When we hear three uneven sounds over two beats where the first is short, the second is long, and the third is short, we can label these sounds with our rhythm syllables *ta di----di*."

(continued)

Table 4.10   Continued

	• T writes the syllables "*ta di----di*" (*not the notation*) on the board • T sings and conducts the "Canoe Song" with rhythm syllables; after each phrase Ss echo-sing with rhythm syllables while clapping the rhythm. • Individual Ss echo the rhythm syllables after T. • T sings a phrase of "Canoe Song" with text; Ss echo with rhythm syllables. • Ss sing "Canoe Song" with rhythm syllables and conduct. • Ss continue the rhythm of the final phrase as an ostinato into the next song (4/4 ♪♩ ♪♩ ⁊ :‖).
Creative movement	"Hill and Gully Rider" CSP: C • T and Ss sing the song while continuing the ostinato. • Ss choose an instrument and create a simple rhythmic ostinato with which to accompany the song. • T and Ss sing and play the game. • Ss compose a rhythmic ostinato for percussion instrument. • Ss compose a melodic ostinato for a pitched instrument. • Ss create a new game movement.

Presentation of music literacy concepts
 	
Describe what you hear with rhythm syllables
	"Come Thru 'Na Hurry"
	CSP: D
	• Ss sing and clap the words.
	• Ss identify where they hear the *ta-di---di* in the song.
	• Ss identify how many times they hear *ta-di---di* in the song.
	• T will have the blank bars prepped on the board, and S fill them in.
	• Ss connect *ta-di---di* pattern to additional related song material:
	  ◦ "Come Thru 'Na Hurry"
	  ◦ "Hill and Gully Rider"
	  ◦ "Riding in the Buggy"
	  ◦ "Weevily Wheat"

SUMMARY ACTIVITIES	
Review lesson outcome Review the new song	"Who Killed Cocky Robin?"

Kodály Today

Table 4.11 Example of Presentation Lesson for Notation

GRADE 4, UNIT 2, ♫ ♪, LESSON 5	
Outcome	Presentation: notate three sounds unevenly distributed over two beats as ♫ ♪
INTRODUCTORY ACTIVITIES	
Warm-up	• Body warm-up • Beat activity "Hoedown," from *Rodeo* by Aaron Copland (1900–1990) • Breathing: Ss practice blowing a balloon and watch how air is released when deflating the balloon. • Resonance: explore a cow sound using low and high voice; make sure Ss are inhaling and exhaling correctly with the support muscles. • Posture: remind Ss of the correct posture for singing.
Sing known songs	"Cedar Swamp" CSP: A • T and Ss sing and pat the beat. • Ss sing with the following ostinato: 2/4 ♫ ♩ | ♫ ♩ :||
Develop tuneful singing Tone production Diction Expression	"Come Thru 'Na Hurry" CSP: F • Ss sing "Come Thru 'Na Hurry" with a "yip" sound. • Ss speak with a "koo" sound; they repeat "koo" sound to known rhythm patterns. • Ss sing "Come Thru 'Na Hurry" with a "koo" sound. • Kodály Choral Library, *Let Us Sing Correctly*, no. 12
Review known songs and rhythmic elements	"Above the Plain" CSP: A • Ss sing the song. • Ss sing the song in canon after four beats. • Ss read the last two phrases from the board with rhythm syllables. 4/4 ♪|♫♫♫♩|♫♫♩ ♪ ♪|♫♫♫♩|♫♫♩ ♪||
CORE ACTIVITIES	
Teach a new song	"C-Line Woman" CSP: A • T sings the song. • Ss identify the number of phrases. (four) • Ss identify the number of beats in each phrase. (four) • T sings each phrase on "loo" and Ss echo with rhythm syllables that T dictates on the board:

(*continued*)

Table 4.11 Continued

	2/4 ♫♫ | ♫𝄽 | ♫♫ | ♫𝄽 | ♫♩ | ♫𝄽 | ♫♩ | ♫𝄽 ‖ • T sings the song on "loo" and Ss label the form (AAA'B). • T sings the song with words while Ss perform the rhythm. • Ss sing the song while keeping the beat.
Presentation of music literacy concepts	"Canoe Song" CSP: A • T and Ss sing "Canoe Song" while performing the rhythm of "C-Line Woman."
Notate what you hear	• Ss sing "Canoe Song" in canon. • T reviews aural presentation: ○ T: "When we hear three uneven sounds over two beats where the first is short, the second is long, and the third is short, we can label these sounds with our rhythm syllables *ta di---di*." • "When the beat is a quarter note, we can represent three sounds over two beats using the traditional notation." 2/4 ♫♩ ♩♫♩ ‖ • "When we write our target pattern, we can use stick notation." 2/4 ▎▎ ▎▕▔▏▎ ‖ • T sings "Canoe Song," stopping after each phrase for Ss to echo with rhythm syllables; T writes the traditional notation as Ss sing. 2/4 ♫♩ ♩♫♩ | ♫♩ ♩♩ ♩ | ♫♩ ♩♫♩ | ♫♩ ♩♩ ‖ • Ss read the rhythm of the song.
Creative movement	"The Jolly Miller" CSP: C • T and Ss sing and play the game. • Compose a rhythmic ostinato for percussion instrument. • Compose a melodic ostinato for a pitched instrument. • Create a new game movement. • Create a new text.

(continued)

Table 4.11 Continued

Presentation of music literacy concepts Notate what you hear	"Riding in the Buggy" CSP: D • Ss sing the refrain of "Riding in the Buggy." • Ss identify the changes needed to transform the last two phrases of "Riding in the Buggy" into "Come Through 'Na Hurry"
Notate what you hear	$\frac{2}{4}$ ♫ ♪|♩ 𝄽 | ♫ ♪|♩ 𝄽 | ♫ ♪|♫♫| ♫ ♪|𝅗𝅥 ‖
	• T will transform the rhythm into "Come Through 'Na Hurry $\frac{2}{4}$ ♫ ♪|♩ ♩ | ♫ ♪|♩ ♩ | ♫ ♪|♩ ♩ | ♫ ♪|𝅗𝅥 ‖ • Ss identify and sing the rhythm syllables of the song. • Ss add an ostinato accompaniment played on a xylophone using ♫ ♪ to any of their known repertoire.
SUMMARY ACTIVITIES	
Review lesson outcomes Review the new song	"C-Line Woman"

Connections to Grade Handbooks

Chapter 2 in each grade handbook addresses repertoire and includes an alphabetized list and a pedagogical list of songs appropriate to the grade. The pedagogically determined list is arranged according to the presentation sequence of music elements to be taught in that grade. The list also indicates the most important focus pattern to be used for teaching a concept. The focus pattern is found in the focus song and is indicated by a star. Normally the phrase containing the focus pattern is also listed. For each musical element we propose songs that have related patterns that may be used to practice the newly learned musical element in different contexts.

Chapter 3 of the handbook supplies teachers with ideas and activities for practicing musical skills. Specific music skills include singing, reading, writing, improvisation, form, part-work, inner hearing, memory, creative movement, instrumental skills, and listening.

Discussion Questions
1. How can teaching tools aid students' ability to read and write music?
2. How does the choice of song repertoire affect the teaching sequence of rhythmic and melodic concepts and elements?
3. Discuss the difference between a concept and an element.
4. Explain the organization of the preparation, presentation, and practice charts.
5. Explain the organization of the pedagogical determined list of songs provided for each grade.
6. How can teaching tools help with teaching elements in a classroom?
7. Discuss this notion: we should not destroy the enjoyment of singing in the classroom by using folk songs and games to develop music literacy skills. Actually spending time teaching music literacy skills is not relevant to today's music students. Music theory concepts should be taught through abstract exercises and worksheets where students learn how to write and practice various scales and intervals and learn traditional notation.

Ongoing Assignment
1. Design a preparation/practice lesson plan for a first grade class. Discuss the resources you used to develop your lesson plan.
2. Design a preparation/practice lesson plan for a third grade class. Discuss the resources you used to develop your lesson plan.
3. Choose a concept to prepare an element to practice for a third grade class. Create a preparation/practice lesson and a presentation lesson.

Bibliography
Aiello, R. "Research in the Perception of Music and the Kodály Method: Establishing a Closer Dialogue." *Bulletin of the International Kodály Society*, 1997, *22*(1): 12–21.

Bamberger, Jeanne. "How the Conventions of Music Notation Shape Musical Perception and Performance." In *Musical Communication*, ed. Dorothy Miell, Raymond Macdonald, and David J. Hargreaves, pp. 143–170. New York: Oxford University Press, 2005.

Barrett, Margaret. "Representation, Cognition and Communication: Invented Notation in Children's Musical Communication." In *Musical Communication*, ed. Dorothy Miell, Raymond Macdonald, and David J. Hargreaves, pp. 117–142. New York: Oxford University Press, 2005.

Bergeson, T. R., and S. E. Trehub. "Infants' Perception of Rhythmic Patterns." *Music Perception*, 2006, *23*(4): 345–360.

Bowman, W. "Cognition and the Body." In *Knowing Bodies, Moving Minds*, ed. L. Bresler, pp. 29–50. Dordrecht, Netherlands: Kluwer, 2004.

Brooks, J. G., and M. G. Brooks. *In Search of Understanding: The Case for Constructivist Classrooms*. Upper Saddle River, NJ: Prentice-Hall, 2001.

Brophy, T. S. "Developing Improvisation in General Music Classes." *Music Educators Journal*, 2001, *88*(1): 34–42.

Bruner, J. *Toward a Theory of Instruction*. Cambridge, MA: Harvard University Press, 1966.

Cevasco, A. M. "The Effects of Mothers' Singing on Full-term and Preterm Infants and Maternal Emotional Responses." *Journal of Music Therapy*, 2008, *45*(3): 273–306.

Chaffin, R., and G. Imreh. "'Pulling Teeth and Torture': Musical and Memory Problem Solving." *Thinking and Reasoning*, 1997, *3*(4): 315–336.

Choksy, Lois, Robert M. Abramson, Avon E. Gillespie, David Woods, and Frank York. *Teaching Music in the Twenty-first Century*. 2nd ed. Upper Saddle River, NJ: Prentice-Hall, 2000.

Cohen, Annabel J. "Music Cognition: Defining Constraints on Musical Communication." In *Musical Communication*, ed. Dorothy Miell, Raymond Macdonald, and David J. Hargreaves, pp. 61–84. New York: Oxford University Press, 2005.

Colwell, Richard, and Carol Richardson, eds. *The New Handbook of Research on Music Teaching and Learning: A Project of the Music Educators National Conference*. New York: Oxford University Press, 2002.

Custodero, L. A. "Singing Practices in 10 Families with Young Children." *Journal of Research in Music Education*, 2006, *54*(1): 37–56. Music Index. Web. Apr. 7, 2013.

Custodero, L. A., and E. A. Johnson-Green. "Caregiving in Counterpoint: Reciprocal Influences in the Musical Parenting of Younger and Older Infants." *Early Child Development and Care*, 2008, *178*(1): 15–39.

Deakin Crick, R., and K. Wilson. "Being a Learner: A Virtue for the 21st Century." *British Journal of Educational Studies*, 2005, *53*(3): 359–374.

Deci, E. L., and R. M. Ryan. *Intrinsic Motivation and Self-Determination in Human Behavior*. New York: Plenum, 1985.

Donaldson, M. *Human Minds: An Exploration*. London: Allen Lane/Penguin Books, 1992.

Dwyer, R. "Critical Music Literacy: Music Education in the 21st Century Building Upon the Kodály Philosophy." *Bulletin of the International Kodály Society*, 2010, *35*(1): 48–52.

Eisner, E. W. *The Arts and the Creation of Mind*. New Haven, CT: Yale University Press, 2002.

Elliott, D. J. *Music Matters: A New Philosophy of Music Education*. New York: Oxford University Press, 1995.

Flavell, J. H. "Metacognitive Aspects of Problem Solving." In *The Nature of Intelligence*, ed. L. B. Resnick, pp. 231–236. Hillsdale, NJ: Erlbaum, 1976.

Fleer, M., and G. A. Quinones. "A Cultural-Historical Reading of 'Children as Researchers.'" In *Childhood Studies and the Impact of Globalization: Policies and*

Practices at Global and Local Levels, ed. M. Fleer, M. Hedegaard, and J. Tudge, pp. 86–107. New York: Taylor & Francis, 2009.

Frazee, Jane, and K. Kreuter. *Discovering Orff: A Curriculum for Music Teachers*. New York: Schott, 1997.

Folkestad, G. "Formal and Informal Learning Situations or Practices vs. Formal and Informal Ways of Learning." *British Journal of Music Education*, 2006, *23*(2): 135–145.

Foulkes-Levy, Laurdella. "Music for Everyone: Pedagogical Tools for All. Part I: Introduction and a Brief History of Solmization Syllables." *Kodály Envoy*, 2006, *32*(3): 15–22.

Foulkes-Levy, Laurdella. "Music for Everyone: Pedagogical Tools for All. Part II: A Comparison of Two Solmization Systems." *Kodály Envoy*, 2006, *32*(4): 5–9.

Good, C., and C. S. Dweck. "Motivational Orientations That Lead Students to Show Deeper Levels of Reasoning, Greater Responsibility for Their Academic Work, and Greater Resilience in the Face of Academic Difficulty." In *Optimizing Student Success in School with the Other Three R's: Reasoning, Resilience, and Responsibility*, ed. R. J. Sternberg and R. F. Subotnik, pp. 39–58. Charlotte, NC: Information Age, 2006.

Goyette, P. "Challenging Your Students' Thinking: Kodály Music Experiences and Bloom's Taxonomy." *Kodály Envoy*, 1986, *12*(3).

Green, L. *How Popular Musicians Learn: A Way Ahead for Music Education*. Aldershot, Hants, UK: Ashgate, 2002.

Green, L. *Music, Informal Learning and the School: A New Classroom Pedagogy*. Aldershot, UK: Ashgate, 2008.

Gromko, J. "Children Composing: Inviting the Artful Narrative." In *Why and How to Teach Music Composition*, ed. M. Hickey, pp.69–90. Reston, VA: Music Educators National Conference, 2003.

Hamann, D. L., ed. *Creativity in the Music Classroom: The Best of MEJ*. Reston, VA: Music Educators National Conference, 1992.

Harris, R. and E. Hawksley. *Composing in the Classroom*. Cambridge, UK: Cambridge University Press, 1989.

Higgins, L., and P. S. Campbell. *Free to Be Musical: Group Improvisation in Music*. Lanham, MD: Rowman & Littlefield, 2010.

Hoffman, Richard, Justin M. London, William Pelto, and John W. White. "Takadimi: A Beat-Oriented System of Rhythm Pedagogy." *Journal of Music Theory Pedagogy*, 1996, *10*: 7–36.

Houlahan, M., and P. Tacka. "An Aural Approach to Harmonic Analysis." *Kodály Envoy*, 1993, *19*(4): 11–19.

Jaffurs, S. E. "The Impact of Informal Music Learning Practices in the Classroom, or How I Learned How to Teach from a Garage Band." *International Journal of Music Education*, 2004, *22*(3): 189–200.

Jorgenson, E. R. *The Art of Teaching Music*. Bloomington: Indiana University Press, 2008.

Juslin, Patrik N. "From Mimesis to Catharsis: Expression, Perception and Induction of Emotion in Music." In *Musical Communication*, ed. Dorothy Miell, Raymond Macdonald, and David J. Hargreaves, pp. 85–116. New York: Oxford University Press, 2005.

Kratus, J. "Growing with Improvisation." *Music Educators Journal*, 1991, *78*(4): 35–40.

Klinger, Rita. *Lesson Planning in a Kodály Setting*. Los Angeles: Organization of American Kodály Editors, 2014.

Klinger, Rita. "A Materials Girl in Search of the Genuine Article." In *World Musics and Music Education: Facing the Issues*, ed. B. Reimer, pp. 205–217. Reston, VA: MENC, 2002.

Kodály, Zoltán. "Let Us Sing Correctly." In *The Selected Writings of Zoltán Kodály*, ed. Ferenc Bánis. London: Boosey & Hawkes, 1974.

Kodály, Zoltán. "Preface to the Volume *Musical Reading and Writing*." In *The Selected Writings of Zoltán Kodály*, ed. Ferenc Bánis, pp. 201–208. London: Boosey & Hawkes, 1974.

Lamont, A., D. Hargreaves, N. A. Marshall, and M. Tarrant. "Young People's Music in and Out of School." *British Journal of Music Education*, 2003, *20*(3): 229–241.

Luce, D. W. "Collaborative Learning in Music Education: A Review of the Literature." *Update: Applications of Research in Music Education*, 2001, *19*(2): 20–25.

Lum, C. H. *Musical Networks of Children: An Ethnography of Elementary School Children in Singapore*. Unpublished Ph.D. diss., University of Washington, 2007.

MacDonald, R.A.R., and D. Miell. "Music for Individuals with Special Needs: A Catalyst for Developments in Identity, Communication and Musical Ability." In *Musical Identities*, ed. R.A.R. MacDonald, D. J. Hargreaves, and D. E. Miell. Oxford: Oxford University Press, 2002.

Maehr, M. L., P. R. Pintrich, and E. A. Linnenbrink-Garcia. "Motivation and Achievement." In *The New Handbook of Research on Music Teaching and Learning: A Project of the Music Educators National Conference*, ed. R. Colwell and C. Richardson, pp. 348–372. New York: Oxford University Press, 2002.

Marsh, K. *The Musical Playground: Global Tradition and Change in Children's Songs and Games*. New York: Oxford University Press, 2008.

Masataka, N. "Preference for Consonance over Dissonance by Hearing Newborns of Deaf Parents and of Hearing Parents." *Developmental Science*, 2006, *9*(*1*): 46–50.

McCaleb, S. P. *Building Communities of Learners: A Collaboration Among Teachers, Students, Families, and Community*. Mahwah, NJ: Erlbaum, 1997.

McPherson, G. E., and S. A. O'Neil. "Students' Motivation to Study Music as Compared to Other School Subjects: A Comparison of Eight Countries." *Research Studies in Music Education*, 2010, *32*(2): 101–137.

MENC. *National Standards for Arts Education: What Every Young American Should Know and Be Able to Do in the Arts*. Reston, VA: Music Educators National Conference, 1994.

Mezirow, J., and Associates. *Learning as Transformation: Critical Perspective on a Theory in Progress*. San Francisco: Jossey-Bass, 2000.

Miell, D., and R. MacDonald. "Children's Creative Collaborations: The Importance of Friendship When Working Together on a Musical Composition." *Social Development*, 2000, *9*(3): 348–369.

Mills, J. *Music in the Primary School*, 3rd ed. Oxford: Oxford University Press, 2009.

Mills, Janet, and Gary E. McPherson. "Musical Literacy." In *The Child as Musician: A Handbook of Musical Development*, ed. Gary McPherson, pp. 155–172. New York: Oxford University Press, 2006.

Miner, Brian. "Fostering Musical Creativity in the Elementary Classroom." *Inquiry* (University of New Hampshire) 2007, 42–47. Music Index. Web. Apr. 7, 2013.

Montgomery, A. "Listening in the Elementary Grades: Current Research from a Canadian Perspective." *Bulletin of the International Kodály Society*, 1993, *18*(1): 54–61.

Nemes, Klára. "The Relative Sol–Fa as Tool of Developing Musical Thinking." *Musicologia*, 1997, *9*: 27–34.

O'Neill, S. A.. "Developing a Young Musician's Growth Mindset: The Role of Motivation, Self-Theories and Resiliency." In *Music and the Mind: Essays in Honour of John Sloboda*, ed. I. Deliège and J. Davidson, pp. 31–46. New York: Oxford University Press, 2011.

O'Neill, S. A., and G. E. McPherson. "Motivation." In *The Science and Psychology of Music Performance: Creative Strategies for Teaching and Learning*, ed. R. Parncutt and G. E. McPherson. New York: Oxford University Press, 2002.

O'Neill, S. A., and Y. Senyshyn. "How Learning Theories Shape Our Understanding of Music Learners." In *MENC Handbook of Research in Music Learning, Vol. 1: Strategies*, ed. R. Colwell and P. Webster. New York: Oxford University Press, 2011.

Patseas, Michalis. "The Use of Relative Solmization in the Countries Using the Fixed Do." *Musicologia* 1997, *9*: 34–39.

Plantinga, J., and L. J. Trainor. "Memory for Melody: Infants Use a Relative Pitch Code." *Cognition*, 2005, *98*(1): 1–11.

Reeve, J. "Why Teachers Adopt a Controlling Motivating Style Toward Students and How They Can Become More Autonomy Supportive." *Educational Psychologist*, 2009, *44*(3): 159–175.

Satterwhite, James Hunter. "Developing Creativity Through Songwriting in Secondary Education Composition Classes." *Dissertation Abstracts International Section A: Humanities & Social Sciences*, 1992, *52*: 3978. Music Index. Web. Apr. 7, 2013.

Scott, S. J. "Making Links Between Research and Instruction: Student's Perception of Contour and Interval While Reading Music Notation." *Kodály Envoy*, 2000, *27*(1): 5–8.

Serafine, M. L. *Music as Cognition: The Development of Thought in Sound*. New York: Columbia University Press, 1988.

Shehan Campbell, Patricia. *Lessons from the World: A Cross-Cultural Guide to Music Teaching and Learning*. New York: Schirmer, 1991.

Shehan Campbell, P. *Songs in Their Heads: Music and Its Meaning in Children's Lives*. New York: Oxford, 1998.

Sloboda, John. *Exploring the Musical Mind: Cognition, Emotion, Ability, Function*. New York: Oxford University Press, 2005.

Sloboda, J. A. *The Musical Mind: The Cognitive Psychology of Music*. Oxford: Clarendon Press, 1985.

Soley, G., and E. E. Hannon. "Infants Prefer the Musical Meter of Their Own Culture: A Cross-Cultural Comparison." *Developmental Psychology*, 2010, *46*(1): 286–292.

Stauffer, Sandra Lee, and Jennifer Davidson. *Strategies for Teaching K–4 General Music*. Reston, VA: Music Educators National Conference, 1996.

Stevens, S. "Creative Experiences in Free Play." *Music Educators Journal*, 2003, *89*(5): 44–47.

Sundin, B., G. E. McPherson, and G. Folkestad. *Children Composing* (in English). Malmö, Sweden: Lund University, Malmö Academy of Music, 1998.

Swanwick, K. *Teaching Music Musically*. London: Routledge, 1999.

Temmerman, N. "An Investigation of the Music Activity Preferences of Pre-School Children." *British Journal of Music Education*, 2000, *17*(1): 51–60.

Wiggins, J. H. "Building Structural Understanding: Sam's Story." *Quarterly Journal of Music Teaching and Learning*, 1995, 6(3): 57–75.

Wiggins, J. "Children's Strategies for Solving Compositional Problems with Peers." *Journal of Research in Music Education*, 1994, *42*(3): 232–252.

Wiggins, J. *Composition in the Classroom: A Tool for Teaching*. Reston, VA: MENC (Music Educators National Conference), 1990.

Wiggins, J. *The Nature of Children's Musical Learning in the Context of a Music Classroom*. Ph.D. diss., University of Illinois at Urbana-Champaign, 1992.

Wiggins, J. H. "The Nature of Shared Musical Understanding and Its Role in Empowering Independent Musical Thinking." *Bulletin of the Council for Research in Music Education*, 2000/01, *143*(Winter): 65–90.

Wiggins, J. *Synthesizers in the Elementary Music Classroom: An Integrated Approach*. Reston. VA: MENC, 1991.

Wiggins, J. *Teaching for Musical Understanding*, 2nd ed. Rochester, MI: CARMU, Oakland University, 2009.

Chapter 5

From Sound to Symbol

A Model of Learning and Instruction for Teaching Music Concepts, Elements, and Skills

> The intuitive experience and enjoyment of music should come first, such that the latter acquisition of formal musical skills occurs inductively, that is, as an integral growth of the child's experience. A good deal of traditional music education has worked deductively: the formal rules have been taught in the abstract, for example, through verbal description or written notation, rather than in the practical context of making the sounds themselves.
>
> David J. Hargreaves, *The Developmental Psychology of Music*, p. 215

Key Questions

- What do we mean by preparation, presentation, and practice of a musical element?
- What are the learning stages of the cognitive phase of instruction?
- What are the learning stages of the associative phase of instruction?
- What are the learning stages of the assimilative phase of instruction?
- How does this learning theory model enhance the construction of music lesson plans?
- How does this learning theory model affect construction of a preparation/practice lesson plan?
- How does this learning theory model affect construction of a presentation lesson plan?

Kodály Today

In the previous chapters, we describe Kodály's philosophy, how to select repertoire, and how to create a music curriculum. In Chapter 4 we suggest a teaching sequence for rhythmic and melodic musical elements. Here we present our model of how music literacy can be systematically developed through a sound-to-symbol orientation to teaching. For decades, music educators have proclaimed the importance of "sound before symbol," but no one has provided a methodology that makes this all-important dictum possible. The purpose of this chapter is to introduce our model of learning and instruction; it is based on the sound-to-symbol maxim, and we explain some of the research at its core.

A common thread in the psychological literature concerning the teaching of music literacy is the "sound before symbol" principle, adopted in music education circles and of paramount importance for teaching music literacy. This idea stemmed from the work of the Swiss educator Heinrich Pestalozzi (1746–1827).[1] His work shaped the efforts of such great American music educators as Lowell Mason (1792–1872), as well as the current teaching methodologies adopted for use by American music teachers. As Patricia Shehan-Campbell and Carol Scott-Kassner write, "The earliest methods used in public school music instruction thus were based on the logic of 'sound before sight' and 'practice before theory'; listening and singing experiences led to an understanding of notation and theory."[2]

The work of the eminent cognitive psychologist Jerome Bruner (b. 1915) has enhanced our understanding of the sound-before-symbol principle. Bruner's "scaffolding" theory proposes that learning may be accomplished using three teaching and learning strategies: enactive, iconic, and symbolic. For example, when students are learning how to read a new melodic pattern they can (1) trace the melodic contour of the new melodic pattern with their arm as they sing the words of the melody or hum the contour (strategy 1, enactive), or (2) point to icons that represent the melodic contour (strategy 2, iconic), or (3) read the traditional notation for this melodic contour on the staff (strategy 3, symbolic).[3] However, this theory of instruction is at its most complex when students move from the iconic stage to the symbolic stage. Although a student's theoretical understanding may be enhanced through this approach, we have no way to document whether students are developing their auditory imagery—their ability to create the sound of the new element mentally without singing or playing. Edwin Gordon's theory of music learning[4] also attempts to expand our understanding of the sound-before-sight principle.

More current research in the field of music perception and cognition suggests that teaching music theory through a sound-to-symbol orientation[5] could be an effective pedagogical approach for conceptualizing musical thought and for building musical knowledge. Lyle Davidson, Larry Scripp, and Patricia Welsh (1988) were the first to recognize the inherent differences between teaching music theory through a symbol (conceptual) and a sound (perceptual) orientation. Results of their studies suggest that teaching music conceptually could negatively affect the ability of students to both internalize (audiate)[6]

From Sound to Symbol

and externalize (represent) their understanding of musical knowledge through Western staff notation (Covington 2005). Similar research by Houlahan and Tacka (2005) supports Davidson and Scripp (1992) while also finding that even expert musicians who have a high level of instrumental expertise but were primarily trained through a symbol-to-sound orientation in their theory and aural skills classes had difficulty notating[7] "Happy Birthday" without any errors. More importantly, they report that expert musicians' aural awareness skills were insufficiently developed to detect errors in their own notations of "Happy Birthday" without the aid of a musical instrument.[8] These findings indicate developing aural awareness is of significant importance for acquiring an understanding of music reading and music writing.

A New Learning Theory Model

The learning theory proposed in this chapter provides a cohesive model for a sound-to-symbol orientation to music. Additionally, it allows us to examine the learning processes associated with acquisition of basic music literacy skills. Our systematic model permits students to develop the ability to read and write music[9] as a consequence of music instruction that is perceptually based. Constructivist and cognitive theories,[10] as well as the work of Kodály scholars,[11] were used as a foundation for this research. Building on the work of these scholars, we have developed a model of instruction and learning that identifies and classifies cognitive scaffolding activities used to facilitate development of music literacy in the music classroom through a sound-to-symbol approach to teaching.[12] Music performance and teaching strategies that engage critical thinking are essential to our model of learning and instruction. Students become active learners not simply learning about the musical concept but additionally learning about the process of their own learning through music performance.[13] It is important to remember that development of music literacy skills is closely linked to repertoire. Although our model of learning promotes music literacy and lets teachers label each stage of learning, music literacy is really about students being able to sing song repertoire musically. Singing and active engagement with high-quality repertoire is the goal.

This learning theory model gives teachers a path that enables students to gain musical knowledge, understanding, comprehension, and mastery of the basic building blocks[14] of music fundamentals. (Recall that in Chapter 4 we presented a melodic and rhythmic learning sequence appropriate for grades one through five.) Additionally students develop musical skills such as reading, writing, improvisation, and composition. Chapter 6 is a detailed examination of what we mean by musical skill development.

Traditional orientations to teaching music theory, musicianship, and ear training, such as that of the Associated Board of the Royal Schools of Music, appear to have limited benefits for developing aural awareness because of the emphasis placed on conceptual learning rather than experiential learning. We have developed a new model for teaching aural awareness skills and music theory through a sound-to-symbol pedagogy. We offer these observations concerning our model:

- Aural awareness is embedded into the process of teaching music theory.
- Singing plays a major role in this model as it helps students internalize music.
- Teaching tools such as rhythmic syllables and solfège syllables are used to develop aural awareness skills.
- Musical examples selected for teaching are broken down into basic rhythmic and melodic patterns or building blocks that can be four to eight beats in length.
- The teaching process begins with simple musical examples and progresses to more difficult examples.
- The music examples become progressively more difficult and include both known and unknown building blocks.
- The teaching pedagogy associated with our model can be used with any age group.[15]

Our model for learning and instruction is divided into three phases of learning: cognitive, associative, and assimilative (see Table 5.1).

Table 5.1

Phase 1: Cognitive Phase (Preparation)
Stage 1: Internalizing Music Through Kinesthetic Activities: Developing Kinesthetic Awareness Ss listen to T singing the new song. Ss perform the new song with movement. Rationale: to match patterns of experience to patterns of music.
Stage 2: Describe What You Hear: Developing Aural Awareness by Responding to Questions Ss aurally analyze the characteristics of the new musical element with T's help. Ss describe the characteristics of the new element. Rationale: to verbalize what they perceive.
Stage 3: Constructing a Representation from Memory: Developing Visual Awareness Ss create a visual representation based on their aural understanding. Rationale: to visually represent what they have heard and verbalized.
Phase 2: Associative Phase (Presentation) Stage 1: Associate the sound of the new element with solfège or rhythmic syllables Stage 2: Associate traditional notation with the sound of the new musical element
Phase 3: Assimilative Phase (Practice) Stage 1: Ss aurally practice the new element in familiar songs and new ones. Stage 2: Ss visually practice the new element in familiar songs and new ones.

- In the cognitive phase, students experience and perceive the new element in a target pattern through kinesthetic, aural, and visual activities, always within the context of performance.
- In the associative phase, students connect their kinesthetic, aural, and visual understanding of the new element in a target pattern and in related patterns by labeling these patterns with solfège or rhythm syllables. Students also learn how to notate these sounds.
- In the assimilative phase, students continue to develop their musicianship skills, practicing the newly learned musical element both aurally and visually.

Cognitive Phase: Preparation

In the cognitive phase, students develop listening and aural awareness skills. The goal is to prepare the necessary conditions for understanding. Here, students experience and perceive the new element in a building block[16] through kinesthetic, aural, and visual activities, always conducted within the context of singing. This phase is a type of multimodal perceptual encoding that strengthens aural awareness.

In the cognitive phase, students learn song material containing the main rhythmic and melodic patterns that will be used for teaching reading and writing. Research reveals that students initially perceive music not as isolated events (note-to-note events) but as patterns according to recognized Gestalt principles for perceptual organization.[17] When teaching, the instructor begins by presenting song material containing the core structural melodic and rhythmic patterns, which can later be extracted. Once presented, each pattern[18] will later provide the musical scaffolding for more advanced melodic and rhythmic patterns and concepts. In our model of learning and instruction, students are guided to compare the characteristics of unknown musical patterns and structures to known musical patterns and structures. This gives them a chance to assimilate, accommodate, and construct music knowledge within familiar stylistic frameworks.

We divide the cognitive phase of learning and instruction into three stages:

Stage 1: internalizing music through kinesthetic activities: developing kinesthetic awareness

Stage 2: describe what you hear: developing aural awareness by responding to questions

Stage 3: constructing a representation from memory: developing visual awareness

Stage 1: Internalizing Music Through Kinesthetic Activities

In this stage, students are taught a selection of core song materials by rote, containing the new element,[19] typically found within a four-beat pattern. The instructor models a kinesthetic motion that focuses the students' attention on the new element within the beat pattern. Movement activities[20] help guide students to hear the new element. The goal is for students to sing while performing a motion that emphasizes the new musical element

Kodály Today

on their own. Students must be able to sing repertoire fluently and independently before beginning stage 1. Sample motions for rhythm are clapping the rhythm of a song or clapping the melodic contour for melody.

Peretz has noted that pitch contour is the first aspect of melody that is stored on hearing a new melody, and contour extraction is "a preliminary and indispensable step to the precise encoding of intervals."[21] This also has a positive effect on short-term musical memory.[22] Cutietta and Booth's research suggests that "the repeated act of performing a piece of music, without the aid of written notation or language-based instruction, can lead to substantive changes in an individual's internal representation of that melody's primary features."[23] Movement, rote learning, and development of musical memory form a foundation for promoting musical literacy.[24]

Examples of Kinesthetic Activities for Rhythm

Here are six examples of kinesthetic activities for internalizing rhythm, which can be practiced in conjunction with singing and inner hearing of the music.

1. Students conduct to feel the meter.
2. Students perform the song while clapping the rhythm.
3. Students learn to sing songs by rote and perform a kinesthetic motion that highlights the new rhythmic element. For example, they may clap the rhythm of the phrase containing the target pattern and keep the beat on their knees for the other phrases of a song.
4. Students perform the song while pointing to pictures or icons showing the number of sounds per beat. We believe this procedure is a kinesthetic activity for the student; no explanation is made as to what these symbols represent. Instructors may guide students to point to imaginary symbols without any reference to the icons.
5. Students perform the new rhythmic pattern with the basic beat. The class may be divided into two groups. One group performs the rhythm pattern and the other performs the beat. This activity may be practiced in a number of combinations, with our suggested order of performance being teacher-class, class-teacher, divided class, and two individuals. The most advanced activity is for individual students to simultaneously perform the beat and rhythm; sing the song while walking the beat and clapping the rhythm.
6. Students inner-hear (sing the song silently in their head) the four-beat phrase of the song containing the new element while clapping the rhythm.

We have found that these activities can be used with students of any age.[25] The repertoire containing the new rhythmic or melodic element is always performed from memory. Performing from memory is important at this stage because subsequent musical reading and writing activities are initially based on melodies that contain similar rhythmic and melodic motives. It is important that students not develop their knowledge of rhythm on the basis of visual clues. Make sure that the students hear the new rhythm pattern being clapped, as opposed to being seen.

Examples of Kinesthetic Activities for Melody
1. Students perform the song and demonstrate the direction of the melodic line with arm motions. These motions should be natural and accompany the text and tempo of the song.
2. Students use simple body signs, for example, touch shoulders for *high* sounds and waist for *low*.
3. Students perform the song and point to a representation that outlines the melodic contour.

Stage 2: Describe What You Hear
The only way we'll know what a student hears is to ask her to tell us what she heard. Therefore, the justification for this stage is to assist students in verbalizing the characteristics of the new rhythmic or melodic element. Through careful questioning by the instructor, the students develop the ability to play back (inner-hear) a particular phrase and describe a specific attribute of the new element contained in the new pattern. For rhythmic elements, the goal is for students to identify the number of sounds on a particular beat or the number of beats a sound lasts. For melodic elements, students must discover the characteristics of the collection of pitches and the relationship between the pitches in the building block. With each question, students audiate the music phrase in order to answer the questions correctly.

Bartholomew states: "To teach the sounds before the signs is to develop musical responsiveness and thought. It is to do more than to present sounds to students. It is to help students develop the sense and the flow of music, to feel its logic, to be part of its unfolding, and to respond to the variety of relationships present in the sounds."[26] Petzold's study concludes that aural perception should precede visual perception and that one must be able to hear music in order to develop skills in music reading.[27] Hewson's work suggests that aural experiences prior to encountering notation facilitates development of sight-singing skills.[28] Results of Gromko and Poorman's recent research support findings that there is a "developmental link between aural perception and what the child chooses to express in writing about musical sounds. These results suggest a developmental link between the ability to discriminate between short tonal patterns and the ability to use musical symbols for pitch."[29]

In stage two, the instructor asks questions that guide students to describe the position and attributes of the new musical element within a four-beat pattern. For rhythmic elements, the goal is for students to be able to identify the number of sounds within a beat. For example, if we are teaching sixteenth notes, students must be able to perceive and identify four sounds on a beat and state on which beat they hear four sounds. To evaluate students' aural awareness of melodic elements, they must be guided to describe and compare the new melodic pitch to previously learned pitches. An important aspect of our teaching

Kodály Today

during this stage is that we provide no visual stimulus for the students that might aid in answering the posed questions. The knowledge developed at this stage is a reinforcement of what has already been embedded in the students' memory during the kinesthetic stage. We are convinced that this "describe what you hear" stage is perhaps the most important aspect of our model of learning experience, as verbalizing the characteristics of the new musical element further embeds their understanding of what they've heard. It establishes a significant connection to the musical element as well as the music they're learning.

Examples of Aural Awareness Questions for Rhythm
Here are sample questions for exploring rhythmic elements that occur on one beat. Perform the target pattern and ask:

- How many beats did we perform?
- On which beat did you hear *the new sound*?[30]
- How many *sounds* did you perform on that beat?
- How would you describe these sounds? (For example, two short sounds, or a long sound followed by two short sounds, etc.)

Here are sample questions for exploring rhythms that last longer than one beat:

- Is there a place in our target pattern where a sound lasts longer than one beat?
- On which beat does it begin?
- For how many beats do we hold the sound?
- How would you describe this sound?

Here are sample questions for exploring uneven rhythm patterns lasting longer than a beat:

- Is there a place in the target pattern where the rhythm is uneven?
- On which beats do you perform the uneven pattern?
- How many sounds do you perform on *those beats*?
- How would you describe these sounds?
- Describe the placement of sounds on *those beats*.

Examples of Aural Awareness Questions for Melody
- How many beats did we perform?
- On what word or beat does *the new melodic pitch* occur?
- Is *the new melodic pitch* higher than or lower than all of the pitches we know?
- Sing the pitches on "loo" (in the target phrase) in descending order from highest to lowest.
- Sing the pitches on "loo" (in the target phrase) in ascending-pitch order from lowest to highest.

Stage 3: Create a Visual Representation of What You Hear

The objective for this stage is to have students construct their own visual representation of the target pattern using the knowledge they gained in stages 1 and 2. Here, we confront students with the music problem or challenge of creating a visual representation of the new pattern. Drawing on knowledge gained through the kinesthetic experience and the aural awareness stage, students construct their own visual representation of the target pattern. As Perkins states, "First, to gauge a person's understanding at a given time, ask the person to do something that puts the understanding to work—explaining, solving a problem, building an argument, constructing a product. Second, what learners do in response not only shows their level of current understanding but very likely advances it."[31]

By connecting the aural awareness stage to the visual stage, the student is allowed time to make the connection between what he or she hears and how to represent it before we label the new element with rhythmic or solfège syllables or notate it on the staff. Jean Bamberger argues, "if the reader of the symbols (teacher/researcher or child) has failed to do the work of constructing the elements, properties, and relations inherent in the framework through which these symbols gain meaning, neither a teacher/researcher reading a child's invented symbol system nor a child reading the privileged symbol systems taught in school can make of the phenomena described by the symbols the particular sense the symbols-makers intend."[32] This approach to teaching is similar to the radical constructivism philosophy, where knowledge and understanding "can only be constructed through a gradual process of disequilibration and accommodation brought about through reflective activity."[33]

Visual awareness activities are a tangible indication of how students understand new concepts. We recommend that once students have completed a visual representation of the target pattern, they should sing the target pattern and point to what they have drawn. The instructor may ask:

- What were the significant factors that contributed to your representation of the target pattern?
- What information does your representation capture?
- Identify known rhythmic and melodic patterns in the target pattern.

How a student represents a target pattern gives the instructor a chance to observe a student's musical development. If a student cannot represent a target pattern at the visual awareness stage, more work in both the kinesthetic and aural awareness stage is required. Observations of students at all levels reveal that initially some may not be able to represent the target phrase accurately, but when asked to point to their representation, their pointing may be correct.

Visual Awareness Activities for Rhythm

During this stage students are asked to create a visual representation of the target pattern containing the new rhythmic element. We suggest using Unifix cubes[34]; this poses

Kodály Today

a challenge and is an opportunity for students to use a three-dimensional object to represent a rhythmic or melodic pattern. Pencil-and-paper is perhaps more appropriate with older students; however, they should not use traditional musical notation. Note that it is not unusual for the students' representation to be similar to what is used for pointing during the kinesthetic stage.

- Students create a visual representation for the specific rhythmic pattern. Encourage them to identify all known rhythmic elements in their representation.
- Students may write the text of a song over the beats in the target pattern.
- Students may write the solfège syllables over each beat to indicate the number of sounds over the beats for a phrase.

Visual Awareness Activities for Melody
- Students create the melodic contour of the target pattern with Unifix cubes.
- Students write the text of the song spatially to show the melodic contour.
- Students write the solfège syllables of the target pattern spatially using a question mark to indicate the placement of the new melodic element.
- More advanced students use horizontal lines to indicate the duration and contour of each note of the melody. This is sometimes referred to as *piano roll notation*.[35] Students may also identify all known elements in their representation.

The three stages of learning in the cognitive phase—kinesthetic, aural, and visual—offer a logical and helpful path to musical understanding and development of critical thinking skills. The cognitive phase is an opportunity for students to understand the characteristics of the new element from a kinesthetic, aural, and visual perspective. Simply stated, it allows students' time to re-envision and reconceptualize their intuitive knowledge; the instructor finds in it a foundation for presenting traditional notation.[36]

We stipulate this instructional order (kinesthetic, aural, and visual) for the awareness stages of learning. Some Kodály instructors believe that the kinesthetic, aural, and visual stages of learning can be addressed in random order. We disagree. Teachers who have used our model of learning and instruction at all levels of education with varied populations of students report that our specified order of presentation is necessary for student comprehension. For example, during the aural stage of learning, no visual aids are used to help students describe the characteristics of the new element. The instructor asks questions to help students develop their aural understanding of a new element. During this stage the teacher does not provide any visual clues to help students; they need to think about what they have heard without the help of a visual aid as this promotes development of audition skills. After describing what they have heard, they must be given time to draw their own representation of the target phrase containing the new element. A student's visual representation offers clues as to how they perceive and audiate the new musical element. It also gives the instructor information on the kinds of questions and activities that could aid students who require additional assistance. Without this assessment opportunity, we lose the chance to recognize the student's current perception of the new element.

Associative Phase: Presentation

The objective for the associative phase of instruction is for students to be able to identify and associate each sound in the building block with a rhythm syllable, or each pitch with a solfège syllable.[37] In the associative phase, students connect their kinesthetic, aural, and visual understanding of the target pattern to solfège or rhythm syllables and staff placement. In the previous cognitive phase, students are guided to inner-hear music examples with texts or with neutral syllables. In the associative phase of instruction, students further develop their understanding by identifying sounds and pitches with rhythm or solfège syllables. We note that in some theory textbooks authors present an overview of the symbols associated with rhythms or present the symbols associated with construction of a major scale and describe how to use solfège syllables to read melodies. Through our research and teaching, we have found that this does afford an understanding of symbols but does not promote sequential development of the sound worlds to which they refer.

The associative phase has two stages.[38]

Stage 1: Label the Sound, Describing What You Hear with Rhythm or Solfège Syllables

First, the instructor guides students to reconsider the critical aural attributes of the target pattern by briefly reviewing the kinesthetic and aural activities only. We then label the sound (or associate the sound) of the target pattern with either rhythm or solfège syllables (and the corresponding hand sign[39]). Studies by Colley, Palmer, and Shehan Campbell have concluded that musical tools such as solfège and rhythmic syllables and hand signs are effective pedagogical devices.[40] The use of musical tools allows students to explore their musical knowledge beyond their starting point, which makes possible new achievements and understanding.[41] Our research indicates that students need time to practice labeling the sound. We strongly advise spending a good portion of time during a presentation lesson and in all music lessons labeling a sound or pitch with syllables. This is most easily accomplished when the instructor sings a target phrase or related phrase with text and students echo but sing with rhythm or solfège syllables.

Stage 2: Notate What You Hear

After associating the newly learned sound with a rhythm or solfège syllable and practicing singing the newly learned musical element by singing the target phrase and related phrases with syllables, we associate traditional notation with the sound of the target pattern.

These two stages in the associative phrase of instruction ensure that students are not introduced to music theory before they can hear what they see and see what they hear.[42]

In our model of learning and instruction, students are taught conceptual information according to their perceptual understandings attained through musical performance. The new musical element is constructed and written using the target pattern and subsequently read with solfège or rhythm syllables. In this manner, writing music "not only provides the readiness for attaining higher levels of learning but also reinforces the ability to read music."[43]

Assimilative Phase: Practice Music Skills

In the assimilative phase, students integrate and reinforce the new musical element in related songs and in conjunction with musical skills both aurally and visually. The instructor guides students to recognize how a new musical element relates to previously learned knowledge within the context of familiar and new musical repertoire. Here students continue to work on aural and visual fluency. As noted by Klinger: "Sometimes referred to as 'reinforcement', this is the time period during which the children's understanding of the rhythm or melody grows, solidifies and deepens. First the newly named element is practiced in well-known materials and familiar contexts. Later it is reinforced in unknown song materials and increasingly difficult music contexts."[44]

The assimilative phase is broken down into two stages. In stage 1, students aurally practice the rhythm or solfège syllables for the new element with music skills; in stage 2 they visually practice the new element with musical skills. In both stages they are developing their aural and visual fluency with solfège syllables, as well as numbers for counting and singing with letter names.

Repertoire that incorporates the newly learned musical element is practiced in conjunction with curriculum goals and musical skills or enriching activities. Among these musical skills:

- Reading known material
- Sight-singing new material
- Writing known material
- Writing unknown material (dictation)
- Improvisation skills
- Composition skills
- Development of musical memory
- Development of audiation skills
- Ear training
- Part work
- Form and analysis
- Listening
- Instrumental experience
- Developing harmonic hearing
- Music theory vocabulary

Throughout the assimilative phase, the newly learned musical element is identified and immediately practiced as additional musical concepts are prepared. As the new element is identified, named, and practiced in the students' repertoire of songs, the instructor should take the opportunity to guide students to recognize familiar musical elements that emerge in the context of each new element. Thus evaluation is built into the process of instruction and is ongoing in each type of lesson.

If our goal is developing music literacy, then regardless of age students need a consistent approach to learning and instruction. Using this perceptual orientation promotes development of aural acuity; students are guided to aurally identify the attributes of the new element and verbalize what they hear, and then reflect on their observations using their own notation. Once the instructor is assured that students can audiate and represent the new element, labeling can take place. Thus our learning theory model fosters a perceptual orientation to instruction and learning that allows for integration of aural observations prior to focusing on notation and traditional representations of musical knowledge.

In our model for developing aural awareness, students become actively engaged not only in performing music, primarily through singing, but also in the learning process. Learners are guided to develop their aural awareness skills as well as to explore how music is organized and perceived as performers, critical thinkers, composers, and listeners. Musical concepts are initially explored through singing, aural analysis, and creating representations. It's only after that initial exploration that sounds are labeled with rhythmic or solfège syllables and notated. This systematic model permits students to develop their aural awareness skills as well as their ability to read and write music as a consequence of music instruction that is perceptually based.

Our approach is to build from generalized understanding to a more particular one. This was explained by Bamberger, who noted:

> The various features of a tune which at first remained unnoticed become liberated from the meld, and this process needs to occur over and over again in different ways: at each stage new entities, new features are made to come into existence, requiring in turn the mental construction of new relations and new coordinating schemata. And as features and relations become accessible for manipulation and scrutiny and are coordinated in new ways, the coordinations form the basis for the construction of stable general structures in terms of which particular, unique instances can be described, compared, and understood.[45]

Following this, one role of the instructor becomes clear: to deconstruct the musical material into melodic and rhythmic building blocks and have students enact them such that they are reconstructed, in order that the musical knowledge becomes operational for them and so the learning process leads to development of aural awareness skills, which form the basis of musicianship.

Applying the Sound-to-Symbol Model to Teaching Music Literacy

A review of commonly used approaches to teaching music literacy reveals they can be formulaic in structure and follow a traditional presentation of music theory concepts, where the development of aural awareness skills is not addressed in any great detail. We suggest that this limits the student's ability to internalize (audiate) music and may be a reason for students having difficulty representing their understanding through music notation. We are convinced that without deliberate development of aural awareness skills, student's musicianship skills are compromised.

We are proposing these *sound-to-symbol principles* for developing music literacy:

- Music performance is at the heart of learning. Music knowledge should be derived through singing. Singing can be understood to also include the ability to internalize or inner-hear a musical score.
- Initially, all musical concepts and elements should be introduced through simple music examples. These are easily learned and scaffold future learning. Students should learn to combine and manipulate these concepts, to read, write, improvise, and compose music that is increasingly complex.
- Many instructors have dismissed simple music examples, such as folksongs, as being unsophisticated and not appropriate for developing aural awareness in older students. We have been able to successfully use these examples with students at all levels, including those attending very elite liberal arts universities. The concept of repeatedly using simple musical examples is connected to cognitive schema theory; it gives us the ability to *think* about a new element, *associate* traditional forms of notation with the element, and *assimilate* this information.
- Students can benefit by being shown how to identify sounds and pitches in music with rhythm and solfège syllables presented entirely sequentially. Our experience suggests that presenting all rhythms or introducing all major scales at once may facilitate conceptual orientation, but it does not promote aural awareness.
- Repetitive exercises that focus on internalizing music, analyzing music by ear, and creating representations of music (without insisting on standard forms of music notation) are a key factor in developing aural awareness.
- Students cannot sight-sing if they cannot read known melodies. Therefore they should be taught how to read known melodies before they read unknown ones.
- Aural awareness skills are necessary for students to develop the ability to successfully write down music they imagine; for this they need to be able first to inner-hear music and then to play it back in their mind.

A Comparison of the Houlahan and Tacka Model of Learning with Current Teaching Approaches Adopted by Kodály Instructors

Most Kodály instructors adopt a model of teaching musical elements that is based on four steps:

1. Prepare
2. Make conscious (or presentation)
3. Reinforce (or practice)
4. Assess

For the basis of comparison, we use the Choksy model of learning associated with the Kodály concept. This model represents the one most closely followed by Hungarian and American Kodály instructors.[46] Here are six critical points of comparison.

First, we offer *an organic model of instruction and learning* that can be used to develop all types of teaching activities and lesson plans.

Teachers who have been immersed in teaching music using the Kodály philosophy of music education intuitively learn to develop lesson plans and activities that promote children's music learning. Finding ways to promote balance among music performance, knowledge of readiness concepts, and music skills is always challenging. Compared to traditional approaches to Kodály pedagogy, we have extended the phases of preparation, presentation, and practice into different stages of learning. Our model supplies teachers with a pathway to teaching music literacy as well as developing music literacy skills. This model of learning and instruction lets teachers plan activities in precise detail for each phase of learning.

Second, we offer *a sequential progression in preparing new musical elements* from kinesthetic to aural and then to visual learning activities.

The Choksy model of learning does emphasize the importance of experiencing the song material before any notation takes place during the preparation phase. Children do not, at this time, see the notation for these songs. They engage in whatever musical activities suit the nature of each song; they may sing softer or louder and determine appropriate dynamics, sing faster or slower and determine appropriate tempo, step the beat, clap an ostinato, perform the song rhythms that are known, and diagram the form. They may play the game, if there is one. In other words, they may engage in all the activities that require only a singing knowledge of the songs.[47]

As noted by Klinger:

During this phase, the children are introduced to repertoire containing the specific melodic or rhythmic components to be introduced. They are invited to sing, dance, play and move to these materials. Nothing conscious is mentioned about the note names or rhythms. Over a period of time, the children are asked to deduce certain things about the note patterns contained in the repertoire. Is there a new note or rhythm in relation to those which are already known? Is it higher or lower? Is it faster or slower? The use of iconic representations of the notes or rhythms in the form of pictures from the songs is often used as a precursor to the understanding of the real musical symbol.[48]

Although we agree with these approaches to teaching, we also believe that the preparation phrase of instruction requires more sequenced activities in combination with performance of music repertoire. In our preparation phase of learning, we offer students a series of activities sequentially guiding them to develop kinesthetic awareness, aural awareness, and finally visual awareness of the new concept or element. We believe that students must work sequentially through these stages; they cannot be presented out of order.

Third, we offer *sequential development of audiation skills* by moving from the kinesthetic to the aural and then to the visual stage of learning.

Students have an opportunity to develop their aural awareness skills and subsequently draw on their perceptual skills in order to begin to construct their own understanding of the new concept. Development of audiation skills is the result of moving through the kinesthetic, aural, and finally visual activities. At each stage of this process, children are engaged through singing and are consistently challenged to use audiation skills. For example, in stage 2, developing aural awareness, the children must replay the melody in their inner ear to answer the questions posed by the teacher. But they must be able to identify the phrase where the new element occurs, and also on which beat. This is a critical step in the learning process. Students cannot create a visual (stage 3) if they cannot audiate the music. Instructors can assess students' aural awareness skills by asking them to create a visual representation of the melody using a form of pre-notation. If students can correctly create a representation of the melody while using auditory imagery, they are in a better position to understand how sounds can be labeled with solfège syllables and traditional notation. It is our contention that if students cannot aurally describe, without any visual aid, such things as the shape of the melodic contour, the number of pitches contained in the contour, the starting pitch, and the final pitch, and sing the pitch collection from the lowest note to the highest note, then their aural awareness skills are compromised and will not develop in tandem with their visual skills.

This work has led us to consider the following. Pointing to an iconic representation of the melodic contour is an effective teaching strategy in the beginning stages of developing students' kinesthetic understanding of a new melodic pattern. However, if the student does not create his or her own visual representation of a melodic contour derived solely from knowledge gained in the aural awareness stage, then presenting notation (whether it be solfège syllables, note names, numbers, or a staff representation of the melodic contour) can create additional complications for teaching students music literacy skills. Strategy 3 (symbolic) of Bruner's instructional theory gains meaning only after students have made two important connections: successful aural analysis of the primary characteristics of the new element, and illustration of their aural understanding in a visual representation using pre-notational graphs. Gromko contends that this kind of activity can "prompt the classification, organization, and connections that enable the child to transform the concrete experience into one that can be represented in icons or symbols."[49] Presenting students with visuals (Bruner's strategy 2, iconic) and subsequently moving to the symbolic stage (Bruner's strategy 3) without developing students' aural awareness shortchanges students' perceptual understanding and may significantly compromise parallel development of aural imagery skills.

Fourth, we offer *a sound-to-symbol orientation to teaching*.

During the presentation phase of learning, Choksy suggests: "Selecting one song in which the new learning is prominent, the teacher will ask adroit questions to lead the children to discover the new element. . . . When the questions have been accurately answered the teacher names and shows notation for the new rhythm or gives the solfa and hand sign for the new note, and shows its notation on staff."[50] In other words, the symbol and the sound are presented together. Choksy does not use traditional note names but rather uses syllables to aurally represent the sound and visually label the sound. At a later stage, students learn the traditional note names. As noted by Klinger about the presentation phase of learning, "When the teacher feels that children have an understanding of the new note or rhythm, and can express this understanding through accurate performance, the sound is tied together with the written symbol and given a name. This is sometimes called 'making conscious' because it brings all that the children already know on a sub-conscious level to a more conscious realm. In contrast to preparation, the presentation of a musical element occurs during one lesson."[51]

The following is from Klinger's book describing a make-conscious presentation procedure for teaching quarter and eighth notes:

A. "Let's sing 'Seesaw.'"
B. "Let's sing again and clap the rhythm." (Class responds, teacher watches and assesses.)
C. "On the board I have drawn the lines that tell us when we have one or two sounds on a beat. Let's clap the rhythm from the board while we sing the song." (Teacher points to the board and watches and listens.)
D. "Today I will tell you the musical names of these symbols. When we have one sound on a beat, we call it 'ta.'" (Teacher points to the symbol I.) "When we have two sounds on a beat, we call it 'ti-ti.'" (Teacher points to the symbol II).
E. "Listen and watch the board while I sing and clap our song for you using these new rhythm names." (Teacher claps under the symbols on the board as she sings.)
F. "Everyone try it with me."[52]

In our model of instruction and learning, we always associate the sound of music with the rhythm or solfège syllable. We do not use visual representations to do this; we simply label the sound. For example, when we are teaching quarter and eighth notes, students must be able to (1) tap the beat, (2) clap the rhythm, (3) perform beat and rhythm, and (4) aurally identify how many sounds occur on each beat. The music instructor labels the new element with rhythm syllables without using any visuals. Once students can aurally identify the new element in the focus pattern with syllables and sing the syllables in the context of the focus and related songs, we can show them how sounds can be represented using traditional notation and how they may use syllables to decode this notation. It is imperative that students spend time listening to music and aural identify rhythms using rhythm syllables. It is very important for them to learn how to notate the sounds and pitches of music with traditional notation.

Fifth, our model of learning and instruction *develops metacognitive skills*.

No matter what concept we are addressing, we always follow the same process for teaching. Students begin to understand and anticipate our procedures, and many times they will figure out the next step in the learning process. For example, during the aural awareness stage they predict the questions we ask. During the visual stage, they offer to help students who might be struggling. This aspect of anticipating procedures and activities related to the learning process is a critical step in cognitive development.

Sixth, our model of learning and instruction has *significant opportunities for assessment*.

Because teachers have a clearer picture of all the steps in learning music, they can assess children's learning using both formative and summative assessments. Our model of instruction assists teachers in evaluation at all stages and phases of the learning and instructional process.

Summary

Taken as a whole, our model of learning and instruction offers teachers a step-by-step roadmap for developing the musical understanding, metacognition, and creativity skills that are relevant for twenty-first-century learning. A feature of this teaching pedagogy is its integration of problem-solving, critical-thinking, and collaborative learning skills into the instruction and learning of music. The Houlahan and Tacka model of learning and instruction promotes simultaneous development of students' performance, musical understanding, and audiation skills, which promotes deeper learning and creativity.

Connections to Grade Handbooks

As previously stated, for each grade we have created a set of unit plans containing five lesson plans for teaching music concepts and elements as well as developing student's musicianship skills. The music lessons follow the model of instruction and learning that we put forward in this chapter.

Discussion Questions
1. What are the three phases of learning a new music element?
2. How are the phases of learning broken into stages?
3. What is the purpose of the kinesthetic stage?
4. What is the purpose of the aural awareness stage?
5. What is the purpose of the visual awareness stage?
6. What are the stages in the associative phase?
7. What are the stages in the assimilative phase?
8. Discuss whether and how the model of learning in this chapter promotes dictation skills and sight-reading skills.

9. Compare and contrast the model of learning presented in this chapter with other models of learning.
10. Discuss whether the model of learning presented in this chapter is too cumbersome for instructors to follow, and whether it is much more effective to present information theoretically and then use it to practice music skills of reading and writing.
11. Discuss the notion that students must be able to write before they can read music.

Ongoing Assignment

1. You have been asked to present a lecture on the Houlahan and Tacka Model of Learning and Instruction for Developing Music Literacy. Develop a PowerPoint presentation for your lecture. Be able to explain how this model of learning might be useful for classroom, instrumental, and choral instruction.

Bibliography

Aiello, Rita. "The Importance of Metacognition Research in Music." In *Proceedings of the 5th Triennial ESCOM Conference,* pp. 656–658. Germany: Hanover University of Music and Drama, 2003.

Amabile, T. M. *Creativity in Context.* Boulder, CO: Westview, 1996.

Anderson, William M., and Patricia Shehan Campbell, eds. *Multicultural Perspectives in Music Education,* 2nd ed. Reston, VA: Music Educators National Conference, 1996.

Bamberger, Jeanne, and Armando Hernández. *Developing Musical Intuitions.* New York: Oxford University Press, 2000.

Bamberger, Jeanne. *The Mind Behind the Musical Ear: How Children Develop Music Intelligence.* Cambridge, MA: Harvard University Press, 1995.

Bamberger, Jeanne. "What Develops in Musical Development?" In *The Child as Musician: A Handbook of Musical Development,* ed. Gary McPherson, pp. 69–72. New York: Oxford University Press, 2006.

Barbe, Walter B., Michael N. Milone, and Raymond H. Swassing. *Teaching Through Modality Strengths: Concepts and Practices.* Columbus, OH: Zaner-Bloser, 1979.

Barkáczi, Ilona, and Csaba PlDh. *Music Makes a Difference: The Effect of Kodály's Musical Training on the Psychological Development of Elementary School Children.* Kecskemét: Zoltán Kodály Pedagogical Institute of Music, 1982.

Barrett, Margaret. "Children's Aesthetic Decision-Making: An Analysis of Children's Musical Discourse as Composers." *International Journal of Music Education,* 1996, 28: 37–62.

Barrett, M. "Freedoms and Constraints." In *Why and How to Teach Music Composition,* ed. M. Hickey, pp. 3–31. Reston, VA: MENC, 2003.

Barrett, Margaret. "Graphic Notation in Music Education." In *Music Education: Facing the Future*, ed. Jack P. Dobbs, pp. 147–153. Christchurch, New Zealand: University of Canterbury, 1991.

Barrett, M. S. "Inventing Songs, Inventing Worlds: The 'Genesis' of Creative Thought and Activity in Young Children's Lives." *International Journal of Early Years Education*, 2006, *14*(3): 201–220.

Barrett, Margaret. "Music Education and the Natural Learning Model." *International Journal of Music Education*, 1992, *20*: 27–34.

Barrett, M. S. "Preparing the Mind for Musical Creativity: Early Music Learning and Engagement." In *Musical Creativity: Insights from Music Education Research*, ed. O. Odena and G. F. Welch, pp. 51–71. Aldershot, UK: Ashgate, 2012.

Bartholomew, Douglas. "Sounds Before Symbols: What Does Phenomenology Have to Say?" *Philosophy of Music Education Review*, 1995, *3*(1): 3–9.

Benward, Bruce. *Music in Theory and Practice*, 2nd. ed., 2 vols. Dubuque, IA: W. C. Brown, 1982.

Berliner, P. F. *Thinking in Jazz: The Infinite Art of Improvisation.* Chicago: University of Chicago Press, 1994.

Boden, M. A. *The Creative Mind: Myths and Mechanisms*, 2nd ed. Abington, UK: Routledge, 2004.

Brindle, Judith. "Notes from Eva Vendrai's Kodály Course." *British Kodály Academy Newsletter*, Spring 2005: 6–11.

Brown, J., et al. "Situated Cognition and the Culture of Learning." *Educational Researcher*, 1989, *18*(1): 32–42.

Bruner, Jerome. *Towards a Theory of Instruction*. Cambridge, MA: Harvard University, 1966.

Burnard, P. "How Children Ascribe Meaning to Improvisation and Composition: Rethinking Pedagogy in Music Education." *Music Education Research*, 2000, *2*(1): 7–23.

Choksy, Lois. *The Kodály Method: Comprehensive Music Education*, 3rd ed. Upper Saddle River, NJ: Prentice-Hall, 1999.

Colley, B. "A Comparison of Syllabic Methods for Improving Rhythm Literacy." *Journal of Research in Music Education*, 1987, *35*(4): 221–235.

Collins, A., J. S. Brown, and A. Holum. "Cognitive Apprenticeship: Making Thinking Visible." *American Educator*, 1991, *15*(3): 6–11, 38–46.

Collins, A., J. S. Brown, and S. E. Newman. "Cognitive Apprenticeship: Teaching the Craft of Reading, Writing and Mathematics." In *Knowing, Learning, and Instruction: Essays in Honor of Robert Glaser*, ed. L. B. Resnick, pp. 453–494. Hillsdale, NJ: Erlbaum, 1989.

Covington, Katherine. "The Mind's Ear: I Hear Music and No One Is Performing." *College Music Symposium*, 2005, *45*: 25–41.

Custodero, L. A. "Intimacy and Reciprocity in Improvisatory Musical Performance: Pedagogical Lessons from Adult Artists and Young Children." In

Communicative Musicality: Exploring the Basis of Human Companionship, ed. S. Malloch and C. Trevarthen, pp. 513–530. Oxford: Oxford University Press, 2009.

Cutietta, Robert A., and Gregory D. Booth. "The Influence of Meter, Mode, Interval Type and Contour in Repeated Melodic Free-Recall." *Psychology of Music,* 1996, *24*(2): 222–236.

Davidson, Lyle, and Larry Scripp. "Surveying the Coordinates of Cognitive Skills in Music." In *Handbook of Research on Music Teaching and Learning*, ed. Richard Colwell, pp. 392–413. New York: Schirmer, 1992.

Davidson, Lyle, Larry Scripp, and Patricia Welsh. "'Happy Birthday': Evidence for Conflicts of Perceptual Knowledge and Conceptual Understanding." *Journal of Aesthetic Education,* 1988, *22*(1): 65–74.

Derry, Sharon J. "Cognitive Schema Theory in the Constructivist Debate." *Educational Psychologist,* 1996, *31*(3/4): 163–174.

Dissanayake, E. "Bodies Swayed to Music: The Temporal Arts as Integral to Ceremonial Ritual." In *Communicative Musicality: Exploring the Basis of Human Companionship*, ed. S. Malloch and C. Trevarthen, pp. 533–544. Oxford: Oxford University Press, 2009.

Dowling, W. J. "Tonal Structure and Children's Early Learning of Music." In *Generative Processes in Music: The Psychology of Performance, Improvisation, and Composition*, ed. J. A. Sloboda, pp. 113–128. Oxford, UK: Clarendon Press, 2001.

Duffy, Thomas M., and David H. Jonassen. *Constructivism and the Technology of Instruction: A Conversation.* Hillsdale, NJ: Erlbaum, 1992.

Eisen, Ann, and Lamar Robertson. *An American Methodology: An Inclusive Approach to Musical Literacy.* Lake Charles, LA: Sneaky Snake, 2002.

Espeland, M. *Compositional Process as Discourse and Interaction: A Study of Small Group Music Composition Processes in a School Context.* Ph.D. diss., Danish University of Education, Copenhagen, 2006. Published by Høgskolen Stord/Haugesund Stord/Haugesund University College, 2007.

Feierabend, John. "Integrating Music Learning Theory into the Kodály Curriculum." In *Readings in Music Learning Theory*, ed. Darrell Walters L. and Cynthia Taggart Crump. Chicago: GIA, 1989.

Feierabend, John. "Kodály and Gordon: Same and Different." *Bulletin of the International Kodály Society,* 1992, *17*(1): 41–50.

Ferguson, L. "The Role of Movement in Elementary Music Education: A Literature Review." *Update: Applications of Research in Music Education,* 2005, *23*(2): 23–33.

Flohr, John, S. C. Woodward, and L. Suthers. "Rhythm Performance in Early Childhood." In *Respecting the Child in Early Music Learning: Eighth International Seminar of the Early Childhood Commission of the International Society for Music Education,* ed. S. Woodward. Cape Town: International Society for Music Education, 1998.

Folkestad, G., D. J. Hargreaves, and B. Linström. "Compositional Strategies in Computer-Based Music-Making." *British Journal of Music Education,* 1998, *15*(1): 83–97.

Frolich, C. "Vitality in Music and Dance as Basic Existential Experience: Applications in Teaching Music." In *Communicative Musicality: Exploring the Basis of Human Companionship,* ed. S. Malloch and C. Trevarthen, pp. 495–512. Oxford: Oxford University Press, 2009.

Gagné, Robert M., and Karen Medsker. *The Conditions of Learning.* Fort Worth: Harcourt Brace College, 1996.

Gardner, Howard. *Frames of Mind: The Theory of Multiple Intelligences.* New York: Basic Books, 1983.

Gardner, H. *The Unschooled Mind: How Children Think and How Schools Should Teach.* New York. Basic Books. 1991.

Gauvain, M., and B. Rogoff. "Collaborative Problem Solving and Children's Planning Skills." *Developmental Psychology,* 1989, *25*: 139–151.

Glover, J. *Children Composing 4–14.* London: Routledge Falmer, 2000.

Gordon, Edwin E. *Learning Sequences in Music: Skill, Content, and Patterns.* Chicago: GIA, 2003.

Gordon, Edwin E. *The Psychology of Music Teaching.* Englewood Cliffs, NJ: Prentice-Hall, 1971.

Gratier, M., and Apter-Danin, G. "The Improvised Musicality of Belonging: Repetition and Variation in Mother-Infant Vocal Interaction." In *Communicative Musicality: Exploring the Basis of Human Companionship,* ed. S. Malloch and C. Trevarthen, pp. 301–327. Oxford: Oxford University Press, 2009.

Gromko, Joyce E. "Children's Invented Notations as Measures of Musical Understanding." *Psychology of Music,* 1994, *22*(2): 136–147.

Gromko, Joyce, and A. Poorman. "Developmental Trends and Relationships in Children's Aural Perception and Symbol Use." *Journal of Research in Music Education,* 1998, *46*(1): 16–23.

Hallam, Susan. "Musicality." In *The Child as Musician: A Handbook of Musical Development,* ed. Gary McPherson, pp. 93–110. New York: Oxford University Press, 2006.

Hargreaves, David J. *The Developmental Psychology of Music.* Cambridge: Cambridge University Press, 1986.

Hetland, Lois. "Learning to Make Music Enhances Spatial Reasoning." *Journal of Aesthetic Education,* 2000, *34*(3–4): 179–238.

Hewson, A. T. "Music Reading in the Classroom." *Journal of Research in Music Education,* 1966, *14*(4): 289–302.

Hodges, Donald A. "The Musical Brain." In *The Child as Musician: A Handbook of Musical Development,* ed. Gary McPherson, pp. 51–68. New York: Oxford University Press, 2006.

Houlahan, Micheál, and Phillip Tacka. "Revisiting 'Happy Birthday': Linking Perceptual Knowledge and Conceptual Understanding in Teaching Music Fundamentals." First European Conference on Developmental Psychology of Music Education, University of Jyväskylä, Finland, Nov. 17–18, 2005.

Jeanneret, N. "Model for Developing Preservice Primary Teachers' Confidence to Teach Music." *Bulletin of the Council for Research in Music Education*, 1997, *133*: 37–44.

Kaschub, M., and J. P. Smith. "A Principled Approach to Teaching Music Composition to Children." *Research and Issues in Music Education*, 2009, *7*(1). http://www.stthomas.edu/rimeonline/vol7/kaschubSmith.htm. Accessed Oct. 27, 2010.

Klinger, Rita. *Lesson Planning in a Kodály Setting: A Guide for Music Teachers*. Los Angeles: OAKE, 2014.

Latten, James Everett. "Exploration of a Sequence for Teaching Intonation Skills and Concepts to Wind Instrumentalists." *Journal of Band Research*, 2005, *41*(Fall): 60–87. Music Index, EBSCOhost (accessed Apr. 7, 2013).

Lehman, A. "Introduction: Music Perception and Cognition." In *The New Handbook of Research on Music Teaching and Learning*, eds. Richard Colwell and Carol Richardson, pp. 443–444. New York: Schirmer, 2002.

Levi, Ray. "Towards an Expanded View of Musical Literacy." *Contributions to Music Education*, 1989, *16*: 34–49.

Louhivuori, Jukka. "Memory Strategies in Writing Melodies." *Bulletin of the Council for Research in Music Education*, 1999, *141*: 81–85.

McPherson, Gary E., and Alf Gabrielsson. "From Sound to Sign." In *The Science and Psychology of Music Performance: Creative Strategies for Teaching and Learning*, ed. Richard Parncutt and Gary E. McPherson, pp. 98–115. New York: Oxford University Press, 2002.

More, Bruce E. "Sight Singing and Ear Training at the University Level: A Case for the Use of Kodály's System of Relative Solmization." *Choral Journal*, 1985, *25*(7): 9–11.

Palincsar, A. S. "The Role of Dialogue in Providing Scaffolded Instruction." *Educational Psychologist* 1986, *21*(1 and 2): 73–98.

Palmer, M. "Relative Effectiveness of Two Approaches to Rhythm Reading for Fourth-Grade Students." *Journal of Research in Music Education*, 1976, *24*(3): 110–118.

Parncutt, Richard. "Prenatal Development." In *The Child as Musician: A Handbook of Musical Development*, ed. Gary McPherson, pp. 1–32. New York: Oxford University Press, 2006.

Peery, J. Craig, Irene Weiss Peery, and Thomas W. Draper, eds. *Music and Child Development*. New York: Springer-Verlag, 1987.

Peretz, I. "Auditory Agnosia: A Functional Analysis." In *Thinking in Sound: The Cognitive Psychology of Human Audition*, ed. S. McAdams and E. Bigand, pp. 199–230. New York: Oxford University Press, 1993.

Perkins, David. *The Intelligent Eye: Learning to Think by Looking at Art*. Santa Monica, CA: Getty Center for Education in the Arts, 1994.

Petzold, R. G. "The Perception of Music Symbols in Music Reading by Normal Children and by Children Gifted Musically." *Journal of Experimental Education*, 1960, *28*(4): 271–319.

Polyanyi, M. *Personal Knowledge: Towards a Post-Critical Philosophy*. Chicago: University of Chicago Press, 1962.

Reifinger, Jr., James L. "The Acquisition of Sight-Singing Skills in Second-Grade General Music: Effects of Using Solfège and of Relating Tonal Patterns to Songs." *Journal of Research in Music Education,* 2012, *60*(1): 26–42. Music Index, EBSCOhost (accessed Apr. 7, 2013).

Reimer, Bennett. "Music as Cognitive: A New Horizon for Musical Education." *Kodály Envoy,* 1994, *20*(3): 16–17.

Rogoff, B. *Apprenticeship in Thinking: Cognitive Development in Social Context.* New York: Oxford University Press, 1990.

Rogoff, B., and J. Lave, eds. *Everyday Cognition: Its Development in Social Context.* Cambridge: Harvard University Press, 1984.

Rozmajzl, M. "Elementary Classroom Teachers: The Challenge of Music Methods Courses." *Kodály Envoy,* 1989, *16*(1–2): 5–10.

Runco, M. A. "The Development of Children's Creativity." In *Handbook of Research on the Education of Young Children,* ed. B. Spodek and O. N. Saracho, pp. 121–134. Mahwah, NJ: Erlbaum, 2006.

Serafine, Mary Louise. *Music as Cognition: The Development of Thought in Sound.* New York: Columbia University, 1988.

Shehan Campbell, P. "Effects of Rote Versus Note Presentations on Rhythm Learning and Retention." *Journal of Research in Music Education,* 1987, *35*(2): 117–126.

Shehan Campbell, Patricia, and Carol Scott-Kassner. *Music in Childhood: From Preschool Through the Elementary Grades.* New York: Schirmer, 1995.

Sinor, Jean. "Musical Development of Children and Kodály Pedagogy." *Kodály Envoy,* 1999, *25*: 9–12.

Sundin, B. "Musical Creativity in Childhood: A Research Project in Retrospect." *Research Studies in Music Education,* 1997, *9*(1): 48–57.

Tafuri, J. "Processes and Teaching Strategies in Musical Improvisation with Children." In *Musical Creativity: Multidisciplinary Research in Theory and Practice,* ed. I. Deliège and G. Wiggins, pp. 134–157. Hove, UK: Psychology Press, 2006.

Tillman, J., and K. Swanick. "Towards a Model of Development of Children's Musical Creativity." *Canadian Music Educator,* 1989, *30*(2): 169–174.

Trehub, Sandra E. "Infants as Musical Connoisseurs." In *The Child as Musician: A Handbook of Musical Development,* ed. Gary McPherson, pp. 33–50. New York: Oxford University Press, 2006.

Vygotsky, Lev. *Mind in Society: The Development of Higher Psychological Processes.* Cambridge, MA: Harvard University, 1978.

Wenger, E. *Communities of Practice: Learning, Meaning, and Identity.* Cambridge: Cambridge University Press, 1998.

Wertsch, J. V., ed. *Culture, Communication, and Cognition: Vygotskian Perspectives.* Cambridge: Cambridge University Press, 1985.

Westerlund, H. "Garage Rock Bands: A Future Model for Developing Musical Expertise?" *International Journal of Music Education,* 2006, *24*(2): 119–125.

Wiggins, J. "Children's Strategies for Solving Compositional Problems with Peers." *Journal of Research in Music Education,* 1994, *42*(3): 232–252.

Wiggins, J. "Compositional Process in Music." In *International Handbook of Research in Arts Education,* ed. L. Bresler, pp. 453–470. Amsterdam: Springer, 2007.

Wiggins, J. "When the Music Is Theirs: Scaffolding Young Songwriters." In *A Cultural Psychology for Music Education,* ed. M. Barrett, pp. 83–114. Oxford: Oxford University Press, 2010.

Chapter 6

Grades 1 Through 5 Teaching Strategies for Rhythmic and Melodic Concepts and Elements

Key Questions

- What is a teaching strategy?
- What are the components of a teaching strategy?
- How does questioning develop metacognition skills?
- What is the connection between a teaching strategy and the model of learning proposed in Chapter 6?

This chapter presents teaching strategies for rhythmic and melodic elements based on the model of learning presented in Chapter 5. Teaching strategies provide a narrative as to how to prepare, present, and practice the basic building blocks of music theory. The teaching strategies are formulaic in structure; ultimately teachers will infuse these strategies with their own creativity to accommodate the changing settings of teaching situations. An important component of the teaching strategies are the questions posed by the teacher during the cognitive phase of learning. The questions offer the metacognitive scaffolding that allows students to understand both the process and the product of teaching. Developing students' music literacy and audiation skills is a primary focus for these teaching strategies.

Lively exchanges on the pedagogical challenges and complexities associated with teaching music literacy frequently occur at national and international forums. Critical assessment of various teaching methods is often obfuscated by emotional arguments defending a solfège system, teaching tools, and techniques associated with a particular methodology. The publication of the *Music Educators Journal* article "An Alternative Orientation to Developing Music Literacy Skills in a Transient Society"[1] and the subsequent responses found in the Readers' Comments, Exception Taken by Jonathan Rappaport, and Author's Response[2] signal an opportunity for music educators to explore anew how the confluence of methodology and pedagogical tools affects the practice of teaching sight-singing and musicianship skills. These two articles reflect the enormous challenges that music teachers struggle with in teaching musical reading and writing: "the goal of simultaneously developing perceptual and conceptual understanding of musical events."[3] As Edward Klonoski writes, "The distinction between perceptual and conceptual understandings lies in the fact that the former entails the processing of external sounds or auditory images; the latter comprises the apprehension of concepts."[4] Teachers generally emphasize one type of understanding over another in their teaching, and they use a pedagogy that has either a perceptual or a conceptual orientation.

Lyle Davidson, Larry Scripp, and Patricia Welsh (1988) first brought forward this dichotomy in arguing that the choice of perceptual or conceptual orientation in teaching music theory can affect a student's ability to represent and internalize their understanding of musical knowledge.[5] A sight-singing methodology with a conceptual or perceptual teaching orientation may have a significant effect on a student's understanding of music notation. Adopting particular solfège and rhythm systems may not be sufficient to support musical understanding. Teaching a particular solfège system through a methodology that is not responsive to cognition research may be a significant factor contributing to the difficulty music students have in acquiring sight-singing and aural skills.

The purpose of this chapter is to explain what a perceptual orientation to teaching music fundamentals through the sequential presentation of rhythm and solfège syllables looks like. We use a *teaching strategy* to identify the approach we recommend for teaching new music elements and concepts.

The template in Table 6.1 is an example of the key components that need to be included within each teaching strategy.

Table 6.1

Element	Concept	Focus Song	Present Syllables	Theory	Traditional Notation	Practice	Additional Songs

Strategies for Teaching Music Elements

The teaching strategies described here supply a sequence of teaching activities that guide students' understanding of specific musical concepts and elements. We cover some of the most important techniques for preparing, presenting, and practicing musical elements.

Two strategies for each grade are included in this chapter. Teaching strategies for all musical elements and concepts in each grade are included in the handbook series.

We begin the teaching strategies with first grade concepts. In this text we assume that students have knowledge of beat, fast and slow, high and low, loud and soft, same and

Kodály Today

different, short and long, and rhythm, and that they understand the words *sound*, *pitch*, and *contour*. These concepts are associated with Kindergarten.

Grade 1 Teaching Strategies

In grade 1, we suggest teaching seven concepts. The order alternates between rhythmic and melodic concepts.

1. Teaching strategy for beat
2. Teaching strategy for melodic contour
3. Teaching strategy for quarter and eighth notes
4. Teaching strategy for a two-note child's chant *so-mi*
5. Teaching strategy for rest
6. Teaching strategy for a three-note child's chant *la-so-mi*
7. Teaching strategy for simple duple meter

Grade 1, Teaching Strategy 1, for Quarter and Eighth Notes

Table 6.2 shows the key components that need to be included in the teaching strategy for quarter note and eighth notes.

Table 6.2

Element	Concept	Focus Song	Present Syllables	Theory	Traditional Notation	Practice	Additional Songs
Quarter and eighth notes	One and two sounds on a beat	"Rain, Rain"	ta, tadi	Note head, stem, beam, stick, and traditional notation	Quarter and paired eighth notes ♩ ♫	Tuneful singing Responsorial singing Phrase same and different	"Bee, Bee, Bumble Bee"; "Queen, Queen Caroline"; "Seesaw"; "Snail, Snail"; "Cobbler, Cobbler"; "Doggie, Doggie"

Cognitive Phase: Preparation

Internalize Music Through Kinesthetic Activities

1. T and Ss sing "Rain, Rain" and perform the beat. Perform the beat by patting knees or touching the heart.

2. T and Ss sing "Rain, Rain" and clap the rhythm.
3. Ss sing the target phrase and point to a representation of the rhythm (see Fig. 6.1).

> • • •• • •• •• •• •   **FIG. 6.1**

4. Ss walk the beat and clap the rhythm while singing the song.
5. Have two small groups of Ss or two individuals perform the beat and rhythm using two different percussion instruments.

Describe What You Hear
1. Assess kinesthetic awareness by allowing the class to perform several kinesthetic activities.
2. The target phrase for aural awareness is the first phrase of "Rain, Rain."
3. T and S sing phrase 1 on "loo" and keep the beat before asking each question.
4. Ss determine the number of beats in the phrase. T: "Andy, how many beats did we tap?" (four)
5. Ss determine which beats had more than one sound. T: "Andy, on which beat did we sing more than one sound?" (beat 3) T: "Andy, how many sounds did we sing on beat 3?" (two)
6. Ss determine the number of sounds on the other beats in the phrase. T: "Andy, if there are two sounds on beat 3, how many sounds did we sing on each of the other beats?" (one) T: "Sing the first phrase with words while keeping the beat and hide the beat with two sounds in your head." The T may repeat the same process with phrase 2.

Create a Visual Representation of What You Hear
1. Assess kinesthetic and aural awareness by allowing the class to perform several of the kinesthetic and aural awareness activities.
2. T hums the target phrase with a neutral syllable and asks Ss to create a visual representation of the target phrase. Ss may use manipulatives. T: "Pick up what you need to recreate what you heard" or "Draw what you heard." T assesses Ss' level of understanding.
3. Ss share their representations with each other.
4. T invites one S to the board to share a representation with the class. If necessary, corrections to the representation can be made by reviewing the aural awareness questions.
5. Ss sing the first phrase of "Rain, Rain" with a neutral syllable and point to their representation. T may place a heartbeat or beat bar below the rhythmic representation on the board.

Kodály Today

Associative Phase: Presentation

Label the Sound
T presents new rhythm syllables.

1. Assess the kinesthetic, aural awareness, and visual awareness activities with phrase 1 of "Rain, Rain."
2. T: "When we hear one sound on a beat we call it 'ta'; when we hear two sounds on a beat we can call them 'tadi.' *Ta*'s and *tadi*'s are called rhythm syllables."
3. T sings "Rain, Rain" with rhythm syllables and Ss echo-sing "*ta ta tadi ta*" as a class and individually.
4. T sings phrase with "loo" and Ss echo-sing with rhythm syllables.
5. Repeat step three with related songs.

Notate What You Hear
T presents the notation for new sounds.

1. T: "We can represent one and two sounds on a beat using traditional notation. We can use a quarter note to represent one sound on a beat. A quarter note has a note head and a stem."
2. T: "We can use two eighth notes to represent two sounds on a beat. Two eighth notes have two note heads, two stems, and a beam."
3. T: "Our first phrase of "Rain, Rain" looks like this:" ♩ ♩ ♫ ♩
4. T: "We can read this rhythm pattern using rhythm syllables."
5. T sings rhythm syllables while pointing to the heartbeats; Ss echo-sing using rhythm syllables while pointing to the heartbeats.
6. Stick notation is an easy way to write rhythmic notation. Stick notation is traditional notation without the note heads for quarter and eighth notes. T: "Our first phrase of 'Rain, Rain' looks like this in stick notation:" ♩ ♩ ♫ ♩ 𝄽 "Sing 'Rain, Rain' with rhythm syllables." Individuals sing and point to the target phrase (the A phrase) on the board as the class sings the song with rhythm syllables.

Assimilative Phase: Practice Music Skills

Aural Practice
These skills should be practiced independently from visual practice.

Singing
- T sings known melodies with words and Ss echo-sing with rhythm syllables.
  T: "I say the other words; you say the rhythm names."
  T: "Rain, rain, go away." (from the song "Rain, Rain")

Ss: "*Ta ta ta di ta.*"
T: "Bee, bee, bumble bee." (from the rhyme "Bee, Bee, Bumble Bee")
Ss: "*Ta ta ta di ta.*"
T: "Queen, queen, Caroline." (from the rhyme "Queen, Queen Caroline")
Ss: "*Ta ta ta di ta.*"
T: "Seesaw up and down." (from the song "Seesaw")
Ss: "*Ta ta ta di ta.*"
T: "Snail snail snail snail." (from the song "Snail, Snail")
Ss: "*Ta ta ta ta.*"
T: "Doggie, doggie, where's your bone?" (from the song "Doggie, Doggie")
Ss: "*Ta di ta di ta di ta.*"
T: "Cobbler, cobbler, mend my shoe." (from the song "Hunt the Slipper")
Ss: "*Ta di ta di ta di ta.*"
T: "Get it done by half past two." (from the song "Hunt the Slipper")
Ss: "*Ta di ta di ta di ta.*"
- Ss read from T's model.
  T: "I'll clap a rhythm; you echo rhythm syllables."

Inner Hearing
- T directs Ss to sing focus song or one of the additional songs and inner-hear the target phrase.

Part Work
- T directs Ss to sing focus song or the additional songs and keep the beat.
- T directs Ss to sing focus song or the additional songs and keep the beat.
- T directs Ss to sing focus song or the additional songs and keep a simple rhythmic ostinato.

Improvisation
- Improvise a question and answer. T gives the question, and Ss answer.

Visual Practice
These skills may be practiced visually. They should not take place without recourse to aural practice.

Reading Activities
- Practice rhythm patterns derived from the focus song and additional songs with Ss using flash cards or the SMART board.
- Ss play Name the Song. T claps the rhythm of a song. One S recognizes the song from hearing the rhythm.
- Matching and inner hearing. Match the name of the song with a rhythm written on the board.

Kodály Today

- Flashcard activities may be used with both stick and staff notation.
    1. Ss read the cards in succession.
    2. Place the cards on the ledge of the chalkboard and perform them in order. Change the order of the cards to have Ss read different patterns, or change the order to move from one song to the next in a lesson. A card may be removed and an individual S may improvise a rhythm to replace the missing pattern.
    3. Have one S draw a rhythm card from a box. A classmate may tell him or her how to perform the rhythm (clapping, jumping, tapping, stamping, blinking, nodding, etc.). The class may echo the rhythm.
- Perform a notated rhythm pattern on an instrument.

Inner Hearing Activities
- T sings a song on a neutral syllable and gives Ss four flash cards; Ss must identify the song and arrange flash cards in the correct order.

Writing Activities
- Ss sing "Snail, Snail" with text and write the rhythm on the board.
- Ss sing "Rain, Rain" with text, and then sing again, clapping the text to compare it with the rhythm of "Snail, Snail" written on the board.
- T points to the rhythm to help Ss determine if both songs have the same rhythm.
- Ss then sing "Rain, Rain" with words. T points to the rhythm and asks whether or not it fits the song.

Improvisation Activities
- Write the rhythm of a four-beat phrase of a known song on the board. Ask Ss to clap the phrase, but change two beats.
- Improvise a new rhythm to one measure or more of a well-known song written on the board. Use "Rain, Rain"; "Bee, Bee"; "Cobbler, Cobbler"; "Doggie, Doggie" (the first two phrases); "Engine, Engine, Number Nine"; "Snail, Snail"; and "We Are Dancing in the Forest."
- T writes a sixteen-beat rhythm pattern on the board in four-beat phrases, leaving the last phrase blank. Ask one S to improvise the final four beats. Write the improvised phrase on the board. This type of activity combines improvisation, reading, and writing.
- T claps a rhythmic question and Ss individually clap an answer. Have the answer choices on the board. Question-and-answer rhythmic conversations can continue as a chain around the class.

Listening
- Andante from Symphony No. 94 "The Surprise Symphony," by Franz Joseph Haydn (1732–1809). Do your very best to teach full names and full dates!

♫♩ | ♫♩ | ♫♩ | ♫♩ | ♫♩ | ♫♩ | ♫ | ♩ ♩ |

Prepare the listening activity by having S recognize the rhythmic patterns found in known songs such as "Bobby Shafto" and "Bounce High, Bounce Low."

"In the Hall of the Mountain King," fourth movement from *Peer Gynt Suite* by Edvard Grieg (1843–1907)

Assessment
- Ss clap the rhythm of "Rain Rain" _____.
- Ss clap and say the rhythm syllables for "Rain Rain." _____.

Sight-Reading
Micheál Houlahan and Philip Tacka. *Sound Thinking: Music for Sight-Singing and Ear Training.* New York: Boosey & Hawkes, 1991. Vol. I, p. 17.

Béla Bartók. *For Children.* Eighty-five pieces originally in four volumes (revised Boosey & Hawkes, 1947). No. 12 and no. 4.

Grade 1, Teaching Strategy 2, for a Two-Note Child's Chant

Table 6.3 shows the key components that need to be included in the teaching strategy for a two-note child's chant.

Table 6.3

Element	Concept	Focus Song	Present Syllables	Theory	Traditional Notation	Practice	Additional Songs
Bichord of the pentatonic scale	Two pitches, one higher and one lower, a skip apart	"Snail, Snail"	*so-mi*	Music staff, lines, and spaces Note head on staff	*so* and *mi* with traditional rhythmic notation	♩ ♫	"Doggie, Doggie"; "Rain, Rain"; "Cobbler, Cobbler"

Cognitive Phase: Preparation

Internalize Music Through Kinesthetic Activities

1. Ss sing and point to a representation of the melodic contour of "Snail, Snail." Figure 6.2 is an example of a representation for the melodic contour of "Snail, Snail."

FIG. 6.2

```
  •        •

       •        •
```

2. Ss sing "Snail, Snail" and show the melodic contour with high and low arm movements.
3. Ss sing "Snail, Snail" with rhythm syllables while showing the melodic contour.

Describe What You Hear
1. Assess kinesthetic awareness by allowing the class to perform several of the activities described above independently.
2. The target phrase for aural awareness is the first phrase of "Snail, Snail." T and Ss sing phrase 1 on "loo" and keep the beat before asking each question.
3. Ss determine the number of beats in the phrase. T: "Andy, how many beats did we tap?" (four)
4. Ss determine the number of different pitches. T sings only the first two beats. T: "Andy, how many different pitches did we sing?" (two)
5. T determines whether Ss can describe the pitches. T: "Andy, describe the pitches." (first is high, second is low) T: "Andy, I'll sing the beginning of 'Snail'; you echo with high and low." T: "Snail snail snail snail." ("High low high low.")

Create a Visual Representation of What You Hear
1. Assess kinesthetic and aural awareness by allowing the class to perform several of the kinesthetic and aural awareness activities.
2. Hum the target phrase with a neutral syllable and ask Ss to create a visual representation of the melody of the target phrase. Ss may use manipulatives. T: "Pick up what you need to recreate what you heard" or "Draw what you heard." T assesses Ss' level of understanding.
3. Ss share their representations with each other.
4. Invite one S to the board to share a representation with the class. If necessary, corrections to the representation can be made by reviewing the aural awareness questions.
5. Ss sing the first phrase of "Snail, Snail" with a neutral syllable and point to their representation, and then sing with known elements: "high low high low."
6. Identify the rhythm of this phrase.

Associative Phase: Presentation

Label the Sound
T presents solfège syllables.

1. Assess the kinesthetic, aural awareness, and visual awareness activities with phrase 1 of "Snail, Snail."

Teaching Strategies: Grades 1 Through 5

2. T: "We can label pitches with solfège syllables. We call the high sound 'so' and the low sound 'mi.' T shows the hand signs spatially.
3. Sing "*so mi so mi*" with hand signs (the first phrase of "Snail, Snail").

4. T sings "*so mi so mi*" with hand signs to individual Ss, who echo the pattern.
5. T: "I'll sing words and you echo solfège names." T: "Snail snail snail snail." Ss: "*so mi so mi*."
6. T labels the interval between *so* and *mi* as a skip.

Notate What You Hear
T presents notation for new pitches.

1. Introduce the "musical steps." T: "*so-mi* looks like this on our steps. From *so* to *mi* is a skip." (See Fig. 6.3.)
2. T can rearrange the solfège syllables according to the pitch contour.
3. "We can write our phrase in traditional notation and put our solfège syllables under the notation." T may direct Ss to write the stick notation and add the solfège syllables.

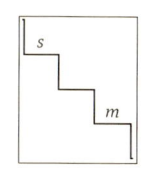

FIG. 6.3

so   mi   so   mi

4. T can at this time begin to place note heads above and below a line so that Ss understand there is a skip between these two notes.
5. Introduce the music staff by making students aware of
   a. Five lines and four spaces
   b. Counting the lines and spaces from the bottom to the top
   c. Distinguishing notes in a space and notes on a line
6. Rule of Placement. (Consider using the finger staff for this activity.) "If *so* is on a space, *mi* is on the next space down. If *so* is on a line, *mi* is on the next line down." (Note: do not address accidentals until students learn instruments.) "If *so* lives on the fifth line, *mi* lives on the fourth line. If *so* lives on the fourth space, *mi* lives on the third space," and so on; *so-mi* looks like Fig. 6.4 on the music staff.

Kodály Today

Fig. 6.4

7. T writes the first phrase of "Snail, Snail" on the staff using several staff placements and Ss sing with solfège syllables and hand signs.
8. Ss sing "Snail, Snail" with rhythm syllables while showing hand signs. (This activity may be difficult for some Ss at first, but it is an accessible and valuable activity.)

Assimilative Phase: Practice Music Skills

Aural Practice
These skills should be practiced independently from visual practice.

Singing
- T sings known melodies with words and S echo-sing with solfège syllables.
  T: "Snail snail snail snail."
  Ss: "*so mi so mi.*"
  T: "Doggie, doggie, where's your bone?"
  Ss: "*so so mi mi so so mi.*"
  T: "Cobbler, cobbler, mend my shoe."
  Ss: "*so so mi mi so so mi.*"
  T: "Get it done by half past two."
  Ss: "*so so mi mi so so mi.*"
- Aural dictation.
  T: "I'll sing on 'loo'; you echo solfège syllables."

Inner Hearing
- T directs Ss to sing focus song or one of the additional songs and inner-hear the target phrase.

Part Work
- Ss sing known songs with a rhythmic ostinato.
- Ss sing known songs in canon.

Improvisation
1. Ss improvise a question and answer. T provides the question (use only *so-mi*); Ss provide answer.
2. Ss improvise four-beat *so-mi* motives using hand signs.
3. Ss improvise *so-mi* melodies to simple four- and eight-beat rhythms using a barred instrument.
4. Ss improvise *so-mi* melodies on barred instruments.

Visual Practice
These skills may be practiced visually. They should not take place without recourse to aural practices.

Reading from Hand Signs
- Ss sing from T's hand signs. T transforms the target pattern into basic four-beat melodic patterns found in student song material. Transform:
Phrase 1 of "Seesaw" into phrase 1 of Rain, Rain"
Phrase 2 of "Seesaw" into phrase 1 of "Doggie, Doggie"
Phrase 1 of "Doggie, Doggie" into phrase 1 of "Cobbler, Cobbler"

Reading Activities
- Practice melodic patterns with Ss reading flash cards derived from the focus and additional songs.
- Perform the same activity on a barred instrument.
- Ss read *so-mi* ostinati and perform them as an accompaniment on barred instruments using known songs.
- Ss sing the first phrase of these songs following the instructor's hand signs: "Rain, Rain"; "Cobbler, Cobbler"; "Doggie, Doggie"; "Snail, Snail"; "This Old Man"; "Apple Tree"; "Teddy Bear."
- Ss read four-beat *so-mi* patterns and play them on a xylophone or bells.
- Ss read "Pala Palita" (Fig. 6.5) and play it on an instrument.

Fig. 6.5 "Pala palita"

Pa - la, pa - li - ta, pa - lo - te, pa - li - tro - que

Note: Reprinted from *Vamos a Cantar* with permission of the Kodály Institute at Capital University.

Inner Hearing
- T gives students four flash cards, and Ss must identify the song and arrange flash cards in the correct order.
- Ss read known songs but inner-hear the phrase containing the new target pattern.

Memory
- Ss read an unknown song with solfège syllables and hand signs. T erases four beats each time and Ss memorize.
- Ss read in two parts from T's hand signs.

Kodály Today

Writing Activities
- Ss write the first four beats of "Snail, Snail" using traditional notation and solfège syllables and then on the staff.

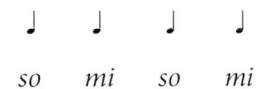

  ♩ ♩ ♩ ♩
  so mi so mi

- Ss write four beats of a known song on a staff using discs on a staff board.
- T labels notes written on the staff with solfège syllables.
- T adds stems to notes written on the staff (stem rule).
- T sings "Snail, Snail" changing beat 3 from one to two sounds. Ss identify the change and write it on the board. They identify the song as "Seesaw" or "Rain, Rain." Consider these examples:
  - T sings the pattern seen above and changes beat 1 from one to two sounds. The pattern is now *so so mi so so mi*. Ss identify the change and write it on the board. Ss identify the song as "Teddy Bear."
  - T sings the pattern and changes beat 2 from one to two sounds. The pattern is now *so so mi mi so so mi*. Ss identify the change and write it on the board. Ss identify the song as "Doggie, Doggie."
- Ss write four-beat *so-mi* patterns and play them on a xylophone or bells (Fig. 6.6).

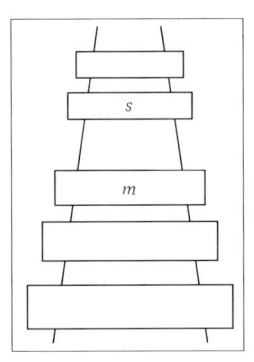

FIG. 6.6

- Write *so-mi* patterns on the staff using a number of placements for the *so-mi* patterns.

Improvisation Activities
- Improvise question-and-answer motives using known rhythms and *so-mi* melodic patterns. Have the question-and-answer choices written on the board.
- Improvise new words to a known song that uses *so-mi*, such as "This Old Man." Have the song written on the board.

Listening Activities
- "Allegro" from the "Toy" Symphony by Leopold Mozart (1719–1787).

Teaching Strategies: Grades 1 Through 5

Assessment
- Ss sing "Rain Rain" with solfège syllables and hand signs _____.
- Ss read "Rain Rain" from notation with solfège syllables and hand signs.

Sight-Reading
Micheál Houlahan and Philip Tacka. *Sound Thinking: Music for Sight-Singing and Ear Training.* New York: Boosey & Hawkes, 1991. Vol. I, pp. 24 and 26.

Here are three teaching strategies, Table 6.4 for the rest, Table 6.5 for a three-note child's chant, and Table 6.6 for duple meter.

Table 6.4

Element	Concept	Focus Song	Present Syllables	Theory	Traditional Notation	Practice	Additional Songs
Quarter rest	Beat with no sound	"Hot Cross Buns"		Quarter note rest	𝄽 or a "z"	*so-mi* Reading and writing in C, F, and G *do* positions	"Bow Wow Wow"; "All Around the Buttercup"; "Pease Porridge Hot"; "Zapatitos blancos"

Table 6.5

Element	Concept	Focus Song	Present Syllables	Theory	Traditional Notation	Practice	Additional Songs
Trichord of the pentatonic scale	Three pitches; a skip between one pair of the pitches	"Bounce High, Bounce Low" or "Snail, Snail"	*la-so-mi*	Staff, lines, spaces, skip between *so* and *mi*; three-note child's chant	*la* with traditional rhythmic notation (add *so* and *mi*)	𝄽 Practice using the rest with different four-beat rhythm patterns extracted from the students' repertoire that also include quarter and eighth notes	"Snail, Snail"; "Bobby Shafto"; "Lucy Locket"; "We Are Dancing in the Forest"

Kodály Today

Table 6.6

Element	Concept	Focus Song	Present Syllables	Theory	Traditional Notation	Practice	Additional Songs
Simple duple meter	Organization of strong and weak beats	"Bounce High, Bounce Low"		Accent; bar lines, measures; double bar line, time signature, strong and weak beats	$\frac{2}{4}$	la-so-mi Reading and writing in C, F, and G *do* positions	"Cobbler, Cobbler"; "Bye Baby Bunting"; "Little Sally Water"

Focus Songs for Grade 1

"Rain, Rain" can be a focus song for quarter and eighth notes (Fig. 6.7).

Fig. 6.7 "Rain, Rain": Focus Song for Quarter and Eighth Notes

Rain, rain, go a-way, come a-gain some oth-er day.
Lit-tle Sus-ie wants to play, rain, rain, go a-way.

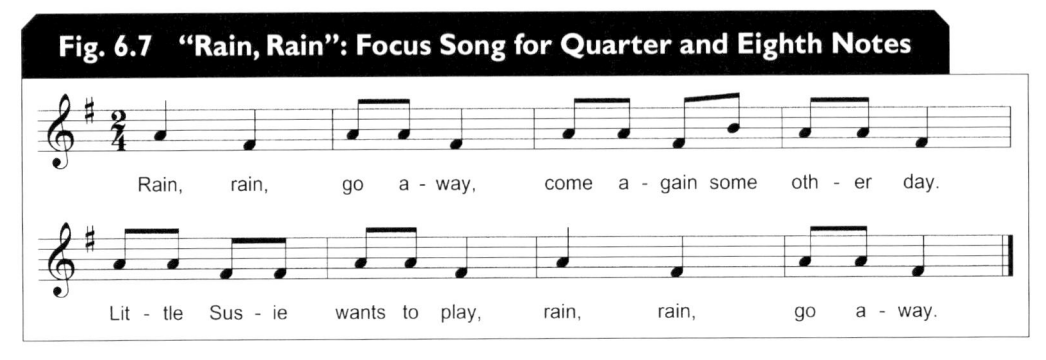

"Snail, Snail" can be a focus song for a two-note child's chant *so-mi* (Fig. 6.8).

Fig. 6.8 "Snail, Snail": Focus Song for a Two-Note Child's Chant *so-mi*

Snail, snail, snail, snail, Go a-round and round and round.

"Hot Cross Buns" can be a focus song for the rest (Fig. 6.9).

Fig. 6.9 "Hot Cross Buns": Focus Song for Rest

Hot cross buns, hot cross buns, one a pen-ny, two a pen-ny, hot cross buns.

"Bounce High, Bounce Low" can be a focus song for a three-note child's chant *la-so-mi* (Fig. 6.10).

Teaching Strategies: Grades 1 Through 5

Fig. 6.10 "Bounce High": Focus Song for a Three-Note Child's Chant

Bounce high, bounce low, bounce the ball to Shi - loh.

"Bounce High, Bounce Low" can also be a focus song for two-beat meter (Fig. 6.11).

Fig. 6.11 "Bounce High": Focus Song for Two-Beat Meter

Bounce high, bounce low, bounce the ball to Shi - loh.

Grade 2 Teaching Strategies

In second grade, we deal with six musical concepts. When teaching them, we alternate between rhythmic concepts and melodic concepts.

1. Teaching strategy for introducing the tonic note of the major pentatonic scale *do*
2. Teaching strategy for half note
3. Teaching strategy for introducing the second degree of the major pentatonic scale *re*
4. Teaching strategy for introducing the sixteenth notes
5. Teaching strategy for the major pentatonic scale
6. Teaching strategy for simple quadruple meter

Grade 2, Teaching Strategy 1, for Introducing the Tonic

Table 6.7 presents the key components that need to be included when teaching the tonic note of the major pentatonic scale.

Cognitive Phase: Preparation

Internalize Music Through Kinesthetic Activities
1. Ss sing "Bow Wow Wow" and keep the beat.
2. Ss sing "Bow Wow Wow" and point to a representation of the melodic contour of phrase 3 ("Little Tommy Tucker's Dog"; Fig. 6.12).

Table 6.7

Element	Concept	Focus Song	Present Syllables	Theory	Traditional Notation	Practice	Additional Songs
Tonic note of the major pentatonic scale	Pitch a skip lower than low *mi* five steps lower than low *so* and six steps lower than *la*	"Bow Wow Wow"	*do*	Tonic note		$\frac{2}{4}$	"Wall Flowers"; "Button You Must Wander"; "Dinah"; "Rocky Mountain"; "Knock the Cymbals"

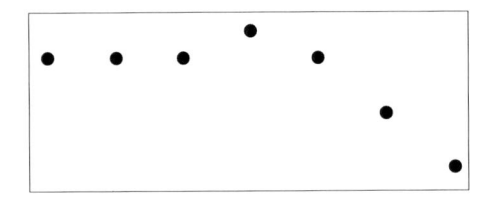

FIG. 6.12

3. Ss sing "Bow Wow Wow" and show the melodic contour.
4. Ss sing "Bow Wow Wow" with rhythm syllables while showing the melodic contour.

Describe What You Hear

1. Assess the kinesthetic awareness.
2. Ss sing the song and clap melodic contour of the target phrase. Each S mirrors and claps the melodic contour with a partner.
3. T and Ss sing phrase 3 on "loo" while keeping the beat before each question.
4. Ss determine the number of beats in the target phrase. T: "Andy, how many beats did we tap?" (four)
5. Ss determine which beat has the new musical element, along with the characteristics of the new musical element on that beat. T: "Andy, which beat has the lowest sound?" (fourth beat, last) T: "Let's sing the phrase on loo but call the last pitch 'low.'" (T demonstrates, pointing to the floor for "low.")
6. Ss determine known musical elements within the phrase.
   T: "Let's sing with hand signs, but on the fourth beat let's sing 'low'. Ss: "*so so so la so mi low*."
7. Call on individual Ss to sing the phrase. (Model the hand signs when singing.)
   T: "Let's sing it again together."

Create a Visual Representation of What You Hear
1. Assess kinesthetic and aural awareness by allowing the class to perform several of the kinesthetic and aural awareness activities.
2. T sings the target phrase with a neutral syllable and asks Ss to create a visual representation of the melody of the target phrase. Ss may use manipulatives. T: "Pick up what you need to recreate what you heard" or "Draw what you heard." T assesses Ss' level of understanding.
3. Ss share their representations with each other.
4. T invites one S to the board to share a representation with the class. If necessary, corrections to the representation can be made by reviewing the aural awareness questions.
5. Ss sing the third phrase of "Bow Wow Wow" with a neutral syllable and point to their representation, and then sing with known elements: *so so so la so mi low*.
6. Ss determine and write the rhythm for "Bow Wow Wow"; add bar lines and a time signature.

Associative Phase: Presentation

Label the Sound
T presents new solfège syllables.

1. Briefly review kinesthetic, aural, and visual awareness.
2. T: "We call the low sound *do*." Present the hand sign.
3. Class and individuals sing phrase 3 of "Bow Wow Wow" with solfège syllables and hand signs.
4. T sings the words of phrase 3 of "Bow Wow Wow" and Ss echo-sing using solfège syllables and hand signs.
5. T echo-sings with at least eight individuals.
6. Ss identify *mi-do* as a skip.

Notate What You Hear
T presents notation for new pitch.

1. On the board place *do* on steps (Fig. 6.13).
2. Write the traditional rhythm notation with solfège syllables.

♫♫♫ ♩
so   so   so   la   so mi do

The class sings the phrase with solfège syllables and hand signs; individuals may come to the board, point to the melody, and sing.

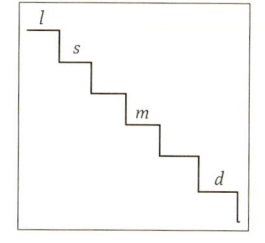

FIG. 6.13

Kodály Today

3. State the Rule of Placement: "If *mi* is on a line, *do* is on the next line below. If *mi* is in a space, *do* is in the space below."
4. Write the melody in the staff and review the Rule of Placement. Everyone points and sings. Write the phrase given above in staff notation. The class sings the phrase with solfège syllables and hand signs; individuals may come to the board, point to the melody, and sing (Fig. 6.14).

Fig. 6.14

Assimilative Phase: Practice Music Skills

Aural Practice
These skills should be practiced independently from visual practice.

Singing
- T sings known melodies with words and Ss echo-sing with solfège syllables.
  T: "I sing the words; you sing the hand signs."
  T: "Little Tommy Tucker's dog." (from "Bow Wow Wow")
  Ss: "*so so so la so mi do.*"
  T: "Let's all go to Mary's house." (from "Wallflowers")
  Ss: "*so so so la so mi do.*"
  T: "Wallflowers, wallflowers." (from "Wallflowers")
  Ss: "*so mi do so mi do.*"
  T: "Old woman, old woman." (from "Deaf Woman's Courtship")
  Ss: "*so mi do so mi do.*"
  T: "Bright eyes will find you, sharp eyes will find you." (from "Button You Must Wander")
  Ss: "*la la la so do la la la so do.*"
  T: "No one in the house but Dinah Dinah." (from "Dinah")
  Ss: "*do do do do do mi so mi so mi.*"
  T: "Rocky mountain, rocky mountain, rocky mountain high." (from "Rocky Mountain")
  Ss: "*do do do mi do do do mi do do mi so so.*"
  T: "Oh law Suzie gal." (from "Knock the Cymbals")
  Ss: "*la la so mi do.*"

- Ss read from T's model.
  T: "I'll sing on 'loo'; you echo solfège syllables." T sings motifs from known songs and Ss sing back with solfège syllables and hand signs.

Inner Hearing
- Ss recognize familiar songs from T's hand signs.
- T sings known fragments of songs, and S sing back with solfège.

Singing Intervals
- T sings the intervals between the notes of the tone set; Ss sing the intervals and identifies whether it is a skip or a step.
- T plays intervals on the piano melodically or harmonically, and Ss identify whether the interval is a skip or step.

Part Work
- Use the third phrase of "Bow Wow Wow" as an ostinato.
- Ss echo-sing four-beat patterns provided by T with solfège syllables and hand signs; begin singing at beat 3 of T's pattern.
- Ss sing pentatonic songs in canon.
- Ss sing pentatonic songs in canon with a rhythmic ostinato.
- Ss sing pentatonic songs in canon with a melodic ostinato.
- Combine a phrase as an ostinato as well as another motif from the song so that two ostinati are being used at the same time. This works with pentatonic music.
- Ss sing a major pentatonic song and T accompanies with a drone made up of *do* or *do-so* played on an instrument.

Improvisation Activities
- T sings a music question with solfège syllables and hand signs and Ss provide an answer. Question ends on *so* and after several repetitions Ss end the activity on *re*. Answer ends on *do*.
- S sings a music question with solfège syllables and hand signs, and another S gives an answer.
- One S improvises a four-beat pattern. The next S begins a four-beat improvisation with the last two beats of the pattern of the first S.

Visual Practice

These skills may be practiced visually. They should not take place without recourse to aural practice.

Kodály Today

Reading from Hand Signs
- Ss sing known song from T's hand signs, including the new solfège pattern.
- Ss sing known song from another S's hand signs, including the new solfège pattern.
- One S reads a motif from T's hand sign and plays on a classroom instrument. T furnishes the starting place on the instrument.

Reading Activities
- Ss read target motifs from the tone ladder.
- Ss read known melodies from the tone ladder.
- Ss read target motif from traditional rhythmic notation and solfège with solfège syllables and hand signs.
- Ss read a known song from traditional rhythmic notation with solfège syllables and hand signs.
- Ss read a known song with solfège syllables and conduct.
- Ss read a known song from staff notation with solfège syllables and hand signs.
- Ss read a known song from staff notation with solfège syllables and conduct.
- transforms target motif into a related pattern.
- Ss read an unknown song with solfège syllables and hand signs.
- Ss read an unknown song with solfège syllables and conduct.
- T shows hand signs and Ss read after two beats in canon with hand signs.
- transforms a known folksong into another folksong.
- Ss read phrases of known song, notated with traditional rhythmic notation and solfège, and play on a classroom instrument.
- Ss read "Bow Wow Wow" from traditional rhythmic notation and solfège.
- Ss read "Bow Wow Wow" from the staff notation.
- Ss read and play selected target phrases on the xylophone or tone bells (Fig. 6.15).

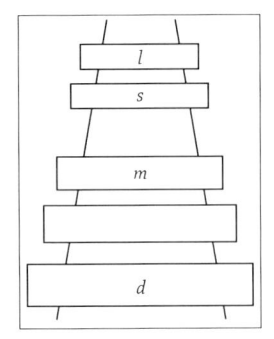

FIG. 6.15

Inner Hearing
- Ss recognize familiar songs from T's hand signs.
- T sings known fragments of songs and Ss sing back with solfège syllables and signs.
- T gives students four flash cards with rhythm, and Ss must identify the song and arrange flash cards in the correct order.

Teaching Strategies: Grades 1 Through 5

- Ss sing known songs but inner-hear the phrase containing the new target pattern.
- Ss sing a song but have to inner-hear the song from a signal provided by T. Ss sing the song aloud when given a signal from the T.

Memory
- Ss read an unknown song with solfège syllables and hand signs. T erases four beats each time and Ss memorize.
- Ss read an unknown song with solfège syllables and conduct. T erases four beats each time and Ss memorize.

Writing Activities
- Ss write all of "Bow Wow Wow" using stick notation with solfège syllables.
- Ss write "Bow Wow Wow" in staff notation.
- Ss write well-known melodic patterns from hand signs using stick or staff notation. Once these patterns are written, play them on the xylophone or bells.
- Ss write the target pattern in stick or traditional rhythmic notation with solfège syllables below.
- Ss write related patterns in stick and traditional rhythmic notation with solfège syllables below.
- Ss write the tone set of a known song on the board as one S or class sings a known song using solfège syllables and hand signs.
- Ss write a known song in stick or traditional rhythmic notation with solfège syllables below.
- Ss fill in the missing measures of a known song with the correct solfège syllables. T may provide the rhythm but not the solfège syllables for the missing measure.
- T sings an unknown song and Ss fill in the missing measures with the correct rhythms and solfège syllables.
- Ss transcribe a song written in rhythmic notation with solfège syllables below into staff notation.
- Ss write tone set of a melody on the tone ladder and on the staff.

Improvisation Activities
- T sings a question phrase with solfège syllables and hand signs that is four beats in long and one S chooses an answering phrase from four patterns written on the board.
- T writes a known folksong in traditional rhythmic notation and solfège but leaves out four beats. Ss read with solfège syllables and one S improvises a four-beat melody that uses the new melodic note.
- Ss improvise a new folksong to a given form and scale. For example, they compose a new melody using the form ABAB. T gives students the A phrase and Ss improvise the B phrase; they should end on *do*.

Kodály Today

Part Work
- Divide the class into two groups. Group 1 sings the song with solfège and hand signs and group 2 taps a rhythmic ostinato that is read from notation.
- Divide the class into two groups. Group 1 sings the song with solfège and hand signs and group 2 sings a melodic ostinato that is read from notation.
- Divide the class into two groups. Group 1 sings the song with solfège and hand signs and group 2 sings a descant with solfège and hand signs that is read from notation.
- Ss read a known song with solfège syllables and hand signs. Divide the class into two groups and perform the activity in canon after two beats, group 1 singing and group 2 clapping in canon.
- Ss read a known song with solfège syllables and conducting. Divide the class into two groups and perform the activity in canon after two beats, group 1 singing and group 2 clapping in canon.
- Ss read a known song with solfège syllables while showing hand signs with left hand and conducting with their right hand. Divide the class into two groups; group 1 performs the activity and group 2 claps rhythm in canon after two beats.
- Ss sing a known song and clap the rhythm of another well-known song simultaneously.
- Ss sing a known song, tap a rhythm from traditional rhythmic notation with the right hand, and tap an ostinato with the left hand.
- Ss sing scales in canon.

Listening Activities
- "Allegro" from Symphony No. 1 by Mozart (1756–1791) (Fig. 6.16).

Fig. 6.16

Sight-Reading Materials
Micheál Houlahan and Philip Tacka. *Sound Thinking: Music for Sight-Singing and Ear Training.* New York: Boosey & Hawkes, 1991. Vol. I, p. 51, nos. 6–7.

Zoltán Kodály. *Kodály Choral Library: 333 Elementary Exercises.* Exercises 7 and 15 explore the *do-mi* interval; exercises 6, 16, 24, 25, 26, 27, 53, and 54 explore the *so-mi-do* intervals; and exercises 28 and 51 explore the *la-so-mi-do* intervals.

Grade 2, Teaching Strategy 2, for Half Note

Table 6.8 shows the key components that need to be included in the half-note teaching strategy.

Table 6.8

Element	Concept	Focus Song	Present Syllables	Theory	Traditional Notation	Practice	Additional Songs
Half note	Note that lasts for two beats	"Here Comes a Bluebird"	ta-ah	ti	♩	do	"Are You Sleeping?"; "Who's That Tapping at the Window?"; "Let Us Chase the Squirrel"; "Phoebe in Her Petticoat"

Cognitive Phase: Preparation

Internalize Music Through Kinesthetic Activities
1. Ss sing "Here Comes a Bluebird" and keep the beat.
2. Ss sing "Here Comes a Bluebird" and clap the rhythm.
3. Ss sing and point to a representation of phrases 2 and 4 (Fig. 6.17).

FIG. 6.17

4. Divide the class into two groups; group 1 performs the beat, and group 2 performs the rhythm. Reverse.
5. Ss sing "Here Comes a Bluebird," walk the beat, and clap the rhythm.

Describe What You Hear
1. Assess the kinesthetic awareness.
2. T and Ss sing phrase 2 on "loo" while performing the beat before each question.

Kodály Today

3. Ss determine the number of beats in phrase 2. T: "Andy, how many beats did we keep?" (eight) T: "Andy, which beat has no sound?" (last one, eight)
4. Ss determine which beat has the new musical element. T: "Andy, where did we sing the longest sound?" (at the beginning) T: "Andy, on which beats did we sing the long sound?" (one and two)
5. T and Ss sing phrase 2 on "loo" and keep the beat. T: "Let's sing on 'loo' and say *long* for beats 1 and 2."
   T: "Let's sing and clap the whole phrase with rhythm syllables and say *long* for beats 1 and 2" (Fig. 6.18).

long		ta di	ta di	ta	ta	ta	
♥	♥	♥	♥	♥	♥	♥	♥

FIG. 6.18

Create a Visual Representation of What You Hear

1. Assess kinesthetic and aural awareness by allowing the class to perform several of the kinesthetic and aural awareness activities.
2. T sings the target phrase with a neutral syllable and asks S to create a visual representation of the target phrase. Ss may use manipulatives.
3. T: "Pick up what you need to recreate what you heard" or "Draw what you heard." T assesses Ss' level of understanding.
4. Ss share their representations with each other.
5. T invites one S to the board to share a representation with the class. If necessary, corrections to the representation can be made by reviewing the aural awareness questions.
6. Ss sing the second phrase of "Here Comes a Bluebird" with a neutral syllable and point to their representation, and then sing with known elements: *long ta di ta di ta ta ta* (rest).

Associative Phase: Presentation

Label the Sound
T presents new rhythm syllables.

1. Quickly review kinesthetic, aural, and visual stages.
2. T: "When we hear one sound lasting for two beats we can call it 'ta-ah.'"
3. T sings the target phrase with "loo" and individuals echo-sing with rhythm syllables.
4. Repeat the third step with related patterns from known songs.

Notate What You Hear
T presents notation for new sound.

1. T: "We can use a half note to represent a sound that lasts for two beats. A half note has a note head and a stem."

Teaching Strategies: Grades 1 Through 5

2. "Our second phrase of 'Here Comes a Bluebird' looks like this; we can read it using our rhythm syllables."

$\frac{2}{4}$ ♩ | ♫ ♫ | ♩ ♩ | ♩ 𝄾 |

3. "When we write the target phrase, we can write using traditional rhythm notation or stick notation."

$\frac{2}{4}$ ♩ | ♫ ♫ | ♩ ♩ | ♩ 𝄾 |

4. "We can read this rhythm pattern using our rhythm syllables."
5. T sings rhythm syllables while pointing to the heartbeats; Ss echo-sing using rhythm syllables while pointing to the heartbeats.
6. "We can count with numbers."
7. T may also explain the "tie" by writing two tied quarter notes to represent the half note.

Assimilative Phase: Practice Music Skills

Aural Practice

These skills should be practiced independently from visual practice

Singing

- T sings known melodies with words and Ss echo-sing with rhythm syllables.
  T: "I sing the words; you sing rhythm syllables."
  T: "Hey, diddledum a day day day."
  Ss: "*ta-ah ta di ta di ta ta ta* (rest)."
  T: "Brother John, brother John."
  Ss: "*ta ta ta-ah ta ta ta-ah.*"
  T: "Who's that tapping at the window?"
  Ss: "*ta-ah ta-ah ta di ta di ta ta.*"
  T: "Who's that knocking at the door?"
  Ss: "*ta-ah ta-ah ta di ta di ta* (rest)."
- Ss read from T's model.
  T: "I'll clap a rhythm; you echo rhythm syllables."
- Ss sing known melodies with rhythm syllables and keep the beat.
- Ss sing known melodies with rhythm syllables and conduct.
- T sings known and unknown motifs and Ss sing back with rhythm syllables.

Part Work

1. T uses the target phrase as an ostinato to accompany a known song.
2. Combine the target phrase as an ostinato as well as another motif from the song so that you are using two ostinatos at the same time.
3. Clap a rhythm; Ss follow in canon after two beats.
4. Ss perform a two-part rhythmic reading exercise. Group 1 performs the upper part and group 2 the lower part. Switch.
5. Ss perform a two-part rhythmic reading exercise. They perform the upper part with right hand and lower part with left hand.

Kodály Today

Improvisation Activities
1. Ss improvise an ostinato that incorporates the new rhythmic pattern.
2. T claps and says the rhythm syllables in a question phrase that uses new pattern, and Ss give an answer.
3. One S claps and says the rhythm syllables in a question phrase that uses new pattern, and another S gives an answer.
4. One S improvises a four-beat pattern. The next S begins a four-beat improvisation with the last two beats from the first S.

Inner Hearing
1. T sings known fragments of songs, and Ss sing back with rhythm syllables and clapping.
2. T sings known fragments of songs, and Ss sing back with rhythm syllables and conducting.

Visual Practice
These skills may be practiced visually. They should not take place without recourse to aural practice.

Reading Activities
- Change one song to another. Ss read and clap the rhythm of the second phrase of "Here Comes a Bluebird" (written on the board). T changes one beat at a time on the board, and Ss clap each change until the eight-beat rhythm is changed to the first eight beats of "Who's That Tapping at the Window?" Ss clap and say the rhythm and identifies the song. Sing with words and rhythm syllables. (Keep at mind that at this stage Ss are reading notation patterns and keeping the beat or clapping the rhythm—not conducting. Duple and quadruple meter are often fluctuating in performance practice. We choose not to introduce the concept of quadruple meter until the end of second grade. You may choose otherwise.
- Ss read in traditional notation. T has "Are You Sleeping?" rhythm on the board in traditional notation, and Ss point and sing with rhythm syllables.
- Ss read in canon. T writes the rhythm of "Are You Sleeping?" on the board; Ss read and clap in canon simultaneously. They perform in canon using two different instruments.
- Ss match song titles to a matching rhythm. T lists the titles of a group of songs on the board that contain half notes. Ss match rhythm patterns associated with these songs to the song titles. These songs all have phrases that contain a half note:
"Here Comes a Bluebird"
"Knock the Cymbals"
"Are You Sleeping?"

- Sing and conduct all of these songs.

Inner Hearing
- Ss recognize familiar songs from T's clapping.
- T sings known fragments of songs, and Ss sing back with rhythm syllables and keep the beat.
- T sings a song on a neutral syllable and gives Ss four flash cards with rhythm patterns. Ss must identify the song and arrange flash cards in the correct order.

Memory
- Ss read an unknown song with rhythm syllables and clap the rhythm. T erases four beats each time, and Ss memorize.
- Ss read an unknown song with rhythm syllables and conduct. T erases four beats each time, and S memorize.

Writing Activities
- T sings the first phrase of "Are You Sleeping?" and Ss sing the phrase back to the T using rhythm syllables. One S writes the rhythm on the board.
- Ss identifies "Knock the Cymbals" from T's clapping and writes rhythm for each phrase. T invites one S to write the last phrase on the board.
- Ss sing "Who's That Tapping?" on "loo"; T claps the rhythm while one S pats the beat. Select four individuals to echo-sing an eight-beat phrase with rhythm names. Direct each S to write his or her phrase on the board.
- Ss write melodies using a tie instead of a half note.
- Introduce the half-note rest.
- Ss write the rhythm of a known listening example through dictation. Class reviews "In the Hall of the Mountain King" from *Peer Gynt* by Grieg and writes these rhythms using this procedure:
Play or sing the music to be written for dictation.
Ss sing the phrase and tap the beat.
Ss sing the phrase and clap the rhythm.
Ss sing the phrase with rhythm syllables.
Ss memorize the musical example.
Simultaneously sing and write the phrase using stick notation.

Improvisation Activities
- Question and answer. T uses the first eight beats of "Who's That Tapping at the Window?" as a rhythmic question on the board, and Ss clap back any possible rhythmic answers. Their answers must contain at least one half note.
- Ss read flashcards in stick notation as a class. They clap flashcards, creating a new rhythm if they are presented with a blank card.

Kodály Today

- Flashcard improvisation. T puts four flashcards on the board. Ss are asked to choose one and clap it as an answer to T's question. Eventually, T takes away flashcards and Ss improvise an original answer.
- One S claps a question phrase and chants rhythm syllables; another S chooses an answering phrase from four patterns on the board. One phrase should be only four heart beats.
- T writes a known folksong in traditional rhythmic notation but leaves out four beats. Ss read and clap the rhythm, and one improvises four-beat rhythms that use new rhythm pattern for the missing measure.

Part Work

- T divides the class into two groups. Group 1 sings the song with solfège and hand signs, and group 2 taps a rhythmic ostinato that is read from notation.
- Ss read a known song with rhythm syllables, and clap the rhythm. Divide the class into two groups and perform the activity in canon after two beats.
- Ss read a known song with rhythm syllables, and conduct. Divide the class into two groups and perform the activity in canon after two beats.
- Ss read a known song with rhythm syllables while tapping the rhythm with the left hand, and conducting with the right hand. Divide the class into two groups and perform the activity in canon after two beat.
- Ss read a known song with rhythm syllables, and clap the rhythm. Divide the class into two groups; one group performs the activity from the beginning of the song, and the other from the end.
- Ss read a known song with rhythm syllables, and conduct. Divide the class into two groups; one group performs the activity from the beginning of the song, and the other from the end.
- Ss read a known song with rhythm syllables while tapping the rhythm with the left hand and conducting with the right hand. Divide the class into two groups; one group performs the activity from the beginning of the song and the other from the end.
- Ss sing a known song and clap the rhythm of another well- known song simultaneously.
- Ss sing a known song, tap a rhythm from traditional rhythmic notation with the right hand, and tap an ostinato with the left hand.

Listening Activities

- "Aase's Death," no. 11 from *Peer Gynt Suite,* Op. 46, by Edvard Grieg (1843–1907). The work uses for note values the quarter note, eighth note, half note, and quarter rest.
- Rondo No. 1 for piano by Béla Bartók (1881–1945). Themes A, B, and C use quarter notes, eighth notes, half notes, and quarter rest.

Teaching Strategies: Grades 1 Through

- Allegretto (Romanze) from Symphony No. 85, "La Reine," by Joseph Haydn (1732–1809).
- "The Great Gate of Kiev," from *Pictures at an Exhibition*, by Modest Mussorgsky (1839–1881).
- "A Short Story," Op. 27, Book 1, No. 13, by Dmitry Kabalevsky (1904–1987). Change the rhythm of "Blue" into the rhythm of "A Short Story."
- "Study for Left Hand," by Béla Bartók (1881–1945), in *For Children*, eighty-five pieces originally in four volumes (revised Boosey & Hawkes, 1947). Uses a half note tied to a quarter note and other half notes. Also uses half note rests in the left hand.

Assessment
- Ss sing focus song with rhythm syllables _____.
- Ss read focus song from notation with rhythm syllables.

Sight-Reading Materials
- Micheál Houlahan and Philip Tacka. *Sound Thinking: Music for Sight-Singing and Ear Training*. New York: Boosey & Hawkes, 1991. Vol. I, pp. 33–56.
- Denise Bacon, *50 Two-Part Exercises*, no.4.
- Zoltán Kodály. *Kodály Choral Library: 333 Elementary Exercises*. London: Boosey & Hawkes, 1963. See no. 89 for reading the half note rest.

Here are four teaching strategies, Table 6.9 for *re*, Table 6.10 for sixteenth notes, Table 6.11 for the major pentatonic scale, and Table 6.12 for simple quadruple meter.

Table 6.9 Teaching Strategy for Introducing the Second Degree of the Pentatonic Scale

Element	Concept	Focus Song	Present Syllables	Theory	Traditional Notation	Practice	Additional Songs
Second degree of the pentatonic scale	Pitch between *mi* and *do*	"Hot Cross Buns"	*re*	Pentatonic trichord *mi-re-do*	*re* on different staff placements	Half note ♩	"Bow Wow Wow"; "All Around the Buttercup"; "Rocky Mountain"; "Ida Red"; "Button You Must Wander"

Teaching Strategy for Sixteenth Notes

Element	Concept	Focus Song	Present Syllables	Theory	Traditional Notation	Practice	Additional Songs
Four sixteenth notes	Four sounds on a beat	"Paw Paw Patch"	*Takadimi*	♬♬ ♩♩♩♩	♬♬	*do* pentatonic triad	"Dinah"; "Dance Josey"; "Old Brass Wagon"; "Tideo"; "Kookaburra"

Table 6.11 Teaching Strategy for a Major Pentatonic Scale

Element	Concept	Focus Song	Present Syllables	Theory	Traditional Notation	Practice	Additional Songs
Major pentatonic scale	Five pitches *do re mi so la* with a skip between *mi* and *so*; ends on *do*	"Rocky Mountain"	*do, re, mi, so, la*	Scale	*do-re-mi-so-la* written on different staff placements	♬♬	"Cut the Cake"; "Knock the Cymbals"; "Button You Must Wander"

Table 6.12 Teaching Strategy for Four-Beat Meter

Element	Concept	Focus Song	Present Syllables	Theory	Traditional Notation	Practice	Additional Songs
Simple quadruple Time signature	Pattern of four beats, one strong and three weak beats within a measure	"Are You Sleeping?"		Bar lines; measures; double bar lines; time signature	$\frac{4}{4}$	*do, re, mi, so, la* *do* pentatonic scale	"Knock the Cymbals"; "Button You Must Wander"

Focus Songs for Grade 2

"Bow Wow Wow" can be a focus song for introducing the tonic note of the major pentatonic scale *do* (Fig. 6.19).

Fig. 6.19 "Bow Wow Wow": Focus Song for Introducing the Tonic Note of the Major Pentatonic Scale *do*

Bow, wow, wow, whose dog art thou? Lit-tle Tom-my Tuck-er's dog bow, wow, wow.

"Here Comes a Bluebird" can be a focus song for half note (Fig. 6.20).

Fig. 6.20 "Here Comes a Bluebird": Focus Song for Half Note

♩ = 104

Here comes a blue-bird through the _ win-dow, hey, did-dle-dum a day day day.

Take a lit-tle? part-ner hop in the gar-den, hey, did-dle-dum a day day day.

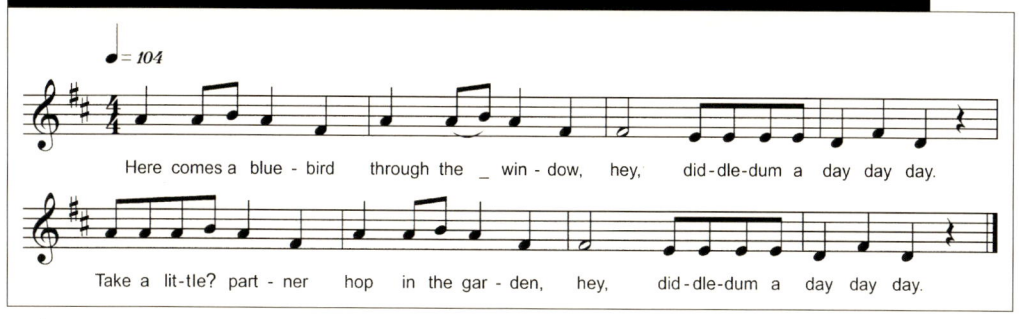

"Hot Cross Buns" can be a focus song for introducing the second degree of the major pentatonic scale *re* (Fig. 6.21).

Fig. 6.21 "Hot Cross Buns": Focus Song for Introducing the Second Degree of the Major Pentatonic Scale *re*

Hot cross buns, hot cross buns, one a pen-ny, two a pen-ny, hot cross buns.

"Paw Paw Patch" can be a focus song for introducing the sixteenth notes (Fig. 6.22).

Fig. 6.22 "Paw Paw Patch": Focus Song for Introducing the Sixteenth Notes

Where, oh where is pret-ty lit-tle Su-sie?

Where, oh where is pre-ty lit-tle Su-sie?

Where, oh where is pret-ty lit-tle Su-sie?

Way down yon-der in the paw paw patch.

...tain" can be a focus song for the major pentatonic scale (Fig. 6.23).

Fig. 6.23 "Rocky Mountain": Focus Song for the Major Pentatonic Scale

Rock-y moun-tain, rock-y moun-tain, rock-y moun-tain high,
When you're on that rock-y moun-tain, hang your head and cry.
Do, do, do, do, do re-mem-ber me,
Do, do, do, do, do re-mem-ber me.

"Are You Sleeping?" can be a focus song for four-beat meter (Fig. 6.24).

Fig. 6.24 "Are You Sleeping?": Focus Song for Four-Beat Meter

Are you sleep-ing, are you sleep-ing,
Broth-er John, Broth-er John?
Morn-ing bells are ring-ing, morn-ing bells are ring-ing,
Ding, ding, dong, ding, ding, dong.

Grade 3 Teaching Strategies

In third grade, we deal with seven musical concepts. We alternate between rhythmic concepts and melodic concepts throughout the year.

1. Teaching strategy for an eighth note followed by two sixteenth notes

2. Teaching strategy for *low la*
3. Teaching strategy for two sixteenth notes followed by an eighth note
4. Teaching strategy for *low so*
5. Teaching strategy for internal upbeat
6. Teaching strategy for *high do*
7. Teaching strategy for external upbeat

Grade 3, Teaching Strategy 1, for an Eighth Note Followed by Two Sixteenth Notes

Table 6.13 shows the key components that need to be included in the eighth note followed by two sixteenth notes teaching strategy.

Table 6.13

Element	Concept	Focus Song	Present Syllables	Theory	Traditional Notation	Practice	Additional Songs
Eighth note followed by two sixteenth notes	Three sounds on a beat, not evenly distributed; the first sound longer than the last two sounds	"Fed My Horse"	ta dimi	Sixteenth note subdivisions of the beat	♪♬	*do* pentatonic	"Ida Red"; "Mama Buy Me a Chiney Doll"; "How Many Miles to Babylon"; "Sailing O'er the Ocean"; "Chickalalelo"; "Skip to My Loo"; "Hogs in the Cornfield"; "Debka Hora"

Cognitive Phase: Preparation

Internalize Music Through Kinesthetic Activities

1. Ss sing "Fed My Horse" and pat the beat.
2. Ss sing "Fed My Horse" and clap the rhythm.
3. Ss sing "Fed My Horse" and point to a representation of the target rhythm on the board (Fig.6.25).

Kodály Today

Fig. 6.25 "San Serafin"

Fed my horse in a pop-lar trough, fed my horse in a pop-lar trough,
Fed my horse in a pop-lar trough. And then caught the whoop-ing cough.
Coy ma-lin-dow, Kill-ko, kill-ko. Coy ma-lin-dow, Kill-ko me.

4. Ss sing "Fed My Horse"; step the beat and clap the rhythm.
5. Have two Ss perform the song on rhythm instruments. One performs the beat, and one performs the rhythm.

Describe What You Hear

1. T assesses kinesthetic awareness: Ss sing "Fed My Horse" and walk the beat.
2. T and Ss sing phrase 2 on "loo" while keeping the beat before each question.
3. One S determines the number of beats in the target phrase. T: "Andy, how many beats did we tap?" (four)
4. S determines the number of sounds on each beat. T: "Andy, which beat had one sound?" (four) T: "Andy, how many sounds are on beat 3?" (two) T: "Andy, how many sounds are on beat 1?" (two) T: "Andy, how many sounds did we sing on beat 2?" (three)
5. S describes the sounds on beat 2. T: "Were the sounds on beat 2 even or uneven?" (uneven) T: "Describe these sounds using the words *long* and *short*." (long short short)
6. T sings "Fed My Horse" as follows and S echo:
   ta di long short short *ta di ta*
7. Small groups and individuals echo-sing with T.
8. All Ss sing phrases 1 and 2 as *tadi long short short tadi ta.*

Create a Visual Representation of What You Hear

1. Assess kinesthetic and aural awareness by allowing the class to perform several of the kinesthetic and aural awareness activities.
2. T hums the target phrase with a neutral syllable and asks Ss to create a visual representation of the target phrase. They may use manipulatives. T: "Pick up what you need to recreate what you heard" or "Draw what you heard." T assesses Ss' level of understanding.
3. Ss share their representations with each other.

4. T invites one S to the board to share a representation with the class. If necessary, corrections to the representation can be made by reviewing the aural awareness questions.
5. Ss sing the first phrase of "Fed My Horse" with a neutral syllable and point to their representation, and then sing with known elements: *ta di "long short short" ta di ta.*
6. Ss determine the solfège syllables for the first four phrases of "Fed My Horse."

Associative Phase: Presentation

Label the Sound
T presents new rhythm syllable.

1. Assess the kinesthetic and aural awareness and visual awareness activities with the focus song "Fed My Horse."
2. T: "We call three sounds on a beat where the first is long and the second and third are short *ta---di-mi.*"
3. T sings the target phrase of "Fed My Horse" with rhythm syllables. Ss echo with rhythm syllables while clapping the rhythm.
   ta di   ta di mi ta di   ta
4. T sings the target phrase of "Fed My Horse" with text; Ss echo with rhythm syllables while clapping the rhythm.
5. T echo-sings with at least eight individuals.

Notate What You Hear
T presents notation for new sound.

1. T: "When the beat is a quarter note, we can use an eighth note followed by two sixteenth notes to represent three sounds unevenly spaced on a beat."
2. "Our first phrase of 'Fed My Horse' looks like this in traditional rhythm notation:" 2/4 ♫ ♫ |♫ ♩ |
3. "Our first phrase of 'Fed My Horse' looks like this in stick notation:"
   2/4 ♫ ♫ |♫ ♩ |
4. "We can read this rhythm pattern using rhythm syllables."
5. It is important to notate examples using a time signature and practice reading these examples with both rhythm syllables and counting with numbers.

Assimilative Phase: Practice Music Skills

Aural Practice
These skills should be practiced independently from visual practice.

Singing
- T sings known melodies with words and Ss echo-sing with rhythm syllables. T: "I sing the words; you sing rhythm syllables."

Kodály Today

T: "Fed my horse in a poplar trough."
Ss: "*ta di ta di mi ta di ta.*"
T: "Down the road and across the creek."
Ss: "*ta di ta di mi ta di ta.*"
T: "Mama buy me a chiney doll."
Ss: "*ta di ta di mi ta di ta.*"
T: "How many miles to Babylon?"
Ss: "*ta di mi ta di ta di ta.*"
- T hums motifs from known songs and Ss sing back with rhythm syllables.
- T: "I'll clap a rhythm; you echo rhythm syllables."

Inner Hearing
- T sings known fragments of songs and Ss sing back with rhythm syllables and clapping.
- T sings known fragments of songs and Ss sing back with rhythm syllables and conducting.

Part Work
- T directs Ss to sing focus song or the additional songs and keep the beat.
- T directs Ss to sing focus song or the additional songs and keep a simple rhythmic ostinato.

Improvisation Activities
- Ss improvise an ostinato that incorporates the new rhythmic pattern.
- T claps and sings a question phrase using the new rhythm pattern; S respond with an answer phrase that uses the new rhythm pattern.
- S claps and says the rhythm syllables in a question phrase that uses the new pattern, and another S provides an answer.

Visual Practice
These skills may be practiced visually. They should not take place without recourse to aural practice.

Reading from Hand Signs
- Ss read from T hand signs known motifs that incorporate the new rhythmic pattern.
- transforms the target pattern into four-beat patterns found in the song material.

Reading Activities
- Ss read target motif from traditional rhythmic notation with rhythm syllables.
- Ss read a known song with rhythm syllables, and clap the rhythm.
- Ss read a known song with rhythm syllables, and conduct.
- Ss read a known song with rhythm syllables while tapping the rhythm with the left hand and conducting with the right hand.

Teaching Strategies: Grades 1 Through 5

- and Ss transform target motif into a related pattern.
- Ss read an unknown song with rhythm syllables, and clap the rhythm.
- Ss read an unknown song with rhythm syllables, and conduct.
- and Ss transform a known folksong into another folksong.
- Ss read the rhythm of a known song, and play on classroom percussion instruments.
- Ss read the rhythm of "San Serafín del Monte" (Fig. 6.26) and play the rhythm on an instrument.

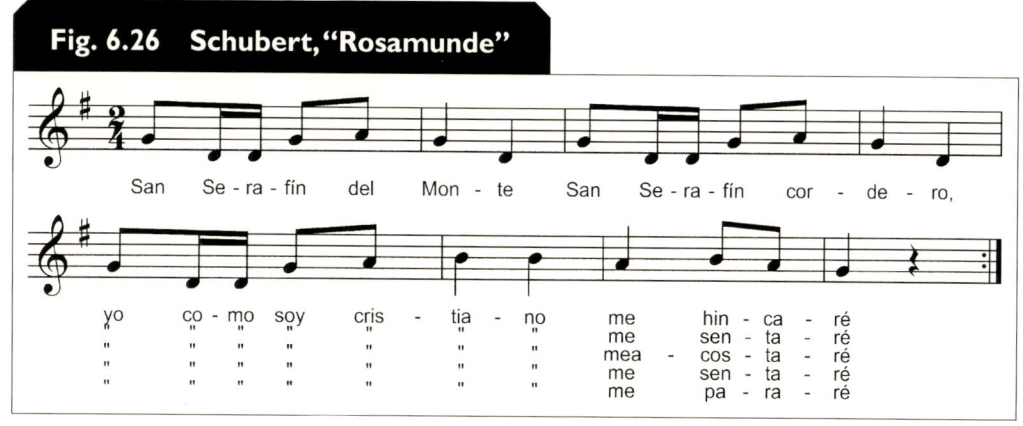

Fig. 6.26 Schubert, "Rosamunde"

San Se-ra-fín del Mon-te San Se-ra-fín cor-de-ro,
yo co-mo soy cris-tia-no me hin-ca-ré
" " " " " " " me sen-ta-ré
" " " " " " " mea-cos-ta-ré
" " " " " " " me sen-ta-ré
" " " " " " " me pa-ra-ré

Note: Reprinted from *Vamos a Cantar* with permission of the Kodály Institute at Capital University.

Inner Hearing
- Ss recognize familiar songs when T performs the rhythm.
- T sings known fragments of songs, and Ss sing back with rhythm syllables while keeping the beat.
- T sings a song on a neutral syllable and gives Ss four flash cards with rhythm patterns; Ss must identify the song and arrange flash cards in the correct order.

Memory
- Ss read an unknown song with rhythm syllables and clap the rhythm. T erases four beats each time, and Ss memorize.
- Ss read an unknown song with rhythm syllables and conduct. T erases four beats each time, and Ss memorize.

Writing Activities
- Ss write phrases 1 and 2 of "Fed My Horse" in stick notation.
- Ss write phrase 1 of "Ida Red" using traditional rhythm notation and perform it on rhythm instruments.
- Ss add bar lines to a given rhythm that includes the new pattern.
- T hums a new melody; Ss must write the rhythm from memory.
- Ss fill in the missing rhythms for a piece of music that is written in traditional rhythmic notation.

Kodály Today

Improvisation Activities
- T claps a question phrase and chants rhythm syllables; Ss choose an answering phrase from four patterns on the board. One phrase should be written as four blank beats to encourage Ss to create their own pattern.
- S claps a question phrase and chants rhythm syllables; another S chooses an answering phrase from four patterns on the board. One phrase should be written as four blank beats to encourage Ss to create their own pattern.
- T writes a known folksong in traditional rhythmic notation but leaves out four beats. Ss read and clap the rhythm, and one S improvises four-beat rhythms that use the new rhythm pattern for the missing measure.
- Ss improvise an ostinato that incorporates the new rhythmic pattern.
- T claps and sings a question phrase using the new rhythm pattern; Ss respond with an answer phrase that uses the new rhythm pattern.
- S claps and says the rhythm syllables in a question phrase that uses the new pattern, and another S provides an answer.
- Ss change rhythm of a first or second grade song.
- S improvises a four-beat pattern. The next S begins a four-beat improvisation with the last two beats used by the first S.

Part Work
- uses the target phrase as an ostinato to accompany a known song.
- combines the target phrase as an ostinato as well as another motif from the song so that two ostinati are used at the same time.
- T claps a rhythm and Ss follow in canon after two beats.
- Ss perform a two-part rhythmic reading exercise. Group 1 performs the upper part and group 2 the lower part. Switch.
- Ss perform a two-part rhythmic reading exercise, the upper part with the right hand and the lower part with the left hand.
- T divides the class into two groups. Group 1 sings the song with solfège and hand signs, and group 2 taps a rhythmic ostinato that is read from notation.
- Ss read a known song with rhythm syllables and clap the rhythm. T divides the class into two groups, to perform the activity in canon after two beats.
- Ss read a known song with rhythm syllables, and conduct. T divides the class into two groups, to perform the activity in canon after two beats.
- Ss read a known song with rhythm syllables while tapping the rhythm with the left hand and conducting with the right hand. T divides the class into two groups, to perform the activity in canon after two beats.
- Ss read a known song with rhythm syllables and clap the rhythm. T divides the class into two groups; one group performs the activity from the beginning of the song and the other from the end.
- Ss read a known song with rhythm syllables, and conduct. T divides the class into two groups; one group performs the activity from the beginning of the song, and the other from the end.

Teaching Strategies: Grades 1 Through 5

- Ss read a known song with rhythm syllables while tapping the rhythm with their left hand and conducting with their right hand. As a challenge, T can divide the class into two groups; one group performs the activity from the beginning of the song and the other in retrograde (from the end).
- Ss sing a known song and clap the rhythm of another well-known song simultaneously.
- Ss sing a known song, tap a rhythm from traditional rhythmic notation with the right hand, and tap an ostinato with the left hand.

Listening Activities

- "Badinerie," from Sonata in b minor BWV 1067, by Johann Sebastian Bach (1685–1750); first phrase.
- *Rosamunde*, ballet music in G major, by Franz Schubert (1797–1828); themes A, B, and C. Theme A (Fig. 6.27).

Fig. 6.27

Kodály Today

[rhythmic notation in 2/4 time - Theme A]

Theme B:

[rhythmic notation in 2/4 time]

Theme C:

[rhythmic notation in 2/4 time]

- Sonata in D minor, K. 64, by Domenico Scarlatti (1685–1757); this piece includes ornamentations that change some of the note values.

Sight-Reading Materials
- Micheál Houlahan and Philip Tacka. *Sound Thinking: Music for Sight-Singing and Ear Training* (Boosey & Hawkes, 1991). Vol. I, pp. 57–70.

Grade 3, Teaching Strategy 2, for *low la*

Table 6.14 provides the key components that need to be included in the *low la* teaching strategy.

Table 6.14

Element	Concept	Focus Song	Present Syllables	Theory	Traditional Notation	Practice	Additional Songs
low la	Pitch a skip lower than *do*	"Phoebe in Her Petticoat"	low la	low la may function as a tonic note; extended pentatonic scale		♫	"Jim Along Josie"; "Old Mr. Rabbit"; "Poor Little Kitty Cat"

Cognitive Phase: Preparation

Internalize Music Through Kinesthetic Activities

1. Ss sing "Phoebe in Her Petticoat" (Fig. 6.28) and point to a representation of the melodic contour at the board.

Teaching Strategies: Grades 1 Through 5

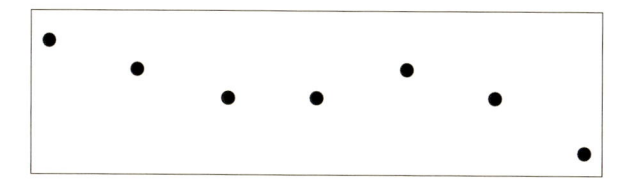

FIG. 6.28

2. Sing "Phoebe in Her Petticoat" and show the melodic contour for the target phrase (phrase 1).
3. Sing "Phoebe in Her Petticoat" with rhythm syllables while showing the melodic contour.
4. Sing "Phoebe in Her Petticoat" in canon.

Describe What You Hear

1. T assesses kinesthetic awareness.
2. T keeps the beat and sings the target phrase on "loo" before asking each question.
3. Ss determine the number of beats. T: "Andy, how many beats did we tap?" (four)
4. Ss determine which beat has the lowest pitch. T: "Andy, which beat had the lowest pitch? (beat 4) T: "Let's sing the phrase on 'loo' but sing 'low' for the lowest note."
5. Ss determine the solfège of known elements and sing "low" for the new note. T: "Sing the first four pitches with solfège syllables and hand signs." (*mi re do do*) Ss identify and sing the remaining solfège syllables of the target phrase, singing "low" on beat 4 and pointing low on beat 4. T: "Is our new sound a step or a skip below *do*?" (skip) Ss sing as a whole group, and then T may select individuals to sing the target phrase.

Create a Visual Representation of What You Hear

1. T assesses kinesthetic and aural awareness by allowing the class to perform several of the kinesthetic and aural awareness activities.
2. T hums the target phrase with a neutral syllable and asks Ss to create a visual representation of the target phrase. They may use manipulatives. T: "Pick up what you need to recreate what you heard" or "Draw what you heard." T assesses Ss' level of understanding.
3. Ss share their representations with each other.
4. T invites one S to the board to share a representation with the class. If necessary, corrections to the representation can be made by reviewing the aural awareness questions.
5. Ss sing the first phrase of "Phoebe in Her Petticoat" with a neutral syllable and point to their representation, and then sing with known elements: *mi re do do re do low*.
6. Ss identify the rhythm for the first phrase of "Phoebe in Her Petticoat."

Kodály Today

Associative Phase: Presentation

Label the Sound
T presents new solfège syllables.

1. T reviews the kinesthetic and aural awareness and visual awareness activities with the focus song "Phoebe in Her Petticoat."
2. T: "When we hear a pitch a skip below *do* we call it *low la*." T shows the hand sign.
  [
3. T sings phrase 1 of "Phoebe in Her Petticoat," with solfège syllables and Ss echo-sing. (*mi-re-do-do-re-do-la,*)
4. T hums target phrase and Ss echo-sing with solfège and hand signs.

Notate What You Hear
T presents notation for new pitch.

1. Present the position of *la,* on the steps (Fig. 6.29).

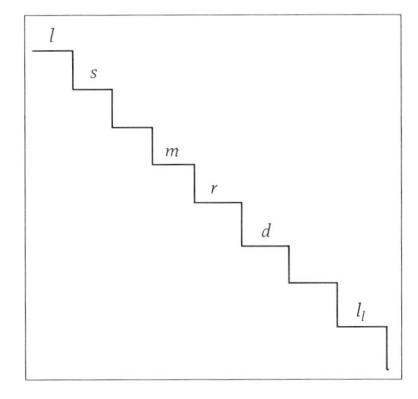

FIG. 6.29

2. T points to target phrase on tone ladder or steps and Ss sing with solfège and hand signs.
3. T presents the target phrase of "Phoebe in Her Petticoat" with rhythmic notation and solfège; Ss sing with solfège and hand signs.
4. T identifies *do–low la* as being a skip of a third.

   $\frac{2}{4}$ ♫ ♫ | ♫♩ |
   mi re do do   re do la,

5. Present the Rule of Placement for *low la* on the staff (consider using the finger staff). If *low la* is in a space, *do* is in the space above; if *low la* is on a line, *do* is on the line above.
6. Present the target phrase of "Phoebe in Her Petticoat" in staff notation. Figure 6.30 is an example of the target phrase written in F-*do*.

Fig. 6.30 "Phoebe" Fragment

Assimilative Phase: Practice Music Skills

Aural Practice
These skills should be practiced independently from visual practice.

Singing
- T sings known melodies with words and Ss echo-sing with solfège syllables.
  T: "I sing the words; you sing the hand signs."
  T: "Phoebe in her petticoat."
  Ss: "*mi re do do re do la,.*"
  T: "Hey Jim along Jim along Josie."
  Ss: "*so so so mi do re re do la, do.*"
  T: "Eating all my cabbage."
  Ss: "*mi mi do la, la, do.*"
  T: "Poor little feller."
  Ss: "*re re do la, do.*"
- Teacher sings motifs on "loo," and Ss echo with solfège syllables.

Inner Hearing
- Recognize familiar songs from T's hand signs.

Singing Intervals
- T sings each interval of the pentatonic tone set on "loo." Ss sing the intervals with solfège syllables and hand signs and identify whether the interval is a skip or a step.
- T plays intervals on the piano melodically or harmonically and one S identifies the intervals as a step or a skip.
- T practices related patterns with Ss that include *low la* with hand signs and solfège syllables.

Part Work
- Use the target phrase as an ostinato.
- Ss echo-sing four beat patterns provided by T with solfège syllables and hand signs, but they begin singing at beat 3 of T's pattern.
- Ss sing the song in canon, if it is a pentatonic song.
- Ss sing the song in canon with a rhythmic ostinato.
- Ss sing the song in canon with a melodic ostinato.
- Ss sing a song and perform two rhythmic ostinati at the same time.

Kodály Today

- Ss sing a major pentatonic song and T accompanies with a drone made up of *do* or *do-so* played on an instrument.
- Ss sing a minor pentatonic song and T accompanies with a drone made up of *low la* or *low la–mi* played on an instrument.

Improvisation Activities

These improvisation suggestions are for the major pentatonic scale using *low la* and not for the minor pentatonic scale.

- T sings a music question with solfège syllables and hand signs, Ss give an answer. Question ends on *so* and after several activities ends on re. Answer ends on *do*.
- S sings a music question with solfège syllables and hand signs and another S gives an answer.
- S improvises a four-beat pattern. The next S begins a four-beat improvisation with the last two beats from that of the first S.

Visual Practice

These skills may be practiced visually. They should not take place without recourse to aural practice.

Reading from Hand Signs
- Ss reads from T hand signs.
- T transforms the target pattern into basic four-beat patterns found in the song material.

Reading Activities
- Ss read "Phoebe in Her Petticoat" in stick notation and staff notation.
- Have Ss play on instruments the first phrase of "Phoebe in Her Petticoat" from staff notation.
- Ss read "Yangtze Boatman's Chanty" in stick notation and in staff notation.
- T changes several measures of the song "Phoebe in Her Petticoat" so that it becomes a reading exercise.
- Ss identify the intervals in a reading exercise as skips or steps.
- Ss read these melodic motifs from solfège or on the staff: *so-mi-re-do-la; la-so-mi-re-do-low la*.
- Ss read the skeleton of known songs (a song "skeleton" is created by deleting repeating notes or passing notes).
- Ss read in Zoltán Kodály's *Choral Library 333 Elementary Exercises* nos. 140, 142, 144, 152, 161, 164, 165, 280, 282, 287, 291, 292, and 295.

Teaching Strategies: Grades 1 Through 5

Inner Hearing
- Ss recognize familiar songs from T's hand signs.
- T sings known phrases of songs on a neutral syllable; Ss echo-sing the phrase with solfège syllables and hand signs.
- T sings a song on a neutral syllable and gives Ss four flash cards with melodic patterns, and Ss must identify the song and arrange flash cards in the correct order.
- Ss sing known songs but inner-hear the phrase containing the new target pattern.
- Ss sing known songs but inner-hear the phrase containing the new target pattern.
- Ss sing a song but have to inner-hear the song from a signal furnished by T. Ss sing the song aloud from a signal provided by T.

Memory
- Ss read an unknown song with solfège syllables and conduct. T erases four beats each time the song is performed and Ss memorize.
- Ss read in two parts from T's hand signs.

Writing Activities
- T writes the tone set of a known song on the board as one S or the class sings a known song with solfège syllables.
- Ss write the target pattern in stick or traditional rhythmic notation with solfège syllables.
- Ss write related patterns in stick and traditional rhythmic notation with solfège syllables.
- Ss fill the missing measures of a known song with the correct solfège syllables. T can provide the rhythm but not the syllables for the missing measure.
- T sings an unknown song and Ss fill in the missing measures with the correct rhythms and solfège.
- Ss transcribe a song written in rhythmic notation and solfège into staff notation.
- Ss transcribe a new melody written in rhythmic notation and solfège to the staff.
- Ss write the tone set of a pentatonic melody and play the notes on a pitched instrument (Fig. 6.31).

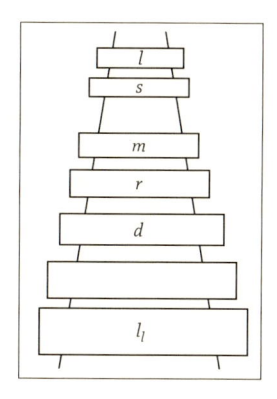

FIG. 6.31

Kodály Today

Improvisation Activities
- T sings a question phrase with solfège syllables and hand signs, and one S chooses an answering phrase from four patterns on the board. One phrase should be blank beats so Ss can create their own rhythm.
- T writes a known folksong in traditional rhythmic notation and solfège but leaves out four beats. Ss read with solfège and one S improvises four-beat melody that uses the new melodic note.
- Ss improvise a new melody to a given form and scale. For example, they compose a new melody using the form ABAB. T gives Ss the A phrase and they improvise the B phrase; the B phrase should end on *do*.

Part Work
- T divides the class into two groups. Group 1 sings the song with solfège syllables and hand signs, and group 2 taps a rhythmic ostinato that is read from notation.
- T divides the class into two groups. Group 1 sings the song with solfège syllables and hand signs, and group 2 sings a melodic ostinato that is read from notation.
- T divides the class into two groups. Group 1 sings the song with solfège syllables and hand signs, and group 2 sings a descant with solfège and hand signs that is read from notation.
- Ss read a known song with solfège syllables and hand signs. T divides the class into two groups and they perform the activity in canon after two beats, group 1 singing and group 2 clapping in canon.
- Ss read a known song with solfège syllables while conducting. T divides the class into two groups and they perform the activity in canon after two beats, group 1 singing and group 2 clapping in canon.
- Ss read a known song with solfège syllables while showing hand signs with the left hand and conducting with the right hand. T divides the class into two groups; group 1 performs the activity, and group 2 claps rhythm in canon after two beats.
- Ss sing a known song and clap the rhythm of another well-known song simultaneously.
- Ss sing a known song, tap a rhythm reading from traditional rhythmic notation with the right hand, and tap an ostinato with the left hand.

Intervals
- Class interval practice through echo singing and hand signs.
  T: "*la, do*."
  Ss: "That's a skip."
  T: "*do re*."

Ss: "That's a step."
T: "*re mi.*"
Ss: "That's a step."
T: "*mi so.*"
Ss: "That's a skip."
T: "*so la.*"
Ss: "That's a step."
T: "*la so.*"
Ss: "That's a step."
T: "*so mi.*"
Ss: "That's a skip."
T: "*mi re.*"
Ss: "That's a step."
T: "*re do.*"
Ss: "That's a step."
T: "*do la,.*"
Ss: "That's a step."

- Practice reading from hand signs typical melodic motifs such as *so-mi-re-do-la,; la-so-mi-re-do-la,.*
- Ss identify intervals from notation of known songs.
- Ss identify intervals from notation of unknown songs.

Listening Activities
"An Evening in the Village," from *Hungarian Sketches*, by Béla Bartók (1881–1945).

Sight-Reading Materials
Micheál Houlahan and Philip Tacka. *Sound Thinking: Music for Sight-Singing and Ear Training.* New York: Boosey & Hawkes, 1991. Vol. I, pp. 71–76.

Zoltán Kodály. *The Kodály Choral Library: 333 Elementary Exercises.* London: Boosey & Hawkes 1963, nos. 140, 142, 144, 152, 161, 164, and 165. Examples in an extended pentatonic scale are nos. 280, 282, 287, 291, 292, and 295. Examples exploring the *re–low la* interval are nos. 57, 58, 59, 60, 62, 64, 66, 73, 83, 86, 93, 94, 95, 96, 97, 98, 100, 102, 105, 106, 107, 108, 109, 111, 113, 115, 116, 118, 120, 121, 125, 127, 128, 129, 135, 136, and 138.

Two-Part Sight-Reading Exercises
Read exercises 22 and 36 from Denise Bacon's *Fifty Two-Part Exercises*.

Five teaching strategies are represented in the following tables: Table 6.15, two sixteenth notes followed by an eighth note; Table 6.16, *low so*; Table 6.17, internal upbeat; Table 6.18, *high do*; and Table 6.19 for an eighth-note external upbeat.

Kodály Today

Table 6.15   Teaching Strategy for Two Sixteenth Notes Followed by an Eighth Note

Element	Concept	Focus Song	Present Syllables	Theory	Traditional Notation	Practice	Additional Songs
Two sixteenth notes followed by an eighth note	Three sounds on a beat; not evenly distributed; the first two sounds shorter than the last sound	"Hogs in the Cornfield"	tika di	Two sixteenth notes followed by an eighth note	♫	la	"Over the River"; "Charlie"; "Hop Old Squirrel"; "Jim Along Josie"; "Skipping Rope Song"; "Sailing O'er the Ocean"

Table 6.16   Teaching Strategy for *low so* (s,)

Element	Concept	Focus Song	Present Syllables	Theory	Traditional Notation	Practice	Additional Songs
low so	Pitch a step lower than *low la*	"Dance Josey"	low so		low so on different staff placements	♫	"Sailing O'er the Ocean"; "Turn the Glasses Over"; "Old MacDonald"; "Walk Along John"

Table 6.17   Teaching Strategy for Internal Upbeats

Element	Concept	Focus Song	Present Syllables	Theory	Traditional Notation	Practice	Additional Songs
Single eighth note (internal upbeat)	Sound that occurs before a strong beat	"Old Mr. Rabbit"	Dependent on where the sound falls in relation to the beat	Internal upbeat		so	"Down Came a Lady"; "Bye Baby Bunting"; "Do, Do Pity My Case"

Table 6.18 Teaching Strategy for *high do* (*d'*)

Element	Concept	Focus Song	Present Syllables	Theory	Traditional Notation	Practice	Additional Songs
high do	Pitch a skip higher than *la*	"Hogs in the Cornfield"	high do	Octave; extended pentatonic scale	high do on different staff placements	Internal upbeat ♫	"Liza Jane"; "I've Lost the Farmer's Dairy Key"; "Riding in a Buggy"; "Tideo"

Table 6.19 Teaching Strategy for External Upbeats

Element	Concept	Focus Song	Present Syllables	Theory	Traditional Notation	Practice	Additional Songs
Eighth note external upbeat	Sound that precedes the strong beat at the beginning of a composition	"I've Lost the Farmer's Dairy Key"	Dependent on where the external upbeat falls in relation to the beat	External upbeat	Quarter and paired eighth notes and single eighth note	do'	"Shoes of John"; "Band of Angels"

Focus Songs for Grade 3

"Fed My Horse" can be a focus song for an eighth note followed by two sixteenth notes (Fig. 6.32).

Fig. 6.32 "Fed My Horse": Focus Song for an Eighth Note Followed by Two Sixteenth Notes

Fed my horse in a pop-lar trough, Fed my horse in a pop-lar trough, Fed my horse in a pop-lar trough. And then he caught the whoop-ing cough. Coy ma-lin-dow. Kill-ko, kill-ko Coy ma-lin-dow, Kill-ko me.

Kodály Today

"Phoebe in Her Petticoat" can be a focus song for *low la* (Fig. 6.33).

Fig. 6.33 "Phoebe": Focus Song for *low la*

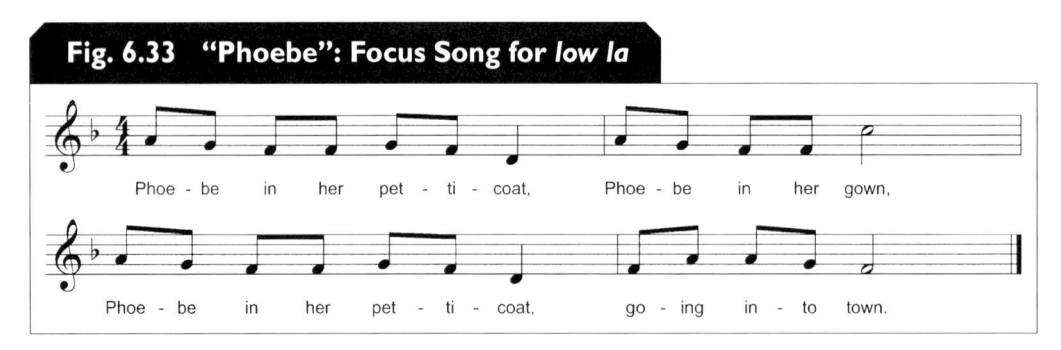

Phoe - be in her pet - ti - coat, Phoe - be in her gown,
Phoe - be in her pet - ti - coat, go - ing in - to town.

"Hogs in the Cornfield" can be a focus song for two sixteenth notes followed by an eighth note (Fig. 6.34).

Fig. 6.34 "Hogs in the Cornfield": Focus Song for Two Sixteenth Notes Followed by an Eighth Note

Hogs in the corn - field, cows chew-in' clo - ver. Tell them pret - ty gals I'm com-ing o - ver.

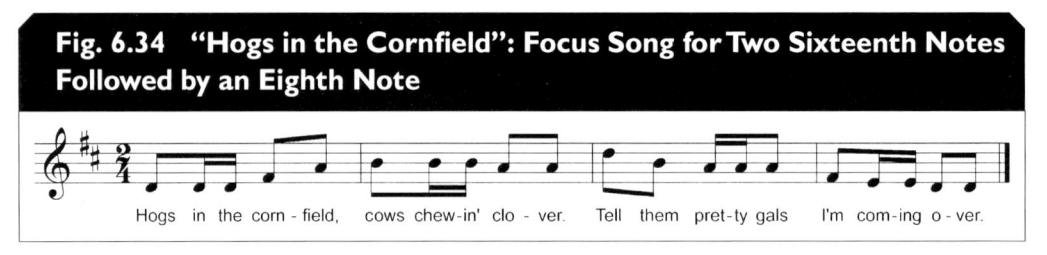

"Dance Josey" can be a focus song for *low so* (Fig. 6.35).

Fig. 6.35 "Dance Josey"

Chick-en in the fence post, can't dance Jo - sey, chick-en in the fence post, can't dance Jo - sey,
Chick-en in the fence post, can't dance Jo - sey, hel - lo Su - san Brown-y - o.

"Old Mr. Rabbit" can be a focus song for internal upbeat (Fig. 6.36).

Fig. 6.36 "Old Mr. Rabbit": Focus Song for Internal Upbeat

Old Mis - ter Rab - bit, you've got a migh - ty ha - bit
Of Jump-ing in my gar - den, and eat - ing all my cab - bage!

"Hogs in the Cornfield" can be a focus song for *high do* (Fig. 6.37).

Fig. 6.37 "Hogs in the Cornfield": Focus Song for *high do*

Hogs in the corn-field, cows chew-in' clo-ver. Tell them pret-ty gals I'm com-ing o-ver.

"I've Lost the Farmer's Dairy Key" can be a focus song for external upbeat (Fig. 6.38).

Fig. 6.38 "Farmer's Dairy Key": Focus Song for External Upbeat

*I've lost the far-mer's dai-ry key, I'm in some la-dy's gar-den.
Do, do, let me out, I'm in some la-dy's gar-den.*

Grade 4 Teaching Strategies

In grade 4, we suggest teaching seven concepts. The order alternates between rhythmic and melodic concepts.

1. Teaching strategy for syncopation
2. Teaching strategy for *la* pentatonic scale
3. Teaching strategy for dotted quarter followed by an eighth note
4. Teaching strategy for *fa*
5. Teaching strategy for three-beat meter
6. Teaching strategy for *ti*
7. Dotted eighth note followed by a sixteenth note

Grade 1, Teaching Strategy 1, for Syncopation

Table 6.20 presents the key components that need to be included in the syncopation teaching strategy.

Cognitive Phase: Preparation

Internalize Music Through Kinesthetic Activities
This kinesthetic procedure may be guided with nonverbal communication. T guides Ss to:

1. sing "Canoe Song" and perform the beat for the target phrase.
2. sing "Canoe Song" and clap the rhythm for the target phrase.

Kodály Today

Table 6.20

Element	Concept	Focus Song	Present Syllables	Theory	Traditional Notation	Practice	Additional Songs
Quarter and eighth notes	Three sounds unevenly distributed over two beats	"Canoe Song"	ta di---di	Syncopation	♫ ♪	high do	"Liza Jane"; "Riding in a Buggy"; "Land of the Silver Birch"; "Alabama Gal"; "Weevily Wheat"; "My Good Old Man"; "Dem Bones"; "John Kanaka Hill"; "Gully Rider"

3. Ss sing "Canoe Song" and point to a representation of the target phrase on the board (Fig. 6.39).

FIG. 6.39

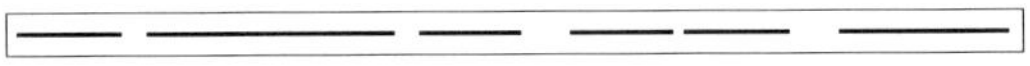

4. Ss sing "Canoe Song" and clap the ostinato:
   2/4 ♫ ♫ | ♩ ♩ :||
5. Ss sing the "Canoe Song." T performs beat and Ss perform rhythm. Switch.
6. T divides the class into two groups; one performs the beat and the other the rhythm while singing. Switch.
7. Ss sing "Canoe Song" while stepping the beat and clapping the text.
8. Ss sing "Canoe Song" while tapping the beat in one hand and rhythm in the other.

Describe What You Hear

1. T assesses kinesthetic awareness by allowing the class to perform several of the activities described above independently.
2. Sing the target phrase using a neutral syllable while performing the beat before asking each question.
3. Ss determine the number of beats in the phrase. T: "Andy, how many beats did you hear?" (four)

Teaching Strategies: Grades 1 Through 5

4. Ss determine the number of sounds on each beat. T: "Andy, which beat has one sound?" (beat 4) T: "Andy, how many sounds did you hear on beat three?" (two) T: "Andy, how many sounds did you hear on beats 1 and 2?" (three) T: "Andy, describe these three sounds." (short, long, short) T: "Let's sing the phrase with *short-long-short* and our rhythm syllables for beats 3 and 4." (*short-long-short-tadi-ta*)

Create a Visual Representation of What You Hear
1. T assesses kinesthetic and aural awareness by allowing the class to perform several of the kinesthetic and aural awareness activities.
2. T sings the target phrase with a neutral syllable and asks Ss to create a visual representation of the target phrase. They may use manipulatives. T: "Pick up what you need to recreate what you heard" or "Draw what you heard." T assesses Ss' level of understanding.
3. Ss share their representations with each other.
4. T invites one S to the board to share a representation with the class. If necessary, corrections to the representation can be made by reviewing the aural awareness questions.
5. Ss sing the first phrase of "Canoe Song" with a neutral syllable and point to their representation.
6. Once Ss have represented the rhythm pattern, they should place heartbeats under the representation to show the placement of the beat. This step can be done later during the presentation if it is too difficult at this time.
7. Ss may identify the solfège syllables of the target phrase (*mi mi re do la, la,*).

Associative Phase: Presentation

Describe What You Hear with Rhythm Syllables
1. T assesses the kinesthetic, aural awareness, and visual awareness activities with phrase 1 of "Canoe Song."
2. T: "When we hear three uneven sounds over two beats where the first is short, the second is long, and the third is short, we can label these sounds with our rhythm syllables *ta di---------di*."
3. T sings the target phrase of "Canoe Song" with rhythm syllables *ta di----di ta di ta*; Ss echo-sing with rhythm syllables while clapping the rhythm.
4. Ss perform the new rhythm with the beat.
5. Ss perform the new rhythm while conducting.
6. T sings a phrase of "Canoe Song" with text or neutral syllable; Ss echo with rhythm syllables while clapping the rhythm.

Notate What You Hear
1. T: "When the beat is equal to a quarter note, we can represent three sounds over two beats using the traditional notation:" ♫ ♪
   "Our target pattern will look like this:"

Kodály Today

$\frac{2}{4}$ ♫ ♪|♫ ♩ |
"When we write our target pattern we can use stick notation."

$\frac{2}{4}$ ♫ ♪|♫ ♩ |
"We can read our target pattern using rhythm syllables and clap the rhythm."

2. Ss read the rhythm of "Canoe Song" with rhythm syllables and clap the rhythm. Individual Ss sing and point to the rhythm of "Canoe Song" on the board as the class sings the song with rhythm syllables and claps the rhythm.
3. T shows Ss how to read with numbers for counting. T: "Sing the 'Canoe Song' with numbers for counting and conduct." Individuals sing and point to rhythm of "Canoe Song" on the board as the class sings the song with numbers and conducts.
4. T explains the concept of syncopation to Ss. T may present other syncopation patterns occurring on a beat.

Assimilative Phase: Practice Music Skills

Aural Practice
These skills should be practiced independently from visual practice.

Singing with Rhythm Syllables
1. Ss echo-sing four-beat melodic patterns containing new rhythm provided by T, with rhythm syllables and clapping the rhythm.
2. Ss echo-sing four-beat melodic patterns containing new rhythm provided by T, with rhythm syllables and conducting.
3. Ss sing "Canoe Round" with rhythm syllables and clap the rhythm.
4. Ss sing "Canoe Round" with rhythm syllables and conduct.
5. T sings motifs containing the new pattern and Ss sing back with rhythm syllables.

Inner Hearing
1. T sings known patterns of songs and Ss sing back with rhythm syllables and clapping.
2. T sings known fragments of songs and Ss sing back with rhythm syllables and conducting.
3. Ss inner-hear a known song while clapping an ostinato that includes a syncopation rhythm.

Part Work
1. Ss use the target phrase as an ostinato to accompany a known song.
2. Ss perform two ostinati to accompany a known song.
3. T claps a rhythm and Ss follow in canon after two beats.
4. Ss perform a two-part rhythmic reading exercise. Group 1 performs the upper part and group 2 the lower part. Switch.
5. Ss performs a two-part rhythmic reading exercise. They perform the upper part with the right hand and lower part with the left hand.

Improvisation Activities
1. T claps and says the rhythm syllables in a question phrase that uses a new pattern, and Ss give an answer.
2. One S claps and says the rhythm syllables in a question phrase that uses the new pattern, and another S gives an answer.
3. Ss change rhythm of a first or second grade song and use a syncopated pattern over two beats.
4. One S improvises a four-beat pattern. The next S begins a four-beat improvisation with the last two beats supplied by the first S.

Visual Practice
These skills may be practiced visually. They should not take place without recourse to aural practice.

Reading from Hand Signs
1. Ss sing known song from T's hand signs, to include the new rhythm pattern.
2. Ss sing known song from another S's hand signs, to include the new rhythm pattern.

Reading Activities
1. Ss read target motif from traditional rhythmic notation with rhythm syllables.
2. Ss read a known song with rhythm syllables and clap the rhythm.
3. Ss read a known song with rhythm syllables and conduct.
4. Ss read a known song with rhythm syllables while tapping the rhythm with the left hand and conducting with the right hand.
5. T and Ss transform target motif into a related pattern.
6. Ss read an unknown song with rhythm syllables and clap the rhythm.
7. Ss read the rhythm of an unknown song with rhythm syllables and conduct.
8. T and Ss transform a known folksong into another folksong.
9. Ss read the rhythm of a known song, and play it on classroom percussion instruments.
10. Ss read a phrase of a known song, with traditional notation and solfège or from the staff, that includes a new rhythmic pattern, and play it on the xylophone or tone bells.
11. Ss read the rhythm of a known song in two or three parts. For example, Ss can sing the rhythm syllables using notes of the tonic chord in major or minor.
12. Ss read the rhythm of a known song in two or three parts. For example, Ss can play the rhythm patterns using notes of the tonic chord in major or minor on the recorder.
13. This ostinato may be sung or played with "Come Thru 'Na Hurry," "Liza Jane," "Riding in a Buggy," and "Weevily Wheat":

do low so do low so do re mi

Kodály Today

Inner Hearing
1. Ss recognize familiar songs from T's clapping.
2. T sings known fragments of songs and Ss sing back with rhythm syllables and keep the beat.
3. T sings a melody on a neutral syllable and provides Ss with four flash cards with the rhythm patterns; Ss must identify the song and arrange flash cards in the correct order.

Memory
1. Ss read an unknown song with rhythm syllables and clap the rhythm. T erases four beats each time and Ss memorize.
2. Ss read an unknown song with rhythm syllables and conduct. T erases four beats each time and Ss memorize.

Writing Activities
1. Ss write the target pattern in stick or traditional rhythmic notation.
2. Ss write related patterns in stick and traditional rhythmic notation.
3. Ss write a known song in stick or traditional rhythmic notation.
4. Ss fill the missing measures of a known song with the correct rhythms.
5. T sings an unknown song and Ss fill in the missing measures with the correct rhythms.
6. Ss notate rhythm patterns furnished by T and add the bar lines and time signature.

Improvisation Activities
1. T claps a question phrase and chants rhythm syllables; Ss choose an answer phrase from four phrases written on the board. One phrase should be four heart beats to encourage Ss to create their own rhythm.
2. One S claps a question phrase and chants rhythm syllables, and another S chooses an answering phrase from patterns on the board. One phrase should be four heart beats to encourage Ss to create their own rhythm.
3. T writes a known folksong in traditional rhythmic notation but leaves out four beats. Ss read and clap the rhythm, and one S improvises four-beat rhythms that use new rhythm pattern for the missing measure. These songs can be used for this activity: "Riding in the Buggy," "Shoo My Love," "Liza Jane," "Alabama Gal," "Come Thru 'Na Hurry," "Hill and Gully Rider," "Weevily Wheat."

Part Work
1. T divides the class into two groups. Group 1 sings the song with solfège syllables and hand signs, and group 2 taps a rhythmic ostinato that is read from notation.
2. Ss read a known song with rhythm syllables and clap the rhythm. Divide the class into two groups and perform the activity in canon after two beats.
3. Ss read a known song with rhythm syllables and conduct. Divide the class into two groups and perform the activity in canon after two beats.

4. Ss read a known song with rhythm syllables while tapping the rhythm with the left hand and conducting with the right hand. Divide the class into two groups and perform the activity in canon after two beats.
5. Ss read a known song with rhythm syllables and clap the rhythm. Divide the class into two groups; one group performs the activity from the beginning of the song and the other from the end.
6. Ss read a known song with rhythm syllables and conduct. Divide the class into two groups; one group performs the activity from the beginning of the song and the other from the end.
7. Ss read a known song with rhythm syllables while tapping the rhythm with the left hand and conducting with the right hand. Divide the class into two groups; one group performs the activity from the beginning of the song and the other from the end.
8. Ss sing a known song and clap the rhythm of another well-known song simultaneously.
9. Ss sing a known song, tap a rhythm from traditional rhythmic notation with the right hand, and tap an ostinato with the left hand.
10. Ss perform "My Paddle" from Denise Bacon's *46 American Folksongs* (p. 16).

Listening Activities
From *Mikrokosmos*, by Béla Bartók (1881–1945), vol. II, no. 40, "The Swine Herd." Listen to the bass part for syncopation.

Sight-Reading Materials
Micheál Houlahan and Philip Tacka. *Sound Thinking: Music for Sight-Singing and Ear Training.* New York: Boosey & Hawkes, 1991. Vol. I, pp. 87–109.

Zoltán Kodály. *Kodály Choral Library: 333 Elementary Exercises.* London and New York: Boosey & Hawkes, 1963. For major keys, see nos. 8, 26, 27, 89, 169, and 184.

Music Theory

It is important for students to learn and understand the concept of the eighth note rest. One way to do this is to write some of the syncopation patterns with eighth note rests and have students read these patterns. The teacher may include eighth note rests in dictation exercises.

Grade 4, Teaching Strategy 2, for *la* Pentatonic Scale

Table 6.21 shows the key components that need to be included in the *la* pentatonic scale teaching strategy.

Table 6.21

Element	Concept	Focus Song	Present Syllables	Theory	Traditional Notation	Practice	Additional Songs
Scale ending on *low la*	Five pitches, *low la do re mi so* with a skip between *low la* and *do* and a skip between *mi* and *so*; ends on *low la*	"Land of the Silver Birch"	*low la do re mi so la*	Scale		Syncopation ♫ ♪	"Canoe Song"; "Sioux Indian Lullaby"; "My Good Ol' Man"; "Liza Jane"; "Whistle Daughter Whistle"; "Gallows Pole"

Cognitive Phase: Preparation

Internalize Music Through Kinesthetic Activities

1. T sings "Land of the Silver" and points to a representation of the melodic contour of the third phrase (Fig. 6.40).

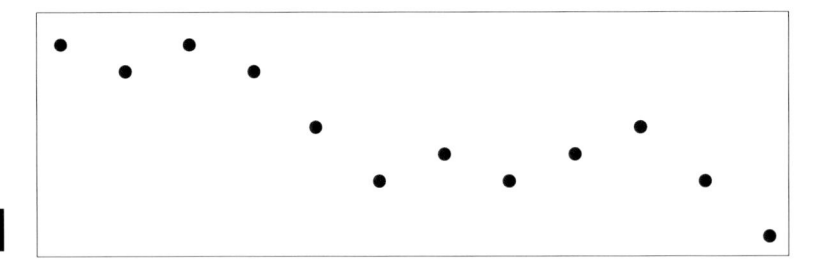

FIG. 6.40

2. T sings phrases 1, 2, and 4; Ss sing and point to the melodic contour of the third phrase.
3. Ss all turn to a partner. Ss sing whole song and clap the melodic contour of the third while matching their partner.
4. Ss sing song with a rhythmic or melodic ostinato.

Describe What You Hear

1. T assesses kinesthetic awareness.
2. Ss sing and clap the contour of phrase 3.

3. Ss get into pairs; one sings phrase 1, one sings phrase 2, and together they mirror-clap phrase 3.
4. T asks Ss to sing the last note with solfège.
5. Ss sing phrase 3 with solfège syllables and hand signs.
6. Individuals sing the phrase with solfège syllables and hand signs.
7. Ss sing all of the notes in the phrase from lowest to highest, with solfège syllables and hand signs.
8. T sings the intervals of the minor pentatonic scale (*la,-do, do-re, re-mi, mi-so, so-la*), and Ss echo-sing either that an interval is a step or that it's a skip.

Create a Visual Representation of What You Hear
1. T assesses kinesthetic and aural awareness by allowing the class to perform several of the kinesthetic and aural awareness activities.
2. T sings the target phrase with a neutral syllable and asks Ss to create a visual representation of the melody of the target phrase. They may use manipulatives. T: "Pick up what you need to recreate what you heard" or "Draw what you heard." T assesses Ss' level of understanding.
3. Ss share their representations with each other.
4. T invites one S to the board to share a representation with the class. If necessary, corrections to the representation can be made by reviewing the aural awareness questions.
5. Ss sing the third phrase of "Land of the Silver" with a neutral syllable and point to their representation.
6. Ss identify the solfège syllables and sing with hand signs.

Create a Visual Representation of the *la* Pentatonic Scale
1. T sings the notes of the minor pentatonic scale.
2. Ss create a visual representation of the *la* pentatonic scale. It is important for them to show the steps and the skips.
3. T invites one S to the board to share a representation with the class. If necessary, corrections to the representation can be made by reviewing the aural awareness questions.

Associative Phase: Presentation

Describe What You Hear with Solfège Syllables
1. T assesses the kinesthetic and aural awareness and visual awareness activities with the focus song "Land of the Silver."
2. T and S sing the target phrase with solfège syllables and hand signs. Ss identify the notes of the target phrase, singing from lowest to highest.
3. T specifically names these notes as a "*la* pentatonic scale," pentatonic because it has five different pitches with a skip between low *la* and *do* as well as *mi-so*, and because the piece of music ends on low *la*.

Kodály Today

4. Ss sing the whole song with solfège and hand signs.
5. Ss perform the new melody with solfège and conduct.
6. T sings phrases of "Canoe Song" with text or neutral syllable; Ss echo with solfège syllables and hand signs.

Notate What You Hear

1. T presents the tone set on the tone ladder.
2. Present the melody with traditional rhythmic notation and solfège. Ss sing with solfège syllables and hand signs.
3. Present the notation for the third phrase of "Land of the Silver Birch."
4. Ss sing target phrase with solfège and hand signs.
5. T writes the target melody with traditional rhythmic notation and solfège. Individuals sing and point to the melody on the board as the class sings the song with solfège syllables and hand signs.
6. Write the target melody with traditional rhythmic notation and solfège. Individuals sing and point to the melody on the board as the class sings the song with solfège syllables and conducts.
7. Write the target melody on the staff. Individuals sing and point to the melody on the board written on the staff as the class sings the song with solfège syllables and hand signs.
8. Write the target melody on the staff. Individuals sing and point to the melody on the board written on the staff as the class sings the song with solfège syllables and conducts.
9. Ss sing phrases of song with letter names. Individuals sing and point to staff notation, and class sings the song with letter names.
10. Present the name of the scale referring to a tone ladder.
    - Ss sing the target phrase with solfège syllables. One S presents the notes on the tone ladder. Identify the steps between the notes of the phrase as steps or skips. T presents the name of the scale.
    - Identify the intervals between the tonic note and each degree of the scale.
11. Present this notation for the *la* pentatonic scale on the staff.
    - T presents the Rule of Placement for *la* pentatonic tone set.
    - Present *la* pentatonic on staff written in several keys, up to two sharps and flats.
    - Ss sing the scale with solfège and hand signs.
    - Ss identify the intervals (steps or skips) between notes of the scale, for example, "*la-do*, skip" (Fig. 6.41).

Fig. 6.41 *la* **Pentatonic Scale**

- At this time T may practice the various pentatonic scales from hand signs. If you choose to do this, focus on the *re* and *mi* pentatonic scales when working with the *la* pentatonic minor scale. The *re* pentatonic scale can be practiced using the songs "I Wonder Where Maria's Gone" and "Older Betty Larkin," or from Kodály's *333 Elementary Exercises* nos. 279 and 330.

Assimilative Phrase: Practice Music Skills

Aural Practice
These skills should be practiced independently from visual practice.

Singing
1. Ss sing "Land of the Silver Birch" with solfège syllables and hand signs.
2. Ss sing "Land of the Silver Birch" with solfège syllables and conduct.
3. T sings motifs from known songs and Ss sing back with solfège syllables and hand signs.
4. T sings *do* pentatonic and *la* pentatonic scales and Ss sing back with solfège syllables and hand signs.
5. Ss sing "Land of the Silver Birch" using solfège syllables while T sings the accompanying second part from the *Sourwood Mountain* collection.

Inner Hearing
1. Ss recognize familiar songs and/or phrases from T's hand signs.
2. T sings known phrases of songs and Ss sing back with solfège syllables.

Singing Intervals
1. T sings the intervals selected from the *la* pentatonic scale; Ss sing the intervals and identify whether each is a skip or a step.
2. T sings the intervals between the tonic note and notes of the minor pentatonic tone set; Ss sing the intervals and identify them.
3. T plays intervals on the piano melodically or harmonically, and one S identifies the solfège syllables and the interval name.
4. Ss sing major and minor pentatonic scales from the same pitch.
5. T sings interval patterns that can be sung with the same solfège. For example, *la-so-mi-re* can be sung with the syllables *re-do-la,-so,*. T can sing *la-so-mi-re* patterns and Ss must sing a perfect fifth below, singing the same solfège syllables, or they can sing with *re-do-la,-so,*. Through this exercise students are practicing real answers.

Part Work
1. T uses the target phrase as an ostinato to accompany known minor pentatonic songs.

Kodály Today

2. Ss echo-sing four-beat patterns provided by the teacher with solfège and hand signs, but begin singing at beat 3 of T's pattern.
3. Ss sing the song in canon, if it is a pentatonic song.
4. Ss sing the song in canon with a rhythmic ostinato.
5. Ss sing the song in canon with a melodic ostinato.
6. T combines a phrase as an ostinato with another motif from the song so that two ostinati are used at the same time. This works with pentatonic music.
7. Ss sing a minor pentatonic song and T accompanies with a drone made up of *low la* or *low la–mi* played on an instrument.
8. Ss sing a minor pentatonic song and T accompanies with *low la* or *low mi*. Reverse.

Improvisation Activities

1. T sings a music question with solfège syllables and hand signs, and Ss give an answer. Question should end on *mi* and the answer on *low la*.
2. One S sings a music question with solfège syllables and hand signs, and another gives an answer. Question should end on *mi* and the answer on *low la*.
3. One S improvises a four-beat pattern. The next S begins a four-beat improvisation with the last two beats from that of the first S.

Visual Practice

These skills may be practiced visually. This should not take place without recourse to aural practice.

Reading from Hand Signs

1. Ss sing known song from T's hand signs, to include the new solfège pattern.
2. Ss sing known song from another S's hand signs, to include the new solfège pattern.
3. Ss read a motif from T's hand sign and play on a classroom instrument. T supplies the starting place on the instrument.

Reading Activities

1. Ss read target motifs from the tone ladder.
2. Ss read known melodies from the tone ladder.
3. Ss read target motif from traditional rhythmic notation and solfège with solfège syllables and hand signs.
4. Ss read a known song from traditional rhythmic notation with solfège syllables and hand signs.
5. Ss read a known song with solfège syllables and conduct.
6. Ss read a known song from staff notation with solfège syllables and hand signs.
7. Ss read a known song from staff notation with solfège syllables and conduct.
8. Ss transform target motif into a related pattern.
9. Ss read an unknown song with solfège syllables and hand signs.
10. Ss read an unknown song with solfège syllables and conduct.

11. T shows hand signs and Ss read in canon after two beats with hand signs.
12. T transforms a known folksong into another folksong.
13. Ss read phrases of known song, notated with traditional rhythmic notation and solfège, and play on a classroom instrument.

Inner Hearing
1. Ss recognize familiar songs from T's hand signs.
2. T sings known phrases of songs and Ss sing back with solfège syllables and signs.
3. T sings a melody on a neutral syllable and gives one S four flash cards with rhythm patterns; S must identify the song and arrange flash cards in the correct order.
4. Ss sing known songs but inner-hear the phrase containing the new target pattern.
5. Ss sing a song but have to inner-hear the song from a signal given by T. Ss sing the song aloud from a signal given by T.

Memory
1. Ss read an unknown song with solfège syllables and hand signs. T erases four beats each time, and Ss memorize.
2. Ss read an unknown song with solfège syllables and conduct. T erases four beats each time, and Ss memorize.

Writing Activities
1. T writes the target pattern in stick or traditional rhythmic notation with solfège syllables.
2. Ss write related patterns in stick and traditional rhythmic notation with solfège syllables.
3. Ss write the tones of a known song on the board as a S or class sings a known song in solfège syllables.
4. Ss write a known song in stick or traditional rhythmic notation.
5. Ss fill the missing measures of a known song with the correct solfège syllables. T can provide the rhythm but not the syllables for the missing measure.
6. T sings an unknown song and Ss fill in the missing measures with the correct rhythms and solfège syllables.
7. Ss transcribe into staff notation a song written in rhythmic notation with solfège syllables.
8. Ss write a scale on the staff and mark the half steps.

Improvisation Activities
1. T sings a question phrase with solfège syllables and hand signs, and one S chooses an answering phrase from four patterns on the board. One phrase should be just four heart beats.

Kodály Today

2. One S sings a question phrase with solfège syllables and hand signs, and another S chooses an answering phrase from four patterns on the board. One phrase should be just four heart beats.
3. T writes a known folksong in traditional rhythmic notation and solfège but leaves out four beats. Ss read with solfège, and one improvises a four-beat melody that uses the new melodic note.
4. Ss improvise a new folksong to a given form and scale. For example, they compose a new melody using the form ABAB. T gives Ss the A phrase, and they improvise the B phrase, to end on *do*.

Part Work

1. T divides the class into two groups. Group 1 sings the song with solfège syllables and hand signs, and group 2 taps a rhythmic ostinato that is read from notation.
2. T divides the class into two groups. Group 1 sings the song with solfège syllables and hand signs, and group 2 sings a melodic ostinato that is read from notation.
3. T divides the class into two groups. Group 1 sings the song with solfège and hand signs, and group 2 sings a descant with solfège and hand signs that is read from notation.
4. Ss read a known song with solfège syllables and hand signs. T divides the class into two groups and perform the activity in canon after two beats, group 1 singing and group 2 clapping in canon.
5. Ss read a known song with solfège syllables and conducting. Divide the class into two groups and perform the activity in canon after two beats, group 1 singing and group 2 clapping in canon.
6. Ss read a known song with solfège syllables while showing hand signs with the left hand and conducting with the right hand. T divides the class into two groups; group 1 performs the activity and group 2 claps rhythm in canon after two beats.
7. Ss sing a known song and clap the rhythm of another well-known song simultaneously.
8. Ss sing a known song, tap a rhythm from traditional rhythmic notation with the right hand, and tap an ostinato with the left hand.
9. Ss sing the *la* pentatonic scale in two- and three-part canons.
10. Ss sing "Sioux Lullaby" from *Sourwood Mountain* (p. 1).

Intervals

1. Ss identify intervals from notation of known songs.
2. Ss identify intervals from notation of unknown songs.
3. Ss read a number of pentatonic scales from the same starting note.

Listening Activities

Béla Bartók, "An Evening in the Village," from *Hungarian Sketches*.

Sight-Reading Materials

Micheál Houlahan and Philip Tacka. *Sound Thinking: Music for Sight-Singing and Ear Training.* New York: Boosey & Hawkes, 1991. Vol. I, pp. 87–109.

Zoltán Kodály. *333 Elementary Exercises.* Nos. 164, 173, 176, 178, 179, 181, and 184.

In *333 Elementary Exercises*, these numbers offer syncopation in minor keys: 151, 169, 184, 313, and 323.

Denise Bacon, *50 Two Part Exercises*, no. 36.

As students develop their knowledge of rhythmic and melodic elements, the teacher may now begin to practice intervals in a more focused manner.

It is important for students to understand that the same interval can have varying solfège syllable interpretations. Teachers should help students understand the difference between a major third and a minor third interval. Comparing parallel keys is an opportunity for students to hear the difference between the major and minor thirds within the context of the perfect fifth interval.

Major and minor seconds should also be studied carefully. They may begin to develop fluency in singing with absolute letter names and neutral syllables without the aid of solfège syllables.

Here are the remaining five teaching strategies. Table 6.22 addresses the dotted quarter note followed by an eighth note; Table 6.23 addresses *fa*; Table 6.24 addresses simple triple meter; Table 6.25 addresses the second degree of the minor scale *t*,; and Table 6.26 addresses the dotted eighth note followed by a sixteenth note.

Table 6.22 Teaching Strategy for a Dotted Quarter Note Followed by an Eighth Note

Element	Concept	Focus Song	Present Syllables	Theory	Traditional Notation	Practice	Additional Songs
Dotted quarter note followed by an eighth note	Two sounds distributed over two beats, the second sound occurring after the second beat	"Liza Jane"	ta--------di	Rule for a dot after a note	Dotted quarter note followed by an eighth note ♩. ♪	low la pentatonic	"John Kanaka Hill"; "Chairs to Mend"; "Long Road of Iron"; "Viva la Musica"; "Above the Plain"; "Hush a Bye"

Kodály Today

Table 6.23 Teaching Strategy for *fa*

Element	Concept	Focus Song	Present Syllables	Theory	Traditional Notation	Practice	Additional Songs
fa	Pitch a whole step below *so* and a half step above *mi*	"Hungarian Canon"	*fa*	Major pentachord and hexachord scale; half step, Bb; major and minor seconds; perfect fourth and fifth and major sixth	*fa* on different staff placements	♩ ♪	"Go Tell Aunt Rhody"; "Chairs to Mend"; "On a Mountain"; "Redbirds and Blackbirds"; "Long Road of Iron"; "Twinkle, Twinkle, Little Star"; "Are You Sleeping?"; "Whistle, Daughter, Whistle"

Table 6.24 Triple Meter

Element	Concept	Focus Song	Present Syllables	Theory	Traditional Notation	Practice	Additional Songs
Triple meter	Organization of one strong and two weak beats	"Rise up, Oh Flame"		Bar lines, measures; double bar line, time signature	$\frac{3}{4}$ time signature	*fa do* pentachord melodies in F major; *fa* = B flat when *do* = F	"Around the Green Gravel"; "America"; "Sweet Betsy from Pike"; "Goodbye Old Paint"

Table 6.25 Teaching Strategy for *low ti*

Element	Concept	Focus Song	Present Syllables	Theory	Traditional Notation	Practice	Additional Songs
ti, the second degree of the minor scale	Pitch a half step below *do*	"The Birch Tree"	*low ti*	Minor pentachord and minor hexachord F#	*low ti* on different staff placement	Triple meter	"The Birch Tree"; "Alfonso Doce"; "Debka Hora"

Table 6.26 Teaching Strategy for a Dotted Eighth Note Followed by a Sixteenth Note

Element	Concept	Focus Song	Present Syllables	Theory	Traditional Notation	Practice	Additional Songs
Dotted eighth note followed by a sixteenth note	Two sounds on one beat, the first being long and the second being short	"Donkey Riding"	ta mi	Subdivision of the beat into sixteenth notes	♪. ♬	*la* pentachord (*low ti*)	"Sail Away Ladies"; "Circle Round the Zero"; "Yankee Doodle"; "Shady Grove"

Focus Songs for Grade 4

"Canoe Song" can be a focus song for syncopation (Fig. 6.42).

Fig. 6.42 "Canoe Song" : Focus Song for Syncopation

My pad - dle's keen and bright, flash - ing with sil - ver,
Fol - low the wild goose flight, dip, dip and swing.

Kodály Today

"Land of the Silver Birch" can be a focus song for the *la* pentatonic scale (Fig. 6.43).

Fig. 6.43 "Land of the Silver Birch": Focus Song for *la* Pentatonic Scale

Land of the sil-ver birch, home of the bea-ver.
Where still the mi-ghty moose wan-ders at will.
Blue lake and rock-y shore, I will re-turn once more,
Boom di-di boom boom, boom di-di boom boom, boom di-di boom boom, boom.

"Liza Jane" can be a focus song for dotted quarter followed by an eighth note (Fig. 6.44).

Fig. 6.44 "Liza Jane": Focus Song for Dotted Quarter Followed by an Eighth Note

Come my love and go with me, Lil' 'Li-za Jane,
Come my love and go with me, Lil' 'Li-za Jane.
O, E-liz-za! Lil' 'Li-za Jane.
O, E-li-za! Lil' 'Li-za Jane.

"Hungarian Canon" can be a focus song for *fa* (Fig. 6.45).

Fig. 6.45 "Hungarian Canon": Focus Song for *fa*

Teaching Strategies: Grades 1 Through 5

"Oh How Lovely Is the Evening" can be a focus song for three-beat meter (Fig. 6.46).

Fig. 6.46 "Oh How Lovely": Focus Song for Three-Beat Meter

O, how love-ly is the eve-ning, is the eve-ning,
When the bells are sweet-ly ring-ing, sweet-ly ring-ing,
Ding, dong, ding, dong, ding, dong.

"The Birch Tree" can be a focus song for *low ti* (Fig. 6.47).

Fig. 6.47 "Birch Tree": Focus Song for *low ti*

See the lone-ly birch in the mea-dow. Cur-ly leaves all dance when the wind blows.
Lu - li loo li the wind blows, Lu - li loo in the mea-dow.

"Donkey Riding" can be a focus song for dotted eighth note followed by a sixteenth note (Fig. 6.48).

Fig. 6.48 "Donkey Riding": Focus Song for Dotted Eighth Note Followed by a Sixteenth Note

1. Were you ev-er in Que-bec, stow-ing tim-ber on a deck,
Where there's a king with a gold-en crown rid-ing on a don-key?
Refrain
Hey, ho! A-way we go, don-key rid-ing, don-key rid-ing,
Hey, ho! A-way we go, rid-ing on a don-key.

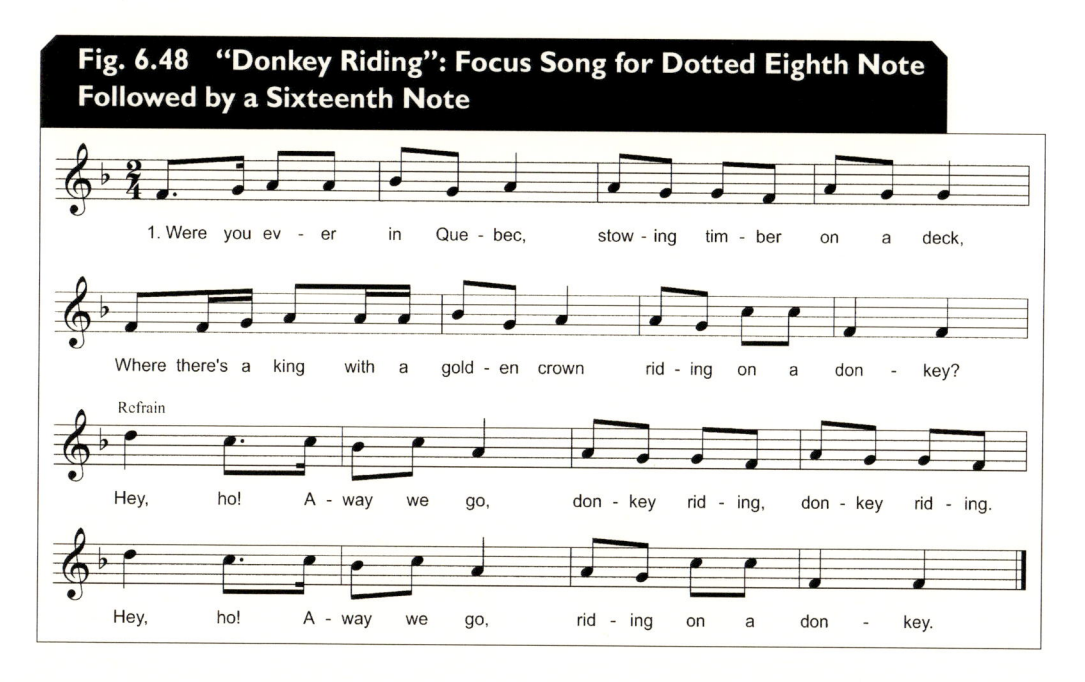

Grade 5 Teaching Strategies

In grade 5, we deal with ten musical concepts alternating between rhythmic concepts and melodic concepts throughout the year.

1. Teaching strategy for major scale
2. Teaching strategy for an eighth note followed by a dotted quarter note
3. Teaching strategy for natural minor scale
4. Teaching strategy for compound meter, part 1
5. Teaching strategy for *si*
6. Teaching strategy for compound meter, part 2
7. Teaching strategy for *fi*
8. Teaching strategy for compound meter, part 3
9. Teaching strategy for *ta*
10. Teaching strategy for *high ti* (major scale)

Grade 5, Teaching Strategy 1, for Major Scale

Table 6.27 presents the key components that need to be included in the major scale teaching strategy.

Table 6.27

Element	Concept	Focus Song	Present Syllables	Theory	Traditional Notation	Practice	Additional Songs
high ti	A series of seven pitches with half steps between the third and fourth degrees and the seventh and eighth degrees	"Alleluia"	*ti*	Major diatonic scale		Dotted eighth followed by sixteenth	"Joy to the World"; "Wake up Canon"; "Sweet Betsy from Pike"; "Alphabet Song (1 and 2)"; "Johnny Has Gone for a Soldier"

Cognitive Phase: Preparation

Internalize Music Through Kinesthetic Activities

1. Ss sing "Alleluia" and imitate T's motions to show the melodic contour.
2. Ss clap "Alleluia" following the contour of the melody with their hands.

Teaching Strategies: Grades 1 Through 5

3. Ss sing "Alleluia" and point to a representation of the melodic contour of phrase 2 at the board.
4. Ss sing "Alleluia" with rhythm syllables while showing the melodic contour (Fig. 6.49).

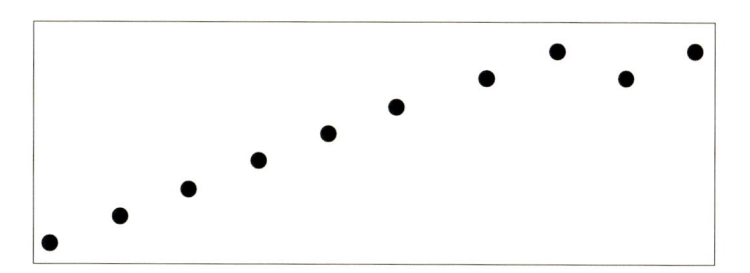

FIG. 6.49

Describe What You Hear

1. T assesses kinesthetic activities with the focus song "Alleluia." T sings phrase 2 while keeping the beat before asking each question.
2. Ss sing and determine the number of beats per phrase and the general direction of the melody. T: "Andy, how many beats are in the second phrase?" (eight) T: "Andy, what is the general direction of the melodic contour?" (it goes up)
3. Ss determine the number of different pitches in the phrase. T: "Andy, how many different pitches did we sing?" (eight) T: "Andy, sing the lowest note of the phrase." T: "Andy, which solfège syllable can we use for that pitch?" (*do*) T: "Andy, sing the highest note of the phrase." T: "Andy, which solfège syllable can we use for that pitch?" (*high do*) T: "Let's sing phrase 1 on solfège and phrase 2 on *loo*." T sings the major scale on "loo" and Ss identify the intervals between the notes as major or minor seconds.

Create a Representation of What You Hear

1. T assesses kinesthetic and aural awareness by allowing the class to perform several of the kinesthetic and aural awareness activities.
2. T sings phrase 2 on "loo" and asks Ss to create a visual representation of the melody of the target phrase. They may use manipulatives. T: "Draw what you heard." T assesses Ss' level of understanding.
3. Ss share their representations with each other.
4. T invites one S to the board to share a representation with the class. If necessary, corrections to the representation can be made by reviewing the aural awareness questions.
5. Ss sing the first phrase of the "Alleluia" with a neutral syllable and point to their representation for the second phrase.
6. T sings the second phrase with rhythm syllables. Ss identify the meter and rhythms; if appropriate, add known solfège syllables.

Kodály Today

Create a Visual Representation of the Major Scale

T follows the process given above to guide Ss in creating a visual representation of the *major* scale. T hums the scale and S echo-sing:

1. T sings the intervals between each pair of notes of the scale, and Ss echo-sing major second or minor second.
2. Ss make a representation of the scale.
3. Ss share their representations.
4. Ss sing the scale on "loo."

Associative Phase: Presentation

Label the Sound

1. T assesses the kinesthetic and aural and visual awareness activities with the focus song "Alleluia."
2. T presents the name and hand sign for the new note: *high ti*.
3. T sings phrase 2 of "Alleluia" with solfège and hand signs.
4. Ss sing back.
5. T hums the second phrase and Ss sing with solfège syllables and hand signs.
6. T sings the pitches of the *major* scale with solfège syllables and hand signs. Ss identify the intervals of the major second and minor second. T specifically names the collection of pitches a "major scale."
7. T sings the major diatonic scale on a neutral syllable ascending. Ss echo with solfège syllables and hand signs.

Notate What You Hear
Second Phrase of "Alleluia"

1. T presents the tone set for "Alleluia" on the tone ladder or steps (Fig. 6.50).

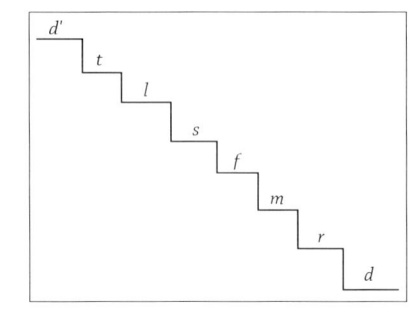

FIG. 6.50

2. T presents the rhythmic notation for "Alleluia" with the solfège syllables.
3. T reviews the Rule of Placement for *ti* on the staff (Fig 6.51).

Teaching Strategies: Grades 1 Through 5

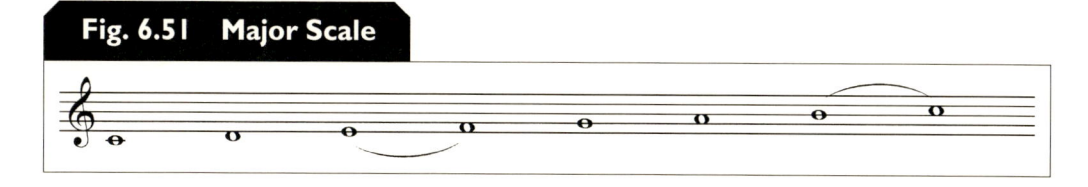

Fig. 6.51   Major Scale

4. T presents the notation for "Alleluia" on the staff.
5. Present the pattern for the major diatonic scale and note the position of the half-step intervals on the tone ladder.

When we write the pitches of "Alleluia" in ascending order, we discover that there are seven adjacent pitches. We can label these pitches with solfège syllables *do-re-mi-fa-so-la-ti–high do,* and scale degree numbers 1-2-3-4-5-6-7-1, respectively. This scale is called the major scale (Table 6.28).

Table 6.28   Labeling Pitches with Solfège Syllables and Scale Degree Number

Solfège Syllables	Corresponding Number
high do	1
ti	7
la	6
so	5
fa	4
mi	3
re	2
do	1

Note that the intervals between *do-re, re-mi, fa-so, so-la,* and *la-ti* are whole steps. The distance between *ti* and *do* and between *mi* and *fa* is a half step. We can refer to whole steps as major seconds (M2) and half steps as minor seconds (m2). (See Table 6.29.)

Table 6.29   Intervallic Distance Between the Notes of the Major Scale

Whole Steps Major Second	Half Steps Minor Second
do-re	ti,-do
re-mi	mi-fa
fa-so	
so-la	
la-ti	

Kodály Today

1. Present Rule of Placement for *ti* on the staff.
2. Present the pattern on the staff. Review rules of placement. Consider presenting the major scale in the F, G, D, and B flat *do* positions.

Assimilative Phrase: Practice Music Skills

Aural Practice
These skills should be practiced independently from visual practice.

Singing with Solfège Syllables
1. Ss sing "Alleluia" with solfège syllables.
2. T sings phrases of several songs containing *high ti* on "loo"; Ss echo the solfège syllables and hand signs.
3. T sings phrases with solfège syllables and Ss echo-sing using letter names.

Inner Hearing
1. T sings known fragments of songs and Ss sing back with solfège syllables and hand signs.
2. T sings known fragments of songs and Ss sing back with solfège syllables and conducting.

Singing Intervals
1. T sings intervals with solfège syllables; Ss echo-sing and identify the intervals as either major or minor seconds.
2. Ss sing and identify the intervals between the tonic note and all of the other scale degrees.
3. T sings the intervals between the tonic note and notes of the major scale tone set; Ss sing the intervals and identify them.
4. T plays intervals on the piano melodically or harmonically, and Ss identify the solfège syllables and the interval name.

Part Work
1. Ss echo-sing four-beat patterns furnished by T with solfège syllables and hand signs but begin singing at beat 3 of T's pattern.
2. Ss sing a song in canon with a rhythmic ostinato.
3. Ss sing a song in canon with a melodic ostinato.

Improvisation
1. T sings descending major scale with a specific rhythm; Ss echo and improvise by singing the ascending major scale with the same or different rhythm.
2. T sings a four-beat question with solfège syllables using the notes of the major scale, including *high ti*, and Ss echo-sing an answer phrase using solfège syllables and hand signs.

3. Ss improvise a new melody based on the form of a known folk song that uses the notes of the major scale.

Visual Practice

These skills may be practiced visually. This should not take place without recourse to aural practice.

Reading from the Teacher's Hand Signs
1. T shows the "Alleluia" using hand signs, and Ss read.
2. T shows known and unknown melodic phrases using hand signs; Ss sing these phrases using solfège syllables and hand signs.
3. T shows typical patterns in major key, and Ss sing back with solfège syllables: *high do ti la; la ti high do; ti so high do.*

Reading Activities
1. Ss read target motifs from the tone ladder with solfège syllables and hand signs.
2. Ss read known melodies from the tone ladder with solfège syllables and hand signs.
3. Ss read target motif from traditional rhythmic notation and solfège with solfège syllables and hand signs.
4. Ss read a known song from traditional rhythmic notation with solfège syllables and hand signs.
5. Ss read a known song with solfège syllables and conducting.
6. Ss read a known song from staff notation with solfège syllables and hand signs.
7. Ss read a known song from staff notation with solfège syllables and conducting.
8. T and Ss transform target motif into a related pattern.
9. Ss read an unknown song with solfège syllables and hand signs.
10. Ss read an unknown song with solfège syllables and conducting.
11. T shows hand signs and Ss read in canon with hand signs after two beats.
12. T and Ss transform a known folksong into another folksong.
13. Ss read phrases of known song, notated with traditional rhythmic notation and solfège, and play on a classroom instrument.
14. Ss read "Alleluia" from traditional rhythmic notation and solfège syllables.
15. Ss read "Alleluia" from staff notation.
16. Ss read known melodies on the staff.
17. Ss read "Heidenröslein" by Johannes Brahms (1833–1897) and listen to recording.
18. Ss read sight-singing examples from *Sound to Symbol* as well as from *Sound Thinking.*
19. Ss read known and unknown melodies with scale degree numbers.

Inner Hearing
1. Ss recognize familiar songs from T's hand signs.
2. T sings known fragments of songs and Ss sing back with solfège syllables and signs.

Kodály Today

3. T sings a melody on a neutral syllable and gives Ss four flash cards with the phrases written in staff notation; Ss must identify the song and arrange flash cards in the correct order.
4. Ss sing known songs but inner-hear the phrase containing the new target pattern.
5. Ss sing a song but have to inner-hear the song from a signal given by T. Ss sing the song aloud when given a signal from the T.

Memory

1. Ss read an unknown song with solfège syllables and hand signs. T erases four beats at a time and Ss memorize.
2. Ss read an unknown song with solfège syllables and conduct. T erases four beats at a time and Ss memorize.

Writing Activities

1. Ss write the target pattern in stick or traditional rhythmic notation with solfège syllables.
2. Ss write related patterns in stick and traditional rhythmic notation with solfège syllables.
3. T or S writes the tones of a known song on the board, as one S or the class sings it in solfège syllables.
4. Ss write a known song in stick or traditional rhythmic notation and solfège syllables.
5. Ss fill the missing measures of a known song with the correct solfège syllables. T can provide the rhythm but not the syllables for the missing segments.
6. T sings an unknown song and Ss fill in the missing measures with the correct rhythms and solfège syllables.
7. Ss transcribe into staff notation a song written in rhythmic notation with solfège syllables.
8. Ss write a scale on the staff and mark the half steps.
9. Ss write "Alleluia" using rhythmic notation and solfège syllables.
10. Ss write "Alleluia" on the staff.
11. Ss write patterns with rhythmic notation and solfège syllables, or on the staff, from the songs "Handsome Butcher," "Roman Soldiers," "Kookaburra," and "Joy to the World."

Improvisation Activities

1. T sings a question phrase with solfège syllables and hand signs, and one S chooses an answer phrase from four patterns on the board. One phrase should be four beats to encourage Ss to create their own phrase.
2. S sings a question phrase with solfège syllables and hand signs, and another S chooses an answer phrase from four patterns on the board. One phrase should be four beats to encourage Ss to create their own phrase.

3. T writes a known folksong in traditional rhythmic notation and solfège syllables but leaves out four beats. Ss read with solfège syllables and improvise a four-beat melody that uses the new melodic note.
4. Ss improvise a new folksong to a given form and scale. For example, Ss compose a new melody using the form ABAB. T provides the A phrase and Ss improvise the B phrase; it should end on *do*.
5. Ss create an alternative ending to a known song. Rhythm can be supplied for Ss.

Part Work
1. T divides the class into two groups. Group 1 sings the song with solfège syllables and hand signs, and group 2 taps a rhythmic ostinato that is read from notation.
2. T divides the class into two groups. Group 1 sings the song with solfège and hand signs, and group 2 sings a melodic ostinato that is read from notation.
3. T divides the class into two groups. Group 1 sings the song with solfège and hand signs, and group 2 sings a descant with solfège syllables and hand signs that is read from notation.
4. T reads a known song with solfège syllables and hand signs. T divides the class into two groups, and perform the activity in canon after two beats, group 1 singing and group 2 clapping in canon.
5. Ss read a known song with solfège syllables and conducting. T divides the class into two groups and perform the activity in canon after two beats, group 1 singing and group 2 clapping in canon.
6. Ss read a known song with solfège syllables while showing hand signs with the left hand and conducting with the right hand. T divides the class into two groups; group 1 performs the activity and group 2 claps rhythm in canon after two beats.
7. Ss sing a known song and clap the rhythm of another well-known song simultaneously.
8. Ss sing a known song, tap a rhythm from traditional rhythmic notation with the right hand and tap an ostinato with the left hand.
9. Ss sing major scale as a two- and three-part canon.
10. Having introduced *ti*, T can now accompany major songs with the tonic, dominant, and subdominant harmonic functions.
11. Sing some of these songs:
    A. "Dear Companion," from *Sourwood Mountain*, by Philip Tacka and Susan Taylor-Howell, pp. 32–33.
    B. "I Will Give My Love an Apple," from *The Owl Sings*, by Susan Taylor-Howell, p. 10.
    C. "Oro, My Bodeen," from *The Owl Sings*, p. 11.
    D. "That Music Enchanting," from *The Magic Flute*, by Wolfgang Amadeus Mozart (1756–1791).

Intervals
1. Ss identify intervals from notation of known songs.
2. Ss identify intervals from notation of unknown songs.
3. Ss are given a starting pitch by T and then sing using solfège syllables from a series of intervals written on the board.
4. Ss read various major and minor scales types from the same starting note.

Listening Examples (Major Scale)
1. Béla Bartók (1881–1945), *For Children*, vol. 1/2 (revised Boosey & Hawkes, 1947).
2. Johannes Brahms (1833–1897), Symphony No. 1, fourth movement, Adagio–Allegro non troppo ma con brio.
3. Edward Jones (1752–1824), "All Through the Night," on album *A Nancy Wilson Christmas*.
4. Moniot d'Arras (ca. 1225), *Ce fut en May*.
5. "In Dulci Jubilo" (1582), recorded by the King's College Choir of Cambridge.
6. Brahms, *Variations on a Theme by Haydn*, Op. 56a. Performed by Magdalena Baczewska and Joanne Polk, 2011.
7. Henry Purcell (1659–1695), "Hornpipe Rigadoon."
8. Johann Sebastian Bach (1685–1750), Minuet in G, from *The Notebook of Ana Magdalena*.
9. Gustav Holst (1874–1934), "Jupiter," from *The Planets*, Op. 32.
10. Thomas Tallis (1505–1585), *Tallis Canon*, St. Patrick's Cathedral, Dublin.
11. Béla Bartók (1881–1945), *Mikrokosmos*, vol. 1, no. 7.
12. Bartók, *Mikrokosmos*, vol. 1, no. 28.
13. Bartók, *For Children*, vol. 1, no. 11.
14. Bartók, *For Children*, vol. 1, no. 5.

Sight-Singing
Micheál Houlahan and Philip Tacka. *Sound Thinking: Music for Sight-Singing and Ear Training*. New York: Boosey & Hawkes, 1991. Vol. 2, pp. 45–49.

Grade 5, Teaching Strategy 2, for an Eighth Note Followed by a Dotted Quarter Note

Table 6.30 shows the key components that need to be included in the eighth note followed by a dotted quarter note teaching strategy.

Cognitive Phase: Preparation

Internalize Music Through Kinesthetic Activities
1. Ss sing "Charlotte Town" and pat the beat.
2. Ss sing "Charlotte Town," determine the meter, and conduct.

Table 6.30

Element	Concept	Focus Song	Present Syllables	Theory	Traditional Notation	Practice	Additional Songs
Eighth note followed by a dotted quarter note	Two sounds distributed over two beats where both sounds occur on beat one	"Charlotte Town"	ta di --------	Review of the rule of the dot	Eighth note followed by a dotted quarter note ♪♩.	Major scale	"All Night, All Day"; "The Erie Canal"; "Billy Boy"; "Great Big Dog"; "Walk Along John"; "Little Johnny Brown"; "Go Down Moses"

3. Ss sing "Charlotte Town" and clap the rhythm.
4. Ss sing "Charlotte Town" and point to a representation of the rhythm on the board (Fig. 6.52).

FIG. 6.52

5. Sing "Charlotte Town" while performing this ostinato:
   $\frac{2}{4}$ ♫ ♫ | ♩ ♩

Describe What You Hear

1. T assesses kinesthetic activities with the focus song.
2. Ss sing the target phrase (phrase 1) using a neutral syllable while keeping the beat before asking each question.
3. T determines the number of beats in phrase one. T: "Andy, how many beats did we keep?" (eight)
4. Ss determine the number of sounds on each beat. T: "Andy, which beats have one sound on them? (beats 2 and 4) T: "Andy, which beats have two sounds?" (beats 1, 3, 5, and 7) T: "Andy, what is different about the two sounds we sing on beats 5 and 7?" (the second sound is longer)

Kodály Today

    5. Ss sing the phrase with rhythm syllables and short-long.
       ta di   ta   ta di   ta   short long---------------   short long---------------

Create a Visual Representation of What You Hear

1. T assesses kinesthetic and aural awareness by allowing the class to perform several of the kinesthetic and aural awareness activities.
2. T hums the target phrase with a neutral syllable and asks S to create a visual representation of the target phrase. They may use manipulatives. T: "Pick up what you need to recreate what you heard" or "Draw what you heard." T assesses Ss' level of understanding.
3. Ss share their representations with each other.
4. T invites one S to the board to share a representation with the class. If necessary, corrections to the representation can be made by reviewing the aural awareness questions.
5. Ss sing the first phrase of "Charlotte Town" with a neutral syllable and point to their representation.
6. T has class determine the meter as well as the solfège syllables for the first phrase of "Charlotte Town."

Associative Phase: Presentation

Label the Sound

1. T assesses the kinesthetic and aural and visual awareness activities with the focus song "Charlotte Town."
2. T: "We label two uneven sounds over two beats where the first is short and the second is long *ta di*---.
3. T sings the target phrase of "Charlotte Town" with rhythm syllables.
4. Ss echo with rhythm syllables while clapping the rhythm or performing the beat.
5. T sings the target phrase of "Charlotte Town" on "loo," and Ss echo with rhythm syllables while clapping the rhythm (Fig. 6.53).

Fig. 6.53

ta di	ta	ta di	ta di	ta di _____	ta di_____
✦	✦	✦	✦	✦ ✦	✦ ✦

Notate What You Hear

1. T presents symbols for two uneven sounds over two beats on the board in traditional notation and then stick notation. Ss immediately clap and echo-sing the target phrase of "Charlotte Town" in rhythm names.
   A. T: "If the beat is a quarter note long, we can write our new rhythm using an eighth note followed by a dotted quarter note."

      Traditional Notation

B. T: "We can also write this phrase using stick notation and solfège syllables."

Stick Notation

♫ | ♩ | ♫ | ♩ | ♫ | ♩. | ♫. |
do do re   mi mi fa   mi do   re low so

Assimilative Phase: Practice Music Skills

Aural Practice
These skills should be practiced independently from visual practice.

Singing with Syllables
1. Ss echo-sing four-beat melodic patterns, containing the new rhythm provided by T, with rhythm syllables and clap the rhythm.
2. Ss echo-sing four-beat melodic patterns, containing the new rhythm provided by T, with rhythm syllables and conduct.
3. T sings phrases of "Charlotte Town" and Ss echo on rhythm syllables.
4. Ss sing "Charlotte Town" on rhythm syllables in canon with T and in small groups.
5. T sings phrases of "All Night, All Day" and Ss echo with rhythm syllables.
6. T claps a rhythm ostinato with a pattern that includes eighth note followed by a dotted quarter note; Ss echo, speaking on rhythm syllables. Example: "All Night, All Day" ostinato pattern.

Inner Hearing
1. T sings known fragments of songs and Ss sing back with rhythm syllables and clap the rhythm.
2. T sings known fragments of songs and Ss sing back with rhythm syllables and conduct.
3. Ss inner-hear known song and clap ostinato that includes new rhythm.

Part Work
1. T uses the target phrase as an ostinato to accompany a known song.
2. T claps a rhythm and Ss follow in canon after two beats.
3. Ss perform a two-part rhythmic reading exercise. Group 1 performs the upper part and group 2 the lower part. Switch.
4. Ss performs a two-part rhythmic reading exercise. They perform the upper part with the right hand and the lower part with the left hand.

Improvisation
1. T claps and says the rhythm syllables in a question phrase that uses the new pattern, and Ss give an answer.

Kodály Today

  2. One S claps and says the rhythm syllables in a question phrase that uses the new pattern, and another S gives an answer.
  3. Ss change rhythm of a first or second grade song and use a *ta di* rhythm pattern over two beats.
  4. One S improvises a four-beat pattern. The next S begins a four-beat improvisation using the last two beats supplied by the first S.

Visual Practice
These skills may be practiced visually. They should not take place without recourse to aural practice.

Reading from Hand Signs
  1. Ss sing known song from T's hand signs to include the new rhythm pattern.
  2. Ss sing known song from another S's hand signs to include the new rhythm pattern.

Reading Activities
  1. Ss read target motif from traditional rhythmic notation with rhythm syllables.
  2. Ss read a known song with rhythm syllables and clap the rhythm.
  3. Ss read a known song with rhythm syllables and conducting.
  4. Ss read a known song with rhythm syllables while tapping the rhythm with the left hand and conducting with the right hand.
  5. Transform target motif into a related pattern.
  6. Ss read an unknown song with rhythm syllables and clap the rhythm.
  7. Ss read an unknown song with rhythm syllables and conducting.
  8. T transform a known folksong into another folksong with the help of students.
  9. Ss read the rhythm of a known song and play it on classroom percussion instruments.
  10. Ss read phrase of a known song with traditional notation and solfège, or from the staff, that includes the new rhythmic pattern, and play on the xylophone or tone bells.
  11. Ss read the rhythm of a known song in two or three parts. For example, they can sing the rhythm syllables using notes of the tonic chord in major or minor.
  12. Ss read the rhythm of a known song in two or three parts. For example, students can play the rhythm patterns using notes of the tonic chord in major or minor on the recorder.
  13. Ss read the rhythmic notation of "Charlotte Town."
  14. T transforms the target pattern into basic four-beat patterns found in the student repertoire.
  15. T transforms the rhythm of phrase 1 of "Charlotte Town" into phrase 2 of "All Night, All Day."
  16. Ss read "All Night, All Day" with rhythmic notation or on the staff.

Inner Hearing
1. Ss recognize familiar songs from T's clapping.
2. T sings known fragments of songs, and Ss sing back with rhythm syllables and keep the beat.
3. T sings a song on a neutral syllable and gives Ss four flash cards with phrases written in rhythmic notation, and Ss must identify the song and arrange flash cards in the correct order.

Memory
1. Ss read an unknown song with rhythm syllables and clap the rhythm. T erases four beats each time, and Ss memorize.
2. Ss read an unknown song with rhythm syllables and conduct. T erases four beats each time and Ss memorize.

Writing Activities
1. Ss write the target pattern in stick or traditional rhythmic notation.
2. Ss write related patterns in stick and traditional rhythmic notation.
3. Ss write a known song in stick or traditional rhythmic notation.
4. Ss fill the missing measures of a known song with the correct rhythms.
5. T sings an unknown song and Ss fill in the missing measures with the correct rhythms.
6. Ss notate rhythm patterns furnished by T and add the bar lines and time signature.
7. Ss write "Charlotte Town" with traditional notation.
8. Ss fill in the missing rhythms to measures of known songs, such as "All Night, All Day."

Improvisation Activities
1. T claps a question phrase and chants rhythm syllables; Ss choose an answer phrase from four patterns on the board. One phrase should be four blank beats to encourage Ss to create their own rhythm.
2. One S claps a question phrase and chants rhythm syllables; another S choses an answer phrase from four patterns on the board. One phrase should be four blank beats to encourage Ss to create their own rhythm.
3. T writes a known folksong in traditional rhythmic notation but leaves out four beats. Ss read and clap the rhythm, and one S improvises four-beat rhythms that use new rhythm pattern for the missing measure:
   A. Ss are given a written rhythmic exercise from a known or unknown song. (Some of the measures contain only "heartbeats" or beat bars.)
   B. Ss perform the rhythm where it is notated, and pat the beat elsewhere.
   C. Ss perform the rhythm where it is notated, and improvise for the missing measures.

Kodály Today

    4. Ss read a four-phrase, sixteen-beat rhythmic composition in ABAC form. Then T erases the C phrase and Ss create a new C phrase using eighth dotted quarter rhythms.

Part Work
1. T divides the class into two groups. Group 1 sings the song with solfège syllables and hand signs and group 2 taps a rhythmic ostinato that is read from notation.
2. Ss read a known song with rhythm syllables and clap the rhythm. T divides the class into two groups, which perform the activity in canon after two beats.
3. Ss read a known song with rhythm syllables and conduct. Divide the class into two groups, and perform the activity in canon after two beats.
4. Ss read a known song with rhythm syllables while tapping the rhythm with the left hand and conducting with the right hand. Divide the class into two groups, and perform the activity in canon after two beats.
5. Ss read a known song with rhythm syllables and clap the rhythm. Divide the class into two groups; one group performs the activity from the beginning of the song and the other from the end.
6. Ss read a known song with rhythm syllables and conducting. Divide the class into two groups; one group performs the activity from the beginning of the song and the other from the end.
7. Ss read a known song with rhythm syllables while tapping the rhythm with the left hand and conducting with the right hand. T divides the class into two groups; one group performs the activity from the beginning of the song and the other from the end.
8. Ss sing a known song and clap the rhythm of another well-known song simultaneously.
9. Ss sing a known song, tap a rhythm from traditional rhythmic notation with the right hand, and tap an ostinato with the left hand.

Listening Activities

Béla Bartók (1881–1945), "An Evening in the Village," from *Hungarian Sketches*, theme 2.

Bartók, *Mikrokosmos*, vol. 3, no. 94.

Zoltán Kodály (1882–1967), "Hungarian Rondo."

Sight-Reading Materials

Micheál Houlahan and Philip Tacka. *Sound Thinking: Music for Sight-Singing and Ear Training.* New York: Boosey & Hawkes, 1991. Vol. I, pp. 71–76, 87–98.

Teaching Strategies: Grades 1 Through 5

Assimilative Phase: Teaching Strategies

Here are teaching strategies for grade 5. Table 6.31 is for teaching the natural minor scale, Table 6.32 is for teaching compound meter using basic patterns, Table 6.33 is for teaching *si*, Table 6.34 is for teaching subdivided compound meter patterns, Table 6.35 is for teaching *fi*, Table 6.36 is for teaching dotted rhythms in compound meter, and Table 6.37 is for teaching *ta*.

Table 6.31 Teaching Strategy for Natural Minor Scale

Element	Concept	Focus Song	Present Syllables	Theory	Traditional Notation	Practice	Additional Songs
	Natural minor scale: a series of eight pitches with half steps between the second and third pitches and the fifth and sixth pitches, and whole steps between all others	"Fly, Fly, Fly (Autumn Canon)" or "Alleluia" in minor	Solfège syllables: low la–low ti–do–re–mi–fa–so–la	Minor scale structure		♪♩	"Ghost of Tom"; "Dona, Dona, Dona"; "Drill Ye Tarriers"; "To Work upon the Railway"; "Sweet William"; "Hashivenu" (w/ solfège syllables); "Come to the Land"; "Tumbalalaika"

Table 6.32 Teaching Strategy for Compound Meter, Part 1, $\frac{6}{8}$ Simple Division

Element	Concept	Focus Song	Present Syllables	Theory	Traditional Notation	Practice	Additional Songs
$\frac{6}{8}$ ♫♩ ♪ ♩. ♪♩	Two pulsations per measure, each pulsation having three micro pulsations	"Row, Row, Row Your Boat"	ta ta ki da ta da	$\frac{6}{8}$ Macro beat Micro beat Compound? (writing not clear on correction)	♫♫ ♩ ♪ ♩. ♪♩	Minor scale	"Wishy Washy"

Kodály Today

Table 6.33 Teaching Strategy for *si*

Element	Concept	Focus Song	Present Syllables	Theory	Traditional Notation	Practice	Additional Songs
si	*si* is a minor second below *la*	"Ah Poor Bird"	*si*	Harmonic minor scale; augmented second		Uneven subdivisions of a beat in $\frac{6}{8}$ meter	"Go Down, Moses"; "Vine and Fig Tree"

Table 6.34 Teaching Strategy for Compound Meter, Part 2, $\frac{6}{8}$ Even Micro Subdivision

Element	Concept	Focus Song	Present Syllables	Theory	Traditional Notation	Practice	Additional Songs
	Two pulsations per measure, each having six micro pulsations	"Morning Is Come"	Subdivision *tavakididama* New rhythm *ta di da*	$\frac{6}{8}$	One eighth note followed by four sixteenth notes	Harmonic minor (*si*)	"The Cherry Tree Carol" (II); "Come Let's Dance"; "Wee Cock Sparra'"

Table 6.35 Teaching Strategy for *fi*

Element	Concept	Focus Song	Present Syllables	Theory	Traditional Notation	Practice	Additional Songs
fi	Major second between *mi* and *fi*	"Drunken Sailor"	*fi*	Dorian mode	*fi* on different staff placements	Rhythm patterns in compound meter	"Scarborough Fair"; "Ground Hog"

Teaching Strategies: Grades 1 Through 5

Table 6.36　Teaching Strategy for Compound Meter, Part 3, 6/8 Uneven Micro Subdivision

Element	Concept	Focus Song	Present Syllables	Theory	Traditional Notation	Practice	Additional Songs
♩.♬	Uneven micro sub-division, where there is a long sound followed by a short sound followed by a long sound	"Early to Bed"	Subdivision *tavakididama* New rhythm *ta di da*	Uneven micro sub-division in 6/8 meter	Sixteenth notes; dotted eighth note, sixteenth note followed by an eighth note ♩.♬	*fi* (Dorian)	"Hashivenu;" "Scarborough Fair"

Table 6.37　Teaching Strategy for *ta*

Element	Concept	Focus Song	Present Syllables	Theory	Traditional Notation	Practice	Additional Songs
ta	Note that is a half-step lower than the seventh degree of a major scale	"Old Joe Clark"	Solfège syllables: *do-re-mi-fa-so-la-ta–high do*	Mixolydian scale structure		♩.♬	"I'm Going Home on a Cloud"; "Git Along Little Doggies"; "Good Morning My Pretty Little Miss"; "The Dying Cowboy"; "The Avondale Mine Disaster"; "The Jam on Jerry's Rocks"; "As I Roved Out"

Kodály Today

Focus Songs for Grade 5

"Alleluia" can be a focus song for major scale (Fig. 6.54).

Fig. 6.54 "Alleluia": Focus Song for Major Scale

[Musical notation with lyrics: Al-le-lu-ia, al-le-lu-ia, Al-le-lu-ia, al-le-lu-ia.]

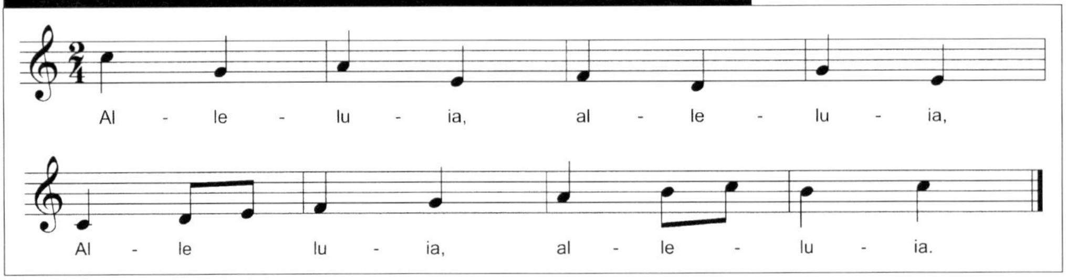

"Charlotte Town" can be a focus song for an eighth note followed by a dotted quarter note (Fig. 6.55).

Fig. 6.55 "Charlotte Town": Focus Song for an Eighth Note Followed by a Dotted Quarter Note

[Musical notation with lyrics: Char-lotte town's burn-ing down. Good-bye! Good-bye! Burn-ing down to the ground. Good-bye Li-za Jane! Ain't ya' might-y sor-ry? Good-bye! Good-bye! Ain't ya' might-y sor-ry? Good-bye, Li-za Jane!]

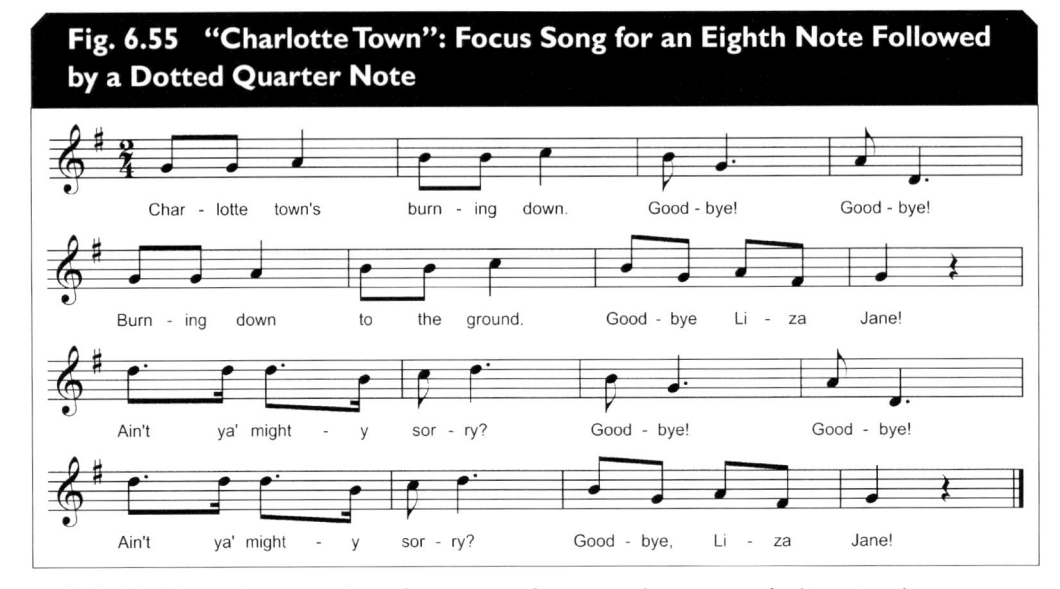

"Alleluia" (in minor) can be a focus song for natural minor scale (Fig. 6.56).

Fig. 6.56 "Alleluia" minor

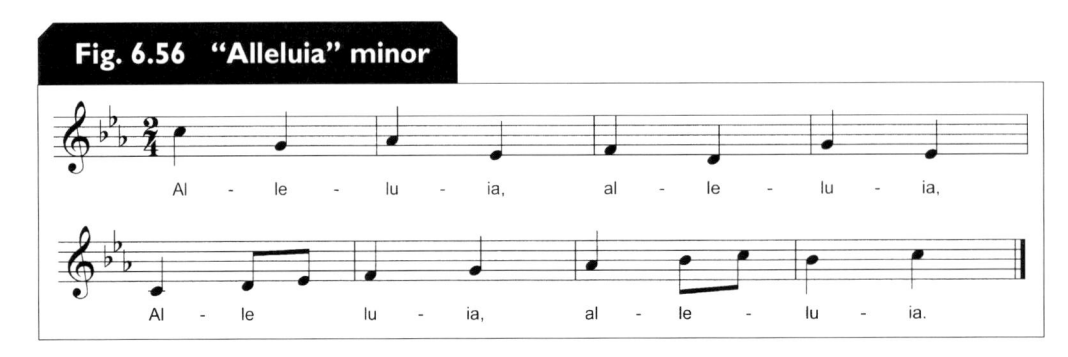

[Musical notation with lyrics: Al-le-lu-ia, al-le-lu-ia, Al-le-lu-ia, al-le-lu-ia.]

"Row, Row, Row Your Boat" can be a focus song for compound meter (patterns in meter; Fig. 6.57).

Fig. 6.57 "Row, Row, Row Your Boat"

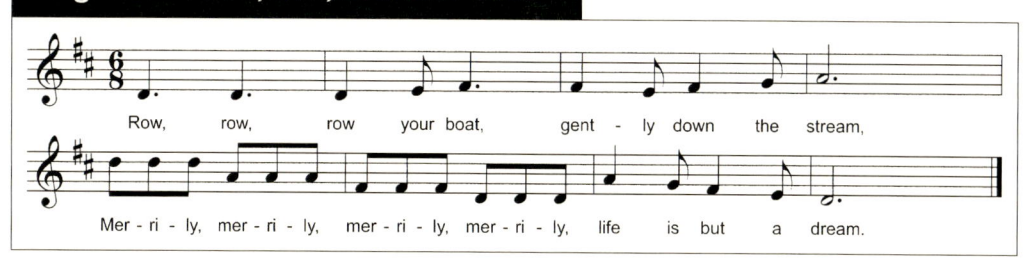

"Ah, Poor Bird" can be a focus song for *si* (Fig. 6.58).

Fig. 6.58 "Ah Poor Bird"

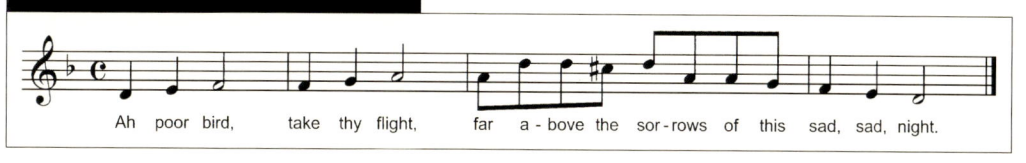

"Morning Is Come" can be a focus song for teaching subdivided patterns in compound meter (Fig. 6.59).

Fig. 6.59 "Morning Is Come"

"Drunken Sailor" can be a focus song for *fi* (Fig. 6.60).

Fig. 6.60 "Drunken Sailor"

Kodály Today

"Early to Bed" can be a focus song for dotted patterns in compound meter (Fig. 6.61).

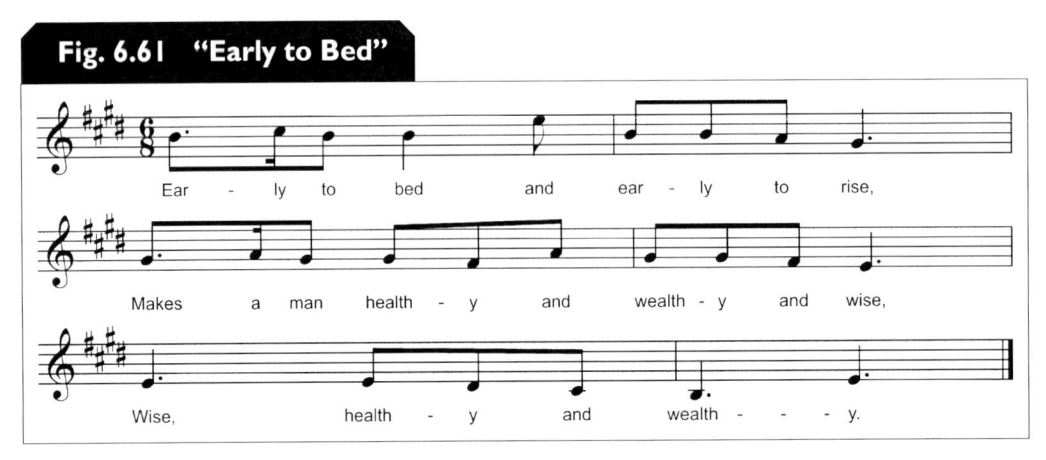

Fig. 6.61 "Early to Bed"

Ear - ly to bed and ear - ly to rise,
Makes a man health - y and wealth - y and wise,
Wise, health - y and wealth - y.

"Old Joe Clark" can be a focus song for *ta* Mixolydian (Fig. 6.62).

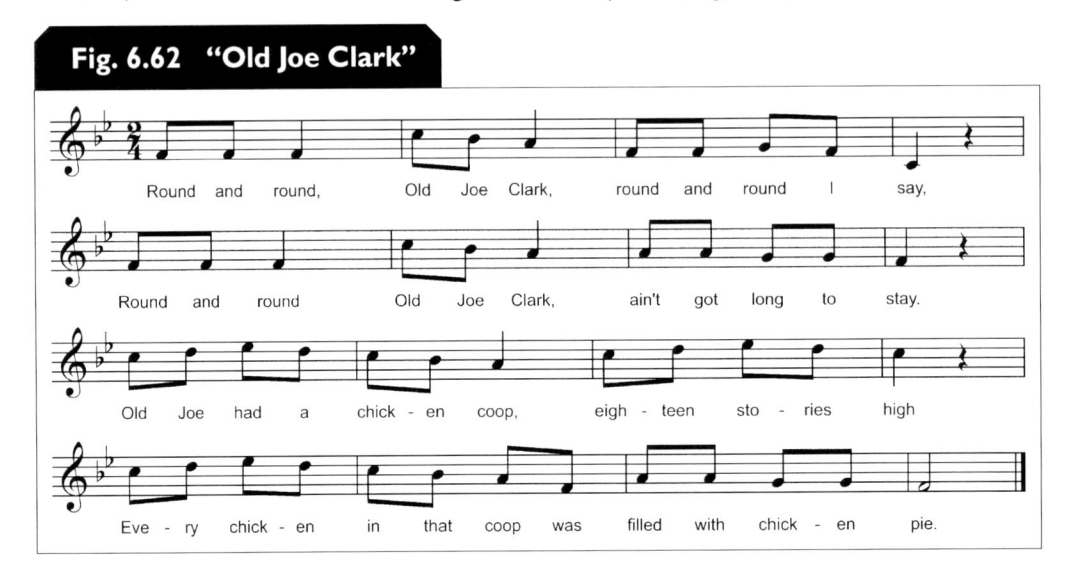

Fig. 6.62 "Old Joe Clark"

Round and round, Old Joe Clark, round and round I say,
Round and round Old Joe Clark, ain't got long to stay.
Old Joe had a chick-en coop, eigh-teen sto-ries high
Eve-ry chick-en in that coop was filled with chick-en pie.

Developing a Lesson Plan Design Based on the Teaching Strategies

The goal of this section is to show how our model of instruction and learning incorporates information for developing musical literacy skills into the preparation/practice and presentation lesson plan designs.

In the cognitive phase of learning, students explore a music concept moving through three stages of learning. In stage 1 students learn to internalize music and construct kinesthetic awareness, in stage 2 they learn to describe the characteristics of the new concept by constructing aural awareness, and in stage 3 they construct a representation of the new concept. Each stage of learning is explored in a lesson plan of its own.

In the associative phase of learning, students learn how to describe the sounds of music with rhythm or solfège syllables and how to translate these sounds into music notation.

Stage 1 is aural presentation of the new rhythmic or melodic syllables and hand signs using known song material that contains the target pattern (the most frequent pattern that contains the new element) and related patterns. Stage 2 is visual presentation of the target pattern using traditional notation. Each stage of learning is explored in its own lesson plan.

In the assimilative phase of learning, students practice and gain fluency through integrating the new element into their vocabulary of other known rhythmic and melodic elements. In stage 1 they aurally practice the rhythm or solfège syllables and hand signs for the new element with music skills. Stage 2 has them visually practice the new element with music skills. Aural practice should take place independently from visual practice, but the latter should never take place without recourse to the former. These stages of learning take place in a concentrated manner over three lessons and may be practiced independently or combined.

Table 6.38a demonstrates how the phases of learning are reflected in different types of lessons.

Table 6.38a   Connecting Lesson Plans to Phases of Learning and Instruction

Phase 1: The Cognitive Phase
Preparation

Lesson 1
Stage 1: Internalizing Music Through Kinesthetic Activities; Constructing Kinesthetic Awareness
Ss listen to T sing the new song.
Ss perform the new song with movement.
Rationale: to match patterns of experience to patterns of music.

Lesson 2
Stage 2: Describe What You Hear: Constructing Aural Awareness by Responding to Questions
Ss aurally analyze the characteristics of the new musical element with the help of T.
Ss describe the characteristics of the new element.
Rationale: to verbalize what they perceive.

Lesson 3
Stage 3: Constructing a Representation from Memory: Constructing Visual Awareness
Ss create a visual representation based on their aural understanding.
Rationale: to visually represent what they have heard and verbalized.

Phase 2: The Associative Phase
Presentation

Lesson 4
Stage 1: Associate the sound of the new element with solfège or rhythmic syllables.

Lesson 5
Stage 2: Associate traditional notation with the sound of the new musical element.

After lesson 5, the new element is now referred to as a *known* element.

(continued)

Table 6.38a Continued

Phase 3: Assimilative Phase
Practice

After the fifth lesson T begins by introducing another new element in Preparation/Practice and Presentation lesson plan cycle. During the practice segments of these lessons, T assimilates the known element.

Stage 1: Ss aurally practice music skills, assimilating the new element, in familiar and new songs.
Stage 2: Ss visually practice music skills, assimilating the new element, in familiar and new songs.

Connecting Lessons Plans to Phases of Learning and Instruction

The lesson plan designs and lesson plans given here represent how students begin the process of understanding the sounds of a new element before learning how to notate the new element. These plans show where the various phases and the stages of learning take place. We include after each plan design a lesson plan segment from an actual lesson plan so you can see how these ideas translate into practical applications in the classroom. For the purposes of showing you examples of lesson plans, we will be using these elements:

New element	Grade 3, Unit 3, *low la*
Known element	Grade 3, Unit 3, eighth note followed by two sixteenth notes
New element	Grade 3, Unit 4, teaching two sixteenth notes followed by an eighth note
Known element	Grade 3, Unit 4, *low la*

Lesson 1: Kinesthetic
Table 6.38b gives a lesson plan template for developing a preparation/practice lesson plan framework for the cognitive phase of learning, stage 1.

   Table 6.39 shows a lesson plan for developing a preparation/practice lesson plan framework for the cognitive phase of learning, stage 1.

Lesson 2: Aural
Table 6.40 shows a lesson plan template for developing a preparation/practice lesson plan for the cognitive phase of learning, stage 2.

   Table 6.41 presents a lesson plan for developing a preparation/practice lesson plan for the cognitive phase of learning, stage 2.

Lesson 3: Visual
Table 6.42 presents a lesson plan template for developing a preparation/practice lesson plan framework for the cognitive phase of learning, stage 3.

Table 6.38b

Outcome	
INTRODUCTORY ACTIVITIES	
Warm-up	
Sing known songs	
Develop tuneful singing Tone production Diction Expression	
Review known songs and elements	
Outcome	
CORE ACTIVITIES	
Teach a new song	
Preparation of new concept Develop knowledge of music literacy concepts Internalize music through kinesthetic activities	Cognitive phase, stage 1 Ss listen to T sing the focus song. Ss perform the focus song with a movement that demonstrates the concept. Rationale: to match patterns of experience to patterns of music.
Creative movement	
Practice music performance and literacy skills Reading and listening	
SUMMARY ACTIVITIES	
Review lesson outcomes Review the new song	

Table 6.39

GRADE 3: UNIT 3, *LOW LA*, LESSON 1	
Outcome	Preparation: internalizing a pitch a skip lower than *do* through kinesthetic activities
	Practice: reading the rhythm of melodies containing an eighth note followed by two sixteenth notes
INTRODUCTORY ACTIVITIES	
Warm-up	
Sing known songs	
Develop tuneful singing Tone production Diction Expression	
Review known songs and melodic elements	
CORE ACTIVITIES	
Teach a new song	
Develop knowledge of music literacy concepts Internalize music through kinesthetic activities	"Phoebe in Her Petticoat" CSP: A • T divides the class and directs them to sing "Over the River" and "Phoebe in Her Petticoat" as partner songs. • Ss sing "Phoebe in Her Petticoat" and keep the beat. • Ss sing the song and clap the melodic contour for the target phrase (phrase 1). • Sing song and point to a representation of the melodic contour on the board. • T selects individuals to come to the board to point to the contour. • Ss find partners (could be the same partner from the game) to mirror one another while clapping the contour. • Sing with rhythm syllables while showing melodic contour. • Ss continue the rhythm of phrase 1 as a rhythmic ostinato into the next song ($\frac{2}{4}$ ♫♫ | ♫ ♩ :‖).
Creative movement	

(continued)

Teaching Strategies: Grades 1 Through 5

Table 6.39 Continued

Practice music performance and literacy skills Reading	
SUMMARY ACTIVITIES	
Review lesson outcomes Review the new song	

Table 6.40

Outcome	
INTRODUCTORY ACTIVITIES	
Warm-up	
Sing known songs	
Develop tuneful singing Tone production Diction Expression	
Review known songs and elements	
CORE ACTIVITIES	
Teach a new song	
Preparation of new concept Develop knowledge of music literacy concepts Describe what you hear	Cognitive phase, stage 2 Describe what you hear Ss aurally analyze the characteristics of the new musical element with the help of T. Ss describe the characteristics of the new element by answering a series of carefully sequenced questions from T. In this way, they can develop their audiation skills during the process of answering questions. Ss must inner-hear the focus phrase to be able to answer T's questions.

(continued)

Table 6.40 Continued

Creative movement	
Practice music performance and literacy skills Writing	
SUMMARY ACTIVITIES	
Review lesson outcomes Review the new song	

Table 6.41

GRADE 3: *LOW LA*, UNIT 3, LESSON 2	
Outcome	Preparation: analyzing repertoire that contains a pitch a skip below *do* Practice: writing musical phrases that contain an eighth note followed by two sixteenth notes
INTRODUCTORY ACTIVITIES	
Warm-up	
Sing known songs	
Develop tuneful singing Tone production Diction Expression	
Review known songs and melodic elements	
CORE ACTIVITIES	
Teach a new song	

(continued)

Table 6.41 Continued

Develop knowledge of music literacy concepts	"Phoebe in Her Petticoat" CSP: A • T directs half the class to continue the ostinato while the remaining **Ss** sing the song. Switch.
Describe what you hear	• Review kinesthetic awareness activities. • T and Ss tap the beat and sing the first phrase on "loo" before asking each question. • T: "Andy, how many beats did we tap?" (four) • T: "Andy, which beat has the lowest pitch?" (four) • T: "Let's sing the phrase on 'loo' but sing 'low' for the lowest note." • T sings the first four pitches on "loo." • T: "Andy, what hand signs do we use to sing those pitches?" (*mi re do do*) • T: "Let's sing our phrase with solfège syllables and hand signs but sing 'low' for our lowest pitch." (*mi re do do re do low*) • Ss sing and point down for the low pitch. • T: "Andy, is our lowest pitch a step or a skip from *do*?" (skip) • Ss sing as a whole group; then T may select individuals to sing the target phrase (*mi re do do re do low*). • Ss sing "Phoebe in Her Petticoat" while T sings "Over the River" as a partner song.
Creative movement	
Practice music, performance, and literacy skills	
Writing	
SUMMARY ACTIVITIES	
Review lesson outcomes	
Review the new song	

Table 6.42

Outcome	
INTRODUCTORY ACTIVITIES	
Warm-ups	
Sing known songs	
Develop tuneful singing	
Tone production	
Diction	
Expression	
Review known songs and elements	
CORE ACTIVITIES	
Teach a new song	
Preparation of new concept Develop knowledge of music literacy concepts Create a representation of what you hear	Cognitive phase Stage 3: constructing a representation from memory; constructing visual awareness. Ss create a visual representation of the focus phrase on the basis of their aural understanding. Rationale: to visually represent what they have heard and verbalized.
Creative movement	
Practice music performance and literacy skills Improvisation	
SUMMARY ACTIVITIES	
Review lesson outcomes Review the new song	

Table 6.43 features a lesson plan for developing a preparation/practice lesson plan framework for the cognitive phase of learning, stage 3.

Lesson Four: Presentation

Table 6.44 presents a lesson plan template for the associative phase of learning, stage 1 (presentation, label the sound).

Table 6.43

GRADE 3: *LOW LA*, UNIT 3, LESSON 3	
Outcome	Preparation: creating a visual representation of a musical phrase containing a pitch a skip below *do* Practice: improvising musical phrases that contain an eighth note followed by two sixteenth notes
INTRODUCTORY ACTIVITIES	
Warm-up	
Sing known songs	
Develop tuneful singing	
Tone production	
Diction	
Expression	
Review known songs and melodic elements	
CORE ACTIVITIES	
Teach a new song	
Develop knowledge of music literacy concepts Create a representation of what you hear	"Phoebe in Her Petticoat" CSP: A • Ss continue the ostinato while singing the song. • Review kinesthetic and aural awareness activities. • T sings the target phrase on a neutral syllable. • T: "Use Unifix cubes to recreate what you heard." • Ss create a visual representation of the target phrase. • Ss share their representations with each other. • Ss make corrections if necessary. • T invites one S to the board to share his or her representation. • Sing on "loo" while Ss point to their own representation. • Ss sing with rhythm syllables and notate rhythm. • Ss sing the song and put away their materials. ➢ Ss sing "Phoebe in Her Petticoat" while T sings "Jim Along Josie" as a partner. Switch.
Creative movement	

(continued)

Kodály Today

Table 6.43 Continued

Practice music performance and literacy skills	
Improvisation	
SUMMARY ACTIVITIES	
Review lesson outcomes Review the new song	"Do, Do Pity My Case"

Table 6.44

Outcome	
INTRODUCTORY ACTIVITIES	
Warm-ups	
Sing known songs	
Develop tuneful singing	
Tone production	
Diction	
Expression	
Review known songs and elements	
CORE ACTIVITIES	
Teach a new song	
Presentation of music literacy concepts	Phase 2: the associative phase: presentation
Describe what you hear with solfège or rhythm syllables	Stage 1: associate the sound of the new element with solfège or rhythmic syllables with a focus pattern
Creative movement	
Presentation of music literacy concepts	Phase 2: the associative phase: presentation
Describe what you hear with solfège or rhythm syllables	Stage 1: associate the sound of the new element with solfège or rhythmic syllables with a related pattern
SUMMARY ACTIVITIES	
Review lesson outcomes Review the new song	

Table 6.45 has a presentation lesson plan for the associative phase of learning, stage 1 (presentation, label the sound).

Lesson Five: Presentation
Table 6.46 presents a lesson plan template for the presentation lesson plan in the associative phase of learning, stage 2 (present the notation).

Table 6.45

GRADE 3: *LOW LA*, UNIT 3, LESSON 4	
Outcome	Presentation: label the pitch a skip below *do* as *low la*
Introductory Activities	
Warm-up	
Sing known songs	
Develop tuneful singing	
Tone production	
Diction	
Expression	
Review known songs and melodic elements	
CORE ACTIVITIES	
Teaching a new song	
Presentation of music literacy concepts Describe what you hear with rhythm or solfège syllables	"Phoebe in Her Petticoat" CSP: A • Ss sing the song. • Review kinesthetic, aural, and visual awareness activities. • T: "When we hear a pitch a skip below *do*, we call it *low la*." (Show sign) • T sings phrase 1 with solfège syllables and hand signs. • Class sings the target phrase with solfège syllables and hand signs. • Approximately six to eight Ss sing the target phrase individually with solfège syllables and hand signs. • Ss perform the rhythm of phrase 1 as a rhythmic ostinato into the next song. (𝟤/𝟦 ♫ ♫ | ♫ ♩ :||)
Creative movement	

(continued)

Kodály Today

Table 6.45 Continued

Presentation of music literacy concepts
 	
Describe what you hear with rhythm or solfège syllables
	"Hey Jim Along"
	CSP: A
	• Ss continue the ostinato while T sings the song.
	• T directs part of the class to continue the ostinato while the remaining Ss sing the song. Switch.
	• Ss sing the target phrase with solfège syllables and hand signs.
	• Ss identify the solfège syllables of the remaining phrases.
	• Ss sing the song with solfège syllables and hand signs.
	• T connects *low la* to other known songs; T and Ss sing these songs with solfège syllables and hand signs:
	   ◦ "Rosie, Darling Rosie"
	   ◦ "Big Fat Biscuit"
	   ◦ "Jim Along Josie"
	   ◦ "Old Mr. Rabbit"

SUMMARY ACTIVITIES	
Review lesson outcomes Review the new song	

Table 6.46

Outcome	
INTRODUCTORY ACTIVITIES	
Warm-up	
Sing known songs	
Develop tuneful singing Tone production Diction Expression	
Review known songs and elements	

(*continued*)

Table 6.46 Continued

CORE ACTIVITIES	
Teach a new song	
Presentation of music literacy concepts	Phase 2: the associative phase: presentation
Notate what you hear	Stage 2: associate traditional notation with the sound of the new musical element in a focus pattern
Creative movement	
Presentation of music literacy concepts	Phase 2: the associative phase: presentation
Notate what you hear	Stage 2: associate traditional notation with the sound of the new musical element in a related pattern
SUMMARY ACTIVITIES	
Review lesson outcomes	
Review the new song	

Table 6.47 features a presentation lesson plan template for the associative phase of learning, stage 2 (presentation, present the notation).

The assimilative phase, stages 1 and 2, takes place during the next units. Stages 1 and 2 are integrated into various sections of lessons of the next units. In our lesson plan structure, we focus on the skills of reading, writing, and improvisation during the next three lessons at the same time as we preparing another new element to be mastered.

Table 6.47

GRADE 3: *LOW LA*, LESSON 5	
Outcome	Presentation: present *low la* in standard and staff notation
INTRODUCTORY ACTIVITIES	
Warm-up	
Sing known songs	
Develop tuneful singing	
Tone production	
Diction	
Expression	

(continued)

Table 6.47 Continued

Review known songs and melodic elements	
CORE ACTIVITIES	
Teaching a new song	
Presentation of music literacy concepts Notate what you hear	"Phoebe in Her Petticoat" CSP: A • T directs part of the class to continue singing "Sailing on the Ocean" while the remaining Ss sing "Phoebe in Her Petticoat." • T reviews aural presentation. • Ss sing song with solfège and hand signs. • Teacher places *la* on the tone ladder. • Ss write the solfège syllables for phrase 1 of the song beneath the standard notation. • Ss read the notation with solfège syllables and hand signs. • T reviews the rule of placement for *low la*. • T writes the first phrase of the song in staff notation (F = *do*, G = *do*). • Ss read the notation with solfège syllables and hand signs. • Ss sing the last phrase of the song with solfège syllables and hand signs as a melodic ostinato into the next song.
Creative movement	
Presentation of music literacy concepts Notate what you hear	"Jim Along Josie" CSP: A • Ss sing with words and conduct. • Ss sing with solfège syllables and hand signs. • T notates the song on the staff and Ss read with solfège and hand signs. • Ss play *do low la do re mi* as a melodic accompaniment on the xylophone for "Jim Along Josie."
SUMMARY ACTIVITIES	
Review lesson outcomes Review the new song	

Lesson Segment for Practicing Reading

We use the preparation/practice lesson plan framework, but note how we focus on practicing reading while preparing the next new element (Table 6.48).

Lesson Segment for Practicing Writing

We use the preparation/practice lesson plan framework, but note how we focus on practicing writing while preparing the next new element (Table 6.49).

Lesson Segment for Practicing Improvisation

We use the preparation/practice lesson plan framework, but note how we focus on practicing improvisation while preparing the next new element (Table 6.50).

Table 6.48

GRADE 3: UNIT 4, TWO SIXTEENTH NOTES, ONE EIGHTH NOTE, LESSON 1	
Outcome	Preparation: internalizing three uneven sounds on one beat (short short long) through kinesthetic activities Practice: reading music with *low la*
INTRODUCTORY ACTIVITIES	
Warm-up	
Sing known songs	
Develop tuneful singing	
Tone production	
Diction	
Expression	
Review known songs and rhythmic elements	
Teach a new song	
Develop knowledge of music literacy concepts	
Internalize music through kinesthetic activities	

(continued)

Table 6.48 Continued

Creative movement	
Practice music performance and literacy skills Reading	"Phoebe In Her Petticoat" CSP: A • Ss sing the song. • Ss sing using solfège syllables and hand signs; Ss places notes on tone ladder. • Ss identify scale. • Ss read from traditional notation and solfège syllables with solfège and hand signs. • Ss read from staff notation with solfège and hand signs. • Ss read the main theme of "An Evening in the Village" from *Hungarian Sketches* by Béla Bartók (1881–1945) from T's hand signs and listen to the melody.
SUMMARY ACTIVITIES	
Review lesson outcomes Review the new song	

Table 6.49

GRADE 3: UNIT 4, TWO SIXTEENTH NOTES, ONE EIGHTH NOTE, LESSON 2	
Outcome	Preparation: aurally analyze repertoire that contains three uneven sounds on one beat. Practice: writing music with *low la*
INTRODUCTORY ACTIVITIES	
Warm-up	
Sing known songs	
Develop tuneful singing Tone production Diction Expression	

(*continued*)

Table 6.49 Continued   Teaching Strategies: Grades 1 Through 5

Review known songs and elements	
CORE ACTIVITIES	
Teach a new song	
Develop knowledge of music literacy concepts	
Describe what you hear	
Creative movement	
Practice music performance and literacy skills Writing	"Phoebe in Her Petticoat" CSP: A • Ss sing the song. • Ss sing the song with solfège syllables. • Ss write the solfège syllables under the rhythmic notation at the board for song. • Ss complete the writing worksheet, filling in the notation for A phrase. • Ss create a melodic ostinato using *mi re do low la* and play it on the xylophone as an accompaniment to "Phoebe in Her Petticoat" and other known songs.
SUMMARY ACTIVITIES	
Review lesson outcomes Review the new song	

Table 6.50

GRADE 3: UNIT 4, TWO SIXTEENTH NOTES, ONE EIGHTH NOTE, LESSON 3	
Outcome	Preparation: creating a visual representation of a musical phrase that contains three uneven sounds on a beat (short short long) Practice: improvising melodic patterns that contain *low la*
INTRODUCTORY ACTIVITIES	
Warm-up	
Sing known songs	

(continued)

Table 6.50 Continued

Develop tuneful singing Tone production Diction Expression	
Review known songs and rhythmic elements	
CORE ACTIVITIES	
Teach a new song	
Develop knowledge of music literacy concepts Create a visual representation of what you hear	
Creative movement	
Practice music performance and literacy skills Improvisation	"Phoebe in Her Petticoat" CSP: A • Ss sing "Phoebe in Her Petticoat." • Ss sing with solfège syllables and hand signs. • Ss identify the form. (ABAC) • Ss place the tone set on the board. One S improvises a new B phrase ending on *so* as the T or another S sings A and C phrases.
SUMMARY ACTIVITIES	
Review lesson outcomes Review the new song	

Connections to Grade Handbooks

In Chapter 3 of each handbook we provide you with all the teaching strategies for that grade.

The teaching strategies may be used as a guide for preparing the focus of lessons for each musical element and concept. Many ideas and activities are offered, certainly more than you could accommodate in your individual lessons; but it is always helpful to vary and work to improve some of the approaches you use in preparing and practicing music elements.

Discussion Questions
1. How do we construct a teaching strategy for each element based on the model of learning presented in this chapter?
2. Discuss the notion that the model of learning in this chapter promotes dictation skills and sight-reading skills.
3. Discuss the role of questioning in developing metacognition skills.
4. Discuss the assessment opportunities that are in-built when using the teaching strategy.
5. How does implementation of the teaching strategy promote independent learning in the classroom?
6. Discuss the notion that the teaching strategies presented in this chapter are too cumbersome for instructors to follow, and that it is much more effective to present information theoretically and then use it to practice the music skills of reading and writing.

Ongoing Assignment
1. Develop teaching strategy plans for your teaching portfolio that are based on the model found in this chapter. Demonstrate how you have infused your teaching strategy with your own creative ideas.

Bibliography
Andress, B. *Music for Young Children*. Fort Worth, TX: Harcourt Brace College, 1998.
Bacon, D. "Kodály Music for Learning Disabled Children." *Bulletin of the International Kodály Society*, 1981, 6(2): 24–25.
Bacon, D. "Survival and Revival of Kodály's Heritage: Back to the Sources." *Bulletin of the International Kodály Society*, 1999, 24(2): 17–23.
Bamberger, J. *The Mind Behind the Musical Ear: How Children Develop Musical Intelligence*. Cambridge: Harvard University Press, 1991.
Barrett, M. S., and J. E. Gromko. "Provoking the Muse: A Case Study of Teaching and Learning in Music Composition." *Psychology of Music*, 2007, 35(2): 213–230.
Barrett, Margaret, and Johannella Tafuri. "Creative Meaning-Making in Infants' and Young Children's Musical Cultures." In *The Oxford Handbook of Music Education*, vol. 1, ed. Gary E. McPherson and Graham F. Welch, vol. 1, pp. 296–314. New York: Oxford University Press, 2012.
Barry, N. H., and V. McArthur. "Teaching Practice Strategies in the Music Studio: A Survey of Applied Music Teachers." *Psychology of Music*, 1994, 22(1): 44–55.

Bergethon, B., E. Boardman, and J. Montgomery. *Musical Growth in the Elementary School*, 6th ed. Fort Worth, TX: Harcourt Brace, 1997.

Boardman, E. L., ed. *Dimensions of Musical Thinking*. Reston, VA: Music Educators National Conference, 1989.

Boardman, E. *Fifty Years of Elementary General Music: One Person's Perspective*. Paper presented at the Music Educator's National Conference, Kansas City, MO, 1996.

Boardman, E. L. "The Generative Theory of Musical Learning" (Part II). *General Music Today*, 1988, 2(2): 3–6, 28–31.

Bresler, L. "The Role of Musicianship and Music Education in the Twenty-First Century." In *Musicianship in the 21st Century: Issues, Trends & Possibilities*, ed. S. Leong, pp. 15–27. Sydney: Australian Music Centre, 2003.

Brown, Kyle D. "An Alternative Approach to Developing Music Literacy Skills in a Transient Society." *Music Educators Journal*, 2003, 90(2): 46–54.

Campbell, P. S., and C. Scott Kassner. *Music in Childhood: From Preschool Through the Elementary Grades*. New York: Schirmer, 1995.

Chen-Hafteck, Lily, and Esther Mang. "Music and Language in Early Childhood Development and Learning." In *The Oxford Handbook of Music Education*, ed. Gary E. McPherson and Graham F. Welch, vol. 1, pp. 261–278. New York: Oxford University Press, 2012.

Choksy, Lois. *The Kodály Method: Comprehensive Music Education*, 3rd ed. Upper Saddle River, NJ: Prentice Hall, 1999.

Daniel, K. "The Kodály Method in Piano Teaching." *Kodály Envoy*, 1991, 18(1): 9–15.

Davidson, Lyle, Larry Scripp, and Patricia Welsh. "'Happy Birthday': Evidence for Conflicts of Perceptual Knowledge and Conceptual Understanding." *Journal of Aesthetic Education*, 1988, 22(1): 65–74.

Deliège, I., and J. Sloboda. *Musical Beginnings: Origins and Development of Musical Competence*. New York: Oxford University Press, 1996.

Dunbar-Hall, P. "An Investigation of Strategies Developed by Music Learners in a Cross-Cultural Setting." *Research Studies in Music Education*, 2006, 26(1): 63–70.

Dunn, R., and K. Dunn. *Teaching Elementary Students Through Their Individual Learning Styles*. New York: Allyn & Bacon, 1992.

Eisen, Ann, and Lamar Robertson. *An American Methodology: An Inclusive Approach to Musical Literacy*. Lake Charles, LA: Sneaky Snake, 2002.

Elkind, D. *The Power of Play: How Spontaneous, Imaginative Activities Lead to Happier, Healthier Children*. Cambridge, MA: Da Capo Press, 2007.

Feierabend, J. *First Steps in Music*. Simsbury, CT: GIA, 1999.

Feierabend, J. M. "Kodály and Gordon: Same and Different." *Bulletin of the International Kodály Society*, 1992, 17(1): 41–50.

Forrai, K. *Music in Preschool*, trans. J. Sinor. Budapest, Hungary: Corvina Press, 1988.

Gardner, H. *Frames of Mind: The Theory of Multiple Intelligence*, 2nd ed. New York: Basic Books, 1993.

Gardner, H. *The Unschooled Mind: How Children Think and How Schools Should Teach.* New York: Basic Books, 1991.

Green, L. *Music, Informal Learning and the School: A New Classroom Pedagogy.* Alder-shot, Hampshire, UK: Ashgate, 2008.

Hargreaves, D. J. "The Development of Artistic and Musical Competence." In *Musical Beginnings: The Origins and Development of Musical Competence*, ed. I. Deliège and J. A. Sloboda, pp. 144–170. Oxford: Oxford University Press, 1996.

Hargreaves, D. *The Developmental Psychology of Music.* Cambridge: Cambridge University Press, 1986.

Hirsh-Pasek, K., and R. M. Golinkoff, with D. Eyer. *Einstein Never Used Flashcards: How Our Children Really Learn—and Why They Need to Play More and Memorize Less.* Emmaus, PA: Rodale Press, 2004.

Houlahan, Micheál, and Philip Tacka. *Sound Thinking: Developing Musical Literacy*, 2 vols. New York: Boosey & Hawkes, 1996.

Jentschke, S., S. Koelsch, and A. D. Friederici. "Investigating the Relationship of Music and Language in Children: Influences of Musical Training and Language Impairment." *Annals of the New York Academy of Sciences*, 2005, *1060*: 231–242.

Kertz-Welzel, A. "Music Education in the Twenty-First Century: A Cross-Cultural Comparison of German and American Music Education Towards a New Concept of International Dialogue." *Music Education Research*, 2008, *10*(4): 439–449.

Klonoski, Edward. "A Perceptual Learning Hierarchy: An Imperative for Aural Skills Pedagogy." *College Music Symposium*, online, 2000, vol. 40.

Leong, S., ed. *Musicianship in the 21st Century: Issues, Trends & Possibilities.* Sydney: Australian Music Centre, 2003.

McNicol, R. *Sound Inventions: 32 Creative Music Projects for the Junior Classroom.* Oxford, UK: Oxford University Press, 1992.

Peery, J. C., I. W. Peery, and T. W. Draper, eds. *Music and Child Development.* New York: Springer-Verlag, 1987.

Phillips-Silver, J., and L. J. Trainor. "Feeling the Beat: Movement Influences Infant Rhythm Perception." *Science*, 2005 *308*(5727): 1430.

Rappaport, Jonathan. "Readers' Comments." *Music Educators Journal*, 2004, *90*(4): 7–11.

Reifinger, Jr., James L. "The Acquisition of Sight-Singing Skills in Second-Grade General Music: Effects of Using Solfège and of Relating Tonal Patterns to Songs." *Journal of Research in Music Education*, 2012, *60*(1): 26–42. Music Index. Web. Apr. 7, 2013.

Scott, S. L. "Integrating Inquiry-Based (Constructivist) Music Education with Kodály-inspired Learning." *Kodály Envoy*, 2008, *35*(1): 4–9.

Serafine, M. L. *Music as Cognition: The Development of Thought in Sound* (Part I). New York: Columbia University Press, 1988.

Sinor, J. "The Ideas of Kodály in America." *Bulletin of the International Kodály Society*, 1986, *11*(2): 23–27.

Strong, A. "Kodály Method Applied to Special Education." *Kodály Envoy*, 1983, *9*(3).

Strong, A. and M. A. Nolteriek. "Multiple Intelligences in the Music Lesson." *Kodály Envoy*, 1995, *22*(1): 4–9.

Swanwick, K. "*Music, Mind and Education*." London: Routledge, 1988.

Tait, M. J. "Teaching Strategies and Styles." In *Handbook of Research on Music Teaching and Learning*, ed. R. Colwell, pp. 525–534. New York: Schirmer, 1992.

Turino, T. *Music as Social Life: The Politics of Participation*. Chicago: University of Chicago Press, 2008.

Welch, G. F., E. Himonides, J. Saunders, I. Papageorgi, C. Preti, T. Rinta, M. Vraka, C. Stephens Himonides, C. Stewart, J. Lanipekun, and J. Hill. *Researching the Impact of the National Singing Programme "Sing Up" in England: Main Findings from the First Three Years (2007–2010). Children's Singing Development, Self-Concept and Sense of Social Inclusion*. London: Institute of Education, University of London, 2010.

Winkler, I., G. P. Háden, O. Ladinig, I. Sziller, and H. Honing. "Newborn Infants Detect the Beat in Music." *Proceedings of the National Academy of Sciences*, 2009, *106*(7): 2468–2471.

Young, V., K. Burwell, and D. Pickup. "Areas of Study and Teaching Strategies in Instrumental Teaching: A Case Study Research Project." *Music Education Research*, 2003, *5*(2): 139–155.

Zentner, M., and T. Eerola. "Rhythmic Engagement with Music in Infancy." *Proceedings of the National Academy of Sciences*, 2010, *107*(13): 5768–5773.

Chapter **7**

Developing Musicianship Skills in the Classroom

Key Questions

- What are the musical skills to be developed in the elementary school?
- How can we promote sequential development of music skills?
- How are musical skills integrated into lesson plans?

In previous chapters, we introduced a model of learning and instruction for teaching music concepts and elements. Our goal in this chapter is to demonstrate how a number of music skills (referred to as *skill areas*) can be developed. These skills are practiced in connection with selected music repertoire as well as musical concepts and elements. The art of practicing music skills in the music classroom should be (1) appropriate to student abilities, (2) varied, and (3) motivating. As newly learned musical elements are practiced, musical skills develop and grow. Development of music skills is related to the students' knowledge of rhythmic and melodic elements. The goal of this chapter is to provide teachers with ideas concerning practice of music skills in lessons that focus on preparation/practice and presentation of music elements.

Musical Skills Practiced in the Classroom

This section identifies some of the most important music skills to be developed in the music classroom.

Singing

This is where students use their singing voices to exhibit correct breathing, posture, range, expression, and intonation.

Inner Hearing

This is the ability to hear a melody inside one's head without any acoustical stimulation. Inner hearing is also known as "audiation."

Movement

This is the ability of students to express space, time, and force using their bodies.

Music Reading

This is the skill where students translate notation (the symbols of music) into the sound of music. The process begins with reading known melodies; this is preparation for sight singing (the ability to read an unknown piece of music). Both familiar and new songs and phrases of songs may be practiced as reading examples. Newly learned musical elements are included with familiar elements in both known and unfamiliar songs and reading examples. For reading purposes, we can simplify a folksong by making a structural reduction of the piece of music for reading. In this way, music teachers can create their own music reading exercises based on the repertoire students are singing in the classroom.

Writing

This is the skill of translating the sound of music into music notation. Music writing may be taught developmentally by using various types of pre-notation, traditional rhythmic notation, or staff notation. We suggest three modes of writing. The first is to allow students to use manipulatives; this is particularly effective with young learners. Manipulatives can include popsicle sticks for writing rhythmic stick notation, disc magnets on a magnetic board for showing the melodic contour, Unifix cubes for constructing rhythms or melodic contours, staff boards and discs, individual erasable lap boards, and SMART Board technology. The second is to have students write at the board by completing a phrase of a song. Teachers may use individual dry erase boards for writing. The third approach is to allow students to use paper and pencil or a computerized notation program.

Improvisation

Improvisation permits students to spontaneously create rhythms, melodies, and movements, as well as new texts to a melody. Within the context of the Kodály philosophy, improvisation is connected to both movement and music literacy. Students can engage in improvisation activities using known musical elements or simply by freely improvising.

Composition

Within the context of the Kodály philosophy, composition permits students to create rhythms and melodies in written form. Generally the composition begins as an improvisation; when students notate an improvisation, it becomes a music composition.

Part Work

By part work we mean the ability to perform two or more activities at the same time. This includes singing while performing the beat, or singing and clapping the rhythm. Another example would be to have students sing a song as they walk the beat and perform the rhythm, that is, three modes of performance occurring at the same time. These preliminary skills are necessary for subsequent performance of musical works in several parts and for development of harmonic thinking. Part-work activities can also include students singing and accompanying themselves on a music instrument.

Form

Form is the phrase structure of a piece of music. Students eventually need to determine the rhythmic and melodic forms of a piece of music both aurally and visually. Determining form begins with identifying same, different, and similar phrases. The ability to recognize and identify form significantly affects development of musical memory as well as how a piece of music is learned.

Memory

Music memory is a critical skill in developing all musical abilities. Teachers need to be cognizant of the fact that nearly all their teaching helps develop both aural and visual memory.

Listening

This is the ability to aurally understand as well as visually analyze a piece of music. Listening skills are developed in a number of ways in the music class, including live classroom performances and recorded musical examples. Providing some information about the life of the composer often makes listening activities more engaging for students.

Conducting

Conducting is the ability to perform the beat to a musical work using standard conducting gestures.

Instrumental Development

This includes the ability to recognize music instruments both visually and aurally as well as to play simple rhythmic and melodic instruments in the elementary classroom.

Harmonic Development

This refers to aurally and visually identifying basic chord progressions related to styles of music.

Terminology

This is the ability to use standard musical terms and symbols to aid the performance as well as the reading and writing of music.

Musical Skills: Sample Curriculum

The music curriculum for each grade includes an outline of music skills to develop in that grade. Here is a sample of a grade four curriculum. It includes recommended musical elements as well as musical skills.

Grade 4 Curriculum Goals

Children as Stewards of Their Music Heritage: Repertoire
Expand song repertoire to add to students' knowledge of children's songs and games, folk music of a variety of cultures, art music, and recently composed music.

- A. The student will be able to relate music to history, to society, and to culture (play games, sing songs from diverse cultures).
    1. Southern Appalachians
    2. American frontier
    3. Native American
    4. African American
    5. Latino
    6. British Isles
    7. Western Europe
    8. Eastern Europe
    9. Mediterranean
- B. The student will be able to connect music to the subject areas of reading, writing, language, and math.

Students as Performers: Singing, Playing Instruments, Movement, and Conducting
Broaden performance skills to include:

A. Singing
   1. Sing songs independently and tunefully.
   2. Learn twenty to twenty-five new songs, canons, and two- and three-part song arrangements of various cultural origins.
   3. Sing ten to fifteen songs with solfège and/or rhythm syllables that include syncopation, dotted quarter note followed by an eighth note, dotted eighth note followed by a sixteenth note, *fa, low ti*, and triple meter.
   4. Learn ten to fifteen songs by sight reading, to include syncopation, dotted quarter note followed by an eighth note, dotted eighth note followed by a sixteenth note, *fa, low ti*, and triple meter.
   5. Learn five to seven two-part songs.
   6. Sing individually and in groups in call and response, verse and refrain, and game songs.
B. Part work
   1. Sing songs or play instruments in a group.
   2. Sing antiphonal songs and call-and-response songs.
   3. Practice intervals simultaneously with hand signs that include *fa* and *low ti*.
   4. Accompany a song with a rhythmic ostinato using these rhythms:
      A. Quarter notes
      B. Eighth notes
      C. Quarter note rests
      D. Sixteenth notes
      E. Eighth note plus two sixteenth notes
      F. Two sixteenth notes followed by an eighth note
      G. Syncopated rhythms
      H. Dotted quarter followed by an eighth note
      I. Dotted eighth followed by a sixteenth note
      J. Triple meter
   5. Accompany a song with a melodic ostinato using *low so, low la, low ti, do, re, mi, fa, so, la,* and *high do*.
   6. Sing simple rhythmic or melodic canons derived from familiar songs.
   7. Perform two-part rhythmic exercises based on rhythms of known songs.
   8. Sing and read two-part songs.
C. Movement
   1. Perform double circle games.
   2. Perform circle games containing square dance patterns.
   3. Perform line dances containing contradance patterns.
   4. Perform basic square dance.
   5. Perform games and dances from various cultures.
   6. Explore games, activities, and movement in personal space or general space.

D. Instruments
1. Demonstrate fourth grade melodic and rhythmic concepts that include syncopation, dotted quarter note followed by an eighth note, dotted eighth note followed by a sixteenth note, *fa, low ti*, and triple meter.
2. Play on classroom instruments such as xylophones, glockenspiels, rhythm instruments, and recorder.
3. Accompany classroom singing on classroom instruments using patterns that include syncopation, dotted quarter note followed by an eighth note, dotted eighth note followed by a sixteenth note, *fa, low ti*, and triple meter.

E. Conducting
1. Conduct repertoire in duple simple, triple meter, compound meter (in two), and quadruple meter.

F. Inner hearing
1. Silently sing melodic motifs or melody from the teacher's hand signs.
2. Silently sing known songs with rhythmic syllables.
3. Silently sing known songs with melodic syllables.
4. Silently read either full or partial rhythms or melodies written in traditional notation with solfège syllables or staff notation.
5. Sing back short known melodic or rhythmic motives from memory using text (if the student recognizes the song it is abstracted from), rhythm syllables, or solfège syllables.

G. Form
1. Continue recognition of phrase forms using question-and-answer, ABAC, and other known forms.
2. Study the form of folksongs, either aurally or through music reading, to include syncopation, dotted quarter followed by an eighth note, dotted eighth note followed by a sixteenth note, *fa, low ti*, and triple meter.

H. Musical memory
1. Sing selected song with melodic patterns using *fa* and *low ti*, and ask students to sing patterns back using hand signs, and again using hand signs and absolute pitch.
2. Sing the starting pitch of a selected song and ask students to sing a melody with absolute letter names while showing hand signs.
3. Students look at a score containing syncopation, dotted quarter note followed by an eighth note, dotted eighth note followed by a sixteenth note, *fa, low ti*, or triple meter; memorize a phrase of the example by silently singing in their head using hand signs.
4. Students may write the melody on staff paper. At a more advanced level, the students can write the example in another key using a different clef.
5. Memorize two-part songs and exercises that include syncopation, dotted quarter note followed by an eighth note, dotted eighth note followed by a sixteenth note, *fa, low ti*, and triple meter.

Students as Critical Thinkers and Problem Solvers: Music Literacy

A. Rhythm elements: in addition to third grade elements, use syncopated rhythms, dotted quarter note followed by an eighth note, dotted eighth followed by a sixteenth note, dotted half note, and triple meter.
   1. Perform songs with rhythm syllables.
   2. Perform ostinati.
   3. Perform rhythmic canons.
   4. Perform two-part rhythmic exercises.
   5. Recognize tunes from clapped rhythm patterns.

B. Melodic elements. In addition to third grade elements, use *fa*, minor pentatonic scale, and *low ti*.
   1. Perform songs with solfège syllables and hand signs.
   2. Perform ostinato.
   3. Perform canons.
   4. Perform two-part melodic exercises from a teacher's hand signs.
   5. Read a two-part melodic exercise from notation.
   6. Recognize tunes hummed by a teacher.
   7. Recognize a tune from a teacher's hand signs.

C. Reading and writing rhythmic elements
   1. Know names and written symbols for syncopated rhythms, dotted quarter followed by an eighth note, dotted eighth followed by a sixteenth note, dotted half note, and triple meter. Students should be able to sing repertoire fluently with rhythm syllables before learning the technical names of notes.
   2. Read with rhythm syllables as well as count with numbers.
   3. Read or write well-known rhythmic patterns with stick notation and traditional rhythmic notation.
   4. Read a two-part rhythmic exercise.
   5. Expand reading and writing of rhythmic and melodic patterns from four to eight to sixteen beats.
   6. Write rhythmic patterns from memory or when dictated by the teacher in stick notation and traditional rhythmic notation.

D. Reading and writing melodic elements
   1. Know the names and written syllables for all solfège notes of the major extended pentatonic scale, minor pentatonic scale, minor pentachord, minor hexachord, and major scale.
   2. Read or write well-known melodic patterns with traditional rhythmic notation and solfège syllables as well as on staff notation.
   3. Write from memory melodic patterns found in focus songs, or write them as dictated by the teacher using stick and solfège syllables, traditional notation, and solfège syllables, or staff notation.
   4. Read a two-part melodic exercise from staff notation.

5. Know the names and written syllables for all solfège notes of the major pentatonic scale, minor pentatonic scale, minor pentachord, minor hexachord, and major scale.
6. Read or write well-known melodic patterns with traditional rhythmic notation and solfège syllables as well on staff notation.
7. Write known songs using traditional rhythmic and staff notation in G-*do,* F-*do,* and C-*do* (major and minor).
8. Apply absolute letter names to simple melodic exercises on the staff in G-*do,* F-*do,* and C-*do* (major and minor).
9. Apply absolute letter names to simple *do, so*, and *la* pentatonic, pentachord, and hexachord melodic exercises on the staff in G-*do*, F-*do*, C-*do*, D-*low la*.

Children as Creative Human Beings: Improvisation and Composition

Expand skills in improvisation and composition to include singing, playing instruments, and moving at the third grade level. Students will be able to carry out:

A. Rhythmic improvisation (based on the rhythmic building blocks of sung repertoire)
   1. Improvise rhythm patterns, of four or eight beats, by clapping and saying rhythm syllables.
   2. Improvise a melodic chain: begin each phrase with the last syllable used by a previous student.
   3. Improvise rhythm patterns of four or eight beats using rhythm instruments.
   4. Improvise a new rhythm to a phrase of a well-known song written in traditional notation.
   5. Improvise question-and-answer motives using known rhythm patterns.
   6. Improvise to a given form.
B. Melodic improvisation (based on the melodic building blocks of sung repertoire)
   1. Improvise melodic patterns of four or eight beats by singing with solfège and hand signs.
   2. Improvise a melodic chain: begin each phrase with the last syllable used by a previous student.
   3. Improvise melodic patterns of four or eight beats using barred instruments.
   4. Improvise short musical motives using known scales.
   5. Improvise major, minor, and modal melodies to simple four- to eight-beat rhythms using the voice or a barred instrument.
   6. Improvise question-and-answer motives using known melodic patterns.
   7. Improvise a two-part melody using hand signs.

Children as Informed Audience Members: Listening

Expand listening repertoire to teach and reinforce fourth grade musical concepts.

Developing Musicianship Skills

1. Recognize musical features in classroom song repertoire, folk music, and masterworks.
2. Recognize rhythmic features in classroom song repertoire, folk music, and masterworks.
3. Recognize melodic features in classroom song repertoire, folk music, and masterworks.
4. Develop awareness of expressive controls, that is, dynamics, tempo, timbre, and their distinctive characteristics in masterworks of various historical periods.
5. Recognize phrase forms in classroom song repertoire, folk music, and masterworks.
6. Recognize tonic, dominant, and subdominant functions.
7. Follow a complete score prepared by the teacher where all known elements will be identified.

Remember that your curriculum goals need to be adjusted according to the frequency of your teaching. Each section of the curriculum includes specific music skills that need to be developed.

Expanding Your Students' Musical Skills

Practicing Rhythm and Melody Through Reading, Writing, and Memory Exercises

Key Questions
- How can we address the prerequisite skills that accompany musical reading and writing?
- How do we practice rhythmic and melodic elements?
- How do we develop our students' writing, reading, and memory skills?
- What reading activities can be used to practice musical elements?
- What types of writing activities can young learners perform?
- What additional learning skills are involved when a student reads or writes music?

Musical reading and writing are skills that lead to comprehensive musicianship. These two skills may be practiced during each music lesson in a manner that does not detract from the enjoyment of making music. Although the terms *reading* and *sight singing* are interchangeable, we make a distinction. We use *reading* when students read known song material and *sight singing* to refer to students' reading unfamiliar musical material. Similarly, we use *writing* when referring to writing known musical patterns; *dictation* refers to writing unknown musical patterns.

We identify specific activities that can be used to practice rhythm and melody once students have a knowledge base of several concepts and elements. Musical reading and writing are fundamental skills that can be built on. For example, a reading exercise can be the basis for an improvisation or musical form activity. The form activity may subsequently evolve into a memory exercise, which can be performed in canon; the canon performance could ultimately progress to a listening activity.

Here we present exercises that can be modified and adapted to any level of instruction. They show a variety of ways to practice rhythmic and melodic elements.

Once you gain the practical experience of working through some of our suggestions, you will undoubtedly begin to develop additional and varied activities by transforming them into inner hearing, memory, and ensemble singing activities.

Approaches to Practicing Rhythm

Here are some ideas as to how to practice rhythm. These activities may be used throughout a lesson plan.

1. Speak or sing the rhythm patterns of well-known songs while tapping the beat.
2. Put the rhythm of a song on the board and allow students to figure out the correct placement of the heartbeats.
3. Speak or sing the rhythm of a pattern or song while conducting.
4. Echo patterns with rhythm syllables.
5. Sing a known or unknown phrase of a song with words, and have the students sing back the phrase with rhythm syllables while keeping the beat or clapping the words.
6. Sing a known or unknown song on a neutral syllable (*loo*), and have the students sing back with rhythm syllables while keeping the beat or clapping the words.
7. Sing a known or unknown song with solfège syllables, and have the students sing back with rhythm syllables while keeping the beat or clapping the words.
8. Play a melody on an instrument, and ask students to sing it back with rhythm syllables while keeping the beat or clapping the words.
9. Play a game where *ta* is placed on the students' head and *ta-di* is placed on their shoulders. The students tap their head and shoulders as they sing a song. Perform this activity slowly. Of course, this can be practiced with other rhythmic combinations.
10. Match song titles to written rhythms. List the titles of four songs on the board. Write a phrase from each of the four songs in rhythmic notation. Students match the rhythm to the title of the song.
11. Sing or clap the rhythm of well-known songs reading from rhythmic notation or staff notation. Inner hearing may be used with this exercise.
12. Ask students to work out the rhythm of an unknown song taught by rote.
13. Identify the meter and rhythm patterns clapped or sung by another person.
14. Read a rhythm from the board, and simultaneously clap it in canon.

15. Error detection. You or a student can write a sixteen-beat rhythm pattern and then clap a slightly different pattern. Another student must identify the phrases and the beats where the changes occur.
16. Clap a four-beat phrase and sixteen-beat rhythm pattern while singing a known song of the same length.
17. Improvise rhythm patterns. First, select a meter and length of beats for the improvisation. For example, a simple task could be to improvise four four-beat phrases. The form can be AABA. Select four students, each to perform a phrase. The first student improvises a four-beat pattern (A). The second student has to remember the pattern and perform it (A). The third student improvises a different pattern (B). The fourth student must remember the A pattern and perform it (A). This exercise can be performed with a number of forms and longer phrases.
18. Improvise rhythm patterns in specified meters. You must specify the phrase length and form (for example, AAAB).
19. Perform a rhythmic canon. We suggest this procedure:
    A. Students say the rhythm syllables while clapping the rhythm.
    B. Instruct students to think the rhythm syllables and clap the rhythm.
    C. Divide the class and have them perform the rhythm in canon.
    D. Two individual students perform the canon.
    E. Challenge individual students to perform the rhythmic canon alone by saying the rhythm syllables but clapping the rhythm in canon at the same time.
20. Transform the rhythm of one song into the rhythm of another. Write the rhythm of a known song on the board but clap a slightly different pattern from the one written. Ask students to identify the phrase and beats that need to be changed to match what was clapped. Continue to do this until the rhythm has been transformed into that of another known song. Once identified, students may sing the transformed song with rhythm syllables.
21. Write a rhythm pattern on the board. After discussing the form, the students may memorize the pattern and write it from memory.
22. Write a known song in rhythmic notation with several missing measures. Students write in the missing measures.
23. Practice rhythmic part work.
    A. Students say the rhythm syllables and clap the rhythm.
    B. Students think the rhythm syllables and clap the rhythm.
    C. Students think and clap the rhythm while you tap it in canon.
    D. Clap the rhythm while the students clap it in canon.
    E. Divide the class into two groups. One half claps the rhythm while the other half claps in canon so that you can observe any students who may be having difficulty.
    F. Individuals may then perform the rhythmic canon saying the rhythm syllables while clapping it in canon.

Kodály Today

24. Rhythm telegraph: clap a four-beat rhythm pattern to a student in a circle, who then passes this pattern on to other students. You may continue to pass several patterns around the circle. The last student may write this pattern on the board.
25. Flashcard activities
    A. Read several flashcards using four-beat patterns written in traditional rhythmic notation in succession.
    B. Place the cards on the ledge of the board, and perform them in order. Change the order of the cards. Have individual students read different patterns by changing the order of the cards. Gradually arrange the order of the cards to move from one song to another in a lesson. A card may be removed and an individual student may improvise a rhythm to replace the missing pattern. By extending the number of phrases involved in this activity, the class may practice different forms.
    C. Have a student draw a rhythm card from a box. Another student may tell her how to perform the rhythm (clapping, jumping, tapping, stamping, blinking, nodding, and so on). The class may echo the rhythm.
    D. Read a series of rhythm flashcards in succession; turn the flashcards upside down, and have the class read them in succession; place the flashcards on the chalk ledge, and have students read them backwards.
    E. Ask students to rearrange a series of flash cards to create a known song.
    F. Students memorize four-, eight-, twelve-, or sixteen-beat patterns from flashcards and sing back with rhythm syllables or write the memorized patterns using stick notation.
26. Read a rhythm pattern as you listen to a piece of music. It is important that the music have a well-defined beat and be simple enough for students to listen to. Baroque pieces are useful for this activity.

Approaches to Practicing Melody

Here are some ideas as to how to practice melody. These activities may be used throughout a lesson plan.

1. Students' piano. Each student becomes a musical pitch and takes a place in order from high to low so that you can "play" the piano by pointing to a student to sing a pitch.
2. Sing known melodies or phrases with solfège syllables and hand signs.
3. Sing known melodies or phrases with solfège syllables and conduct.
4. Sing a known song with solfège syllables and hand signs reading traditional rhythmic notation with solfège or staff notation.
5. Sing a known song or phrase with solfège syllables or letter names and hand signs, and have the students echo.

Developing Musicianship Skills

6. Sing a known song with text, and have the students echo with hand signs and solfège syllables or letter names.
7. Echo patterns with solfège syllables and hand signs.
8. Show a melody with hand signs or finger staff, and have the students sing back with solfège syllables and hand signs.
9. Show a melody with hand signs or finger staff, and have the students sing back with letter names and hand signs.
10. Hum a known song or phrase and have the students echo back with hand signs and solfège syllables or letter names.
11. Match song titles to written rhythmic notations and solfège. List the titles of four songs on the board. Write a phrase from each of the four songs in rhythmic notation and solfège. Students match the notation to the title of the song.
12. Point to a melody on the staff or tone ladder, and have the students sing with hand signs and solfège syllables or letter names.
13. Sing a phrase with rhythm syllables, and have the students echo sing the phrase with solfège syllables or letter names.
14. Play a melody on recorder, and have the students sing with solfège syllables or letter names.
15. Show a pattern with hand signs, or point to a tone chart or tone ladder. Ask an individual student to sing the pattern.
16. Error detection. Write a known song with rhythmic notation and solfège and then hum a slightly different version. Students must identify the phrases and the beats where the changes occur.
17. Sing a melody or play a melody on the piano, and have the students sing in canon with solfège syllables, letter names, or rhythm syllables.
18. Flashcard activities
    A. Read several flashcards using four-beat patterns written in traditional rhythmic notation and solfège in succession.
    B. Place the cards on the ledge of the chalkboard, and perform them in order. Change the order of the cards. Have individual students read different patterns by changing the order of the cards. Gradually arrange the order of the cards to move from one song to another in a lesson. A card may be removed and an individual student may improvise a rhythm to replace the missing pattern. Various forms may be practiced by extending the number of phrases involved in this activity.
    C. Ask students to rearrange a series of flash cards to create a known song.
    D. Students memorize four-, eight-, twelve-, or sixteen-beat patterns from flashcards and sing back with syllables or write the memorized patterns.
19. Perform a two- or three-part canon: play a melody on piano, and have group 1 sing in canon after two measures; or add another group and sing as a three-part canon.

Kodály Today

20. Students read a music example with solfège syllables; at a given signal from you, students switch to singing with absolute letter names.
21. Divide class into two groups; each group reads a pentatonic melody of the same phrase structure and phrase length simultaneously.
22. Improvise melodic patterns. First, select a meter and length for the improvisation. For example, a simple task could be to improvise four four-beat phrases. The form can be AABA. Select four students, each to perform a phrase. The first student improvises a four-beat pattern (A). The second student has to remember the pattern and perform it (A). The third student improvises a different pattern (B). The fourth student must remember the A pattern and perform it (A). This exercise can be performed with a number of forms and longer phrases.
23. Improvise melodic patterns in specified meters. You must specify the phrase length and form (for example, AAAB).
24. Play a melody on piano, and have the students play it back immediately.
25. Sing a melody in retrograde.

Procedures for Developing Reading and Sight Reading Skills

Before students can read unknown rhythm and melodies (sight reading) they need to be able to read known rhythms and melodies. Here are activities that can be used for developing students' rhythmic and melodic reading and sight-reading skills. Depending on the ability of the students, some of these steps outlined below can be skipped.

Reading the Rhythm of a Known Song

For the first activity, we have selected "Let Us Chase the Squirrel" (Fig. 7.1).

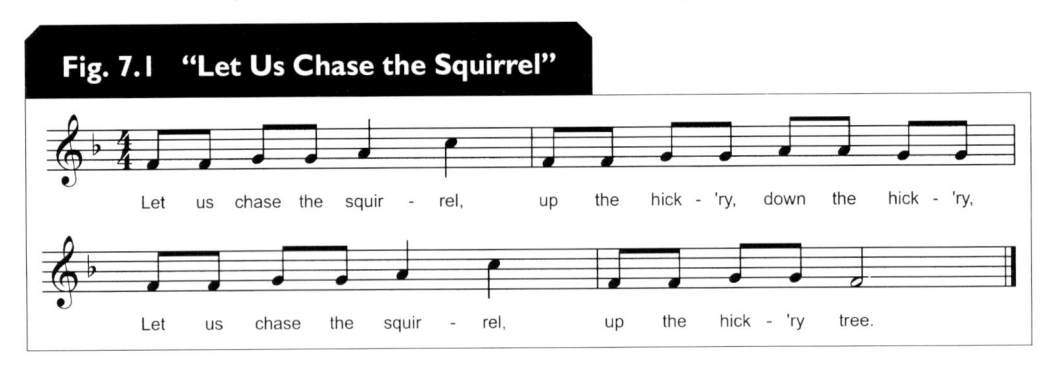

Fig. 7.1 "Let Us Chase the Squirrel"

1. Sing the song and tap the beat.
2. Sing the song with rhythm syllables.
3. Tap as Ss keep the beat, and read the rhythm of the complete song or the rhythm of a specific phrase, using inner hearing or aloud.
4. Tap the beat:
   A. Ss read phrases 1 and 3 and T reads phrases 2 and 4 in succession.
   B. T reads phrases 1 and 3 and Ss read phrases 2 and 4 in succession.

By guiding students to read using this procedure, you teach them to become aware of the form and structure of the song.

Reading Known Melodies from Hand Signs

Before reading melodies from notation, it is helpful and easier for students to read known melodies from hand signs. Here is a process to be used to practice reading known melodies from hand signs.

1. Ss sing the song and keep the beat.
2. T sings the melody phrase by phrase on a neutral syllable and Ss sing with rhythm syllables and conduct. Or Ss can sing the melody with rhythm syllables and conduct from memory.
3. T sings the melody on a neutral syllable and Ss sing with solfège syllables and hand signs. Or Ss can sing the melody with solfège syllables and hand signs from memory.
4. Ss read the melody from the T hand signs using inner hearing.
5. Ss sing the melody from the T hand signs with solfège syllables.

Reading Known Melodic Patterns and Intervals from Hand Signs or Notation

Provide opportunities for students to read typical melodic patterns and intervals, found in the repertoire, from hand signs and from notation. Once target patterns from song material have been learned, practice reading and writing these patterns and related patterns. For example, after students learn the pentatonic trichord *la-so-mi* we need to consider how to practice the intervals formed by these three notes. The *mi-la* interval, though not difficult to sing, is difficult to read.

The *mi-la* interval is common to a number of children's chants, yet making students conscious of this melodic turn requires some careful but logical preparation. Students should be able to sing several or all of these songs in their entirety and know the solfège syllables *so-mi* and *la*: "Rain Rain," "Doggie, Doggie," "Little Sally Water," "Bye Baby Bunting," "No Robbers Out Today," "Johnny's It," "Nanny Goat," and "Fudge, Fudge."

The *mi-la* interval usually occurs on the second beat within a four-beat song phrase. Students may be guided to read the *mi-la* pattern if the teacher manipulates known *mi-so* and *so-la* melodic patterns. Here are suggestions for easily getting students to read and perform the *mi-la* interval. Please note that what is presented is only a portion of a lesson plan.

1. Ss read the pattern seen in Figure 7.2 silently while showing hand signs, and then they sing aloud. T asks Ss individually to sing and show hand signs.

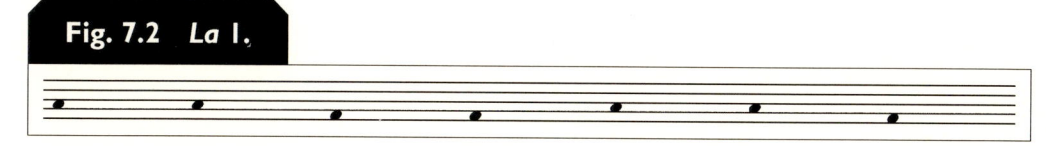

Fig. 7.2 La l.

Kodály Today

2. T changes the pattern: "I'm going to see if I can trick you." Ss read the pattern in Figure 7.3 silently while showing hand signs and then sing aloud. T asks Ss individually to sing and show hand signs.

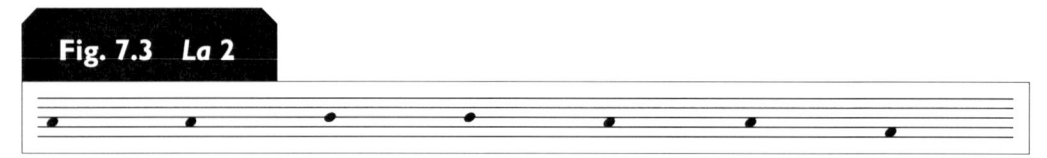

Fig. 7.3   La 2

3. T changes the pattern: "I'm going to see if I can trick you again." Ss read the pattern in Figure 7.4 silently while showing hand signs and then sing aloud. T asks Ss individually to sing and show hand signs.

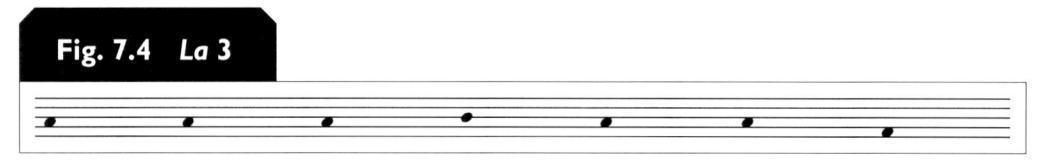

Fig. 7.4   La 3

4. T changes the pattern: "I'm going to see if I can trick you again." Ss read the pattern in Figure 7.5 silently while showing hand signs and then sing aloud. T asks Ss individually to sing and show hand signs.

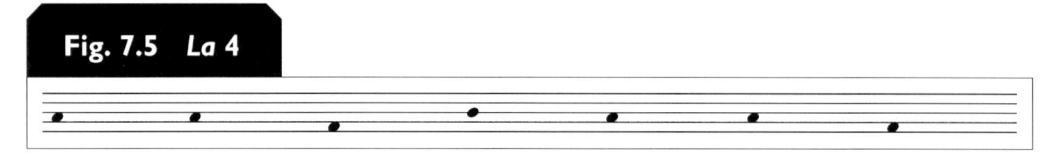

Fig. 7.5   La 4

5. T says, "That reminds me of a song we know." (T has a choice of many songs; see below.) Once the song is identified, Ss sing it with solfège syllables.

The *mi-la* pattern occurs in the second phrase of "Rain, Rain" and "Doggie, Doggie." The *mi-la* pattern occurs throughout "Doggie, Doggie," "Little Sally Water," "Bye Baby Bunting," "No Robbers Out Today," "Ring Around the Rosie," "Johnny's It," "Nanny Goat," and "Fudge, Fudge."

Two-hand Sign Singing

The teacher shows a series of intervals using both hands to show hand signs; students have to read from the teacher's hand signs in two groups. Two-hand sign singing is helpful in developing accurate intonation. We recommend using Kodály's publication from his Choral Method series, *Let Us Sing Correctly*, for examples of repertoire that use this kind of activity.

Reading a Known Melody of a Song from Traditional Rhythmic Notation and Solfège

We use "Bounce High, Bounce Low" (Fig. 7.6) to illustrate the process.

Developing Musicianship Skills

Fig. 7.6 "Bounce High, Bounce Low"

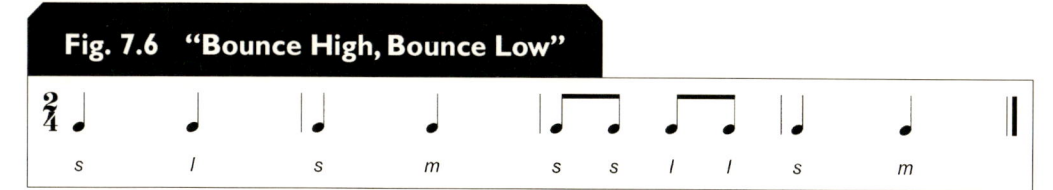

```
2/4  s   l   s   m   s s l l   s   m
```

1. Ss sing the known song with rhythm syllables.
2. T points to the notation, keeping the beat while Ss read the rhythm with rhythm syllables and clap the rhythm.
3. Ss locate the highest and lowest notes.
4. T provides the starting pitch and may have Ss sing the tone set.
5. Ss read from the melody, from T's hand signs with inner hearing. T may hum an occasional note to help them.
6. Ss read and perform the exercise aloud, singing with solfège syllables and hand signs.
8. Ss perform the exercise aloud singing with solfège syllables and hand signs.
9. Ss perform the exercise aloud, singing on a neutral syllable.

Reading a Known Melody from Staff Notation

Prepare both melodic and rhythmic patterns to help students read a new song from staff notation. You can use familiar songs to prepare the intervals and the tone set of the new song. The steps outlined above may be used when reading from staff notation. For example, the tone set of "Bye, Bye Baby" prepares the *so-mi-re-do* tone set of "Let Us Chase the Squirrel" (Fig. 7.7).

Fig. 7.7 "Let Us Chase the Squirrel"

Let us chase the squir - rel, up the hick - 'ry, down the hick - 'ry,
Let us chase the squir - rel, up the hick - 'ry tree.

1. Ss sing the known songs with rhythm syllables.
2. T points to the notation, keeping the beat while Ss read (using inner hearing) the rhythm syllables and clap the rhythm.
3. T points to the notation, keeping the beat while Ss clap the rhythm.
4. Ss sing the known song with solfège syllables.
5. Ss locate the highest and lowest notes.
6. T provides the starting pitch and may have Ss sing the tone set.
7. Ss read from the melody from T's hand signs.

Kodály Today

8. T reviews the Rule of Placement for Ss, and they read the notes of the melody from the tone set written on the staff.
9. Ss show the hand signs and use their inner hearing while T points to keep the beat. T may hum an occasional note to help them.
10. Ss read the known song from the staff aloud, singing with solfège syllables and hand signs.
11. Ss perform the exercise aloud, singing on a neutral syllable.

Reading a Two-part Known Melody from Rhythmic Notation with Solfège Syllables

1. Ss sing the known song with rhythm syllables and solfège syllables.
2. T points to the notation of the upper part, keeping the beat while Ss read the rhythm syllables and clap the rhythm.
3. T points to the notation of the lower part, keeping the beat while Ss read the rhythm syllables and clap the rhythm.
4. Ss clap the upper part and T claps the lower part. Reverse.
5. T divides the class into two groups. One group claps the upper part and the other claps the lower part. Reverse.
6. Ss read the upper part from T's hand signs.
7. Ss read the lower part from T's hand signs.
8. Ss read the upper part from T's hand signs while T sings the lower voice. Reverse.
9. Ss read the upper part with hand signs while T sings the lower voice. Reverse.
10. T divides the class into two groups; one sings the upper part and the other the lower part. Reverse.
11. One S sings the upper voice part and shows the hand signs for the lower part. Reverse.

Reading a Two-part Known Melody from Staff Notation

1. Ss sing the known song with rhythm syllables and solfège syllables.
2. T points to the notation of the upper part, keeping the beat while Ss read the rhythm syllables and clap the rhythm.
3. T points to the notation of the lower part, keeping the beat while Ss read the rhythm syllables and clap the rhythm.
4. Ss clap the upper part and T claps the lower part. Reverse.
5. T divides the class into two groups. One claps the upper part and the other claps the lower part. Reverse.
6. Ss read the upper part from T's hand signs.
7. Ss read the lower part from T's hand signs.
8. Ss read the upper part from T's hand signs while T sings the lower voice. Reverse.
9. Ss locate the highest and lowest notes.
10. T provides the starting pitch and may have Ss sing the tone set.

11. T reviews the Rule of Placement for Ss, and they read the notes of the upper and lower parts from the tone set written on the staff.
12. Ss read the upper part with hand signs while T sings the lower voice. Reverse.
13. T divides the class into two groups. One sings the upper part and the other the lower part. Reverse.
14. One S sings the upper voice part and shows the hand signs for the lower part. Reverse.

As a preliminary exercise, the teacher can arrange known folksongs where the melody is divided between two voice parts. The voice part that is not performing the melody can clap or sing a simple rhythmic or melodic ostinato.

Changing a Reading Activity into a Sight-Singing Activity
We suggest this procedure:

1. T puts the song "Old Mother Witch" on the board using traditional notation and solfège syllables written under the notation.
2. T claps and says the rhythm syllables.
3. T sings with solfège syllables and hand signs.
4. T transforms the song, changing one beat at a time and having Ss identify where the change occurred.
5. T then sight-sings the new melody.
   A. T asks, "How many beats are in each measure?"
   B. T has the students read the rhythm.
   C. T compares and contrasts measures 3, 5, 6, and 7.
   D. Ask Ss to sing the exercise in their heads and show hand signs.
   E. T sings the entire exercise. Challenge Ss to strive for accuracy.
6. Ss sing the new sight-reading melody in canon.

Inner Hearing (Audiation) and Its Significance for Practicing Musical Skills

Developing inner-hearing skills is one of the most important music activities a music teacher can develop in the music classroom. Singing with solfège syllables promotes this critical musicianship skill. As students' inner-hearing abilities develop, they will hear melodies without any acoustic stimulus. This is important for students singing in choirs or for instrumentalists. Here are some techniques for developing inner hearing:

1. Ss sing a melody with solfège, and T indicates where they should sing the melody silently.
2. Ss read from a score, but T indicates where they should sing silently with inner hearing.
3. T shows a melody with hand signs. Ss sing back the melody.
4. T sings or and plays a melody and Ss have to remember the first note of the melody played. This exercise can be extended from short to longer motifs.

Kodály Today

5. Ss sing a series of notes and T plays another series above or below what Ss sing. They must identify the solfège for each interval of the melody sung or performed by T.
6. Ss sing a series of notes and T plays another series above or below what Ss sing. They sing the melody performed by T, and he or she sings the melody performed by Ss.

Inner hearing can be practiced in several ways. Here are specific inner-hearing activities that can be used in the classroom. We suggest you connect inner hearing to as many activities as possible (see Fig. 7.8).

1. Prior to reading a musical example aloud, T allows Ss to sing through the example silently (inner-hear) while performing a beat.
2. Ss sing a song aloud, and at a signal from T they inner-hear a phrase or portion of a phrase. For younger Ss, use a puppet or symbol as a signal for them to inner-hear or to sing aloud.
3. Ss recognize a song from hearing T clap its rhythm.
4. Ss recognize a song from traditional rhythmic notation or staff notation on the board without hearing it performed aloud.
5. Ss recognize a song from T's hand signs.
6. Ss recognize a song from T pointing to solfège syllables on the steps.
7. Ss sing a melody with solfège syllables, and T indicates where they should sing the melody silently.
8. Ss read from a score, but T indicates where they should sing silently with inner hearing.
9. T sings or plays a melody, and Ss have to remember the first note of the melody played. This exercise can be extended from short to longer motifs.
10. Ss sing a well-known song as T claps a four-beat ostinato. Ss repeat the song and clap the T's ostinato.
11. Ss sing a series of notes and T plays another series above or below the first. Ss must identify the intervals of the solfège of the melody sung or performed by T.
12. T points to a song on the tone ladder and Ss must sing back each phrase from memory.

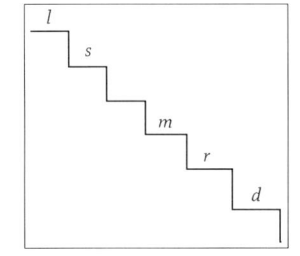

FIG. 7.8 SOLFÈGE STEPS

Developing Musicianship Skills

General Considerations for Sight-Singing Unknown Melodies

Sight-singing is different from reading in that students have not technically sung the sight-singing example; therefore, these exercises need careful preparation. We suggest that students begin by reading known melodies and gradually transform the known melody in an unknown melody.

Physical Activities That Prepare Sight Singing
Prepare students to read a musical example by performing physical activities such as echo clapping the rhythms of the example, tracing the melodic contour of the melody, or singing melodic motives from the sight-singing example with solfège syllables and hand signs.

Reading from the Board
Begin sight singing by guiding students to read from the board or from a SMART Board. We suggest that you point to the beats (not to each note) and, prior to singing aloud, ask students to sing or read in their heads (inner-hear). After they have read through the example silently, they may sing it aloud. It's usually easier for students to read from the board; after they can successfully do that, they can read from a worksheet.

Begin with Short Phrases
Beginning reading exercises should use short musical phrases. Read a complete phrase; do not stop on each beat. Reading examples or exercises should be slightly easier than the rhythmic and melodic elements being studied.

Read Known Melodies and Melodic Phrases First
Begin by first reading songs that are familiar to students. You can always transform the known melody into a new melody, or into another known melody.

Allow Students to Be Independent
Avoid guiding the students too much by always tapping the rhythm or the beat for every sight-singing example. Work to develop independent readers who can read without your help.

The Performance
Students need to be reminded that although they are sight-singing (something that is usually challenging), they must attempt to make their performance musical. Before each sight-singing exercise, practice basic rhythmic and melodic patterns from the exercise with the students. Difficult rhythms can be practiced with an appropriate rhythmic ostinato or with the subdivision of the beat. Sing these preparatory exercises in the same key as the reading example. A useful approach for developing sight-singing skills is for students to read the melodic turns of the melody from hand signs without rhythm. The melodic contour for the song "Dinah" would look like this:

do-mi-so-mi
do-mi-re-do
do-mi-so-mi
re-mi-re-do

Kodály Today

By preparing the tone set, students can better read the sight-singing example with solfège syllables and rhythmic notation. We prepare each sight-singing example to help students perform the example musically. Exercises may be sung with solfège syllables, letter names, and neutral syllables. Once students are comfortable with the stylistic characteristics of the repertoire they are singing, it is also important to practice sight-singing repertoire with words.

This is a procedure that may be applied to sight-reading new material using traditional notation and solfège:

1. T identifies all of the rhythmic and melodic elements that need to be practiced in advanced of the sight reading. T selects and sings known songs that contain these elements.
2. T makes Ss aware of the meter of the sight reading, choosing an appropriate tempo.
3. T asks Ss to think through the entire rhythm.
4. Ss clap the rhythm with rhythm syllables. Exercises can be repeated, asking Ss to conduct and say the rhythm syllables.
5. T reviews the tone set and the final note of the sight-reading example.
6. Ss use hand signs while inner-hearing the melody.
7. Ss sing the exercise with solfège syllables and hand signs.
8. Ss sing the example using a neutral syllable.

This procedure may be used for sight-reading new material from the staff:

1. T identifies all of the rhythmic and melodic elements that need to be practiced in advanced of the sight reading. He or she selects and sings known songs that contain these elements.
2. T makes Ss aware of the meter of the sight reading, choosing an appropriate tempo.
3. Ask Ss to think through the entire rhythm.
4. Ss clap the rhythm with rhythm syllables. Exercises can be repeated, asking Ss to conduct and say the rhythm syllables.
5. T reviews the Rule of Placement for the tone of the piece of music.
6. Ss sing the scale of the sight-reading example.
7. Ss inner-hear the melody with hand signs.
8. Ss sing the melody with solfège syllables and hand signs.
9. Ss sing the example using a neutral syllable.

Sight-singing exercises may be memorized and notated. Practice reading melodic patterns using or not using a rhythm pattern. The teacher may devise a variety of ways to practice a reading exercise, for example, reading the melody backwards, reading a unison melody while clapping a rhythmic ostinato, or for a challenge singing a melody in canon

Developing Musicianship Skills

at the fifth with only the first voice given. Our text on music fundamentals, *From Sound to Symbol,* includes an audio CD and interactive skill development DVD and web-based supplementary materials for eleven chapters. The web-based supplementary materials include many examples that can be used for sight singing and sight-reading.

Activities for Developing Writing Skills

The ability to discern individual pitches, vocally reproduce them, and echo rhythm patterns is prerequisite for writing music accurately. Writing a melody involves the skills of memory and inner hearing. Students need to know and understand the rhythmic and melodic content of any piece of music they are trying to write; most young students have difficulty taking both rhythmic and melodic dictation at the same time. Dictation is a skill and can therefore be broken down into incremental steps: writing beats, echoing activities, and determining solfège syllables are pre-dictation skills. Writing should begin with notation of known melodies before we begin to working on notating new melodies. Here are activities that can be used for developing student's rhythmic and melodic writing skills. Depending on students' abilities and frequency of instruction, some of the steps outlined below may be skipped.

Writing Beats

Ask students to mark the beats on their desks, moving from left to right as the teacher sings and marks beats on the board. Mark the beats according to the number of phrases in the song and the number of beats per phrase. For example, "Rocky Mountain" has four phrases of eight beats. A beat chart for "Rocky Mountain" is shown in Figure 7.9.

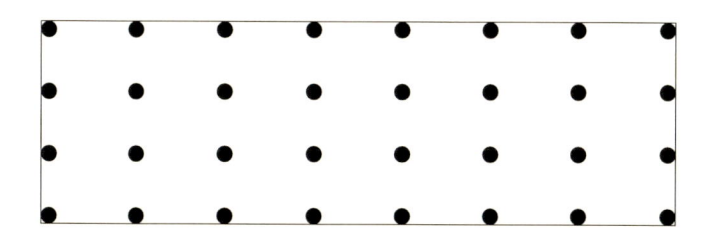

FIG. 7.9 BEAT CHART

Ask a student to come to the board and point to a beat chart while you and the class sing a song, or have the students create such a chart as they sing it.

Writing a Known Rhythmic Pattern Abstracted from Song Material
1. T sings the song and keeps the beat.
2. Ss sing the phrase and clap the beat.
3. Ss sing the phrase and clap the rhythm.
4. Ss sing the phrase with rhythm syllables.
5. Ss can draw a representation of the rhythm.

Kodály Today

6. T reviews how to write various sounds on the beat.
7. Ss write the phrase with stick notation.
8. Ss add note heads.
9. Ss read notation with rhythm syllables.

Writing a Known Melodic Pattern Using Traditional Rhythmic Notation and Solfège Syllables

1. T sings the song and keeps the beat.
2. Ss sing the phrase and clap the beat.
3. Ss sing the phrase and clap the rhythm.
4. Ss sing the phrase with rhythm syllables.
5. Ss can draw a representation of the rhythm.
6. T reviews how to write various sounds on the beat.
7. Ss write the phrase with stick notation.
8. Ss add note heads.
9. Ss read notation with rhythm syllables to check for errors.
10. Ss sing the known phrase with solfège syllables and hand signs.
11. Ss sing the example and add solfège syllables.

Writing a Known Melodic Pattern Using Traditional Rhythmic Notation and Solfège Syllables

1. T sings the song and keeps the beat.
2. Ss sing the phrase and clap the beat.
3. Ss sing the phrase and clap the rhythm.
4. Ss sing the phrase with rhythm syllables.
7. Ss write the phrase with stick notation.
8. Ss add note heads.
9. Ss read notation with rhythm syllables to check for errors.
10. Ss sing the known phrase with solfège syllables and hand signs.
11. Ss sing the example and add solfège syllables.
12. T reviews the Rule of Placement for notes and practices the placement of notes on the staff. T may also use the hand staff.
13. Ss sing the example as they place the note heads on the staff.
14. Ss sing, and they add the stems.

Writing a Known Melody Using Traditional Rhythmic Notation and Solfège Syllables

1. T sings the song and keeps the beat.
2. Ss sing the song with rhythm syllables from memory.
5. Ss can draw a representation of the rhythm.

6. T reviews how to write various sounds on the beat.
7. Ss write the phrase with stick notation.
8. Ss add note heads.
9. Ss read notation with rhythm syllables to check for errors.
10. Ss sing the song with solfège syllables and hand signs from memory.
11. Ss sing the example and add solfège syllables to the rhythmic notation.

Writing a Known Melody on the Staff
Depending the ability of the students, some of these steps can be skipped.
1. Ss sing the song and keep the beat.
2. Ss sing the phrase and clap the beat.
3. Ss sing the phrase and clap the rhythm.
4. Ss sing the phrase with rhythm syllables.
5. Ss identify the meter and sing the phrase with rhythm syllables and conduct.
6. Ss can draw a representation of the rhythm.
7. T reviews how to write various sounds on the beat.
8. Ss write the phrase with stick notation.
9. Ss add note heads, meter, and bar lines.
10. Ss read notation with rhythm syllables.
11. Ss sing the known phrase with solfège syllables.
12. Ss sing the example and write in the solfège syllables beneath the rhythmic notation.
13. T reviews the Rule of Placement for Ss for a given *do* position.
14. Ss sing song with solfège syllables and point to notes on the finger staff.
15. Ss write the note heads on the staff and then add the stems.
16. Ss sing the notation with solfège and hand signs.

Here are samples of other writing activities that can be used for writing known or unknown melodies.

1. T presents the rhythmic notation of a known melody with some measures missing rhythmic notation. Ss must complete the missing notation for the unknown melody.
2. T presents the rhythmic notation of a known melody with some measures missing rhythmic notation. Ss must complete the missing notation.
3. T presents the rhythmic notation and solfège of a known melody with some measures missing rhythmic notation and solfège. Ss must complete the missing notation.
4. T presents the notation of a known melody with some measures missing rhythms and notes. Ss must complete the missing notation.
5. T presents the note heads for rhythms and has Ss add stems and bar lines for the unknown melody.

Kodály Today

6. T presents solfège syllables and has Ss add the note heads and stems as well as bar lines.
7. T presents rhythmic notation and bar lines and has Ss add solfège syllables.
8. T presents notes of the melody on the staff and has Ss add stems and bar lines for the unknown melody.

Examples of Writing Activities

Choose a song or rhyme and challenge the students to figure out the rhythm or the solfège syllables. This activity can be performed at any level of instruction. For example:

"Engine, Engine, Number Nine"
1. T has Ss chant with words.
2. T has Ss chant with rhythm syllables.
3. T or a S writes after Ss say the rhythm syllables.

"Seesaw" (first phrase): "Seesaw up and down"
1. T sings with words.
2. T sings with rhythm syllables.
3. T or a S writes after Ss say the rhythm syllables.

Translating the Solfège Syllables of a Melody into Notation

The teacher sings a melodic turn on a neutral syllable and the students echo (see Figs. 7.10a and 7.10b).

1. Ss sing it again and clap the rhythm.
2. Ss sing the melodic turn with rhythm syllables.
3. T guides Ss in determining the solfège syllables.
    A. "What is the solfège syllable for the last pitch?"
    B. "What is the solfège syllable for the first pitch?"
4. T writes the pattern with disks and then plays or sings using a neutral syllable.
5. T then changes one beat of the pattern, e.g., *so so so so mi.*
6. S sing the new pattern.

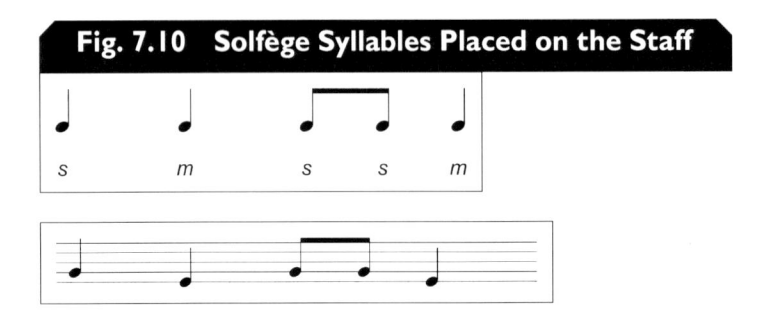

Fig. 7.10 Solfège Syllables Placed on the Staff

| s | m | s | s | m |

Dictation (Writing More Complex Unknown Melodies)

The ability to take dictation is linked to development of musical memory, inner hearing, and reading and writing skills. Memory is essential for dictation. As we have already indicated, initial writing activities should be based on patterns that the students have memorized. As their memory develops, you can formulate longer examples for practicing dictation. We are convinced that students should perform the melody before notating it so you may be certain students are hearing it accurately. We also believe that the material for dictation should be familiar to them. Dictation examples that are derived from folk music or notating a variant of a known folksong help ensure familiarity.

A Procedure for Rhythmic Dictation
1. T plays a melody on the piano while Ss establish the meter and the number of bars.
2. T plays and Ss conduct.
3. Ss conduct and sing the melody using rhythm syllables.
4. Ss write the rhythm.
5. One S writes the rhythm on the board.
6. T plays once more while the Ss sing and follow their score.

A Procedure for Melodic Dictation
1. T prepares the key of the dictation with hand signs and staff notation.
2. T shows typical melodic patterns extracted from the melody used for dictation, and the Ss sing with solfège syllables and then letter names. At the beginning stages of formal dictation, T may also give the Ss a score with bar lines and selected notes or rhythms filled in to help the Ss' memory.
3. T plays the melody on the piano or another instrument.
4. Ss determine the meter.
5. Ss sing the extract and keep the beat.
6. Ss sing the dictation and conduct.
7. Ss sing the dictation and clap the rhythm.
8. Ss sing the dictation with rhythm syllables and conduct.
9. Ss determine the final note and the beginning note as well as some or all of scale or mode, melodic cadences, melodic contour, patterns, and meter.
10. Ss sing the melody with solfège syllables and hand signs.
11. T provides Ss with the absolute letter name for the first note of the piece.
12. Ss sing the melody using absolute letter names while showing hand signs.
13. Ss write the melody without any assistance from the teacher.
14. One S writes the melody on the board.
15. Ss sing the melody from their score. This melody may be used to practice other skills, such as transposing it into other keys or practicing the intervals in the melody.

Activities for Developing Musical Memory

Musical memory plays an important role in accurate singing. The ability to recall a pattern or a musical phrase is critical for musical reading and writing.

Kodály Today

There are three ways to memorize a music example:

1. From hand signs
2. From staff notation
3. By ear

Memorizing from Hand Signs

Hand signs help students learn and understand melodic contours. A sequence of hand signs evokes the memory of melodic patterns.

1. T shows typical melodic patterns and asks Ss to sing patterns back, starting with short patterns such as *so-la-so-mi* or *mi-fa-mi-re-mi*.
2. Once the melodic patterns are mastered, the class can progress to singing four- and eight-beat melodies.
3. T selects a pentatonic melody and shows it with hand signs. T challenges Ss to sing the melody in canon immediately, using solfège syllables or absolute letter names. Extend this activity by asking them to write the melody from memory.
4. T may also give the starting pitch and ask Ss to sing a melody with absolute letter names while showing hand signs.

Memorizing from Staff Notation

1. Ss look at a score and memorize a phrase of the musical example by silently singing in their head using rhythm syllables, solfège syllables, and hand signs.
2. Ss should identify the form.
3. Ss may write the memorized melody on staff paper. At a more advanced level, they can write the example in another key using a different clef.

Memorizing by Ear

Memorizing by ear is more difficult than memorizing from notation as it involves no visual aids. Melodies used for memorizing by ear should be simpler than those used with notation. Selected phrases should be played on the piano or another instrument and sung a few times by the students. The procedures given here may be used for both rhythmic and melodic memorization. You should sing the musical example and ask students to identify or perform them in sequence. Be certain to sing the musical example prior to asking students to determine each point.

1. Ss identify the meter.
2. Ss sing the example with rhythm syllables.
3. Ss identify the ending and starting pitches.
4. Ss sing the example and conduct.
5. Ss sing the example with hand signs.
6. Ss sing the example with absolute pitch names and hand signs.

Developing Musicianship Skills

7. Ss write the exercise.
8. T plays it back on the piano as one S writes the exercise on the board; T and Ss check for errors. Later, the example may be transposed. Ss can sing the example with letter names in another key, or they can write it on the staff in a different key.

T may also play pentatonic or diatonic canons and ask the Ss to sing it back in canon on "loo" or on solfège syllables while memorizing the example. At a more advanced level, Ss may sing back the canon at a different interval.

Memorizing Two-Part Musical Examples

Once students have gained experience in unison memory work, they can begin to memorize two-part extracts. Accompaniments may be drawn from a rhythmic pattern, a rhythmic or melodic ostinato, chord roots, a contrapuntal melodic line, or typical cadential idioms in modal or harmonic music. Memory work may also include three- and four-part work.

1. Class sings the selected extracts in two parts.
2. Ss memorize one part silently, using rhythm and solfège syllables.
3. Ss sing the part out loud while conducting.
4. Ss practice the other part following steps 1 through 3.
5. T divides the class into two groups. One sings the upper part and the second sings the lower part. Reverse.
6. One S can sing one part and show the hand signs for another.
7. T writes both parts of the musical example.
8. T sings one part and plays the other on the piano.

Discussion Questions
1. What do we mean when we say that rhythmic and melodic elements need to be practiced?
2. How can we connect skill areas such as development of musical memory and inner hearing to teaching musical reading and writing? Provide specific examples.
3. Discuss the notion that the most successful way for students to read and write music is through constant practice, using lots of drills. Several computer programs could be incorporated into the music lesson so students develop their reading and writing ability.
4. What is the difference between reading and sight singing?
5. What is the difference between writing and dictation?

Ongoing Assignment

1. When we present an element to students in a focus pattern, it is important that we practice additional patterns containing the element on another beat or surrounded by known elements. Choose an element that you are going to teach next year from

Kodály Today

your first, third, and fifth grade classes. List the steps that you would use to practice a variation of this pattern through reading and writing activities.
2. How can you extend the reading and writing activities given above to develop inner hearing, memory, sight singing, and dictation activities?
3. Describe how you would teach a new piece of music to your students through sight singing.

References

Here are two useful references for practicing rhythm and melody through reading, writing, and memory exercises.

Houlahan, Micheál, and Philip Tacka. *Sound Thinking: Music for Sight-Singing and Ear Training*. 2 vols. New York: Boosey & Hawkes, 1991.

Houlahan, Micheál, and Philip Tacka. *From Sound to Symbol: Fundamentals of Music Theory*. New York: Oxford University Press, 2011.

Practicing Form, Improvisation, and Composition

Key Questions

1. What is musical form?
2. How do we develop the concept of form in the elementary classroom?
3. What is the difference between improvisation and composition?
4. What do we mean by kinesthetic, aural, and visual improvisation activities?
5. What types of rhythmic and melodic improvisation activities can be used with all grade levels?

Developing a Sense of Musical Form

Teaching the structure of a song (form) begins early in a student's musical education. As students learn to clap the rhythm of songs and sing in tune using correct breathing and dynamics, they are already learning phrasing and dynamics—both significant aspects of musical form. The phrase of music containing the new musical element as well as the teaching of tonality, melodic contour of phrases, cadences, and range of notes are all aspects of form.

Teaching form begins in the early childhood classroom with understanding of same, different, and similar. These simple concepts lead to understanding and ternary forms, a prerequisite for understanding larger sonata and symphonic forms. Give students many examples of music forms to recognize through singing. Here are some strategies.

1. T and class work together to determine the form of a folksong; T notates this form on the board.
2. Ss sing a folksong; one S identifies the form and writes it on the board.
3. Ss sing a song and write the form as a dictation exercise.
4. T writes several forms on the board (ABAC, AAvBA, etc.). T sings several folksongs for Ss, and has them classify the folksongs according to the forms on the board.
5. One S writes several forms on the board and sings folksongs for the class. The class subsequently classifies the folksongs according to the forms on the board.

Developing Musicianship Skills

Activities That Emphasize Structure and Form

Understanding musical form is closely linked to developing musical memory, reading, writing, improvisation, composition, and inner-hearing skills. Here are activities that lead students to recognize the structure of songs. Any of these activities can be further expanded into composition and improvisation activities.

Possible Sequence for Teaching Form to Students

1. Same and different. T guides Ss to discover:
    A. The number of phrases in a song
    B. The number of beats in each phrase
    C. Whether phrases are the same or different
2. Class uses letters to identify same and different phrases in simple songs. For young Ss, T may call an A phrase "apple" and a B phrase "banana." Phrases that are nearly the same are referred to as *variants*. The rhythmic form can be different from the melodic form.
3. T introduces repetition and repeat sign. Teach Ss how to read music using repeat signs.
4. T explains that first and second endings are simply another way to use the repeat sign and to emphasize form. Use of first and second endings may be explained as a kind of musical shorthand. Consider the song "Great Big House in New Orleans" (Fig. 7.11). "Great Big House in New Orleans" may also be written with first and second endings, as in Figure 7.12.

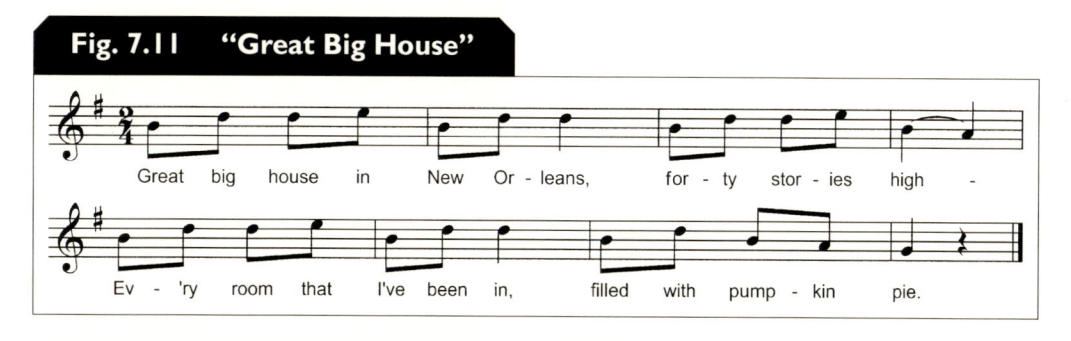

Fig. 7.11 "Great Big House"

Fig. 7.12 "Great Big House" Ending F

5. T uses letter names to identify the form in more complex songs. Ss should be guided to aurally and visually recognize simple song forms such as AABA, ABAB, and ABAC. Understanding form is valuable in helping them develop their musical memory. For example, "Great Big House in New Orleans" is in ABAC. This form is clearly audible when performed with a breath every two measures.

Kodály Today

6. Question and answer. There are many excellent examples of folksongs with period structure. When exploring period structure, T uses songs that have the structure AAv, or AB, where the final A ends on the dominant note and the Av phrase ends on the tonic note. Consider the song "Love Somebody," which is written in the key of F major. The final note of the first line is a C and is the dominant note in the key of F. The final note of the second line is an F, the tonic note in the key of F major.

7. Identifying forms. It is also possible for Ss to identify the form of short compositions using repertoire from other cultures. The following examples for singing and identifying form are from the *Kodály Choral Library: 333 Elementary Exercises*:

   AABBv: nos. 185, 187, 188, 198, 199, and 204.

   AAvBAv: nos. 176 and 202.

   AA5A5Av: no. 277. (The A theme is repeated up a fifth. This theme can be sung with the same solfège syllables used in the A section because the intervallic structure is identical.)

   AA5A5A: no. 280.

   AB5AvBv: no. 284.

   Another form that may be practiced is A5A. This is typical of the old-style Hungarian folksong in which the two sections can be sung with the same solfège syllables as the intervallic structure. See an example in no. 314. The classroom practice of performing this type of exercise is a helpful bridge to structures found in contemporary music.

"Love Somebody" (Fig. 7.13) is a simple musical example in which we can see the relationship between harmony and form. To demonstrate the form of "Love Somebody," divide the class into two groups. One sings the first half of the song and the other may sing the second half. Allow students to aurally compare the melodic material in each part of the period, by considering

   A. The number of measures in each part
   B. The opening and closing notes of each phrase
   C. The relationship between the two phrases (one is open and one is closed, or one is finished and one is unfinished)
   D. Period structure in classical music.

Fig. 7.13 "Love Somebody"

Developing Musicianship Skills

After introduction of the major and minor scales, students should begin to sing repertoire connected to classical music. Singing folksongs with an AAv or AB question-and-answer form offers a connection to singing period structures in classical music. Begin teaching period structure forms using the AA' model, where A ends on the dominant and A' ends on the tonic note. This can be extended to other forms such as AB. Later, students can identify period structure forms using AA' or AB, where the A ends on the third of the dominant triad.

Here is a process that can be used.

1. Ss sing the song in solfège syllables and conduct.
2. Ss sing the song and identify the form.
3. T sings the song and Ss identify the harmonic functions or chord tones.
4. T divides the class into two groups. One sings the melody while the other sings the harmonic functions or chord roots.
5. T discusses the period form of the song. Determine the form, the opening and closing notes of each phrase, and the relationship between each pair of phrases.
6. Ss sing the song and carefully listen to the aspects of the music discussed above.
7. After learning the song, Ss could improvise a new answer phrase to the first part of the period. This exercise may be made more demanding if Ss have to improvise a phrase not related to the material of the first phrase.
8. Cadences. Ss should be introduced to the types of cadence. This is especially important once they have a basic knowledge of triads. They need to identify whether the cadence sounds closed or open; we need to compare cadences to one another in a piece of music.
9. Modulating period structures. Ss can perform period structures that involve modulations. The easiest ones to analyze are those that involve a modulation from the minor key to the major key, as this does not entail a change of *do* position and they are easiest to read. T and Ss can then analyze modulating period structures that move from the tonic key to the dominant.
10. Binary form. Ss can be introduced to the concept of binary form using simple classical repertoire. It is a good idea to use repertoire that includes two periods. Ss should analyze each period as well as relate the two periods to one another. It will be important to note that sometimes the final cadence in the first period can be considered closed but when viewed from the complete example it acts as a half cadence. Although Ss can sing the examples we will give here, it is important to play them on the piano. Use uppercase letters for analyzing large-scale forms. The musical examples for listening activities (note that Ss who are good performers may also perform them) are
    A. Binary form: J. S. Bach (1685–1750), Partita No. 1 in B flat major, BWV 825; or J. S. Bach, Minuet in G from the *Anna Magdalena Notebook*.

B. Ternary form. This is represented by the letters ABA. There are many examples of ABA form in the classical repertoire. Sometimes the second section of ternary form is shorter than the first section; in this case we may use the letters AbA. We have successfully used these two examples of ternary to play for students: Frederick Chopin (1810–1849), Mazurka in C major Op. 33, No. 3; and J. S. Bach (1685–1750), "Musette," from the *Anna Magdalena Notebook*.
C. Trio form. This is a combination of binary and ternary forms. We normally find it in the third movement of classical symphonies. It exists as a type of ternary form, however each section of the ABA is larger and can include mood and tempo changes.
D. Rondo. There are many fine examples of this form (ABACABA) to listen to, sing, and analyze. It is important that Ss have an understanding of a "theme" as well as the appearance of the episode (at least two) to establish rondo form. Examples of rondo form are Joseph Haydn (1732–1809), String Quartet in C major, Op. 33, No. 2; and Beethoven (1770–1827), last movement of Piano Sonata in G, Op. 14, No. 2.
E. Variation form. Many examples are available for analysis. It's most helpful to choose examples that Ss can sing, which enables them to more easily identify the technique used for analysis. Variation form can easily become the basis for their own improvisations and composition in the classroom. Example: Ralph Vaughan Williams (1872–1958), *Variations of Greensleeves*.
F. Complex music forms. Depending on the Ss' music background, it may be appropriate to undertake the study of more complex musical forms. We advise that before listening to or analyzing complex forms, Ss should be able to sing themes from the work so they can aurally analyze different sections of music. Consider: for *sonata allegro form*, W. A. Mozart (1756–1791), his sonatas; for *fugues, tonal and real answers*, J. S. Bach (1685–1750), "Fugue" from the Toccata and Fugue in D minor for Organ; for *concerto form*, Mozart, Horn Concerto No. 4 in E flat, K. 495, rondo movement; for *symphony form*, Joseph Haydn (1732–1809), Symphony No. 104 in D major, movement 1.

Activities Developing Improvisation and Composition

Improvisation, the art of composing extemporaneously, and composition, the art of formulating and writing music, are both integral components of the Kodály approach to teaching. Improvisation and composition extend and develop student creativity and musicianship. Improvisation can take many forms. Often young students invent words and melodies quite naturally. Substituting words in a song and choosing motions to accompany a song are initial forms of improvisation.

It is wise to set the parameters for improvisation simply and clearly so everyone can perform the task. Another basic rule for improvisation is that the students must keep the beat without changing the original tempo. An improvisation game should not be stopped. The activity proceeds until everyone has had a turn. At the same time the teacher can observe and assess which students might need additional help with a particular concept.

Making up movements to accompany songs and changing the words to a song will encourage young students' spontaneity and creativity. The classroom atmosphere for such activities should be free and gamelike, so students can make an error without becoming embarrassed. In a gamelike setting, students may be encouraged to have fun while putting their musical skills into practice immediately and instinctively.

Once students have an understanding of typical rhythmic and melodic patterns in songs, they are prepared to improvise and compose music on the basis of musical concepts. Rhythmic and melodic elements as well as form may be practiced through improvisation activities. Teachers should consider the students' age and assess the class's level of understanding to determine appropriate improvisation activities. If possible, some type of improvisation activity should accompany each musical element learned.

The activities described here can be turned into composition exercises by writing down the improvisations. Remember that all improvisation activities should be related to repertoire. For example, we can ask students to improvise question-and-answer forms only if they have performed and analyzed folksongs that contain question-and-answer forms.

Activities that involve improvising rhythmic elements are usually the first to be incorporated into music lessons. What follows are kinesthetic, aural, and visual activities that aid in practicing rhythm and developing improvisation skills. Kinesthetic improvisation activities involve using our bodies to create a new movement sequence to accompany a song. Aural improvisation activities do not include any notation. Visual improvisation activities involve using notation.

Kinesthetic Activities for Improvising Rhythms

Begin with simple activities. Movements to accompany songs, changing the words to a song, echo clapping, and echo singing should be used with young students to encourage spontaneity and creativity.

1. T improvises a motion to a rhyme suggested by the text.
2. T improvises a motion to the beat. Or one S may select a motion for the class to imitate, such as clapping, jumping, patting, tapping, and so on.
3. Adding to the chain improvisation game. A chain improvisation is a game where Ss sit in a circle and improvise a four-beat rhythmic phrase. Once the beat is established and the game begins around the class, the momentum established by the beat should not be interrupted for a hesitation or error. The

Kodály Today

improvisation continues until all Ss have had a turn. An important aspect of this type of activity is that it teaches Ss to make quick decisions. In many cases these decisions are intuitive, which indicates that the musical elements in question have been completely internalized.
  A. One S performs a four-beat pattern.
  B. Another S performs the pattern and adds another four-beat pattern. The next S repeats the patterns and adds his or her own four-beat pattern.
  C. The game continues until someone makes a mistake.

A simplified version of the chain improvisation game is
  A. One S performs a four-beat pattern.
  B. Another S performs the last two beats of the first pattern and adds two more beats. The next S repeats the last two beats from the previous pattern and adds his or her own two beats.
  C. The game continues until someone makes a mistake.
4. T improvises a motion for the rhythmic form of a folksong. For example, Ss may say the rhythm syllables while walking in a circle, clockwise for the A phrases and counterclockwise for the B phrase.
5. Ss perform a body canon using finger snaps or hand claps in a four-beat pattern. One S leads and the class follows.
6. Ss improvise a two-beat rhythmic ostinato using body motions such as clapping hands for beat 1 and patting knees for beat 2.

Aural Activities for Improvising Rhythms

1. T improvises a rhythmic ostinato to a song. One S can compose a rhythmic ostinato to a song. Initially these should be with simple two-beat ostinati.
2. T improvises a rhythmic ostinato using Orff instruments.
3. T improvises rhythms according to a given form.
4. Question-and-answer improvisation:
   A. Clap a four-beat rhythmic question to one S; he or she must respond by clapping back a four-beat answer.
   B. Ss may do this exercise without naming any of the rhythms. Later, they can clap their answer and say rhythm syllables. Question-and-answer conversations can continue as a chain around the class.
5. First and second endings: after working with question-and-answer rhythms, T may move to songs having first and second endings. T or one S performs the rhythm through the first ending, and another S performs the repeat of the rhythm but improvises a second ending. This type of activity involves memory development along with the improvisation.
6. Class creates a new rhythmic composition based on a form provided by T.
   A. T gives Ss an A phrase (question) that is four beats long and asks them to improvise a B phrase (answer). This may be turned into a larger improvisation exercise using the form ABAC.

Developing Musicianship Skills

   B. T may specify a longer composition, an AABA form.
   C. This could be performed as a group activity or could be performed by an individual S. This exercise should be based on song material the class is studying.
7. Four volunteers are each given a letter of the form AABA. Each S improvises four beats; T may supply the tempo.
8. T improvises short rhythmic canons.
9. Given a rhythmic skeleton, Ss add more complex rhythms but without changing the length of the phrase.
10. Ss sing a known melody in a different meter.

Visual Activities for Improvising Rhythm
1. Improvising a new ending or a new measure:
   A. T puts an easy rhythm on the board and erases one measure. Have one S perform the rhythm and improvise the rhythm of the missing measure.
   B. T writes the rhythm of that song on the board but erases the last two measures.
   C. Individual Ss may clap the rhythm while saying the rhythm syllables and improvise the final two measures.
2. Fill-in improvisation:
   A. Place a series of four flash cards on the board.
   B. Three of the flash cards have a rhythm written on them; one card is blank.
   C. Ask Ss to clap flash cards 1, 2, and 4 while one S improvises a four-beat rhythm pattern for flash card 3. (In beginning this activity, consider putting four beats on the third card and ask the S to change only one beat.)
3. Improvising to a given form:
   A. Once Ss can identify quarter and eighth notes, T can move on to improvisation activities that deal with form.
   B. T writes a rhythm on the board. Ss clap the rhythm.
   C. T names the phrases A and B.
   D. T erases the B phrase.
   E. T asks how many beats are in the A phrase.
   F. T asks how many beats should be in the B phrase.
   G. T suggests repeating the A phrase for phrase 3. T or one S may write it on the board.
   H. Ask individuals to improvise a new B line and write it. Have the class repeat lines 2 and 4, clapping the new rhythm and saying rhythm syllables.
   I. If the letter names A and B seem to be too abstract for Ss, use pictures of fruits such as apples and bananas instead of letters.
   J. After this exercise, use a similar procedure to work with ABAB form.

Kodály Today

Improvising Melodies

Activities that involve improvising melodic elements can be more demanding than rhythmic improvisation. Again there are three types of improvisation: kinesthetic, aural, and visual.

Kinesthetic Activities for Improvising Melodies

1. Improvising new motions to a song. In "That's a Mighty Pretty Motion," one S may select a motion for the class to imitate, such as clapping, jumping, patting, tapping, and so on.
2. Class improvises new motions that fit the melodic form for the song. For example, Ss may sing "Hot Cross Buns" while walking in a circle, clockwise for the A phrases and counterclockwise for the B phrases.
3. Ss perform a body canon using finger snaps or hand claps in a four-beat pattern as T sings a song. One S leads and the class follows.
4. In primary grades, T uses the song "Snail, Snail" and improvises motions for the snail. T should consider substituting the word "cat" or "squirrel" for snail and improvise appropriate motions.

Aural Activities for Improvising Melodies

1. Improvising text. Ss may improvise words with simple melodies. For example, T may sing a question to one S using the notes *so-mi*, and the S improvises an answer using the same notes (Fig. 7.14).

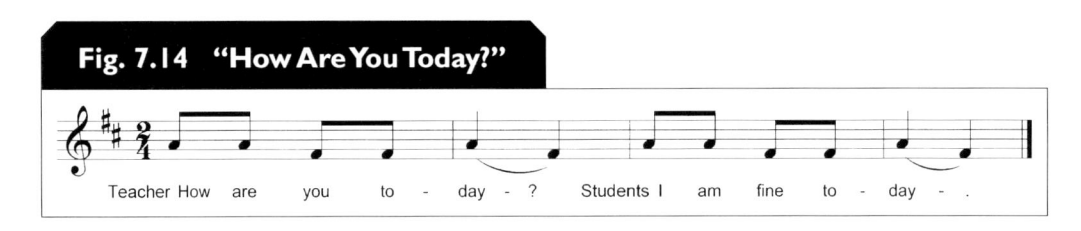

Fig. 7.14 "How Are You Today?"

Teacher How are you to - day - ? Students I am fine to - day - .

2. Substitute text. Consider the song "Teddy Bear." Ask Ss to substitute words for "Teddy Bear" like "buzzing bee" or "kitty cat."
3. T improvises a melodic ostinato to accompany pentatonic songs. T asks Ss to improvise a melodic ostinato to a known pentatonic melody. It is important for T to limit the number of solfège syllables that Ss will improvise with. For example, they might begin to improvise with just two or three notes of the pentatonic scale.
4. A chain improvisation game:
    A. One S performs a four-beat melodic pattern made up of quarter notes. Another performs this pattern but changes one beat.

B. One S performs a four-beat melodic pattern. Another performs this pattern and adds a four-beat pattern. The next S repeats the new patterns and adds his or her own. The game is played until someone makes a mistake.
5. Question and answer:
   A. T establishes the beat. Sing a four-beat melody, and have Ss respond with a different four-beat melody.
   B. T sings a pattern and asks Ss to change one beat. (This can also be done visually, which may be easier for some Ss.)
   C. As Ss become more proficient, T lengthens the phrase or changes the tempo. This leads to performance of melodic conversations. Question-and-answer conversations can continue as a chain around the class. It is best to begin the exercise using these forms and ending notes:
   A ends on *so* A ends on *do*
   A ends on *re* B ends on *do*
   A ends on *so* B ends on *do*
   A ends on *re* B ends on *do*
   D. In exercises 261, 266, 271, and 272 of *Kodály Choral Library: 333 Elementary Exercises*, the question ends on *so* and the answer ends on *do*.
   E. In *Kodály Choral Library: 333 Elementary Exercises*, nos. 240, 247, 250, 252, 253, 257, 258, and 260 have the question ending on *re* and the answer ending on *do*.
6. First and second endings:
   A. After working with question-and-answer melodies, T may move to songs with first and second endings.
   B. T or S performs a melody through the first ending, and another S performs the repeat of the melody but improvises a second ending.
   C. This type of activity develops musical memory as well as the ability to improvise.
7. Ss improvise a melody using the retrograde of a given pattern: *do-mi-so-la* in retrograde is *la-so-mi-do*. These particular solfège patterns are found in the song "Rocky Mountain."
8. Presented with a melody, Ss improvise a sequence based on it. T should set the parameters. In the example of Figure 7.15, T may sing the first and third measures, and one S could sing the second and fourth measures following the sequence, singing a step down.

Fig. 7.15 Singing a Pattern

9. Sing a known melody with another meter.

Kodály Today

Visual Activities for Improvising Melodies

1. Fill-in a four-beat pattern:
   A. Improvising with solfège notes. T writes a rhythmic pattern on the board and puts solfège syllables under certain rhythms. Ss have the choice of filling in the missing rhythms with solfège.
   B. One S may sing the melody but improvise in the blank measure. T may provide the rhythm. It is best to begin with a very simple rhythm before moving on to more complex ones. T writes a simple melody on the board but leaves one measure blank. Have one S sing the melody but improvise the blank measure. The rhythm for this measure may be improvised by S or specified by T.
   C. Begin with a very simple rhythm before moving on to more complex structures.
2. Students may arrange cards with rhythms and melodies to create a new song.
3. Improvising a melody to a given rhythmic pattern. Have one S improvise solfège syllables to a given rhythmic pattern.
4. Place a series of four flash cards on the board.
   A. Three of the flash cards have a rhythm and solfège syllables written on them, and one has only a rhythm written on it.
   B. Ask Ss to sing the flash cards with hand signs and improvise a new melody for the flash card with only the rhythm written on it.
5. Ss may improvise a melody to a given scale.
6. Improvisation with form. T improvises using the form of a composition. "Hot Cross Buns" is in AABA form. One S may sing the A sections of this song but improvise the B section.
7. Flash cards. Cards with rhythmic and melodic patterns may be arranged by Ss to create a new song.
8. Improvising a melodic ostinato to a given melody:
   a. Sing a song with a melodic ostinato.
   b. Each S may improvise a new ostinato for the folksong. Ask several Ss to perform their ostinato together while singing the song.
9. T presents the notation of a known melody on the staff with some of the measures missing rhythms and notes. Ss must complete the missing notation for the unknown melody.
10. Ss perform a known melody in another meter.
11. Ss improvise a new melody to a given form.
12. Ss improvise a new melody to a given text.

Improvisation on Classroom Instruments

With enough experience in singing a folksong repertoire and performing simple melodic and rhythmic improvisations as echo activities, students may begin improvising new endings to songs they have learned in class. They can then be guided to improvise a new ending to a known song on an instrument. The suggestions seen here are helpful.

Allow students to choose from two to four melodic turns that you provide. These suggestions can be written using rhythmic notation with solfège syllables beneath or in staff notation.

- Consider furnishing a few starting notes and or a specific rhythm for the beginning of the improvisation.
- With experience, allow Ss to improvise a new ending to a song without T's guidance.
- Guide Ss in activities that encourage them to perform a known melody in another meter.
- Guide Ss to improvise a new melody to a given form.
- Guide Ss to improvise a new melody to a given text.

Composition Techniques
Depending on the time constraints of the music lesson, the teacher might occasionally use standard compositional techniques and incorporate them into improvisation and composition activities in a lesson. These compositional devices can make some valuable connections to twentieth- and twenty-first-century music repertoire. Here are some compositional techniques that you can use in the music classroom.

Motivic Device
The teacher writes known rhythmic patterns from a folksong on the board. This could be done through rhythmic dictation or through a memory game. Ask students to choose some of the patterns and rearrange them, but use one rhythm pattern as a motivic device; it should appear several times as a unifying motif in the composition. "Liza Jane" is an example of a song built around several important rhythmic motives.

Changing Meter
The students perform a folksong that has changing meter, tapping the accented beats and clapping the unaccented ones. Write the folksong without bar lines and ask them to create a new composition using the concept of changing meter. They can also compose another melody to accompany the new rhythmic structure. A musical example is Dave Brubeck (1920–2012), "Three to Get Ready."

Ostinato
Students sing a folksong with a rhythmic ostinato. Each student should devise a new ostinato accompaniment for the folksong. Ask several students to clap their ostinatos together while singing the song. They notate their ostinato. A musical example is "Ostinato" from *Mikrokosmos*, vol. 6, no. 146, by Béla Bartók (1881–1945).

Musical Fragmentation, Octave Displacement
1. Ss memorize a rhythmic pattern of sixteen beats aurally.
2. Ss notate the pattern.
3. Ss add accents to the notated rhythmic pattern.

Kodály Today

4. Two Ss clap the pattern; one S claps only the accented beat.
5. The Ss score their composition for two instruments. One instrument plays only the accented beats; the other plays the remainder.
6. The Ss could also compose a melody for the rhythmic pattern.
7. Play a familiar melody. Then select notes to play in another octave. Perform the result.

A musical example is "Greeting Prelude" (a version of "Happy Birthday") by Igor Stravinsky (1882–1971), with octave displacement.

Variation
1. The Ss sing a known folksong.
2. Ask the Ss to compose variations on a song or theme.
3. Compare and contrast the compositions by the Ss.

Musical examples are Morton Gould (1913–1996), *American Salute*; Roy Harris (1898–1979), "Welcome Party," from *Folk Song Symphony No. 4* (1940); Igor Stravinsky (1882–1971), "Finale," from *Firebird Suite*; Zoltán Kodály (1882–1967), *Peacock Variations*; Benjamin Britten (1913–1976), *The Young Person's Guide to the Orchestra* (a set of variations based on the beginning of Henry Purcell's "Rondo" from *Abdelazer*); Norman Dello Joio (1913–2008), Piano Sonata No. 3 (the first movement is a theme and variation based on the Gregorian chant "De Angelis").

Singing Pentatonic Scales from the Same Starting Pitch
Practice singing the pentatonic scales all from the same starting pitch. Once students gain confidence and facility, they can sing several or all of these scales in canon. For example, once group one has sung the major (*do*) pentatonic scale, they can sing the *re* pentatonic scale from the same starting pitch as the major pentatonic scale, while group two follows in canon.

Singing Pentatonic Tone Clusters
Singing pentatonic tone clusters is a way to introduce students to the aural sounds of tone clusters. For example, divide the students into six groups. Five groups sing and sustain the notes of the pentatonic scale while the sixth group sings a pentatonic song; the sustained tone cluster serves as an accompaniment.

Singing Symmetrical Scales
In upper grades, students may practice singing vocal etudes composed of the whole tone and octatonic scales. The whole tone scale is formed by a sequence of major second intervals, and the octatonic scales are formed by using a sequence of alternating major and minor seconds that create symmetrical scales. Theses scale can begin with either a minor second or a major second interval.

Developing Musicianship Skills

A music example of the octatonic scale is "Harvest Song," violin duo no. 33, by Bartók.

Singing a Series of Complex Intervals Composed of Major Seconds, Minor Thirds, and Perfect Fourths

With the introduction of the pentatonic scale, children can sing complex melodies with solfège syllables if the teacher reinterprets notes with known solfège syllables by using a pivot note. (This is the same concept as using a pivot chord for modulations in harmony.) The teacher can begin to practice this technique once children can sing major seconds, minor thirds, and perfect fourth intervals. It is important to initially practice these intervals in a given tonality. Later, introduce students to melodies that do not have a clear tonal center.

A helpful way to practice singing melodies without a clear tonal center is to sing a known pentatonic folksong but change the tonality for each measure. To accomplish this, the last pitch of each measure will be the starting pitch for solfège syllables of the next measure. For example, in "Great Big House in New Orleans" we can change the tonality of the piece by singing the first few measures as *mi-so-so-la = mi-so-so = mi-so-so-la = mi-re*, etc. The last pitch for each measure becomes the new pitch for the next measure but is sung with the beginning solfège syllable for that measure.

Tone Row and Serial Techniques
1. Ss choose a set of notes from a well-known song.
2. T asks Ss to write the notes in a tone row (prime order). (Ss will not be using a complete tone row.)
3. T and Ss explore the concept of retrograde and inversion using this tone row. T can introduce them to pieces of music that demonstrate the techniques described above. For example, "The Lamb," by John Tavener (1944–2013), can be used to explore the concepts described here with children. It is also interesting to note that this piece uses bitonality.
4. T can show very complex tone rows by using hand signs.

Musical examples are Alban Berg (1885–1935), Violin Concerto, movement 1 (there is a clear statement of the tone row after the introduction); Arnold Schoenberg (1874–1951), String Quartet No. 4, movement 3; and Anton Webern (1883–1945), Symphony, Op. 21, movement 2.

Polytonality
1. Class practices singing partner songs in the same or different keys.
2. Class practices singing songs in canon at the octave, fifth, fourth, etc.

Musical examples are Arthur Honegger (1892–1955), "March," from *King David*; Benjamin Britten (1913–1976), "There Is No Rose," from *A Ceremony of Carols*; and Charles Ives (1874–1954), *Three Places in New England*, movement 2.

Implementation of these ideas will depend on the students' reading and writing skills. (The same techniques can be used in conjunction with new musical elements learned.) Here are additional compositional techniques that can be integrated into the curriculum.

1. Ss write a melody using these techniques:
   - Augmentation of the rhythm patterns
   - Diminution of the rhythm patterns
   - Mirror inversion of a melody
   - Mirror inversions written from different starting notes
   - Melodic sequence using a complete phrase or motif
   - Transposition of folksongs into various modes
   - Using a selected group of notes in a predetermined order and creating a composition using a rhythm, from a folksong or other music

All of these rhythmic, melodic, and form activities may be extended and varied, taking into account the level and abilities of the students. Ostinati, both rhythmic and melodic, may be created and incorporated into the performance of many simple and complex folksongs. Possibilities are limitless when the music class is conducted in an atmosphere of creativity and spontaneity.

Discussion Questions
1. Describe the difference between an improvisation and a composition exercise.
2. How can you develop students' kinesthetic, aural, and visual improvisation abilities in the classroom?
3. Discuss whether students should be allowed to compose music freely in the classroom using their own ideas and forms of expression, and whether activities based on the suggestions of this chapter are only another form of reading and writing and do not help students with creative skills.

Ongoing Assignment
1. Review the goals for form and improvisation/composition for each grade.
2. Choose an element that you are going to teach next year from your first, third, and fifth grade classes. List the steps that you would use to practice this element through form, improvisation, and composition.
3. How can you extend the improvisation and composition activities in this section of the chapter to develop inner hearing, memory, sight singing, and dictation activities?

References
Here are references that can be used for practicing form, improvisation, and composition.

Improvisation

Alperson, Philip A. "On Musical Improvisation." *Journal of Aesthetics and Art Criticism*, 1984, *43*(1): 17–29.

Burnard, Pamela. "The Individual and Social Worlds of Children's Musical Creativity." In *The Child as Musician: A Handbook of Musical Development*, ed. Gary McPherson, pp. 353–375. New York: Oxford University Press, 2006.

Pressing, Jeff. "Improvisation: Methods and Models." In *Generative Processes in Music: The Psychology of Performance, Improvisation and Composition*, ed. John Sloboda, pp. 129–179. Oxford: Clarendon Press, 2001.

Composition

Barrett, Margaret. "Children's Aesthetic Decision Making: An Analysis of Children's Musical Discourse as Composers." *International Journal of Music Education*, 1996, *28*: 37–62.

Bitz, Michael Eric. "A Description and Investigation of Strategies for Teaching Classroom Music Improvisation." Ph.D. thesis, Columbia University, 1998.

Bramhall, David. *Composing in the Classroom*. New York: Boosey & Hawkes, 1989.

Brophy, Timothy S. "The Melodic Improvisations of Children Ages Six Through Twelve: A Developmental Perspective." Ph.D. thesis, University of Kentucky, 1998.

Bunting, R. "Composing Music: Case Studies in the Teaching and Learning Process." *British Journal of Music Education*, 1987, *4*(1): 25–52.

Bunting, R. "Composing Music: Case Studies in the Teaching and Learning Process." *British Journal of Music Education*, 1988, *5*(3): 269–310.

Campbell, L. *Sketching at the Keyboard*. London: Stainer & Bell, 1998.

Chatterley, A. *The Music Club Book of Improvisation Projects*. London: Stainer & Bell, 1978.

Csikszentmihalyi, M. "Society, Culture, Person: A Systems View of Creativity." In *The Nature of Creativity*, ed. R. J. Sternberg, pp. 325–339. New York: Cambridge University Press, 1988.

Dowling, W. Jay. "Tonal Structure and Children's Early Tonal Learning of Music." In *Generative Process of Music: The Psychology of Performance, Improvisation, and Composition*, ed. John Sloboda, pp. 113–129. New York: Oxford University Press, 2001.

Hamann, Donald L., ed. *Creativity in the Music Classroom: The Best of MEJ*. Reston, VA: Music Educators National Conference, 1992.

Harris, Ruth, and Elizabeth Hawksley. *Composing in the Classroom*. Cambridge, UK: Cambridge University, 1990.

Herboly-Kocsár, Ildikó. *Teaching of Polyphony, Harmony and Form in Elementary School*, ed. Lilla Gábor, trans. Alexander Farkas. Kecskemét: Zoltán Kodály Pedagogical Institute, 1984.

Houlahan, Micheál, and Philip Tacka. *Sound Thinking: Music for Sight-Singing and Ear Training*. Vol. 2. New York: Boosey & Hawkes, 1991.

Lin, Yu-Sien. "Fostering Creativity Through Education: A Conceptual Framework of Creative Pedagogy." *Creative Education*, 2011, *2*(3): 149–155.

Kodály, Zoltán. "A Hundred Year Plan." In *The Selected Writings of Zoltán Kodály*, 1974.

Kodály, Zoltán. "Preface to *Musical Reading and Writing* by Erzsebet Szőnyi." In *The Selected Writings of Zoltán Kodály*, 1974.

Kodály, Zoltán. "The Role of the Authentic Folk Song in Music Education 1966." *Bulletin of the International Kodály Society*, 1985, *10*(1): 15–19. Also found as "Folk Song in Hungarian Music Education." *International Music Educator*, 1967, *15*: 486–490.

Kodály, Zoltán. "Who Is a Good Musician?" In *The Selected Writings of Zoltán Kodály*, 1974.

Kratus, J. "The Use of Melodic and Rhythmic Motives in the Original Songs of Children Aged 5 to 13." *Contributions to Music Education*, 1985, *12*: 1–8.

Laczó, Z. "A Psychological Investigation of Improvisation Abilities in the Lower and Higher Classes of the Elementary School." *Bulletin of the Council for Research in Music Education*, 1981, *66, 67*: 39–45.

McNicol, R. *Sound Inventions: 32 Creative Music Projects for the Junior Classroom*. Oxford, UK: Oxford University Press, 1992.

Mead, Virginia Hoge. *Dalcroze Eurhythmics in Today's Classroom*. New York: Schott, 1994. See also *Music Educators Journal*, September 1993, January 1995, November 1996, November 1997, and November 1999.

Sloboda, John, ed. *Generative Processes in Music: The Psychology of Performance, Improvisation, and Composition*. New York: Oxford University Press, 2001.

Smith, B., and W. Smith. "Uncovering Cognitive Process in Music Composition: Educational and Computational Approaches." In *Music Education: An Artificial Intelligence Approach*, ed. M. Smith, A. Smaill, and G. Wiggins, pp. 56–72. New York: Springer-Verlag, 1994.

Szabó, Helga. *Énekes improvizáció az iskolában* [*Vocal Improvisation in the Elementary School*]. In *Hungarian*. Vols. I–V. Budapest: Zeneműkiadó Vállalat, 1977.

Szabó, Helga. *Vocal Improvisation in the School IV: Canon, Imitation and Fugue*, trans. Judit Pokoly. Kecskemét: Zoltán Kodály Pedagogical Institute, 1984.

Tillman, June, and Keith Swanwick. "Towards a Model of Development of Children's Musical Creativity." *Canadian Music Educator*, 1989, *30*(2): 169–174.

Upitis, Rena. *"Can I Play You My Song?" The Compositions and Invented Notations of Children*. Portsmouth, NH: Heinemann, 1992.

Webster, Peter. "Creativity as Creative Thinking." *Music Educators Journal*, 1990, *76*(9): 22–28.

Wiggins, Jackie. "Children's Strategies for Solving Compositional Problems with Peers." *Journal of Research in Music Education*, 1994, *42*(3): 232–252.

Wiggins, Jackie. *Composition in the Classroom: A Tool for Teaching*. Reston, VA: Music Educators National Conference, 1990.

Winner, Ellen, Lyle Davidson, and Larry Scripp. *Arts PROPEL: A Handbook for Music*. Cambridge, MA: Harvard Project Zero and Educational Testing Service, 1992.

Winters, G., and J. Northfield, *Starter Composing Packet*. Essex, UK: Longman, 1992.

Integrating Listening into a Music Lesson

Although we already have a string quartet the mass of students do not know what can be gained by listening to this superior kind of music. Only a few of them listened to the beautiful performance of Schubert's Quartet in A Minor, though with its richness of feelings this work is of outstanding value in cultivating the heart. For such works it is worth going on long pilgrimages. And yet it was played here on the premises—and they did not listen.

Zoltán Kodály, "Good Musician?" p. 198

Individual singing plus listening to music (by means of active and passive well-arranged experiences) develops the ear to such an extent that one understands music one has heard with as much clarity as though one were looking at a score; if necessary—and if time permits—one should be able to reproduce such a score.

Kodály, "Musical Reading," p. 204

It is not enough to listen once, fleetingly, to great works; one has to prepare for them and to follow the notes through the pages both before and after hearing them in order to implant them abidingly in one's mind. Personal participation is worth more than anything else.

Kodály, " Good Musician," p. 198

Key Questions
- How can we develop students' listening skills on the basis of folksong repertoire?
- How can we reinforce musical elements through listening experiences?
- How do we prepare students to listen to more extended examples of art music?

For Kodály, a primary goal of a music education is "to make the masterpieces of world literature public property, to convey them to people of every kind and rank."[1] Accordingly, incorporating fine examples of music literature into music lessons is something all music teachers ought to consider. Using singing and music literacy as a means of opening the world of music literature to students is a primary goal of Kodály-inspired music education: "The final purpose of all this must be to introduce pupils to the understanding and love of great classics of past, present and future."[2]

In order for students to listen to music attentively, we have to find the pedagogical process whereby their singing and active music making lead to an understanding of the music we select for listening. The idea is to understand the various principles of teaching music literature and to inspire the teacher to collect examples and repertoire for their own teaching situations. A goal of this chapter is to give teachers examples of music listening activities that they may incorporate into their own teaching.

Kodály Today

What Listening Repertoire Should Be Included in a Music Curriculum?

Because most music teachers have only a few lessons a week with their students, the selection of music to use for a listening activity is important. Here are some guidelines to use in selecting music literature for the classroom:

1. Select music of the well-known composers.
2. Music must have musical appeal for the students.
3. Music should be developmentally appropriate, relevant to specific age groups.
4. Live performances are best. Solo and small ensemble performances by the teacher or another student(s) should be a staple of music lessons.
5. Knowledge of music literacy should be correlated with some examples used for music listening.
6. Music should be selected from different style periods.
7. Try to include a number of genres of music in your music curriculum.
8. Consider using examples that highlight different solo instruments as well as a variety of small and large ensembles. Learning the instruments of the orchestra should be built into the music curriculum.
9. Try to select short pieces of music so the students can listen to complete examples. We also believe that at several points throughout their musical education students should experience listening to complete music examples while following a score. This might be accomplished when the teacher performs a known song for the students and they follow a score with the music written in staff notation including phrasing and dynamics. It is also helpful for the teacher to create a listening map or score for these, examples. The score should include notation that the students can sing or perform in some manner as they listen and follow. In this way students connect their conscious knowledge of musical elements with the listening experience. The score should include:
    Rhythms that students can sing
    Melodies that students can sing
    Information that might include another voice line
    Indication of dynamics
    Instrumentation
    Inclusion of the form

Figure 7.15a is an example of a simplified score, from Bartók's For Children, vol. 4, no. 32, for students to follow. It may be used in grades four or five once students can read and follow the rhythmic notation as they listen. As students' skills progress, they can listen to longer pieces of music. They can identify and sing segments or phrases of listening examples. In Figures 7.15b and 7.15c, Bartók's "An Evening in the Village" is presented as a listening map. Once students have learned about the la pentatonic scale, they may follow this score and sing along with the recording. In the figures the score is presented as a basic treble and bass outline of the work.

10. Ideally, it is best to introduce students to live performance of songs or instrumental compositions at the earliest stages of musical learning. Folk and ethnic instruments may be used to accompany songs for listening as well as songs for singing and performance. The teacher or older students who perform instrumentally may supply the initial listening experiences for students. Later, students who are studying instruments can demonstrate them for the rest of the class. Consider the activities described in the next section.

Fig. 7.15a

Fig. 7.15b

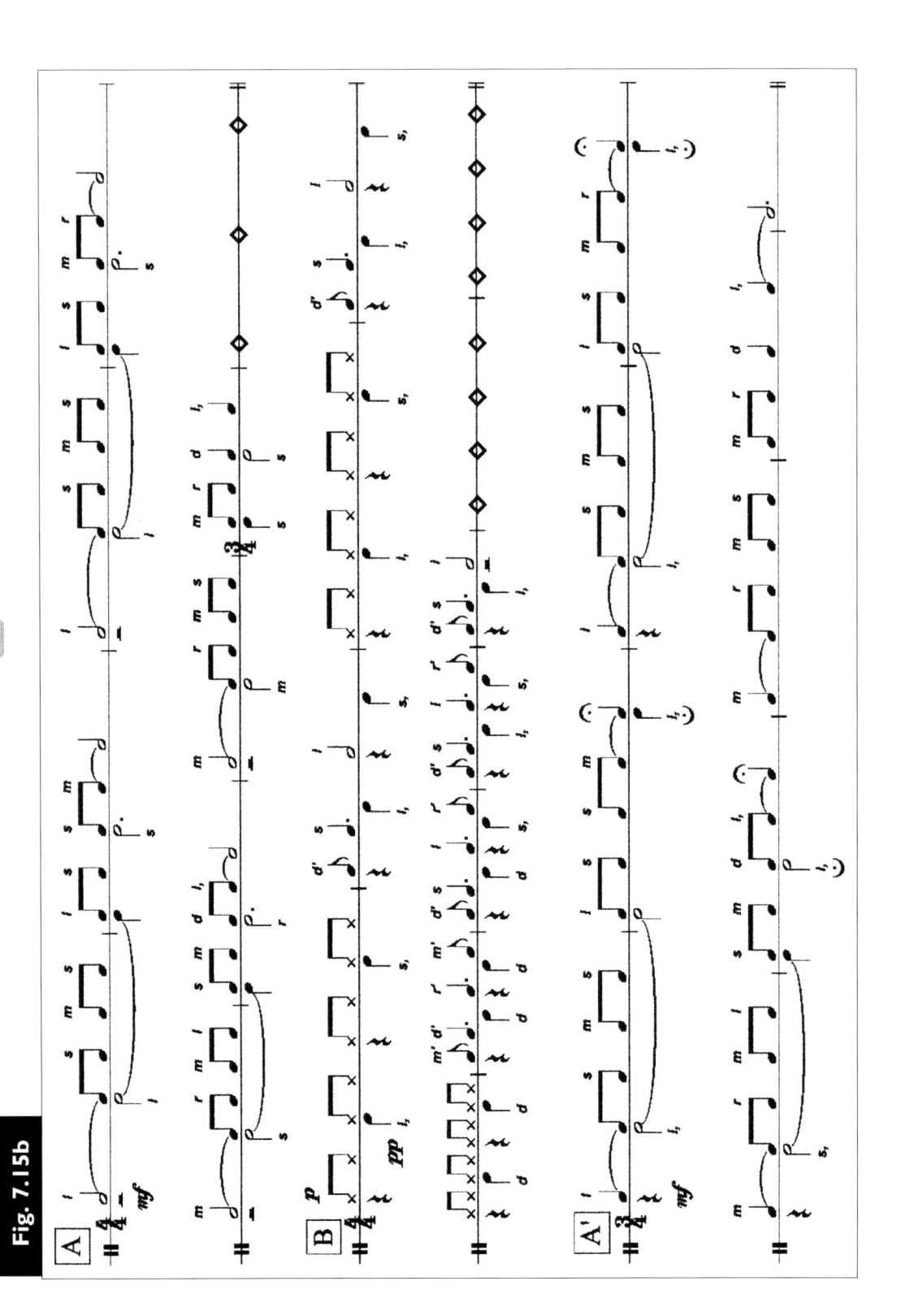

Fig. 7.15b

From Folk Music to Art Music

There has been an emphasis, perhaps even an overemphasis, on the role of the folksong in the Kodály concept. Much has been said about the rationale for basing a curriculum on folksongs. As we've stated, Kodály was convinced that folksongs were the ideal vehicle for leading the student to an appreciation and understanding of the works of the great composers. He believed that students should be taught folk music and that folk music ought to lead to the introduction of art music and composed music.

When teachers become aware of the possibilities inherent in folksong materials, they can skillfully guide students to an understanding of art music. Consider the intellectual capacity and interests of your students and determine the many types of music they will enjoy.

We believe it is important to use art music examples containing melodic and rhythmic fragments that may be isolated for easy recognition. Such works may be orchestral, or works that can be performed by the students. The musical examples employed in the *Juilliard Repertoire Project* provide music from all eras that is within the student's vocal capabilities. Students' attention should be directed to the musical example they are listening to, and not simply to the life of the composer or historical facts surrounding the composition of the work. Although historical facts and stories may be interesting to some older students, young students need to be more actively engaged in listening and performing.

Using folksongs as listening examples,

1. T sings a folksong to Ss at the close of music lessons. These songs may be taught in a subsequent lesson.
2. T plays known folksongs on a musical instrument such as a recorder or dulcimer.
3. Older Ss may perform a folksong. Those with more secure musical execution can perform materials in several parts or in canon.
4. Ss listen to the actual composition that includes the folksong.

Introducing Short Listening Excerpts Based on Musical Elements

This section offers two procedures for incorporating listening activities into music lessons.

1. T sings a theme from a musical example to Ss. They memorize the theme by singing the melody on a neutral syllable. Then T plays the piece of music for Ss and has them raise their hands when they hear the theme.
2. T sings a theme to the class and repeats it over several sessions of instruction. Ss memorize the theme and figure out the known melodic or rhythmic elements in the theme. Then T plays the piece of music for Ss. As reading and writing skills develop, T will be able to use art music themes for memory work, sight reading, dictation, and writing.

3. Table 7.1 contains a brief list of suggested listening examples that may be used to augment and enliven the teaching of musical elements. Additional examples have already been integrated throughout the text for specific musical elements (see Tables 7.2 and 7.3).

Table 7.1

Composer	Composition	Related Song for Classroom Performance
Samuel Barber (1910–1981)	*Excursion No. 3*	"Streets of Laredo"
Ludwig Beethoven (1770–1827)	*Symphony No. 9, Movement 4*	"Ode to Joy"
Georges Bizet (1838–1875)	*L'Arlésienne Suite No. 1*	"March of the Three Kings"
Lucian Cailliet (1891–1985)	*Theme and Variations on "Pop Goes the Weasel"*	"Pop Goes the Weasel"
Aaron Copland (1900–1990)	*Appalachian Spring*	"Simple Gifts"
Aaron Copland (1900–1990)	*A Lincoln Portrait*	"Springfield Mountain"
Aaron Copland (1900–1990)	*Billy the Kid*	"The Old Chisholm Trail"
Morton Gould (1913–1996)	*American Salute*	"When Johnny Comes Marching Home"
Charles Ives (1874–1954)	*Fourth of July Symphony*	"America"
Charles Ives (1874–1954)	*Symphony No. 2*	"Camptown Races," "Columbia the Gem of the Ocean," "Turkey in the Straw"
Charles Ives (1874–1954)	*Variations on "America"*	"America"
Gustav Mahler (1860–1911)	*Symphony No. 1 "The Titan," Movement 2*	"Frere Jacques" (in minor)
Harl McDonald	*Students' Symphony, Movement 1*	"London Bridge," "Baa, Baa, Black Sheep"
Harl McDonald	*Students' Symphony, Movement 3*	"The Farmer in the Dell," "Jingle Bells"
Wolfgang Mozart (1756–1791)	*Twelve Variations on "Ah vous dirai je maman"*	"Twinkle, Twinkle Little Star"

(continued)

Table 7.1 Continued

Composer	Composition	Related Song for Classroom Performance
Franz Schubert (1797–1828)	*Trout Quintet*	"The Trout"
William Schumann (1910–1992)	*New England Triptych*	"Chester," "When Jesus Wept"
Jean Sibelius (1865–1957)	*Finlandia*	"Finlandia"
Peter Tchaikovsky (1840–1893)	*Little Russian Symphony*	"The Crane"
Ralph Vaughn-Williams (1872–1958)	*Fantasia on Greensleeves*	"Greensleeves"

Table 7.2

Concept	Composer	Musical Composition
Slow-fast	Corelli	Concerto Grosso in F Major Op. 6, Introduction and Movement 1
	Wagner	Overture to *The Flying Dutchman*
Loud-soft	Beethoven	Symphony No. 7, Movement 1 (note the sudden contrasts in dynamics; "Egmont" Overture)
High-low	Banchieri	*Counterpoint to the Animals*
Natural pulse in duple meter	Joplin	*Rags*
Natural pulse in triple meter	Bach	Brandenburg Concerto No. 2 in F major
Call and response	Gabrielli	*Brass Choir Compositions*
Rhythmic ostinato	Beethoven	Symphony No. 7, Movement 2
Pentatonic themes	Mozart	Clarinet Quintet, Movement 1 *so-mi-re-do*
	Grieg	*Peer Gynt Suite*, "Morning" *so-mi-re-do-mi-so-mi-re-do*
	Bach	D major Suite, "Gigue" *so-do-mi-re*
	Handel	Water Music Suite No. 2, "Alla Hornpipe" *low so–do-re-mi-do* Sequential themes *re-mi-do-re-so-re-mi-do-re-so-re* etc.

(continued)

Table 7.2 Continued

	Composer	Composition
	Mozart	Symphony No. 1 *do-mi-ssss-ssss-mi-do*
	Dvorak	Symphony No. 5 "New World" Movement 2 *mi-so-so-mi-re-do-re-mi-so-mi-re* *mi-so-so-mi-re-do-re-mi-re-do-do*
Diatonic themes	Copland	*Appalachian Spring* "Simple Gifts" in Theme and Variation form
	Mahler	Symphony No. 1, Movement 2 "Frere Jacques" in minor
	Tchaikovsky	Symphony No. 4, Movement 4, "The Birch Tree"

Table 7.3

Composer	Composition	Program
Wagner (1813–1883)	Overture to *The Flying Dutchman*	"Storm Music"
Mussorgsky (1839–1881)	*Pictures at an Exhibition*	"Gnomes"
Saint-Saens (1835–1921)	*Carnival of the Animals*	"The Swan," "The Elephant"
Saint-Saëns (1835–1921)	*Danse Macabre*	"Ghosts," "Goblins"
Vivaldi (1678–1741)	*Four Seasons*, "Summer"	"Storm"
Vivaldi (1678–1741)	*Four Seasons*, "Winter"	"Sliding on Ice"
Grieg (1843–1907)	*Peer Gynt Suite*, "Morning" and "In the Hall of the Mountain King"	"Sunrise" Scary movements
Menotti (1911–2007)	*Amahl and the Night Visitors*	Opera selections
Prokofiev (1891–1953)	*Peter and the Wolf*	The wolf, the duck, the hunter

A Teaching Strategy for Music Listening

The same care and attention used for selecting song repertoire for the classroom must also be used in selecting music listening examples. Once the selections are made for music listening, consider this question: "How can I prepare the students to listen to this piece of music with understanding?" The same process used in teaching new musical elements and concepts (the cognitive, associative, and assimilative phases of learning) can be used for presenting a listening example.

Here are guidelines for use in developing a teaching strategy for listening to a piece of music.

Teacher Preparation Activities for Music Listening
1. Choose a piece of music that you and the music students will enjoy.
2. Listen to the piece of music many times without and with a score.
3. Analyze the piece of music. Identify:
   - Character of the music
   - Dynamic changes
   - Form
   - Thematic material
   - Key changes
   - Harmonic structure
   - Meter, metric changes, rhythmic patterns, ostinati, tempo changes
   - Compositional devices
   - Instrumentation, texture
   - Programmatic elements
4. Decide which themes the students may sing. They do not have to read every theme they are listening to. They can also memorize a theme by rote and sing it on a neutral syllable. Sometimes the key of the listening example will need to be transposed for the students to perform it.
5. Review the students' knowledge of performance repertoire and try to find connections between this repertoire and the piece of music you are going to use for listening. It is important for them to compare and contrast different styles of music.
6. Decide what concepts and elements you want to teach.
7. Decide what you want to teach the students about this piece of music during the year, or whether you are going to return to this composition in a future grade. Beginning listening experiences should be short. Young students do not necessarily need to hear an entire movement.

Presentation Activities for Listening
1. Decide how many times you are going to play the music example and what students are going to be actively engaged in as they listen repeatedly to the piece of music.

2. There should be a different focus for each repeated listening. Music teachers can also design listening maps for students as well as worksheets that will help them organize their knowledge of the listening example. Another useful teaching strategy is for the teacher to create a simplified score for singing.

Follow-Up Activities

Determine follow-up activities. For example, if students have listened to the Andante from Symphony No. 94 by Joseph Haydn, then they could be asked to write another variation on the theme.

Listening to one piece of music could logically lead to listening to another piece of music. For example, in the "Spring" section of Haydn's oratorio *The Seasons,* the theme from the Andante movement of Symphony No. 94 is sung. Robert Schumann's *Exercises Etudes in the Form of Free Variations on a Theme of Beethoven* can be played for students once they have listened to the Andante from Beethoven's Symphony No. 7.

From Folk Music to Art Music: A Sample Listening Activity

Here is an example demonstrating how the music teacher can move from a folksong to a listening activity. The listening activity pairs the Russian folksong "The Crane" with the principal theme from the final movement of Symphony No. 2, the "Little Russian," by Peter Tchaikovsky (1840–1893).

Students learn the Russian folksong "The Crane" with solfège and rhythm syllables (Fig. 7.16).

Fig. 7.16 "The Crane"

They sing "The Crane" with piano accompaniment (Fig. 7.17).

Kodály Today

Fig. 7.17

The Crane

Tchaikovsky

They read Theme A from the symphony and discover where it deviates from the folksong (Fig. 7.18).

Fig. 7.18

Developing Musicianship Skills

They listen to a complete recording of the movement.

In Figure 7.19, the listening activity is based on the "Finale" (Allegro con fuoco) of Symphony No. 4 by Peter Tchaikovsky (1840–1893) and the Russian folksong "The Birch Tree." The B theme of the symphonic fourth movement, written in sonata rondo form, is based on the folksong "The Birch Tree."

Fig. 7.19 Finale, Allegro con fuoco, Movement 4, from Symphony No. 4 by Peter Tchaikovsky (1840–1893)

Students should be able to sing "The Birch Tree" with text, solfège, or rhythm syllables. They should be able to perform song in canon.

The teacher should sing the B theme for students so that they can aurally identify how Tchaikovsky changed the original folksong in his symphony.

Students should read the B theme. They compare the B theme to "The Birch Tree" and discover that he switches the time signature from duple meter to quadruple meter and adds an extra two beats of rest per phrase. Students should sing the B theme in canon.

The next listening activity is based on the "Farandole" (Allegro vivo e deciso) of *L'Arlésienne Suite* by Georges Bizet (1838–1875).[3]

Preparation Activity

1. The main themes are seen in Figures 7.20 and 7.21

Fig. 7.20

Fig. 7.21

2. Table 7.4 is an outline of the form for the "Farandole" and may be used to create a listening map for students.

Table 7.4

Form	Explanation
A	The A section is in a minor tonality Simple presentation of theme Two part canon
B	The B section is in a major tonality
A'	A' is in minor
B'	B' is in minor
A"	A" is in minor with more thematic development
B"	B" is in minor with thematic development
C	C combines parts A and B in a major tonality
Coda	The coda uses a portion of the B theme in a major tonality

3. Here are the concepts we want to teach from the listening example:
   - Practicing dotted eighth and sixteenth note patterns
   - Practicing dotted quarter and eighth note patterns
   - Canonic imitation
   - Variation
   - Themes played as partner songs
   - Transforming melodies from major to parallel minor and vice versa
   - Accompanying a major and minor melody with chord roots
4. These folksongs may be used to reinforce rhythmic and melodic concepts:
   - "Big Fat Biscuit" (dotted eighth note and sixteenth note patterns)
   - "Shady Grove" (dotted eighth note and sixteenth note patterns)
   - "Liza Jane" (partner song with "Tideo," dotted quarter and eighth note patterns)
   - "Tideo" (partner song with "Liza Jane")
   - "Hey, Ho, Nobody Home" (minor tonality canon)
   - "Are You Sleeping?" (can be used to demonstrate how we accompany a song with tonic and dominant chord roots; this song may also be transposed into the parallel minor and accompanied with chord roots *la* and *mi*)
     1. Develop a listening chart as a guide for your listening.
     2. You can now create a simplified listening chart for your students based on your listening chart.

Music teachers can also design listening maps for students as well as worksheets that will help students organize their knowledge of the listening example (see Table 7.5).

Developing Musicianship Skills

Table 7.5

Form	Description	Theme Instrument(s)	Accompaniment	Mode	Tempo	Dynamics
A	Theme A	Full orchestra	None	Minor	Slow march	*ff: fortissimo*
	Two-part canon	Woodwinds, horns, strings	None	Minor	Slow march	*ff: fortissimo*
	Transition	None	Tambourine	None	Lively and fast	*pp: pianissimo*
B	Theme B	Flute and clarinet	Strings and tambourine	Major	Lively and fast	*pp: pianissimo*
	Theme B	Flute and clarinet	Bassoon, horn, sweeping strings, and tambourine	Major	Lively and fast	*mf: mezzo-forte with crescendo*
	Theme B	Flute, clarinet, and One oboe	Bassoon, horn, strings, and tambourine	Major	Lively and fast	*f: forte with crescendo*
	Theme B	Flute, clarinet, and Two oboes	Bassoon, horn, sweeping strings, and tambourine	Major	Lively and fast	*ff: fortissimo with crescendo*
	Theme B	Flute, clarinet, oboes, bassoons, and strings	Horns, trumpets, trombones, timpani, tambourine, and double bass	Major	Lively and fast	*ff: fortissimo*
A'	Theme A	Oboes, clarinets, bassoons, horns, and strings	None	Minor	Lively and fast	*ff: fortissimo*
B'	Theme B	One flute, then two flutes	Strings and tambourine	Minor	Lively and fast	*p: piano*
A"	Theme A development	Oboes, clarinets, bassoons, horns, and strings	None	Minor	Lively and fast	*ff: fortissimo*
B"	Theme B development	One flute, then two flutes, then one oboe	Strings, tambourine, clarinets, horn	Minor	Lively and fast	*p: piano with crescendo*

(continued)

Table 7.5 Continued

	Theme B development	Flutes, oboes, one clarinet, and violins	All other instruments	Minor	Lively and fast	*mf: mezzo-forte* with crescendo
	Transition from minor to major	Flutes, oboes, clarinets, and violins	All other instruments except tambourine	Minor to major	Lively and fast	*ff: fortissimo*
C	Both A and B themes as partner song	Flutes, oboes, clarinets, and high strings on B theme; two horns, two trumpets, and one trombone on A theme (in major mode)	All other instruments	Major	Lively and fast	*fff: fortississimo*
	Both A and B themes as partner song	Flutes, oboes, clarinets, and high strings on B theme; two horns, two trumpets, and one trombone on A theme (in major mode)	All other instruments	Major	Lively and fast	*ffff: fortissississimo*
Coda	Portion of B theme is used	Flutes, oboes, clarinets, violins violas, and cellos	All other instruments	Major	Lively and fast	*ffff: fortissississimo*

5. Decide how many times you are going to play the music example and what the students are going to be actively engaged in as they listen repeatedly to the piece of music. There should be a different focus for each repeated listening. Music teachers can also design listening maps for students as well as worksheets that will help students organize their knowledge of the listening example. Another useful teaching strategy is for the teacher to create a simplified score for singing (Table 7.6). You can also create a simplified score for singing for students. Figure 7.22 is a score that can be used to perform the work in three parts. This section is the "C" portion of the work.

Table 7.6

First listening	• In previous lessons Ss have memorized themes A and B singing on a neutral syllable. • T and Ss review singing theme A and theme B. • Ss listen to the piece of music.	Sixth listening	• Ss sing "Are You Sleeping?" in solfège. • Ss determine the tonic and dominant chord root tones. • One-half sing song and other half sing chord roots. • Listen to the orchestral work.
Second listening	• Sing "Shady Grove"; perform the rhythm saying rhythm syllables. • Sing "Liza Jane"; perform the rhythm saying rhythm syllables. • Prepare and sight-read theme A with solfège syllables. • Listen and count the number of times theme A occurs.	Seventh listening	• Read theme B. • Determine tonic and dominant chord roots for theme B. • Combine both parts. • Listen and count the number of times theme B occurs.
Third listening	• Review theme A with rhythm and solfège syllables. • Ss write rhythm of theme A from memory. • Listen and tap rhythm of theme A when it occurs.	Eighth listening	• Prepare and sing theme B; transform theme B into the parallel minor key. • Rewrite theme B in minor tonality by adding accidentals • Listen and count how many major statements of B and how many minor statements of B are in the piece
Fourth listening	• Sing "Hey, Ho, Nobody Home." • Identify as minor. • Sing again in two-part canon. • Ss read theme A in unison and sing in two-part canon. • Listen.	Ninth listening	• Sight-read theme A in minor. • Sight-read theme B in minor. • Ss listen and count when each theme occurs in each tonality.
Fifth listening	• Ss read theme A and then prepare and sight-sing theme A extension. • Ss sing "Are You Sleeping?" and transform to parallel minor. • Ss sing eight measures of theme A and transform into parallel major. • Ss listen and count how many times theme A occurs in a major tonality.	Tenth listening	• Ss sing "Liza Jane" and "Tideo" as partner songs. • Ss read theme A in major, and theme B in major; Ss sing both themes as a partner song. • Ss sing combined themes with I-V harmony in three groups of students. See score. • Listen to form map.

Kodály Today

Fig. 7.22

6. Create worksheets for selected listening lessons. An example (Fig. 7.23):
   L'Arlésienne Suite:
   Farandole, Allegro vivo e deciso
   Georges Bizet
   Worksheet 1
   1. Read the A section with solfège syllables. (Hint: it is a minor modality!)
   2. T: "What are the characteristic rhythmic elements in this theme?"
   3. T: "How many times do you hear the theme? Keep track!"

Fig. 7.23

L'Arlésienne Suite:
Farandole. Allegro vivo e deciso
Georges Bizet
Worksheet 2

Developing Musicianship Skills

1. Sing the A section in canon after two beats.
2. T: "Which instruments do you hear playing this canon?" (see Fig. 7.24)

Fig. 7.24

L'Arlésienne Suite:
Farandole, Allegro vivo e deciso
Georges Bizet
Worksheet 3
1. Sing the B section with solfège syllables.
2. T: "How many times do you hear this entire section? Keep track!"
3. Identify the tonic and dominant chord roots that accompany this melody.
4. Design follow-up activities for your listening lesson (see Fig. 7.25).

Fig. 7.25

A good follow-up piece of music to listen to after this example is the "Funeral March," *Feierlich und gemessen*, from Symphony No. 1 in D by Gustav Mahler (1860–1911). In this example (Fig. 7.26) the familiar folksong "Are You Sleeping?" appears in a variation in the minor key. This theme is accompanied by a melodic ostinato based on the tonic and dominant chord root tones.

Fig. 7.26

Discussion Questions
1. What do we mean by the term *listening*?
2. How is the skill of listening connected to development of music literacy?
3. How is the skill of music literacy connected to development of listening?
4. Discuss the notion that it is more important for students to enjoy listening to music and avoid spending time in learning how to read or write themes from the listening example.
5. Discuss whether young students should be able to identify selected musical compositions, memorize facts about the life of the composer, and identify specific themes and orchestral instruments.

Ongoing Assignment
1. Choose a piece of classical (art) music to present to your third grade students next year. Analyze the piece of music, decide what elements you can teach the students on the basis of their knowledge of music, and find songs from their repertoire list that will prepare elements found in the art music example. Develop a set of listening exposures and work sheets for the art music example. Include a listening chart that the students can follow. Describe how you can return to this piece of music in another grade with another set of listening exposures that match the students' knowledge of music literacy.

References
Here are references that can be used for listening.

Choksy, Lois. *The Kodály Method II: Folksong to Masterwork.* Upper Saddle River, NJ: Prentice-Hall, 1999.

Espeland, Magne. "Music in Use: Responsive Music Listening in the Primary School." *British Journal of Music Education*, 1987, *4*(3): 283–297.Heidsiek, Ralph G. "Folk Quotations in the Concert Repertoire." *Music Educators Journal*, 1969, *56*(1): 51–53.

Herboly-Kocsár, Ildikó. "The Place, Role and Importance of Art Music in School." *Bulletin of the International Kodály Society*, 1993, *18*(1): 41–44.

Kerchner, J. L. "Creative Music Listening." *General Music Today*, Fall 1996, *10*(1): 28–30.

Montgomery, Amanda. "Listening in the Elementary Grades: Current Research from a Canadian Perspective." *Bulletin of the International Kodály Society*, 1993, *18*(1): 54–61.

Rappaport, Jonathan C. *New Pathways to Art Music Listening: A Kodály Approach Appropriate for All Age Levels.* Marlborough, NH: Pro Canto Press, 1983.

Rodriquez, C. X., and P. R. Webster. "Development of Children's Verbal Interpretive Responses to Music Listening." *Bulletin of the Council for Research in Music Education*, 1997, *134*: 9–30.

Shehan Campbell, Patricia. "Beyond Cultural Boundaries: Listening as Learning Style." *Bulletin of the International Kodály Society*, 1994, *19*(1): 49–60.

Shehan Campbell, Patricia, and Bonnie C. Wade. "Learning Through Engaged Listening." In *Teaching Music Globally: Experiencing Music, Expressing Culture*, ed. Patricia Shehan Campbell. New York: Oxford University Press, 2004.

Developing the Three Primary Musical Skill Areas

Key Questions
- What are the primary skill areas?
- How can we accommodate musical skill areas into the preparation/practice lesson plan format?
- How can we accommodate musical skill areas into the presentation lesson plan format?
- How can we accommodate musical skill areas into the initial practice lesson plan format?

We designate three skill areas—reading, writing, and improvisation—as being the most important. The other musical skills addressed in this chapter are all dependent on the ability to read, write, and improvise. Therefore we use these three skill areas as a means of developing all other skill areas. These skills become the basic building blocks for other musical skills such as improvisation, composition, memory, ensemble singing, and listening.

In the preceding sections, we showed how reading and writing activities can be expanded to include development of additional musical skills. For example, when students are asked to read a new song or the theme from an art music example, these skill areas may be developed in conjunction with reading.

- Ss can identify the form of the example.
- Ss memorize the example after sight-reading the melody.
- Ss can inner-hear sections of the melody.
- Ss can notate motifs from the melody sung by the T in stick or staff notation.
- Ss can compose a variant of the sight-reading example.
- Ss may improvise an ostinato to accompany the musical example.
- Ss can play the ostinato on rhythm instruments.
- Ss may listen to a recording of a listening example.

When the students are asked to complete a writing activity, many skill areas can be developed. For example, the teacher may write a well-known song on the board but ask the students to complete two measures.

- Ss can identify the form of the example.
- Ss can inner-hear sections of the melody.
- Ss can notate motifs from the melody sung by the T in stick or staff notation.

- Ss compose a variant of the sight-reading example.
- Ss may create an ostinato to accompany the musical example.
- Ss may compose an alternative ending to the song.
- Ss may perform their variation on a melodic instrument.

When students are asked to *improvise*, additional skill areas are developed. For example, the instructor may write a well-known song on the board but ask students to improvise two measures.

- Ss write the newly improvised measures.
- Ss can identify the form of the example. After one S completes the two measures, Ss can compare and contrast the variation to the original (include a discussion of form).
- T can select one example improvised by a class member, and Ss memorize the newly improvised melody.
- Ss can inner-hear sections of the melody.
- Ss can notate motifs from the melody sung by the T in stick or staff notation.
- Ss compose a variant of the sight-reading example.
- Ss may create an ostinato to accompany the newly composed melody.

Developing Music Skills in a Music Lesson Plan

In previous sections of this chapter, we have presented specific information for developing musical skills that may be incorporated into the preparation/practice, presentation, and practice lesson plan formats. The goal of this section is to show how musical skills may be incorporated into lesson plan formats.

We have provided

- Ways to practice rhythmic elements and eighteen suggestions for practicing melodic elements.
- A sequential approach for reading a known rhythm or melody from staff notation as well as sight-reading unknown rhythms and melodies.
- Examples of written activities for writing known melodies and procedures for dictation of unknown rhythms and melodies.
- Activities for developing memorizing by ear, from hand signs, and from staff notation. Also included in this section are strategies for memorizing two-part musical examples.
- Classroom activities that emphasize structure and form and how these activities are closely linked to memory, reading, writing, inner hearing, improvisation, and composition. Many kinesthetic, aural, and visual activities for rhythmic and melodic improvisation are included.

Developing Musicianship Skills

- Examples of how to develop the students' ensemble singing. Included is a discussion of how to teach a two-part musical example. Closely related to development of ensemble singing is development of harmonic hearing.

Creating Lesson Plans That Develop Students' Musical Skills

This chapter furnishes teachers with a wealth of information about developing students' music skills. We suggest reviewing lesson plans in the preceding chapter to see how music skills are developed and also to determine if there are other opportunities for musical skill development during a lesson. For example, can a reading activity be linked to a listening activity, or a memory activity, or form analysis? When students sing known songs with syllables, teachers can create a variation of the melody so that students can aurally decipher (with the help of rhythm or solfège syllables) the melody of the new variation. Of course, we also have to be very mindful of how much or how little time we have for each segment of the lesson and try not to spend too much of it on one segment but rather move musically from one section of the lesson to another.

Table 7.7 presents a Preparation/Practice Lesson Plan Template that shows how the information for this chapter can now be used to modify a lesson plan design.

Table 7.7 Preparation/Practice Lesson Plan Template

Outcome	
INTRODUCTORY ACTIVITIES	
Warm-up	
Sing known songs	Known song: "Here Comes a Bluebird" CSP A Sing with text and play the game. Ensemble work: sing and perform a two-beat ostinato. Reading: Ss read melodic motifs from the song shown from T's hand signs. Sing with rhythm syllables. Ensemble singing: sing song in canon after two beats.
Develop tuneful singing Tone production Diction Expression	Tuneful singing: develop singing skills through beautiful singing, vocal warm-ups, breathing exercises.

(continued)

Table 7.7 Continued

Review known songs and melodic elements	
CORE ACTIVITIES	
Teach a new song	New song: "Down Came a Lady" CSP D Teach "Down Came a Lady," in preparation for teaching $\frac{4}{4}$ meter. Form: Ss identify the form of the melody. Memorization: Ss memorize the song.
Develop knowledge of music literacy concepts	Known song: "Paw Paw Patch" CSP D T provides Ss with a series of discovery learning activities that will develop their knowledge of four sounds on a beat (sixteenth notes) through known songs. Ensemble or part work: all of the following activities develop the ability to use more than one skill at the same time. A. Sing "Paw Paw Patch" and keep the beat. B. Sing and clap the rhythm. C. Sing and point to a representation of phrase 1. _ _ _ _ _ _ _ _ _ _ D. Sing "Paw Paw Patch," walk the beat, and clap the rhythm.
Creative movement	"Great Big House" CSP F# Movement: focus on sequential development of age-appropriate movement skills. Creativity: Ss create their own movements for the game.
Practice music performance and literacy skills	Known song: "Frosty Weather" CSP A Ss reinforce their knowledge of *re* working on the skill areas selected from reading and writing, form, and memory, through known songs found in the alphabetized repertoire list. Singing: sing song tunefully. Memory: aural/oral dictation; T hums motifs from "Frosty Weather." Ss sing back with solfège syllables and hand signs. Writing: Ss write a section of the melody in stick or staff notation. Sight-singing: Ss sight-sing a variation of "Frosty Weather" composed by T.

(continued)

Developing Musicianship Skills

Table 7.7 Continued

	Ensemble singing: Ss sing "Frosty Weather" in canon after two beats. Improvisation: Ss improvise a new A phrase. Inner hearing: Ss sing "Frosty Weather" with solfège syllables and hand signs but inner-hear *re*.
Outcome	
SUMMARY ACTIVITIES	
Review lesson outcomes Review the new song	

Table 7.8 presents a Presentation Lesson Plan Template that shows how the information for this chapter can now be used to modify a lesson plan design.

Table 7.8 Presentation Lesson Plan Design Template for Notating the Sound

Outcome	
INTRODUCTORY ACTIVITIES	
Warm-up	
Sing known songs	"Rocky Mountain" CSP D Ss demonstrate their prior knowledge. Sing with text. Sing rhythm syllables. Sing with solfège syllables. Ensemble work: Ss sing in canon after two beats; Ss create an ostinato. Reading: Ss read from staff notation and sing rhythm or solfège syllables.
Develop tuneful singing Tone production Diction Expression	Tuneful singing: develop singing skills through beautiful singing, vocal warm-ups, breathing exercises.

(continued)

Kodály Today

Table 7.8 Continued

Review known songs and melodic elements	
CORE ACTIVITIES	
Teach a new song	Teach "Ida Red," using an appropriate method of presentation selected from the repertoire list for the grade. Form: Ss identify the form of the song. Memory work: Ss memorize the solfège syllables of "Ida Red."
Develop knowledge of music literacy concepts	"Paw Paw Patch" CSP D Reading and writing: Review the aural awareness stage questions. Use the rhythm syllables to identify the new element. Review the visual awareness activities and associate traditional notation with the visual representation. Read with rhythm syllables. Identify another song that includes the target pattern motif or a closely related pattern. Review the aural awareness and visual awareness activities as above.
Creative movement	"Great Big House" CSP F# Movement: focus on sequential development of age-appropriate movement skills. Creativity: Ss create their own movements for the game.
Practice music performance and literacy skills	"Cumberland Gap" CSP F# Echo-sing rhythm syllables to phrases from "Cumberland Gap." Error recognition activity: change the rhythm into "Dinah." T writes the rhythm of "Dinah" on the board but claps the rhythm of "Old Brass Wagon." Ss identify where the discrepancies occur and write the correction. Identify the form. Improvise with sixteenth notes on the basis of the rhythmic form.

(continued)

Table 7.8 Continued

	Listening: read the rhythm of one or both of these examples and then listen to a recording: "Solfegetto" for piano by C.P.E. Bach "Prelude in C Minor" from Book 1 of the *Well-Tempered Clavier*, by J. S. Bach
Outcome	
Summary Activities	
Review lesson outcomes Review the new song	

Connections to Grade Handbooks

In the handbooks that accompany this book, we have included unit plans for each grade level to serve as a guide for accomplishing curriculum goals. As well as including repertoire for teaching and listing the musical elements to be prepared, practiced, and presented, these units also include activities for developing the musical skill areas.

Discussion Questions

1. How are the skill areas of reading, writing, and improvisation related to all other skill areas?
2. How can the various musical skills be incorporated into the preparation/practice, presentation, and practice lesson plan formats? Provide specific examples.

Ongoing Assignment

1. Design a preparation/practice lesson plan for a first grade class. Discuss how you have incorporated specific musical skills into your lesson plan.
2. Design a preparation/practice lesson plan for a third grade class. Discuss how you have incorporated specific musical skills into your lesson plan.

Bibliography

Bernstrof, Elaine. "Music and Language: Sound Features for Teaching Literacy." *Kodaly Envoy*, 2008, *34*(3): 26–29. Music Index. Web. Apr. 7, 2013.

Bilhartz, T. D., R. A. Bruhn, and J. E. Olson. "The Effect of Early Music Training on Child Cognitive Development." *Journal of Applied Developmental Psychology*, 1999, *20*(4): 615–636.

Campbell, P. S. "Global Practices." In *The Child as Musician: A Handbook of Musical Development*, ed. G. McPherson, pp. 415–438. Oxford: Oxford University Press, 2006.

Campbell, P. S. *Songs in Their Heads: Music and Its Meaning in Children's Lives.* New York: Oxford University Press, 1998.

Choksy, Lois. *The Kodály Method II: Folksong to Masterwork*. Upper Saddle River, NJ: Prentice-Hall, 1999.

Cuskelly, J. "Musicianship and Contemporary Research and Practice." *Bulletin of the International Kodály Society*, 2007, *32*(1): 19–29.

Custodero, L. A. "Singing Practices in 10 Families with Young Children." *Journal of Research in Music Education*, 2006, *54*(1): 37–56.

Custodero, L. A., P. R. Britto, and J. Brooks-Gunn. "Musical Lives: A Collective Portrait of American Parents and Their Young Children." *Journal of Applied Developmental Psychology*, 2003, *24*(5): 553–572.

Espeland, Magne. "Music in Use: Responsive Music Listening in the Primary School." *British Journal of Music Education*, 1987, *4*(3): 283–297.

Gransee, C. "Reading Literacy and Musical Literacy Instruction Share Similar Educational Principles." *Kodály Envoy*, 2005, *31*(3): 4–8.

Green, L. *Music, Informal Learning and the School: A New Classroom Pedagogy*. Aldershot, UK: Ashgate, 2008.

Herboly-Kocsár, I. "How to Choose Materials for Musicianship Classes in Kodály Courses." *Kodály Envoy*, 1993, *20*(1): 49–52.

Herboly-Kocsár, Ildikó. "It Can Be a Joy Not a Torture. Music Dictation with Frames." *Bulletin of the International Kodaly Society*, 2004, *29*(1): 35–39.

Herboly-Kocsár, Ildikó. "The Place, Role and Importance of Art Music in School." *Bulletin of the International Kodály Society*, 1993, *18*(1): 41–44.

Houlahan, M., and P. Tacka. "Developing Harmonic Hearing." *Kodály Envoy*, 1993, *19*(3): 10–13.

Hultberg, C. "Approaches to Music Notation: The Printed Score as a Mediator of Meaning in Western Tonal Tradition." *Music Education Research*, 2002, *4*(2): 185–197.

Ittzés, M. "Pedagogical Consequences of Research in Ethnomusicology and Linguistics in Kodály's Oeuvre." *Bulletin of the International Kodály Society*, 2004, *29*(1): 3–14.

Ittzés, Mihály. "Zoltán Kodály's Messages in Canon Form." *Bulletin of the International Kodaly Society*, 2012, *37*(2): 17–21.

Jacobi, Bonnie S. "Kodály, Literacy, and the Brain: Preparing Young Music Students to Read Pitch on the Staff." *General Music Today*, 2012, *25*(2): 11–18. ERIC. Web. Mar. 4, 2013.

Kerchner, J. L. "Creative Music Listening." *General Music Today*, Fall 1996, *10*(1): 28–30.

Klinger, Rita. "Introducing Part Music to Children." *Kodaly Envoy*, 1989, *15*(4): 21–23.

Kratus, J. "A Developmental Approach to Teaching Music Improvisation." *International Journal of Music Education*, 1995, *26*: 27–38.

Luckey, N. J. "The Creative Process and the Kodály Approach." *Kodály Envoy*, 1986, *13*(1).

Mason, Emily. "Idea Bank: Using Kodály to Promote Music Literacy Skills." *Music Educators Journal*, 2012, *99*(1): 28–31. Music Index. Web. Apr. 7, 2013.

Mithen, S. *The Singing Neanderthals: The Origins of Music, Language, Mind and Body.* London, UK: Weidenfeld & Nicholson, 2005.

Montgomery, Amanda. "Listening in the Elementary Grades: Current Research from Canadian Perspective." *Bulletin of the International Kodály Society*, 1993, *18*(1): 54–61.

Rappaport, Jonathan C. *New Pathways to Art Music Listening: A Kodály Approach Appropriate for All Age Levels.* Marlborough, NH: Pro Canto Press, 1983.

Rodriguez, C. X., and P. R. Webster. "Development of Children's Verbal Interpretive Responses to Music Listening." *Bulletin of the Council for Research in Music Education*, 1997, *134*: 9–30.

Shehan-Campbell, Patricia. "Beyond Cultural Boundaries: Listening as Learning Style." *Bulletin of the International Kodály Society*, 1994, *19*(1): 49–60.

Shehan Campbell, Patricia, and Bonnie C. Wade. "Learning Through Engaged Listening." In *Teaching Music Globally*. New York: Oxford University Press, 2004.

Sinor, J. "Musical Development of Children and Kodály Pedagogy." *Kodály Envoy*, 2014, *40*(3): 17–20.

Stefanova, Maria. "Developing Critical Thinking and Assessment in Music Classrooms." *American String Teacher*, 2011, *61*(2): 29–31. Music Index. Web. Apr. 6, 2013.

Szőnyi, E. "Musical Reading and Writing" (3 vols.) New York: Boosey & Hawkes, 1974–1979.

Thompson, William Forde, and E. Glenn Schellenberg. "Listening to Music." In *MENC Handbook of Musical Cognition and Development*, ed. Richard Colwell. New York: Oxford University Press, 2006.

Trehub, S. E., A. M. Unyk, S. B. Kamenetsky, D. S. Hill, L. J. Trainor, J. L. Henderson, and M. Saraza. "Mothers' and Fathers' Singing to Infants." *Developmental Psychology*, 1997, *33*: 500–507.

Upitis, R., K. Smithrim, and B. Soren. "When Teachers Become Musicians and Artists: Teacher Transformation and Professional Development." *Music Education Research*, 1999, *1*(1): 23–35.

Vinden, D. "At First I Was to Sing Only." *Bulletin of the International Kodály Society*, 2008, *33*(2): 29–31.

Waluga, Anna. "From Folk Music to Art Music." *Bulletin of the International Kodály Society*, 2006, *31*(2): 28–32.

Welch, G. F., E. Himonides, J. Saunders, I. Papageorgi, C. Preti, T. Rinta, M. Vraka, C. Stephens-Himonides, C. Stewart, J. Lanipekun, and J. Hill. *Researching the Impact of the National Singing Programme "Sing Up" in England: Main Findings from the First Three Years (2007–2010). Children's Singing Development, Self-Concept and Sense of Social Inclusion.* London: Institute of Education, University of London, 2010.

Chapter **8**

Technology in the Kodály Classroom

Key Questions

- How do we choose and assess music technology for the Kodály classroom?
- What are some of the important technology resources available to teachers for use in the Kodály classroom?
- What are some of the important technology resources available to students for use in the Kodály classroom?
- How do we design Kodály-based lessons for the interactive white board?

There has been exponential growth in technology applications for the music classroom during the last decade, and teachers are sometimes bewildered as to how to manage and integrate the most promising technological developments into their classroom teaching. These advances include growth in applications to aid in music notation and sound recording as well as development of hardware and use of the internet as a means of communication. Music teachers also contend with the fact that sometimes children's knowledge of technology can be superior to their own and that "the rise of new media technology (e.g., computers and the internet) and the emergence of new musical styles contribute to an increasing variety of musical development in the fields of composition, performance, listening, and preferences. Therefore, parents and teachers should be aware that their students' musical development may differ considerably from their own."[1]

The goal of this chapter is to review some of the most promising technology that can be of use to the Kodály music teacher and the students. However, our main focus will be on applying the interactive white board to teaching in the music classroom. Remember that "when we speak of using technology, many of us tend to restrict the conversation to technologies that are very new or those used by a minority of teachers. This is unfortunate because we often forget how powerful certain commonly used technologies can be."[2] Hughes and Potter advocate that teachers make small adjustments to their teaching when incorporating technology into the classroom; in their view, this will be a more effective strategy than trying to include too much technology in teaching.[3]

We cannot lose sight of the fact that our goal in the music classroom is to develop the multiple dimensions of a child's musicianship. If there are some technology applications than can help teachers and students become more successful in attaining their musical goals, we need to make a good faith effort to learn about them and use them in our teaching. We need to keep in mind that the goal of using technology should be to develop and encourage a child's music development and understanding.

We organize this discussion around these headings:

- How to Choose and Assess Music Technology for the Kodály Classroom
- Technology Resources for the Kodály Classroom
- Technology Resources for the Kodály Student
- Kodály-Based Lessons for the Interactive White Board
- Sample Kodály Lesson Plan Incorporating Technology

How to Choose and Assess Music Technology for the Kodály Classroom

Now more than ever, greater demands are being placed on teachers to include new technology in their curriculum, but knowing where to begin and identifying instructional enhancements that are meaningful and relevant for today's students can be overwhelming. After all, not much more than a decade ago it was normal practice for music teachers to use flip charts, handmade listening maps, overhead projectors, and hand-drawn icons; today's elementary-age students may not relate well to these materials and methods. In light of the technology available today, they may even seem quaint and old fashioned. Twenty-first-century students are far more comfortable with digital media as a platform for learning, entertainment, and social interaction. Understanding the need for appropriate classroom technology and knowing where to begin the process of selecting it are two very different things. We offer a number of ideas as a jumping-off point.

- Attend music technology sessions at professional conferences. This is an opportunity to learn what people are successfully doing in the field. Ask the presenters how the technology interfaces with their music curriculum.
- Pay attention to product reviews in professional journals. Review technology on producers' websites. Search for YouTube videos demonstrating use of the technology.

- Visit the classrooms of other colleagues. Find out what is working for your colleagues and see firsthand how it plays out in the classroom.
- Review materials from the Technology Institute for Music Education (TI:ME) at www.ti-me.org. They offer many resources for cutting-edge ideas. Their website features blogs, available technology courses, information on their annual conference, publications, and much more.

In a perfect educational world, if teachers wanted to acquire a piece of technology for their students, they would simply obtain it. The reality is that schools and districts don't always have funds available for these projects. There are, however, a number of foundations and institutions willing to invest the capital needed for teachers to implement technology in the schools. There are several types of organizations offering donations or grants for classroom technology:

- Charitable foundations. These are not connected to any corporation and generally have specific prerequisites for sponsoring a project.
- Corporate foundations. Many large corporations are eager to invest in local communities, sometimes sponsoring their own private foundations to support community works or K–12 schools.
- Local businesses. Local businesses often seek to give back to the communities in which they are based. Contact major businesses in the area to see if they are interested in supporting educational initiatives.
- Nontraditional. Modern trends in donations have reversed many traditional roles, giving the private donor more control over how money is spent. For example, with organizations such as Donors Choose (www.donorschoose.org), teachers have the opportunity to make a case for classroom projects they would like to implement, and donors may give any amount to the project that most inspires them.

When researching hardware and software for the music classroom, think about how it fits within the categories of curriculum and pedagogy, practicality, classroom considerations, and musical value. The questions given here will help you assess the quality of the technology you are considering and guide you in making the best decisions possible for your students.

Curriculum and Pedagogy
- Can it be blended into a Kodály curriculum that is already in place?
- Does it enhance the work of the teacher?
- When students interact with the technology, do they get immediate feedback on their work?
- Will it aid in the flow of a lesson, or possibly bog down the pacing?
- Does it have a clear application in the classroom?

Practicality
- Is it user-friendly? How much so?
- What is the cost-benefit ratio?
- Does the manufacturer extend a trial offer?
- Are the product reviews positive? What are other consumers saying?

Classroom Considerations
- Is it for use by the teacher, the student, or both?
- Does it enhance the student's learning?
- Does it have age-appropriate animations that would be engaging to a modern student?
- How is the quality of the audio?
- Is it designed for a classroom, a small group, or the individual student?
- Can all age groups use it?

Musical Value
- Will it develop awareness of music, or is it simply a game or activity?
- Will it encourage critical listening?
- Will it enhance the experience of the music?
- Will students become better musicians because of it?

There are many wonderful examples of technology that apply beautifully to music education in general, but not every product is appropriate for a Kodály classroom setting. Although a music theory program appropriate for elementary-aged children could be a wonderful tool for individual students, how will the software integrate with sequential lessons and engage the entire class? Will the sequencing of concepts align with an already established curriculum? Music theory software programs tend to hyperfocus on one small element of musical literacy rather than teaching literacy in the context of actually making music. They may be entertaining and appropriate for use at home or on the part of the classroom teacher. But generally, they do not support the Kodály teacher. The best pieces of technology for a Kodály classroom are those that encourage music making with the voice and with the body, that do not distract from but rather support the lesson and the concept at hand, and that can be blended and integrated without any loss of pacing in the lesson.

Technology Resources for the Kodály Classroom

In this section we explore technology resources specifically for the teacher's use. There are many music-teaching resources available, but those selected here have direct application to Kodály inspired teaching. They have been chosen because they are practical, efficient, and functional, and they can interface effectively with the lesson plan model laid out in this book. These resources are all easily integrated and used often in the classroom.

Hardware

Tablets

Tablets can have a multitude of functions in the classroom, especially when using apps. If tablets are not available in your school, check to see if your classroom teachers have a set available for their grade level. It may be possible to upload your selected music apps to the tablets so that students may practice music concepts during their free time outside of music class. It may also be worth exploring the possibility of borrowing the tablets during music classes.

The teacher may also use a tablet to video-record class activities for assessment. Remember to get permission from school administration as well as parents before you video any child in a music lesson. With permission, the teacher may also upload these videos as "unlisted" to YouTube to be shared privately with parents. This can make economic and effective use of the device since it can be accomplished with only one tablet. A tablet may be used to take pictures of student dictations, visual representations of melodic or rhythmic concepts, and other creative projects for assessment. This can be far more efficient than keeping files of hard copies of student work, and in the case of students' written representations it documents progress throughout a semester or year. Videos and pictures of student work can be organized in individual files by student or class to present to parents, teachers, or administrators. These files can be easily archived to show student growth over a longer period of time.

Smart Phones, iPods, Minitablets

In the absence of a tablet, a smart phone or iPod can be used for some of the same functions. Some teachers may even prefer the smaller size since it can be more quickly taken out and put away. Minitablets are also a good alternative to full-size tablets; they're more economical than their larger counterparts and afford some of the same advantages as the smart phone or iPod as well as the full-size tablet.

Recording Microphone

A computer's internal microphone may be inadequate for making recordings in a class setting. Recording microphones are a far better option; they span the price range from very affordable to extremely expensive, although for a very reasonable price teachers can acquire a microphone that will produce good-quality recording depending on the need. These microphones can be used to record singing or playing by a class or a special ensemble, so that students can assess their own performance. The recordings may also be used to increase community support through sharing with parents, administrators, and colleagues.

Consider including these recordings in podcasts, to share with students and the larger school community what is happening in your classroom. If you're not familiar with podcasting, think of it as a type of multimedia digital radio show for the internet. Student-oriented or student-created podcasts also offer a way for students to create real-life connections with music outside of the school day. Creating a podcast does not need to be complicated; in fact, all you need to get started is a computer, a microphone, a website to host your files, and basic recording software such as GarageBand or Audacity. There is also software available specifically for recording and publishing podcasts, notably ePodcast Producer, Propaganda, and WebPod Studio. Podcasts can be a successful way to make a unique connection with teachers, parents, and administrators to help them better understand the value of music in schools.

Document Camera

Document cameras can be used simply as a projection tool, similar to an old-fashioned overhead projector, though with the ability to project onto a screen any object (including three-dimensional ones) placed under the camera. The teacher could place sheet music under the camera for students to read. Students can also assemble visual representations they have made with Unifix cubes on the projection surface. Teachers can project student work, and so on. Depending on the model, the teacher may also audio- and video-record anything placed beneath the camera.

Smart Board, Promethean ActivBoard, MimioTeach

These models of interactive whiteboard (to be discussed later in the chapter) can be used as extremely effective tools for student interactivity and engagement. An interactive whiteboards can be a significant investment in the classroom. If a Smart Board or a Promethean ActivBoard is too expensive a purchase for your school, consider the more cost-effective, though slightly less versatile, MimioTeach. This product, a bar that can be placed on any white board, interfaces with a computer and projector to make the white board function interactively.

Software and Apps

Audacity, GarageBand

Audio recording software of this kind can be used by teachers to record and edit student performances, create podcasts, generate song accompaniments and practice recordings, edit song tracks, etc. GarageBand comes standard with newly purchased Mac computers and can be purchased for PCs. Audacity is a free download available for Mac or PC.

DropBox, Evernote, LiveBinders

These products allow you to store information (DropBox can be used for particularly large files) and access it anywhere using most devices. Teachers can use the software to store their digital song collections, teaching videos, music, important documents, etc.

iRetrieval

This software, which can be purchased online, is a great resource for entering and organizing your folksong collection online. With iRetrieval you can create a customizable database that allows you to store, search, and print your song analyses. More information can be found at www.iretrievaldatabase.com.

Technology in the Kodály Classroom

MimioStudio Software, SMART Notebook
This software, created specifically for each interactive board, is used for interactive presentations. Techniques for using this type of software will be discussed later in the chapter.

Explain Everything
This is an app available for iPad that allows the user to animate, annotate, and narrate presentations. This could be used to add drama to lessons by creating animated presentations of musical concepts, or even by prerecording short lessons that a substitute teacher could use.

Websites

Blogger, Wordpress, Edublogs
These three websites are free platforms for building personal blogs. Blogs are an excellent way to stay connected with students, family, colleagues, and the community. Blogs do not require long expository writing; they can be used to share short and simple "blurbs" about what is happening in the classroom, pedagogical techniques you use, special projects completed by students, etc. Add pictures, sound recordings of students, links to videos of classroom activities, and anything else that effectively communicates exactly what happens in the classroom.

DropBox, Evernote, LiveBinders
See Software and Apps above.

Edmodo
Using Edmodo, teachers can start discussions, post practice materials, and share calendars, quizzes, and assignments. Edmodo can help keep students accountable and create a space that is specific for each class and ensemble.

Facebook
If a teacher is looking for more interactivity with students, then a classroom Facebook page is a solution. This can be an appropriate place for teacher and students to start conversations about classroom topics, share photos of classroom activities, and disseminate information about the music program in your school.

Twitter
Think of Twitter as microblogging or instant messaging to the masses. Each message a user posts is limited to 140 characters, including punctuation and spaces. People use Twitter as a means to share quick updates and short thoughts or commentary. As a teacher, Twitter can be used in a number of ways. You can send notices to parents about rehearsals, concerts, programs, etc. It can be a way for parents, teachers, and community to hear your thoughts on teaching and music education. If you have little time to maintain a blog,

Twitter is a good alternative; the school community can still know your thoughts and it only takes a matter of seconds to share them.

Prezi

Prezi is a presentation website that functions similarly to PowerPoint. The difference is that Prezi has sharp, creative, and sometimes whimsical transitions from one slide to the next. It is also possible to embed sounds clips, music, and video into Prezi. Prezi may be most effective for teaching songs and for lessons that present or notate musical concepts.

Technology Resources for the Kodály Student

In this section we explore technology resources specifically for student use. Some of these resources may be the same as those listed in the previous section, but with different recommendations for their application. These products and websites have been selected because of how they help develop children's music perception, cognition, and performance skills, and also because of their efficiency, effectiveness, and relevance to Kodály teaching.

Hardware

Tablets

As stated in the previous section, there are many uses for a personal tablet in the classroom, but within the context of a Kodály lesson this may be more specifically and narrowly defined. In a Kodály lesson the student should be able to use the device as a small part of the lesson and not be drawn into using it for more than a brief moment. This way, making music with the voice and the body stays central and the technology is used as a means to this end. Consider using the tablet in visual lessons as a tool for creating representations of rhythmic or melodic concepts (Doodle Buddy, or a similar drawing app works well for this). Make connections to literacy for younger students by reading an animated story. Individual students can pass the tablet for sight-reading exercises using digital flashcards, swiping from one example to the next (compositions created in Finale can be viewed, printed, and played through their app Finale SongBook).

Smart Phones, iPods, Minitablets

Smart phones and iPods can be used for many of the same functions as the tablet, the main difference being the size. The benefit of using these devises with students is that they are easily held in smaller hands. Students can hold an iPod and record themselves singing an assessment exercise, they can video-record a group performance in class to share with their teachers and families, and they can play the digital instruments available for purchase through the iTunes App Store.

There are hundreds of exciting and engaging music apps available for smart phones and tablets, but choose very carefully: many of the apps that are available may not be appropriate for a Kodály lesson. Considerations are that apps appropriate for this style of teaching should encourage the child to use the voice, they must only take a matter of seconds to use, the tablet should be easily shared among students, and the app should not draw attention away from the main objectives of the lesson.

SMART Board, MimioTeach, Promethean ActivBoard
Interactive white boards, which will be discussed later in the chapter, are extremely effective tools in increasing student engagement, differentiation, and understanding. There are endless ways for students to interact with the board. Interactive boards can blend seamlessly into classroom instruction and make it possible to streamline materials and manipulatives.

Software and Apps

GarageBand, Audacity
Just as the teacher is able to use Audacity and GarageBand for recording projects in the classroom, so may students. Depending on their age, students need some amount of independence when it comes to running and using the software, especially if it has a clear and simple interface. They may run them from a computer or interactive white board; GarageBand may be used as well on an iPad or iPod. Students may also use this recording software to create podcasts on topics such as a composer or a particular piece of music.

MimioStudio Software, SMART Notebook
If an interactive white board is available in the classroom, students can immerse themselves in the software that comes with the product to gain deeper understanding and engagement in musical concepts.

Digital Instruments
Digital instruments, such as the Percussive line available for iPad and iPhone, are fun and authentic-sounding substitutes for their real-life counterparts. Some students in the class may play the real, acoustic instruments while others play the instrument on a tablet.

There is an incredible amount of valuable music education software and apps available for students; however, much of it has been designed with the individual student in mind and not the classroom. These programs may be appropriate and helpful for substitute teachers, or for individual practice outside of class time.

Music Ace Series
This software contains interactive music lessons that develop music reading and performance skills. Teachers should be aware that many of the concepts in Music Ace are not necessarily sequenced in the traditional Kodály format, and care should be taken to choose appropriate topics.

Morton Subotnick's Making/Playing/Hearing Music
The Morton Subotnick series mixes short animated lectures and games to teach and reinforce basic concepts.

JoyTunes Recorder Master
JoyTunes is a popular app for iPhone and iPad created for practice on the recorder. The app is creative and well animated and engages students by activating games only when they play the recorder.

Note Squish and Flashnote Derby
These apps were created for students to learn or reinforce their knowledge of the notes on the treble, bass, and C-clefs.

A Jazzy Day, Melody Street Series
These are interactive apps for children to explore various instruments and styles of music.

Websites

Blogger, Wordpress, Edublogs, Facebook
Blogs and social media have been included in this section because for the student they can accomplish the same purpose as for the teacher. Not only will a blog inform your community about what is happening in the classroom, it can also keep students connected outside of the school day. Make pages specific for grade levels or ensembles and encourage students to leave comments, post videos of songs being studied in lessons, critique recordings of their class performances, create short blog posts for their parents and classmates to read, etc. The more involved students become in music when they are not in school, the more it will legitimize the subject in their mind. Blogs and social media can be a powerful tool in this way.

Edmodo
Along the same lines, Edmodo enables students to participate in class discussions, practice songs and concepts with materials posted by the teacher, take quizzes, and complete assignments. This will aid in keeping learning fresh and holding students accountable to what is happening in the classroom. Edmodo is also a great exercise in building skills for a twenty-first-century workplace, where emphasis is on collaboration, teamwork, cooperation, and exchange of innovative ideas.

Kodály-Based Lessons for the Interactive White Board

We are grateful for Nick Holland, music specialist at the St. Paul School in Baltimore, for contributing this section on Kodály-based lessons for the interactive whiteboard to this chapter. (Nick studied with us in the Texas State Program and is currently creating

SMART Board lessons based on the lesson plans and Houlahan and Tacka model of learning found in this publication.)

SMART Boards and other interactive white boards have stood out as an effective instrument in educating students but also an important connection to practical classroom technology. They create avenues for differentiation of concepts in ways that have not been possible in the past, and as Kodály educators we find this an integral aid to pedagogy and curriculum. However, maintaining the integrity of a Kodály-based curriculum and effectively assimilating the use of an interactive white board is a slippery slope on which it is far too easy to fall. Many times kinesthetic or aural teaching activities become visual; musical discovery is overshadowed by the discovery of technology, or teaching becomes centered on the activity with one student at the board, rather than including an entire class. How, then, should lessons be designed for use with an interactive white board to differentiate teaching and increase interactivity for all students, yet keep the concepts of a Kodály education at its core? The answer is simple: *teach before tech*. In other words, the most effective music teaching considers pedagogy first and technology second, and then only as a means of supporting the instruction that is already in place. Keeping this model in mind while designing lessons will create a classroom environment that is rich with focused and active teaching, practical use of technology, and student-centered instruction.

It is important to understand exactly what role an interactive board plays in the context of a lesson. As previously stated, the board should support the teaching currently in place, rather than dominate it. Effective teaching uses the interactive board only at key points in the teaching process to cement student understanding of a concept. Observe the placement of the interactive board in Table 8.1, the segment from a lesson plan focusing on the *la* pentatonic scale.

After the students have experienced music making in multiple ways, the board is used as an aid for understanding. Students are already able to demonstrate the contour of the phrase before they are invited to board, and only then as a confirmation of knowledge that they have already discovered. In the video example of this lesson segment (see Video 8.1 on the companion website ⏵), notice for how many minutes the students explore kinesthetic awareness before the SMART Board is brought into the picture.

The most effective approaches used on an interactive board are virtually the same as what is used in traditional Kodály teaching. The point made by Hughes and Potter in the beginning of the chapter remains true and can be expanded even further: small adjustments to technology are a more effective strategy than radical adjustments. Small and meaningful additions of technology are far more effective than radical additions to, or replacement of, traditional music teaching methods. Because a piece of technology is new and cutting-edge does not necessarily mean that tried-and-true methods of teaching must also be changed; it simply means they can now be enhanced by new possibilities as a result of technology. There is no need to stop using icons as a means to visualize melodic contour simply because they've always been used. Feltboards, however, have

Kodály Today

Table 8.1

Develop knowledge of music literacy concepts Internalize music through kinesthetic activities	"Land of the Silver Birch" CSP: D • Ss sing the song and keep the beat. • T directs one group of Ss to sing phrase 4 as a melodic ostinato while the remaining Ss sing the song. • T directs Ss to sing in two-part canon after eight beats. • Ss sing the song and show the phrases with their bodies. • Ss sing the target phrase (phrase 3) and keep the beat. • Ss inner-hear the target phrase and show the melodic contour. • Ss sing the target phrase on a neutral syllable and clap the melodic contour. • Ss turn and face partners, sing, and show melodic contour as a pair, each mirroring the other's claps. • Ss repeat the previous step with a new partner. • Ss sing the song and direct their attention to T at the board. • Ss sing the target phrase and point to the melodic contour while T taps the windows of the representation on the board (as T taps the windows, they will open to reveal the representation of the contour). *Land of the Silver Birch* [image of covered grid] • Ss sing the target phrase and tap the melodic contour on the board, opening and closing the windows. *Land of the Silver Birch* [image of grid with melodic contour revealed]

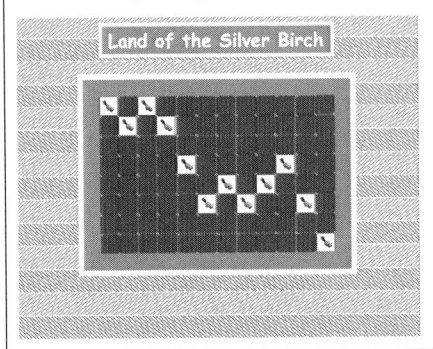

lived their lives, and although they relate to twentieth-century teaching, they do not relate to twenty-first-century students. The core of the pedagogy will always remain the same; the teaching is what should constantly be reevaluated and updated.

Incorporating use of an interactive white board into each step in Houlahan and Tacka's model of instruction and learning outlined in this book (kinesthetic, aural, visual, presentation, practice) demands particular design elements for the most targeted application to each approach. For example, elements used to design an interactive lesson targeting aural instruction will differ from elements used to design a lesson focusing on notation. Interactive lessons must stay true to the method with which a lesson is being taught; aural teaching must remain strictly aural, visual strictly visual, etc. The next sections outline ideas to aid in designing well-classified lessons focused on kinesthetic, aural, and visual teaching and methods for presentation and practice. Keep in mind that what makes use of an interactive white board, or any other piece of technology for that matter, most successful is not how the teacher uses the board but rather how the teacher applies a strong base of pedagogy. Designing with these principles in mind will make it possible to include technology in a way that is meaningful for students, and where the teacher will not feel forced to compromise pedagogy or the organization of curriculum.

Using the SMART Board to Develop Kinesthetic Awareness of a Music Concept or Element

We should point out that a major pitfall of any kind of technology is that it is far too easy to engage one student at a time at the expense of excluding the rest of the class, or draw attention away from what is being taught and focus on the piece of technology itself. The music should be more engaging than the technology, and to accomplish this, three simple rules for designing kinesthetic activities on an interactive white board should be followed:

1. Make it highly interactive
2. Keep it simple and intuitive
3. Keep it quick

It should go without saying that interactive white boards were created to be interactive; unfortunately, this is not always the case. The most engaging element of these lessons should be the interactivity. This is what draws students to participate and keeps their attention focused on the task at hand. Additionally, this level of interactivity and engagement adds an entirely new layer of kinesthetic understanding. They are not simply touching an icon; they are manipulating, moving, feeling, and changing an icon as a result of their action. Experiencing music at this level of kinesthetic activity becomes an intrinsic reward for students.

Exactly how objects are manipulated should be left to the discretion of the teacher, but a student looking at what the teacher has created should understand intuitively how it works. Keeping the page simple and the screen clear of distracting objects and words

Kodály Today

works best. With as few objects as possible on the screen, there is less room for confusion on the part of students and more room for understanding. This is partially what makes products like the iPad so successful: they are functional, are simple, and can be used with little or no instruction. Lessons for the interactive white board should be the same, and kinesthetic lessons even more so.

The most successful lessons will be interactive and intuitive; however, they will also engage the highest number of students for the shortest time possible. Kinesthetic activities for the interactive board should be designed so that the task at hand can be accomplished quickly in order to hold student interest and engagement. Depending on the age of the students, the activity should take no longer than a few seconds.

In Illustrations 8.1 and 8.2 we see an example from a lesson focusing on kinesthetic awareness of quarter and eighth notes. Students sing the target phrase of the song and tap the raindrops to the rhythm of the words. As the raindrops are tapped, they fall off the bottom of the screen.

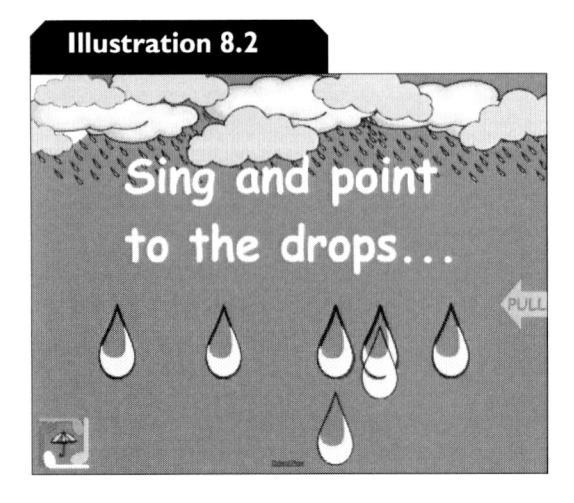

Illustration 8.1

Illustration 8.2

This follows the three guidelines for kinesthetic activities on an interactive board:

1. It is interactive. Interactivity and complexity are not synonymous; a highly interactive learning can be as simple as tapping a raindrop and having it fall off the screen.
2. It is simple and intuitive. Words and background are unobtrusive, the focal point of the page is the rhythmic representation, and with little or no verbal explanation students understand what they should do.
3. It is quick. It takes only a matter of seconds for the task to be completed before another student comes to the board to perform the same activity.

Using the SMART Board to Develop the Aural Awareness of a Music Concept or Element

In the Houlahan and Tacka approach to preparation, aural awareness brings together the learning from the previous kinesthetic and aural lesson(s) to create a verbal description of the new concept that demonstrates student knowledge. Designing lessons for an interactive white board focusing on aural preparation can be difficult, simply because when teaching aurally the aim is to engage critical listening skills without any visual aid. Using the board in the aural awareness preparation lesson requires great care, because doing so in the wrong way will weaken and confuse the aural perception of musical concepts. It is vital that the manner in which the board is used remain well compartmentalized from kinesthetic and visual teaching. Keeping two guidelines in mind will help focus instruction on aural analysis of the music:

1. Activate students' ears, not their eyes.
2. Choose one or two significant questions to present on the board.

In designing lessons for the interactive board, it is very easy to engage students visually or physically rather than aurally. After all, the interactive board is an inherently visual and tactile tool, which is all the more reason to think out of the box and design so as to support critical listening and still take advantage of the interactive qualities of the board. Consider adding sound clips rather than visual cues to confirm answers to aural questions, add recordings of the target phrase that students may replay if necessary, etc. Essentially, when a student looks at the page and does not have to sing to produce an answer, the activity is visual and not aural. If a student looks at the page and must use the voice to answer a question, the activity is aural. Be very objective about creating aural activities with the white board, and consider carefully whether they activate students' ears or their eyes. In the end, and depending on the concept or age of the students, the teacher may determine if it would more beneficial not to use the board at all. This may sometimes be preferable.

If you decide to use the board in the aural preparation stage of teaching, keep the pages from becoming needlessly complicated. In order to streamline teaching and

Kodály Today

hold student focus, choose one or two critical questions in the aural process and highlight them with the board. This will keep students' attention on singing and listening and reinforce the key questions in the process. Read the following aural awareness questions concentrating on four sixteenth notes, using "Paw Paw Patch" (phrase 1) as a focus song, and determine where would be the most appropriate place to use the board:

1. T: "How many beats did we tap?"
   Ss: "Four."
2. T: "Which beat had the most sounds?"
   Ss: "Beat 3."
3. T: "How many sounds are on beat 3?"
   Ss: "Four."
4. T: "If beat 3 has four sounds, how many sounds are on each of the other beats?"
   Ss: "Two."
5. T: "Let's sing the phrase with rhythm syllables and keep the beat, but sing our four sounds on beat 3 with *loo*."

In this case, the teacher could put the questions on the board, beginning with question number one. Just remember, reading the questions will distract students from answering. To promote audiation skills, the students should not see the answers.

Students should not see anything on the board until they are able to articulate what they hear. In the example of Illustration 8.3, for teaching *low la*, students sing phrase one of "Phoebe in Her Petticoat" while keeping the beat. They see only the words on the screen.

Illustration 8.3

How many beats are in the phrase?

Phoebe in her petticoat

Once students have identified that there are four beats in the phrase, the beats will appear on the screen (Illust. 8.4):

Technology in the Kodály Classroom

Illustration 8.4

[Interactive screen: "How many beats are in the phrase?" showing "Phoebe in her petticoat" with four beat icons and Phoebe character images]

The students sing the phrase again, and the teacher asks them to identify the beat on which we hear the lowest pitch (Illust. 8.5).

Illustration 8.5

[Interactive screen: "Which beat has the lowest sounding pitch?" showing "Phoebe in her petticoat" with four beat icons]

After students have identified that beat 4 has the lowest pitch, they may drag the icon of Phoebe from the top circle to the bottom, which reveals what is seen in Illustration 8.6.

Illustration 8.6

[Interactive screen: "Which beat has the lowest sounding pitch?" showing "Phoebe in her petticoat" with "Beat 4" label revealed]

This example meets the three requirements for successful interactive aural teaching. Nothing in the example presents information to students that they have not already discovered on their own. And to discover and eventually see the information, they are directed to use their ears and not their eyes. Two very simple, but significant, questions are chosen to emphasize the musical concept and are appropriately placed to strengthen understanding. The example seen in Video 8.2 ▶, with third grade students working through the aural awareness process for *low so*, also demonstrates these three guidelines for interactive aural teaching.

Using the SMART Board to Develop Visual Awareness of a Music Concept or Element

In the Houlahan and Tacka approach to preparation, visual awareness brings together the learning from the previous kinesthetic and aural lessons to create a product (a visual representation) that demonstrates student knowledge. This is accomplished by having students create a representation of a target phrase with Unifix cubes, buttons, poker chips, popsicle sticks, pencil and paper, etc. In creating an interactive lesson for visual awareness, the teacher should not abandon these traditional methods; the task is to enhance these methods with use of the interactive board. The suggestions for interactive kinesthetic and aural lessons should still be implemented, but simply carried out to the next logical step, which is a physical creation. For example, an effective interactive visual lesson is still simple and intuitive, just as in kinesthetic and aural awareness, and it also encourages critical listening skills; additionally it creates a visual product that represents the musical concept being taught. To accomplish this, keep in mind these three suggestions for interactive visual awareness:

1. Incorporate the guidelines for kinesthetic and aural interactive awareness.
2. Set up pages so they are completely student-operated.
3. What is on the board should be representative of whatever the class is using to create their individual visual representations.

To create a visual representation of a musical concept, students must first be able to demonstrate the knowledge kinesthetically and describe it aurally. This is why, as stated above, lessons for interactive visual awareness should be embedded with kinesthetic and aural preparation activities in mind. In using Kodály approach according to the Houlahan and Tacka model, we find that the learning is cumulative, and designing for interactive lessons should be the same. Design in ways that will challenge students to continuously activate their previously acquired knowledge. This yields a group of students who are consistently thinking as well as engaged in the learning process, and it ultimately produces engaged musicians.

It is conceptually important for students to create their representation without assistance from the teacher; therefore the students' visual representation activity should be set up so this can be accomplished. The interactive "visual" lesson associated with the Houlahan and Tacka model is no different; what is on the screen should be simple and intuitive enough that students will need little or no instruction to complete it. For the concept to have the

Technology in the Kodály Classroom

proper emphasis, students have to be able to turn an event entity (the music) into a concrete representation; and if the activity on the screen is confusing, incomplete, too busy, distracting, or needlessly difficult then it may not be possible for them to demonstrate their level of understanding. Set students up for success by keeping pages simple and clear enough that they will be able to complete the activity without assistance or explanation.

One way to accomplish this is to design the activity on the board to represent the manipulatives that students are using in class. If the class is using buttons to create a visual representation, then the activity on the board should use something that looks like a button to create a representation. Look at the example in Illustration 8.7 of an interactive visual lesson teaching *re*.

Illustration 8.7

After reviewing kinesthetic and aural awareness activities, students are asked to create a visual representation of phrase 1 using some type of manipulative (e.g., Unifix cubes). After materials have been distributed and students begin work, one student is invited to the board to create a representation of the melodic contour of the three pitches in phrase 1 of "Hot Cross Buns." Without saying anything other than the words on the screen, students understand the task and produce an adequate representation. (See Illustration 8.8.)

Illustration 8.8

What should be avoided are methods of creating that are not congruent, such as asking a student to draw a representation while the class is using Unifix cubes. This example also follows the previously outlined suggestions: it supports earlier learning by building on kinesthetic and aural skills, and it is simple enough for students to be able to complete without assistance. Video 8.3 ⊙ also demonstrates these three guidelines for interactive visual teaching. In the video, fourth grade students have just finished reviewing kinesthetic and aural awareness of *fa* and are about to engage in the visual activity.

Using the SMART Board to Present the Name of a Music Concept or Element

In the Houlahan and Tacka model of learning and instruction, presentation is a two-step process. First, label the sound, which means presenting the solfège or rhythm syllables for the new element and aurally synthesizing the information with other known songs. Second, present the traditional name and notation in the following lesson; here the teacher combines aural understanding with the symbol of the musical element. How the interactive white board is used for each step is quite different, as with the method of presentation. It is conceptually necessary that lessons for each step in the process be designed carefully so that there is no crossover between aural and visual presentation. Interactive lessons that label the sound are minimal in visual activities and instead place heavy emphasis on critical listening and aural identification through singing. Interactive lessons that present the notation of a musical element are visual and have more emphasis on reading and writing. In either case, the same ideas must be maintained in order to create successful interactive lessons:

1. Allow the board to facilitate musical discovery.
2. The board should engage students in musical activity that leads to presentation of information.

Using the SMART Board to Label the Sound

As with teaching aural awareness, it would be far too easy at this point in the teaching process to employ the interactive board as a visual tool, rather than for an activity to develop hearing. In the Houlahan and Tacka model of learning and instruction, the point of associative phase 2 is for students to use their ears to associate the song's sounds and pitches with rhythm or solfège syllable that's just been presented. The teacher, then, must determine how to incorporate a piece of hardware that is inherently visual with teaching that is inherently aural. The teacher can simply have the correct spelling for the rhythm syllable or a picture of the hand sign with the solfège syllable. In the end, it may be that the interactive white board is not appropriate for this stage of teaching, a decision that is perfectly acceptable.

Using the SMART Board to Present the Notation of a Music Concept or Element

When presenting notation of a musical element, the teacher should embed all the characteristics of the element that students have been made aware of up to this point in the design of these lessons. All the characteristics should be incorporated into the lesson. However, the aspects that make this lesson more interactive are the two points presented earlier in this section: (1) allow the board to facilitate musical discovery and (2) let it engage the students in musical activity, not simply presentation of information.

A page created for presenting notation offers visual opportunities for student interaction at the board and for practicing music skills. Most importantly, it leads students to learn the notation of the music concept. Take a portion from a *fa* presentation lesson for example (Illust. 8.10–8.12). Illustration 8.10 shows the blank tone ladder; students must articulate where *so, fa, mi, re,* and *do* belong. Once students are able to sing it and show where they belong, they may compare their answers to one presented on the SMART Board. At this point, students must be able to identify whole steps and half steps between the pitches; they may check their answers by erasing the circles beneath the tone ladder (see Illust. 8.11).

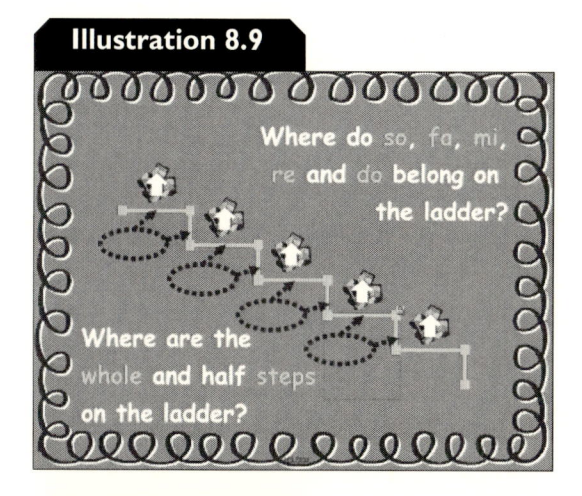

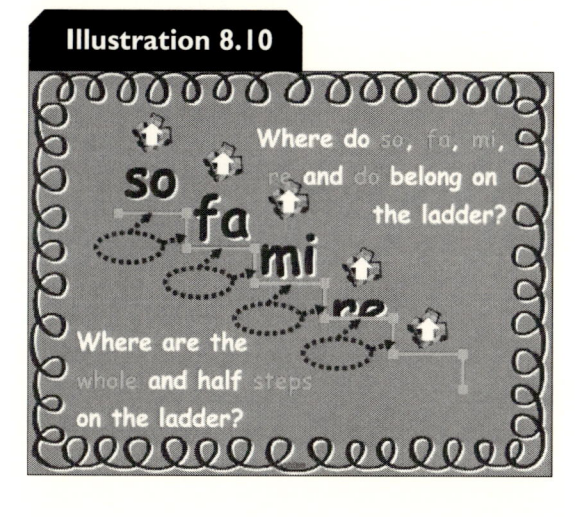

Illustration 8.9

Where do so, fa, mi, re and do belong on the ladder?

Where are the whole and half steps on the ladder?

Illustration 8.10

so
fa
mi
re

Where do so, fa, mi, re and do belong on the ladder?

Where are the whole and half steps on the ladder?

Kodály Today

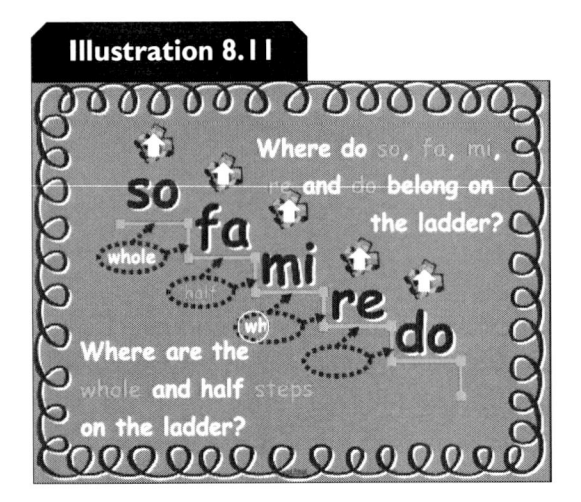

> **Illustration 8.11**
>
> Where do so, fa, mi, re and do belong on the ladder?
>
> so
> fa
> mi
> re
> do
>
> whole
>
> Where are the whole and half steps on the ladder?

Illustrations 8.10–8.12 involve making music in three ways: (1) with the voice, (2) through the musical interactivity on the board, and (3) conducting musical assessment as a result of students' actions at the board. This is a comprehensive process for presentation of notation. Whether working with melodic or rhythmic concepts, older students or younger students, there should be a high level of interactivity and a significant amount of singing and performance leading to musical discovery.

Using the SMART Board to Practice Music Concepts or Elements

An important thing to remember in designing Kodály-inspired lessons using the interactive board is that the pedagogy does not change. Whether a teacher chooses to use traditional teaching methods or to incorporate technology, the most basic elements of a Kodály classroom always remain constant: students should be singing, reading, writing, or improvising with the new musical concept. How these activities are presented may vary, but how musical elements and concepts are taught stays the same. Combining traditional pedagogical techniques with effective use of an interactive board can increase engagement and depth of understanding. Students should be making connections, synthesizing information, evaluating performance, and creating new material; effective practice exercises will take advantage of one or more of these activities. Using an interactive white board can increase student engagement and aid immensely in students' cognitive processing.

Reading

Effective reading exercises should consistently increase the level of effort required of students. For example, after they successfully read a rhythm or melody, it may be modified and immediately reread with the new changes. Continue modifying the rhythm or melody until it turns into another song (known or unknown) or a motif from a piece of classical music. This is an effective way to practice reading. To take it to another level and make it more interactive, the teacher can hide these changes and modifications beneath "ink layers," animated objects, icons embedded with sound, links to recordings or websites, etc. Students are most engaged when they don't see these changes coming; they want to figure out what the teacher will change next and how they will see it. (Check your software's tutorials for specific help with how to create some of these effects.) Not only are these effects intriguing to students, they also help with visual processing. For example, if students are instructed to rearrange the form of a song and read it, then instead of the teacher erasing and rewriting or relabeling, students can see the entire phrase literally move from one place on the screen to another. Or in asking students to read a phrase in retrograde, the teacher can actually rotate the phrase to be read backwards. Since reading exercises are essentially visual, this can be incredibly helpful. In summary, reading exercises built for the interactive board should:

- Enable a teacher to make several quick and simple changes to rhythms or melodies
- Include hidden changes (animations and effects available with the software) to aid in modifying rhythms or melodies

Writing

In terms of construction, interactive writing practice is less complex and more student-operated. Interactive writing practice may look and function just like a traditional writing activity, but what distinguishes the interactive lesson from the traditional is how the teacher and students can manipulate rhythmic and melodic elements on the board. The teacher should aim to build a writing page with

- Elements that can be manipulated
- A layout that is clear and intuitive
- Prompts (aural or visual) that can help students discover and execute changes

Including these elements in the structure of a writing activity encourages and trains students to be more independent in their musicianship. Illustrations 8.12 and 8.13 are taken from a writing activity targeting two sixteenth notes and an eighth note (taka di). Students sing the song ("Over the River") with rhythm syllables while pointing to or tapping the beats. When they are ready, they come to the board and fill in each beat with the correct rhythm. If they need to hear a phrase again, they can tap the correlating number on the right side of the screen; it is embedded with a sound clip of that particular phrase. Once students have finished, they may erase their work to reveal the correct answer.

Illustration 8.12

Kodály Today

Illustration 8.13

The layout is clear; the blank beats should be filled in with the rhythms. There are objects that can be manipulated; students write on top of the blank beat bars and can erase the phrases to reveal a final answer. There are aural prompts included in the page that they can use to help them discover what belongs in the blank beats. In this way, the teacher is able to walk away from the board and students can complete the whole task with very little verbal instruction.

Video 8.4 ▶ demonstrates first graders practicing writing rest with the focus song "Hot Cross Buns." The structure of the page is very similar to that of the previous example: clear structure, elements that can be modified, and aural cues.

Improvisation

Involving students in improvisation activities can be intimidating. Improvisation can be as simple as writing a new verse to a song, creating beat motions, or substituting an alternative rhythm in one beat of a phrase. As long as students are creating something new and making their own decisions while demonstrating mastery of a skill, they are improvising. Improvisation activities should be easy to understand. When students are asked to make critical choices in the moment, too much visual or aural stimulation can be confusing. A successful interactive improvisation activity will have only a few objects on the screen; elements may be added to increase the level of complexity.

The difference between interactive and traditional methods of improvisation may not be significant, which is perfectly acceptable. The main difference will be how the teacher uses the board. In other words, incorporate the extra elements that increase student effort creatively and in a way they will not expect (see the Reading section of this chapter for suggestions). The most authentic improvisation happens when students do not anticipate the changes that are coming. In the beginning stages of improvisation, the teacher should

Technology in the Kodály Classroom

guide them to make some kind of choice. A solid improvisation activity will look very similar to a reading activity but play out to the next logical step: students create their own changes in the rhythm or melody. Here is how a good interactive improvisation sequence could be laid out:

1. Ss read the rhythm of a song from the board (Illust. 8.14).

Illustration 8.14

2. T modifies the rhythm of phrase 2. Ss read the changes.
3. T modifies the rhythm of phrase 3. Ss read the changes.
4. T modifies the rhythm of phrase 4. Ss read the changes (Illust. 8.15).

Illustration 8.15

5. T asks phrase 1 as a "question"; Ss use phrase 2, 3, or 4 as an "answer" (Illust. 8.16).

Kodály Today

Illustration 8.16

6. T takes away the possible answers one by one (Illust. 8.17).

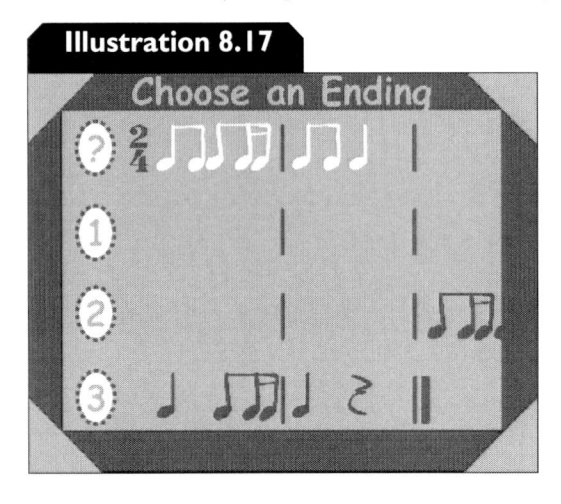

Illustration 8.17

7. Ss create their own answer" (Illust. 8.18).

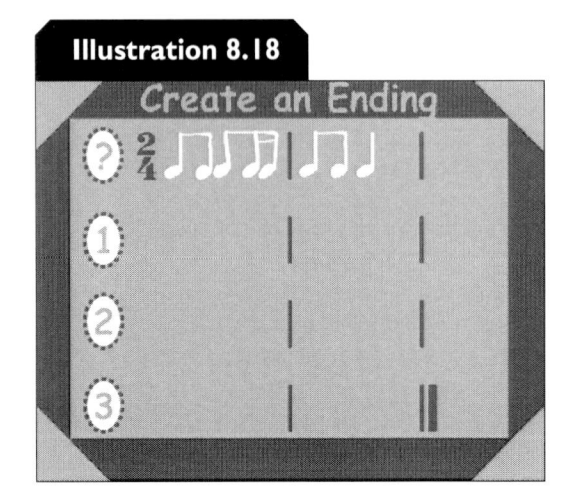

Illustration 8.18

This interactive improvisation lesson works because:

- It is simple to the eye.
- It is free of extraneous distractions.
- It has several hidden elements to increase the difficulty and raise this from a simple reading exercise to improvisation.

Best Practices

A number of techniques for successful integration of an interactive board have been presented. There are some simple principles that teachers should follow to create effective interactive lessons.

- Above all, activities should exercise musicianship. Pages need to be more than attractive and nice to look at; they must also serve a pedagogical purpose.
- The board is secondary to the music. Music should always be the center of activity, not the board.
- Keep pages simple.
- Ensure that pages have interactive elements.
- Strive to create user-friendly lessons where the teacher is able to step aside and allow students to operate the board.

Remember, the difference between traditional teaching methods and an interactive board may not always be great. When students are engaged, their understanding of musical concepts and elements is deeper and practicing can be more focused on the musical element being studied. When the concepts of Kodály teaching remain uncompromised and at the core of the lesson, the interactive board is being used effectively. Interactive white boards are a tool and a means to an end; they should be used not as a trendy device but rather as an instrument to aid in the training of solid musicianship.

Sample Kodály Lesson Plan Incorporating Technology

The lesson plan in Table 8.2 is grounded in the Houlahan and Tacka model of learning and instruction and infused with simple and direct applications of technology. Comments in the left-hand column are suggestions for student use of technology, and comments in the right-hand column are suggestions for teacher use of technology. Remember that these are suggestions, not instructions. If you are new to technology or to thinking about technology in this context, then pace yourself by choosing one idea that would be practical for your own unique teaching situation. If the technology supports the teaching and student understanding of musical concepts, then use it. If technology weakens pedagogy that has already proven to be strong, then it may not be suitable. Always measure your use of technology against your end goal, which is to create stronger musicians with an intrinsic love for the subject. If a particular piece of technology helps us to reach that goal, we should use it.

Table 8.2

STUDENT

GRADE 4: *LA* PENTATONIC, LESSON 1	
Outcome	Preparation: internalize the *la* pentatonic scale through kinesthetic activities Practice: read again four-beat patterns
INTRODUCTORY ACTIVITIES	
Warm-up	*Valse* in Db Major, Op. 64, No. 1 ("Minute Waltz"), Frederic Chopin (1810–1849) http://www.youtube.com/watch?v=yN7TvQdnZNU Body warm-up Breathing exercise Beat/movement activity
Sing known songs	"Above the Plains" CSP: A Ss sing the song in canon. Ss sing "Above the Plains" while T sings in canon. "I Lost the Farmer's Dairy Key"

TEACHER

> Create a playlist of all recorded music in the lesson with iTunes or another media player.

> Use QR codes in lesson plans to link to recorded music. Scan and play from a smart phone or tablet connected to a sound system.

> Students may use software such as Audacity or Garage Band to record themselves individually or as a class to use for partner songs.

	CSP: D
	Ss sing and conduct.
	Ss may briefly play the game as time allows.
	Ss perform the rhythm of the last four beats as a rhythmic ostinato into the next song (2/4 ♫♫ | ♩ ♩ :||)
	Ss may select unpitched instruments on which to perform the rhythm.
Develop tuneful singing	"Cocky Robin"
	CSP: A
	T and Ss sing the first verse of "Cocky Robin."
	Ss sing the song with a light and resonant hum.
	T will conduct Ss to sing with various musical elements (crescendo/decrescendo, staccato/legato, etc.).
	Ss will sing the last eight beats as a melodic ostinato into the next song ("it was I, oh it was I. . . ")
Review known songs and elements	"Canoe Song"
	CSP: A
	T will direct part of the class to sing the song while the rest continue the ostinato. Switch.
	Ss sing the song in three-part canon.
	Ss sing the song in three-part canon with rhythm syllables.
	Ss read the rhythm from the board.
	Ss chant phrase 4 of the song on *do* and *so* of the next song (D and A) while T sings "Liza Jane."

> Create reading examples with software made for use with an interactive white board such as SMART Notebook. Add appropriate manipulations or animation.

> Record students singing the chant as accompaniment for use while teaching the new song. Use recording software, or the recording function within SMART Notebook.

(continued)

Table 8.2 Continued

	CORE ACTIVITIES
Teach a new song	"Liza Jane" CSP: F# Ss continue the ostinato while T sings the song. Ss step the beat and show the phrases of the song with their bodies. Ss identify the number of phrases in the song (four). Two or three Ss take turns tracing the phrases on the board while T sings. Ss identify the number of beats in each phrase (eight). Two or three Ss take turns tracing the beats on the board while T sings. T sings the song, pausing after each phrase for Ss to identify and label the form (AA'BB'). T sings first four beats; Ss sing the last four beats of each phrase. Ss sing phrases 1 and 2; T sings 3 and 4. Switch.
Develop knowledge of musical literacy concepts	"Land of the Silver Birch" CSP: D Ss sing the song. T will direct Ss to sing in two-part canon. Sing "Land of the Silver Birch" and point to a representation of the melodic contour of the target phrase (phrase 3) at the board.
Internalize music through kinesthetic activities	

X	X							
	X	X						
			X					
				X	X			
			X	X				
						X		
							X	
								X

> Use an interactive white board to reveal one musical element at a time (phrases, beats, form) that students can use to trace or fill in.

> Students use an interactive white board to trace phrases, beats and label the form of the song.

> Use an interactive board to create melodic or rhythmic representations

> Students manipulate animated objects on the interactive board while singing.

		Ss will sing the target phrase and clap the melodic contour. Ss turn and face partners, sing, and show melodic contour as a pair, each mirroring the other's claps. Ss will sing the song with rhythm syllables while showing the melodic contour. Ss sing "Land of the Silver Birch" while reading and performing the rhythm of "Weevily Wheat" from the board. Ss identify and select the correct song from a list on the board.
	Creative Movement	"Weevily Wheat" CSP: A Ss sing the song with rhythm syllables. Ss sing the song and move into position for the game. Ss sing and play the game. Ss create a rhythmic accompaniment. Ss continue their accompaniment into the next song.
	Practice of music performance and literacy skills: Reading	"Hill and Gully Rider" CSP: C T sings the song as Ss continue the ostinato. T directs some of the Ss to continue the ostinato while the remaining sing the song. Ss read the traditional notation. $\frac{2}{4}$ ♫♫ | ♩ ♩ | ♫ ♩ | ♩ ξ | ♫ ♫ | ♩ ♩ | ♫ ♩ | ♩ ξ ‖ Transform rhythmic notation into "Canoe Song." Ss read the changes and identify the song.

Callouts (top):
- Create the rhythm of the song using notation software for students to read either from an interactive white board or tablet.
- Take pictures and save student compositions with a camera or tablet for later assessment.
- Utilize the capabilities of the interactive board to modify the rhythm of the song.
- Use a camera, smart phone, or tablet to video record students performing each variation of the rhythm for later assessment.
- Videos may also be uploaded to YouTube as "unlisted". Provide a link to parents to view their child.

Callouts (bottom):
- Students read from an interactive board or tablet with notation software.
- Students click the correct song to automatically play an embedded sound, link to a website, or trigger another animation.
- Students dictate their composition onto an interactive white board or tablet using notation or drawing software.

(continued)

Table 8.2 Continued

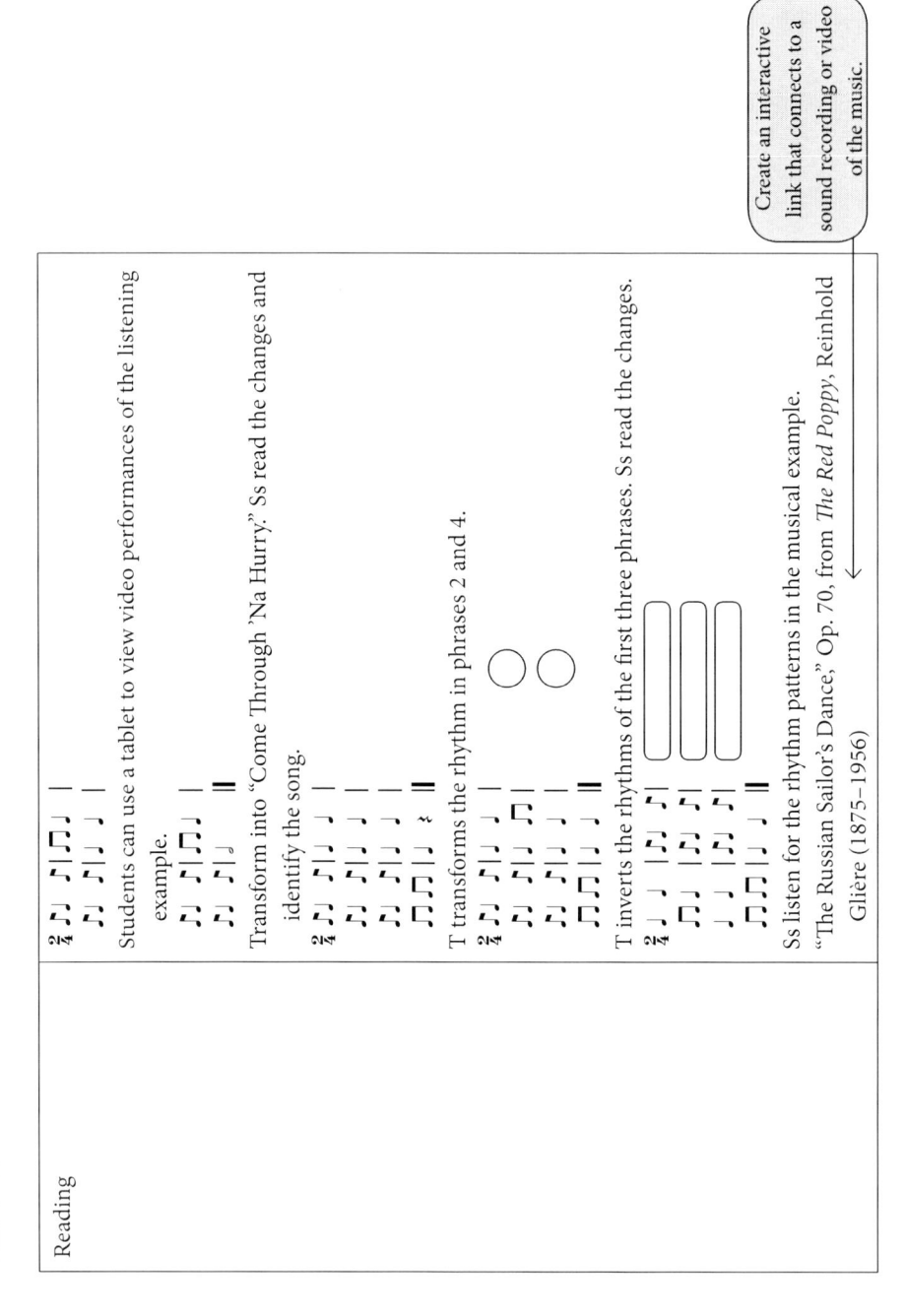

| Reading | $\frac{2}{4}$ ♩♪ ♪♩ \| ♪♩♩♩ \|
 ♩♩ ♪♩♩♩ \| ♪♩♩ ≡

 Students can use a tablet to view video performances of the listening example.
 ♩♩ ♪♩♩♩ \|
 ♩♩ ♪♩ ≡

 Transform into "Come Through 'Na Hurry." Ss read the changes and identify the song.
 $\frac{2}{4}$ ♩♩ ♪♩♩♩ \|
 ♩♩ ♪♩♩♩ \|
 ♩♩♩♩ ♪ ≡

 T transforms the rhythm in phrases 2 and 4.
 $\frac{2}{4}$ ♩♩ ♪♩♩♩ \|
 ♩♩ ♪♩ ♩ \|
 ♩♩♩♩♩♩ ≡

 T inverts the rhythms of the first three phrases. Ss read the changes.
 $\frac{2}{4}$ ♩♩ \| ♪♩ ♪♩ \|
 ♩♩ \| ♪♩ ♪♩ \|
 ♩♩ \| ♪♩ ♪♩ ≡

 Ss listen for the rhythm patterns in the musical example.
 "The Russian Sailor's Dance," Op. 70, from *The Red Poppy*, Reinhold Glière (1875–1956) | Create an interactive link that connects to a sound recording or video of the music. |

> Send students away with a paper containing QR codes linking to YouTube videos of music heard that day in class and the notation (rhythmic or melodic) to any listening examples of classical music which were read.

> Increase outside involvement by adding quality recordings of music from warm-ups, new songs, or any listening examples from class that day to a teacher website or blog. Students visit and make comments or add links to videos they've found of the same music.

http://www.youtube.com/watch?v=x9EphP0u2xg

SUMMARY ACTIVITIES

Review lesson outcomes	Read ♪♩♪ in various songs
Review the new song	"Liza Jane"

437

Discussion Questions
1. How can use of technology in the music classroom facilitate student learning?
2. What are some of the most effective technology resources available to teachers?
3. What are some of the most effective technology resources available to students?
4. How does technology make music knowledge more relevant for the twenty-first-century student?

Ongoing Assignment
1. Choose a concept to prepare and practice. Include several examples of technology you could use in your teaching.
2. Identify a music teacher who incorporates technology successfully into the classroom. Discover how the music curriculum has been enhanced by use of technology on the part of both the teacher and the students.

Bibliography
Bannan, N., and S. Woodward. "Spontaneity in the Musicality and Music Learning of Children." In *Communicative Musicality: Exploring the Basis of Human Companionship,* ed. S. Malloch and C. Trevarthen, pp. 465–494. Oxford: Oxford University Press, 2009.

Bjørkvold, J. R. *The Muse Within: Creativity and Communication, Song and Play from Childhood Through Maturity.* New York: HarperCollins, 1992.

Burns, Amy M. "Integrating Technology into Your Elementary Music Classroom." *General Music Today,* 2006, *20*(1): 6–10.

Finney, J., and P. Burnard. *Music Education with Digital Technology.* London & New York: Continuum International, 2007.

Foulkes-Levy, L. "Art Music for Musicianship Training: Welcome to the World Wide Web." *Kodály Envoy,* 2010, *36*(3): 6–9.

Gembris, H. "The Development of Musical Abilities." In *The New Handbook of Research on Music Teaching and Learning,* R. Colwell and C. Richardson (ed.), pp. 487–509. New York: Oxford University Press, 2002.

Himonides, E., and R. Purves. "The Role of Technology." In *Music Education in the 21st Century in the United Kingdom: Achievements, Analysis and Aspirations,* ed. S. Hallam and A. Creech, pp. 123–140. London: Institute of Education, 2010.

Hughes, M., and Potter, D. *Tweak to Transform: Improving Teaching—a Practical Handbook for School Leaders.* Bodmin, UK: Network Educational Press, 2002.

Kassner, K. *Effects of Computer-Assisted Instruction in a Mastery Learning/Cooperative Learning Setting on the Playing Abilities and Attitudes of Beginning Band Students.* Doctoral dissertation, University of Oregon, 1992.

Kassner, K. "Funding Music Technology." *Music Educators Journal,* 1998, *84*(6): 30–35.

Lejeune, Tanya. "In Harmony with Technology: SMART Board Assessments in the Kodály Classroom." *Kodály Envoy,* 2013, *39*(2): 19–21.

Litterst, G. F. "Smokin' Technology for Your Studio (Recording CDs for Student Use)." *American Music Teacher*, Aug.–Sept. 2003, *53*: 82–93.

Seddon, F. A., and Biasutti, M. "Evaluating a Music E-Learning Resource: The Participants' Perspective." *Computers & Education*, 2009, *53*(3): 541–549.

Southcott, Jane, and RenDe Crawford. "The Intersections of Curriculum Development: Music, ICT and Australian Music Education." *Australasian Journal of Educational Technology*, 2011, *27*(1): 122–136.

Swanwick, K. "Musical Technology and the Interpretation of Heritage." *International Journal of Music Education*, 2001, *37*: 32–43.

Webster, P. "Computer Based Technology and Music Teaching and Learning." In *The New Handbook of Research on Music Teaching and Learning*, R. Colwell and C. Richardson (ed.), pp. 416–462. New York: Oxford University Press, 2002.

Wise, Stuart, Janinka Greenwood, and Niki Davis. "Teachers' Use of Digital Technology in Secondary Music Education: Illustrations of Changing Classrooms." *British Journal of Music Education*, 2011, *28*(2): 117–134.

Chapter 9

Applying the Kodály Concept to the Elementary Choir

Key Questions

- How do you structure auditions for a children's choir?
- What activities should be included in a choral lesson plan?
- What are the steps involved in teaching choir students to hear and sing two-part repertoire?
- How can you use the sequence for teaching part singing to arrange folksongs for your children's choir?
- What are the various ways of teaching part music in a choral setting to children?
- What are the factors in selecting choir music for a children's choir?

In this chapter we address appropriate teaching strategies and techniques for the choral setting. We offer ideas for auditioning students, ideas for choral rehearsal activities, repertoire and activities for developing part-singing and music literary skills in the choral setting. There is a discussion on how to teach simple two-part repertoire song materials by note or rote as well as a section on developing harmonic hearing in the elementary choir. Many of the teaching strategies suggested in the chapter are applicable to the music classroom as well as the choir. The reality is that a Kodály-inspired classroom setting may also be considered a choral setting, and vice versa. Both the classroom and the choral rehearsal should enhance development of musicianship skills. We believe that although every teacher will ultimately create his or her own measureable goals and outcomes, some helpful objectives are still in order:

1. Students should learn to artistically perform a body of repertoire that includes different styles of music.
2. They should learn to perform artistically with their own voice, alone and in a choral setting, with good intonation.
3. They should learn how to follow a choral director and the meaning of cues and conducting gestures.
4. They should develop their ability to read unison and part music.
5. They should develop aural awareness skills.
6. They should learn to become independent singers.
7. Conductors should remember that they are responsible for balancing rehearsing and teaching in the choral setting.

Auditioning Students for an Elementary Choir

Developing students' ability to participate in a choir begins in the music classroom. A sequenced music curriculum shaped by the Kodály concept develops a student's performance and musicianship skills alike, and it provides them with the abilities and expertise to participate in a school choir. Teachers should view the elementary choir as an extension of the music classroom and the music classroom as an extension of the elementary choir. Understanding this unique relationship will foster successful choral rehearsals and help music programs gain distinction. Carrying out this philosophy in everyday teaching will enable all students to grow artistically. If the classroom music teacher is also the choral director then they will understand how to select children to participate in a choir.[1]

It is important to be able to assess the singing ability of the students participating in a school choir. Whether a choir is auditioned or not, you should create a profile of every choir member, to include such things as

1. Voice range
2. Musicality
3. Rhythmic ability, ear training, and rhythm clapping
4. Melodic ability, ear training, and sight singing

Voice Range

Students' comfortable voice ranges in the fourth to sixth grade lie between middle C and high D or E. Students with training can sing A below middle C or up to high F or G. Using the second phrase of the song "Alleluia" (Fig. 9.1), ask students to sing the melody, beginning on different pitches until you can figure out the vocal range of each student.

Fig. 9.1 "Alleluia"

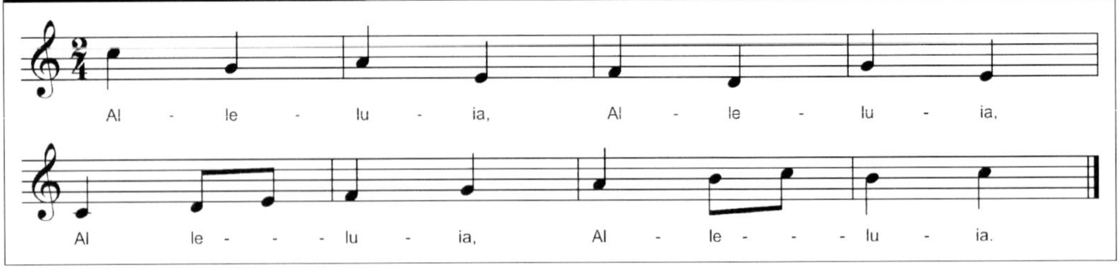

[musical notation: two-line score in 2/4 time with text "Al-le-lu-ia, Al-le-lu-ia," for each line]

Begin singing this in the key of C major and progress to other keys. This will help determine strong soprano and alto singers. The information you gain may also be useful in selecting exercises to develop the vocal range of your students.

Musicality

Ask students to sing some of their favorite repertoire to determine if they can sing songs with differing character and whether they have the ability to change the dynamics or mood of a song. Students who exhibit considerable musicality can be selected as team leaders in their sections, or they can also be asked to model during the rehearsal.

Rhythmic Ability, Ear Training, and Rhythm Clapping

Determine a student's ability to clap known and unknown rhythms and whether the student can sing known repertoire with rhythm syllables while conducting. A background in music reading should permit the student to read rhythms from both rhythmic notation and a melody written in staff notation.

Test for two types of rhythmic ability: (1) to clap back rhythmic patterns musically that are abstracted from their repertoire of songs studied in the classroom, and (2) to echo-clap more complicated rhythmic patterns that are contained in contemporary styles of music. We suggest using the rhythm pattern sequence discussed in this text to determine rhythmic aptitude. It is important to identify whether a student can keep a beat with one hand and tap the rhythm with the other. Rhythmic memory may be determined by asking the students to clap back several rhythmic patterns. Understanding students' rhythmic abilities gives the teacher an idea of what rhythmic training needs to be addressed as well as the kind of repertoire that can be selected for both the classroom and the choral performance. To determine a student's ability to sight-read rhythm patterns, we suggest using the pedagogical lists for grades two through five. This will furnish a progressive repertoire to determine students' ability to sing known repertoire with rhythm syllables and to read known rhythms. In this way you can determine the collective aptitude of the choir.

Melodic Ability, Ear Training, and Sight Singing

Determine a student's ability to sing known and unknown melodic patterns. This may include figuring out if students can sing known repertoire with solfège syllables and hand signs, and if they can read these melodic patterns from hand signs, rhythmic notation, and solfège syllables written beneath and from a score in simple keys such as D, C, F, G, D, and B-flat. Students with previous musical training could sing with absolute letter names.

Test for two types of melodic ability: (1) to musically echo melodic patterns taken from their classroom repertoire, and (2) to echo-sing more complex melodic patterns contained in contemporary music. Use the melodic pattern sequence discussed in the book to determine students' melodic ability. Understanding their ability to securely sing a melody gives you an idea of what melodic training is needed to address the choral and classroom song repertoire. To determine a student's ability to sight-read melodic patterns, use the pedagogical lists for grades two through five. This will help you determine their ability to learn melodies in various styles.

Seating Arrangement for the Choir

Some teachers prefer to begin the choral rehearsal outside the choir room so that students can walk or freely move while singing known songs as they move to their designated seats. Make sure the students are singing in a well-ventilated room and have a space the size of another student between them. If adequate space is not available, be creative in allowing students ample space to move and sing. Remember that their seated location need not be the same as their standing singing location. Use the same seating arrangement that will be used during a concert performance. You can decide where the upper voices or lower voices sit or stand. For three-part music, it may be effective to position the first upper voices in the center of the choir, the second upper voices to the left of this group, and lower voices on the right. To strengthen individual singing and voice parts, it may be advantageous to have the students change their position in the choir. There are a number of philosophies regarding this topic.

Seating Arrangement of Students Within a Section of the Choir

It is often amazing how changing the place of two students in a choir can make a difference in the sound! Try to listen to each voice in relationship to the ones around it. Begin by breaking the choir into their initial groups (S, A, B, etc.). Ask the entire section to sing one of the phrases you are working on from the repertoire, and move among them. If you have the time, give them a designation such as "flute" (the lighter voices—usually a little breathier and having more of the higher partials) or "oboe" (the voices that have a little more "bite" in the sound and with more of the lower partials). Try to make sure that within the section the students stand in an alternating arrangement—no two flutes or oboes standing together. Listen to them in groups of two, three, or four, and eventually the whole group. The students can help determine which sound is better as you move them around. Make sure that your leader is in the center of the section, or if it is a very strong voice then in the middle of the section on the back row.[2] The real skill you're trying to develop is the students' ability to listen.

Choral Rehearsal Activities

In addition to learning and performing repertoire, we suggest that a number of activities be included in every choral lesson.

Body Posture: Physical Warm-ups and Developing Good Posture

Choir should begin with brief physical warm-ups for both the body and the face to encourage proper singing posture. Body warm-up exercises can include stretches, or making circles with various parts of the body. Facial warm-up exercises can include mimicking certain facial expressions; massaging of the neck, jaw, cheeks, and chin; and exploring lip and tongue trills or buzzes. Include how to stand or sit in a chair correctly during rehearsal, and how to position the feet, legs, hips, shoulders, arms, and head while singing.

It is sometimes helpful for students to lead these activities themselves, as they often pay more attention to each other that way. Guide students in moving their bodies as expressively as possible, even in warm-up exercises. Practice good posture and focus on developing a loose jaw and relaxed throat and facial muscles. Sometimes it is useful to give students an image that will help them sing with the desired effect.

Respiration: Breathing Exercises

Begin to develop proper breathing technique. This includes working on correct use of the diaphragm to understand the breathing mechanism. Students may explore this by lying on the floor with a book on their waistline to observe the correct way to breathe. During this part of the rehearsal, students should practice sustained breathing exercises as well as staggered breathing. Another exercise is to have them stand against a wall and feel their back muscles expand with each breath.

Phonation Exercises

These exercises demonstrate proper vocal production/placement. Typically, choral directors work on humming exercises as well as abdominal pulsing.

Vocalizations

During an initial portion of the choir rehearsal, students learn how to gently stretch and warm up the voice. Begin these exercises moving from the head voice down into the lower register to warm up the voice, paying particular attention to moving through the passaggio. Singing warm-up exercises using solfège syllables helps develop singing technique. Remember, if we simply remove the consonant before each solfège syllable, we're left with the vowels so important in vocal training. This is another justification for using solfège syllables to enhance vocal technique. These exercises may be sung in major or minor as well as in various modes. Rhythm patterns found in the repertoire can also be incorporated into these exercises to add variety and enhance secure rhythmic as well as melodic precision.

Students can then move on to singing sequences that involve articulators (the lips, teeth, and tip of the tongue) to acquire clear articulation of consonants and pure vowel sounds. During these exercises, it is important to make sure that a student's jaw lowers correctly. This is an ideal time for students to work on both vowel and consonant sounds.

In-Tune Singing Exercises

Choral directors may use *Let Us Sing Correctly*[3] by Zoltán Kodály as a resource. The work is a series of progressive two-part exercises that may be used reading from either notation or hand signs to develop in-tune singing. In the Foreword, Kodály explains that proper intonation in singing matches the acoustic intervals, not the tempered, and that the singing teacher or choral director should not depend on a piano for pitch. He examines the use of part singing and solfège for developing good intonation.

Additionally, a teacher may sing different types of scales, such as pentachord, hexachord, pentatonic, major, and minor ascending and descending, and in canon using solfège syllables or pure vowels. Students may also be guided to sing a melody from the director's hand signs. Folksongs may be used as well and sung in solfège to develop in-tune singing. Practice these songs in the keys of D, E-flat, and E. Singing songs like "Rocky Mountain" or "Liza Jane" works well because they are pentatonic, repetitive, and memorable. These songs can be accompanied by a tonic drone, or by a sustained tonic and dominant drone, and they can also be sung in canon.

Developing a choir's "sound" is most easily achieved by working on well-known song repertoire. Working with well-known songs allows the teacher extra time to focus on things like phrasing, as well as working on developing a beautiful tone quality through vowel unification.

Developing Music Literacy Skills

During this phase of the rehearsal, the conductor can continue to develop students' knowledge of music literacy. We suggest that teachers continue to use folksongs during this section of the rehearsal as a basis for developing literacy skills and knowledge of rhythms and tonalities. The folksong repertoire used in this section of the rehearsal could also be featured on a choral program. We recommend checking our other publications: *Sound Thinking: Music for Sight-Singing and Ear Training, Vols. I and II*, published by Boosey & Hawkes; and *From Sound to Symbol: Fundamentals of Music*, published by Oxford University Press. *From Sound to Symbol* covers all basic rhythmic and melodic elements found in choral repertoire, but with a unique, sound-to-symbol approach that explores concepts through the sound of music before explaining how symbols are used. Students actively and methodically explore music by listening, performing, thinking critically, and composing, learning the rudiments of music theory in the process. This book carefully introduces music teachers to the concept of developing a student's sense of hearing—a vital component in being a member of a choir.

Because of time constraints, teachers generally spend more time teaching repertoire and less time developing students' knowledge relating to music literacy and broad-based musicianship skills in the choral rehearsal. Finding ways to develop both performance and music literacy skills is a key requirement for creating effective choral programs that have a lasting musical impact on students. The overall goal is to enable the students to become effective choir participants and informed audience members.

Developing the Skill of Part Singing

Preparing students for two- or three-part singing should take place from the earliest stages of a student's musical education. The strategies presented in this chapter constitute a foundation to approach part-singing with confidence and can be used in both the music classroom and the choral rehearsal. These activities give the teacher the means to prepare and practice musical elements at several levels of sophistication and difficulty. By incorporating these activities into the music class, the teacher enlivens the vocal music program while encouraging precise and critical awareness of musical elements in conjunction with performance practice.

Components of a Choir Rehearsal

Table 9.1 is a template that can be used during a choir rehearsal.[4] It is important to remember that the choral rehearsal should be considered an extension of the music classroom.

Table 9.2 is a sample choral lesson plan.

Developing Part Work Skills in the Choral Rehearsal

The goal of developing part work is for students to sing their own part correctly and in tune while listening attentively to the other part(s) and understanding the relationship between their part and the other(s).

Here is a sequence of activities to be used when teaching part work skills, as they impart ease and order, to enable students to perform part music. Teachers may choose to apply all of these techniques to both pentatonic and diatonic music, although we would recommend that students practice first with pentatonic material and then later with diatonic. We're convinced that pentatonic song material promotes more accurate intonation.

Table 9.1 Choral Rehearsal Plan

GRADE X: UNIT TITLE, LESSON X	
Outcome	Preparation/presentation Practice:
INTRODUCTORY ACTIVITIES	

Body warm-up
Breathing exercises
Vocal warm-ups
	The class begins with body warm-ups and breathing exercises.
	    Sing known songs to develop performance skills of Ss. Great time to use canons in the class.
	    This is a good opportunity to focus on phonation exercises based on the repertoire being sung in this section of the lesson.

Develop tuneful singing	Here T can develop tuneful singing strategies based on the materials Ss are singing. T can focus on resonance, vowels, and agility exercises. It is important to consider how to develop two-part singing. These exercises should develop logically from folksongs that Ss are singing.
Rehearsing materials	T rehearses music repertoire, working on such things as rhythm, melody, phrasing, and text.
CORE ACTIVITIES	
Teach new repertoire	T can teach a new song, canon, or repertoire to Ss using note or rote approaches to teaching.
Preparation/presentation of music concepts and elements	T can prepare and present a new rhythmic or melodic element. He or she should use the model of learning presented in the book and follow the same sequence of activities but using a faster pace.
Creative movement	T may play a singing game or practice a known song or a song with a movement activity to keep Ss actively engaged.

Performing repertoire	T practices known rhythmic and melodic elements in combination with music skills that include:
	    Singing
	    Inner hearing
	    Developing musical memory
	    Reading and sight reading
	    Writing and dictation
	    Part work
	    Playing instruments
	    Listening
	
	These skills should be practiced where possible both aurally (no score) and visually (use of score).

(continued)

Kodály Today

Table 9.1 Continued

	SUMMARY ACTIVITIES
Review	T focuses on performance of known material.
Lesson objectives	
Review new song	

Table 9.2 Sample Choral Lesson Plan

GRADE 6: UNIT X, LESSON X, VOCAL PLAN	
Outcome	Rehearsal of new repertoire: "Liza Jane" (three-part piece), arr. G. Krunnfusz, from score, Alliance Publications AP-1151 Preparation/presentation: low la (extended do pentatonic) through the song "Canoe Round" Practice: eighth and sixteenth note combinations by reading and writing known patterns from memory Performing: "Kookaburra," arr. C. Curtright, Boosey & Hawkes
INTRODUCTORY ACTIVITIES	
Body warm-up Posture and breathing	• Body warm-up Shoulder rolls/rotations Body stretching • Breathing: eagle spread (vocal warm-up ideas from Kenneth Philips, *Teaching Kids to Sing*, Schirmer, 1994) Ss stand and place their hands behind their heads with fingers interlocked; elbows are extended outward to the sides. Ss exhale by bending over from the hips while keeping the elbows outward (using "sshh" on exhalation). Ss say, "Over and exhale." Ss stand slowly and inhale through pursed lips while keeping the elbows back. Say "Up and inhale." Ss exhale while standing, elbows back, keeping the chest elevated and the abdominal muscles consciously contracting upward and inward. Say, "Up and inhale." Ss inhale while standing with elbows drawn back. Say, "Up and inhale." T always begins the breathing motion cycle with Ss exhaling.
Vocal warm-up Sing known canons or songs	Tallis Canon "All Praise to Thee" • Phonation Ss hum with lips together and clenched teeth. T notes vibrations in nose. Ss hum with lips together and teeth as far apart as possible. T notes vibrations in throat and whether sound is too dark.

(continued)

Table 9.2 Continued

Develop tuneful singing Resonance Vowels Agility Two-part singing	"Hungarian Canon" • Ss sing the melody with "ning" • Ss sing the melody with "viva" • T shows melody with right hand and bass accompaniment using *do* or *so* harmonic accompaniments.
Rehearsing materials	"Liza Jane" (three-part piece), arr. G. Krunnfusz from score, Alliance Publications AP-1151 • T sings soprano line and plays the other two parts on the piano. • T and Ss discuss the form, texture, meter, rhythm, and tonality of "Liza Jane." • T: "How many times do you hear 'come my love and go with me'?" T performs again for Ss. • T: "Sing this phrase with rhythm syllables, and conduct." • T: "Sing this phrase with solfège syllables and hand signs." • T: "Sing this phrase with 'loo' and hand signs." • T has Ss sing those words for the beginning of the first and second phrases while T sings the rest of the song. • T has Ss sing the entire first and second phrases as T sings third and fourth phrases. • T and Ss sing entire song while keeping beat. • T presents score to Ss. They identify the sections they have sung, and sing with rhythm and solfège syllables. • T sings soprano line and plays the other two parts on the piano as Ss follow score.
CORE ACTIVITIES	
New song: choral (to begin preparation of syncopation)	"Hill and Gully Rider" (unison piece) CSP: A • T performs song for Ss and they identify the form, meter, and tonality. • Ss memorize the refrain. • T sings melody and Ss sing "Hill and Gully" refrain while keeping beat in different ways. • Ss sing their same part and clap the rhythm of their part. • Ss stand and keep beat in their feet while clapping the way the words go. T is still singing the "verses" at this point. • T invites Ss to sing the first four phrases of the song.

(continued)

Table 9.2 Continued

| Preparation/present: *low la* Develop knowledge of music concepts and elements | Internalizing music through kinesthetic activity
• T sings while keeping beat. Ss keep beat too.
• Ss sing and draw the phrases.
• T: "How many phrases were there?"
• T and Ss sing.
• One S answers. (four)
• T and Ss sing while keeping beat, and T draws phrases on board.
• T: "How many beats do we have in each phrase?"
• T and Ss sing again.
• One S answers. (four)
• T sings first phrase and points to a melodic contour of song on board.
• T and Ss sing first phrase while pointing to melodic contour.
• T: "On the first and third phrase we are going to point to the melodic contour, and on phrases 2 and 4 we will sing without pointing."
• Ss stand and clap melodic contour while facing T and pretending fingertips touch.
• Ss clap melodic contour while singing, but this time their eyes are closed.
• Each S faces a partner and repeats the process with the partner.
• Ss put left hand behind back and clap melodic contour with the partner's hand.
• Ss return to seat while singing. They have to be in seat by the end of the song.

Describing what you hear
• T and Ss sing first phrase on "loo."
• T: "How many beats are in the first phrase?"
• T and Ss sing again.
• T answers. (four)
• T: "On which beat do we sing the highest sound?"
• T and Ss sing again.
• S answers. (beat 1)
• T: "Where do we sing the lowest sound?"
• T and Ss sing again.
• S answers. ("and" of beat 3 and beat 4)
• T: "How many different sounds do we have?"
• T and Ss sing phrase again.
• S answers. (four)
• T: "Andy, sing the different notes from highest to lowest." |

(continued)

Table 9.2 Continued

	• T hums from the highest to lowest; Ss must sing whether T is singing a step or skip. • T hums the pattern *mi-mi-re-do* and Ss identify notes with solfège. • T sings *mi-mi-re-do* and hums the last sound; asks Ss about this sound. "What can you tell me about the sound I hummed?" They will identify this note as a skip from *do* and it is the lowest sound. • T: "Let's sing the tone set *mi-re–low do*." • T: "Let's sing the song using solfège and 'low' for the lowest note." • Ss draw visual representation of the phrase. • Ss trade with partner and point while singing. • Ss discuss their drawings with one another. Presentation syllable • T: "Now let's sing the first phrase on solfège, calling our last sound 'low.'" • T and Ss sing first phrase on solfège, calling new pitch "low." • T: "What can you tell me about the interval *do-low*?" • T and Ss sing tone set from highest to lowest. • Ss: "It's a skip." • T: "When we have a skip from *do*, we call it (low) *la*." • Ss sing the song with solfège and hand signs. Presentation notation • T puts tone ladder on board and Ss sing the tone set from *mi* to *low la*. • T sings first phrase on "loo" and Ss echo on solfège while T points to tone ladder on the board. • T shows location of the notes on the staff and Ss sing phrases 1 and 3 from T pointing to staff while T sings phrases 2 and 4. • T and Ss sing through entire song, making sure to sing phrases 1 and 3 on solfège with hand signs and phrases 2 and 4 on "loo." Transition
Creative movement	"Turn the Glasses Over" (performed in key of sight reading) CSP: T and Ss sing song while forming circle • T and Ss play game. Transition

(*continued*)

Table 9.2 Continued

Practice	"Ida Red," from *46 Two-Part American Folksongs* CSP: X • T sings "Ida Red" as Ss clap a rhythmic ostinato using the rhythms of the first phrase of "Turn the Glasses Over." • Ss sing "Ida Red" with rhythm syllables and clap the ostinato. • Ss read the rhythm of "Ida Red" with rhythm syllables and clap the ostinato. • Ss sing with words and keep clapping ostinato; T sings the second part of "Ida Red." • Ss and T switch parts. • T divides class into two groups: one sings the upper line and the other sings the lower line. • T transforms rhythm of "Ida Red" into the rhythm of "Kookaburra."
	SUMMARY ACTIVITIES
Performance	"Kookaburra," arr. C. Curtright, Boosey & Hawkes • Ss read the rhythm of "Kookaburra" off the board on rhythm syllables. • Ss recognize and sing unison. • T has Ss keep beat and sing in a two-part canon. • T has Ss sing in a three-part canon while keeping beat. • Ss perform the arrangement of "Kookaburra."

1. T demonstrates activity and class imitates.
2. Class demonstrates and T imitates.
3. T divides the class into two groups and has each perform its own part. Switch.
4. T divides the class into two ensembles, each performing its own part.
5. Have two Ss perform, each performing his or her own part. Repeat this with several other pairs of Ss.
6. One S in a pair performs and the other follows in canon with clapping, with hand signs, or by pointing to a score in canon.

The part-work sequence outlined below also helps teachers and students with ideas for arranging folksongs, and perhaps their own compositions.

Keeping a Beat
Sing a folksong while marching, walking, or in some way moving to the beat. Performing a song while keeping the beat requires students to concentrate on two tasks at the same time. This activity is valuable in both the classroom and the choral rehearsal.

Keeping a Beat and Demonstrating Music Comparatives
Once students can sing and perform the beat both accurately and musically, add the task of altering tempo and dynamics. To accomplish this, they will need a strong foundation in being able to demonstrate such music comparatives as slow and fast, high and low, loud and soft, duple meter beat (marching), and compound meter beat.

Call-and-Response or Antiphonal Singing
Although students perform only one phrase of music in a call-and-response song, they must eventually learn to sing both phrases if they are going to be able to sing rhythmically and musically. Developing this ability requires audiation practice (using inner hearing). Call-and-response singing may be applied to folksongs (you may also think of call and response as responsorial singing). Some simple examples of call-and-response songs are "Skin and Bones," "Charlie over the Ocean," and "Pizza, Pizza."

Pointing to a Beat
Perform or point to a visual of the beat in a song while singing. This "tracking" ability promotes more fluent music reading and reading in general. Students may also keep the beat by performing it on a percussion instrument.

Clapping the Rhythm
Sing a song while clapping the rhythm. This can be accomplished in a number of ways. Students need to perform this activity musically and always according to the phrase. They may sing while clapping (we suggest clapping with two fingers) the rhythm, or performing the rhythm on a percussion instrument. Two students may perform a simple folksong, one performing the beat while the other performs the rhythm; use different timbres for beat and rhythm. The teacher may write the rhythm of a known song on the board and place the beat below the rhythmic notation. Two students can go to the board and perform the song, with one pointing to the beat and the other pointing to the rhythm.

Tapping on Specified Beat
When students are singing familiar melodies, ask them to tap on the strong beats while singing. Or they might tap on the rests in a known song, or the beginning of each phrase. This activity may also be done with a musical instrument.

Singing the Final Note of a Composition
The teacher sings a known melody but does not sing the final note; students must fill it in. This activity helps them understand the tonal strength of each note. An interesting

activity is to have them explore alternative endings to known compositions. This strengthens their understanding of harmonic functions and voice leading.

Finding the Tonic Note of a Composition

This exercise can be performed with known songs, known canons, or a new song. The teacher sings a known song to the students and stops in the middle. Students must identify the tonic of the melody. They sing a canon, and the teacher signals a pause; then they must sing the tonic note.

Creating Organ Points on a Specified Beat

Guide students to sing on the first note of each phrase of a known composition on a neutral syllable, or sustain a note for the length of the phrase. This could be the tonic note of the known melody. This activity is most successful when the teacher demonstrates the sustained note singing as the students sing the song prior to students singing the accompaniment.

Rhythmic Ostinato

An ostinato is a repeated rhythmic or melodic motif used to accompany a song. Here is a procedure for performing a rhythmic ostinato. Singing songs with hand-clapping movements can also be included in this category. For example, the singing game "Four White Horses" has specified hand-clapping movements to perform while singing the song. Depending on the age of the students, you may use several ostinatos together.

To begin, the students sing the melody while the teacher claps a rhythmic ostinato or sings a melodic ostinato. (It is important when teaching students about rhythms that the students not develop their knowledge of rhythm on the basis of visual clues. The teacher should always make sure the students *hear* the new rhythm pattern being clapped, as opposed to seeing it.)

1. Ss sing the melody while T claps a rhythmic ostinato or sings a melodic ostinato.
2. Ss and T exchange parts.
3. T divides Ss into two groups; one sings and the other performs the ostinato. Switch tasks.
4. Two Ss perform the work.
5. One S sings while performing the second part. More advanced Ss can perform the ostinato on percussion.

Performing Rhythm Canons Based on Simple Rhythms

These canons are based on simple rhymes or rhythms of very simple melodies. Begin the canon after one measure. Rhythm syllables can be used to perform the canons. It is useful to practice both types of canons with familiar material before moving to unknown repertoire. Although the rhythm of many folksongs can work well when performed in canon, the best songs for this type of activity are those that have a rest at the end of every phrase. A good example is "Bow Wow Wow." Perform the canon with two timbres.

1. T and class.
2. Class and T.
3. T divides the class into two groups, each performing its own part. Switch.
4. Two small ensembles, each performing their own part
5. Two Ss, each performing their own part
6. Have the Ss begin to clap the rhythm of a simple song; T can clap in canon. Once Ss are comfortable with hearing the canon, T and Ss can reverse roles. Canons may be performed kinesthetically, aurally, visually, or using a combination of techniques.

Performing a Kinesthetic Canon

The teacher performs a rhyme with a beat motion for every four beats. The students follow in canon, performing the rhythm as well as the beat motion. For example, say "Ali Baba Forty Thieves" while tapping four beats. Say "Ali Baba Forty Thieves" and tap the beats on different parts of your body, and have students imitate. Once students are proficient at this activity, perform it in canon after four beats with text. The teacher could also perform a rhythm and have students clap it back after two or four beats.

Performing a Visual Rhythm Canon with Rhythm Syllables

The goal of this activity is for students to read a rhythm in canon. The canon can be performed with the teacher and students, or with just the students performing the canon. To perform a rhythm canon visually, have students read rhythm flash cards of the rhyme or melody to be used for the canon. The teacher should keep a steady pulse but show the card quickly and move on to the next card while the students are still performing the rhythm of the first card. In other words, give the students a brief look at all cards in succession. The speed of this process may be increased so that the students are always saying something different from what they are seeing. Students should perform the canon reading with rhythm syllables.

Performing an Aural Rhythm Canon with Rhythm Syllables

Aural canons can be more challenging to perform than visual canons. Aural rhythm canons are performed without the aid of notation. If a motion is attached to a phrase, the exercise is simple to perform. Echo clapping is a preliminary preparation for aural canon work. This task can be made more complex by having students clap back the rhythm while chanting or singing the rhythm syllables.

Performing Simple Canons Based on Rhythms of Simple Folksongs

These canons are based on the rhythms of very simple melodies. Rhythm syllables can be used to perform the canons. Here is a procedure for performing a rhythmic canon.

Kodály Today

1. T performs the song with actions and words.
2. Ss sing the song with rhythm syllables and keep the beat.
3. Ss say rhythm syllables while clapping the rhythm.
4. Ss think the rhythm syllables and clap the rhythm.
5. T taps the rhythm using a drum or wood block; Ss clap and say the rhythm syllables beginning after four beats.
6. T writes the canonic part below the notation of the song. T asks, "Where should we begin writing the second part? What should be written in the empty measures?"
7. T and Ss may perform "Bow Wow Wow" in canon after two beats.
8. Challenge one S to sing "Bow Wow Wow" while pointing to the notation in canon.

Drones

Students sing a folksong as the teacher accompanies their singing with a tonic drone. As students gain fluency with this technique, they can sing a drone made up of the tonic and dominant notes to accompany known pentatonic melodies.

Pentatonic and diatonic melodies are a good basis for developing functional and harmonic thinking. For *do*-centered and *la*-centered pentatonic songs, accompany the song by having a group of students sustain the tonal center while the class performs the song. This pitch is the chord root note of the tonic triad. These songs may also be accompanied by a drone made up of *do-so* or *do-mi-so* (major tonic triad) for *do* pentatonic repertoire and *la-mi* or *la-do-mi* (minor tonic triad) for *la* pentatonic repertoire. Be mindful that sustained pitches tend to go flat.

Melodic Ostinato

Students accompany known songs with melodic ostinatos. Melodic ostinati should be based on the melodic building blocks of known song repertoire.

Combining Drones and Melodic Ostinatos

Divide the class into groups. One group sings the folksong. Another group or groups will accompany the folksong with a drone composed of the tonic note, or tonic and dominant notes; yet another group sings a melodic ostinato.

Three-Part Singing

Here are examples of pieces of music that can be created from a simple folksong:

1. Sing a melody with two complementary melodic ostinati.
2. Sing a pentatonic melody in canon and add a melodic ostinato.
3. Sing a melody in canon and add a third voice that sings a descant. Kodaly's "Ladybird" is an example of this compositional technique.
4. Rhythmic ostinatos work well with all of these techniques.

Discovering an Ostinato as the Students Sing a Known Song
The students sing a song while the teacher taps a rhythmic ostinato or sings the ostinato on one note. Students discover the ostinato and write it on the board.

Discovering an Ostinato as the Students Sight-Read a Song
Have the students sight-sing an unknown melody while the teacher taps a rhythmic ostinato or sings the ostinato on one note. Students discover the ostinato and write it down.

Two-Part Hand Sign Singing (Note Against Note)
Guide students to sing in two parts from a teacher's hand signs. Using pentatonic musical examples before moving to diatonic will ensure more secure intonation. Initially, begin and end the exercise with the same notes.

1. Ss hold one tone in one voice while the other voice performs a simple melody. Switch parts.
2. T shows a simple canon from hand signs (signs both parts simultaneously).
3. Ss perform two individual melodies holding one note against another voice. (One melody is more stationary than the other.)
4. Ss perform two individual lines.

Singing Simple Melodies as Canons with Text
All pentatonic songs may be sung in canon. Choose simple folksongs. The teacher may begin to sing the melody and the students follow in canon after one measure. Carefully select pentatonic songs that may be performed as canons. Initially the canon should begin on the same pitch as what the first part is singing. These songs meet this criterion:

"Down Came a Lady": the second part begins after four beats.
"I See the Moon": the second part begins after two or four beats.
"Bow Wow Wow": the second part begins after two beats.

Canons may also be performed with words or with rhythm or solfège syllables. Once students have mastered singing simple pentatonic songs, they can sing pentachord, hexachord, and major and minor canons. Remember that canons may be performed aurally (without the aid of notation) or visually (using notation).

Partner Songs
Remember that all pentatonic songs can be performed in canon and can be performed together. For example, half the class may perform the song "Liza Jane" while the other half performs "Rocky Mountain." Here are additional examples of partner songs:

"Dinah" and "Bounce High"
"Bow Wow Wow" and "I See the Moon"

"Land of the Silver Birch" and "Who Killed Cocky Robin"
"Liza Jane" and "Come Through 'Na Hurry"
"Liza Jane," "Come Through 'Na Hurry," "All Around the Brickyard," and "Dinah"

Singing a Known Song and Clapping Rhythmic Motives as an Accompaniment
Guide students to sing one song while reading and clapping the rhythms of another known song. For example, they may sing "Rocky Mountain" while reading and clapping the rhythm of "Tideo." The teacher might ask students to read from the board a series of four-beat rhythms abstracted from a known song, or typical rhythms found in the repertoire being sung by students.

Another variation on this technique is for the teacher to label the phrases of a song or a series of rhythms with a number and the students sing a known song and clap according to a given number sequence (for example, 1, 4, 3, 2). In other words, they have to sing a known song, look at the number, and clap the corresponding phrase. This requires considerable concentration. It is always best that these activities lead to music making rather than being mere technical exercises.

Singing and Tapping a Known Pentatonic Melody
Create a two-part arrangement of a pentatonic folksong. Have the upper voice perform phrase 1 and the lower voice phrase 2. Create a rhythmic ostinato or accompaniment for the voice that is not singing. Divide the class into two groups. When group one begins, group two will perform the rhythmic accompaniment. It is important for the students to sing the complete melody fluently with solfège syllables and hand signs so that when they are clapping their part of the composition, they are also listening to the other voice part for the example to be performed musically.

Singing Simple Pentatonic Melodies as Canons With Solfège Syllables
All pentatonic songs may be sung in canon. Choose simple folksongs. Begin singing the melody with solfège syllables; the students follow in canon after one measure. Once students have mastered singing simple pentatonic songs, they can sing pentachord, hexachord, and major and minor canons. Remember that canons may be performed aurally (without notation) or visually (using notation).

Sight Singing and Clapping in Canon
Guide students to sight-sing an unknown melody and clap the rhythm in canon after one measure. This helps them develop the facility of looking at two lines of music at the same time.

Singing Pentatonic Scales in Canon
Students can now sing major and minor pentatonic scales in two or more parts. Begin the canon after two notes. These are excellent activities for developing intonation.

Singing a Pentatonic Melody While Singing Pentatonic Scales in Canon
Divide the class into three groups. One sings a pentatonic melody in canon, and the others may sing a pentatonic scale in two or more parts. These are excellent activities for developing secure intonation.

Singing Simple Pentatonic Folk Songs in Three Parts
In this activity, the class is divided into two groups. Perform the pentatonic folksong as a two-part canon. Once the students can perform the two parts with ease, the teacher may sing in canon with the students to create a third part.

Sing Simple Pentatonic Melodic Motives and Melodies in Canon at the Octave, Fourth, and the Fifth with Solfège Syllables
Once students can sing simple melodies in canon, the teacher can add another challenge for students. Give the starting pitch of a well-known song, and sing or play in canon in unison, and then a fifth above. Students will enjoy figuring out the puzzle as to how the teacher performed the canon. The teacher can sing the example using the same solfège as the students. Even though the teacher and students are technically singing in two keys, the canon can be sung using the same solfège syllables. Of course, students can also discover other solfège possibilities with the aid of the teacher. A simple way to think about this exercise is to perform "Hot Cross Buns" in canon, having students sing the melody with *do-re-mi*; the teacher can sing at a canon of a fifth using the notes *do-re-mi* or *so-la-ti*.

Repertoire for Developing Part Work and Music Literacy

Choral directors should select repertoire for concerts that children will enjoy singing and can also be used for developing their performance and music skills. Sometimes repertoire is chosen that will be taught by rote to children while other repertoire is chosen that can be taught by note. The following repertoire suggestions are examples sources and examples of repertoire that can be performed by children's choirs.

The list of songs in Figure 9.2, selected from *150 American Folk Songs*, may be easily adapted for developing part work skills and can be performed by children's choirs.

The songs in Figure 9.3, selected from *Sail Away: 155 American Folk Songs*, may also be easily adapted for children's choirs.

Here are excellent sources of music for children's choir.

Bacon, Denise. *46 Two-Part American Folk Songs for Elementary Grades*. Columbus, OH: Capital University, Kodaly Center of America, 1973.
Bolkovac, Edward. *150 Rounds for Singing and Teaching*. New York: Boosey & Hawkes, 1996.
Bolkovac, Edward. *Sing We Now Merrily*. New York: Boosey & Hawkes, 2007.

Figure 9.2 Selections from *150 American Folk Songs*

Song	Performance Suggestions
All Night, All Day	Perform this song as a partner song with "Swing Low, Sweet Chariot."
Band of Angels	The students may extend the song by singing the numbers backwards.
Blow Boys Blow	Audience participation
Cape Cod Girls	Divide class into two groups and perform as a call and response song.
Cock Robin	Accompany the song with a *la* drone and have soloists sing the verses.
Cradle Hymn	Expressive singing
Dance Josey	Perform in canon after two beats.
Deaf Woman's Courtship	Dramatization: the boys begin singing loudly but get softer and softer; girls begin singing softly and get louder. The instructor should explain that in this song the word "smoking" refers to smoking meat and the word "carding" means combing and cleaning wool.
Father Grumble	Use soloists and a dramatization.
Grey Goose	Expressive singing
Hold My Mule	Perform in canon after two beats.
I'm Goin' Home on a Cloud	Expressive singing
Liza Jane	Solo and chorus. The song may be performed in canon at two or four beats.
Mary Had a Baby	Perform as a canon after four beats.
Mister Frog Went a Courtin'	This song tells a story; different soloists may be used.
Mister Rabbit	Use two soloists and perform the song as a call and response. It may also be performed in canon after four beats.
Most Done Ling'ring Here	Sing in call and response style; the call may be given by different soloists.
Old Bald Eagle	Divide class up into two groups and perform as a call and response song.
Old Joe Clark	Expressive singing
Old Sow	Two students may sing solos: one sings the first phrase, the second sings the second phrase, and the group sings phrases three and four.
Paw Paw Patch	Expressive singing; perform play party dance
Riddle Song	Use a soloist for the second verse
Riding in a Buggy	1. Use soloists for each verse. 2. Perform the verse and chorus simultaneously.
Sailing O'er the Ocean	Divide the chorus and have each half alternate every two measures.
Sailor's Alphabet	Use one soloist for each letter of the alphabet.
Sweet William	Expressive singing
Turn the Glasses Over	Divide the chorus and have each half alternate every four measures.

Figure 9.3 Selections from *Sail Away: 155 American Folk Songs*

Song	Performance Suggestions
Amasee	Call and response
Birds Courtin' Song	Two groups, alternate singing verse by verse
Bob-A-Needle	Call and response
Boney	Solo and chorus
Chicka-hanka	Alternate singing between two groups
Didn't My Lord Deliver Daniel	Solo and chorus
Down in the Valley	Group 1 sings the song and Group 2 sings the harmonic chord roots
Go Tell It on the Mountain	Two groups for verse and refrain
Great Big House in New Orleans	Two-part canon after the second measure.
Hammer Ring	Two groups for call and response
Jack, Can I Ride?	Two soloist plus choir
Just from the Kitchen	Solo and chorus
La Bella Hortelana	Part work and rhythmic accompaniments
Lemonade	Dialogue song between two groups
Lucy Locket	Two part canon after the second measure
Pizza Pizza	Call and response
Santy Anna	Solo and chorus
Ser Come el Aire Libre	Sing in two parts
Skin and Bones	Call and response and dramatization
Snail, Snail	Two-part canon after the second measure
Stew Ball II	Call and Response
Witch Witch	Use the first two bars as a melodic ostinato

Taylor-Howell, Susan. *The Owl Sings: 22 Folk Songs Arranged for 2 or 3 Voices*. Organization of American Kodály Educators, 1997.

Tacka, Philip, and Susan Taylor-Howell. *Sourwood Mountain: 28 North American & English Songs Arranged for Two Voices*. Organization of American Kodály Educators, 1986.

Here are examples of choral pieces to use with children's choir for performance as well as development of music literacy skills.

Beat in Simple Meter
"Rocky Mountain," from *Sourwood Mountain, 28 North American & English Songs Arranged for 2 Voices,* arr. P. Tacka and S. Taylor-Howell, Organization of American Kodály Educators, 1986.

"Cripple Creek," arr. E. Crocker, Jenson Publications, 1981.

Beat in Compound Meter
"Kitty of Coleraine," arr. E. Thiman, Boosey & Hawkes, 1983.

"Oh Dear, What Can the Matter Be?" arr. R. Robinson, Warner Bros., 2000.

Quarter and Eighth Notes
"Appalachian Sleepytime," from *Sourwood Mountain, 28 North American & English Songs Arranged for 2 Voices,* arr. P. Tacka and S. Taylor-Howell, Organization of American Kodály Educators, 1986.

"Long, Long Ago," T. Bayly, arr. J. Leavitt, *A Cappella Songs for Treble Chorus,* Hal Leonard, 1995.

A Beat with No Sound
"Fancie," by B. Britten, Boosey & Hawkes, 1965.

"Da Pacem Domine," by M. Franck, arr. M. Goetze, Boosey & Hawkes, 1985.

Three-Note Children's Chant
"Bye Baby Bunting," arr. M. Williams, *Two-Part American Songs* (Bicinia Americana), Southern Music, 1977.

Two-Beat Meter
"Cripple Creek," arr. E. Crocker, Jenson, 1981.

"Rocky Mountain," from *Sourwood Mountain, 28 North American & English Songs Arranged for 2 Voices,* arr. P. Tacka and S. Taylor-Howell, Organization of American Kodály Educators, 1986.

Half Note
"Mary Had a Baby," from *Sourwood Mountain, 28 North American & English Songs Arranged for 2 Voices,* arr. P. Tacka and S. Taylor-Howell, Organization of American Kodály Educators, 1986.

"Da Pacem Domine," by M. Franck, arr. M. Goetze, Boosey & Hawkes, 1985.

Subsets of the Major Pentatonic Scale
(mi re do)

"Rocky Mountain," from *Sourwood Mountain, 28 North American & English Songs Arranged for 2 Voices,* arr. P. Tacka and S. Taylor-Howell, Organization of American Kodály Educators, 1986.

"Laugh, Ha, Ha," *150 Rounds for Singing and Teaching,* ed. E. Bolkovac and J. Johnson, Boosey & Hawkes, 1996.

(*do re mi*)
"Are You Sleeping?" ed. E. Bolkovac and J. Johnson, Boosey & Hawkes, 1996.
"The Dodger," arr. A. Copland, Boosey & Hawkes, 1950.

(*so mi re do*)
"For All the Saints" (Sine Nomine), by R. Vaughan Williams, *The English Hymnal,* Oxford University Press, 1906.

(*do re mi so*)
"Scotland's Burning," *150 Rounds for Singing and Teaching,* ed. E. Bolkovac and J. Johnson, Boosey & Hawkes, 1996.

Sixteenth Notes
"Ching-a-Ring Chaw," arr. A. Copland, Boosey & Hawkes, 1954.
"The Drunken Sailor," arr. E. Crocker, Jensen, 1980.

The Major Pentatonic Scale—*do* Pentatonic—*la so mi re do*
"The Sally Garden," arr. B. Britten, Boosey & Hawkes, 1962.
"Fiddle Dee Dee," arr. M. Williams, *Two-Part American Songs (Bicinia Americana),* Southern Music, 1977.

Four-Beat Meter
"Da Pacem Domine," by M. Franck, arr. M. Goetze, Boosey & Hawkes, 1985.
"Sakura," arr. DeCourmier, Lawson-Gould, 1997.

Eighth and Sixteenth Note Combinations
"The Drunken Sailor," arr. E. Crocker, Jensen, 1980.
"Une Poule Blanche," arr. S. Donahue, Alliance, 1998.

Low la (*la,*)
Round no. 6, "Hungarian," *150 Rounds for Singing and Teaching,* ed. E. Bolkovac and J. Johnson, Boosey & Hawkes, 1996.
"Chickalileeo," from Sourwood Mountain, *28 North American & English Songs Arranged for 2 Voices,* arr. P. Tacka and S. Taylor-Howell, Organization of American Kodály Educators, 1986.

Sixteenth and Eighth Note Combinations
"I Bought Me a Cat," arr. A. Copland, Boosey & Hawkes, 1950.
"Pick a Bale of Cotton," arr. B. Bertaux, Boosey & Hawkes, 1985.

Low so (so,)
"Laugh, Ha, Ha," *150 Rounds for Singing and Teaching*, ed. E. Bolkovac and J. Johnson, Boosey & Hawkes, 1996.
"Make New Friends," *150 Rounds for Singing and Teaching*, ed. E. Bolkovac and J. Johnson, Boosey & Hawkes, 1996.
"Brother Martin," *150 Rounds for Singing and Teaching*, ed. E. Bolkovac and J. Johnson, Boosey & Hawkes, 1996.
"The Hart, He Loves the High Wood," from *Firsts and Seconds*, arr. W. Appleby, Oxford University Press, 1960.

High do (do')
"Annie Laurie," arr. Rentz, BriLee Music, 2000.
"Old Abram Brown," from *Friday Afternoons*, by B. Britten, Boosey & Co., 1936.

External Upbeat
"The Ash Grove," arr. T. Steffy, Tetra Continuo Music Group, 1993.
"The Sally Garden," arr. B. Britten, Boosey & Hawkes, 1962.

Syncopation
"Didn't My Lord Deliver Daniel?" arr. Emerson, Jensen, 1992.
"Elijah Rock," arr. J. Hairston, Bourne, 1955.

la Pentatonic Scale
"The Birch Tree," *150 Rounds for Singing and Teaching*, ed. E. Bolkovac and J. Johnson, Boosey & Hawkes, 1996.
"Didn't My Lord Deliver Daniel?" arr. Emerson, Jensen, 1992.

so Pentatonic Scale
"A Mince Pie or a Pudding," source E. Andrews, *The Gift to Be Simple*, J. J. Augustin, 1940 http://kodaly.hnu.edu.
"Handsome Molly," source Frank Proffit, Folk-Legacy Records, FSA-1, 1962, http://kodaly.hnu.edu.

Dotted Quarter Followed by an Eighth Note
"Annie Laurie," arr. Rentz, BriLee Music, 2000.
"Da Pacem Domine," by M. Franck, arr. M. Goetze, Boosey & Hawkes, 1985.

fa
"Are You Sleeping?" *150 Rounds for Singing and Teaching*, ed. E. Bolkovac and J. Johnson, Boosey & Hawkes, 1996.
Round no. 4, "Hungarian," *150 Rounds for Singing and Teaching*, ed. E. Bolkovac and J. Johnson, Boosey & Hawkes, 1996.

"Da Pacem Domine," by M. Franck, arr. Goetze, Boosey & Hawkes, 1985.
"Friendship Song," arr. Rao, Boosey & Hawkes, 1991.

Three-Beat Meter
"The Ash Grove," arr. T. Steffy, Tetra Continuo Music Group, 1993.
"Jesu, Joy of Man's Desiring," by J. S. Bach, arr. P. Liebergen, Carl Fischer, 1991.

low ti
"For the Beauty of the Earth," by J. Leininger, Alliance Music, 1995.

la Pentachord
"Before Rain," Betty Bertaux, Boosey and Hawkes (OC 3B6 192).

Dotted Eighth Followed by a Sixteenth Note
"Clementine," arr. J. Eliot, BriLee, 2006.
"The Dodger," arr. A. Copland, Boosey & Hawkes, 1950.

Major Scale
"The Echo Child," by R. Thompson, Thorpe, 1992.
"Jubilate Deo," by M. Praetorius, arr. Rao, Boosey & Hawkes, 1987.

Eighth Note Followed by a Dotted Quarter Note
"In the Village," by B. Bartók, arr. Suchoff, Boosey & Hawkes, 1960.
"Shenandoah," arr. M. Goetze, Boosey & Hawkes, 1986.

Natural Minor Scale
"Johnny Has Gone for a Soldier," arr. C. Moore, Somerset Press, 1987.
"I Will Give My Love an Apple," Betty Bertaux (OC 3B6 370).
"The Little Horses," arr. A. Copland, Aaron Copland Fund for Music, 1965.

Harmonic Minor
"Prayer for the Norwegian Child," by R. Artman, Schirmer, 1987.

Dorian Mode
"Scarborough Fair," arr. Emerson, Jensen, 1983.
"Haul Away Joe," source J. Colcord, *Songs of American Sailormen,* Oak, 1964 http://kodaly.hnu.edu.

Mixolydian Mode (*ta*)
"Waters Ripple and Flow," arr. D. Taylor, J. Fischer & Bro., 1926.
"The Golden Willow Tree," arr. A. Copland, Boosey & Hawkes, 2000.

How to Teach Simple Two-Part Song Arrangements

When teaching students to sing in two parts, build on their prior knowledge. It is a good idea to select two-part arrangements where students already know the melody; now they will be learning an arrangement of the folksong. Many of these folksongs can include some or all of these compositional techniques.

- A rhythmic or melodic ostinato to accompany the folksong
- Including a tonic, or tonic and dominant drone that may be sung as an accompaniment
- The melody line to be shared between the upper and lower voices
- Songs including imitation

Teaching the Second Part to a Known Song by Rote

Students should already be able to sing songs with rhythmic and melodic ostinato as well as sing songs in canon before learning simple two-part songs. Here is a suggested teaching procedure for teaching a two-part song arrangement.

1. T sings the unfamiliar part or harmony while playing the melody on the piano or performing with one S.
2. T asks Ss questions based on the performance of the song:
    A. "How many phrases are there in this arrangement?"
    B. "Did the two parts begin and end each phrase together?"
    C. "Did both parts have the same text?"
    D. "How would you describe the tune of the harmony line?"
    E. "Did both parts begin and end on the same pitch?"
3. T sings the harmony line phrase by phrase and Ss repeat. This can be done with rhythm or solfège syllables or on a neutral syllable if Ss have not learned all the solfège or rhythm syllables. This is easiest when done with text. T performs the melody on the piano for each phrase as Ss learn the harmony line phrase by phrase.
4. Ss and T sing the harmony line while T plays the melody line on the piano.
5. Ss sing the harmony line while T sings the melody line. Switch parts.
6. T divides the class into two groups. Group A sings the harmony and group B sings the melody. Switch parts.

Teaching the Second Part to a Known Song by Note

Here is a teaching procedure for working with a two-part song arrangement.

1. All Ss should know the main melody.
2. T may sing the unfamiliar part or harmony while playing the melody on the piano, or have several Ss perform the known melody.
3. T asks Ss questions based on the performance of the song.

A. "How many phrases are there in this arrangement?"
   B. "Did the two parts begin and end each phrase together?"
   C. "Did both parts have the same text?"
   D. "How would you describe the tune of the harmony line?"
   E. "Did both parts begin and end on the same pitch?"
4. T hums the harmony line while pointing to the contour on the board. Ss repeat and point to the contour. T repeats the harmony but Ss have to repeat each phrase and indicate the contour with their hands. They sing and draw the contour of the harmony line as T sings the melody line.
5. T and Ss identify the rhythm and solfège syllables of the harmony line phrase by phrase and Ss repeat.
6. Ss are presented with the score and clap and say the rhythm of the melody with rhythm syllables or numbers for counting. T prepares the staff placement for *do* and Ss read the harmony line with solfège syllables.
7. T sings the melody and T perform the harmony line with solfège syllables.
8. Ss perform the harmony line with neutral syllables and then learn to sing the text with T's help.
9. Ss sing the harmony line while T sings the melody. Switch parts.
10. T divides the class into two groups. Group A sings the harmony and group B sings the melody using solfège syllables and then text. Switch parts.

Teaching a Simple Two-Part Song by Rote

Students should already be able to sing and perform songs with rhythmic and melodic ostinati, perform in canon, and perform simple two-part folksong arrangements prior to learning a two-part song that is not familiar.

1. T performs the new two-part song by singing one part and playing the other on the piano, or by singing and having one S sing the second part, or by playing a recorded performance.
2. T asks Ss questions based on the performance of the song. Have Ss perform the song again and ask Ss for their response to these questions:
   A. "How many parts are there in this arrangement?"
   B. "What did you notice about the form of the piece?"
   C. "How many phrases are there in this arrangement?"
   D. "Did the two parts begin and end each phrase together?"
   E. "Did both parts have the same text?"
   F. "Did both parts begin and end on the same pitch?"
   G. "Which is the harmony line?"
   H. "How would you describe the tune of the harmony line?"
3. T sings one part and plays the second part on the piano phrase by phrase while Ss repeat the sung part from memory.
4. Ss and T sing the first part while T plays the second part on the piano.

5. T sings the second part and plays the first part on the piano, phrase by phrase, and Ss repeat from memory. T hums or plays the first part as Ss are singing the second part phrase by phrase.
6. Ss and T sing the second part while T plays the first part on the piano. Ss sing the second part while T plays the first part on the piano.
7. Ss sing the second part while T sings the first part. Switch parts.
8. T divides the class into two groups. Group A sings the top part and group B sings the second. Switch parts.

Teaching a Simple Two-Part Song by Note

Here is a teaching procedure for working with a two-part song arrangement.

1. T sings one part of the arrangement while playing the second part on the piano or performing with another S. Switch.
2. T asks Ss questions based on the performance of the song:
   A. "Where did you hear the melody?" Or "Which voice had the new melody?"
   B. "How many phrases are there in this arrangement?"
   C. "Did the two parts begin and end each phrase together?"
   D. "Did both parts have the same text?"
   E. "How would you describe the tune of the harmony line?"
   F. "Did both parts begin and end on the same pitch?"
3. T sings the melody line phrase by phrase and Ss repeat. This can be done with rhythm or solfège syllables or on a neutral syllable if Ss have not learned all the solfège or rhythm syllables. This is done most easily with text.
4. Ss sing the melody line with syllables and text.
5. Ss sing the melody line and T hums the second part. T sings the second part with text.
6. T sings the harmony line phrase by phrase and Ss repeat. This can be done with rhythm or solfège syllables or on a neutral syllable if Ss have not learned all the solfège or rhythm syllables. This is done most easily with text.
7. Ss perform the harmony line on their own. They perform it a second time as T sings the melody line.
8. Ss sing the harmony line while T sings the melody line. Switch parts.
9. T divides the class into two groups. Group A sings the harmony and group B sings the melody. Switch parts.

Developing Harmonic Hearing in the Elementary Choir

The next section offers more advanced part-work ideas and teaching techniques for developing harmonic hearing in the elementary choir. It is important that students develop their sense of harmonic hearing so that they can hear the harmonic progressions used in

The Kodály Concept and the Elementary Choir

the choral repertoire they are singing. Harmonic motion has a significant impact on the understanding of form.

Singing Folksongs in Thirds and Sixths

As students begin to learn music of other cultures, they will discover the stylistic traits of this repertoire. Guide them in recognizing familiar elements in this repertoire, but also in discovering a greater variety of musical elements. Singing folksongs in thirds and sixths is another skill in developing part work (see Fig. 9.4, "Vamos a Belen").

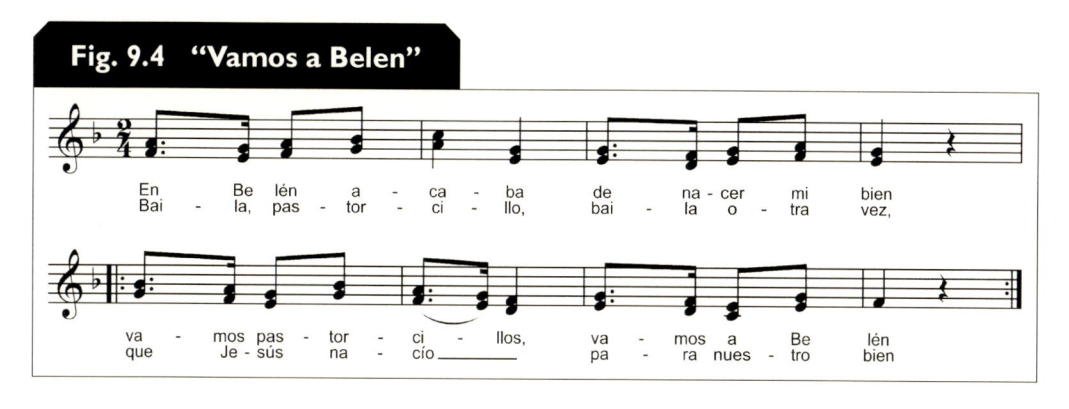

Fig. 9.4 "Vamos a Belen"

En Be - lén a - ca - ba de na - cer mi bien
Bai - la, pas - tor - ci - llo, bai - la o - tra vez,

va - mos pas - tor - ci - llos, va - mos a Be - lén
que Je - sús na - ció___ pa - ra nues - tro bien

Accompanying Melodies with Tonic and Dominant Chord Roots (Harmonic Functions)

As students add the solfège syllables *fa* and *ti* to their melodic vocabulary, they begin to discover the need for a note other than *do* in major and *la* in minor melodies for their accompaniments. While students are singing known pentachord, hexachord, and diatonic melodies, the teacher should quietly hum the functional notes (chord roots) *do* and *so* for *do*-centered pieces (see Fig. 9.5, "Laugh, Ha, Ha").

Fig. 9.5 "Laugh, Ha, Ha"

Humming *la* and *mi* for *la*-centered Pieces

Once the students are familiar with these accompanying pitches, the teacher can guide them to discover the solfège syllables of the new accompanying notes and introduce the terms *tonic function* and *dominant function* (see Fig. 9.6, "Ah Poor Bird").

Fig. 9.6 "Ah Poor Bird"

Accompanying Melodies with Tonic, Dominant, and Subdominant Chord Roots (Harmonic Functions)

When students sing folksongs, especially those from Germany, many times the bass part outlines the notes of the tonic, subdominant, and dominant functions.

The subdominant chord root may be introduced once students have had sufficient practice with tonic and dominant chord roots. The procedures outlined for presenting and practicing the tonic and dominant chord roots are the same for the subdominant chord roots. While the students sing melodies that contain clear tonic, subdominant, and dominant function triads, the teacher may hum or play the appropriate chord root on the piano. In this way, they are led to discover that the subdominant chord root in major is *fa* and the subdominant chord root in minor is *re*. The melodies in Figure 9.7 help focus attention on the subdominant chord root.

Fig. 9.7 "White Sand and Grey Sand"

Practice Suggestions
- Ss sing familiar songs while T sings or plays the functional notes or chord roots as an accompaniment.
- Ss sing familiar songs while showing with hand signs when the functional note or chord root in the melody changes.
- Individual Ss sing familiar songs while showing hand signs for the functional note or playing the functional notes on the piano.
- Ss identify the tonic, subdominant, and dominant functions of unknown melodies sung or played by T.
- Ss transpose melodies into their parallel major or minor key and sing them with the corresponding functions.
- Ss may be presented with sight-reading materials that include a melody and an accompaniment built on the tonic, subdominant, and dominant functions. These materials can also be used for dictation, memory work, and analysis of the harmonic basis of the melodies.
- Ss relate harmonic functions to their knowledge of form.

These exercises are very important for developing harmonic thinking. Being able to harmonize melodies with the chord roots of tonic, dominant, and subdominant functions develops another very important skill in our students, the ability to sense when chords change in music.

Triads and Their Respective Functions

After students are thoroughly familiar with the tonic, subdominant, and dominant functions, they can be introduced to the concept of triads. Explain the meaning of root, third, and fifth of a triad and how a triad is classified as either major or minor. Show how the tonic, subdominant, and dominant notes and the triads built on them define a key.

Canons in major and minor keys with clearly defined triads at the cadence furnish appropriate literature for initial experiences in analyzing harmony. Initially, the music material should be restricted to primary triads. Looking at both the melodic lines and the harmonic aspects of music is essential for students' understanding of harmonic concepts. They should memorize canons and discover the harmonic functions of the melody. Then draw their attention to individual melodic lines, or melodic lines that are sounded together to create triads. These triads should be abstracted from the music material and sung by the class. Students should be guided to hear major and minor triads within the context of the perfect fifth interval. Students should sing triads beginning with the root, then the fifth, and finally the third.

For example, sing the major tonality canon in Figure 9.8 in four parts, and accompany each line with tonic or dominant notes.

Kodály Today

Fig. 9.8 "Canon in G Major"

- The fourth line of this canon uses the tonic and dominant notes.
- Ss sing the notes that are circled and T explains that the circled notes are referred to as a major triad when they are performed together. Triads are composed of three notes: the root (*do*), the third (*mi*), and the fifth (*so*). The root of the triad is the note on which the triad is based, so that in the root position the third of the triad is a note positioned a third above the root, and the fifth is a note positioned a fifth above the root.
- Ss sing the canon again and pause on the circled triads. Ss listen for each note of the triad as it is being sung.

Sing the minor tonality canon in Figure 9.9 in four parts, and accompany each line with tonic or dominant notes.

Fig. 9.9 "Canon in G Minor"

- The fourth line of this canon uses the tonic and dominant notes.
- Ss sing the notes that are circled and T explains the concept of a minor triad. Minor triads are composed of three members: the root (*la*), the third (*do*), and the fifth (*mi*). The root of the triad is the note on which the triad is based, so in the root position the third of the triad is a note positioned a third above the root, and the fifth is a note positioned a fifth above the root.
- Ss sing the canon again and pause on the circled triad. Ss listen for each note of the triad as it is being sung.

Using the same techniques for preparing and practicing the tonic, subdominant, and dominant triads, the teacher may introduce augmented and diminished triads. Explain the idea of primary and secondary triads. The triads built on the II, III, VI, and VII degrees can be shown to be related to one of the primary triads and have the same function. The II and VI belong to the subdominant class, and III and V to the dominant. Chord VI can also belong to the tonic class.

Introducing Triad Inversions and Singing Harmonic Progressions

Once students have an understanding of root position primary triads, the teacher may introduce the concept of the inversion of triads. Introducing triad inversions does not involve a great deal of explanation if students understand the character and tonality of the triad. First-inversion triads have the third in the bass; second-inversion triads have the fifth in the bass. Examples from the musical literature should be used to introduce the concept of inversion of triads. It is best to concentrate on isolating triad inversions melodically and then harmonically. The same procedures outlined at the beginning of this chapter should be used.

Introduction of triad inversions should also include this practice:

- The tonic, subdominant, and dominant triads in root position, first inversions, and second inversions in a triad sequence such as:
  1-1V-V-1- I6-IV6-V6-I6/4–V-I This chord progression may be written initially with solfège syllables. Depending on time, consider introducing or practicing figured bass. Students could sing a chord progression from Roman numerals and figured bass or from the bass line written on the staff with a figured bass. The progression would be directly related to choral work being practiced.
  Discuss the intervals included in these triads, for example, major triad, first inversion (*mi-so–high do*)
  mi-so minor third
  mi–high do minor sixth
  so–high do perfect fourth

The choral director may explore singing progressions in three parts using root position and inversions. Guide students in discovering that singing certain chords in inversion is easier than singing each chord in root position. Once they understand inversions,

Kodály Today

three-part chordal progressions may be used as warm-up exercises and as accompaniments to their songs.

Accompanying Melodies with Chord Inversions

Students can now create their own accompaniments to melodies using notes other than the bass note of the tonic, subdominant, and dominant chord roots. For example, in a major key the third of the tonic chord, *mi*, can substitute for *do*, and the third of the dominant chord, *ti*, can substitute for *so*. In a minor key the third of the tonic minor, *do*, can substitute for the tonic note *la* and the third note of the dominant chord, *si*, can substitute for the dominant note *mi*. The goal is for students to create interesting bass lines using root and first inversions.

Discovering Bass Lines

The teacher plays a two-part melody on the piano; students listen and show the melodic contour of the lowest voice with arm motions.

1. Ss discover the direction of the bass line.
2. Ss discover the rhythm of the bass line.
3. Ss sing the bass line with solfège syllables.
4. Ss sing both parts.

Suggested Teaching Procedure

See Figure 9.10.

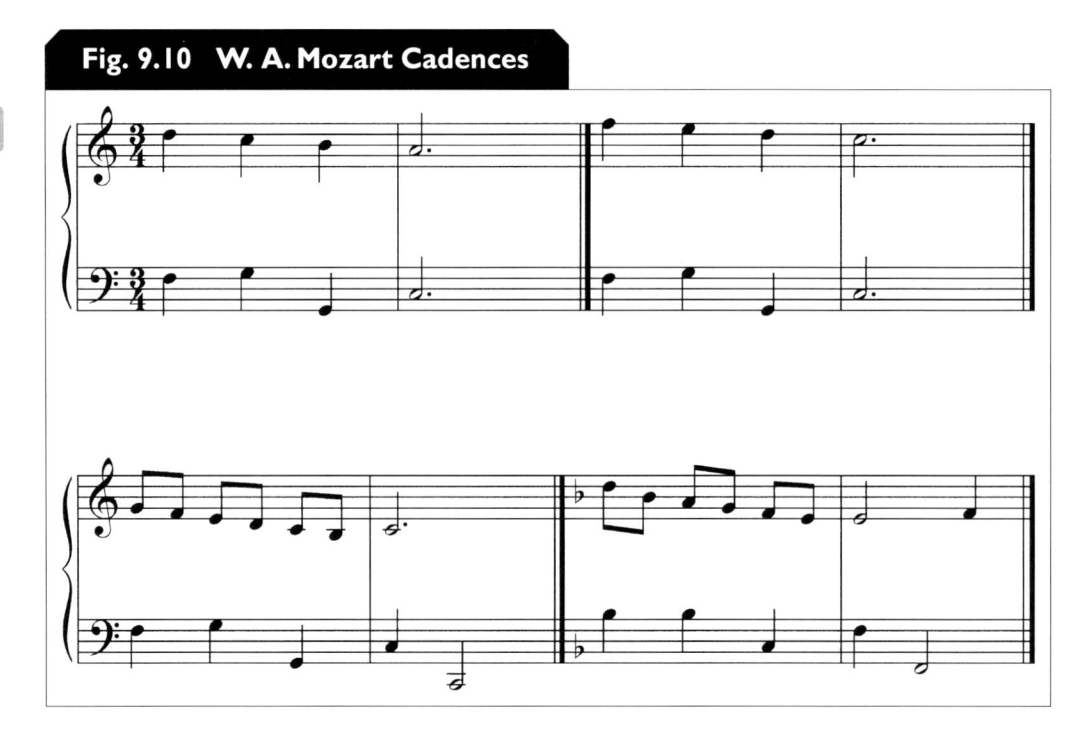

Fig. 9.10 W. A. Mozart Cadences

The Kodály Concept and the Elementary Choir

1. T sings the upper voice and plays the lower voice on the piano.
2. T plays both melodies on the piano while Ss show the melodic contour of the lowest part.
3. Ss write the melody and trace the melodic contour of the bass part. Those who are more advanced may be encouraged to add the rhythm and melody to the bass part.
4. T plays short two-part cadential examples on the piano. Ss sing back the bass line with solfège syllables. These examples should include the tonic, subdominant, and the dominant notes in the lower voice.
5. Ss listen to examples using more than one note in the lower part. They must be able to differentiate single or simultaneously sounded notes in the accompaniment.

Singing Pentatonic Major, Minor, and Modal Scales in Canon

- Ss sing different pentatonic scales(*do, re, mi, so* and *la* pentatonic scales) in canon. This can be done in two to five parts. Figure 9.11 illustrates a pentatonic scale beginning on *do* and performed in four parts. The same technique can be used with other types of pentatonic scales.

Fig. 9.11

- Sing pentatonic scales in ascending and descending succession from the same starting pitch. Begin on a selected pitch, for example, D. Sing the pentatonic scale up from that pitch, change the top pitch to the new scale as directed by the = sign, and follow the arrows. This can also be performed in canon.

Kodály Today

Fig. 9.12

d'	=	r'		m'	=	s	l	=	d
		d'		r'			s		
l				d'		m			l
s		l				r		m	s
		s		l		d		r	
m				s				d	m
r		m				l,			r
d		r	=	m		s,	=	l,	d
↑									
	Ascending	↑		Descending	↓		Same Pitch	=

- Sing major and minor scales using solfège syllables or letter names in canon; begin after two notes. Perform the scales in three-part canon.
- Sing major and minor scales from the same starting note in canon. Using solfège syllables, sing the major scale beginning on *do* and starting on the pitch D; then sing the minor scale beginning on *la*, beginning on the same starting pitch. In this way, Ss perform the major scale followed by its parallel minor scale.
- Perform modal scales in canon.
- Perform modal scales ascending and descending from the same starting pitch. This may also be performed in canon.
- T divides the class into three parts and gives each part a note of the major triad to sing. T asks all groups to call this note *mi*. T instructs the groups to sing "Hot Cross Buns" with solfège syllables. Ss will be singing the simple song in three parts in parallel major chords. This exercise may be repeated using a minor triad and starting on *la*.

The teacher can explore sound colors with the students using a number of techniques. Divide the class and have the students:

- Sing pentatonic scales, sustaining each note of the scale. Use this to accompany a pentatonic song.
- Sing pentachord and hexachord scales, sustaining each note of the scale. Use this to accompany a hexachord song.
- Sing pentachord and hexachord scales, sustaining each note of the scale.

Selecting Repertoire for Children's Choir

It is important to know how to select appropriate and successful pieces of music for a children's choir. Take time to analyze the music of great composers of children's repertoire. For example, spend time analyzing the choral works of Kodály. You will find a rich source of excellent materials and techniques, and thus be able to evaluate other pieces of music. Search for choral works composed and arranged by such composers as Mary Goetze and Betty Bertaux.

The Kodály Concept and the Elementary Choir

These criteria should be considered by teachers in selecting choral materials.

- Is the material of good quality? If you are unsure as to how to select quality material, familiarize yourself with the works of recognized composers for children's choirs. Begin to analyze and sing some of the choral compositions of Kodály. It will become apparent how his style of composition and his folksong arrangements provide excellent models for composing children's choral works.
- Select all types of repertoire for your choir, including the Medieval, Renaissance, Baroque, Classical, Romantic, and Modern eras of composition.
3. Will the students enjoy singing the text of the choral piece? The text should be meaningful to them.
4. Is the vocal line for each voice part interesting for them to sing?
5. Does the range of the song work for the them?
6. Is this an easy, challenging, or difficult piece for the choir? Look at the melodic turns, rhythms, harmony, voice leading, and modulation. Avoid simplified scores, or repertoire that has been simplified for children's choir.
7. How difficult is the part singing?
8. What role does the piano accompaniment play in the performance?

Types of Works

The selection of repertoire should include the types described below.

Folk Songs Taught by Note and Rote
Pentatonic, diatonic, and modal folksongs may be memorized and used for developing music literacy and inner-hearing skills. These songs should be recycled many times in a number of concert programs. For example:

- Sing as a unison song
- Sing and play the game
- Perform with an ostinato
- Perform in canon
- Perform as a partner song
- Perform as a two-part arrangement
- Perform as a three-part arrangement

Canons
Singing canons should be a part of every concert program. Sometimes canons can be used for teaching music literacy concepts.

Part Music Taught by Rote
Generally this material will be taught primarily by rote, but of course the teacher should take every opportunity to use students' knowledge of music literacy when learning this material.

Kodály Today

Part Music That Will Be Taught by Note

It is important to include part music repertoire that can be taught by note. This will include more advanced pieces of repertoire where students will not be familiar with the melodic line. Here are some excellent basic sources for repertoire for children's choir.

Bibliography for Selecting Repertoire

Bacon, Denise. *46 Two-Part American Folk Songs for Elementary Grades.* Columbus, OH: Capital University, Kodaly Center of America, 1973.

Bolkovac, Edward. *150 Rounds for Singing and Teaching.* New York: Boosey & Hawkes, 1996.

Bolkovac, Edward. *Sing We Now Merrily.* New York: Boosey & Hawkes, 2007.

Erdei, Peter, and Katalin Komlos. *150 American Folk Songs to Sing, Read and Play.* Collected principally by Katalin Komlos. New York: Boosey & Hawkes, 1974.

Locke, Eleanor G. *Sail Away: 155 American Folk Songs to Sing, Read and Play.* New York: Boosey & Hawkes, 1981.

Tacka, Philip, and Susan Taylor-Howell. *Sourwood Mountain: 28 North American & English Songs Arranged for Two Voices.* Organization of American Kodaly Educators, 1986.

Taylor-Howell, Susan. *The Owl Sings: 22 Folk Songs Arranged for 2 or 3 Voices.* Organization of American Kodaly Educators, 1997.

Trinka, Jill. *Folk Songs, Singing Games and Play Parties.* 4 vols. Chicago: GIA, 2006. Vol. 1: *My Little Rooster*. Vol. 2: *Bought Me a Cat*. Vol. 3: *John, The Rabbit*. Vol. 4: *The Little Black Bull*.

Wilson, Harry. *Old and New Rounds and Canons.* Shawnee Press.

Score Preparation and Teaching a Choral Composition

All choral directors should prepare the score from the perspective of performers, conductors, and teachers. Choral directors should be able to sing all lines of the music fluently and artistically. In addition, all music should be prepared as a sing-and-play, playing one part on the piano and singing the other. The goal here is for the director to create an aural image of the score in the students' ear. The director should make sure that he or she can sing all lines with solfège, neutral syllables, and text. In addition, the director should be competent singing each voice part and playing the other parts on the piano at the same time. Here is a sample checklist of things to do.

1. *Analyze the rhythms of the main themes.* Write out the main themes of the choral piece and analyze the rhythms of these themes. Note all tempo markings. Check to determine if some of these rhythm patterns can be used as part of the vocal warm-ups. Decide on the rhythms that can be taught by note or rote. Make sure you can clap all rhythms and say the rhythm syllables or count with a number

system. And be sure you can sing one part with rhythm syllables while tapping the other voice parts.

2. *Analyze the tonal content.* Analyze the key of the compositions. Identify any modulations in the composition. Phrase all lines of music, note dynamic markings, and be able to sing them with solfège syllables and letter names. Sing one line and show the other lines with your hand signs. Sing one line and play the other lines on the piano. Identify themes that can be used for vocal warm-ups. Pay attention to any articulation or tempo markings.

3. *Form.* Determine the form of the music composition by identifying all the phrases in the composition. Pay particular attention to sections of the composition that are repeated or modified. Identify sections of the compositions that contain variations.

4. *Analyze the harmony of the composition.* Analyze all the harmonic intervals in the composition created by the voice parts. Analyze the composition and understand the chord structure of the composition, paying particular attention to harmonic motion and cadences. Typical chord progressions found in the music can then be used in the vocal warm-up section of the composition.

5. *Dynamics.* Review all the dynamic markings in the composition. Review carefully the relationship between text and dynamics.

6. *Tempo.* Review all the tempo markings in the composition. Review carefully the relationship between text and dynamics. Review to determine correct tempo interpretation. Analyze the harmonic tempo as part of tempo information.

7. *Text.* Review the text. Look carefully at how the music brings out the meaning of the text. Check carefully for vowel modifications, pure vowels, or diphthongs. Check to see what consonants need careful preparation. Review carefully the relationship between text and dynamics and the composer's setting of a text or compositional tools used to set the text.

8. *Accompaniment.* Analyze the accompaniment. Review how the accompaniment doubles the voice part or how it supports the melody.

9. *Conduct.* Figure out how to conduct the score. Practice how you will do so during rehearsal as well as during a concert. Prepare cut-offs and cues very carefully. It is important to practice facial expressions and eye contact in front of a mirror. Be prepared to inner-hear the composition and conduct from memory. Keep these considerations in mind while you are conducting:
   A. Check your posture as well as the height of your arms and hand positions.
   B. Be sure your conducting is precise and easy for the students to follow.
   C. Constantly review the size and style of your conducting pattern.
   D. Practice giving pitches from a tuning fork.

E. Remember that your preparatory beat must show the character, tempo, dynamics, and mood of the music.
F. Establish eye contact with members of the choir before you start to conduct.
G. Use your right hand to give beats, but use the left hand for phrasing, dynamics, entrances, cues, and cut offs.

Deciding How to Teach a Score

Next, determine the best strategy for teaching the score. Look at the score and figure out how to deconstruct it so that the students can reconstruct it for themselves. Develop long-term strategies on how you will teach a piece of music over a number of rehearsals. Make an effort to address students' music literacy, musical skill development, history of the composition, and understanding of the style of the composition.

Preparing the Music During the Vocal Warm-ups

It is important to prepare a music composition during the vocal warm-ups. This can include practicing selected intervals in the piece and using challenging rhythmic patterns to practice vocalizes.

Teaching the Main Themes of the Composition

Find the best way to teach each composition. Depending on students' skill and knowledge of music, the music may be taught by rote or by note. Sometimes teachers can teach a composition from hand signs, tone steps, or the score. It is important that students be prepared to hear and read the main themes.

Singing in Two or More Parts

Common intervallic patterns can be practiced during the vocal warm-up of the choral rehearsal by using two-part hand sign singing. Create two-part rhythmic and melodic exercises for students to clap or sing. These exercises should contain the music skeleton of the main themes of the composition.

Guidelines for Teaching a New Piece of Music

1. How can you prepare the music in your breathing, vocal warm-up, and intonation exercises?
2. Regardless of how you are teaching the score (by note or rote), it is important to provide every student with a copy of the music. Be certain that the score includes measure numbers.

3. Determine which sections of the score you will teach kinesthetically, aurally, or visually. Determine which sections you can teach by note or rote with the students.
4. Every time you sing for students, it is important to do it with a light and pure tone. Male teachers should sing in their falsetto range.

Teaching a More Difficult Two-part Song Arrangement by Note

Here is a teaching procedure for working with a two-part song arrangement. It uses kinesthetic, aural, and visual activities as well as note and rote processes.

1. T sings one part with text and performs the other part on the piano or with one S. Reverse.
2. T asks Ss questions based on the performance of the song.
   A. "How many phrases are there in this arrangement?"
   B. "Did the two parts begin and end each phrase together?"
   C. "Did both parts have the same text?"
   D. "How would you describe the tune of the harmony line?"
   E. "Did both parts begin and end on the same pitch?"
3. T hums the melody line and points to the contour of the melody on the board. Ss repeat and point to the contour. T repeats the exercise but Ss have to repeat each phrase and indicate the contour with their hands. They sing and draw the contour of the melody.
4. Ss identify the rhythm and solfège syllables of melody line phrase by phrase and sing with rhythm syllables while clapping the rhythm or singing with hand signs.
5. Ss are presented with the score and clap and say the rhythm of the melody with rhythm syllables and numbers for counting. T prepares the staff placement for the tonic *do*, and Ss read the melody line with solfège syllables.
6. One S sings the score with neutral syllables.
7. One S sings the text.
8. Class repeats steps 1–7 for the second part of the melody or the harmony line.
9. Ss perform the harmony line with neutral syllables and then learn to sing the text with T's help.
10. Ss sing the harmony line while T sings the melody line using solfège and then text. Switch parts.
11. T divides the class into two groups. Group A sings the harmony and group B sings the melody using solfège and then text. Switch parts.

Students need to learn that a director's gestures mean something. They need to learn to follow them in order to create the best live performance settings.

Discussion Questions

1. The goal of conducting a choir is to prepare students for several concert performances every year. Teach students their parts as quickly as possible using a CD so that you can work on the performance of the repertoire. Comment.
2. What is the difference between teaching and rehearsing in the choir class?
3. What are some of the key steps in developing part-work and musicianship skills in the choral rehearsal?

Ongoing Assignment

1. Select a folksong in major or a minor key. Create several arrangements of this folk song based on the part-work sequence outlined in this chapter.
2. Visit an elementary school choir and analyze the materials being used.
3. Listen to recordings of Kodály's choral repertoire for students and find performances on some of these works on YouTube. Make a list of some of the choral techniques that he uses in his compositions. Can you use these ideas to create your own arrangements of folksongs?

Bibliography

American Academy of Teachers of Singing. "Teaching Children to Sing: A Statement by the American Academy of Teachers of Singing," 2002. Retrieved from http://www.americanacademyofteachersofsinging.org.

Bárdos, L. "On Kodály's Children's Choruses. Part One." *Bulletin of the International Kodály Society*, 1979, 4(1): 32–47.

Bárdos, L. "On Kodály's Children's Choruses. Part Two." *Bulletin of the International Kodály Society*, 1979, 4(2): 36–43.

Bárdos, L. "On Kodály's Children's Choruses. Part Three." *Bulletin of the International Kodály Society*, 1980, 5(2): 44–53.

Bárdos, L. "On Kodály's Children's Choruses. Part Four." *Bulletin of the International Kodály Society*, 1981, 6(1): 27–35.

Bárdos, L. "On Kodály's Children's Choruses. Part Five." *Bulletin of the International Kodály Society*, 1981, 6(2): 26–35.

Bárdos, L. "On Kodály's Children's Choruses. Closing Part (Six)." *Bulletin of the International Kodály Society*, 1982, 7(1): 20–36.

Bartle, J. A. *Sound Advice: Becoming a Better Children's Choir Conductor*. New York: Oxford University Press, 2003.

Bertaux, B. "Suitable Choral Music Selection Criteria for Children's Chorus." *Kodály Envoy*, 1980, 6(2).

Bolkovac, Edward. "Good Intonation: Ear or Voice?" *Bulletin of the International Kodály Society*, 1998, 23(2): 21–25.

Bradford, Cynthia Bayt. "Developing a Sequential Curriculum for Middle School Choir." *Kodály Envoy*, 2005, *31*(2): 8–11.

Broeker, Angela. "An Interview with Six Successful Elementary School Choral Directors." *Choral Journal*, 2006, *46*(10): 38–48.

Brumfield, S. "Choral Arranging in the Music Classroom (You Can Do It Too!)." *Kodály Envoy*, 2006, *32*(2).

Coleman, R. "Dynamic Intensity Variations of Individual Choral Singers." *Journal of Voice*, 1994, *8*(3): 196–201.

Cox, James. "The ABC's of Choral Rehearsal Structure." *Kodály Envoy*, 1988, *15*(2): 22–26.

Darazs, A. "Developing Musicianship in Choral Rehearsals." *Kodály Envoy*, 1978, *5*(1).

Deibler, J. B. "Application of the Kodály Concept: The Children's Choir." *Kodály Envoy*, 2014, *40*(3): 15–16.

Edwards, M. "The Choral Rehearsal and the Singing Experience as a Conserving Activity." *Bulletin of the International Kodály Society*, 2003, *28*(2): 31–37.

Fenton, W. C. "Improving Choral Tone Through Solfège." *Bulletin of the International Kodály Society*, 1993, *18*(1): 33–36.

Goetze, M. "Children's Singing Voices." *Kodály Envoy*, 1981, *7*(4).

Herboly-Kocsár, Ildiká. "How to Choose Materials for Musicianship Classes in Kodály Courses." *Kodály Envoy*, 1993, *20*(1): 49–52.

Herboly-Kocsár, Ildiká. "The Kodály Concept and 20th Century Music." *Bulletin of the International Kodály Society*, 1981, *6*(1): 17–27.

Ittzés, Mihály. "Music Pedagogical Works of Kodály and Their Relation with European Art Music." *Bulletin of the International Kodály Society*, 1977, *2*: 5–12.

Ittzés, Mihály. "Zoltán Kodály Singing Exercises: A Summary." *Bulletin of the International Kodály Society*, 1995, *20*(1): 50–53.

Jaccard, Jerry. "Intonation Begins in Kindergarten: The Art and Science of Teaching Music Acoustically." *Kodály Envoy*, 2014, *40*(3): 60–67.

Kodály, Zoltán. "Children's Choirs." In *Selected Writings of Zoltán Kodály*, 1974, 119–126.

Nemes, Lászlá Norbert. "A New Generation of Hungarian Music Pedagogues in the Service of Safeguarding the Tradition of Kodály-Based Music Pedagogy in Hungary." *Bulletin of the International Kodály Society*, 2009, *34*(2): 42–46.

Pohjola, Erkki. "The Tapiola Sound and Kodály." *Bulletin of the International Kodály Society*, 1993, *18*(2): 41–50.

Rao, Doreen. "Choral Singing and Musical Experience: Developing the Artist in Every Child." *Kodály Envoy*, 1986, *12*(4): 12–19.

Sataloff, R. T., and J. Spiegel. "Laryngoscope: The Young Voice." *NATS Journal*, 1989, *45*(3): 35–37.

Szabá, Miklás. "Problems of Interpretation in Kodály's Choral Music." *Bulletin of the International Kodály Society*, 1983, *8*(1): 15–18.

Ternström, S. "Hearing Myself with the Others—Sound Levels in Choral Performance Measured with Separation of One's Own Voice from the Rest of the Choir." *Journal of Voice*, 1994, 8(4): 293–302.

Thomasson, Donna. "Younger Singers Singing on Pitch and with Tone Quality—It's Elementary!" *Choral Journal*, March 2007, 47(9): 85–87. Music Index, EBSCOhost (accessed Apr. 7, 2013).

Wicks, Darren. "Modern Vocal Pedagogy: Implications for Educators Who Employ the Kodály Concept." *Bulletin of the International Kodály Society*, 2007, 32(1): 43–51.

Chapter 10

Sequencing and Lesson Planning

> Every lesson should be built in such a way that at its end the child should feel his strength increased rather than any sense of tiredness; moreover he should look forward to the next.
>
> Zoltán Kodály, "Preface to the Volume *Musical Reading and Writing by ErzsDbet Szönyi*"

Key Questions

- How does a philosophy of music education influence individual music lessons?
- What are the key components of a lesson plan?
- What is the connection between curriculum goals, teaching strategies, and lesson plans?
- How can we musically transition between the sections of a lesson?
- How do we evaluate a lesson plan?
- How many lessons does it take to teach a specific musical concept or element?
- Why do we define musical concepts prior to teaching specific musical elements?
- Are there activities or procedures that can be consistent in every music lesson?
- What can constitute new learning in every music lesson?
- What activities can be used to practice known musical concepts and elements?
- How can practice activities be varied so that they are interesting rather than repetitive exercises or drills?
- How can a music teacher come to an understanding of how a young learner thinks?

Kodály Today

- How can a music teacher guide a student's perceptual understanding of a sound and pitch event?
- What modes of learning are necessary for students to come to an understanding of a particular musical concept or element?
- How can we adapt lesson plans to be more inclusive and meet the needs of all students?

Kodály provides a fitting comment linking artistry in music making and the importance of excellent teaching techniques: "It is not technique that is the essence of art, but the soul. As soon as the soul can communicate freely, without obstacles, a complete musical effect is created. Technique sufficient for a free manifestation of the child's soul can easily be mastered under a good leader in any school."[1] A primary objective of this text is to supply teachers with the tools to create and implement lesson plans that lead to musical artistry in every student. The lesson plans we present are a framework and should be considered as a structure into which to infuse the teacher's own artistry and creativity. With the handbooks and this publication, we have given teachers helpful tools for creating lesson plans:

1. Music curriculum for each grade. Each grade handbook includes a curriculum that focuses on developing a student's knowledge of repertoire, performance skills, critical-thinking skills, improvisation/composition skills, and listening skills to guide students in becoming informed audience members.
2. Teaching strategies for each grade. Each grade handbook includes the strategies that address music concepts and elements for that particular grade. Strategies include all the necessary steps for preparing, presenting, and practicing elements. Included in these strategies are a number of listening and sight-reading examples.
3. Unit plans for each grade. We have created individual unit plans for teaching music concepts and elements for each grade. These unit plans can be organized by month or by year depending on how often you see your classes during the week. There are about six to eight units addressed in each grade; each unit addresses a particular musical concept or element.

Unit plans have three sections. Section one gives the repertoire of songs for the entire unit. The repertoire is used to prepare and practice the musical elements in that unit. Table 10.1 is an example of section one of a unit plan.

Section two of a unit plan includes the musical skills of reading, writing, improvisation, movement, and listening addressed over the five lessons. Although there are additional musical skills, we believe that reading, writing, and improvisation anchor all other music skills addressed in lessons. For example, reading includes the skills of inner hearing, form, and memory; writing can include the skills of form, reading, and inner hearing. Table 10.2 is an example of section two of a unit plan.

Table 10.1 Song Repertoire

SONG REPERTOIRE

	Known Songs	Songs for Tuneful Singing	Songs to Review Known Rhythmic Elements	Songs to Prepare Next New Concepts: *fa*	Songs to Prepare Concepts: ♩ ♪	Creative Movement	Songs to Practice Known Elements: *la* Pentatonic Scale
Lesson 1	"Riding in the Buggy" "Chairs to Mend"	"Above the Plain"	"Canoe Song"	"Hungarian Canon"	"Liza Jane"	"Bump up Tomato" (new song)	"Land of the Silver Birch"
Lesson 2	"Come Thru 'Na Hurry" "Chairs to Mend"	"Hey, Ho, Nobody Home"	"Gallows Pole"	"Hungarian Canon"	"Liza Jane"	"John Kanaka"	"Land of the Silver Birch"
Lesson 3	"Hill and Gully Rider" "Hungarian Canon"	"Above the Plain"	"Cocky Robin"	"Redbirds and Blackbirds"	"Liza Jane"	"Rabbit and Possum"	"Land of the Silver Birch"
	Known Songs	Songs for Tuneful Singing	Songs to Review Known Rhythmic Elements	Songs to Prepare Next New Concepts: *fa*	Songs to Present Concepts: ♩♪	Creative Movement	Songs to Present Concepts: ♩♪
Lesson 4	"Riding in the Buggy" "Redbirds and Blackbirds"	"Hey, Ho, Nobody Home"	"C-Line Woman"	"Go Tell Aunt Rhody"	"Liza "Jane"	"Long Road of Iron"	"Chairs to Mend"
Lesson 5	"Weevily Wheat" "Go Tell Aunt Rhody"	"Hush-a-Bye"	"Gallows Pole"	"Whistle Daughter, Whistle"	"Liza Jane"	"John Kanaka"	"Liza Jane"

Table 10.2 Musical Skills

	Lesson 1	Lesson 2	Lesson 3	Lesson 4	Lesson 5
Reading	Ss read "Land of the Silver Birch" and additional *la* pentatonic songs with hand signs from steps, tradition notation with solfège, and then staff notation.				Ss read the rhythm of "Liza Jane" from tradition rhythm notation.
Writing		Ss write "Land of the Silver Birch" with hand signs from steps, traditional notation with solfège, and then staff notation.			Ss write the rhythm of "Liza Jane" using tradition rhythm notation.
Improvisation			T sings a question phrase written on the board; Ss sing an answer phrase that ends on *low la*.		
Movement	"Bump up Tomato" or "John Kanaka"	"John Kanaka"	"Rabbit and the Possum"	"Long Road of Iron"	"John Kanaka"
Listening	Béla Bartók (1881–1945) "Evening in the Village," from *Hungarian Sketches*				

Section three of the unit plan is a sequence of five individual lesson plans that guide teachers to prepare new musical elements, practice known elements, and carefully present the new element by both labeling the sound and presenting the notation. The five lesson plans are designed to allow students to engage and explore music literature and build on these experiences to learn musical concepts and elements, always within the context of performance. The outcomes for all five lessons are derived from activities suggested in the teaching strategies (Chapter 6).

Note that although the first three lessons focus on preparing the new element by developing kinesthetic, then aural, and then visual awareness, we are also practicing known musical elements through reading, writing, and improvisation activities. Table 10.3 is a simple chart that correlates lesson plans with the Houlahan and Tacka model of learning and instruction.

Table 10.3   Learning Phase and Lesson Plans

Learning Phase	Lesson Plan
Cognitive phase of learning for new element and the assimilative phase of learning for known concept	Lesson 1: kinesthetic preparation of a new element and practice of reading with known element (preparation/practice lesson)
	Lesson 2: aural awareness of a new element and practice of writing with known elements (preparation/practice lesson)
	Lesson 3: visual awareness of a new element and practice of improvisation with known lesson (preparation/practice lesson)
Associative phase of learning for new element	Lesson 4: presentation of syllables for a new element (preparation lesson) Lesson 5: presentation of how to notate a new element (preparation lesson)
Assimilative phase of learning for the new element (this now is labeled familiar element)	This becomes the practice segment of lesson 1 of the next element to be taught (preparation/practice lesson)

Lesson Plans and Learning Outcomes

The accompanying handbooks to *Kodály Today* furnish teachers with lesson plans for each grade. Every lesson plan has one or two stated outcomes. A preparation and practice outcome is stated in each of the three preparation/practice lessons; a presentation outcome is stated for each of the two for the presentation lessons. Depending on your teaching situation, the outcomes need to be restated or reframed as behavioral objectives. In both cases, the statement must address what the student will be able to do. Creating and planning outcomes is fundamental to successful music learning in every lesson. The stated outcome describes student activities that advance learning. We suggest that teachers include the outcomes as well as the behavioral objectives for every lesson. Outcomes should be stated specifically; each outcome needs a focus. In a series of music lessons, there should be outcomes for performance (singing, moving, and playing instruments), conducting, developing critical thinking skills through music literacy, improvisation/composition, and listening. Of course, the teacher will take every opportunity to develop all skill areas.

The more specifically the outcomes are stated, the easier it is for teachers to devise questions that prompt students' participation in the learning activities and the development of cognitive skills. Here is a list of sample general outcomes that the teacher may use or modify when writing lesson plans. The goal of these examples is to give teachers a list of outcomes that delineate student learning in the classroom.

- Memorize repertoire.
- Tunefully sing while performing the beat.
- Inner-hear known songs, and rhythmic and melodic motifs.
- Sing selected songs and clap the rhythm.
- Sing selected songs and point to the melodic contour.
- Aurally identify the beat on which a new rhythmic sound occurs.
- Aurally identify the beat on which a new melodic pitch occurs.
- Create a visual representation of a target phrase containing the new element.
- Label a rhythmic motif with rhythm syllables.
- Label a melodic motif with solfège syllables and hand signs.
- Write known rhythms using stick notation.
- Write rhythmic motifs of known songs with traditional notation.
- Write rhythmic motifs of unknown songs with stick notation.
- Write rhythmic motifs of unknown songs with traditional notation.
- Write melodic motifs of known songs using traditional rhythmic notation with solfège syllables beneath or on the staff.
- Write melodic motifs of unknown songs using traditional rhythmic notation with solfège syllables beneath or using staff notation.
- Sing selected songs using rhythm syllables.
- Sing selected songs using solfège syllables and hand signs.
- Read the rhythm of known songs written in traditional rhythmic notation with rhythm syllables.
- Read the melody of known songs written in traditional notation with solfège syllables beneath as well as staff notation using solfège syllables and hand signs.
- Read new songs written in traditional notation with solfège syllables beneath as well as staff notation with solfège syllables and hand signs.

- Improvise/compose music with the newly learned musical element to a given form.
- Improvise/compose an ostinato using the new element to accompany a known song.
- Improvise/compose a new ostinato and play it on a classroom instrument to accompany a known song.
- Improvise/compose new words to a known song.
- Create a new melody for a known song text.
- Identify known rhythmic or melodic elements in listening examples.
- Identify the form of known and unknown music compositions.
- Memorize rhythmic or melodic motifs.
- Memorize unison melodies.
- Memorize two-part examples.
- Develop part-work skills.
- Identify known rhythmic and melodic elements in a listening example.
- Identify the form of a listening example.

Lesson Plans for the Cognitive Phase of Instruction and Learning

The goal of the cognitive phase of learning and instruction is to prepare students to recognize patterns encountered in their song repertoire. At the same time, vocal production and musicianship skills are developed. The cognitive phase of instruction addresses three modes of learning:

1. Developing kinesthetic awareness, that is, internalizing music through kinesthetic activities
2. Developing aural awareness, or analyzing what you hear
3. Developing visual awareness, or constructing a representation from memory

The cognitive phase of instruction and learning cannot be rushed; time invested in the preparation of every concept and element through all the modalities of learning will help avoid confusion.

The Preparation/Practice Lessons

The goal of preparation/practice lessons is to prepare a new concept and element and practice known musical elements. That is to say, each preparation lesson has an instructional context (preparation) and a reinforcement context (practice). This dual structure and focus gives students time to process their kinesthetic, aural, and visual understandings of the new concept, while creating opportunities to further enhance their musical skills by practicing previously learned musical elements. In Chapter 7 we defined the three primary musical skill areas as reading, writing, and improvisation and showed how

Kodály Today

they were related to all other musical skills. These three skills become the focal points for the practice segment of the preparation/practice lessons. There are three preparation/practice lesson plans in the cognitive phase:

1. Lesson 1 centers on kinesthetic awareness of a new melodic or rhythmic concept and practice of known melodic or rhythmic elements through reading. We try to connect the reading activity to a listening example.
2. Lesson 2 develops the students' aural awareness by directing them to answer questions about the new melodic or rhythmic concept, and in the second portion, to practice known melodic or rhythmic elements through writing.
3. Lesson 3 is an assessment of the students' visual awareness of a new melodic or rhythmic concept, and in the second portion, practice of known melodic or rhythmic elements through improvisation and composition.

Lesson 1: Developing Kinesthetic Awareness of a New Concept and Practicing Known Elements Through Reading

During a kinesthetic preparation/practice lesson, the instructor reviews several songs containing the new element in a variety of patterns for students in a stylistically appropriate manner. Although several songs are performed, one song with one particular phrase is selected to focus the students' attention on the new musical element. The teacher models a kinesthetic motion that focuses the students' attention on the new element, and the students respond in the same way. This is a fixed opportunity for students to interact with the musical element and it also gives the teacher a chance to observe student interaction. Movement enhances the performance (e.g., clapping the rhythm or clapping showing a melodic contour, or by pointing to icons on the board). The teacher should guide students through these kinesthetic activities until they can sing and perform independently.

During the practice section of the lesson, the instructor reinforces and further develops the students' understanding of previously learned musical elements through a reading activity. This reading practice section may also include assessment activities to help the teacher identify which students require additional help.

Here are sample lesson outcomes for developing kinesthetic awareness of a new rhythmic or melodic concept and practicing known rhythmic or melodic concept through reading. The outcomes (of the kinesthetic preparation/practice lesson) need to be customized by relating them to specific songs. (For the sake of clarity, not all of the music skills outcomes are listed here.)

Lesson Outcomes
1. Outcomes for performance
   A. Students will review known repertoire through singing, playing on instruments, movement, and conducting.
   B. Students will develop tuneful singing skills focusing on breathing, tone production, diction, and expression.

2. Outcomes for performance and demonstration of musical concepts and elements
   A. Students will review known rhythmic or melodic elements.
   B. Students will demonstrate their understanding of a new rhythmic or melodic concept kinesthetically:
      i. Singing and keeping a beat
      ii. Singing and clapping the rhythm
      iii. Singing and pointing to a representation of new rhythmic or melodic concept in a four- or eight-beat target pattern and a related pattern
      iv. Singing and performing beat and rhythm simultaneously, or, for melodic concepts, singing with rhythm syllables while clapping the melodic contour
3. Outcomes for learning new repertoire
   A. Students will learn a new song or game to broaden their song repertoire.
   B. Students will learn a new song that will be used to teach rhythmic and melodic concepts.
4. Outcomes for movement development
   A. Students will practice the movement skill of _____ while playing the singing game.
   B. Students will create a new movement activity to a known song.
   C. Students will create a new melody for a singing game.
   D. Students will create a rhythmic or melodic accompaniment for a known singing game.
5. Outcomes for musical skill development
   A. Students will practice reading rhythmic or melodic elements using syllables, rhythmic notation with solfège syllables written beneath, or staff notation.
   B. Students will sight-read an unknown melody containing familiar rhythmic and melodic elements.
   C. Students will sight-read an unknown melody of a piece of art music containing familiar rhythmic and melodic elements.
   D. Students will identify the form of the reading example.
   E. Students will memorize the reading example.
   F. Students will develop their inner hearing skills.
   G. Students will develop their part work skills.

When placed in a lesson plan, these activities will take the format seen in Table 10.4.

Lesson 2: Developing Aural Awareness of a New Element and Practicing Known Elements Through Writing

During this lesson, students construct an aural understanding of the new musical element. The goal is to aurally identify and describe the new musical concept and distinguish it from familiar ones. Aural awareness depends on information students gained

Kodály Today

Table 10.4 Lesson 1, Preparation/Practice Lesson

Outcome	Preparation: internalize two sounds on one beat, the first long and the second short, through kinesthetic activities.
	Practice: reading melodic patterns that include *low ti*.
INTRODUCTORY ACTIVITIES	
Warm-up	• Body warm-up
	• Beat activity
	Symphony No. 4 in A, "Italian," first movement, "Allegro vivace," by Felix Mendelssohn (1809–1847)
	• **Breathing:** **Ss** practice blowing a balloon and watch how air is released when deflating the balloon.
	• **Resonance:** explore a cow sound using low and high voices. Make sure **Ss** are inhaling and exhaling correctly with the support muscles.
	• **Posture:** remind **Ss** of the correct posture for singing.
Sing known songs	"Oh How Lovely Is the Evening"
	CSP: E
	• **Ss** sing the song in canon.
	"Michael, Row the Boat Ashore"
	CSP: E
	• **T** and **S** sing the song and keep the beat.
Develop tuneful singing Tone production Diction Expression	"Sail Away, Ladies"
	CSP: G-sharp
	• Sirens. **Ss** imitate the sound of a siren with the voice. Challenge them to make soft and loud, high and low, long and short sirens, and sirens that ascend, descend, or do both.
	• **Ss** pretend to fall off a cliff and say "aaaahhhhhhhhhh!"
	• **T** tosses a ball from one **S** to another, and they follow the movement of the ball with their voices.
	• **Ss** sing the song.
	• **T** directs one group of **Ss** to chant "sail away" ($\frac{2}{4}$ ♩♫ :||) on *do* while another group sings the song. Switch.
	Kodály Choral Library, *Let Us Sing Correctly*: select exercises that use the solfège syllable *ti* in introduction of the volume.

(*continued*)

Sequencing and Lesson Planning

Table 10.4   Continued

Review known songs and rhythmic elements	"Autumn Canon" CSP: E • **Ss** sing the song. • **Ss** sing with rhythm syllables and clap the contour of the melody. • **Ss** sing in canon with rhythm syllables. • **T** sings each phrase of "Weevily Wheat," "Riding in a Buggy," "Come Thru 'Na Hurry," and "Hill and Gully Rider"; **Ss** echo-sing each phrase singing with rhythm syllables while tapping the beat both as a class and individually.
CORE ACTIVITIES	
Teach a new song	"Wake Up! Canon" CSP: B • **T** sings the song. • With each repetition, **T** discloses the rhythm of another phrase until **Ss** are singing the song completely with rhythm syllables. • **Ss** sing in canon with **T**. • **Ss** sing the song in two-part canon with one another.
Develop knowledge of musical literacy concepts Internalize music through kinesthetic activities	"Donkey Riding" CSP: D • **Ss** sing the song and continue the ostinato. • **Ss** sing the song while clapping the rhythm and stepping the beat. • **Ss** sing the song and keep the beat for phrase 1. • **Ss** sing the song and clap the rhythm of phrase 1. • **Ss** sing and point to a representation of phrase 1. ——————— • Half the class keeps the beat, and the half other clap the rhythm of phrase 1. Switch. • Six to eight **Ss** come to the board to tap the rhythm of phrase 1.
Creative movement	"Zudio" CSP: D • *Note: this will be a new song.* • **T** sings the song as **Ss** continue the beat. • **T** sings while **Ss** find a partner and move into a double line. • **T** sings and demonstrates the game. • **Ss** play while **T** sings. • After two or three cycles, **Ss** must sing with **T** in order to continue the game. • **Ss** sing the song and move to board.

(continued)

Kodály Today

Table 10.4 Continued

Practice music performance and literacy skills Reading	"The Birch Tree" CSP: A • **Ss** sing the song. • **Ss** read the song from the tone ladder. • **Ss** read the song from standard rhythmic notation. • **Ss** read the song from staff notation. • **T** adds two measures of rest at the end of each phrase. **Ss** read the changes.
	• **T** modifies phrase 1, and **Ss** read the changes (shown here in rhythmic notation): $\frac{2}{4}$ ♫ ♫ | ♫ ♩ | ♫ ♫ | ♩ ♩ | dd t,t, l,l,l, dd t,t, l, t, ♫ ♫ | ♫ ♫ | ♩ ♩ | 𝄽 𝄽 | mmsm rr dd t, l, ♩. ♪ | ♩ ♫ | ♩ ♩ | 𝄽 𝄽 | t, d r dd t, l, ♩. ♪ | ♩ ♫ | ♩ ♩ | 𝄽 𝄽 ‖ t, d r dd t, l, • **T** modifies phrase 2. **Ss** read the changes: $\frac{2}{4}$ ♫ ♫ | ♫ ♩ | ♫ ♫ | ♩ ♩ | ddt,t, l,l,l, ddt,t, l, t, ♫ ♩ | ♫ ♩ | ♫ ♫ | ♩ ♩ | drm drm mrd t, l, l, ♩. ♪ | ♩ ♫ | ♩ ♩ | 𝄽 𝄽 | t, d r dd t, l, ♩. ♪ | ♩ ♫ | ♩ ♩ | 𝄽 𝄽 ‖ t, d r dd t, l, • **T** copies the second phrase into the third and erases phrase 4: $\frac{2}{4}$ ♫ ♫ | ♫ ♩ | ♫ ♫ | ♩ ♩ | ddt,t, l,l,l, ddt,t, l, t, ♫ ♩ | ♫ ♩ | ♫ ♫ | ♩ ♩ | drm drm mrd t, l, l, ♫ ♩ | ♫ ♩ | ♫ ♫ | ♩ ♩ | drm drm mrd t, l, l, • **Ss** listen to "Children's Games," from *For Children*, vol. 1, no. 8, by Béla Bartók (1881–1945) and identify the "A" and "B" sections in the music. **Ss** then sing the sections they recognize with the recording.

(continued)

Table 10.4 Continued

SUMMARY ACTIVITIES	
Review lesson outcomes Review the new song	"Wake Up! Canon" CSP: B • Ss sing in canon with T.

through their kinesthetic activities in the previous lesson. Questions need to be formulated that focus their attention on the attributes of the phrase that contains the new musical element.

The practice activities in an aural preparation lesson address the skill of writing. The practice section of the lesson may also be thought of as an assessment activity to help the instructor identify students who require extra help in learning a particular concept.

Here are sample lesson outcomes for developing aural awareness of a new rhythmic or melodic concept and practicing known rhythmic or melodic concepts through writing. The outcomes (for the aural preparation/practice lesson plan) need to be customized by relating them to specific songs and phrases.

Lesson Outcomes
1. Outcomes for performance
   A. Students will review known repertoire through singing, playing on instruments, movement, and conducting.
   B. Students will develop tuneful singing skills focusing on breathing, tone production, diction, and expression.
2. Outcomes for performance of demonstration of musical concepts and elements
   A. Students will review known rhythmic or melodic elements.
   B. Students will demonstrate their understanding of a new rhythmic or melodic concept aurally:
      i. Sing and keep a beat
      ii. Sing and clap the rhythm
      iii. Sing and point to a representation of new rhythmic or melodic element in a four- or eight-beat target pattern and related pattern
      iv. Sing and perform beat and rhythm simultaneously, or, for melodic concepts, singing with rhythm syllables while clapping the melodic contour
      v. Verbally describe the characteristics of the new concept and element
3. Outcomes for learning new repertoire
   A. Students will learn a new song or game to expand their knowledge of repertoire.
   B. Students will learn a new song that will later be used to teach rhythmic and melodic concepts.

4. Outcomes for movement development
   A. Students will practice the movement skill of _____ while playing the singing game.
   B. Students will create a new movement activity to a known song.
   C. Students will create a new melody for a singing game.
   D. Students will create a rhythmic or melodic accompaniment for a known singing game.
5. Outcomes for musical skill development
   A. Students will write the rhythm of a known melody containing familiar rhythmic elements with traditional rhythmic notation.
   B. Students will write the rhythm of an unknown melody containing familiar rhythmic elements with traditional rhythmic notation.
   C. Students will write a known melody or phrase containing familiar rhythmic and melodic elements with traditional notation and solfège or on the staff.
   D. Students will write an unknown melody or phrase containing familiar rhythmic and melodic elements with traditional notation and solfège or on the staff.
   E. Students will identify the form of the writing example.
   F Students will memorize the writing example.
   G. Students will develop their inner hearing skills.
   H. Students will develop their part work skills.

When placed in a lesson plan, these activities will take the format seen in Table 10.5.

Table 10.5 Unit 8, Dotted Eighth and Sixteenth Note, Lesson 2

Outcome	Preparation: analyze repertoire that contains two sounds on one beat, the first being long and the second short.
	Practice: write a six-beat melody containing *low ti*.
INTRODUCTORY ACTIVITIES	
Warm-up	• Body warm-up • Beat activity "Hoedown," from *Rodeo*, by Aaron Copland (1900–1990) • Breathing: **Ss** practice blowing a balloon and watch how air is released when deflating the balloon. • Resonance: explore a cow sound using low and high voices. Make sure **Ss** are inhaling and exhaling correctly with the support muscles. • Posture: remind **Ss** of the correct posture for singing.

(*continued*)

Table 10.5 Continued

Sing known songs	"Rise Up, Oh Flame" CSP: D • **Ss** sing the song and keep the beat. • **Ss** sing the song in canon. "Wake Up! Canon" CSP: A • **Ss** sing the song in two- and three-part canon.
Develop tuneful singing Tone production Diction Expression	"Sourwood Mountain" CSP: G-sharp • **Ss** sing the song in canon after four beats. • **Ss** sing using voiced consonants: b, d, g, and J using rhythm patterns of "Sourwood Mountain" Kodály Choral Library, *Let Us Sing Correctly*: select from exercises that use the solfège syllable *ti* in the introduction of the volume.
Review known songs and rhythmic elements	"Viva Viva la Musica!" CSP: B • **Ss** sing the song. • **Ss** sing the song in canon. • **Ss** sing the song with rhythm syllables. • **T** sings each phrase; **Ss** echo-sing each phrase singing with rhythm syllables while tapping the beat both as a class and individually.
CORE ACTIVITIES	
Teach a new song	"Alleluia" CSP: D • **T** sings song. • **Ss** discover the form. • **Ss** read the rhythm as **T** sings song. • **Ss** sing the song without assistance. • **T** and **Ss** sing the song in canon. • **Ss** sing the song in canon with each other after four beats.
Develop knowledge of musical literacy concepts	"Donkey Riding" CSP: D • **Ss** sing "Donkey Riding." • Review kinesthetic awareness activities.

(*continued*)

Kodály Today

Table 10.5 Continued

Describe what you hear	T and Ss sing phrase 1 on "loo" and keep the beat before asking each of these questions: • T: "Andy, how many beats did we keep in phrase 1?" (eight) • T: "Andy, which beats have one sound?" (4 and 8) • T: "Andy, how many sounds did we sing on beat 1?" (two) • T: "Andy, are the two sounds on beat 1 even or uneven?" (uneven) • T: "Andy, describe the sounds on beat 1." (the first is long and the second is short) • T: "Sing this phrase with 'long' and 'short' for beat 1 and rhythm syllables for all the rest." (*long-short tadi tadi ta tadi tadi tadi ta*) • Ss step the beat and sing the rhythm syllables of phrase 1, with "long" and "short" for beat 1.
Creative movement	"Circle 'Round the Zero" CSP: F-sharp • Ss sing the song and play the game. • Compose a rhythmic ostinato for a percussion instrument. • Compose a melodic ostinato for a pitched instrument. • Create a new game movement. • Create a new text.
Practice music performance and literacy skills Writing	"The Birch Tree" CSP: A • Ss sing the song. • Ss sing phrase 1 with solfège syllables and hand signs. • Ss write in the solfège syllables for phrase 1 under standard rhythmic notation. • Ss write the tone set for phrase 1 of the song on the staff in A = *la* and D = *la*. • Ss write the tone set for phrase 1 of the song on the staff in E = *la*. T sings the tone set as is and Ss identify that the "F" sounds incorrect. The interval between E and F is a small step or minor second; it should be a major second. T introduces the sharp sign and the letter name for F-sharp. Students read the melody from the staff where E = *la* with solfège syllables and hand signs, and then with letter names and hand signs. • Ss sing the song in canon with letter names. • Ss create ostinato on xylophones to accompany any or all of these songs.

(*continued*)

Table 10.5 Continued

	SUMMARY ACTIVITIES
Review lesson outcomes Review the new song	"Alleluia" CSP: D • T and Ss sing the song in canon.

Lesson 3: Developing Visual Awareness of an Element and Practicing Known Elements Through Improvisation and Composition

In the context of the Houlahan and Tacka model of learning and instruction, "visual" means that the students show the teacher their understanding of the new musical element by creating a visual representation. This representation is based on information learned from the kinesthetic and aural awareness stages, as well as from their intuitive knowledge. By following these three stages of instruction (kinesthetic, then aural, and then visual), we find that perception leads to conceptual information and ultimately to musical understanding. By connecting the aural stage to the visual stage, the students are allowed time to make the connection between what they hear and how to represent it. After this beginning "visual" portion of the lesson, the practice activities in the subsequent portion of the lesson plan focus on improvisation/composition. The practice section of the lesson may also include assessment activities to help the teacher identify students who require extra help.

Here are sample lesson outcomes for developing visual awareness of a new rhythmic or melodic concept and practicing known rhythmic or melodic concepts through improvisation and composition. As with the other lessons, these outcomes (for the visual preparation/practice lesson plan) need to be customized by relating them to specific songs and phrases. (For purposes of clarity, not all music skill outcomes are listed.)

Lesson Outcomes
1. Outcomes for performance
    A. Students will review known repertoire through singing, playing on instruments, movement, and conducting.
    B. Students will develop tuneful singing skills focusing on breathing, tone production, diction, and expression.
2. Outcomes for performance and demonstration of musical concepts and elements
    A. Students will review known rhythmic or melodic elements.
    B. Students will demonstrate their understanding of a new rhythmic or melodic concept visually by
        i. Singing and keeping a beat
        ii. Singing and clapping the rhythm
        iii. Singing and pointing to a representation of a new rhythmic or melodic element in a four-beat target pattern and in related patterns.

Kodály Today

     iv. Singing and performing beat and rhythm simultaneously, or, for melodic concepts, singing with rhythm syllables while clapping the melodic contour
     v. Verbally describing the characteristics of the new concept
     vi. Creating a visual representation of the target pattern
3. Outcomes for learning new repertoire
   A. Students will learn a new song or game to broaden their knowledge of repertoire.
   B. Students will learn a new song that will later be used to teach rhythmic and melodic concepts.
4. Outcomes for movement development
   A. Students will practice the movement skill of _____ while playing the singing game.
   B. Students will create a new movement activity to a known song.
   C. Students will create a new melody for the text of a singing game.
   D. Students will create a rhythmic or melodic accompaniment for a known singing game.
5. Outcomes for musical skill development
   A. Students will practice reading rhythmic or melodic elements using syllables, rhythmic notation, rhythmic notation with solfège syllables written beneath, or staff notation.
   B. Students will improvise a melody aurally containing familiar rhythmic and melodic elements.
   C. Students will improvise a melody visually containing familiar rhythmic and melodic elements.

When placed in a lesson plan, these activities will take the format seen in Table 10.6.

Table 10.6   Unit 8, Dotted Eighth and Sixteenth Note, Lesson 3

Outcome	Preparation: create a visual representation of two sounds on one beat, the first being long and the second being short.
	Practice: improvise a six-beat melody containing *low ti*.
INTRODUCTORY ACTIVITIES	
Warm-up	• Body warm-up • Beat activity "Hoedown," from *Rodeo*, by Aaron Copland (1900–1990) • Breathing: **Ss** practice blowing a balloon and watch how air is released when deflating the balloon. • Resonance: explore a cow sound using low and high voices. Make sure **Ss** are inhaling and exhaling correctly with the support muscles. • Posture: remind **Ss** of the correct posture for singing.

(continued)

Table 10.6 Continued

Sing known songs	"Pretty Saro" CSP: C • **Ss** sing and conduct the beat. "Alleluia" CSP: D • **Ss** sing the song; **Ss** sing the song in canon.

Develop tuneful singing
Tone production
Diction
Expression
	"Shady Grove"
	CSP: E
	• **Ss** sing the song.
	• **Ss** sing the song on the syllable "koo."
	• **Ss** read from **T**'s hand signs.
	$\frac{4}{4}$ ♩ ♩ ♩ ♩ | ♩ ♩ ♩ 𝄽 :|
	   r d r m r d r
	• **T** directs part of the class to sing the melodic motif as an accompaniment while the remainder sing the song. Switch.
	• **T** renames the solfège syllables (*re = low la*) and **Ss** sing from **T**'s hand signs:
	$\frac{4}{4}$ ♩ ♩ ♩ ♩ | ♩ ♩ ♩ 𝄽 :|
	   l, s, l, t, l, s, l,
	• **Ss** sing the song again slowly, while keeping the beat.
	Kodály Choral Library, *Let Us Sing Correctly*: select from exercises that use the solfège syllable *ti* in the introduction of the volume.

Review known songs and rhythmic elements	"The Birch Tree" CSP: A • **T** sings the song while **Ss** continue the melodic ostinato. • **Ss** sing the song with rhythm syllables. • **T** sings each phrase of the song and **Ss** echo-sing with rhythm syllables both as a class and individually. • **T** sings each phrase of "Weevily Wheat," "Riding in a Buggy," "Come Thru 'Na Hurry," and "Hill and Gully Rider"; **Ss** echo-sing each phrase singing with rhythm syllables while tapping the beat both as a class and individually.

(continued)

Table 10.6 Continued

CORE ACTIVITIES	

Teach a new song	"Johnny Has Gone for a Soldier"
	CSP: D
	• T sings the song and accompanies on an instrument.
	• Ss read from T's hand signs:
	$\frac{4}{4}$ ♩ ♩ | ♩ ♩ |
	    l m l m
	♩ ♩ | ♩ ♩ |
	    s m s m
	♩ ♩ | ♩ ♩ |
	    l m l m
	♩ ♩ | ♩ - ‖
	    l s m
	• Ss hum the melodic motif from the board as T sings the song again. Ss may also transfer the ostinato to instruments.
	• T sings the first verse while Ss continue the melodic motif
	• Ss label the form of the song. (ABCD)
	• Ss sing when ready.

Develop knowledge of musical literacy concepts Create a visual representation of what you heard	"Donkey Riding" CSP: D • Ss sing the song. • Review kinesthetic and aural awareness activities. • Ss use manipulatives to create a representation of the rhythm of the target phrase. • Ss share their representations with each other. • T invites one S to the board to share a representation with the class. If necessary, corrections can be made by reviewing aural awareness questions. • Ss sing the target phrase and point to the representation. • Ss identify all known elements in the song and place them on the board.
Creative movement	"Mamalama" CSP: G • *Note: this will be a new song.* • T sings each phrase; Ss echo. • T demonstrates how to play the game. • T and Ss sing and play the game.

(continued)

Table 10.6 Continued

Practice music performance and literacy skills
Improvisation
	"The Birch Tree"
	CSP: A
	• Ss sing the song.
	• Ss read the song from staff notation.
	• Ss identify the tone set of phrase 1. (*low la low ti do re mi*)
	• Ss sing a *la* pentachord from low to high to low.
	• T writes a four beat melody on the board using notes from the *la* pentachord. Ss read:
	$\frac{2}{4}$ ♫♫ | ♩ ♩ ‖
	  l,t,dr m m
	• T writes the pitches backwards. Ss read:
	$\frac{2}{4}$ ♫♫ | ♩ ♩ ‖
	  mrdt, l, l,
	• T writes two additional melodies for Ss to read:
	$\frac{2}{4}$ ♫♫ | ♩ ♩ ‖
	  l,t,d t, l, l,
	$\frac{2}{4}$ ♫♫ | ♩ ♩ ‖
	  rrdd t, l,
	• T uses the first melody as a "question" and Ss sing any of the remaining three as an "answer."
	• Ss may also create their own melody using notes from the *la* pentachord as an answer.
	• Ss perform their answers on xylophones.
	• Ss create their own compositions by putting several of their improvisations together.

SUMMARY ACTIVITIES	
Review lesson outcomes Review the new song	"Johnny Has Gone for a Soldier" CSP: D • Ss sing song • T and Ss sing the song as T plays the second part on the piano from the two-part arrangement of the song by Denise Bacon, *46 Two-Part American Folk Songs* p. 61.

Lesson Plans for the Associative Phase of Learning and Instruction

Lessons four and five are the two presentation lessons in the associative phase. The goal of the first presentation lesson (number four) is to label the new sound with rhythm syllables or the new pitch with solfège syllables. The goal of the second presentation lesson (five) is to present the notation for the new element. Here are sample outcomes for the first presentation lesson plan. As with the previous lessons, the outcomes (for the first presentation lesson plan) may need to be somewhat customized to relate them to specific songs and phrases.

Lesson 4: Labeling the Sound of the New Melodic or Rhythmic Element

Lesson Outcomes
1. Outcomes for performance
    A. Students will review known repertoire through singing, playing on instruments, movement, and conducting.
    B. Students will develop tuneful singing skills focusing on breathing, tone production, diction, and expression.
2. Outcomes for performance and demonstration of musical concepts and elements
    A. Students will review known rhythmic or melodic elements.
    B. Students will demonstrate their kinesthetic, aural, and visual understanding of a new musical element.
    C. Students will sing the new sound with rhythm syllables.
    D. Students will sing the new pitch with solfège syllables and hand signs. The teacher names the new rhythm syllables aurally or sings the new solfège syllable and shows the hand signs for the new melodic element in the target pattern (no visual).
3. Outcomes for learning new repertoire
    A. Students will learn a new song or game to broaden their knowledge of repertoire.
    B. Students will learn a new song that will be used to teach rhythmic and melodic concepts.
4. Outcomes for movement development
    A. Students will practice the movement skill of _____ while playing the singing game.
    B. Students will create a new movement activity to a known song.
    C. Students will create a new melody for a singing game.
    D. Students will create a rhythmic or melodic accompaniment for a known singing game.

When placed in a lesson plan, these activities will take the format seen in Table 10.7.

Sequencing and Lesson Planning

Table 10.7 Unit 8, Dotted Eighth and Sixteenth Note, Lesson 4

Outcome	Presentation: label two sounds on one beat, the first being long and the second short, with rhythm syllables (*ta---mi*)
INTRODUCTORY ACTIVITIES	
Warm-up	• Body warm-up • Beat activity
	"Andante," Piano Concerto No. 21, W. A. Mozart (1756–1791) • Breathing: **Ss** practice blowing a balloon and watch how air is released when deflating the balloon. • Resonance: explore a cow sound using low and high voices. Make sure **Ss** are inhaling and exhaling correctly with the support muscles. • Posture: remind **Ss** of the correct posture for singing.
Sing known songs	"Coffee Canon" CSP: C • **Ss** sing the song and conduct; **Ss** sing in canon. "Johnny Has Gone for a Soldier" CSP: D • **Ss** sing the song. • Individual **Ss** sing verses of song.
Develop tuneful singing Tone production Diction Expression	"Michael, Row the Boat Ashore" CSP: D • **Ss** sing the song; **Ss** sing and conduct. • **Ss** sing with solfège syllables reading from **T**'s hand signs. • **Ss** hum the song. • **Ss** sing song with lip trills. Kodály Choral Library, *Let Us Sing Correctly*: select from the exercises that use the solfège syllable *ti* in the introduction of the volume.
Review known songs and rhythmic elements	"John Kanaka" CSP: D • **Ss** sing the song. • **Ss** sing song with rhythm syllables. • **T** sings each phrase; **Ss** echo-sing each phrase with rhythm syllables while tapping the beat.

(continued)

Table 10.7 Continued

	CORE ACTIVITIES
Teach a new song	"Alphabet Song" CSP: D • **T** sings the song and **Ss** identify the meter. • **Ss** conduct while **T** sings the song. • **Ss** identify the form of the song. (ABCD) • **Ss** sing all phrases of the song with assistance from **T**.
Presentation of music literacy concepts Describe what you hear with rhythm syllables	"Donkey Riding" CSP: D • **Ss** sing the song. • Review kinesthetic, aural, and visual awareness activities. • **T**: "We call two uneven sounds on one beat where the first is long and the second is short *ta---mi*." • **T** sings the first phrase using rhythm syllables. **Ss** echo. • **T** sings the first phrase to six or eight **Ss**; **Ss** echo-sing the target phrase with rhythm syllables. • **Ss** step the beat and sing the entire song with rhythm syllables.
Creative movement	"Zudio" CSP: D • **Ss** sing and play the game. • Compose a rhythmic ostinato for a percussion instrument. • Compose a melodic ostinato for a pitched instrument. • Create a new game movement. • Create a new text.

Presentation of music literacy concepts
 	
Describe what you hear with rhythm syllables
	"London Bridge Is Falling Down"
	CSP: S
	• **Ss** sing the song.
	• **Ss** sing phrase 1 with rhythm syllables.
	• **Ss** sing the entire song with rhythm syllables.
	• **Ss** connect new learning to related song material. **T** sings individual phrases from the following songs with text; **Ss** echo-sing with rhythm syllables while tapping the beat both as a class and individually.
	  ○ "Sail Away, Ladies"
	  ○ "Sourwood Mountain"
	  ○ "Shady Grove"
	  ○ "Michael, Row the Boat Ashore"

(*continued*)

Table 10.7 Continued

	SUMMARY ACTIVITIES
Review lesson outcomes	"Alphabet Song"
	CSP: D
Review the new song	• **Ss** sing the song and conduct.

Lesson 5: Presenting the Notation

Here are sample outcomes for lesson five, the second presentation lesson plan. They need to be customized by relating them to specific songs and phrases.

Lesson Outcomes
1. Outcomes for performance
   A. Students will review known repertoire through singing, playing on instruments, movement, and conducting.
   B. Students will develop tuneful singing skills focusing on breathing, tone production, diction, and expression.
   C. Students will notate the new sound with stick notation and traditional rhythmic notation.
   D. Students will notate the new pitch with traditional rhythmic notation and solfège syllables and on the staff.
2. Outcomes for performance and demonstration of musical concepts and elements
   A. Students will review known rhythmic or melodic elements.
   B. Students will sing the target pattern and related patterns with rhythm syllables or solfège syllables and hand signs.
   C. Students will be able to notate sounds and pitches. For a rhythmic element, the teacher will present the time signature and rhythmic notation for the target pattern and related pattern. For a melodic element, the teacher will present the target pattern and related pattern on the tone ladder, rhythmic notation with solfège syllables written beneath, and the new element in the target pattern.
3. Outcomes for learning new repertoire
   A. Students will learn a new song or game to develop knowledge of repertoire.
   B. Students will learn a new song that will be used to teach rhythmic and melodic concepts.
4. Outcomes for movement development
   A. Students will practice the movement skill of _____ while playing the singing game.

Kodály Today

B. Students will create a new movement activity to a known song.
C. Students will create a new melody for the text of a singing game.
D. Students will create a rhythmic or melodic accompaniment for a known singing game to be played on classroom.

When placed in a lesson plan, these activities will take the format seen in Table 10.8.

Table 10.8 Unit 8, Dotted Eighth and Sixteenth Note, Lesson 5

Outcome	Presentation: notate two sounds on one beat, the first being long and the second being short, with a dotted eighth and sixteenth note.
INTRODUCTORY ACTIVITIES	
Warm-up	• Body warm-up • Beat activity "Allegro Adagio," *Brandenburg Concerto No. 3* in G Major, BWV 1048, by J. S. Bach (1685–1750) • Breathing: **Ss** practice blowing a balloon and watch how air is released when deflating the balloon. • Resonance: explore a cow sound using low and high voices. Make sure **Ss** are inhaling and exhaling correctly with the support muscles. • Posture: remind **Ss** of the correct posture for singing.
Sing known songs	"Oh How Lovely Is the Evening" CSP: D • **Ss** sing in canon and conduct. "Alphabet Song" CSP: D • **Ss** sing in canon and conduct.
Develop tuneful singing Tone production Diction Expression	"Shady Grove" CSP: E • **Ss** sing song. • **Ss** sing the song on a "koo" syllable while clapping the contour. • **Ss** sing song with solfège syllables reading from **T's** hand signs. Kodály Choral Library, *Let Us Sing Correctly*: select exercises that use the solfège syllable *ti* in the introduction of the volume.

(continued)

Sequencing and Lesson Planning

Table 10.8   Continued

Review known songs and rhythmic elements	"Debka Hora" CSP: D • **Ss** sing the song and continue the ostinato. • **Ss** sing with rhythm syllables and conduct. • **Ss** read the rhythm from the board with rhythm syllables and conduct. • **Ss** conduct and sing the song.
CORE ACTIVITIES	
Teach a new song	"Sweet Betsy from Pike" CSP: D • **T** sings the song and accompanies on an instrument while **Ss** listen. • **Ss** trace the phrases on the board while **T** sings the song. • **Ss** label the form of the song while **T** sings again. (ABCDD') • **T** adjusts the accompaniment pattern to fit the next song.
Presentation of music literacy concepts Notate what you hear	"Donkey Riding" CSP: D • **Ss** sing and keep the beat. • **Ss** sing song and clap rhythm. • **Ss** sing phrase 1 with rhythm syllables. • **T:** "When we have a long sound followed by a short sound on one beat, we can notate it with a dotted eighth note and one sixteenth note when the beat is a quarter note." • **T** writes the rhythm on the board. • **Ss** may practice writing dotted eighth and sixteenth notes on the board. • **Ss** read phrase 1 of the song from the board in standard rhythmic notation with rhythm syllables: $\frac{2}{4}$ ♫♫ | ♫♩ | ♫♫ | ♫♩ ‖ • **T** shows students how to read phrase 1 of the song from the board written in standard rhythmic notation with numbers for counting. **Ss** sing with numbers and conduct.
Creative movement	"Mamalama" CSP: G • **T** and **Ss** sing the song and play the game. • Compose a rhythmic ostinato for a percussion instrument. • Compose a melodic ostinato for a pitched instrument. • Create a new game movement. • Create a new text.

(continued)

Table 10.8 Continued

Presentation Notate what you hear	"London Bridge Is Falling Down" CSP: A • **Ss** sing song. • **Ss** sing song with rhythm syllables and keep the beat. • **Ss** read the rhythm of "London Bridge" from the board with rhythm syllables and conduct as well as sing using counting numbers while conducting. **Ss** write the rhythm of the first phrase on a worksheet. • **T** transforms the rhythm into other related song material: 　○ "Circle 'Round the Zero" 　○ "Michael, Row the Boat Ashore" 　○ "Shady Grove" 　○ "Sourwood Mountain" • **Ss** create an ostinato that uses a dotted eighth followed by a sixteenth note, write the pattern on the board, and perform it as an ostinato to accompany any or all of these songs.
SUMMARY ACTIVITIES	
Review lesson outcomes Review the new song	"Sweet Betsy from Pike" CSP: D • **Ss** sing song.

Assimilative Phase of Learning

The assimilative phase of learning normally takes place in the second half of the first three preparation/practice lessons of the subsequent musical element. If there is time in the teacher's schedule, some instructors add a sixth lesson, where the song repertoire and patterns from the presentation phase may be used again to reinforce the new musical element. You may want to review the practice activities in Tables 10.9, 10.10, and 10.11.

Table 10.9 is an example of a lesson plan that includes reading practice activities in the portion of the lesson plan marked "Practice Music Performance and Literacy Skills: Reading."

Table 10.10 is an example of a lesson plan that includes writing practice activities in the portion of the lesson plan marked "Practice Music Performance and Literacy Skills: Writing."

Table 10.11 is an example of a lesson plan that includes improvisation practice activities in the portion of the lesson plan marked "Practice Music Performance and Literacy Skills: Improvisation."

Sequencing and Lesson Planning

Table 10.9 Unit 2, *high ti* and Dotted Eighth Note and Sixteenth Notes, Lesson 1

Outcome	Preparation: internalize *high ti*, the major scale, through kinesthetic activities
	Practice: read four beat patterns that include dotted eighth and sixteenth notes
INTRODUCTORY ACTIVITIES	
Warm-up	"Les Toreadors," from *Carmen*, by Georges Bizet (1838–1875), Allegro • Body warm-up • Beat activity • Breathing: **Ss** practice breathing exercises. • Resonance: imitate the sound of a siren with the voice. Challenge the **Ss** to make soft and loud, high and low, long and short sirens, and sirens that just go up, just come down, or do both. • Posture: remind **Ss** about correct posture for singing.
Sing known songs	"Sail Away, Ladies" CSP: F-sharp • **Ss** sing song and keep the beat. • **T** provides an ostinato, and **Ss** sing song. • **Ss** sings song and class sings refrain.
Develop tuneful singing Tone production Diction Expression	"Johnny Has Gone for a Soldier" CSP: D • **Ss** sing song with text. • **T** introduces tempo markings, and **Ss** find the appropriate one to use for singing song. Kodály Choral Library, *Let Us Sing Correctly*: select exercises that use the solfège syllable *ti* from the introduction of the volume.
Review known songs and elements	"The Birch Tree" CSP: A • **Ss** sing the song with text. • **Ss** sing the song with solfège syllables and hand signs. • **T** sings individual phrases, and **Ss** sing with solfège syllables and hand signs both as a class and individually. • **T** sings phrases of "Alfonso Doce," "Debka Hora," "Three Rogues," "Coffee Canon," "Morning Is Come," or other known songs that use the solfège syllables *la so fa mi re do low ti low la* and *low so*; **Ss** echo-sing using solfège syllables and hand signs both as a class and individually.

(continued)

Table 10.9 Continued

CORE ACTIVITIES	
Teach a new song	"Charlotte Town" CSP: F • **Ss** sing the song with text. • **T** writes the text of the song on the board. **T** sings and **Ss** indicate the phrase marks and identify the form. • **Ss** sing the song with text. • **Ss** sing the song and play a game similar to "Come Thru 'Na Hurry" as they sing.
Develop knowledge of music literacy concepts Internalize music through kinesthetic activities	"Alleluia" CSP: D • **Ss** sing "Alleluia" with text. • **Ss** sing the second phrase and point to a representation of the melodic contour at the board. • **Ss** sing "Alleluia" and show the melodic contour of the second phrase. • **Ss** sing phrase 2 of "Alleluia" with rhythm syllables while showing the melodic contour.
Creative movement	"Rabbit and the Possum" CSP: D • **Ss** sing song and play the game. • **Ss** create their own movements to the song to reflect form. • **Ss** create their own rhythmic accompaniment to game.
Practice music performance and literacy skills Reading	"Donkey Riding" CSP: F • **Ss** sing song. • **Ss** sing song with rhythm syllables. • **Ss** read the rhythmic notation of song with rhythm syllables. • **Ss** read the rhythmic notation counting with numbers and conducting. • Make a transition in the notation of "Donkey Riding" to the theme for *Variations on a Theme, St. Anthony's Chorale by Haydn*, by Johannes Brahms (1833–1897). • **Ss** sing the "St. Anthony's Chorale" with rhythm syllables and then solfège syllables and hand signs as they listen to the recording.
SUMMARY ACTIVITIES	
Review lesson outcomes Review the new song	"Charlotte Town" CSP: F • **Ss** sing the song with text.

Table 10.10 Unit 2, *high ti* and Dotted Eighth Note and Sixteenth Notes, Lesson 2

Outcome	Preparation: internalize *high ti*, the major scale, through kinesthetic activities
	Practice: read dotted eighth and sixteenth four-beat patterns
INTRODUCTORY ACTIVITIES	
Warm-up	"Les Toreadors," from *Carmen*, by Georges Bizet (1838–1875), Allegro
	or
	T may select a contemporary composition for movement. • Body warm-up • Beat activity • Breathing: **Ss** practice breathing exercises. • Resonance: imitate the sound of a siren with the voice. Challenge the **Ss** to make soft and loud, high and low, long and short sirens, and sirens that just go up, just come down, or do both. • Posture: remind **Ss** about correct posture for singing.
Sing known songs	"Viva la Musica!" CSP: D "Charlotte Town" CSP: F • **Ss** sing song and conduct. • **Ss** sing in canon. • Two **Ss** sing in canon. • **Ss** sing song and **T** accompanies with tonic, subdominant, and dominant chord roots on a musical instrument.
Develop tuneful singing Tone production Diction Expression	"Alphabet Song" CSP: D • **T** introduces tempo markings to **Ss**; **Ss** determine the appropriate one to use for the song. Kodály Choral Library, *Let Us Sing Correctly*: select exercises that use the solfège syllable *ti* from the introduction of the volume.
Review known songs and elements	"When I First Came to This Land" CSP: F • **Ss** sing song with text. • **Ss** sing song with solfège and hand signs. • **T** sings phrases and **Ss** sing with solfège syllables and hand signs.

(*continued*)

Table 10.10 Continued

	• T sings phrases of "The Birch Tree," "Alfonso Doce," "Debka Hora," "Three Rogues," "Coffee Canon," "Morning Is Come," or other known songs that use the solfège syllables *la ss fa mi re do low ti low la* and *low so*; **Ss** echo-sing using solfège syllables and hand signs.
CORE ACTIVITIES	
Teach a new song	"Camptown Races" CSP: A • **T** sings song. • **T** sings song. **Ss** create a score indicating the meter and bar lines. • **T** sings song. **Ss** identify the form. • **T** sings song and **Ss** follow a score that includes text. • **Ss** sing song.
Develop knowledge of music literacy concepts Describe what you hear	"Alleluia" CSP: D • **Ss** sing song. • **T** assesses the kinesthetic activities with the focus song "Alleluia." Sing phrase 2 while keeping the beat before asking each question below. • **Ss** sing and determine the number of beats per phrase and the general direction of the melody.

	• **Ss** sing the second phrase on "loo" before **T** asks each of these questions:
	  • **T**: "Andy, how many beats are in the second phrase?" (eight)
	  • **T**: "Andy, what is the general direction of the melodic contour?" (it goes up)
	 • Determine the number of different pitches in the phrase:
	  • **T**: "Andy, how many different pitches did we sing?" (8)
	  • **T**: "Andy, sing the lowest note of the phrase."
	  • **T**: "Andy, which solfège syllable can we use for that pitch?" (*do*)
	  • **T**: "Andy, sing the highest note of the phrase."
	  • **T**: "Andy, which solfège syllable can we use for that pitch?" (*high do*)
	 • **T** sings the major scale on "loo" and **Ss** identify all intervals as major or minor seconds.
	 • **Ss** sing song in canon.

(continued)

Table 10.10 Continued

Creative movement	"Rabbit and the Possum" CSP: D • Ss sing song and play game. • Compose a rhythmic ostinato for a percussion instrument. • Compose a melodic ostinato for a pitched instrument. • Create a new game movement. • Create a new text.
Practice music performance and literacy skills Writing	"Donkey Riding" CSP: F • Ss sing song and conduct. • Ss sing the song with rhythm syllables and clap the rhythm. • Ss write the last phrase of the song with rhythmic notation and solfège syllables beneath. • Individual Ss sing verses of song.
SUMMARY ACTIVITIES	
Review the lesson outcomes Review the new song	"Camptown Races" CSP: A • Ss sing song.

Table 10.11 Unit 2, *high ti* and Dotted Eighth Note and Sixteenth Notes, Lesson 3

Outcome	Preparation: create a visual representation for *high ti*, major scale. Practice: improvise a four-beat rhythm using ♪♫
INTRODUCTORY ACTIVITIES	
Warm-up	"Les Toreadors," from *Carmen*, by Georges Bizet (1838–1875), Allegro or T selects a contemporary composition for movement. • Body warm-up • Beat activity • Breathing: Ss practice breathing exercises. • Resonance: imitate the sound of a siren with the voice. Challenge the Ss to make soft and loud, high and low, long and short sirens, and sirens that just go up, just come down, or do both. • Posture: remind Ss about correct posture for singing.

(*continued*)

Table 10.11 Continued

Sing known songs	"The Birch Tree" CSP: A "Camptown Races" CSP: A • **Ss** sing song. • **Ss** sing song in canon if appropriate.
Develop tuneful singing Tone production Diction Expression	"Wake Up! Canon" CSP: A • **Ss** sing song. • **Ss** practice singing a phrase of a song and **T** has them repeat it a minor second higher. Use a pure vowel sound. Each time **T** repeats, **Ss** can sing another on another vowel sound. • **T** continues to work on dynamic and tempo markings. • **Ss** hum song and **T** plays the tonic and dominant chord roots on an instrument. Kodály Choral Library, *Let Us Sing Correctly*: select from *ti* exercises in introduction of the volume.
Review known songs and elements	"Debka Hora" CSP: A • **Ss** sing. • **Ss** sing with rhythm syllables and keep the beat. • **T** claps each phrase; **Ss** echo with rhythm syllables. • **T** sings phrases of "The Birch Tree," "Alfonso Doce," "Three Rogues," "Coffee Canon," "Morning Is Come," or other known songs that use the solfège syllables *la so fa mi re do low ti low la* and *low so*; **Ss** echo-sing using solfège syllables and hand signs both as a class and individually.
	CORE ACTIVITIES
Teach a new song	"Colorado Trail" CSP: F-sharp • **T** sings song. • **Ss** identify the meter and form. • **Ss** create their own score for the music indicating the bar lines and form.

(continued)

Table 10.11 Continued

Develop knowledge of music literacy concepts Create a representation of what you hear	"Alleluia" CSP: D • **Ss** sing song. • **T** assesses kinesthetic and aural awareness by allowing the class to perform several of the kinesthetic and aural awareness activities. • **T** sings phrase 2 on a neutral syllable and asks **Ss** to create a visual representation of the melody of the target phrase. **Ss** may use manipulatives. **T**: "Pick up what you need to recreate what you heard" or "Draw what you heard." **T** assesses **Ss**' level of understanding. • **Ss** share their representations with each other. • **T** invites one **S** to the board to share a representation with the class. If necessary, corrections to the representation can be made by reviewing the aural awareness questions. Identify the meter. • **Ss** sing the second phrase of "Alleluia" with a neutral syllable and point to the representation. • **T** hums the notes of the major scale and asks **Ss** to change their visual representation to show the major and minor seconds. • **Ss** sing song in canon.
Creative movement	"Mamalama" CSP: F • Compose a rhythmic ostinato for a percussion instrument. • Compose a melodic ostinato for a pitched instrument. • Create a new game movement. • Create a new text.
Practice music performance and literacy skills Improvisation	"Donkey Riding" CSP: F • **Ss** sing song. • **T** claps a rhythmic question based on the new rhythm pattern and **Ss** provide an answer. Use rhythmic phrases of "Donkey Riding." **Ss** clap back their answer and say rhythm syllables.
	• **Ss** compose a rhythmic composition based on a given form. The A phrase can be the rhythm from the first four measures of "Donkey Riding." • **T** sings known folk song with rhythm syllables. **Ss** sing back but include a more advanced rhythmic element. For example, **T** sings "Rain, Rain" on rhythm syllables and **Ss** substitute *ta mi* for *ta di*.

(continued)

Table 10.11 Continued

SUMMARY ACTIVITIES	
Review lesson outcomes Review the new song	"Colorado Trail" CSP: F-sharp • **Ss** sing song.

Transitions in Lesson Plans

Transitions are the portion of the lessons where the students are guided to move between sections of a lesson plan. Transitions are often the cement that holds the various segments of a lesson together. Transitioning between songs and activities can become an interesting activity in itself that helps tie, and often holds, the lesson together. It can be used to move students from one activity to another in a music lesson. In this section, we present some sample transition activities that may be used to enliven a creative music lesson plan.

Transitions may be thought of as conscious and unconscious: in conscious transitions the students are aware that they are moving between songs or activities, whereas in unconscious transitions the teacher guides them to different activities. Spend time analyzing the repertoire and materials you will be using in the lesson. This will allow you to see possible connections in the repertoire. Transitions should be logical. When they are properly planned, they add the elements of surprise, creativity, and magic to a lesson. Many of the best transitions are musical; if you are transitioning into a segment of a lesson where the focus is rhythm, use a rhythmic activity such as an ostinato to move to the next segment of the lesson, and if you are transitioning into a melodic segment of the lesson, you could use a melodic ostinato to move to the next section of your lesson. Therefore we have three types of transitions.

1. Connecting several lessons
2. Connecting several sections in a lesson
3. Moving from one section of a lesson to another

Transitions That Connect Several Lessons

Here are examples of transitions that can be used over a series of lessons.

1. Teaching a new song over several lessons
   A. Sing the song as a listening activity.
   B. Discover the form of a song.
   C. Read the rhythm of the new song.
   D. Read the melody of the new song written in rhythmic notation with solfège syllables beneath.

Sequencing and Lesson Planning

   E. Read the new song from staff notation.
   F. Sing the song as a partner song with another known song.
2. Teaching a game over several lessons
   A. Sing the song as a listening activity.
   B. Memorize the song by rote.
   C. Learn the game associated with the song. This may take place over several lessons.
   D. Create a new movement to accompany the singing game.
3. Teaching a second part to a known folksong
   A. Sing and memorize a folksong.
   B. Teacher sings the second voice part to a folksong.
   C. Students learn to sing the second voice part to a folksong.
   D. Students learn to sing both voice parts.
4. Teaching a new piece of art music over several lessons
   A. Sing some themes of an art music example. Listen to these themes.
   B. Create a listening map or chart that illustrates the form of the listening example.
   C. Identify the main instruments that play in the section of music.
   D. Create a listening score for the piece of music. Remember that in the listening score you can notate the major themes and instruments. You do not have to include all measures, but indicate the measures that are not notated.

Transitions That Connect Several Segments in a Lesson

1. Story line connection
   A. Connecting lessons using a story line is most often successful in the early childhood classroom or first grade. Connections are made throughout the lessons as the teacher builds a story uniting all of the songs used during the lesson. All the songs in a lesson can be woven into the story line that connects them. For example, in grade one "Lucy Locket" might take a trip to Music Land to find her pocket. The king of Music Land is King Heart Beat, and he always walks to the beat and sings all of his songs with the beat. The queen of Music Land is the Queen of Words, and she always walks to the words. You can imagine how captivating this story becomes for students!
   B. Use songs that have the same form. When selecting songs for your lesson plans, include songs that have the same form. Students can point to a generic form map that can be used to connect several activities. For example, when teaching a new song, sing songs during the introduction of the lesson that use the same form as that of the new song. This will help you move seamlessly from one activity to another.
   C. Sing songs in the same tonality or related tonalities. Make sure to sing songs in the same keys. This is particularly important when moving from a piece of music in a major key to a minor key. There are times when we sing the

song in the related key but other times we might need to sing the song in the parallel keys. It is important to establish new keys tonally.
    D. Songs may also be used to prepare the singing of a new song. Keeping the same tonality between known and unknown will help secure students' listening and singing skills.
    E. When moving from a creative movement activity to a reading, writing, or improvisation activity, you should keep the subsequent game song in the same key as the reading, writing, or improvisation activities, as this helps with intonation and makes the transition between lesson segments smooth and accessible.
2. Use songs that have the same meter.
    A. When teaching an aural awareness activity addressing rhythm, singing known songs in the same meter as the aural awareness activity helps student focus and subsequent attentiveness.
3. Use the same key or *do* placement on the staff for all sections in a lesson. A particular scale written on the staff can be used throughout a lesson for different melodies. This provides a point of focus for the students.
4. Use the same rhythmic ostinato from one segment of a lesson to another to accompany singing.
5. Use the same melodic ostinato from one segment of a lesson to another to accompany singing.
6. Sing songs that share the same rhythmic motif from one segment of a lesson to another to accompany singing.
7. Sing songs that share the same melodic motif from one segment of a lesson to another to accompany singing.

Transitions Between One Segment of a Lesson and Another

1. Using specific directions
    A. Give students directions using the melody of a song they are about to sing.
    B. Nonverbal directions.
    C. Give students directions without any verbal language. This might be as simple as having students sing a known song while the teacher motions to the students to form a circle to play the game.
2. Unconscious rhythmic connections
    A. Sing several songs with the same time signature and tempo.
    B. Sing several songs that have the same rhythmic motifs.
    C. Conduct a song and ask students to keep conducting while you sing the next song in the lesson.
3. Unconscious melodic connections
    A. Sing several songs in the same tonality.
    B. Sing several songs in the same tonality and scale range.

  C. Sing several songs that have the same recurring melodic motifs.
  D. Sing several songs having the same character or mood. Students will not be made aware of this at this time in the lesson.
4. Conscious rhythmic connections
  A. Use rhythmic connections in songs to move from one segment of the lesson to another. Students are made aware of these rhythmic connections.
  B. Sing several songs with the same time signature.
  C. Sing songs that share the same tempo.
  D. Sing songs that share rhythmic motifs; for example, think of the syncopated rhythmic pattern that connects the "Canoe Song" and "Liza Jane."
  E. A rhythmic motif from one song may become an ostinato for another song.
  F. Transform the rhythm of one song into another song.
  G. Clap the rhythm of a folksong, and have students follow in canon. Begin to transform this rhythm into the rhythm of another folksong.
5. Conscious melodic connections

Teachers use melodic connections in songs to move from one segment of the lesson to another. Students are made aware of these melodic connections.

1. Sing several songs in the same tonality. Preparation for this type of activity may be accomplished by pointing to the tone steps or staff ladder.
2. The teacher connects two songs by using the same melodic motive; for example:
  A. "Bow Wow Wow" and "Hot Cross Buns" share the *mi re do* motif at the end.
  B. "Tideo" and "Great Big House" share the *mi so so la mi so so* melodic motif.
3. Structural reductions
  A. You can use structural reductions of folksongs to move from one song to another. To make a structural reduction, write the notes that occur on each beat in a phrase. Do not include passing notes. The structural reduction (for example, *so la so mi* is the structural reduction of the first four beats of "Lucy Locket") is the same as the first phrase of "Bounce High, Bounce Low." Finding these links between songs can build a powerful connection for students.
4. Structural reductions and partner songs
  A. Sing the structural reduction of one song and use it as a partner with another song, for example, "Liza Jane" and "Ridin' in a Buggy."
5. Melodic transformations
  A. Transform the melodic phrase of one song into a phrase of another song.
6. Melodic motifs
  A. Use a melodic motif in a song as a melodic ostinato for another song.
7. Canon
  A. For older students, show the hand signs of a known song and ask the students to follow in canon. Then transform the known song into another song.
8. Harmonic functions

Kodály Today

    A. Divide the class into two groups. One group performs the song; the other performs the functional chord root tones. As one group continues to repeat the functional chord root tones, you can use hand signs and have students sing another melody that shares the same harmonic rhythm as the first melody.
9. Character of repertoire
    A. Sing several songs having the same character or mood.
10. Form connections
    A. Unconscious connections
        i. Sing several songs that have the same rhythmic form. For example, "All Around the Buttercup" and "Let Us Chase the Squirrel" share the same form.
        ii. Sing several songs that have the same melodic form.
    B. Conscious connections
        i. Sing several songs that have the same rhythmic form. Students will identify the forms of these songs.
        ii. Sing several songs that have the same melodic form. Students will identify the forms of these songs.

Here are two versions of the same lesson plan: Table 10.12 contains no transitions and Table 10.13 includes the same lesson plan with transitions. We have bolded the new transitional activities. Transitions should not detract from the lesson but instead allow the teacher to move smoothly from one segment of the lesson to another.

Table 10.12   Unit 2, Syncopation ♪♩ ♪, Lesson 1

Outcome	Preparation: internalize three sounds unevenly distributed over two beats through kinesthetic activities.
	Practice: Reading known songs that include *high do*.
INTRODUCTORY ACTIVITIES	
Warm-up	• Body warm-up • Beat activity Sinfonia No. 8, BWV 794, J. S. Bach (1685–1750) • Breathing: **Ss** practice blowing a balloon and watch how air is released when deflating the balloon. • Resonance: explore a cow sound using low and high voices. Make sure **Ss** are inhaling and exhaling correctly with the support muscles. • Posture: remind **Ss** of the correct posture for singing.

(continued)

Table 10.12 Continued

Sing known songs	"Hill and Gully Rider"
	CSP: C
	• **Ss** sing the song in canon after four beats.
	"I Lost the Farmer's Dairy Key"
	CSP: D
	• **Ss** sing the song with a simple ostinato. $\frac{2}{4}$ ♩ ♩ | ♫ ♩ :|
	• **Ss** continue the ostinato into the next song.
Develop tuneful singing	"Riding in the Buggy"
Tone production	CSP: D
Diction	• **T** sings the song while **Ss** continue the ostinato.
Expression	• **Ss** sing song with a "koo" sound.
	• **Ss** sing the song while **T** shows these hand signs for accompanying melody:
	$\frac{4}{4}$ ♩ ♩ ♩ ♩ | ♩ ♩ ♩ ♩ ||
	d m r s d m r d
	• **Ss** sing the solfège syllables of the accompanying melody while **T** sings the song (**T** may sign while singing to help **Ss**).
	• **T** directs part of the class to sing the melodic motif while the remainder sing the song. Switch.
	Kodály Choral Library, *Let Us Sing Correctly*, no. 9
Review known songs and rhythmic elements	"I Am Walking in the Shoes of John"
	CSP: C
	• **Ss** sing the song and show the strong and weak beats.
	• **Ss** read from traditional rhythmic notation from the board.
	• **T**: "A note that comes before the strong beat of a phrase is called an 'upbeat' or a 'pickup.' When we have an upbeat at the *beginning* of a song, we call it an _____." (external upbeat)
	• **T** sings each phrase of "The Jolly Miller," "Old Mr. Rabbit," and "I Lost the Farmer's Dairy Key"; **Ss** echo-sing each phrase, singing with rhythm syllables both as a class and individually.
	CORE ACTIVITIES
Teach a new song	"Land of the Silver Birch"
	CSP: D
	• **T** and **Ss** show beat of the song as **T** sings.
	• **T** sings and points to the phrases again; **Ss** join.
	• **T** sings the first phrase and **Ss** label the phrase as "A."
	• **T** continues to sing, stopping for **Ss** to label each phrase.
	• **T** and **Ss** sing song.

(continued)

Table 10.12 Continued

Develop knowledge of music literacy concept Internalize music through kinesthetic activity	"Canoe Song" CSP: A • T and **Ss** sing "Canoe Song" in unison; **Ss** sing "Canoe Song" while T sings in canon. • **Ss** stand and sing while clapping the rhythm and stepping the beat. • **Ss** sing and point to a representation of the target phrase on the board: __ _____ __ __ __ _____ (target phrase) • T directs half the class to sing and pat the beat and half to sing and clap the rhythm by pointing to "B" or "R" on the board; **Ss** switch parts. • Individuals sing, perform rhythm, and beat while singing. • T divides the class into two groups and directs **Ss** to sing in canon.
Creative movement	"Come Thru 'Na Hurry" CSP: F • As **Ss** sing the song, T chooses individuals to play instruments. • One plays the steady beat; one plays the subdivision. • Compose a rhythmic ostinato for a percussion instrument. • Compose a melodic ostinato for a pitched instrument. • Create a new game movement. • Create a new text.
Practice of music performance and literacy skills Reading	"Hogs in the Cornfield" CSP: D • **Ss** sing the song. • **Ss** sing phrase 2 with solfège syllables and hand signs. • **Ss** read the solfège syllables from the board with standard rhythmic notation and solfège syllables. • **Ss** read from staff notation. • **Ss** read Kodály Choral Library, *333 Elementary Exercises*, no. 327. • T writes the tone set on the board and prepares **Ss** to read *For Children*, vol 1, no. 5, by Béla Bartók (1881–1945). • T creates a score for **Ss** that indicates all known elements with rhythmic notation and solfège syllables. If the solfège has not been taught, T can include the rhythmic notation. • T sings the Bartók melody on "loo" in the parallel minor as a transition by singing the next melody.

(*continued*)

Table 10.12 Continued

	SUMMARY ACTIVITIES
Review lesson outcomes Review the new song	"Land of the Silver Birch" CSP: D • **Ss** sing song and **T** sings in canon.

Table 10.13 Unit 2, Syncopation ♩♪ ♪, Lesson 2

Outcome	Preparation: analyze repertoire that contains three sounds unevenly distributed over two beats.
	Practice: write patterns from known songs that include *high do*.
	INTRODUCTORY ACTIVITIES
Warm-up	• Body warm-up • Beat activity Sinfonia No. 8, BWV 794, J. S. Bach (1685–1750) • Breathing: **Ss** practice blowing a balloon and watch how air is released when deflating the balloon. • Resonance: explore a cow sound using low and high voices. Make sure **Ss** are inhaling and exhaling correctly with the support muscles. • Posture: remind **Ss** of the correct posture for singing.
Sing known songs	"John Kanaka" CSP: A • **Ss** sing the song and keep the beat. • **Ss** continue the beat into the next song. "Hogs in the Cornfield" CSP: D • **Ss** sing the song and pat the beat. • **Ss** sing the song and conduct. • **Ss** sing the song with inner hearing and conduct.
Develop tuneful singing Tone production Diction Expression	"Come Thru 'Na Hurry" CSP: F • **Ss** sing the song. • **Ss** sing with a "koo" sound. • Lip trills. **T** directs **Ss** to then use lip trills to sing the song. Kodály Choral Library, *Let Us Sing Correctly*, no. 10

(continued)

Table 10.13 Continued

Review known songs and rhythmic elements	"Old Mr. Rabbit" CSP: F • **T** and **Ss** sing the song. • **Ss** sing the song and perform the strong and weak beats. • **Ss** are instructed to sing only upbeats and the first beat of each phrase. • **Ss** identify the song as containing an internal upbeat. • **Ss** sing and conduct the song. • **T** sings each phrase of "Paw Paw Patch", "Tideo," "Ida Red," and "Chickalalelo"; **Ss** echo-sing each phrase singing with rhythm syllables both as a class and individually.
CORE ACTIVITIES	
Teach a new song	"Land of the Silver Birch" CSP: D • **T** and **Ss** keep the beat while **T** sings the song alone. • **T** sings while **Ss** point to the phrases. • **T** sings, **Ss** show strong and weak beats; **Ss** identify meter.
Develop knowledge of musical literacy concept Describe what you hear	"Canoe Song" (round) CSP: D • **Ss** sing song. • Review kinesthetic activities. • **T** and **Ss** sing phrase 1 (the target phrase) on "loo" and tap the beat before **T** asks each question. Determine the number of beats in the phrase. • **T**: "Andy, how many beats did we tap?" (four) Determine the number of sounds on each beat. • **T**: "Andy, how many sounds did we sing on beat 4?" (one) • **T**: "Andy, how many sounds did we sing on beat 3?" (two) • **T**: "Andy, how many sounds did we sing on beats 1 and 2?" (three) • **T**: "Andy, were our three sounds even or uneven?" (uneven) • **T**: "Andy, describe our three uneven sounds on beat 3 with the words *short* and *long*." (short, long, short) • **T**: "Let's sing our phrase like this: *short long short tadi ta*. • **T**: "I'll sing words and you echo *short long short* and rhythm syllables." • The class then, as individuals, echo-sing with **T**. • **T** eventually sings the text for each phrase; **Ss** echo-sing with *short long short* and the appropriate rhythm syllables.

(continued)

Sequencing and Lesson Planning

Table 10.13   Continued

Creative movement	"Weevily Wheat"
	CSP: A
	• As **Ss** sing the song, **T** will choose individuals to play instruments.
	• One plays the steady beat; one plays the subdivision.
	• One continues the ostinato: ($\frac{4}{4}$ ♪♪ ♪♪ ≻ ‖)
	• Compose a rhythmic ostinato for percussion instrument.
	• Compose a melodic ostinato for a pitched instrument.
	• Create a new game movement.
	• Create a new text.
Practice music performance and literacy skills Writing	"Hogs in the Cornfield"
	CSP: D
	• **T** presents the song on the board, leaving phrase 2 blank.
	• **Ss** sing the song with solfège syllables and hand signs.
	• **Ss** complete the writing worksheet. (Songs may be written with rhythmic notation with solfège syllables beneath or in staff notation.)
	• **Ss** may complete other known songs with *high do* as time allows.
	• **Ss** create an ostinato on xylophones that includes *high do la* and *so*; they use the ostinato to accompany any of their known songs.
	SUMMARY ACTIVITIES
Review lesson outcomes Review the new song	"Land of the Silver Birch"
	CSP: D
	• **Ss** sing the song and **T** sings the second part from *Sourwood Mountain*, p. 6.

General Considerations for Planning Lessons

Here are suggestions of a general nature and of relevance for evaluating lesson planning.

In General

1. Outcomes for every lesson should come from the focus of the lesson plan. For example, in our model of learning and instruction, lesson one has two outcomes, one on kinesthetic preparation of a new concept and the second addressing practice through reading a known concept.
2. Tuneful singing should always be a primary goal of any lesson.

3. Work to select the best song material for each class and make sure that you enjoy this material. You should have at least three to six songs in a thirty-minute lesson. Memorize all the song material that you are going to use.
4. Remember that every new song you teach should be introduced appropriately.
5. When teaching a new element, the selected repertoire must contain known rhythmic or melodic patterns.
6. Work with both a rhythmic and a melodic element in every lesson (as per our lesson plan structure). Remember that when you abstract a pattern or motif from a song you should always sing the song again to put it back in the context of performance and to give students the experience of enjoying the song.
7. Continuously work to be certain you have selected the best songs for preparing, presenting, and practicing a particular musical element.
8. Remember that there should be a focus to each section of the lesson, one that you can assess informally and formally.
9. Know your materials. Analyze the materials for each lesson from an analytical, performance perspective and from a pedagogical one.
10. Try to use a variety of repertoire for the lesson.
11. One activity should also prepare or lead (transition) to the next activity.
12. Remember to include periods of relaxation and concentration (this is built into our lesson plan format). The pace of a lesson is critical. Veteran teachers constantly tell us that it is better to teach faster than slower. Students will follow you if you're moving.
13. Provide the students with plenty of individual experiences in the classroom. Work from group participation to calling on individual students to perform.
14. Music skill activities such are reading, writing, and composition should always be sequentially presented.
15. Begin and end every lesson with tuneful singing.
16. Although reading and writing are not always the focus of every lesson, try to include an aspect of one or the other in each lesson.
17. Remember to develop all music skills.

Evaluating a Lesson Plan
1. All learning should stem from enjoyment of singing songs, chanting rhymes, and playing games. The overarching goals of a music lesson should be tuneful singing, listening, and enjoyment of music. Musical concepts and elements are taught to enhance the enjoyment of music.
2. Reading and writing should be addressed during every lesson. Even if students read or write only a small motive from a song, they develop a deeper understanding and appreciation of the song. There should be opportunities for both reviewing and reinforcing musical elements and concepts.
3. A good lesson plan should reveal clear answers to these questions:
    A. Was the lesson presented musically?

B. What were the primary and secondary outcomes of the lesson?
C. How were the outcomes of the lesson achieved?
D. How many songs and games were used in the lesson?
E. Was there enough individual work in the lesson?
F. Were students able to sing the repertoire musically?
G. Did the students sing the material with different tempi, and did they find the correct character for each piece of music?
H. Did the teacher keep the beat gently with a hand drum to control the tempo for the song?
I. Were the ostinatos musical? Did they distract from the musicality of the lesson?
J. What activities used in conjunction with the song material led students to an understanding of the goals of the lesson?
K. Was there an emphasis on singing and making music?
L. Were a sufficient variety of songs used in the lesson?
M. Were the goals of the lesson achieved?
N. Was new material prepared and presented clearly in the lesson?
O. Was there a logical sequence and pacing in the lesson?
P. Did students have the necessary knowledge and skills for the lesson to be successful?
Q. Was the music teacher able to phrase questions correctly?
R. Was there a focus for every section of the lesson?
S. Did the teacher spend the right amount of time on every segment of the lesson?
T. Was the culmination of the lesson clear?
U. Were there periods of relaxation and concentration in the lesson?
V. What musical skills were developed in the lesson?
W. Were the students active collectively and individually during the lesson?
X. Did the lesson plan offer an opportunity to assess student progress?
Y. Was the lesson enjoyable for the students?
Z. Did the lesson begin and end with singing?

Evaluating Your Teaching
1. Did I select the most appropriate repertoire to teach the new element?
2. Did I select the correct musical element to teach?
3. Did one song lead to another with an appropriate transition?
4. Did the students have the prerequisite skills to understand the new element?
5. Were my teaching strategies for teaching every outcome specific? Did I review what the students already knew, and did I reinforce new information?
6. Could students independently demonstrate their new understanding?
7. When working with the rhythmic or melodic elements of a song, did we sing the song as a performance one more time to ensure the musicality of the lesson?

Adapting Lesson Plans for the Inclusive Classroom

Differently abled and gifted and talented children have needs unlike those of other learners, and this poses a variety of challenges for the music teacher. The Houlahan and Tacka model of learning and instruction can be adapted to help teachers deal with learners of all kinds in the music classroom. Since our model of learning and instruction is based on a constructivist philosophy, we believe that it possesses myriad opportunities to develop the music potential for all learners in the music classroom. It is important to help children with learning disabilities engage in the process of making music as well as learn how to express themselves musically. All activities developed for the special learner should work well in a larger group setting.

Special Needs Students

Here we offer generic guidelines for teaching students with special needs. It is important to recognize every student's specific learning needs and create learning strategies for that student.

Evaluate Your Own Philosophy of Teaching

Try to evaluate your own philosophy concerning teaching the special needs student. We should view students with special needs as those who can engage in music activities and develop knowledge of music concepts and music skills.

Communicate

Remember that you are not alone when teaching the student with special needs. Consult with classroom teachers and other professionals in the school who can furnish guidance for working with such students. It is also important to communicate with parents concerning their child. Most important, don't forget to speak to students about how they are doing in your music class. Most students with special needs will have an individualized educational program (IEP) or 504 plan on file at the school. Take time to read these reports. They will help you in understanding individual needs and developing teaching activities that address their strengths.

Plan in Advance

Once you have created your lesson plan, figure out strategies for including special needs learning in the music-making process in your classroom; consult the classroom teacher to determine what skills (social, emotional, physical, intellectual) you can reinforce during the music class.

Make Seating Arrangements

Create a seating arrangement for all your music classes. Students with special needs should be paired with children who will have the patience to explain and help them through these activities. It is important that you provide a model for all students in the class while paying particular attention to students with special needs.

Give Positive Reinforcement
Give all students positive reinforcement in the music classroom. Take time to explain to students how they will be rewarded when they participate and follow the rules of the music classroom. When possible, try to set activities so students with special needs have an option in choosing their performance activity.

Promote Predictability
A hallmark of the Houlahan and Tacka model of lesson planning and the accompanying process of teaching is predictability; this is particularly valuable, if not wholly necessary, for students with special needs. The teacher should be able to analyze and break down or split tasks for the children ,and also know when to skip procedures or add more steps for certain students. This is an important scaffolding device for all children, but especially for students with special needs. Try to follow the sequence of instruction for each activity in the lesson plans. After a while, the children will be able to predict what will happen next in the lesson.

Use Songs That Share Stylistic Elements
We recommend that teachers use repertoire having rhythmic and melodic building blocks in common. This is highly important for the special learner. It will be easier for them to sing this repertoire, as it will become predictable.

Make Directions and Visual Cues Clear
Guide students and explain all directions clearly. Sometimes using large gestures or a visual can help clarify your expectation for students in the music classroom. If you're uncomfortable with movement and you want students to keep a beat, show a picture of a drum; if you want students to sing, show students a picture of someone singing. In our approach to teaching, we use icons in the initial stages of learning to help students with reading and writing activities, but you might have to keep using icons for students with special needs. To address specific needs, consider using colorful images and large-size print for instructions.

Model Expected Behavior
One approach to modeling behavior is to choose students who will succeed with the activity before you ask a student with special needs to participate. Sometimes you need to pair another class member with a special needs student to help with music activities during the music lesson.

Use Instruments
Use instruments as a means of informing students about expectations. For example, you might consider using a slide whistle to signal when to stand and when to sit. A melodic

instrument might work to tell students to freeze at a particular activity or return to their seats. Have a "cue" for students who are being disruptive during your music class. It is important to continue teaching but give a disruptive student a visual clue so that he or she can change behavior.

Attend to Pacing

It is important for students with special needs to have time to digest what you are teaching. If you are asking them to perform a certain activity, give them enough time and space to do it.

Use Puppets

Use puppets to help students repeat an activity, or encourage tuneful singing, or even learn the words of a song. Match the movement of the puppet's mouth to your own so students will make connections concerning pronunciation, articulation, and tuneful singing in general.

Teaching Performance Skills with Special Needs Students

Repetition is important in all teaching, but particularly so when dealing with the special needs student. When teaching a new song, sing it several times before asking a question concerning its text or a musical element. We believe it best to introduce the song without accompaniment to avoid distracting students with special needs. If you ask a question and a student gives an answer, consider responding "Thank you, let's check" and singing the song again to verify the response. When asking students to play a rhythm instrument to keep a beat, you might want a special needs learner to put his or her hands around or on top of a drum as you play so as to feel the sensation of the sound.

Consider using visuals with words to help students memorize the text of songs. Choose a key word or phrase printed underneath a picture. Leave these song charts in a corner of the music room so students can review during their play time.

Use Peer Helpers

When teaching folk dances or games, try to assign a student who can grasp and explain instructions to a student having special needs. Consider modifying the tempo and plan for repetition of an activity. With every repetition, you can ask a student to explain what is happening in the game. Sometimes you might have to practice the steps of the dance without singing the song. If you follow the game sequence suggested in the book, you will find that you can engage more of the students with special needs because of the sequence. Remember to give them adequate time and practice to process game directions. Reward a helper by allowing the student to choose a favorite song, class activity, or game.

Move from Physical Activity to Symbolic Activity

Students with special needs learn faster when they explore a concept physically before moving to a more abstract representation of the concept. In teaching a concept such as beat, it is important that students experience singing and moving to the beat before you ask them to point to icons that represent the beat. To understand a concept such as fast and slow beats, it is valuable for the special needs student to see a visual that implies awareness of fast and slow (a picture of a rabbit or a turtle). Passing a ball around a circle to the beat is a difficult task for young learners, but it's a concrete way for students to make connections between tempo and keeping the beat.

Use Tools and Visual Aids

Use a variety of tools and visual aids when teaching students rhythm or melodic concepts. Try these ideas for bringing students to awareness of rhythm and subsequently teaching them rhythmic concepts and elements.

- Echo-sing melodies with a neutral syllable before asking students to clap a rhythm or the way the words go.
- Clap rhythm patterns.
- Tap rhythm patterns.
- Play rhythm patterns on an instrument.
- Use icons such as a clapping hand to indicate that students should clap the rhythm.

Try these ideas for bringing students to awareness of melody and subsequently teaching melodic concepts and elements.

- Echo-sing melodies with a neutral syllable before asking students to show or point to a melodic contour.
- Use hands or arm motions to show melodic contours.
- Point to icons arranged to illustrate the shape of a musical phrase.
- Use pitched instruments to perform simple melodic phrases.

Engage as Many of the Senses as Possible

It is important to engage the various learning modalities of students; this is especially important for the special needs learner. In the Houlahan and Tacka method of learning and instruction, kinesthetic, aural, and visual learning activities are the core of the learning experience in the music classroom. In our model, we begin with a kinesthetic activity, move to an aural activity, and then work with a visual one. This specified sequence of learning events brings significant opportunities for working with special needs students. When asking students to demonstrate their aural understanding by answering a question, be certain that your question is connected to a kinesthetic activity you've seen the student perform. Likewise, when we ask students to create a visual representation of their aural understanding, this resulting representation should connect with and therefore demonstrate the students' kinesthetic and aural understanding.

Perform an Activity with the Teacher or a Small Group
Ask a special needs student to perform an activity with the teacher or in a small group. In this text, we advocate following teaching strategies in a specified order; working through this process has also been especially valuable in working with students with special needs.

First begin with a class activity. Then perform the activity with a smaller group of students. Finally, work with one student to share the performance or creation with the class.

Designate a Space to Escape
Sometimes a special needs student can feel overwhelmed with an activity. We should allow the student to go to a "safe space" in the music classroom. A visual placed on the wall can be comforting because the special needs student knows exactly where the safe space is. Such students also feel a sense of ownership in their learning if they can show appropriate decision making in going to the safe place and then returning to the activity when they feel comfortable.

Assess
Modify your assessment rubrics for special needs learners. The goal is to document the improvements and accomplishments of your students as well as being able to use this information to continue to challenge and engage students in a meaningful way. In addition to assessing knowledge of concepts and skills make sure that you include such items as a student's attitude towards their peers, teacher, and the music class.

Gifted and Talented Students

Gifted and talented students can be just as demanding to teach as students with special needs, and often more so. It is important to have techniques and activities so that you can steadily challenge these student's abilities.

Knowing Your Students
Students who are gifted have their own strengths and challenges. Work with the classroom teacher to find out what these strengths and challenges are.

Advance Planning
Once you have created your lesson plan, think ahead and figure out strategies for creating more demanding (but not impossible) tasks for the gifted students to perform in your classroom. Consult with the classroom teacher to find out what types of activities the gifted and talented students are working on so that you can reinforce these skills in the music classroom.

Performance and Improvisation
Find ways to challenge gifted and talented students during performance and improvisation activities. They should be encouraged to perform as soloists with simple rhythmic or

melodic instruments. They can often improvise their own rhythmic accompaniment for their singing.

Student as Teacher
Give talented students an opportunity to assume the role of the teacher. For example, they can sing greetings to other students. Use them to demonstrate a particular movement in a game or to sing a particular phrase correctly.

Challenging Music Tasks
Ask students to perform songs on their own for other students. Use a talented student to provide a rhythmic accompaniment to class singing. In addition to asking students to create a new text or work to a well-known song, ask them to accompany themselves with a beat on a rhythmic instrument or movement activity. It is important to steadily challenge gifted children through acceleration.

Mentors
Pair gifted and talented students with other students in the class who need extra help with a task.

Students as Readers
Use gifted and talented students to read the story that is to be used during a lesson.

Music Instruments
Ask students to create rhythmic instruments that can be used in the classroom.

Bilingual Students

We offer here some general guidelines for teaching bilingual students. It's important for you to have an understanding of each student's specific learning needs and create unique learning strategies for that student. Keep reading the research and educational suggestions pertaining to teaching bilingual students. Evaluate your own philosophy concerning the teaching of the bilingual learner. Consult with the class teacher and other professionals in the school for guidance as to how to teach bilingual learners in the music classroom, and take the time to communicate with parents about their child. Don't forget to speak to students directly about how they are doing in your music class!

Once you have created your lesson plan, develop strategies to include bilingual learners in the music-making process in your classroom. Consult with the classroom teacher as to what skills you can reinforce during the music class. It is helpful to pair bilingual learners with students who have the patience to explain and help them through music activities whether in English or their native language. Offer all students positive reinforcement in the music classroom. In some instances, it is appropriate to take the time to explain to students how they will be rewarded if they follow the rules of the music classroom. If something has worked particularly well, reward the student and the class by allowing the bilingual students to select a performance activity of their own.

Our sequence of lesson plans and overall process of teaching is predictable; this is helpful for bilingual learners. When you follow the specified sequence of instruction in the lesson plans, after a while the students will be able to predict or guess what comes next in the lesson. Work to communicate with clear directions. Develop a list of terms that you can use in both English and the native language of other students in your classroom. Remember to use easy-to-read colors and large print for instructions.

Connections to Grade Handbooks

In the accompanying handbooks for this series, we offer teachers a detailed lesson plan addressing procedures for preparing to teach specified musical elements, labeling the sound of the new element, presenting the notation, and practicing newly learned concepts as well as develop musical skills. The handbooks are written according to grade level. A handbook includes five to eight teaching units, every unit containing five sequenced lessons addressing a specified musical element. The unit plans also include an overview of repertoire required to teach the elements, the music skills being developed in the units, and five sequenced lesson plans for teaching a new concept or musical element.

Discussion Questions
1. What are the primary learning outcomes for each lesson?
2. How are lesson outcomes related to each segment of the lesson?
3. How are lesson plans constructed for each phase of learning?
4. Discuss the kinds of transitions you can use in your teaching.

Ongoing Assignment

1. Choose a concept to prepare and an element to practice for a first grade class. Write the outcomes for each type of lesson. Include titles of songs you will be using.
2. Choose a concept to prepare and an element to practice for a third grade class. Write the outcomes for each type of lesson. Include titles of songs you will be using.
3. Review several lesson plans that you have designed. Indicate how you will move smoothly from one activity to another.
4. Review several lesson plans that you have designed. Indicate how you would adapt these lessons for use in the inclusive classroom.

Bibliography

Boshkoff, Ruth. "Lesson Planning the Kodály Way." *Music Educators Journal*, October 1991, *78*(2): 30–34.

de Frece, Robert. "Planning for Success: Optimizing Your Teaching." *General Music Today*, 2010, *24*(1): 32–40. Music Index. Web. Apr. 7, 2013.

Feierabend, J. M. "Skill Levels: The 'Other' Sequence." *Bulletin of the International Kodály Society*, 1989, *14*(2): 13–15.

Gargiulo, R. M., and D. Metcalf. *Teaching in Today's Inclusive Classrooms: A Universal Design for Learning Approach* (2nd ed.). Belmont, CA: Wadsworth, 2013.

Johnson, Cecile. "From One Activity to the Next—Making Your Lessons Flow." *Kodály Envoy*, 2013, *39*(3): 18–21.

Klinger, Rita. *Lesson Planning in a Kodály Setting*. Los Angeles: OAKE, 2014.

Leithold, S. "Classroom Connections: Translating the Standards into Effective Scope and Sequence." *Kodály Envoy*, 1999, *25*(2): 9–10.

Pippart, J. "Maintaining Interest in Middle School (A Typical Lesson Plan)." *Kodály Envoy*, 1983, *10*(1).

Regelski, Thomas A. "On 'Methodolatry' and Music Teaching as 'Critical' and Reflective Praxis." *Philosophy of Music Education Review*, 2002, *10*(2): 102–124.

Scott, Sheila J. "Constructivist Perspectives for Developing and Implementing Lesson Plans in General Music." *General Music Today*, 2012, *25*(2): 24–30.

Wiggins, G., and J. McTighe. *Understanding by Design*. Alexandria, VA: Association for Supervision and Curriculum Development, 1998.

Zemke, Lorna, Sr. "How to Get Started with Lesson Planning." *Keeping up with Kodály Concepts in Music Education*, November–December 1974, *1*(1): 3–8.

Chapter 11

Teaching Musicianship Skills Starting in the Upper Grades

> Anyone who studies carefully these one hundred lessons cannot stray from the path to good musicianship. Nor should he despair at not having completed them by the age of twelve; he can still win laurels. Even an adult musician will experience renewed discovery through studying these lessons, which may indeed overcome many small shortcomings in his proficiency.[1]
>
> Zoltán Kodály, "Preface to the volume *Musical Reading and Writing* by Erzsébet Szőnyi," in *The Selected Writings*, p. 204

Key Questions

- What do we include in a music curriculum for older students who are beginning their study of music?
- What are some of the basic lesson designs that can be used when teaching an older student who is beginning to study music?
- How does the sequence for teaching rhythmic and melodic elements to older beginners differ from that for younger students?
- How do we select song repertoire and materials to teach an older student who is new to the study of music?
- How do we teach an appropriate repertoire to these beginning music learners?

The previous chapters have set forth a pedagogy for teaching music beginning in grade one and moving sequentially through the elementary grades. Occasionally teachers face the challenge of working with students in grades four, five, or beyond who have not been taught according to the Kodály concept, and who in some cases have never had classroom music instruction. Consequently, the students' knowledge of repertoire, performance skills in singing, playing instruments, and movement skills, as well as their knowledge of music literacy and improvisation require an approach appropriate for their age. Our approach to teaching older beginners is to offer them an accelerated program of instruction that allows them to catch up with those who have had instruction throughout their elementary education. We are addressing two populations of students. Consider a group of students who come into a grade four or five class and have never had music lessons taught according to the Kodály concept, or another group who have received music lessons from a variety of teachers, teaching approaches, and philosophies.

In developing curriculum goals for the older beginner, the instructor may have to modify curriculum expectations several times during the course of instruction. Clearly, a fourth grade class that has never had sequential music literacy training will not be able to cover the same topics as a fourth grade class that has. The song repertoire should remain appropriate to the fourth grade students, but the concepts and musical elements may need to include rudimentary concepts. The first goal is therefore to assess the knowledge of the students and design a curriculum plan for the class.

Occasionally an instructor may have to teach a group of students who have had some music training. Although this situation can be more complex than teaching students who have never had music training based on the Kodály concept, there will be some similarities between the groups. Here are a curriculum summary and goals that can be modified to teach both these populations.

Curriculum Summary

Students as Stewards of Their Cultural Heritage

Students should experience a varied repertoire of music that includes folk music, art, contemporary and patriotic music, as well as music representative of local and international cultures. They should learn to embrace or understand their musical heritage and the musical roots of others. They should relate music to history, society, and culture through the use of singing and playing games from diverse cultures.

Students as Performers

Students should be able to sing tunefully. Repertoire may include folksongs, echo songs, canons, and two- and three-part arrangements in a group as well as individually, and it may include accompanying themselves using rhythmic and melodic ostinato. They should also be adept with simple instruments for accompaniment. Rhythmic ostinati may include eighth, quarter, dotted rhythms, half note, four sixteenth notes, and eighth-note-sixteenth-note variations. Students should be able to conduct in $\frac{2}{4}$ $\frac{3}{4}$ and $\frac{4}{4}$ and keep the beat in compound meter. Repertoire can include a melodic range of trichords, tetrachords, pentachords, and pentatonic scales in both major and minor keys.

Students as Critical Thinkers

We can increase students' literacy skills by having them read and write melodic and rhythmic patterns up to eight beats in length by using more complex rhythms such as eighth, quarter, dotted rhythms, half note, four sixteenth notes, and eighth-note-sixteenth-note variations. Melodic and rhythmic patterns should be chosen from known song material. Melodically, students should be able to distinguish between first and second endings, and phrase variants. Inner-hearing activities and sight-singing simple melodies using major and minor pentachords, hexachord, and pentatonic as well as major and minor scales should form a portion of the curriculum.

Students as Creative Human Beings

Students should improvise or compose rhythmic patterns and accompaniments using known forms, rhythms, and simple melodies and build on known musical concepts to increase their knowledge of the material in a way that is both creative and meaningful to them.

Students as Informed Audience Members

Students should integrate different styles and genres of music through guided listening and movement activities, and by relating listening examples to core concepts. They should learn to recognize learned melodic and rhythmic patterns, phrasing, and musical artistry in music they hear both in the classroom and in their everyday life. We should provide opportunities to hear live music as well as recorded music examples that include the rhythmic and melodic elements they have learned. Listening to music examples while following a simple score is also important; this can be as simple as following the score of a folksong performed by the teacher or following the score of a simple instrumental work where the teacher has reduced it to a one-line score that includes the central features of the work. These scores should be written and based on the musical concepts and elements students have addressed in class, to include numerous style periods, biographical details of composers, and information on the instruments of the orchestra.

Here we present a sample curriculum template of what can be accomplished in teaching older beginners.

Curriculum Guide

I. Repertoire: Children as Stewards of Their Cultural and Music Heritage

Develop a song repertoire to add to students' knowledge of folk music from various cultures (with emphasis on America), art music, and composed music.

II. Performance: Students as Performers

Broaden performance skills to include the following:

Singing
1. Learn twenty to twenty-five new folksongs, canons, and two- and three-part song arrangements of various cultures.
2. Sing ten to fifteen songs with rhythm and solfège syllables.
3. Sing seasonal and holiday songs.
4. Learn five two- and three-part songs from the classical or folk/contemporary repertoire.
5. Learn and play at least five game songs.
6. Learn eight songs through sight reading.
7. Learn songs in preparation for beginning intermediate musical concepts and elements.

Part Work
1. Accompany a song with a rhythmic ostinato.
2. Accompany a song with a melodic ostinato.
3. Sing simple rhythmic or melodic canons derived from familiar songs.
4. Sing both individually and in groups call and response, echo singing, game songs, verse and refrain, partner songs, simple canons, and simple two-part pieces.
5. Perform two-part rhythmic exercises based on rhythmic motifs derived from known songs.
6. Sing in two parts from:
   A. Hand signs with one part moving at a time.
   B. Two-part material and exercises written with traditional rhythmic notation, with solfège syllables written beneath, or from known songs written in staff notation.

Creative Movement
1. Perform partner games that use more complex directions.
2. Perform circle games containing square dance formations.
3. Perform line dances containing contradance patterns.
4. Perform basic square dances.
5. Perform games and dances from various cultures.
6. Perform partner clapping and body percussion games.
7. Perform double line games.
8. Conduct duple, simple, and compound meter, triple meter, and simple quadruple meter.

Instruments
1. Students demonstrate melodic and rhythmic concepts on classroom instruments.
2. Accompany singing on classroom instruments.
3. Play instruments independently or in a group.
4. Play music accompaniments that reflect various world cultures on unpitched percussion instruments.

III. Music Literacy: Students as Critical Thinkers

Rhythmic Elements
1. Perform the beat in simple duple, triple, and quadruple meter as well as compound meter.
2. Count using rhythm syllables and numbers for whole, half, quarter, eighth, and sixteenth notes and rests.
3. Understand simple rhythms in compound meter.
4. Conduct patterns in duple, triple meter, and quadruple meters.

Melodic Elements
Sing these melodic patterns and scales with solfège syllables and hand signs:

1. Major trichord
2. Pentatonic bichord, trichord, tetrachord, scales
3. Major pentachord and hexachord scales
4. Major extended pentachord, hexachord, and pentatonic scales
5. Minor pentachord, hexachord, and minor pentatonic scales
6. Major scale
7. Minor scale

Reading Rhythms
1. Read well-known rhythmic patterns found in students' repertoire, from stick notation, traditional rhythmic notation, and staff notation.
2. Extend the length of reading exercises from four to eight to sixteen beats.
3. Sight-read rhythmic phrases and songs with rhythm syllables.
4. Sight-read two-part rhythmic exercises.

Writing Rhythms
1. Write well-known rhythmic patterns found in students' repertoire, using stick notation, traditional rhythmic notation, and staff notation.
2. Write rhythmic patterns from memory or when dictated by the teacher.
3. Extend the writing of rhythmic patterns from four to eight to sixteen beats.

Reading Melodies
1. Read well-known melodic patterns found in students' repertoire, from hand signs, stick notation, traditional rhythmic notation with solfège syllables, and staff notation.
2. Extend the length of melodic patterns students read from four to eight to sixteen beats.
3. Sight-sing unknown melodic phrases and songs with solfège syllables and absolute letter names.

Writing Melodies
1. Write well-known melodic patterns found in students' repertoire, from hand signs, stick notation, traditional rhythmic notation with solfège syllables, and staff notation.
2. Write melodic patterns found in focus songs from memory or when dictated by the teacher using stick notation, traditional notation with solfège syllables, and staff notation.
3. Extend the length of melodic patterns students write from four to eight to sixteen beats.

Inner Hearing
1. Silently sing "inside" from the teacher's hand signs.
2. Silently sing known songs with melodic syllables.
3. Silently sing either full or partial rhythms or melodies written in stick notation, traditional rhythmic notation with solfège syllables or staff notation.
4. Sing back short melodic or rhythmic motives from memory using text, rhythm syllables, or solfège syllables.
5. Sing known songs silently:
   A. While performing the beat or rhythm of the song
   B. Without performing the beat or rhythm of the song
6. Recognize songs, rhythm patterns, or melodic patterns from stick or staff notation.

Form
1. Students analyze the phrase form of folksongs.
2. Students sing call and response songs.
3. Students perform question-and-answer phrases in songs.

IV. Improvisation/Composition: Students as Creative Human Beings

Rhythmic Improvisation
1. Improvise rhythms with known rhythm syllables using simple song forms.
2. Improvise movements that reflect the rhythmic form of the song.
3. Write a simple rhythmic composition, and improvise a rhythmic accompaniment or an ostinato.

Kodály Today

4. Create short rhythmic patterns using quarter notes, eighth notes, quarter rests, sixteenth notes, dotted quarter note followed by sixteenth notes, and sixteenth notes followed by dotted quarter notes.
5. Read an exercise and improvise an alternative ending.
6. Improvise empty measures within a four-measure phrase of music.

Melodic Improvisation
1. Broaden skills in improvisation and composition to include singing, playing instruments, and moving.
2. Improvise melodies with known solfège syllables using simple song forms.
3. Improvise movements that reflect the form of the song.
4. Write a simple melody and compose a rhythmic accompaniment or an ostinato.
5. Echo-sing simple melodic patterns, and then improvise singing in question-and-answer format.
6. Improvise a melodic chain; begin each phrase with the last syllable of the previous melodic turn.
7. Read an exercise and improvise an alternative ending.
8. Sing simple major melodies in a minor tonality.

V. Listening: Students as Informed Audience Members

1. Broaden the listening repertoire to reinforce musical concepts.
2. Identify a variety of instruments, voices, and dynamic levels.
3. Identify typical musical features in folk music and masterworks repertoire.
4. Listen to live performances.
5. Listen to recorded performances.
6. Identify phrase structure in classroom song repertoire, folk music, and masterworks.

Getting Started

When beginning to teach older students consider these recommendations.

- Develop a repertoire of songs that you can teach during the first few weeks of class.
- Broaden the song repertoire to include repertoire you can use throughout the year.
- Develop a series of vocal warm-up and singing exercises for students that you can build on.
- Develop a rhythmic sequence of elements.
- Develop a melodic sequence of elements.
- Integrate the sequence of rhythmic and melodic elements.
- Develop a process for teaching repertoire.
- Develop a lesson plan design.
- Develop techniques for practicing rhythm and melodies.
- Develop techniques for practicing various skill areas.

Selecting Song Repertoire for Older Beginners

Selection of musical materials is critical to the success of teaching older beginners. Repertoire should develop students':

- Knowledge of the selected repertoire
- Vocal skills
- Music literacy skills
- Movement skills
- Basic instrumental skills
- Creative skills
- Listening skills

The criteria for selecting song material are wide-ranging. Consider these recommendations.

- Songs should have an aesthetic and musical appeal.
- Songs should be developmentally appropriate for the students.
- Songs should be selected to reflect the cultural makeup of the classroom.
- Songs should also be selected for teaching specific musical concepts. The sequence of elements should be determined by their frequency of appearance in the repertoire. Elements can be isolated from phrases or motives of songs. Simple folksongs may be used without the text.

From these criteria, we can develop a repertoire list for the older beginner. Here is a sample of songs that can be used during the first few weeks of class with older beginners:

Song	Source
"Alabama Gal"	*150 American Folk Songs*, no. 107
"Are You Sleeping?"	*150 Rounds*, p. 5
"Birch Tree"	*150 Rounds*, p. 7
"Canoe Round"	*150 Rounds*, p. 38
"Charlotte Town"	*From Sound to Symbol*, p. 86
"Dance Josey"	*150 American Folk Songs*
"Dinah"	*Sound to Symbol*, p. 72
"Great Big House"	*Sail Away*, no. 19
"Hungarian Canon"	*From Sound to Symbol*, p. 112
"Ida Red"	*150 American Folk Songs*, no. 38
"Kookaburra"	*150 Rounds for Singing and Teaching*
"Old Brass Wagon"	*Kodály Today*
"Paw Paw Patch"	*150 American Folk Songs*, no. 140
"Rocky Mountain"	*150 American Folk Songs*, no. 35

Next we present an alphabetized list of songs that can be used throughout the year in the older beginner classroom. We have chosen songs from easily available sources. Many of

Kodály Today

these songs can be found in our *From Sound to Symbol*. The newly revised second edition (2011) includes an audio CD, an interactive skill development DVD, and web-based supplementary materials for eleven chapters. The book covers all basic rhythmic and melodic elements, but with a unique, sound-to-symbol approach that explores concepts through the sound of music before explaining how symbols are used. Students actively and methodically explore music by listening, performing, thinking critically, and composing, learning the rudiments of music theory in the process.

Song	Source
"A la Rueda de San Miguel"	*El Patio de Mi Casa*
"Alabama Gal"	*150 Folk Songs*, no. 107
"All Praise to Thee"	*150 Rounds*, p. 3
"Alleluia"	*150 Rounds*, p. 2
"Are You Sleeping?"	*150 Rounds*, p. 5
"Aunt Rhody"	*150 Folk Songs*, no. 95
"Birch Tree"	*150 Rounds*, p. 7
"Bounce High" (performed on a neutral syllable)	*Sail Away*, no. 5
"Bound for the Promised Land"	*Sail Away*, no. 127
"Canoe Round"	*150 Rounds*, p. 38
"Charlie over the Ocean"	*150 Folk Songs*, no. 26
"Charlotte Town"	*From Sound to Symbol*, p. 86
"Cocky Robin"	*150 Folk Songs*, no. 56
"Cotton Eyed Joe"	*150 Folk Songs*, no. 43
"De Colores"	*Sail Away*, no. 121
"The Deer Chase"	*Sail Away*, no. 120
"Dinah"	*From Sound to Symbol*
"Down in the Valley"	*Sail Away*, no. 103
"Down to the Baker's Shop"	*150 Folk Songs*, no. 104
"Early to Bed"	*150 Rounds*, p. 15
"Gallows Pole" (melody)	*From Sound to Symbol*, p. 264
"Great Big House"	*Sail Away*, no. 19
"Here Comes a Bluebird"	*150 Folk Songs*, no. 32
"Hey Ho"	*150 Rounds*, p. 24
"Hungarian Canon"	*From Sound to Symbol*, p. 112
"Ida Red"	*150 Folk Songs*, no. 38
"I've Been to Harlem"	*150 Folk Songs*, no. 80
"Jim Along Josie"	*150 Folk Songs*, no. 51
"Kis kece lanyom" (melody)	*From Sound to Symbol*, p. 253
"Land of the Silver Birch"	*The Kodály Method*
"Liza Jane"	*150 Folk Songs*, no. 71
"London Bridge"	*150 Folk Songs*, no. 105
"The Longest Train"	*Sail Away*, no. 126
"Lucy Locket"	*Sail Away*, no. 6
"Mama, Buy Me a Chiney Doll"	*150 Folk Songs*, no. 39
"My Momma Told Me"	*150 Folk Songs*, no. 124
"Oh, How Lovely Is the Evening"	*150 Rounds*, p. 39
"Paw Paw Patch"	*150 Folk Songs*, no. 140

Musicianship Skills in the Upper Grades

"Phoebe in Her Petticoat"	*Kodály Today*, p. 330
"Rain, Rain" (sung on "loo")	*150 Folk Songs*, no. 5
"Rocky Mountain"	*150 Folk Songs*, no. 35
"Rosie Darling, Rosie"	*150 Folk Songs*, no. 19
"Row, Row, Row Your Boat"	*150 Rounds*, p. 42
"Scotland's Burning"	*150 Rounds*, p. 43
"Shake Them 'Simmons Down"	*Sail Away*, no. 28
"Show Me the Way"	*150 Folk Songs*, no. 64
"Skin and Bones"	*Sail Away*, no. 57
"Sleep Little One"	*Sail Away*, no. 117
"Slovak Folk Song"	*From Sound to Symbol*, p. 258
"Snail, Snail" (melody)	*Sail Away*, no. 4
"Sweet William"	*150 Folk Songs*, no. 139
"Twinkle, Twinkle"	*Sound to Symbol*, p. 119
"When Jesus Wept"	*Sound Thinking*, p. 64
"Who's That Tapping at the Window?"	*150 Folk Songs*, no. 15
"Witch, Witch"	*Sail Away*, no. 1
"The Zebra Run"	*Sail Away*, no. 114

References for Selecting Songs for Older Beginners

Bolkovac, Edward, and Judith Johnson. *150 Rounds for Singing and Teaching.* New York: Boosey & Hawkes, 1996.

Erdei, Peter, and Katalin Komlás. *150 American Folk Songs to Sing, Read and Play.* New York: Boosey & Hawkes, 1974.

Houlahan, Micheál, and Philip Tacka. *From Sound to Symbol: Fundamentals of Music.* New York: Oxford University Press, 2011.

Locke, Eleanor G. *Sail Away: 155 American Folk Songs.* London: Boosey & Hawkes, 1988.

Montoya-Stier, Gabriela. *El Patio de Mi Casa.* Chicago: GIA, 2008.

Considerations, Techniques, and Procedures for Developing Older Students' Singing Skills

Posture

1. Balance the head. To accomplish this, the face should look straight ahead. Try several exercises, such as moving the head up and down and sideways to relax the head and neck muscles. Stand with your back against a wall and make sure that your head and the heels of your feet are touching the wall. The head should feel suspended as if you are a puppet or a balloon. Keep the spine straight.
2. Explain the correct seating position:
   Shoulders should be relaxed and rotated toward the back.
   Neck muscles should be relaxed.
   Tongue should be relaxed in the bottom of the mouth.

Kodály Today

   Spine should be extended.
   Rib cage is lifted.
   Sit at the edge of the chair when singing.
   Feet are on the floor,
   Hands are on the legs.
   Eyes are on the conductor.
3. Explain the correct standing position:
   Shoulders should be relaxed and rotated toward the back.
   Neck muscles should be relaxed.
   Tongue should be relaxed in the bottom of the mouth.
   Spine should be extended.
   Rib cage is lifted.
   Feet are on the floor.
   Arms should dangle freely at the sides; hands should be relaxed at the sides.
   Knees should be relaxed and very slightly bent.
   Feet should be firmly placed on the ground and roughly ten to twelve inches apart. Feet should be slightly apart, a shorter distance than the width of the shoulders. Weight should be on the balls of the feet. Eyes should be focused on the conductor.

Body Warm-up
1. Body stretches. Shoulders should be kept down as you reach for the stars; each hand should alternate with the other.
2. Shaking arms. Extend your arms in front of the body, and shake each arm separately.
3. Shoulder roll. Roll each shoulder separately, making a circle.
4. Shrugging shoulders. Shrug your shoulders, hold the position for several counts, and then release.
5. Head rolls. Drop your head to the left shoulder and trace a half circle, moving your chin toward your chest and right shoulder.
6. Neck stretch. Drop the right ear to the right shoulder and then the left ear to the left shoulder. Move your neck, making a yes-or-no motion.
7. Facial stretch. Act surprised.
8. Drop your jaw and say "mah, mah, mah" several times.
9. Knee flex. Arms should be extended forward and hands should be relaxed; gently bounce your body and flex the knees.
10. Wiggle toes. Wiggle your toes inside your shoes.

Breathing
1. Correct breathing posture. Students lie on the floor with a book placed on their abdominal muscles. When inhaling, the book rises, and when exhaling, the book lowers. Students should stand and place a hand on the abdominal muscles.

They should then exhale and inhale, paying attention to abdominal muscles without raising their shoulders. They need to be encouraged to take in a deep breath through their nose and mouth, not a shallow one. Sometimes it is useful for them exhale air against the palm of their hand.
2. Awareness of the diaphragm and other abdominal muscles for breathing. These exercises will help students with understanding the use of the abdominal muscles for breathing:
Show students how to sip through a straw correctly and expand their waist.
Show students how to release air using a "sss" or hissing sound.
Show students how to release air using the word "ha."
Guide the students in yawning, as this opens up the back of the throat and relaxes the voice.
3. Sighing is a gentle way of using a higher voice. Try sighing a few times, starting each sigh a little higher than the last.
4. Practice breathing. Have students breathe in through the nose for four counts, hold for four counts, and exhale through mouth for four counts. Extend the number of counts.

Resonance
1. Use of sirens. Have the students imitate the sound of a siren with the voice. Challenge them make soft and loud, high and low, long and short sirens, sirens that just go up, just come down, or do both.
2. Falling off a cliff. Tell students to pretend they're falling off a cliff, to say "aaaahhhhhhhhhh!"
3. Short vowel sounds. Have students practice singing the short vowels with known songs. For example, they can sing the song "Bingo" but instead of spelling out the word they sing each of the short vowel sounds.

Tone Production
1. Lip trills. Direct students to use lip trills to sing a known song.
2. Humming. Have them hum known melodies.
3. Pure vowel sounds. They sing with known solfège syllables and hand signs.
4. Vowel scales. Teach students to unify vowel sounds by singing descending scales using a major pentatonic or pentachord scale on "mee," "meh," "mah," "moh," and "moo."
5. Combination vowels. Students sing the sequence of OH-OO-AH on notes of the pentatonic scale. For example, they sing the three vowel sounds on *mi*, then *re*, and finally *do*. Pay attention to the jaw on each of the vowel sounds. Have them keep repeating but singing a minor second higher each time.
6. Extending vocal range. Students practice singing a phrase of a song and repeating it a minor second higher. Use a pure vowel sound; each time they repeat they can sing another on another vowel sound.

7. Students sing while pointing to a vowel sound chart:
   A Ah
   E Eh
   I Ee
   O Oh
   U Oo smaller
   Students sing a known song and point to the vowels on a chart; this focuses their attention on sound production.
8. Students sing songs with solfège syllables. They practice singing melodic patterns.

Diction
1. Tongue twisters sung. Students will gain flexibility by singing tongue twisters on one pitch and repeat as a minor second. They repeat the exercise by moving up a minor second on each repetition.
2. Tongue twisters sung in two voice parts. Students gain flexibility by singing tongue twisters at the interval of a fourth or fifth.
3. Unvoiced consonants. Students say the unvoiced consonants *p, t, k*, using rhythm patterns derived from song repertoire.
4. Voiced consonants. Students sing a song on a voiced consonant (*m, n, ng, v*). Then they sing songs using voiced consonants *b, d, g*, and *j* using rhythm patterns from known songs.
5. Melodic patterns with an "inner smile." Ask students to keep their lips closed and form an inner smile. Ask them to echo-sing, using this position.
6. Diphthongs. Students practice singing diphthongs (dominant vowel sound and a lesser vowel sound). For example, they practice saying and singing on a pitch:
   "How now brown cow?"
   "The rain in Spain stays mainly in the plain."
7. Singing using a sustained *m* or *n*. Ask students to sing the sequences "moo-moh," "mah-meh-mee," and "noo-noh-nah-neh-nee" on a sustained note or using notes of the pentatonic scale.
8. Vowel scales. Teach unifying vowel sounds by singing ascending and descending pentatonic, pentachord, hexachord, major, and minor scales on "mee," "meh," "mah," "moh," and "moo."

Tuneful Singing
1. Remember to include working with major and minor melodies containing *low la*. In a minor context, the *re-* in a minor setting will be sung closer to the *do* than in a major setting, and the interval between *low la* and *do* will be a much darker-sounding minor third interval. Work with more melodic ostinatos and descants. Students may begin to work with simple canons using a smaller range of notes. Students may also begin to sing simple two-part arrangements

of folksongs. More challenging harmonically based arrangements may be appropriate, depending on the skill level of the students.
2. Singing phrases of songs on an OH sound. Students sing phrases of songs on an OH and make sure that the tone is very light and relaxed.
3. Singing with dynamic markings. Students should sing known melodies using the correct dynamic names and terms:

pp pianissimo

p piano

mp mezzo piano

mf mezzo forte

f forte

ff fortissimo

It is best to sing songs using two very different dynamics (e.g., forte and piano).
4. T sings songs using two-part hand signs. Students sing in two parts from teacher's hand signs.
5. Singing longer phrases. Students sing known songs but combine two phrases into one phrase.
6. Tempo markings. Students should be taught the Italian terms and English meanings for tempo markings.
7. Practice staggered breathing with students. They sing on one pitch using the word "loo." Students must learn to breath quietly and enter softly after each breath to maintain the sound and vowel color.
8. Staccato and legato. Students practice singing songs legato and staccato.
9. Crescendo and decrescendo. Students should sing songs using crescendo and decrescendo.

Sample Rhythmic Sequence of Music Concepts and Elements

Tables 11.1 and 11.2 show a sample rhythmic sequence of rhythmic concepts and elements appropriate for the older beginner. The same teaching strategies used with younger students may be followed when working with older beginners. We have defined the concept for only the most challenging rhythmic elements.

Sample Melodic Sequence of Music Concepts and Elements

Table 11.3 is a sample teaching sequence addressing melodic elements appropriate for the older beginner. The same teaching strategies used with younger students may be followed when working with older beginners. It is important to remember that if necessary, the teacher must spend more time developing the students' singing voices before introducing any melodic concepts. We have defined the concept for only the most challenging rhythmic elements.

Kodály Today

Table 11.1

Rhythm/Theory	Corresponding Concept	Rhythm Syllables	Songs
Beat			"Rocky Mountain" "Zudio" "Tideo" "Sailing on the Ocean"
Simple duple, triple, and quadruple meter			"Dance Josey" $\frac{2}{4}$, "How Lovely Is the Evening" $\frac{3}{4}$ "Are You Sleeping?" $\frac{4}{4}$
Form			"Canoe Song" (ABAC)
Dynamics			"Charlotte Town"
Rhythm			"Tideo" "Great Big House"
Quarter and eighth notes and rests	One and two even sounds on a beat	*ta, ta di*	"Are You Sleeping?" "Rocky Mountain" "Great Big House" "Liza Jane" "I've Been to Haarlem" "Scotland's Burning" "Sur le Pont d'Avignon" Without text: "Snail, Snail" "Lucy Locket"
Meter $\frac{2}{4}$ $\frac{3}{4}$ $\frac{4}{4}$	Patterns of strong and weak beats Bar lines, measures		$\frac{2}{4}$ "Rocky Mountain" $\frac{3}{4}$ "Oh How Lovely Is the Evening," canon $\frac{4}{4}$ "Great Big House"
Half note and half note rest	One sound that lasts for two beats		"I Got a Letter"
Dotted half note	One sound held for three beats		"Oh How Lovely Is the Evening"

Table 11.2

Teaching sixteenth notes	Four even sounds on a beat	*takadimi*	"Dinah" "Tideo" "Kookaburra" "Who's That Tapping at the Window?"
Sixteenth note combinations made up of one eighth note and two sixteenth notes or two sixteenth notes and one eighth note	Three sounds on a beat; the first sound is longer than the last two sounds, long sound followed by two short sounds Three uneven sounds on a beat; the last sound is held longer than the first two sounds, two short sounds followed by a long sound	*tadimi* *taka di*	"Car Song" "John Cuko" "Kookaburra" "Draw Me a Bucket of Water" "ZumGaliGali" "Jim Along Josie"
Internal upbeats	Internal phrase begins with unstressed beats		"Fed My Horse" "Over the River"
External upbeats	External phrase begins with unstressed beats		"Good Bye Old Pain"
Syncopation	Three uneven sounds over two beats, one short, one long, and one short	*ta di---di*	"Hill and Gully Rider" "Alabama Gal" "Land of the Silver Birch"
Dotted quarter followed by eighth note	Two uneven sounds over two beats where the first sound lasts a beat and a half	*ta--------di*	"Liza Jane" "Birch Tree"
Dotted eighth followed by a sixteenth note	Two uneven sounds on one beat; the first sound is three times longer than the second	*tami*	"Shady Grove"
Sixteenth note followed by a dotted eighth	Two uneven sounds on one beat; the first sound is shorter than the second	*taka--*	"Shake Them 'Simmons Down"
Eighth note followed by a dotted quarter	Two uneven sounds over two beats where the first sound lasts half a beat and the second sound lasts a beat and a half	*ta di---*	"Charlotte Town"

(continued)

Table 11.2 Continued

Eighth note rest			
6/8 meter with even division		ta taki da ta da	"Row, Row, Row Your Boat"
6/8 meter with uneven divisions		ta di da	"Early to Bed"
Triplet	Three sounds on a beat in simple meter	taki da	"Every Night When the Sun Goes Down"
Duplet	Two sounds on one beat in compound meter	ta di	"A la Rueda de San Miguel"

Table 11.3

Elements	Concept	Solfège Syllables	Songs
Major trichord (begin to work on absolute letter names)	Three adjacent pitches	do-re-mi	"Great Big House" "Au Clair de la Lune" "Long Legged Sailor" "The Boatman" "Dinah" "Fed My Horse"
Bichord and trichord of the pentatonic scale		so-mi la-sol-mi	"Dinah" "Pizza, Pizza"
Pentatonic tetrachord		do-re-mi-so	"Dinah"
Pentatonic scale		do-re-mi-so-la	"Rocky Mountain" "Hill and Gully Rider"
Major pentachord, hexachord		do-re-mi-fa-so do-re-mi-fa-so-la	"Old Woman" "Alabama Gal" "When I First Came to This Land"
Major extended pentachord, hexachord, and pentatonic scales		la-sol-mi-re-do–low la–low so	"Dance Josey" "Turn the Glasses Over"

(continued)

Table 11.3 Continued

Elements	Concept	Solfège Syllables	Songs
Minor pentatonic scale		*low la–do–re–mi–so*	"Land of the Silver Birch"
Minor extended pentatonic scale		*low so–low la–do–re–mi–so–la–high do*	"Canoe Song"
Scales based on permutations of the pentatonic scale		*so* pentatonic scale	*Sound Thinking*, pp. 66–67
Major scale	Eight adjacent pitches with a half step between the third and fourth and the seventh and eighth scale degrees of the scale	*do–re–mi–fa–so–la–ti–do*	"Alleluia" "Kookaburra" "Viva La Musica"
Natural minor scale	Eight adjacent pitches with a half step between the second and third and fifth and sixth degrees of the scale	*low la–ti–do–re–mi–fa–sol–la–ti–do*	"Sweet William" "Drill Ye Tarriers"
Harmonic minor scale		*low la–ti–do–re–mi–fa–si–high la*	"Ah Poor Bird"
Melodic minor scale		*low la–ti–do–re–mi–fi–si–la high la–so–fa–mi–re–do–ti–low la*	"Who Can Sail"
Dorian mode	Eight adjacent pitches with a half step between the second and third and the sixth and seventh degrees of the scale	*re–mi–fa-sol-la-ti–high do–high re* or *low la–ti–do–re–mi–fi–sol–la*	"Drunken Sailor" "Scarborough Fair"

(continued)

Table 11.3 Continued

Elements	Concept	Solfège Syllables	Songs
Mixolydian	Eight adjacent pitches with a half step between the third and fourth and the sixth and seventh degrees of the scale	low so–la,-ti-do-re-mi-fa-so or do-re-mi-fa-sol-la-ta–high do	"Old Joe Clark" "Every Night When the Sun Goes Down"
Harmonic functions			"Jim Along Josie" *150 American Folk Songs*, no. 51
Primary chords			*Sound Thinking*, vol. II, p. 106, no. 1 "Oh How Lovely Is the Evening" *150 Rounds*, p. 139
Dominant seventh chord			*Sound Thinking*, p. 107 "Music Alone Shall Live"

A Sample Integrated Sequence of Melodic and Rhythmic Elements for Teaching Older Beginners

Here is a suggested teaching sequence including song repertoire and some choral repertoire for the older beginning music student. Depending on the singing ability of the students, the music instructor might spend more time on teaching rhythmic elements while developing the students' singing voices.

1. In-tune singing
   A. "Rocky Mountain"
   B. "Rosie Darling, Rosie"
   C. "Hey Ho, Nobody Home"
2. Steady beat
   A. "Ida Red"
   B. "London Bridge"
   C. "Dinah"
3. Rhythm
   A. "Are You Sleeping?"
   B. "Ida Red"
   C. "Dinah"

D. "Tideo"
   E. "Great Big House"
4. Beat in duple and compound meter
   A. Compound
      i. "Skin and Bones"
      ii. "The Miller of Dee"
      iii. "Row, Row, Row Your Boat"
   B. Duple
      i. "Rocky Mountain"
      ii. "Great Big House"
      iii. "Dinah"
5. Simple duple, triple, and quadruple meter
   A. Simple duple
      i. "Charlotte Town"
      ii. "Birch Tree"
      iii. "Canoe Song"
   B. Triple
      i. "America"
      ii. "When Jesus Wept"
      iii. "Early to Bed"
   C. Quadruple
      i. "Frère Jacques"
      ii. "Low Bridge"
      iii. "Sweet William"
6. Form
   A. "Are You Sleeping?"
   B. "Rocky Mountain"
   C. "Dinah"
   D. "Ida Red"
7. Dynamics
   A. "Birch Tree"
8. Teaching quarter and eighth notes rests
   A. "Are You Sleeping?"
   B. "Rocky Mountain"
   C. "Great Big House"
   D. "'Liza Jane"
   E. "I've Been to Haarlem"
   F. "Scotland's Burning"
   G. "Mrs. Jenny Wren," by Arthur Baynon; text by Rodney Bennett (Boosey)
9. Pentatonic bichord and trichord
   A. "Witch, Witch" (bichord)
   B. "A Tisket, a Tasket" (trichord)

Kodály Today

10. Major trichord *do-re-mi*
    A. "Hot Cross Buns" (melody)
    B. "Rocky Mountain"
    C. "Dinah"
    D. "Here Comes the Bluebird"
    E. "Long Legged Sailor"
    F. "Celtic Cradle Song," arranged by Robert Hugh (#HL 08744430, Hal Leonard Corporation)
    G. "Three French Folksongs," arr. by Geoffrey Edwards (Heritage Music Press)
11. Pentatonic tetrachord
    A. "Dinah"
    B. "Bought Me a Cat"
    C. "Sleep My Baby," arrangement of "Suo-Gan," folksong by Alex Rowley (Boosey and Hawkes)
    D. "Kyrie," arr. by Ruth Elaine Schram, on an Antonín Dvorák (1841–1904) melody
12. Pentatonic scale
    A. "Rocky Mountain"
    B. "Ida Red"
    C. "Songs of a Summer Afternoon," arrangement of "Blue Bird," by Emily Crocker (Hal Leonard Corporation)
13. Begin work on absolute letter names
    A. "Dinah"
    B. "Ida Red"
    C. "Rocky Mountain"
14. Major pentachord scale
    A. "Ode to Joy"
    B. "When the Saints Go Marching In"
15. Major hexachord scale
    A. "Alabama Gal"
    B. "Twinkle, Twinkle, Little Star"
    C. "Show Me the Way"
    D. "Coffee Grows on White Oak Trees"
    E. "Dormi, Dormi," by Mary Goetze (Boosey & Hawkes)
16. Half note and half note rest
    A. "Here Comes a Bluebird"
    B. "Aunt Rhody"
    C. "Are You Sleeping?"
    D. "Hey, Ho, Nobody Home"
17. Whole note:
    A. "Aunt Rhody" (in $\frac{4}{4}$ or $\frac{4}{2}$ meter)
    B. "Velvet Shoes," by Randall Thompson (E. C. Schirmer Music)

Musicianship Skills in the Upper Grades

18. Dotted half note:
    A. "Down in the Valley"
    B. "Au Clair de la Lune"
19. Counting with numbers
    A. "Rocky Mountain"
    B. "Are You Sleeping?"
    C. "Hush Little Minnie"
20. Sixteenth notes (in groupings of four)
    A. "Paw Paw Patch"
    B. "Dance Josey"
    C. "Kookaburra"
    D. "Old Brass Wagon"
21. Teaching sixteenth-note combinations made up of one eighth note and two sixteenth notes or two sixteenth notes and one eighth note
    A. "Jim Along Josie"
    B. "Ida Red"
    C. "Mama, Buy Me a Chiney Doll"
    D. "Aussie Animals," by David Lawrence, based on "Kookaburra" (Studio 224)
22. Continue to work on absolute letter names
    A. "Rocky Mountain"
    B. "Bow Wow Wow"
    C. "Cotton Eyed Joe"
23. Major extended pentachord, hexachord, and pentatonic scales
    A. "Rocky Mountain"
    B. "Old Lady Sittin' in the Dining Room"
    C. "Mary Had a Baby" (use of *low la* in major tonality)
    D. "The Sally Gardens," by Benjamin Britten, text by William Yeats (Boosey; uses *high do*)
    E. "Sail Away," arr. by Susan Brumfield (Colla Voce Music; uses *high do*)
    F. "Chatter with the Angels," arr. by Charles Collins (Boosey & Hawkes)
24. Syncopation
    A. "Liza Jane"
    B. "Dog and Cat"
    C. "My Mommy Told Me"
25. Minor pentachord scale
    A. "Birch Tree"
    B. "Kis kece Lanyom" (*From Sound to Symbol*)
26. Dotted quarter note followed by an eighth note
    A. "Birch Tree"; see also "The Little Birch Tree," arr. by Mary Goetze (Boosey and Hawkes)
    B. "Hey, Ho"
    C. "Chairs to Mend"

27. Minor hexachord scale
    A. "Slovak Folk Song" (*From Sound to Symbol*, p. 258)
28. Minor pentatonic scale
    A. "Canoe Round"
    B. "Land of the Silver Birch"
29. Major scale
    A. "Alleluia"
    B. "All Praise to Thee"
    C. "Viva la Musica"
    D. "De Colores"
    E. "Sleep Little One"
    F. "The Deer Chase"
    G. "Friendship Song," arr. by Doreen Rao (Boosey & Hawkes)
30. Dotted eighth note followed by a sixteenth note
    A. "London Bridge"
    B. "Charlie over the Ocean"
    C. "Old Joe Clark," arr. by Judy Herrington and Sara Glick (Pavane)
    D. "Goin' to Boston," arr. by Shirley W. McRae (Plymouth Music)
    E. "Sail Away," arr. by Susan Brumfield (Colla Voce Music)
31. Minor scale
    A. "Old Abram Brown," by Benjamin Britten (Boosey)
    B. "Bound for the Promised Land"
    C. "The Longest Train"
    D. "A Daffodil, Too," by B. Wayne Bisbee
32. Compound meter
    A. "De Colores"
    B. "Sleep, Little One, Sleep"
    C. "The Zebra Run"
    D. "To Work upon the Railway"
    E. "May Song," by Franz Schubert, ed. by Doreen Rao (Boosey & Hawkes)

Teaching Songs

Develop a process for teaching songs to older students. Generally speaking, there are only two ways to teach them song repertoire: by note or by rote.

General Suggestions for Teaching Songs by Rote
1. Sing the song for the students using your head voice; do not overuse vibrato.
2. Ask questions relating to the text or specific musical elements. This strengthens listening and analytical skills, as well as the students' ability to memorize. A student's aural awareness and ability to analyze what is sung may be developed simultaneously with that of older students. Questions must be specific. Sing the song or phrase of the song before asking each question. This

enables the students to hear it several times before they sing and permits a better grasp of melodic contours and rhythmic complexities.
3. Have the students repeat selected phrases. This focuses attention on a difficult interval or rhythmic pattern. Melodic and rhythmic discrimination abilities are developed and practiced through singing.
4. Challenge older beginners' ability to concentrate. Ask the students to perform a rhythmic or melodic ostinato while you sing the song.

General Suggestions for Teaching Songs by Note
1. Show the students the musical score.
2. Sing the song for them using your head voice.
3. Sing the song and ask the students to follow the score. Focus their attention on the text or on the melodic contour.
4. Ask questions relating to the text or specific musical elements. This strengthens listening and analytical skills, as well as the students' ability to memorize. Aural skill and analysis may be developed simultaneously with older beginners. Again, questions need to be specific. Sing the song or phrase of the song before asking each question. This enables the students to hear the song several times before they sing and permits a better grasp of melodic contours and rhythmic complexities.
5. Have the students repeat selected phrases. This focuses attention on a difficult interval or rhythmic pattern. Melodic and rhythmic discrimination abilities are developed and practiced through singing.
6. Challenge older beginners to concentrate. Ask the students to perform a rhythmic or melodic ostinato while the instructor sings the song.

Initially the teacher may sing songs in the class and the students should have pencil and paper ready for drawing the phrase marks and beats within each phrase. This simple task is an opportunity for you to sing the song many times before asking the students to sing the song on their own. When you are singing a new song, students should listen and perform one of these three activities:

1. Tapping the beat
2. Drawing the phrases of the song in the air
3. Conducting the meter

You may ask the students to draw the phrases and mark the beats during the first performances of the song. This keeps the students on task as they listen to the song. These procedures engage students in doing two things at the same time: listening and writing.

Teach them the concepts of phrase and phrase mark, beat, meter, and form as soon as possible.

We believe that singing in tune should be developed before melodic elements are introduced. Therefore, rhythmic elements may be introduced while working on the students' vocal skills. In general, presentation of rhythmic elements is similar to that used when

Kodály Today

teaching younger students; however, presentation of melodic elements is different. Because of the frequency of the *mi-re-do* motif in older students' song repertoire, the *mi-re-do* pattern can be the first pattern introduced to students rather than the *so-mi* pattern. Several songs are suggested in the sequence of rhythmic and melodic elements. Remember that singing simple songs leads to better intonation and makes learning concepts more clear.

Lesson Design

The same types of lesson plans as described in Chapter 10 ("Sequencing and Lesson Planning") can also be used with older beginners. However for older beginners, there needs to be more attention on developing vocal skills throughout the lesson. The preparation/practice lesson plan may be modified to permit the instructor to work on developing the students' intonation while working on specific rhythmic concepts and elements.

Framework for Lesson Plan Outline

The lesson plan outline in Table 11.4 may be used for teaching older beginners. It is a blend of all other lesson plans used with the beginning music student. New musical

Table 11.4 Sample Lesson Plan for Older Beginners

GRADE X, LESSON X	
Outcome	Preparation: Practice:
INTRODUCTORY ACTIVITIES	
Warm-up Develop tuneful singing	• Body warm-up • Breathing • Beat activity • Intonation exercises
Performance	Sing and review known songs. Sing known canons. Teach new song material.
Music theory through performance	Focus on preparation, presentation, and practice of melodic and rhythmic elements.
Creative movement	Focus on movement and creativity.
Music skill development	Focus on music skill development of a known element.
SUMMARY ACTIVITIES	
Review Lesson objectives Review new song	

elements should be reinforced in every section of the lesson plan. This enables students to reinforce a new concept through practice exercises, sight singing, memory work, dictation, and part singing.

What follows is a brief explanation of the lesson plan design for older beginners.

Vocal Warm-up
The class begins with a body warm-up, which develops breathing as well as beat movement. This can be achieved by playing to the students a piece of music that has a well-defined beat. You can lead the students in a rote movement activity that incorporates breathing activities and breath control.

Sing Known Songs
Work on the performance aspect of singing as students perform known repertoire. You can also begin to work on part singing during this section of the lesson.

Tuneful Singing
Develop and practice tuneful singing strategies based on the materials students are singing.

Review Known Songs
Practice singing known repertoire with rhythm or melodic solfège syllables.

Teach a New Song
Teach students a new song or canon by note or rote.

Music Theory Through Performance
Prepare and later present a new rhythmic or melodic element. Use the model of learning presented in the book, and follow the same sequence of activities but at a faster pace.

Creative Movement
Perform a known song or singing game with the class.

Musical Skill Development
Practice known rhythmic and melodic elements in combination with the music skills, to include

- Singing
- Inner hearing
- Developing musical memory
- Reading and sight-reading skills
- Writing and dictation skills
- Part work

- Improvisation
- Instrumental skills
- Listening skills
- Practice where possible both aurally (no score) and visually (use of score)

Review Activities
During this stage of the lesson, you review the main outcomes with the students.

Preparation Activities
Table 11.5 provides a brief synopsis of ideas for teaching rhythm and melody.

Table 11.5

Echo clapping	Clap the rhythm of a melody or a rhythmic pattern.
Melodic contour and rhythm	T demonstrates the melodic contour of the song while clapping the rhythm.
Perform rhythm and beat at the same time	T divides the class into two groups, one group performing the rhythmic pattern, the other keeping the beat. This activity may be practiced in several combinations: 1. T/class 2. Class/T 3. Divided class 4. Two individual Ss 5. Ss keeping the beat with one hand and tapping the rhythm with the other 6. Ss performing the rhythm and beating at the same time
Conduct	Sing and conduct at the same time.
Aural analysis	Identify which beat or beats contain the new rhythmic element.
Visual representation	Create a beat chart and write solfège syllables on each beat to indicate the number of sounds within the beat.

Practice Activities
Table 11.6 gives a synopsis of ideas for practicing both rhythm and melody.

Practice Activities for Rhythm
Practice sessions can be made more efficient by using a variety of performance techniques. Practicing in small groups is valuable for students on many levels. We know that, in addition to sharpening their listening skills by evaluating each other's performance, students who practice with their peers are far more secure in their performance when called on in class. Table 11.7 is a summary of ideas for practicing rhythm.

Table 11.6

Melodic contour	Ss demonstrate the melodic contour of a melody with arm motions. Motions should be natural and appropriate to the text and tempo of the song.
Melodic contour and rhythm	Ss demonstrate the melodic contour while clapping the rhythm of a melody.
Echo singing	Ss sing melodic patterns sung or played by T.
Writing	Ss write the rhythm of a melody spatially.
Aural analysis	Ss identify which beat or beats contain the new melodic element.
Visual representation	Ss create a representation of the melodic contour.

Table 11.7

Rhythm syllables	Ss sing a melody with rhythm syllables while tapping the beat.
Conducting	Ss sing with rhythm syllables while conducting.
Echo singing	Ss echo-sing rhythm syllables to a rhythm pattern clapped by T.
Aural dictation	Ss identify the meter and rhythm patterns clapped or sung by T.
Writing	Ss change a rhythm pattern from a given pattern into a new rhythm pattern. In pairs, one S writes a sixteen-beat pattern and then claps a slightly different pattern. The other S must identify where the changes occur.
Improvise rhythm patterns	Ss select a meter and length for the pattern, then determine the rhythmic form to use (for example, ABA or ABAB).
Writing	Ss memorize a phrase of a melody and write it from memory.
Perform a rhythmic canon	1. Say rhythm syllables while clapping the rhythm. 2. Think the rhythm syllables and clap the rhythm. 3. Clap the rhythm in canon with someone else. 4. Perform the rhythmic canon by yourself. Clap one part with one hand and the other part with the other.

Practice Activities for Melody

Developing ear-training abilities and mastering sight singing normally takes many hours of practice. These sessions can be made more efficient by using a variety of practice techniques. Practicing in small groups is valuable for students on many levels. In addition to sharpening their listening skills by evaluating each other's performances, students who practice with their peers are far more secure in their performance when called on in class. Table 11.8 is a summary of ideas and teaching techniques for practicing melody.

Table 11.8

Conducting	Ss sing using solfège syllables and conduct.
Hand signs	Ss sing using solfège syllables and show hand signs.
Rhythm and hand signs	Ss sing using solfège syllables while showing hand signs.
Sight singing from hand signs	Ss sing using solfège syllables or show hand signs for a pattern; ask another S to sing it back.
Memory	Ss memorize an exercise and notate it without referring to the book. First analyze the form by looking for repetition and similar patterns. This helps simplify the task.
Error detection	Ss select a phrase of music. One S plays the selection, deliberately making a melodic mistake. Another S follows the score and locates the error.

Developing Music Skills

The same processes outlined in Chapter 7 ("Developing Musicianship Skills in the Classroom") can be used or modified for teaching older students.

Reading and Sight-Reading Rhythms

Sight-reading rhythms should be practiced only when students have well-developed audiation skills. It is best that students read known rhythms before tackling unknown examples. It is also best to begin sight-singing exercises by reading variations of known song material. Table 11.9 presents sample procedures for sight-reading rhythms.

The procedures set out in Table 11.10 may be used for sight-reading melodic examples.

Writing and Dictation

Dictation is closely linked to development of musical memory, inner hearing, and reading and writing skills. Memory is an essential skill for being able to take musical dictations. Students must to be able to sing known repertoire with hand signs, rhythm syllables,

Table 11.9

Prior to sight singing	T practices basic rhythmic patterns from the sight-reading exercise with Ss. Difficult rhythms patterns should be practiced with known song material
Sight singing	1. T and Ss discuss the meter and an appropriate tempo for performance. 2. T and Ss determine the form and identify rhythmic motifs. 3. Ask Ss to inner-hear the rhythm with rhythm syllables. 4. Ss chant the exercise with rhythm syllables and keep the beat.
Memorize	Memorize the example and notate it if appropriate.
Practice	T should devise a variety of ways to practice a reading exercise. For example: Ss read the rhythm backwards while clapping a rhythmic ostinato.

Table 11.10

Prior to sight singing	T practices basic rhythmic and melodic patterns from the sight-reading exercise with Ss. They should sight read from T's hand signs, tone ladder, rhythmic notation, and solfège or from the staff. Difficult rhythms should be practiced with a suitable rhythmic ostinato or subdivision of the beat. Sing these preparatory exercises in the same key as the reading example. Exercises should be sung in solfège, letter names, and neutral syllables.
Sight singing	1. T and Ss discuss the meter and key. Determine an appropriate tempo. 2. T and Ss determine the form. Look for repeated patterns. 3. Ss chant the rhythm with rhythm syllables. 4. Ss think through the melody with solfège and hand signs. 5. Ss sing the exercise with solfège and hand signs.
Memorize	Memorize the example and notate it if appropriate.
Practice	T should devise a variety of ways to practice a reading exercise. For example, read the melody backwards; or read a unison melody while clapping a rhythmic ostinato.

and solfège syllables before they begin to notate these known melodies using traditional rhythmic notation and staff notation. Beginning dictations should be based on known patterns that have been memorized. As the students' memory expands, the teacher can begin more formal dictation practice. Initially, the students should sing the melody before attempting to notate it. In this way, the instructor can determine whether the students are

Kodály Today

hearing the example accurately. Initial dictation repertoire can be based on simple folk music. Later, music of other styles may be added.

The procedures set out in Table 11.11 may be used for rhythmic dictation.

The procedures found in Table 11.12 may be used for melodic dictation.

Table 11.11

Prepare the meter	Prepare the meter by singing known folksongs.
Sing typical rhythmic patterns found in the dictation	Sing typical melodic patterns found in the dictation. Ss sing using rhythm syllables and letter names. During beginning stages of formal dictation, T may also give Ss a score with the bar lines indicated and certain notes or rhythms filled in to aid their memory.
Perform the melody	T performs the exercise on the piano. It is best to sing a rhythmic dictation so Ss can hear the full length of all notes.
Aural analysis	Ss determine the meter, how many measures, and the form.
Ss perform	Ss sing the melody using rhythm syllables.
Ss write	Ss write the melody from memory.
Ss perform	Ss sing the melody from their score.

Table 11.12

Prepare the key	Prepare the key with hand signs and with reading notes of the tone set from staff notation. Use known folksongs to practice difficult rhythms.
Sing typical melodic patterns	Sing typical melodic patterns found in the dictation. Ss sing using solfège syllables and letter names. During beginning stages of formal dictation, T may also give Ss a score with the bar lines indicated and certain notes or rhythms filled in to aid their memory.
T performs the melody	T performs the melody on the piano or another instrument.
Aural analysis	Ss determine the final note and the beginning note as well as some or all, as appropriate, of the mode, melodic cadences, melodic contour, patterns, and meter.
Ss perform	Ss sing the melody using solfège syllables and absolute letter names.
Ss perform	Ss sing the melody using rhythm syllables and hand signs.
Ss write	Ss write the melody from memory.
Ss perform	Ss sing the melody from their score. This melody may be used to practice additional skills; T transposes it into other keys or practice the intervals in the melody.

Developing Musical Memory

Musical memory plays an important role in singing accurately and being able to recall a pattern for the purpose of dictation. Memorizing by ear is more difficult than memorizing from notation because no visual aid is present. Melodies used for memorizing by ear should be easier than those with notation. Extracts should be played on the piano or another instrument and sung a few times before allowing students to write. In Table 11.13 are general procedures that may be used for memorizing both rhythmic and melodic examples.

Table 11.13

Prepare the example	T plays a melody on the piano; Ss determine the meter and the number of bars.
T performs	T plays the musical example while Ss conduct.
Ss perform	Ss conduct and sing using rhythm syllables.
Ss write	Ss write the dictation with stick or traditional notation.
T plays the musical example	T plays the musical example while Ss check their written work.

Once students have gained experience with unison works, they can begin to memorize two-part extracts. Accompaniments may be drawn from a rhythmic pattern, a rhythmic or melodic ostinato, chord roots, a contrapuntal melodic line, or typical cadential idioms in harmonic or modal music. Table 11.14 offers a sequence of activities for developing a student's musical memory.

Table 11.14

Memorize from hand signs	1. T shows typical melodic patterns and ask Ss to sing patterns back, starting with short patterns such as *so-la-so-mi* or *mi-fa-mi-re-mi*. 2. Once melodic patterns can be echoed with ease, guide Ss to sing four- and eight-beat melodies. 3. Show a melody in hand signs. Select pentatonic melodies or rounds. Ss sing the melody in canon using solfège or absolute letter names and write the example from memory. 4. Sing a known melody with absolute letter names while using hand signs.
Memorize from staff notation	1. Memorize a short fragment of a musical example from a score using hand signs. 2. T sings the unknown part of a musical example. Ss memorize and sing the motifs. 3. Ss write the melody on staff paper. At a more advanced level, they can write the example in another key using a different clef.

(continued)

Table 11.14 Continued

Memorizing by ear	T plays a melody on the keyboard, and Ss 1. Identify the meter 2. Sing with rhythm syllables 3. Sing and conduct 4. Identify the ending and starting pitches 5. Sing with hand signs 6. Sing with absolute pitch names and hand signs 7. Write or play it back on the piano (the example may be transposed)
Memorizing two-part examples	1. Sing the two-part example. 2. Memorize one part silently using solfège syllables. 3. Sing that part out loud while conducting. 4. Practice the other part following steps 1 through 3. 5. Sing both parts in a group and then as solos, using both solfège syllables and note names. 6. Sing one part and play the other on the piano, or sing one part and show the second part with hand signs. 7. Write both parts of the extract.
Error detection	Select a phrase of music. One S plays the selection, deliberately making a melodic mistake. Another S follows the score and locates the error.

Part Work

Both singing and playing part music are important aspects of musical training. This enables the student to learn to hear several voices simultaneously. The procedures set out in Table 11.15 may be used for developing two-part singing.

A Few Final Considerations for Teaching Older Beginners

Here are a few considerations for dealing with older students who are beginning their study of music. We thank Julie Arend, choral director at Dobie Middle School in the Austin Independent School District in Austin, Texas, for her suggestions. Julie's perspective is realistic, and we know from having worked with her that she speaks from the perspective of someone who has very fine musicianship and real dedication to the profession.

- Spend a considerable amount of time on rote teaching (retention is almost nil in the beginning), and make a point of insisting that they learn the repertoire.
- Show students how to clap musically, using two fingers in the right hand to tap on the left hand.

Musicianship Skills in the Upper Grades

Table 11.15

Perform	Sing folksongs or other exercises while clapping the beat or the rhythm.
Perform	Sing folksongs, dividing the singing by phrases in call-and-response style. This enables group 1 to hear what group 2 sings, and vice versa.
Ensemble work	Add a rhythmic ostinato and sing using rhythm syllables.
Develop two-part singing	1. Ss sing while T claps the rhythm. 2. Ss and T exchange parts. 3. Divide the Ss into two groups; one group sings and another performs the rhythm. 4. Two Ss perform the work. 5. One S may sing one voice while playing the other voice on the piano. 6. Ss clap a series of rhythmic patterns while singing a known song. 7. Sing in two parts from hand signs. This helps Ss see the intervals spatially. 8. Sing simple pentatonic folksongs in canon. 9. Sing a well-known song, and at the same time clap various rhythms indicated by T. Ss may also read an exercise while T improvises an extended rhythmic ostinato. Ss must sing and listen at the same time, and then try to recall the rhythmic pattern. T should begin this task with simple, familiar patterns. 10. Sing one part and clap the second part simultaneously.
Performing two-part music	1. If the two-part selection is a folksong, T teaches the song first either by rote or from the music, and then the second part. 2. T divides the class into two groups. Group 1 sings the top line while group 2 sings the bottom. Reverse. 3. Group 1 sings the bottom line and group 2 claps the top. Reverse. 4. Perform the work as a group and then with soloists. Individuals may then sing any part while clapping the other, or they may sing one part and play the other part on the piano.

- Take time to show students how to hold rhythm sticks and use them musically.
- Show students how to put the beat in their feet; this gets them moving, and movement generates good vocal development.
- You may also have to practice saying the words of a folksong and have them repeat back (many times, often enough), phrase by phrase. This significantly helps students with diction. It is also important to explain the text of a song to students. For younger students, this isn't much of an issue, but in our experience older students want to know about the song.

Kodály Today

- Practice hand signs, without singing. You can sing the song with solfège syllables and students can demonstrate the hand signs. This technique works well with older students.
- Take nothing for granted. Don't assume that they know information. Always double-check whether they know something.

Discussion Questions
1. What are some of the general considerations in teaching songs to older beginners?
2. How does the choice of songs you use in your classroom affect the teaching sequence of rhythmic and melodic elements for older beginners?
3. Discuss the notion that we should avoid teaching singing and developing music literacy skills to older beginners. Older beginners need intellectual challenges. Because they have not previously learned basic concepts associated with music theory, the teacher should teach music theory and music appreciation and music history to these students.

Ongoing Assignment

1. The principal of your school has just informed you that you will be teaching music to fifth grade next year. Unfortunately, none of these students have had any previous experience with music. Develop a teaching philosophy and curriculum goals for these students.
2. Develop a repertoire of songs and games suitable for teaching older students.
3. Develop a lesson plan to teach older students the quarter and eighth note as well as the quarter note rest and tuneful singing.
4. Develop a lesson plan to teach your students the *do* pentatonic scale and practice $\frac{2}{4}$ meter using quarter note, eighth note, and half note.

Bibliography

Bacon, Denise. *50 Easy Two-Part Exercises: First steps in A cappella Part singing Using Sol-fa and Staff Notation*. 3rd ed. Clifton, NJ: European American Music Corporation, 1980. Originally published 1977.

Bacon, Denise. *46 Two-Part American Folk Songs for Elementary Grades*. Wellesley, MA: Kodály Center of America, 1973.

Bidner, Sara Baker. "A Folk Song Approach to Music Reading for Upper Elementary Levels Based on the Kodály Method." Ph.D. thesis, Louisiana State University and Agricultural and Mechanical College, 1978.

Bodolay, Laurdella. "Solfège for Adult Beginners." *Kodaly Envoy*, 1984, 10(3): 17–19.

Choksy, Lois. *The Kodály Method Comprehensive Music Education*. 3rd ed. Upper Saddle River, NJ: Prentice-Hall, 1999.

Crock, Winifred Woodward. "Thoughts on the Older Beginner." *American Suzuki Journal*, Spring 2005, *33*: 29–31. Music Index, EBSCOhost (accessed Apr. 7, 2013).

Eisen, Ann, and Lamar Robertson. *Directions to Literacy*. Lake Charles, LA: Sneaky Snake, 2005.

Herboly-Koscár, Ildiká. *Teaching of Polyphony, Harmony and Form in Elementary School*, trans. Alexander Farkas, revised by Lilla Gabor. Kecskemét: Zoltán Kodály Pedagogical Institute, 1984.

Houlahan, Micheál, and Philip Tacka. *From Sound to Symbol: Fundamentals of Music Theory*. New York: Oxford University Press, 2011.

Houlahan, Micheál, and Philip Tacka. "Sequential Order for the Preparation, Presentation, Practice and Evaluation of Rhythmic and Melodic Concepts." *Journal of Music Theory Pedagogy*, 1990, *4*(2): 243–268.

Houlahan, Micheál, and Philip Tacka. "Sound Thinking: A Suggested Sequence for Teaching Musical Elements Based on the Philosophy of Zoltán Kodály for a College Music Theory Course." *Journal of Music Theory Pedagogy*, 1990, *4*(1): 85–110.

Houlahan, Micheál, and Philip Tacka. *Sound Thinking: Developing Musical Literacy*. 2 vols. New York: Boosey & Hawkes, 1995.

Houlahan, Micheál, and Philip Tacka. *Sound Thinking: Music for Sight-Singing and Ear Training*. 2 vols. New York: Boosey & Hawkes, 1991.

Mantie, Roger. "Learners or Participants? The Pros and Cons of 'Lifelong Learning.'" *International Journal of Community Music*, Dec. 7, 2012, *5*(3): 217–235. Music Index, EBSCO-host (accessed Apr. 7, 2013).

Papageorgi, I., A. Creech, E .Haddon, F. Morton, C. De Bezenac, E. Himonides, J. Potter, C. Duffy, T. Whyton, and G. Welch, "Perceptions and Prediction of Expertise in Advanced Musical Learners." *Psychology of Music*, 2010, *38*(1): 31–66.

Virágh, Gábor. "Teaching Advanced Ideas with Simple Materials: Ideas for Teaching Older Students." *Bulletin of the International Kodaly Society*, 2000, *25*(2): 14–24.

Chapter 12

Evaluation and Assessment

There is an important distinction between evaluation and assessment. The primary function of assessment in music education is to provide feedback to students about the quality of their growing musicianship. Learners need constructive feedback about why, when, and how they are or are not meeting musical challenges in relation to musical standards and traditions. Overall, the assessment of students' achievement gathers information that benefits students directly in the form of constructive feedback. Assessment also provides useful data to teachers, parents, and the surrounding educational community. Building on the accumulated results of continuous assessments, evaluation is primarily concerned with grading, ranking, and other summary procedures for purposes of students' promotion and curriculum evaluation.

D. J. Elliott, Praxial Music Education, p. 13

Key Questions

- What is the purpose of teacher assessment?
- What criteria should be used in assessing a music teacher?
- What is the purpose of student assessment?
- What criteria should be used in assessing a student?
- What are the components of a student profile chart?
- How can we develop scoring rubrics to assess a student's progress in the music classroom?

In previous chapters we laid out a comprehensive planning process for teaching music concepts and elements. In this chapter we address how to assess student learning and develop strategies to improve learning on the basis of this information. Additionally, we also provide assessments to measure the effectiveness of an instructor's planning and teaching in the music classroom.

Supervisors or principals are generally responsible for evaluating music teachers. Often music teachers do not furnish their administrators with the information necessary to evaluate their work effectively. Once a supervisor understands a teacher's philosophy and curriculum goal for the music program, it is easier to conduct a constructive assessment that will ultimately result in growth and recognition of a music program.

Educators want to make a difference in the lives of the students. Most teachers want to know: How am I doing? Am I making a difference? Are the students benefiting? How will the results of an assessment of both the teacher and the students assist the growth of my music program? Assessment and evaluation have become increasingly important to every facet of education in the past two decades. Every aspect of a child's education undergoes examination and analysis. Clearly, evaluation should be ongoing and built into the music curriculum and program. The information given here is vital to developing better teaching strategies and to the continued growth and development of the music program.

Assessing the Effectiveness of Music Teaching

Hiring music teachers who are excellent musicians and who can demonstrate how to use both their voice and their ability to play several instruments is essential to the development and growth of a music program. Music teachers who are going to teach in a school or school system who have embraced the Kodály concept for teaching music should have a good understanding of the Kodály philosophy, knowledge of the basic components of music curriculum, and understanding of how to create teaching strategy as well as lesson plans. Before hiring a Kodály music teacher, the supervisor should check to see if the music teacher understands[1]:

- The Kodály philosophy
- Children's musical developmental characteristics during elementary school years
- How to construct a music curriculum and adapt it to meet state or regional standards
- How to select music repertoire, including folk music, art music, and recently composed music, for both the classroom and the elementary choir
- The child's voice
- The characteristics and stylistic elements of children's songs, including knowledge of scales, meter, rhythms, motivic structure, and form
- How to teach diverse learners
- The main types of children's singing games and the physical maturity necessary to play them
- How to develop children's music skills, including singing, playing instruments, and movement

- Professional literature on children's musical development
- The stylistic elements of art music, including knowledge of scales, meter, rhythms, motivic structure, and form
- How to teach music using a sound-to-symbol orientation
- How to assess learning

In addition to conducting an interview, it's equally important for a supervisor to evaluate a candidate's musicianship abilities. Candidates should be required to perform vocal and instrumental repertoire, demonstrate how they would teach both rhythmic and melodic concepts, and conduct a vocal ensemble.

In this chapter we present assessment rubrics for evaluating an instructor's ability to plan and teach. Music teachers can use these to reflect on their own teaching practices and plan accordingly. The assessments can also be appropriately modified and used by a music supervisor or a school principal.

The assessment tool for evaluating music teaching is divided into five sections:

1. Curriculum planning
2. Evaluation of a lesson plan format
3. Lesson evaluation
4. Instructor's musicianship assessment
5. Assessment of student learning

Section one, curriculum planning, evaluates an instructor's ability to plan for long-term teaching. Evidence indicating that lesson planning is built on the students' prior knowledge is essential to the design of a well-structured lesson, as well as to the various teaching strategies used throughout the lesson. This evaluation also takes place before the lesson. These rubrics offer teachers the opportunity for self-reflection and ultimately better teaching practices.

Section 2, evaluation of a lesson plan format, assesses an instructor's ability to plan individual lessons. Lesson plans built on the students' prior knowledge is fundamental to the design of a well-structured lesson, as well as the various teaching strategies that are used throughout the lesson. There should be a connection between the instructor's philosophy of music, curriculum goals, the design of unit plans and lesson plans, and assessment tools. The assessment rubrics we have included (Table 12.1) evaluate a teacher's ability to plan lessons. This evaluation may take place before the lesson observation. Our rubrics offer teachers a continuing opportunity for self-reflection and teaching improvement.

Section 3, instructor's musicianship, evaluates the instructor's ability to transform a script of a lesson into practice. This evaluation requires the evaluator to observe the lesson.

Section 4, lesson evaluation, assesses the pedagogical decisions that a teacher makes during the lesson to ensure maximal student learning. This evaluation takes place during the lesson.

Section 5, assessment of student learning, evaluates the assessment tools the instructor uses throughout the lessons to evaluate students' knowledge of the objectives for the lesson. It also assesses the students' participation during the lesson.

Table 12.1 is our *assessment tool for evaluating music teaching*. It may be used by teachers or supervisors to assess a music lesson. This evaluation takes place before the lesson.

Table 12.1 Assessment Tool for Evaluating Music Teaching

Name:	School district:
Grade observed:	Supervisor:
Date:	

SECTION 1: CURRICULUM PLANNING

	Criteria	Comments
Highly effective 4	Curriculum planning fosters appropriate learning goals and active musical behaviors as evidenced by the teaching resource portfolio.	
Effective 3	Curriculum planning does not always foster appropriate learning goals and active musical behaviors and occasionally detracts from planning behaviors as evidenced by the teaching resource portfolio.	
Developing 2	Curriculum planning does not always foster appropriate learning goals and active musical behaviors and detracts from planning behaviors as evidenced by the teaching resource portfolio.	
Ineffective 1	Curriculum planning does not foster appropriate goals and active musical behaviors.	

SECTION 2: EVALUATION OF A LESSON PLAN FORMAT

Behavioral Objectives

	Criteria	Comments
Highly effective 4	Behavioral objectives describe appropriate active musical behaviors within the lesson.	
Effective 3	Behavioral objectives do not always describe appropriate active musical behaviors within the lesson and occasionally detract from the lesson.	
Developing 2	Behavioral objectives do not always describe appropriate active musical behaviors within the lesson and detract from the lesson.	
Ineffective 1	Behavioral objectives do not describe appropriate active musical behaviors.	

(*continued*)

Table 12.1 Continued

Selection of Music Material		
	Criteria	**Comments**
Highly effective 4	Selection of music material is always appropriate.	
Effective 3	Selection of music material is not always appropriate and occasionally detracts from the lesson.	
Developing 2	Selection of music material is not always appropriate and detracts from the lesson.	
Ineffective 1	Selection of music material is not appropriate.	
Instructor's Understanding of Students' Prior Knowledge		
	Criteria	**Comments**
Highly effective 4	There is evidence that behavioral objectives are built on Ss' prior knowledge.	
Effective 3	It is not always evident that behavioral objectives are built on Ss' prior knowledge, and this occasionally detracts from the lesson.	
Developing 2	It is not always evident that behavioral objectives are built on Ss' prior knowledge, and this detracts from the lesson.	
Ineffective 1	Behavioral objectives are not built on Ss' prior knowledge.	
Sequence of Teaching Strategies		
	Criteria	**Comments**
Highly effective 4	Sequence of teaching strategies is always evident.	
Effective 3	Sequence of teaching strategies is not always evident and occasionally detracts from the lesson.	
Developing 2	Sequence of teaching strategies is not always evident, and this detracts from the lesson.	
Ineffective 1	Sequence of teaching strategies is not evident.	

(*continued*)

Table 12.1 Continued

Musical Transitions Between Teaching Segments		
	Criteria	Comments
Highly effective 4	Musical transitions are always evident.	
Effective 3	Musical transitions are not always evident, and this occasionally detracts from the lesson.	
Developing 2	Musical transitions are not always evident, and this detracts from the lesson.	
Ineffective 1	Musical transitions are not evident.	
Alternating Periods of Concentration and Relaxation		
	Criteria	Comments
Highly effective 4	There is a balance between periods of concentration and relaxation skills being taught in the lesson.	
Effective 3	There is some imbalance between periods of concentration and relaxation skills being taught in the lesson, and this occasionally detracts from the lesson.	
Developing 2	There is an imbalance between periods of concentration and relaxation skills being taught in the lesson, and this detracts from the lesson.	
Ineffective 1	There is an imbalance between periods of concentration and relaxation skills.	
SECTION 3: INSTRUCTOR'S MUSICIANSHIP		
Musicality		
	Criteria	Comments
Highly effective 4	Musicality is evident.	
Effective 3	Musicality errors occur, and this occasionally detracts from the lesson.	
Developing 2	Musicality errors detract from the lesson.	

(*continued*)

Table 12.1 Continued

Ineffective 1	Musicality errors consistently detract from the lesson.	
Conducting			
	Criteria	Comments
Highly effective 4	Conducting skills are evident.	
Effective 3	Conducting errors occur, and this occasionally detracts from the lesson.	
Developing 2	Conducting errors occur, and this detracts from the lesson.	
Ineffective 1	Conducting is not evident.	
Functional Keyboard Skills			
	Criteria	Comments
Highly effective 4	Functional keyboard skills are evident.	
Effective 3	Errors in functional keyboard skills occur, and this occasionally detracts from the lesson.	
Developing 2	Errors in functional keyboard skills detract from the lesson.	
Ineffective 1	Functional keyboard skills are not evident.	
Instrumental Skills			
	Criteria	Comments
Highly effective 4	Instrumental skills are evident.	
Effective 3	Errors in instrumental skills occur, and this occasionally detracts from the lesson.	
Developing 2	Errors in instrumental skills detract from the lesson.	
Ineffective 1	Instrumental skills are not evident.	
SECTION 4: LESSON EVALUATION			
Appropriate Starting Pitches for Songs			
	Criteria	Comments
Highly effective 4	Appropriate starting pitch of songs is evident.	
Effective 3	Appropriate starting pitch is not always correct, but this does not detract from the lesson.	

(*continued*)

Table 12.1 Continued

Developing 2	Appropriate starting pitch is not always correct, and this detracts from the lesson.	
Ineffective 1	Appropriate starting pitch is not correct.	
Appropriate Tempo for Songs		
	Criteria	Comments
Highly effective 4	Appropriate tempo of songs is evident.	
Effective 3	Appropriate tempo of songs is not always logical, but this does not detract from the lesson.	
Developing 2	Appropriate tempo of songs is not always logical and detracts from the lesson.	
Ineffective 1	Appropriate tempo of songs is not logical.	
In-tune Singing		
	Criteria	Comments
Highly effective 4	Sequenced teaching strategies for teaching in-tune singing are evident.	
Effective 3	Sequenced teaching strategies for teaching in-tune singing are not always evident, but this does not detract from the lesson.	
Developing 2	Sequenced teaching strategies for teaching in-tune singing are not always evident, and this detracts from the lesson.	
Ineffective 1	Sequenced teaching strategies for teaching in-tune singing are not evident.	
Development of Students' Musical Skills		
	Criteria	Comments
Highly effective 4	There is a balance among the musical skills being taught in the lesson.	
Effective 3	There is some imbalance among the musical skills being taught in the lesson, and this occasionally detracts from the lesson.	
Developing 2	There is an imbalance among the musical skills being taught in the lesson, and this detracts from the lesson.	
Ineffective 1	There is an imbalance among musical skills.	

(continued)

Table 12.1 Continued

	Flexibility in Adaptation of Lesson Plans	
	Criteria	**Comments**
Highly effective 4	Flexibility and adaptation of lesson plan is always appropriate.	
Effective 3	Flexibility and adaptation of lesson plan is not always appropriate, and this sometimes detracts from the lesson.	
Developing 2	Flexibility and adaptation of lesson plan is not always appropriate, and this occasionally detracts from the lesson.	
Ineffective 1	Flexibility and adaptation of lesson plan is not appropriate.	
	Appropriate Pacing of Lessons	
	Criteria	**Comments**
Highly effective 4	Appropriate pacing of lesson is present.	
Effective 3	Appropriate pacing of lesson is not always present, and this occasionally detracts from the lesson.	
Developing 2	Appropriate pacing of lesson is not always present, and this detracts from the lesson.	
Ineffective 1	Appropriate pacing of lesson is not present.	
	Questioning Technique	
	Criteria	**Comments**
Highly effective 4	Questioning technique is always effective.	
Effective 3	Questioning technique is not always effective, and this occasionally detracts from the lesson.	
Developing 2	Questioning technique is not always effective, and this detracts from the lesson.	
Ineffective 1	Questioning technique is not effective.	
	Error Correction of Students	
	Criteria	**Comments**
Highly effective 4	Error correction is evident.	
Effective 3	Error correction is not always evident, and this occasionally detracts from the lesson.	

(*continued*)

Table 12.1 Continued

Developing 2	Error correction is not always evident, and this detracts from the lesson.	
Ineffective 1	Error correction is not evident.	
Classroom Management/Discipline		
	Criteria	Comments
Highly effective 4	Appropriate classroom management is evident.	
Effective 3	Appropriate classroom management is not always evident, and this occasionally detracts from the lesson.	
Developing 2	Appropriate classroom management is not always evident, and this detracts from the lesson.	
Ineffective 1	Appropriate classroom management is not evident.	
	Technology	
	Criteria	Comments
Highly effective 4	Use of technology fosters appropriate learning goals and active musical behaviors.	
Effective 3	Use of technology does not always foster appropriate learning goals and active musical behaviors, and this occasionally detracts from the lesson plan.	
Developing 2	Use of technology does not always foster appropriate learning goals and active musical behaviors, and this detracts from the lesson plan.	
Ineffective 1	Use of technology does not foster appropriate learning goals and active musical behaviors.	
	SECTION 5: ASSESSMENT OF STUDENT LEARNING	
	Assessment of Student Participation	
	Criteria	Comments
Highly effective 4	75% or more of students are participating successfully in observed activities.	
Effective 3	50% or more of students are participating successfully in observed activities.	
Developing 2	25% or more of students are participating successfully in observed activities.	
Ineffective 1	Fewer than 25% of students are participating successfully in observed activities.	

(*continued*)

Table 12.1 Continued

Teacher Assessment of Students		
	Criteria	Comments
Highly effective 4	Appropriate S assessment tools are evident.	
Effective 3	Appropriate S assessment tools are not always evident, and this somewhat detracts from assessment of the Ss.	
Developing 2	Appropriate S assessment tools are not always evident, and this detracts from assessment of the Ss.	
Ineffective 1	Appropriate S assessments are not evident.	

Developing a Class Profile Summarizing the Child's Achievement

Most teachers assess student learning three or four times during the academic year, depending on the assessment philosophy of the school. Normally teachers evaluate student performance four times a year. One way to capture student achievement is by using a class profile summary sheet. This enables the teacher to document the level of success in the classroom as well as develop strategies for improving students' musical skills. Table 12.2 gives an example of a class profile. Each class profile should include

1. Grading period
2. Outcomes for grading period
3. Assessment activities for grading period
4. Alphabetized list of students' names with their individual scores for each assessment activity

Table 12.2

Name _____
Grade _____
Term _____

Outcomes	*Activities*	*Indicators*
Knowledge of music repertoire	Drawing on S's knowledge of music repertoire	S sings a selection of songs that he or she chooses from memory, making no mistakes.
		S sings a selection of songs that he or she chooses from memory, making few mistakes that only occasionally detract from the overall performance.

(*continued*)

Table 12.2 Continued

		S sings a selection of songs that he or she chooses from memory, making mistakes that detract from the overall performance.
		S cannot choose a selection of songs and sing them from memory.
Performance (national standards 1, 2, 7, 8, 9)	Singing	S performs, making no mistakes.
		S performs, making few mistakes that only occasionally detract from the overall performance.
		S performs, making mistakes that detract from the overall performance.
		S cannot perform.
	Ensemble performance — Singing in choir	S performs, making no mistakes.
		S performs, making few mistakes that only occasionally detract from the overall performance.
		S performs, making mistakes that detract from the overall performance.
		S cannot perform.
	Movement	S performs, making no mistakes.
		S performs, making few mistakes that only occasionally detract from the overall performance.
		S performs, making mistakes that detract from the overall performance.
		S cannot perform.
	Instrument performance	S performs, making no mistakes.
		S performs, making few mistakes that occasionally detract from the overall performance.
		S performs, making mistakes that detract from the overall performance.
		S cannot perform.

(continued)

Table 12.2 Continued

	Evaluating music performance	S can evaluate the quality of his or her performance.
		S can evaluate the performance, but the description lacks some details.
		S can describe the performance as good or not good, but the description lacks details.
		S cannot describe the quality of his or her performance.

Grading period
Outcomes for grading period (List all outcomes for the grading period: reading, writing, singing, etc.)
Assessment activities for the grading period (List the outcomes you will test for this specific grading period)
Alphabetized list of student names and assessment activity scores for the grading period
Reflection on student learning and implications for future teaching

Assessment and Evaluation of Students: Student Profiles

This chapter provides several assessment and evaluation indicators, as well as rubrics to assess music students. The purpose of assessment in the music classroom is to evaluate the students'

- Knowledge of music repertoire: children as cultural stewards
- Performance skills: children as performers
- Music literacy skills: children as critical thinkers
- Creative skills: children as composers and improvisers
- Listening skills: children as listeners

Data Collection: Formative Assessment

There are many opportunities to assess a student's progress throughout a lesson. Teachers generally assess the performance of the whole class while observing individual children who may require more individualized attention during a lesson. This is known as a "formative" assessment. Teaching and learning activities are modified or adjusted during the lesson. For example, during the introduction of a preparation/practice lesson, the teacher can assess children's singing, as well as their knowledge of known concepts. Using the lesson plan model that we provide affords a number of opportunities for individual singing to assess performance. Because of time constraints, the music teacher may decide to

Evaluation and Assessment

evaluate certain areas of the curriculum such as singing, reading, writing, and creativity. When assessments become part of the regular practices of classroom teaching, it is easier to notice deficiencies and develop strategies to improve student learning.

In some cases, a teacher may decide to conduct an assessment during a music lesson. In others, it may be helpful to have a time other than the music lesson to assess student learning. Assessment may be done as a group activity, or if the teacher is unsure of a child's skills, it may be conducted individually. Singing may be assessed during a music lesson at various times throughout the lesson. Assessment of reading, writing, and improvisation may be done as part of the practice activities for a lesson. A worksheet that deals with a class activity may also function as a more formal assessment activity for child.

As previously stated, formative assessment is informal assessment of the students' work during the class lesson. A student's work is not graded but rather observed during formative assessments. Here, a music instructor can assess a student's progress during the course of teaching a lesson. This allows teachers to address their instructional approach to improve classroom instruction on the spot. In general, the instructor may assess the performance of the class while observing those students who need more individual attention. The approach to teaching we describe in this book promotes many opportunities for assessment. Data collection for assembling a student's profile chart based on formative assessment may take several forms. During the course of a lesson the instructor may assess

- Repertoire: during the introduction of the lesson, the instructor can observe the students' knowledge of musical repertoire on the basis of their ability to sing song segments or whole songs independently.
- Performance: during the core activities of the lesson, the instructor can easily observe and then assess the students' performance abilities.
- Creative skills: in the segments of the lesson dealing with performance and development of music skills, the instructor can assess the students' ability to improvise or compose music with known rhythmic and melodic elements.
- Critical thinking, music literacy: during the segment of the lesson dealing with performance and preparation of the new musical concept and performance and development of music skills, the instructor can assess music literacy skills. For example, in the visual awareness stage of preparing a new musical element, the instructor asks the students to create a representation of the target phrase containing that element. These representations may be collected and evaluated.
- Listening skills: during the segments of the lesson on performance and development of music skills, the instructor can assess the students' ability to recognize music with known rhythmic and melodic elements.

Data Collection: Summative Assessment

Summative assessment occurs at the end of teaching a particular musical concept or element. It is a more formal evaluation of the students' understanding of a certain music concept. Student profile charts may be used to document student achievement and assessment.

Consider developing a profile chart for each student in your class, where you can record information concerning student achievement. Here we give a sample of areas of assessment to be included in a student profile chart, on the basis of national content standards and the music curriculum presented in this text. We present this as a sample profile chart; it may easily be modified for individual teaching situations.

Repertoire
To document the students' knowledge of music repertoire, the rubrics for evaluation may be written in a manner that lets students evaluate their own performance or the performance of their peers.

Performance
To document the students' singing, movement, and instrumental abilities, again, rubrics may be written that allow students to evaluate their own performance or the performance of their peers. The student's profile can include a recording of individual or group singing or instrumental playing.

Music Literacy
Assess the students' knowledge of rhythmic and melodic elements through reading and writing activities. Assessments should focus on the rhythmic and melodic elements included in each grade. Examples may be included of written work consisting of visual representations for melodic and rhythmic elements, written work done in traditional rhythmic notation and staff notation, and work done on the computer.

Creative Skills
This area helps document the students' ability to improvise or compose music. It requires rubrics that address the students' ability to use known rhythmic and melodic elements within specific forms. Examples of composition assignments using traditional rhythmic notation, staff notation, or work on computers may be included.

Listening and Describing
An assessment of listening enables the instructor to evaluate the students' aural analysis and visual analysis skills. Instructors may wish to document whether students can sing the principle themes of a musical composition, use a listening map, or identify specific music compositions.

Cross-Curricular Instruction
An evaluation can be made of the students' ability to identify and understand the connection between music and other subject areas in addition to the repertoire they are performing. Cross-curricular instruction might also include information presented by instructors of related subject areas.

Step One: Developing an Assessment Profile Chart for Each Child

Developing an assessment profile chart for each child in the class enables the teacher to record information concerning student progress and growth. You need not assess every skill area. Choose those skills that are important for children and your music program. This individual assessment profile keeps track of and records a child's understanding. It permits teachers to develop additional teaching strategies to improve learning. Here we give suggestions that may be included in the general comment section of the child profile.

The profile may contain a section recording individual assessments of student learning. It is probably best to assess a student's understanding of every concept addressed in a particular grade. Sometimes a teacher will have time to do only four assessments and may decide to combine the testing of two concepts.

Each section should contain an assessment for singing, reading, writing, and improvisation. Include space to record comments. A class profile can be developed where the name of the child and the recorded grade for singing, reading, writing, and improvisation are logged. This information allows the instructor to see where adjustments in teaching and or lesson planning need to be made. Assessment allows teachers to plan on the basis of their children's learning and responses. Sometimes we forget that assessment is not just judgment; it is a call to action on the part of the teacher to plan accordingly in the future. Table 12.3 is a sample of how the various components may be assessed.

Table 12.3

Assessment of Singing	
Criteria	**Comment**
Sing while clapping or tapping the beat.	
Sing while clapping the rhythm of a melody or rhyme.	
Sing while playing a musical game with the correct sequence of movements.	
Sing while playing simple rhythmic instruments.	
Assessment of Reading Skills	
Criteria	**Comment**
Read known rhythms written in tradition rhythmic notation.	
Read known melodies from hand signs.	
Read known melodies written in traditional rhythmic notation with solfège syllables beneath.	
Read known melodies from staff notation.	

(continued)

Table 12.3 Continued

Assessment of Writing Skills	
Criteria	Comment
Write known rhythms using tradition rhythmic notation.	
Write the tone set of a piece of music on the staff.	
Write known melodies using traditional rhythmic notation with solfège syllables written beneath.	
Write known melodies on the staff.	
Assessment of Creative Skills	
Criteria	Comment
Sing new words to a familiar melody or create new words for a known rhyme or chant.	
Sing a song and improvise beat motions.	
Improvise by clapping a four-beat rhythm pattern.	
Improvise a four-beat rhythm pattern on a percussion instrument.	
Improvise a rhythmic ostinato.	
Improvise a melodic ostinato.	
Improvise to a given form.	

Step Two: Assessment Activities

For each component of the assessment, the teacher must decide what activities will be assessed. Table 12.4 is just a sample assessment chart. These first charts are more basic; the charts/rubrics will become more involved in the following pages.

Table 12.4

Performance: assessment of singing	Comments
Music literacy: assessment of reading	Comments
Creative skills: melodic composition	Comments

Step Three: Designing More Specific Activities

Once the teacher has decided what skills and activities will be used for assessment, he or she can design a more specific assessment profile. Depending on the time, teachers can select some or all of these matters to be assessed:

- Knowledge of repertoire
- Performance

Evaluation and Assessment

- Music literacy
- Creative skills
- Listening

Within each category, the teacher can determine what skills need to be assessed. This depends on the concepts or unit plans being studied by students.

Table 12.5 is a sample of an individual assessment profile with the activity for assessing children's knowledge of a music concept.

Table 12.5

Name Class Date of assessment Concept		
Criteria		**Comments**
Advanced 4	S sings repertoire tunefully, making no errors.	
Proficient 3	S sings repertoire tunefully, making a few errors in singing that do not detract from the overall performance.	
Basic 2	S sings repertoire, making errors that detract from the overall performance.	
Emerging 1	S does not sing tunefully.	

Step Four: Creating Assessment Rubrics

Once assessment activities have been determined, we need a scoring rubric to help evaluate the information that has been collected. We can use assessment of tuneful singing to demonstrate how we can create assessment rubrics for evaluation.

Assessment of tuneful singing may be done during the class lesson. When we assess tuneful singing, we observe what the child is able to demonstrate through singing. Assessment of tuneful singing will change for each concept; here we present an example of an assessment rubric for singing. It is important to determine whether the student actually used the singing voice in tune, or whether sang out of tune in the singing voice, or was using a speaking voice (obviously this would be out of tune). The teacher may wish to include this information in the comment section of the rubric. The two sections are important because the teacher can use this information accurately to describe a child's performance when talking to a parent. It gives the "grade," but it also makes room for intangibles to be documented in the comments section.

Kodály Today

We prefer a four-point rubric, but sometimes teachers might choose to use a three-point rubric instead. All of the rubrics in this chapter can be modified, so the teacher can use a three-point scale.

Samples of Assessment Rubrics

The following tables are sample rubrics that demonstrate what assessment tools look like for singing, reading, writing, and improvisation in the music class. These assessments are from grade two and are used to evaluate students' understanding of *do* within their song repertoire.

Table 12.6 is an example of a tuneful singing rubric for the musical element *do*.

Table 12.6

Student name: _____

Date: _____

Class: _____

Criteria	Levels	Comments
S sings "Bow Wow Wow" on text with accurate intonation, pure vowel sounds, clear pronunciation, and balanced posture, giving a musically sensitive performance that shows evidence of excellent vocal technique.	Advanced 4	
S sings "Bow Wow Wow" on text with mostly accurate intonation, primarily pure vowel sounds, some use of clear pronunciation, and balanced posture, giving an overall musical performance.	Proficient 3	
S sings "Bow Wow Wow" on text with some accurate intonation, few pure vowel sounds, unclear pronunciation, and generally poor posture, giving a performance that lacks musicality.	Basic 2	
S sings "Bow Wow Wow" on text without accurate intonation, pure vowel sounds, clear pronunciation, or tall posture, giving a performance that lacks musicality and shows evidence of poor vocal technique.	Emerging 1	

Evaluation and Assessment

Table 12.7 is an example of a reading rubric for the musical element *do*.

Table 12.7

Student name: _____
Date: _____
Class: _____

Criteria	Levels	Comments
S sings the third phrase of "Bow Wow Wow" with solfège syllables and hand signs reading from the staff notation or traditional rhythm notation, making no errors.	Advanced 4	
S sings the third phrase of "Bow Wow Wow" with solfège syllables and hand signs reading from the staff notation or traditional rhythm notation, making only a few errors that do not detract from the performance.	Proficient 3	
S sings the third phrase of "Bow Wow Wow" with solfège syllables and hand signs reading from the staff notation or traditional rhythm notation, making errors that detract from the performance.	Basic 2	
S does not sing the third phrase of "Bow Wow Wow" with solfège syllables and hand signs, reading from the staff notation or traditional rhythm notation.	Emerging 1	

Table 12.8 is an example of a writing rubric for the musical element *do*.
Table 12.9 is an example of an improvisation rubric for the musical element *do*.

Table 12.8

Student name: _____ Date: _____ Class: _____		
Criteria	**Levels**	**Comments**
S writes a four-beat melodic motif with solfège syllables underneath the traditional notation of the third phrase of "Bow Wow Wow," making no errors.	Advanced 4	
S writes a four-beat melodic motif with solfège syllables underneath the traditional notation of the third phrase of "Bow Wow Wow," making only a few errors that do not detract from the writing activity.	Proficient 3	
S writes a four-beat melodic motif with solfège syllables underneath the traditional notation of the third phrase of "Bow Wow Wow," making errors that detract from the writing activity.	Basic 2	
S does not write a four-beat melodic motif with solfège syllables underneath the traditional notation of the third phrase of "Bow Wow Wow."	Emerging 1	

Table 12.9

Student name: _____ Date: _____ Class: _____		
Criteria	**Levels**	**Comments**
S improvises a four-beat melodic motif with solfège syllables that include *do*, making no errors.	Advanced 4	
S improvises a four-beat melodic motif with solfège syllables that include *do*, making few errors, which do not detract from the performance.	Proficient 3	

(continued)

Table 12.9 Continued

S improvises a four-beat melodic motif with solfège syllables that include *do*, making errors that detract from the performance.	Basic 2	
S does not improvise a four-beat melodic motif with solfège syllables that include *do*.	Emerging 1	

Connections to Grade Handbooks

In each grade handbook, we have included a set of assessments for evaluating all musical elements and concepts addressed in that grade for tuneful singing, reading, writing, and improvisation. The rubrics may be modified to include more assessment activities, according to the information presented in this chapter.

Discussion Questions
1. Discuss the role of assessment in the music class.
2. How do we assess the students' musical knowledge in the music classroom? Provide examples of each kind of assessment.
3. Discuss the notion that there is inadequate time to assess student learning during two thirty-minute lessons every week. Music is meant to be a fun activity, and assessment has no part in a music curriculum.

Ongoing Activities

1. For all of the classes that you will be teaching next year, develop a student profile sheet, formal assessment activities, and the accompanying rubrics. Include the profile sheets and assessment tools in your teaching portfolio.
2. Imagine that you are having a conference with a parent from a third grade class at the end of your next year at a new school. In preparation for the meeting, develop a detailed profile for that parent's student. Explain to the parent how the child is succeeding in your music class and what the implications are for the child's learning across the curriculum.
3. Because of your incredible success in the classroom, you have been asked to become the head of the music of your school. As part of your responsibilities, you must evaluate teachers' resource portfolios, their lesson plans, and musicianship skills, and evaluate a lesson taught by the teachers in your department. How will you prepare for evaluation of music instructors under your supervision?

Bibliography

"Arts in Education Program." Harvard University, n.d. http://www.gse.harvard.edu/masters/aie.

Black, Paul, Christine Harrison, Clare Lee, Bethan Marshall, and Dylan Wiliam. *Assessment for Learning: Putting It into Practice*. Buckingham, UK: Open University Press, 2003.

Boyle, David J., and Rudolf E. Radocy. *Measurement and Evaluation of Musical Experiences*. New York: Schirmer, 1987.

Boyle, J. "Evaluation of Music Ability." In *Handbook of Research on Music Teaching and Learning*. ed. R. Colwell, pp. 247–265. New York: Schirmer, 1992.

Colwell, Richard. "Preparing Student Teachers in Assessment." *Arts Education Policy Review, 1998, 99*(4): 29–36.

Daniel, R. "Self-Assessment in Performance." *British Journal of Music Education*, 2001, *18*: 215–226.

Elliott, D. J. *Praxial Music Education: Reflections and Dialogues*. New York: Oxford University Press, 2005.

Freed-Garrod, J. "Assessment in the Arts: Elementary-Aged Students as Qualitative Assessors of Their Own and Peers' Musical Compositions." *Bulletin of the Council for Research in Music Education*, 1999, *139*: 50–63.

"Harvard Project Zero." Harvard University, n.d. http://www.pz.harvard.edu.

Herboly-Kocsár, Ildiká. *Teaching of Polyphony, Harmony and Form in Elementary School*, ed. Lilla Gábor, trans. Alexander Farkas. Kecskemét: Zoltán Kodály Pedagogical Institute, 1984.

Herman, Joan L., Pamela R. Aschbacher, and Lynn Winters. *A Practical Guide to Alternative Assessment*. Alexandria, VA: Association for Supervision and Curriculum Development, 1992.

Hickey, Maude. "Assessment Rubrics for Music Composition." *Music Educators Journal* 1999, *85*(4): 26–33.

Kassner, K. "Would Better Questions Enhance Music Learning?" *Music Educators Journal*, 1998, *84*(4): 29–36.

Lehman, P. "Curriculum and Program Evaluation." In *Handbook of Research on Music Teaching and Learning*, ed. R. Colwell, pp. 281–294. New York: Schirmer, 1992.

McPherson, G. E., and W. Thompson. "Assessing Music Performance: Issues and Influences." *Research Studies in Music Education*, 1998, *10*(1): 12–24.

Mitchell, Nancy. "Assessment and Evaluation as Discussed in Provincial Elementary Music Curriculum Documents." *Canadian Music Educator/Musicien Educateur au Canada*, 2012, *54*(1): 33–36. Education Research Complete. Web. Mar. 2, 2013.

Scott, Sheila J. "Assessing Student Learning Across the National Standards for Music Education." *General Music Today*, 1999, *13*(1): 3–7.

Scott, Sheila J. "The Construction and Preliminary Validation of a Criterion-Referenced Music Achievement Test Formulated in Terms of the Goals and Objectives of a

Kodály-Based Music Curriculum." *Bulletin of the International Kodály Society*, 1992, *17*(1): 26–32.

Scott, S. J. "Developing Long-Term Plans for Student Assessment Within a Kodály-Based Context for Music Education." *Kodály Envoy*, 2003, *30*(1), 8–12.

Scott, Sheila J. "Rethinking the Roles of Assessment in Music Education." *Music Educators Journal*, 2012, *98*(3): 31–35. Education Research Complete. Web. Mar. 4, 2013.

Smith, J. "Using Portfolio Assessment in General Music." *General Music Today*, 1995, *9*(1): 8–12.

Stefanova, Maria. "Developing Critical Thinking and Assessment in Music Classrooms." *American String Teacher*, May 2011, *61*(2): 29–31. Music Index, EBSCOhost (accessed Apr. 6, 2013).

Wells, R. "The Student's Role in the Assessment Process." *Teaching Music*, October 1998, *6*(2): 32–33.

Winner, Ellen. *Arts PROPEL: An Introductory Handbook*. Boston: Harvard Project Zero and Educational Testing Service, 1991.

Winner, Ellen, Lyle Davidson, and Larry Scripp, eds. *Arts PROPEL: A Handbook for Music*. Boston: Harvard Project Zero and Educational Testing Service, 1991.

Chapter 13

Organizing Your Teaching Resources for the Elementary Classroom

Key Questions

- What are the key components of a teaching resource folder?
- What should be included in a teaching portfolio?

This chapter supplies ideas for organizing your teaching resources, and it also summarizes how to access information regarding teaching and assessments. We suggest that teachers create a teaching resource folder divided into specific sections. In preceding chapters, we presented valuable information pertaining to developing a philosophy of teaching, curriculum, students' music skills, and approaches to teaching music concepts and elements. This can be organized into your professional portfolio and resource folder. Additionally, information collected from conference presentations and in-service workshops can be filed into your portfolio.

We suggest organizing all of this information in a teaching resource folder for every grade. The information in it can also be used to create a teaching portfolio for each grade level. A teaching resource folder is therefore a resource that a teacher keeps to organize information that pertains to teaching. A teaching portfolio contains current documents that teachers use for planning, teaching, and assessing aspects of the music program. Both the teaching resource folder and the teacher portfolio can be grade-specific.

What Are the Components of a Teaching Resource Folder?

A teaching resource folder contains practical information that an instructor will use for teaching music. The information contained in each section of this portfolio should be updated throughout your professional career. When you attend a professional development workshop, update your teaching resource folder with the information you've collected. Create two sections in your resources binder: one for teaching and the other for information pertaining to assessment. You may choose to develop a hard-copy or an electronic version of the folder.

Section 1 pertains to key components of a teaching resource folder:

- Your philosophy of education, as well as samples of teaching philosophies created by other teachers
- Samples of various music curriculums
- Songs to be used in teaching singing as well as music concepts and elements
- Techniques for developing the singing voice
- Techniques for developing movement skills
- Techniques for developing students' instrumental skills
- Strategies for teaching music concepts and elements
- Techniques for practicing form, rhythmic and melodic improvisation/composition, part singing, and listening
- Information pertaining to technology
- Information pertaining to children's choir
- Samples of unit plans and lesson plans
- Assessments and rubrics
- Resource materials, video, iTunes lists, and recordings

Table 13.1 links the divisions of the resource folder to chapters in *Kodály Today* as well as to the accompanying grade handbooks.

Table 13.1

Components of a Teaching Portfolio	Related Chapter in *Kodály Today* and Accompanying Handbooks
Teaching philosophy	Chapter 1 Chapter 1 in the Grade Handbooks
Curriculum	Chapter 1 Chapter 2 in the Grade Handbooks
Repertoire	Chapter 2 Chapter 2 in the Grade Handbooks

(continued)

Table 13.1 Continued

Components of a Teaching Portfolio	Related Chapter in *Kodály Today* and Accompanying Handbooks
Techniques for developing the singing voice	Chapter 3 Chapter 4 in the Grade Handbooks
Techniques for developing movement skills	Chapter 3 Chapter 3 in the Grade Handbooks
Techniques for playing instruments	Chapter 3 Chapter 3 in the Grade Handbooks
Strategies for teaching music concepts	Chapter 6 Chapter 4 in the Grade Handbooks
Techniques for developing music skills	Chapter 7 Chapter 3 in the Grade Handbooks
Getting started: lesson plans for the first few weeks of class	Chapter 7 Chapter 5 in the Grade Handbooks
Unit and lesson plans for teaching concepts and skills	Chapter 7, 10 Chapter 5 in the Grade Handbooks
Information pertaining to technology	Chapter 8
Information on children's choirs	Chapter 9
Assessments and rubrics for assessing teaching effectiveness	Chapter 12
Resource materials, video, iTunes lists, and recordings to be used in your teaching	

Teaching Portfolio

A teaching portfolio should contain evidence of successful teaching as well as information to help teachers reflect on and improve their teaching. Some teachers have created a teaching portfolio for each grade they teach. Supervisors and principals can use these portfolios to help them understand the breadth of the work that goes on in a music classroom and subsequently better evaluate the work of the music teacher. These portfolios can also be created electronically. Here are the suggested areas of a teaching portfolio.

Statement of Teaching Philosophy and Reflective Practice

The first component of your teaching portfolio is a statement concerning your philosophy of music education. This statement lays out a rationale for the inclusion of music in the curriculum and should be linked to the school's mission, vision, and philosophy statement. The philosophy statement gives the instructor a basis for developing realistic curriculum goals and lesson plans. In Chapter 1, we present a brief summary of Zoltán Kodály's philosophy of music education that may provide a model for developing your personal philosophy of music education. In each grade's music handbook, we include questions you can use to develop a music curriculum; we also have included our curriculum for each grade, reflecting our teaching philosophy.

Curriculum Goals

Once you have developed a philosophy statement, it will be easier to determine your curriculum goals. Curriculum goals are broad in nature and should incorporate the same language as your philosophy statement. Your music curriculum for each grade should meet local, state, and national standards as well as reflect the teaching philosophy of the school. For example, curriculum goals for teaching music may include:

- Repertoire for developing singing, instrumental performance, and movement
- Performance goals for developing singing, ensemble singing, movement, and playing instruments
- Music literacy goals for teaching music concepts and elements as well as development of music skills
- Creative goals, which include development of improvisation and composition skills
- Listening goals
- Curricular connections to other disciplines

You may wish to look at the emerging discussions on Core Curriculum Standards and design your curriculum to reflect these standards. In the handbooks, you will find a sample curriculum for each grade that you may use as the basis for developing your own.

Repertoire for Teaching

In this section of your portfolio, keep a list of songs arranged by each grade level and then further arranged by music concept or element. In selecting repertoire, you may want to ask yourself these questions.

- How many songs should be used for developing singing and movement skills?
- How many songs should be multicultural?
- How many songs need to be included for specific holidays, seasonal songs, commemoration days, and patriotic celebrations?
- Which songs are best used for linking music literacy and reading literacy?
- How many songs should you include that will be listening experiences for the students? They will not be required to sing these songs.
- What songs will represent different musical styles, such as pop, jazz, rock, or rap? In other words, how will you address the songs students listen to outside of school? You may find it tricky trying to connect this type of music to developmentally appropriate musical practices (particularly music literacy), but consider doing so because it will make things in the music classroom more relevant to what is happening with current popular forms of music.

Techniques for Developing Specific Skill Areas Such as Form, Rhythmic and Melodic Improvisation, Part Singing, and Listening

This section of the portfolio lists strategies and activities for developing appropriate reading, writing, inner hearing, and improvisation/composition skills.

Unit Lesson Plans for Teaching Concepts, Elements, and Skills

This section of your resource binder can include the unit plans that you will need to teach in each grade. A unit plan should have four sections:

1. List of repertoire required for five lesson plans
2. List of music skills developed in each lesson
3. Five lesson plans for teaching each concept and element
4. Copy of the worksheets you will need for each unit

Assessment of Students

This should include:

- Assessment rubrics for all the concepts and skills you want to assess
- Individual student profiles
- Class profiles

Assessment of Teacher

Include a self-evaluation of your work with previous evaluations from supervisors. This gives you an opportunity to show supervisors how you are developing as a music teacher.

Discussion Questions

1. What components should be included in a teaching resource portfolio for early childhood music?
2. Review the national and state standards for early childhood music education in your state. How do these standards have an impact on a music curriculum?
3. Interview a successful early childhood music instructor in your community and find out what his or her long-term and short-term plans for music instruction entail.
4. Identify web resources that could be useful for music instructors.

Ongoing Assignment

1. Imagine that you have been hired by a school to teach early childhood music. Create a teaching resource portfolio binder, and tab the binder according to the teaching portfolio components. This is an ongoing assignment, and you will be adding to this portfolio as you progress through the chapters in the book.
2. Speak to a music teacher. Find out how the teacher keeps track of all of the resources used in the music lessons.

Bibliography

Anderson, Erin, ed. *Campus Use of the Teaching Portfolio: Twenty-Five Profiles.* Washington, DC: American Association for Higher Education, 1993.

Cambridge, Barbara, ed. *Electronic Portfolios: Emerging Practices in Student, Faculty, and Institutional Learning.* Washington, DC: American Association for Higher Education, 2001.

Choksy, Lois, Robert M. Abramson, Avon E. Gillespie, David Woods, and Frank York. *Teaching Music in the Twenty-First Century*, 2nd ed. Upper Saddle River, NJ: Prentice-Hall, 2000.

Drake, Susan M. *Planning the Integrated Curriculum: The Call to Adventure.* Alexandria, VA: Association for Supervision and Curriculum Development, 1993.

Gault, B. "A Resource List of Kodály-Related Publications." *Kodály Envoy*, 2004, *30*(3): 9–10.

Houlahan, M., and P. Tacka. "The Kodály Concept: Expanding the Research Base." *Bulletin of the International Kodály Society Journal*, 1994, *19*(1): 34–43.

Hutchings, Pat, ed. *The Course Portfolio: How Faculty Can Examine Their Teaching to Advance Practice and Improve Student Learning.* Washington, DC: American Association for Higher Education, 1998.

Lund, F. "Quality Kodály Materials." *Kodály Envoy*, 1979, *5*(4).

Murray, John P. *Successful Faculty Development and Evaluation: The Complete Teaching Portfolio.* Washington, DC: ERIC Clearinghouse on Higher Education, 1997.

Ratliff, M. "Reflections on the Kodály Concept of Music Education." *Kodály Envoy*, 2005, *31*(2): 6–7.

Seldin, Peter. *The Teaching Portfolio: A Practical Guide to Improved Performance and Promotion/Tenure Decisions*, 3rd ed. Bolton, MA: Anker, 2004.

Notes

Introduction
1. Christian, *The Pendragon*, 1980, pp. 298–299.
2. Ibid., pp. 298–299.
3. Elliott, *Praxial Music Education*, 2005, p. 12.
4. Elliott, *Music Matters*, 1995, p. 271.
5. Dolloff, "Elementary Music Education," 2005, p. 283.
6. See also Gardiner and Fox, "Letter to the Editor," 1996, p. 284.
7. Szabá, *The Kodály Concept*, 1969.
8. Kodály, "Bartók the Folklorist," *Selected Writings*, 1974, p. 107.
9. Kodály, "Ancient Traditions," *Selected Writings*, 1974, p. 175.
10. Kokas, *Joy Through the Magic of Music*, 1999.
11. McPherson, *The Child as Musician*, 2012. See also *The Oxford Handbook of Music Education*, vols. 1 and 2.
12. "Education for Life and Work," 2012.

Chapter 1
1. Houlahan and Tacka, *Zoltán Kodály*, 1998.
2. Eősze et al., "Zoltán Kodály," 2002.
3. Kodály, [Bicinia Hungarica—Foreword], *Selected Writings*, [1937] 1974, p. 215.
4. Kodály, "333 olvaságyakorlat." *Selected Writings*, [1943] 1974.
5. Kodály, "Ötfokú zene," *Selected Writings*, [1945 and 1947] 1974, p. 221.
6. Kodály, "Hungarian Music Education," *Selected Writings*, 1974, pp. 152–155.
7. Kodály, "Hundred Year Plan," *Selected Writings*, 1974, p. 160.
8. Szőnyi, *Musical Reading*, 1974, p. 22.
9. Kodály, "A zenei írás-olvasás," *Selected Writings*, 1974, pp. 201–205.
10. Kodály, "Let Us Sing Correctly," *Selected Writings*, 1974, pp. 216–219.
11. Ádám, "Influence of Folk Music," 1965, pp. 11–18.
12. Kodály, "Beethoven's Death," *Selected Writings*, 1974, p. 77.
13. Ibid., p. 122.
14. Kodály, "Inauguration," 1985, p. 9.
15. Kodály, "Music in the Kindergarten," *Selected Writings*, 1974, p. 130.
16. Kodály, "Children's Choirs," *Selected Writings*, 1974, p. 121.
17. Kodály, *Selected Writings*, 1974, p. 206.

Notes

18. Kodály, "Two Part Exercises," *Selected Writings*, 1974, p. 225.
19. Kodály, "Children's Choirs," *Selected Writings*, 1974, p. 124.
20. Ibid., 120.
21. Kodály, "Beethoven's Death," *Selected Writings*, 1974, p. 76.
22. Kodály, "Good Musician," *Selected Writings*, 1974, p. 199.
23. Mills, *Music in the Primary School*, 1991.
24. Ibid., p. 121.
25. Crawford Seeger, *American Folk Songs*, 1953, p. 21.
26. Kodály, "Role of the Folksong," *Selected Writings*, 1974, p. 36.
27. Ibid., p. 120.
28. Kodály, "Music in the Kindergarten," *Selected Writings*, 1974, p. 141.
29. Kodály, "Children's Choirs," *Selected Writings*, 1974, p. 122.
30. Kodály, "Introduction to *Music Education*," *Selected Writings*, 1974, p. 206.
31. Kodály, "Introduction to *Musical Reading*... by Erzsébet Szőnyi," *Selected Writings*, 1974, p. 204.
32. Kodály, "Good Musician," *Selected Writings*, 1974, p. 193.
33. Kodály, "Sing Correctly," *Selected Writings*, 1974, p. 216.
34. Kodály, [Bicinia Hungarica—Foreword], *Selected Writings*, [1937], 1974, p. 215.
35. Kodály, "Solfège Competition," *Selected Writings*, 1974, p. 163.
36. Kodály, "Two-Part Exercises," *Selected Writings*, 1974, p. 224.
37. Kodály, "Good Musician," *Selected Writings*, 1974, p. 196.
38. Ibid., p. 193.
39. Kodály, "Music in the Kindergarten," *Selected Writings*, 1974, p. 151.
40. Kodály, "Pentatonic Music," *Selected Writings*, 1974, p. 221.
41. Kodály, "Children's Games," *Selected Writings*, 1974, p. 46.
42. Kodály, "National Importance," *Selected Writings*, 1974, p. 156.
43. Kodály, "Bartók the Folklorist," *Selected Writings*, 1974, p. 106.
44. Kodály, "Good Musician," *Selected Writings*, 1974, p. 197.
45. Ibid., p. 196.
46. Kodály, "Role of Authentic Folksong," 1985, p. 15.
47. Kodály, "Good Musician," *Selected Writings*, 1974, p. 198.
48. Kodály, "Preface to *Musical Reading*," *Selected Writings*, 1974, p. 204.
49. Pink, *A Whole New Mind*, 2006.
50. Consortium of National Arts Education Associations, *National Standards*, 1994.
51. http://www.corestandards.org.
52. Coleman, *Guiding Principles*, 2011.
53. Wiggins, McTighe, *Understanding by Design Guide*, 2012. Wiggins, McTighe, *Unpacking*, 2011.

Chapter 2

1. Kodály, "Music in the Kindergarten," *Selected Writings*, 1974, p. 145.
2. Kodály, "Children's Games," *Selected Writings*, 1974, pp. 46–47.

Notes

3. Kodály, *Bulletin . . . Kodály Society*, 1985, p. 18.
4. Kodály, "Authentic Folksongs," *Bulletin . . . Kodály Society*, 1985, p. 18.
5. Ibid., p. 18.
6. Ibid., p. 16.
7. Kodály, "Ancient Traditions," *Selected Writings*, 1974, p. 177.
8. Kodály, "Authentic Folksongs," *Bulletin . . . Kodály Society*, 1985, p. 18.
9. Kodály, "Pentatonic Music," *Selected Writings*, 1974, p. 221.
10. Kodály, "Hundred Year Plan," *Selected Writings,* 1974, p. 161.
11. Ibid., p. 161.
12. Kodály, "Children's Choirs," *Selected Writings*, 1974, p. 126.
13. Kodály, "Pentatonic Music," *Selected Writings,* 1974, p. 221.
14. Lund, *Research and Retrieval,* 1981, pp. 4–10.
15. See Epstein and Rappaport, *Kodály Teaching,* 2000.

Chapter 3

1. The additional sources at the end of this chapter provide more comprehensive information on vocal development.
2. We recommend Pearse, S*ound Singing,* 2000, for ideas on the teaching of singing.
3. Kodály, "Let Us Sing Correctly," *Selected Writings*, 1974, p. 216.
4. Kardos, *Foundations of Education*, 1972.
5. Kodály, Énekeljünk Hungary, 1941.
6. Kontra, *Let Us Try to Sing Correctly*, 1995.
7. Kodály, "Children's Choirs," *Selected Writings*, 1974, p. 123.
8. Kodály, "Two-Part Exercises," *Selected Writings*, 1974, p. 224.

Chapter 4

1. Kodály, "Preface to *Musical Reading and Writing,*" *Selected Writings*, 1974, p. 203. Kodály quotes Émile Artaud's 1878 *Solfège Universel.*
2. Kodály, "Let Us Sing Correctly," *Selected Writings*, 1974, p. 217.
3. Klinger, *Lesson Planning*, 2014, p. 52.
4. Hoffman et al., "Takadimi," pp. 7–30. Throughout this text, we cite this approach to teaching rhythm. From our own work with university as well as elementary school students, we are strongly convinced that it is a superior system for rhythmic reading and hearing.
5. Describing these melodies as pentatonic is not necessarily correct. It is important to realize that the sound of the pentatonic melody derives from the use of perfect fourth, major second, and perfect fifth intervals. For example, if we sing a *do–low la* interval in music using a diatonic melodic turn it would be *do ti low la*, but if we were to sing *do–low la* using a pentatonic turn it would be *do–low so–low la*. Therefore, to be completely accurate, we may state that we are teaching the students the *notes* of the pentatonic scale; however this is different from singing a true pentatonic melody.

Notes

Chapter 5

1. McPherson and Gabrielsson, "From Sound to Sign," 1992, pp. 99–115.
2. Shehan Campbell and Scott-Kassner, *Music in Childhood*, 1995, p. 9.
3. Bruner, *Towards a Theory of Instruction*, 1966.
4. Gordon, *Learning Sequences in Music*, 1994, 2003.
5. A symbol-to-sound orientation to learning a language would correspond to teaching through rules and grammar, while a sound-to-symbol orientation corresponds to learning a language through immersion.
6. Aural awareness, described as "the internal mental processing of musical relationships," is also known as inner hearing or audiation.
7. We note that in two types of notation (pre-notation and standard) errors occurred in the same place. This might be an indication as to the abilities of the stakeholders to "think in sound" without the use of an instrument. We also note that this expertise is more important for orchestral or choral directors who need this skill than for musicians who use technology for notation purposes.
8. The majority of stakeholders in our studies repeatedly asked to check what they had written using a keyboard to detect errors.
9. To enable students to read and write music, the instructor should (1) identify song repertoire containing the target and related rhythmic and melodic patterns that are initially four beats in length, and (2) sequence these patterns on the basis of frequency of occurrence in song material.
10. Perkins, *Intelligent Eye*, 1998.
11. Choksy, *Kodály Method*, 1999, pp. 171–173.
12. Brindle, "Notes from Eva Vendrai," 2005, pp. 6–11.
13. Aiello, "Importance of Metacognition," 2003, p. 656.
14. Bamberger, *Developing Musical Intuitions*, 2000.
15. We have tested our model of teaching for more than fifteen years with various student populations, including students at Eastman School of Music, Rochester, New York; Georgetown University, Washington, DC; Millersville University, Millersville, Pennsylvania; Texas State University, San Marcos, Texas; and in Texas schools in the Austin Independent School District, Houston Independent School District, and Siccoro Independent School District, El Paso.
16. We use the term *building block* as coined by Jeanne Bamberger (2000); this type of a musical chunk has also been referred to as a "comprehending pattern" by Gary McPherson (2006, 165).
17. Dowling, "Tonal Structure," 1988, pp. 113–128.
18. We use the word *pattern* to distinguish a particular musical motive. For example, a pattern could be a four-beat phrase of two quarter notes followed by two eighth notes followed by a quarter note. In this "pattern" the "concept" would be recognition of two sounds on one beat. The musical "element" would be the two eighth notes.
19. It is currently a practice of national, state, and local curriculums to specify the order and presentation of musical elements. For example, for rhythmic elements the instructor first presents quarter and eighth notes. For melodic elements, the

instructor first presents the solfège syllables *so* and *mi,* followed by *la* and then *do.* The order of elements is determined by their frequency in song repertoire.
20. By "movement activities" we mean singing games as well as gestures and movements that imitate the text of a song or highlight the melodic contour or rhythmic pattern of a phrase.
21. Peretz, "Auditory Agnosia, 1993, pp. 199–230.
22. According to Jukka Louhivuori, there is an intrinsic link between the stability of melodic formulas and the capacity of short-term memory. Therefore the main role of the instructor should be to solidify melodic and rhythmic formulas and schemes typical for specific music cultures. "Memory Strategies," 1999, pp. 81–85.
23. Cutietta and Booth, "Influence of Meter," 1996, pp. 222–236.
24. Levi, "Towards an Expanded View," 1989.
25. Simple melodies can be used to teach complex ideas. For example, when working with older students we might use simple major pentachord and hexachord melodies notated in alto or tenor clef. The musical example may be simple and easy, but the task is made more complex by using clefs.
26. Bartholomew, "Sounds Before Symbols," 1995, pp. 3–9.
27. Petzold, "Perception of Music Reading," 1960, pp. 271–319.
28. Hewson, "Music Reading," 1966, pp. 289–302.
29. Gromko and Poorman, "Developmental Trends" 1998, pp. 16–23.
30. The *new sound* may also refer to something specific, for example, the number of sounds on specific beats. The instructor might ask, "On which beat did you sing four sounds?"
31. Perkins, *Intelligent Eye,* 1998.
32. Bamberger, *Mind Behind,* 1995, p. 282.
33. Derry, "Cognitive Schema Theory," 1996, pp. 163–174.
34. Unifix cubes are small, interlocking plastic cubes that are often used in elementary grades to reinforce math concepts.
35. Piano roll notation uses horizontal lines to indicate the pitch and duration of sounds.
36. Davidson and Scripp, "Surveying the Coordinates," 1992, p. 407.
37. This is different from stage 3 of the "cognitive stage," where students use pre-notation and not traditional music symbols.
38. To view an example of this type of teaching activity, access http://www.oup.com/us/companion.websites/9780199751914/instructor/video/chapter3/3_1a/ and view video 3.1, "Analyze What You Hear."
39. Hand signs offer visual and physical motions, which develop the ability to inner-hear. Similar to "silent reading" in written language, mental imagery plays an increasingly important role in establishing musical literacy skills, such as "inner hearing" or "hearing with the eyes." Relative solmization is discussed in relation to other systems in More's "Sight Singing," 1985, pp. 9–11.
40. Colley, "Comparison of Syllabic Methods," 1987, pp. 221–235. See also Palmer, "Relative Effectiveness," 1976, pp. 110–118; and Shehan Campbell, "Effects of Rote," 1987, pp. 117–126.

Notes

41. Davidson and Scripp, "Surveying the Coordinates," 1992, p. 407. See also Brown, "Situated Cognition," 1990, pp. 32–34; and Polyanyi, *Personal Knowledge,* 1962.
42. Benward has aptly described this sound-into-notes and notes-into-sound transference as developing the "seeing ear" and the "hearing eye." Benward, *Music and Theory,* 1981, p. 100.
43. Gordon, *Learning Sequences in Music,* 1980, 25.
44. Klinger, *Lesson Planning,* 2014, p. 2.
45. Bamberger, *Mind Behind,* 1995, p. 265.
46. See Brindle, "Notes from Eva Vendrei," 2005, pp. 6–11. See also Choksy, *Kodály Method,* 1999. Both the article and the book have procedures for teaching music elements on the basis of the preparation, presentation, and practice model.
47. Choksy, *Kodály Method,* 1999, pp. 171–172. See also Eisen and Robertson, *American Methodology,* 1997.
48. Klinger, *Lesson Planning,* 2014, p. 2.
49. Gromko, "Student's Invented Notations," 1994, p. 146.
50. See Choksy, *Kodály Method,* p. 172.
51. Klinger, *Lesson Planning,* 2014, p. 2.
52. Ibid., p. 27.

Chapter 6
1. Brown, "Alternative Orientation," 2003, pp. 46–54.
2. Rappaport, "Readers Comments," 2004, pp. 9–11.
3. Klonoski, "Perceptual Learning," 2000, p. 1.
4. Ibid., p. 4.
5. Davidson et al., "'Happy Birthday,'" 1988, pp. 65–74.

Chapter 7
1. Kodály, "Hundred Year," *Selected Writings,* p. 160.
2. Kodály, "Authentic Folk Song," *Bulletin. . . Kodály Society,* 1985, p. 18. Also found as "Folk Song in Hungarian Music Education," *International Music Educator,* March 1967, *15*: 486–490.
3. The following outline of a teaching strategy was developed at the Texas State University 2003 Kodály Certification Program by students of level 3, John Gillian, and Micheál Houlahan.

Chapter 8
1. Gembris, "Development of Musical Abilities," 2002, pp. 489–490.
2. Litterest, "Smokin' Technology," 2003, p. 82.
3. Hughes and Potter, *Tweak to Transform,* 2002, p. 45.

Chapter 9
1. This narrative includes excellent suggestions from Bartle, *Sound Advice*, 2003.
2. This suggestion comes from one of our students, Jan McFarland, of the Sicorro School District in El Paso, Texas. She has her Kodály certification from the program at Texas State University, San Marcos.
3. Kodály, *Let Us Sing Correctly*, 1952.
4. This narrative includes ideas and suggestions from Bridges, *Sing Together,* 2008.

Chapter 10
1. Kodály, "Children's Choirs," in *Selected Writings*, 1974, pp. 121–122.

Chapter 11
1. Zoltán Kodály. "Preface to *Musical Reading and Writing* by ErzsDbet Szőnyi." In *Selected Writings*, p. 204.

Chapter 12
1. Forrai, *Music in Preschool,* 1995.

Song Index

"Aase's Death," no. 11 from *Peer Gynt Suite*, Op. 46 (Grieg), 244
"Above the Plain," 178*t*, 179*t*, 182*t*, 281*t*
"A Don Chin Chino," 65*fig.*
"Ah Poor Bird," 302*t*, 305*fig.*, 470*fig.*, 557*t*
"Alabama Gal," 268*t*, 272, 555*t*, 556*t*, 560
"A la Rueda de San Miguel," 556*t*
"Alfonso Doce," 283*t*
"All Around the Brickyard," 458
"All Around the Buttercup," 82*t*, 245*t*
Allegretto (Romanze) from Symphony No. 85, "La Reine" (Haydn), 245
"Alleluia"
    and auditioning for elementary choir, 441–42
    in dotted eighth and sixteenth notes lesson, 499*t*
    as focus song for grade five, 304*fig.*
    in grade five teaching strategy for major scale, 286–92
    in grade five teaching strategy for minor scale, 301*t*
    in *high ti* lesson plan, 514*t*, 516*t*
    as major diatonic scale, 67*fig.*
    and sequence for older beginners, 557*t*, 562
"Alleluia Minor," 304*fig.*
"All Night, All Day," 295*t*, 297, 298
"All Praise to Thee," 562
"Alphabet Song," 286*t*, 508*t*, 509*t*
"America," 282*t*, 559
American Salute (Gould), 370
"Apple Tree," 227
"Are You Sleeping?"
    as focus song for grade two, 248*fig.*
    and "Funeral March," Feierlich und gemessen, Symphony No. 1 in D, 393
    in grade two teaching strategy for half notes, 242, 243
    moving to listening activity from folksong, 388
    in preparation/practice lesson plan, 78*t*

    and sequence for older beginners, 554*t*, 558, 559, 560, 561
    in teaching strategy for *fa*, 282*t*
"Around the Green Gravel," 282*t*
"As I Roved Out," 303*t*
"Au Clair de la Lune," 556*t*, 561
"Aunt Rhody," 68*fig.*, 282*t*, 560
"Aussie Animals" (Lawrence), 561
"Autumn Canon," 495*t*
"Avondale Mine Disaster, The," 303*t*

"Badinerie," from Sonata in b minor BMW 1067 (Bach), 255
"Band of Angels," 265*t*
"Bee, Bee, Bumble Bee"
    in grade one teaching strategy for quarter and eighth notes, 218*t*, 221, 222
    presenting, by acting out text, 115
    for voice modulation, 107*fig.*
"Big Fat Biscuit," 145*t*, 318*t*, 388
"Billy Boy," 295*t*
"Birch Tree, The"
    in dotted eighth and sixteenth notes lesson, 496*t*, 500*t*, 503*t*, 505*t*
    as grade four focus song, 285*fig.*
    in *high ti* lesson plan, 513*t*, 518*t*
    moving to listening activity from folksong, 387
    and sequence for older beginners, 555*t*, 559, 561
    in teaching strategy for *low ti*, 283*t*
"Boatman, The," 556*t*
"Bought Me a Cat," 560
"Bounce High, Bounce Low"
    and developing sight reading skills, 344–45
    as focus song for grade one, 231*fig.*
    as *la so mi* pentatonic trichord, 66*fig.*
    as partner song, 457
    as song with narrow range, 108*fig.*
    and structural reductions, 523

Song Index

"Bound for the Promised Land," 562
"Bow Wow Wow"
    as canon, 457
    as circle game, 125
    as focus song for grade two, 246–47
    in grade two teaching strategy for tonic note of major pentatonic scale, 231–33, 234, 235, 236, 237
    and labeling four sounds on beat with rhythm syllables, 82*t*
    melodic connections and, 523
    as partner game, 128
    as partner song, 457
    performing rhythm canons based on simple rhythms, 455
    in preparation/practice lesson plan including music skills, 141*t*
    in presentation lesson plan including music skills, 144*t*
    and sequence for older beginners, 561
    in teaching strategy for second degree of pentatonic scale, 245*t*
Brandenburg Concerto No. 3 in G Major, BMV 1048, Allegro adagio (Bach), 510*t*
"Button You Must Wander," 234, 245*t*
"Bye Baby Bunting," 264*t*
"Bye Bye Baby," 85*t*

"Camptown Races," 516*t*, 517*t*
"Canoe Round," 562
"Canoe Song"
    as grade four focus song, 283*fig.*
    in grade four teaching strategy for *la* pentatonic scale, 274*t*, 276
    in grade four teaching strategy for syncopation, 267–70
    in sample presentation lesson for labeling sounds, 180*t*
    in sample presentation lesson for notation, 183*t*
    and sequence for older beginners, 554*t*, 557*t*, 559
    in transitions lesson plan, 526*t*, 528*t*
"Canon in G Major," 472*fig.*
"Car Song," 555*t*
"Cedar Swamp," 182*t*
"Celtic Cradle Song" (Hugh), 560
"Chairs to Mend," 281*t*, 282*t*, 561
"Charlie over the Ocean," 127–28, 264*t*, 562
"Charlotte Town"
    as focus song for grade five, 304*fig.*
    in grade five teaching strategy for eighth note followed by dotted quarter note, 294–97, 298, 299
    in *high ti* lesson plan, 514*t*
    and sequence for older beginners, 554*t*, 555*t*, 559
"Chatter with the Angels" (Collins), 561
"Cherry Tree Carol, The," 302*t*
"Chickalileeo," 180*t*, 249*t*
"Circle Round the Zero," 283*t*, 500*t*
"Clap Your Hands Together," 86*t*
"C-Line Woman," 182*t*, 184*t*
"Cobbler, Cobbler"
    in grade one teaching strategy for quarter and eighth notes, 218*t*, 221, 222
    in grade one teaching strategy for two-note child's chant, 226, 227
    presenting, by acting out text, 115
"Coffee Canon," 507*t*
"Coffee Grows on White Oak Trees," 560
"Colorado Trail," 518*t*, 520*t*
"Come Let's Dance," 302*t*
"Come Through 'Na Hurry"
    as double-line game, 130
    in grade four teaching strategy for syncopation, 271, 272
    as partner song, 458
    in sample presentation lesson for labeling sounds, 182*t*
    in sample presentation lesson for notation, 181*t*, 184*t*
    in transitions lesson plan, 526*t*, 527*t*
"Come to the Land," 301*t*
"Cotton Eyed Joe," 301*t*
"Crane, The," 385–87
"Cuckoo," 103
"Cumberland Gap," 78*t*, 83*t*, 399*t*
"Cut the Cake," 86*t*

"Daffodil, Too, A" (Bisbee), 562
"Dance Josey"
    as grade three focus song, 266*fig.*
    and labeling four sounds on beat with rhythm syllables, 82*t*, 83*t*
    and notating four sounds on beat with four sixteenth notes, 86*t*
    in sample lesson plan for preparing *high do*, 178*t*
    and sequence for older beginners, 554*t*, 556*t*, 561
    in teaching strategy for *low so*, 264*t*
"Deaf Woman's Courtship," 234

"Dear Companion," from *Sourwood Mountain* (Tacka and Tayor-Howell), 293
"Debka Hora"
  in dotted eighth and sixteenth notes lesson, 511*t*
  in grade three teaching strategy for eighth note followed by two sixteenth notes, 249*t*
  in *high ti* lesson plan, 516*t*
  in teaching strategy for *low ti*, 283*t*
"De Colores," 562
"Deer Chase, The," 562
"Dem Bones," 268*t*
"Dinah"
  as *do* pentatonic tetrachord, 66*fig.*
  as *do* pentatonic trichord, 64*fig.*
  in grade two teaching strategy for tonic note of major pentatonic scale, 234
  and labeling four sounds on beat with rhythm syllables, 83*t*
  and notating four sounds on beat with four sixteenth notes, 86*t*
  as partner song, 457, 458
  and sequence for older beginners, 555*t*, 556*t*, 558, 559, 560
"Do, Do Pity My Case," 143*t*, 264*t*
"Dog and Cat," 561
"Doggie, Doggie"
  in grade one teaching strategy for quarter and eighth notes, 218*t*, 221, 222
  in grade one teaching strategy for two-note child's chant, 226, 227, 228
"Dona, Dona, Dona," 301*t*
"Donkey Riding"
  in dotted eighth and sixteenth notes lesson, 495*t*, 499*t*, 504*t*, 508*t*, 511*t*
  as grade four focus song, 285*fig.*
  in *high ti* lesson plan, 514*t*, 517*t*
  in teaching strategy for dotted eighth note followed by sixteenth note, 283*t*
"Dormi, Dormi" (Goetze), 560
"Down Came a Lady," 264*t*, 398*t*, 457
"Down in the Valley," 561
"Draw Me a Bucket of Water," 555*t*
"Drill Ye Tarriers," 301*t*, 557*t*
"Drunken Sailor," 302*t*, 305*fig.*, 557*t*
"Dying Cowboy, The," 303*t*

"Early to Bed"
  as focus song for grade five, 306*fig.*

  in grade five teaching strategy for compound meter, 303*t*
  and sequence for older beginners, 556*t*, 559
"Engine, Engine, Number Nine"
  in grade one teaching strategy for quarter and eighth notes, 222
  presenting, by acting out text, 115
  and tone production, 103
  for voice modulation, 108*fig.*
  writing development activities, 354
"Erie Canal, The," 295*t*
"Evening in the Village, An," from *Hungarian Sketches* (Bartók)
  in grade five teaching strategy for eighth note followed by dotted quarter note, 300
  in grade four teaching strategy for *la* pentatonic scale, 280
  in grade three teaching strategy for *low la*, 263
  listening map, 378–79*fig.*
  in reading practice lesson segment, 322*t*
  simplified score, 377*fig.*
"Every Night When the Sun Goes Down," 556*t*, 558*t*

"Farandole" (Allegro vivo e deciso), *L'Arlésienne Suite* (Bizet), 387–88, 392–93
"Fed My Horse"
  as grade three focus song, 265*fig.*
  in grade three teaching strategy for eighth note followed by two sixteenth notes, 249–52, 253
  in preparation/practice lesson plan including music skills, 142*t*
  and sequence for older beginners, 555*t*, 556*t*
"Finale" (Allegro con fuoco), Symphony No. 4 (Tchaikovsky), 387
"Finale," from *Firebird Suite* (Stravinsky), 370
"Firefly," 143*t*
"Fire in the Mountain," 144*t*
"Fly, Fly, Fly (Autumn Canon)," 301*t*
For Children, vol. 4, no. 32 (Bartók), 377
"Four White Horses," 454
"Frère Jacques," 559
"Friendship Song" (Rao), 562
"Frosty Weather," 398–99*t*
"Fugue" from the Toccata (Mozart), 362
Fugue in D minor for Organ (Mozart), 362
"Funeral March," Feierlich und gemessen, Symphony No. 1 in D (Mahler), 393

Song Index

"Gallows Pole," 274t
"Ghost of Tom," 301t
"Git Along Little Doggies," 303t
"Go Down Moses," 295t, 302t
"Goin' to Boston" (McRae), 562
"Goodbye Old Paint," 282t, 555t
"Good Morning My Pretty Little Miss," 303t
"Great Big Dog," 295t
"Great Big House"
    as double-circle game, 129
    melodic connections and, 523
    in musicianship skills preparation/practice lesson, 398t
    in musicianship skills presentation lesson, 399t
    in preparation/practice lesson plan, 79t
    and sequence for older beginners, 554t, 556t, 559
    teaching form, 359
"Great Gate of Kiev," from *Pictures at an Exhibition* (Mussorgsky), 245
"Green Gravel," 85t, 86t
"Greeting Prelude" (Stravinsky), 370
"Ground Hog," 302t
"Gully Rider," 268t

"Harvest Song," violin duo no. 33 (Bartók), 371
"Hashivenu," 301t, 303t
"Here Comes a Bluebird"
    as choosing game, 127
    as focus for grade two, 247*fig.*
    in grade two teaching strategy for half notes, 239, 240, 241, 242
    and labeling four sounds on beat with rhythm syllables, 82t
    in musicianship skills preparation/practice lesson, 397t
    and notating four sounds on beat with four sixteenth notes, 84t
    in preparation/practice lesson plan including music skills, 141t
    in presentation lesson plan including music skills, 144t
    and sequence for older beginners, 560
"Hey, Ho, Nobody Home"
    moving to listening activity from folksong, 388
    and sequence for older beginners, 558, 560, 561
"Hey Jim Along," 318t
"Hill and Gully Rider"
    in grade four teaching strategy for syncopation, 272
    in sample choral lesson plan, 449t
    in sample presentation lesson for labeling sounds, 181t
    and sequence for older beginners, 555t, 556t
    in transitions lesson plan, 525t
"Hoedown," from *Rodeo* (Copland), 179t, 182t, 498t, 502t
"Hogs in the Cornfield"
    as grade three focus song, 266–67
    in grade three teaching strategy for eighth note followed by two sixteenth notes, 249t
    in preparation/practice lesson plan including music skills, 141t, 142t
    in presentation lesson plan including music skills, 144t
    in sample lesson plan for preparing *high do*, 178t
    in teaching strategy for *high do*, 265t
    in teaching strategy for two sixteenth notes followed by eighth note, 264t
    in transitions lesson plan, 526t, 527t, 529t
"Hop, Old Squirrel," 124, 144t, 264t
"Hot Cross Buns"
    as acting-out game, 125
    as focus song for grade one, 230*fig.*
    as focus song for grade two, 247*fig.*
    improvising melodies, 366, 368
    and labeling four sounds on beat with rhythm syllables, 82t
    melodic connections and, 523
    in preparation/practice lesson plan, 79t
    and sequence for older beginners, 560
    in teaching strategy for second degree of pentatonic scale, 245t
    as trichord, 63*fig.*
"How Are You Today?," 366*fig.*
"How Lovely Is the Evening," 554t
"How Many Miles to Babylon," 249t
"100 Dves terv" [A Hundred Year Plan] (Kodály), 17–18
"Hungarian Canon," 282t, 284*fig.*, 449t
"Hungarian Rondo" (Kodály), 300
"Hunt the Cows," 140t
"Hushabye," 67*fig.*, 281t
"Hush Little Minnie," 78t, 79t, 561

"Ida Red"
    in grade three teaching strategy for eighth note followed by two sixteenth notes, 249t, 253
    and labeling four sounds on beat with rhythm syllables, 82t

Song Index

    in musicianship skills presentation lesson, 399*t*
    in sample choral lesson plan, 452*t*
    in sample presentation lesson for labeling sounds, 180*t*
    and sequence for older beginners, 558, 559, 560, 561
    in teaching strategy for second degree of pentatonic scale, 245*t*
"I Got a Letter," 554*t*
"I Lost the Farmer's Dairy Key," 525*t*
"I'm Going Home on a Cloud," 303*t*
"In the Hall of the Mountain King" (Grieg), 223, 243
"I See the Moon," 457
"I've Been to Haarlem," 129–30, 554*t*, 559
"I've Lost the Farmer's Dairy Key," 265*t*, 267*fig.*
"I Will Give My Love an Apple," from *The Owl Sings* (Taylor-Howell), 293
"I Wonder Where Maria's Gone," 277

"Jam on Jerry's Rocks, The," 303*t*
"Jim Along Josie"
    in associative phase preparation/practice lesson, 318*t*
    in associative phase presentation lesson, 320*t*
    as circle game, 126
    in grade three teaching strategy for *low la*, 256*t*, 259
    in presentation lesson plan including music skills, 145*t*
    in sample lesson plan for preparing *high do*, 178*t*
    and sequence for older beginners, 555*t*, 558*t*, 561
    in teaching strategy for two sixteenth notes followed by eighth note, 264*t*
"John Cuko," 555*t*
"John Kanaka," 178*t*, 268*t*, 281*t*, 507*t*, 527*t*
"Johnny Has Gone for a Soldier," 286*t*, 504*t*, 505*t*, 513*t*
"Jolly Miller," 179*t*, 183*t*
"Joy to the World," 286*t*

"Kis kece Lanyom," 561
"Knock the Cymbals," 234, 242, 243
"Kookaburra," 452*t*, 555*t*, 557*t*, 561
"Kyrie" (Schram), 560

"Lamb, The" (Tavener), 371
"Land of the Silver Birch"
    as grade four focus song, 284*fig.*
    in grade four teaching strategy for *la* pentatonic scale, 274–76, 277

    in grade four teaching strategy for syncopation, 268*t*
    in lesson for interactive whiteboard, 416*t*
    as partner song, 458
    and sequence for older beginners, 555*t*, 557*t*, 562
    in transitions lesson plan, 525*t*, 527*t*, 528*t*, 529*t*
"La Patita," 64*fig.*
"Laugh, Ha, Ha," 469*fig.*
"Lemonade," 108*fig.*
"Les Toreadors," *Carmen* (Bizet), 513*t*, 515*t*, 517*t*
"Let Us Chase the Squirrel"
    and developing sight reading skills, 342–46
    and development of beat movement sequence, 124
    in preparation/practice lesson plan including music skills, 140*t*, 141*t*
    in presentation lesson plan including music skills, 144*t*
"Little Birch Tree, The" (Goetze), 561
"Little Johnny Brown," 295*t*
"Little Russian," Symphony No. 2 (Tchaikovsky), 385–87
"Little Sally Water," 127
"Liza Jane"
    as grade four focus song, 284*fig.*
    in grade four teaching strategy for *la* pentatonic scale, 274*t*
    in grade four teaching strategy for syncopation, 268*t*, 271, 272
    moving to listening activity from folksong, 388
    as partner song, 458
    in sample choral lesson plan, 449*t*
    and sequence for older beginners, 554*t*, 555*t*, 559, 561
    and structural reductions, 523
    in teaching strategy for dotted quarter noted followed by eighth note, 281*t*
    in teaching strategy for *high do*, 265*t*
"London Bridge"
    in dotted eighth and sixteenth notes lesson, 508*t*, 512*t*
    as line game, 128
    and sequence for older beginners, 558, 562
"Lonesome Road," 66–67
"Longest Train, The," 562
"Long Legged Sailor," 556*t*, 560
"Long Road of Iron," 281*t*, 282*t*
"Love Somebody," 360
"Low Bridge," 559
"Lucy Locket," 63*fig.*, 523, 554*t*

Song Index

"Mama, Buy Me a Chiney Doll," 81*t*, 249*t*, 561
"Mamalama"
    in dotted eighth and sixteenth notes lesson, 504*t*, 511*t*
    in *high ti* lesson plan, 519*t*
"March," from *King David* (Honegger), 371
"Mary Had a Baby," 561
"May Song" (Schubert), 562
Mazurka in C major Op. 33, No. 3 (Chopin), 362
"Michael, Row the Boat Ashore," 507*t*
Mikrokosmos (Bartók), 300
"Miller of Dee, The," 559
Minuet in G from *Anna Magdalena Notebook* (Bach), 361
"Morning Is Come," 302*t*, 305*fig.*
"Mrs. Jenny Wren," 559
"Musette," from *Anna Magdalena Notebook* (Bach), 362
"Music Alone Shall Live," 558*t*
"My Good Old Man," 268*t*, 274*t*
"My Mommy Told Me," 561

New Mexico March (Sousa), 177*t*

"Ode to Joy," 560
"Oh How Lovely Is the Evening"
    in dotted eighth and sixteenth notes lesson, 494*t*, 510*t*
    as grade four focus song, 285*fig.*
    and sequence for older beginners, 554*t*, 558*t*
"Oh When The," 560
"Old Abram Brown" (Britten), 562
"Old Betty Larkin," 145*t*, 277
"Old Brass Wagon," 177*t*, 561
"Old Joe Clark"
    as example of Mixolydian mode, 70
    as focus song for grade five, 306*fig.*
    in grade five teaching strategy for *ta*, 303*t*
    and sequence for older beginners, 558*t*, 562
"Old Lady Sittin' in the Dining Room," 561
"Old MacDonald," 264*t*
"Old Mother Witch," 347
"Old Mr. Rabbit"
    in associative phase preparation/practice lesson, 318*t*
    as grade three focus song, 266*fig.*
    in grade three teaching strategy for *low la*, 256*t*
    in preparation/practice lesson plan including music skills, 140*t*
    in presentation lesson plan including music skills, 143*t*, 145*t*
    in sample lesson plan for preparing *high do*, 177*t*, 178*t*, 179*t*
    in sample presentation lesson for labeling sounds, 180*t*
    in teaching strategy for internal upbeats, 264*t*
    in transitions lesson plan, 528*t*
"Old Woman," 556*t*
"Oliver Twist," 116
"On a Mountain," 282*t*
"Oro, My Bodeen," from *The Owl Sings* (Taylor-Howell), 293
"Ostinato" from *Mikrokosmos,* vol. 6, no. 146 (Bartók), 369
"Over the River," 142*t*, 264*t*, 555*t*

"Pala Palita," 227*fig.*
Partita No. 1 in B flat minor, BWV 825 (Bach), 361
"La Patita," 64*fig.*
"Paw Paw Patch"
    and aural awareness development using SMART Board, 420
    as focus song for grade two, 247*fig.*
    and labeling four sounds on beat with rhythm syllables, 82*t*
    in musicianship skills preparation/practice lesson, 398*t*
    in musicianship skills presentation lesson, 399*t*
    and notating four sounds on beat with four sixteenth notes, 85*t*
    in preparation/practice lesson plan, 79*t*
    and rhythm syllables, 161
    and sequence for older beginners, 561
Peacock Variations (Kodály), 370
"Phoebe in the Her Petticoat"
    in associative phase preparation/practice lesson, 315*t*, 317*t*
    in associative phase presentation lesson, 320*t*
    and aural awareness development using SMART Board, 420–21
    in cognitive phase preparation/practice lesson, 310*t*, 313*t*
    as grade three focus song, 266*fig.*
    in grade three teaching strategy for *low la*, 256–59, 260
    in improvisation practice lesson segment, 324*t*
    in preparation/practice lesson plan including music skills, 141*t*

Song Index

    in presentation lesson plan including music skills, 144*t*
    in reading practice lesson segment, 322*t*
    in sample lesson plan for preparing *high do*, 178*t*
    in writing practice lesson segment, 323*t*
Piano Concerto No. 21, "Andante" (Mozart), 507*t*
Piano Sonata in G, Op. 14, No 2 (Beethoven), 362
Piano Sonata No. 3 (Joio), 370
"Pizza Pizza," 108–9, 556*t*
"Poor Little Kitty Cat," 256*t*
"Prelude in C Minor," from *Well-Tempered Clavier* (Bach), 401*t*
"Pretty Saro," 503*t*

"Queen, Queen Caroline," 218*t*, 221

"Rabbit and Possum," 514*t*
"Rain, Rain"
    and development of beat movement sequence, 123
    as focus song for grade one, 230*fig.*
    in grade one teaching strategy for quarter and eighth notes, 218–20, 222, 223
    in grade one teaching strategy for two-note child's chant, 227, 228, 229
"Redbirds and Blackbirds," 282*t*
"Riding in the Buggy"
    in grade four teaching strategy for syncopation, 268*t*, 271, 272
    in sample presentation lesson for labeling sounds, 179*t*
    in sample presentation lesson for notation, 184*t*
    and structural reductions, 523
    in teaching strategy for *high do*, 265*t*
    in transitions lesson plan, 525*t*
"Ring Around the Rosy," 125
"Rise Up, Oh Flame," 282*t*, 499*t*
"Rocky Mountain"
    beat chart, 351*fig.*
    as focus song for grade two, 248*fig.*
    in grade two teaching strategy for tonic note of major pentatonic scale, 234
    improvising melodies, 367
    and linking common rhythmic elements to rhythm syllables, 160
    in major pentatonic scale, 62*fig.*
    in musicianship skills presentation lesson, 399*t*
    in preparation/practice lesson plan including music skills, 141*t*

    in presentation lesson plan including music skills, 144*t*
    and sequence for older beginners, 554*t*, 556*t*, 558, 559, 560, 561
    and teaching by rote through questioning, 113–14
    in teaching strategy for second degree of pentatonic scale, 245*t*
Rondo alla Turca (Mozart), 78*t*, 81*t*
Rondo No. 1 for piano (Bartók), 244
Rosamunde (Schubert), 253*fig.*, 255
"Rosie, Darling Rosie," 145*t*, 318*t*, 558
"Row, Row, Row Your Boat," 301*t*, 304–5, 556*t*, 559

"Sail Away" (Brumfield), 561, 562
"Sail Away, Ladies," 283*t*, 494*t*, 513*t*
"Sailing O'er the Ocean," 249*t*, 264*t*, 554*t*
"St. Anthony's Chorale," *Variations on a Theme* (Brahms), 514*t*
"Sally Gardens, The" (Britten), 561
"San Serafin," 250*fig.*
"Santo Domingo," 65*fig.*
"Scarborough Fair"
    as example of Dorian mode, 71*fig.*
    in grade five teaching strategy for compound meter, 303*t*
    in grade five teaching strategy for *fi*, 302*t*
    and sequence for older beginners, 557*t*
"Scotland's Burning," 554*t*, 559
"Sea Shell," 78*t*, 81*t*
"Seesaw"
    in grade one teaching strategy for quarter and eighth notes, 218*t*, 221
    in grade one teaching strategy for two-note child's chant, 227, 228
    as pentatonic bichord, 63*fig.*
    as *so-mi* pentatonic bichord, 65*fig.*
    writing development activities, 354
"Shady Grove"
    in dotted eighth and sixteenth notes lesson, 503*t*, 510*t*
    moving to listening activity from folksong, 388
    and sequence for older beginners, 555*t*
    in teaching strategy for dotted eighth note followed by sixteenth note, 283*t*
"Shake Them 'Simmons Down," 555*t*
"Shoes of John"
    in sample presentation lesson for labeling sounds, 180*t*
    in teaching strategy for external upbeats, 265*t*
    in transitions lesson plan, 525*t*

Song Index

"Shoo My Love," 272
"Short Story," Op. 27, Book 1, No. 13 (Kabalevsky), 245
"Show Me the Way," 560
Sinfonia No. 8, BWV 794 (Bach), 524*t*, 527*t*
"Sioux Indian Lullaby," 63*fig.*, 274*t*
"Skin and Bones," 64*fig.*, 66*fig.*, 559
"Skipping Rope Song," 264*t*
"Skip to My Loo," 249*t*
"Sleep Little One," 562
"Sleep My Baby" (Rowley), 560
"Slovak Folk Song," 562
"Snail, Snail"
    as focus song for grade one, 230*fig.*
    in grade one teaching strategy for quarter and eighth notes, 218*t*, 221, 222
    in grade one teaching strategy for two-note child's chant, 223–26, 227, 228
    improvising melodies, 366
    and sequence for older beginners, 554*t*
    as winding game, 125
"Solfegetto" (Bach), 401*t*
Sonata in D minor, K. 64 (Scarlatti), 256
"Songs of a Summer Afternoon" (Crocker), 560
"Sourwood Mountain," 499*t*
"Star Light, Star Bright," 113
String Quartet in C major, Op. 33, No 2. (Haydn), 362
String Quartet No. 4, movement 3 (Schoenberg), 371
"Study for Left Hand" (Bartók), 245
"Sur le Pont d'Avignon," 554*t*
"Surprise" Symphony, Allegretto (Haydn), 84*t*
"Surprise" Symphony, Andante (Haydn), 222
"Sweet Betsy from Pike"
    in dotted eighth and sixteenth notes lesson, 511*t*, 512*t*
    in grade five teaching strategy for major scale, 286*t*
    in teaching strategy for triple meter, 282*t*
"Sweet William," 301*t*, 557*t*, 559
"Swine Herd, The," from *Mikrokosmos* (Bartók), 273
Symphony, Op. 21, movement 2 (Webern), 371
Symphony No. 1, "Allegro" (Mozart), 238
Symphony No. 104 in D major, movement 1 (Haydn), 362
Symphony No. 4 in A, "Italian," Movement 1, Allegro vivace (Mendelssohn), 494*t*

"Teddy Bear," 227, 228, 366
"That Music Enchanting," from *The Magic Flute* (Mozart), 293

"That's a Mighty Pretty Motion, 366
"There Is No Rose," from *A Ceremony of Carols* (Britten), 371
"This Old Man," 227, 228
"Three French Folksongs" (Edwards), 560
Three Places in New England, movement 2 (Ives), 371
"Three to Get Ready" (Brubeck), 369
"Tideo"
    and labeling four sounds on beat with rhythm syllables, 83*t*
    melodic connections and, 523
    moving to listening activity from folksong, 388
    and notating four sounds on beat with four sixteenth notes, 85*t*
    in sample presentation lesson for labeling sounds, 180*t*
    and sequence for older beginners, 554*t*, 555*t*, 559
    in teaching strategy for *high do*, 265*t*
"Tisket, a Tasket, A," 127–28, 559
"To Work upon the Railway," 301*t*, 562
"Toy" Symphony, Allegro (Mozart), 228
"Tumbalalaika," 301*t*
"Turn the Glasses Over," 264*t*, 451*t*, 556*t*
"Twinkle, Twinkle, Little Star," 68*fig.*, 282*t*, 560

"Vamos a Belen," 469*fig.*
Variations of Greensleeves (Williams), 362
"Velvet Shoes," (Thompson), 560
"Vine and Fig Tree," 302*t*
Violin Concerto, movement 1 (Berg), 371
"Viva la Musica!"
    in dotted eighth and sixteenth notes lesson, 499*t*
    in *high ti* lesson plan, 515*t*
    and sequence for older beginners, 557*t*, 562
    in teaching strategy for dotted quarter noted followed by eighth note, 281*t*

"Wake Up!" canon
    in dotted eighth and sixteenth notes lesson, 495*t*, 497*t*
    in grade five teaching strategy for major scale, 286*t*
    in *high ti* lesson plan, 518*t*
"Walk Along John," 264*t*, 295*t*
"Wall Flowers," 126, 234
"We Are Dancing in the Forest," 222
"Wee Cock Sparra," 302*t*
"Weevily Wheat," 180*t*, 268*t*, 271, 272, 529*t*

Song Index

"Welcome Party," from *Folk Song Symphony No. 4* (Harris), 370
"When I First Came to This Land," 515*t*, 556*t*
"When Jesus Wept," 559
"Whistle Daughter Whistle," 274*t*, 282*t*
"White Sand and Grey Sand," 470*fig.*
"Who Can Sail," 557*t*
"Who Killed Cocky Robin?"
    and labeling four sounds on beat with rhythm syllables, 82*t*, 83*t*
    as partner song, 458
    in sample presentation lesson for labeling sounds, 180*t*, 181*t*
"Who's That Tapping at the Window?," 60*fig.*, 243, 555*t*
"Wishy Washy," 301*t*
"Witch, Witch," 559

"Yankee Doodle," 283*t*

"Zebra Run, The," 562
"Zudio," 495*t*, 508*t*, 554*t*
"ZumGaliGali," 555*t*

Subject Index

absolute letter names, 155
a capella singing, 100
accompaniment
    clapping rhythmic motives as, 458
    and score preparation, 479
acting out games, 120, 125, 127
acting out text, presenting songs by, 114–15
Aeolian Mode, 69, 70
American folk music, 56
anhemitonic pentatonic scales, 62
antiphonal singing, 108–9, 116, 453
apps, 409, 410–11, 413, 414
Arend, Julie, 572
d'Arezzo, Guido, 25, 155
art music, folk music and, 380
arts, in curriculum based on Kodály Method and national content standards, 38
assessment, 576–77. *See also* evaluation
    class profile summarizing student achievement, 586–88
    connection to grade handbooks, 595
    creating rubrics, 593–94
    of music teaching, 577–86
    opportunities in learning theory model, 208
    sample rubrics, 594–97
    of special needs students, 536
    student profiles, 588–97
    in teaching portfolio, 604
    in teaching strategy for quarter and eighth notes, 222–23
    in teaching strategy for two-note child's chant, 229
assimilative phase
    in learning theory model, 194*t*, 195, 202–4, 307, 308*t*
    lesson plans for, 512–20
    in teaching strategy for eighth note followed by dotted quarter note, 297–301
    in teaching strategy for eighth note followed by two sixteenth notes, 251–56
    in teaching strategy for half notes, 241–45
    in teaching strategy for *la* pentatonic scale, 277–81
    in teaching strategy for *low la*, 259–63
    in teaching strategy for major scale, 290–94
    in teaching strategy for quarter and eighth notes, 220–23
    in teaching strategy for syncopation, 270–73
    in teaching strategy for tonic note of major pentatonic scale, 234–38
    in teaching strategy for two-note child's chant, 226–30
associative phase
    in learning theory model, 194*t*, 195, 201–2, 306–7
    lesson plans for, 506–12
    preparation/practice lesson plan template for, 314–17*t*
    presentation lesson plan template for, 317–20*t*
    in teaching strategy for eighth note followed by dotted quarter note, 296–97
    in teaching strategy for eighth note followed by two sixteenth notes, 251
    in teaching strategy for half notes, 240–41
    in teaching strategy for *la* pentatonic scale, 275–77
    in teaching strategy for *low la*, 258
    in teaching strategy for major scale, 288–90
    in teaching strategy for quarter and eighth notes, 220
    in teaching strategy for syncopation, 269–70
    in teaching strategy for tonic note of major pentatonic scale, 233–34
    in teaching strategy for two-note child's chant, 224–26
Audacity, 410, 413
audiation skills. *See* inner hearing
auditions, for elementary choir, 441–44
aural awareness. *See also* inner hearing
    in cognitive phase of learning, 197–98, 200
    learning theory model for, 192–94
    in preparation/practice lessons, 493–501
    using SMART Board to develop, 419–22

Subject Index

aural practice
    in teaching strategy for eighth note followed by dotted quarter note, 297–98
    in teaching strategy for eighth note followed by two sixteenth notes, 251–52
    in teaching strategy for half notes, 241–42
    in teaching strategy for *la* pentatonic scale, 277–78
    in teaching strategy for *low la*, 259–60
    in teaching strategy for major scale, 290–91
    in teaching strategy for quarter and eighth notes, 220–21
    in teaching strategy for syncopation, 270–71
    in teaching strategy for tonic note of major pentatonic scale, 234–38
    in teaching strategy for two-note child's chant, 226

Bach, C.P.E., "Solfegetto," 401*t*
Bach, Johann Sebastian
    "Badinerie," from Sonata in b minor BMW 1067, 255
    Brandenburg Concerto No. 3 in G Major, BMV 1048, Allegro adagio, 510*t*
    Minuet in G from *Anna Magdalena Notebook*, 361
    "Musette" in G from *Anna Magdalena Notebook*, 362
    Partita No. 1 in B flat minor, BWV 825, 361
    "Prelude in C Minor," from *Well-Tempered Clavier*, 401*t*
    Sinfonia No. 8, BWV 794, 521*t*, 524*t*
bad taste, 21–22
Bamberger, Jean, 199, 203
Bartholomew, Douglas, 197
Bartók, Béla
    For Children, vol. 4, no. 32, 377
    "Evening in the Village, An," from *Hungarian Sketches*, 263, 280, 300, 322*t*, 378–79*fig.*
    "Harvest Song," violin duo no. 33, 371
    Kodály and, 16
    Mikrokosmos, 300
    "Ostinato" from *Mikrokosmos, vol. 6, no. 146*, 369
    Rondo No. 1 for piano, 245
    "Study for Left Hand," 245
    "Swine Herd, The," from *Mikrokosmos*, 273
bass lines, 474–75
beat
    in choir rehearsal part work, 453
    in developing movement sequence, 123–24
    and incorporating instruments into curriculum, 136
    repertoire for, in compound meter, 462
    repertoire for, in simple meter, 462
    writing, 351

Beethoven, Ludwig van, Piano Sonata in G, Op. 14, No. 2, 362
behavior
    and evaluation of lesson plan format, 579*t*
    Kodály training's effect on, 2
    modeling, for special needs students, 533
Berg, Alban, Violin Concerto, movement 1, 371
bilingual students, 537–38
binary form, 361
Bizet, Georges, "Farandole" (Allegro vivo e deciso), *L'Arlésienne Suite*, 387–88, 392–93
Blogger, 411, 414
blogs, 411, 414
body warm-up exercises, 101, 132–34
Booth, Gregory D., 196
Bowman, Wayne, 14
Brahms, Johannes, "St. Anthony's Chorale," *Variations on a Theme*, 514*t*
breathing
    in choral rehearsal, 444
    exercises, 102
    and singing skills in older beginners, 550–51, 553
    stagger, 106
Britten, Benjamin, "There Is No Rose," from *A Ceremony of Carols*, 371
Brubeck, Dave, "Three to Get Ready," 369
Bruner, Jerome, 192

cadence, 361
call-and-response singing, 108–9, 116, 453
cameras, document, 410
canon(s)
    in children's choir repertoire, 477
    in choir rehearsal part work, 454–59
    pentatonic major, minor, and modal scales in, 475–76
    and transitions, 523
    with triads, 471–73
chase games, 120–22, 127–28
chest voice, 106–10
Chevé, Émile, 157
child's chant
    grade one focus song for three-note, 230–31
    grade one focus song for two-note, 230*fig.*
    grade one teaching strategy for three-note, 229*t*
    grade one teaching strategy for two-note, 223–30
    repertoire for three-note, 462
child's piano, 157
choir. *See* elementary choir
Choksy, L., 207

Subject Index

Choksy model of learning, 204–8
choosing games, 120, 127
Chopin, Frederick, Mazurka in C major Op. 33, No. 3, 362
choral composition, teaching, 478–82
chord inversions, 474
circle games, 120, 125–26
classical music, association between folk music and, 55
classroom management, 585t
cognitive phase
    in learning theory model, 194t, 195–201, 306, 307t
    lesson plans for, 491–505
    preparation/practice lesson plan template for, 309–16t
    in teaching strategy for eighth note followed by dotted quarter note, 294–96
    in teaching strategy for eighth note followed by two sixteenth notes, 249–51
    in teaching strategy for half notes, 239–40
    in teaching strategy for *la* pentatonic scale, 274–75
    in teaching strategy for *low la*, 256–57
    in teaching strategy for major scale, 286–88
    in teaching strategy for quarter and eighth notes, 218–19, 223–24
    in teaching strategy for syncopation, 267–69
    in teaching strategy for tonic note of major pentatonic scale, 231–33
Collected Songs for Schools [*Iskolai DnekgyüjtemDny I-II*] (Kodály & Kerényi), 17
combination vowels, 103, 551
comfortable starting pitch, 61
Common Core Standards, 39–40
complex intervals, 371
composition
    activities for developing, 362–65
    in curriculum based on Kodály Method and national content standards, 38
    in grade one sample curriculum, 34
    in grade four musicianship skills sample curriculum, 336
    improvisation and, 369
    in Kodály's philosophy of music education, 26
    as musical skill to be developed in classroom, 331
    practicing known elements through, 501–5
    references for, 373–74
compound meter
    grade five focus song for, 304–5
    grade five focus song for dotted patterns in, 306fig.
    grade five focus song for subdivided patterns in, 305fig.
    grade five teaching strategy for, 301t, 302t, 303t
    repertoire for beat in, 462
comprehensive music education, 20–27
conducting
    and evaluation of instructor's musicianship, 582t
    in grade one sample curriculum, 31
    in grade four musicianship skills sample curriculum, 334
    and score preparation, 479–80
conscious rhythmic connections, 523
content standards for music education, national, 37–39
contrived music, 22
Copland, Aaron, "Hoedown," from *Rodeo*, 179t, 182t, 498t, 502t
correcting students, 106–7
creativity. *See also* movement
    assessment of, 589, 590, 592t
    connection to grade handbooks, 145–46
    and curriculum for upper grades, 542, 545–46
    in grade one sample curriculum, 34
    in Kodály-based curriculum, 29
    in Kodály's philosophy of music education, 26
    as part of comprehensive music education, 21
critical thinking skills
    assessment of, 589
    and curriculum for upper grades, 542, 544–45
    in grade one sample curriculum, 31–33
    in Kodály-based curriculum, 29
    in Kodály's philosophy of music education, 24–25
    as part of comprehensive music education, 21
cross-curricular instruction, 590
cultural heritage, students as stewards of, 21–22, 28–29, 30, 53, 541
culture, in curriculum based on Kodály Method and national content standards, 39
curriculum
    based on Kodály Method and Common Core Standards, 39–40
    based on Kodály Method and national content standards, 37–39
    building framework of, 28–29
    evaluation of, 578, 579t
    goals in teaching portfolio, 603
    incorporating instruments into, 136–37
    Kodály's philosophy on music in, 19
    listening, 376–77
    for musicianship skills in upper grades, 541–46
    pentatonic music in, 56–57
    prompt questions for tailoring, 35–37
    repertoire analysis and connections to, 73

Subject Index

curriculum (*Cont.*)
    sample, for developing musicianship skills, 332–37
    sample, for grade one, 29–35
    selecting songs for, 57–59
    technology and, 407
Curwen, John, 25, 155
Cutietta, Robert A., 196

Davidson, Lyle, 192–93, 217
descending melodic patterns, 108
diatonic scales, 67–68, 164
dictation
    activities for developing writing, 351, 354–55
    developing, in older beginners, 568–70
diction
    and singing skills in older beginners, 552
    and teaching singing, 104
digital instruments, 413
diluted music, 22
diphthongs, 104, 552
do
    moveable, 25, 155
    sample assessment rubric for, 594–97
document cameras, 410
dominant chord roots, accompanying melodies with, 469, 470
do pentatonic scale, 66, 157*fig.*, 463
Dorian modal scale, 69, 70–71, 465
do system of somization, 25
dotted eighth note
    grade four focus song for, followed by sixteenth note, 285*fig.*
    preparation/practice lesson for sixteenth note and, 494–97*t*, 498–501*t*, 502–5*t*
    presentation lesson for sixteenth note and, 507–9*t*, 510–12*t*
    repertoire for, followed by sixteenth note, 465
    teaching strategy for, followed by sixteenth note, 283*t*
dotted quarter note
    grade four focus song for, followed by eighth note, 284*fig.*
    grade five focus song for eighth note followed by, 304*fig.*
    grade five teaching strategy for eighth note followed by, 294–301
    repertoire for eighth note followed by, 465
    teaching strategy for, followed by eighth note, 281*t*
double-circle games, 122, 129–30
double-line games, 122, 130

drones, 456
DropBox, 410
dynamic markings
    and score preparation, 479
    and singing skills in older beginners, 553
    and teaching tuneful singing, 105

ear, memorization by, 356–57
ear training, and auditioning for elementary choir, 442, 443
Edmodo, 411, 414
Edublogs, 411, 414
eighth note combinations, elementary choir pieces with, 463
eighth note rest, 273
eighth notes. *See also* dotted eighth note
    focus song for, followed by two sixteenth notes, 265*fig.*
    focus song for two sixteenth notes followed by, 266*fig.*
    grade one focus song for, 230*fig.*
    grade one teaching strategy for, 218–23
    grade three teaching strategy for, followed by two sixteenth notes, 249–56
    grade four focus song for dotted quarter note followed by, 284*fig.*
    grade five focus song for, followed by dotted quarter note, 304*fig.*
    grade five teaching strategy for, followed by dotted quarter note, 294–301
    repertoire for, 462
    repertoire for, followed by dotted quarter note, 465
    repertoire for combinations with sixteenth notes, 463
    in sequence for teaching rhythmic elements, 163
    teaching strategy for dotted quarter note followed by, 281*t*
    teaching strategy for two sixteenth notes followed by, 264*t*
elementary choir
    applying Kodály concept to, 440–41
    auditions, 441–44
    rehearsal activities, 444–59
    repertoire for part work and music literacy, 459–65
    score preparation and teaching choral composition, 478–82
    seating arrangement, 443–44
    selecting repertoire, 476–78
    teaching two-part song arrangements, 466–76
Elliott, David, 1, 53–54, 153, 576

Subject Index

enactive teaching and learning strategy, 192
error correction, 584–85t
evaluation. *See also* assessment
    in curriculum based on Kodály Method and national content standards, 38
    of lesson plan, 530–31
    of teaching, 531
Evernote, 410
Explain Everything app, 411
external upbeats
    focus song for, 267*fig*.
    repertoire for, 464
    teaching strategy for, 265t

fa
    grade four focus song for, 284*fig*.
    repertoire for, 464–65
    teaching strategy for, 282t
Facebook, 411, 414
fi
    grade five focus song for, 305*fig*.
    grade five teaching strategy for, 302t
fifth grade. *See* grade five
finger staff, 157
first grade. *See* grade one
Flashnote Derby, 414
focus songs, 80
    for grade one, 230–31
    for grade two, 246–48
    for grade three, 265–67
    for grade four, 283–85
    for grade five, 304–6
Folk Songs, Singing Games, and Play Parties (Trinka), 74
folk songs and music
    art music and, 380
    authenticity in, 55–56
    and children as stewards of cultural heritage, 21
    in children's choir repertoire, 477
    of closely related cultures, 56
    David J. Elliott on, 53
    Kodály on art music and, 26
    Kodály's use of, 16
    moving to listening activity from, 385–93
    performance and notation of, 73–74
    and repertoire development, 54–55
    singing, in thirds and sixths, 469
    singing simple pentatonic, in three parts, 459
    and teaching basic rhythmic and melodic patterns, 175–76

form
    activities emphasizing structure and, 359–62
    connections, 524
    and curriculum for upper grades, 545
    developing, 358–59
    in grade one sample curriculum, 33
    in grade four musicianship skills sample curriculum, 334
    melodic, in repertoire analysis, 72
    as musical skill to be developed in classroom, 331
    and score preparation, 479
formative assessment, 588–89
four-beat meter
    focus song for introducing, 248*fig*.
    repertoire for, 463
    teaching strategy for, 246t
fourth grade. *See* grade four
fragmentation, 369–70
From Sound to Symbol (Houlahan and Tacka), 446

games. *See* singing games
GarageBand, 410, 413
Gardiner, Martin F., 2
German letter names, 155
gifted and talented students, 536–37
Glover, Sarah, 155
Gordon, Edwin, 192
Gould, Morton, *American Salute*, 370
grade one
    focus songs for, 230–31
    teaching strategy for quarter and eighth notes, 218–23
    teaching strategy for two-note child's chant, 223–30
grade two
    focus songs for, 246–48
    sample assessment rubrics for *do*, 594–97
    teaching strategy for four-beat meter, 246t
    teaching strategy for half note, 239–46
    teaching strategy for introducing tonic, 231–38
    teaching strategy for major pentatonic scale, 246t
    teaching strategy for second degree of pentatonic scale, 245t
    teaching strategy for sixteenth notes, 246t
grade three
    focus songs for, 265–67
    teaching strategies for, 248–49
    teaching strategy for eighth note followed by two sixteenth notes, 249–56
    teaching strategy for external upbeats, 265t
    teaching strategy for *high do*, 265t

Subject Index

grade three (*Cont.*)
 teaching strategy for internal upbeats, 264*t*
 teaching strategy for *low la*, 256–63
 teaching strategy for *low so*, 264*t*
 teaching strategy for two sixteenth notes followed by eighth note, 264*t*
grade four
 focus songs for, 283–85
 sample curriculum for musicianship skills, 332–37
 teaching strategy for dotted eighth note followed by sixteenth note, 283*t*
 teaching strategy for dotted quarter note followed by eighth note, 281*t*
 teaching strategy for *fa*, 282*t*
 teaching strategy for *la* pentatonic scale, 273–81
 teaching strategy for *low ti*, 283*t*
 teaching strategy for syncopation, 267–73
 teaching strategy for triple meter, 282*t*
grade five
 focus songs for, 304–6
 teaching strategy for compound meter, 301*t*, 302*t*, 303*t*
 teaching strategy for eighth note followed by dotted quarter note, 294–301
 teaching strategy for *fi*, 302*t*
 teaching strategy for major scale, 286–94
 teaching strategy for natural minor scale, 301*t*
 teaching strategy for *si*, 302*t*
 teaching strategy for *ta*, 303*t*
greetings, singing, 110
Grieg, Edvard
 "Aase's Death," no. 11 from *Peer Gynt Suite*, Op. 46, 245
 "In the Hall of the Mountain King," 223, 243
Gromko, J., 197, 206

half notes
 focus song for, 247*fig*.
 grade two teaching strategy for, 239–46
 repertoire for, 462
hand signs, 25, 156
 and developing sight reading skills, 343, 344, 611n39
 memorization from, 356
 in teaching strategy for eighth note followed by dotted quarter note, 298
 in teaching strategy for eighth note followed by two sixteenth notes, 252
 in teaching strategy for *la* pentatonic scale, 275, 276, 277, 278–80
 in teaching strategy for *low la*, 260, 262, 263
 in teaching strategy for major scale, 288, 291, 292, 293
 in teaching strategy for syncopation, 271
 in teaching strategy for tonic note of major pentatonic scale, 236
 in teaching strategy for two-note child's chant, 227
 two-part singing, 457
Hargreaves, David J., 191
harmonic functions, 469, 470, 523–24
harmonic hearing, developing, in elementary choir, 468–69
harmonic instruments, 137–38
harmonic minor scale, 465
harmonic progressions, and triad inversions, 473–74
harmony
 as musical skill to be developed in classroom, 332
 and score preparation, 479
Harris, Roy, "Welcome Party," from *Folk Song Symphony No. 4*, 370
Haydn, Franz Joseph
 Allegretto (Romanze) from Symphony No. 85, "La Reine," 245
 String Quartet in C major, Op. 33, No 2., 362
 "Surprise" Symphony, Allegretto, 84*t*
 "Surprise" Symphony, Andante, 222
 Symphony No. 104 in D major, movement 1, 362
head voice, 106–10
hemitonic pentatonic scales, 62
Hewson, A. T., 197
high do
 focus song for, 267*fig*.
 repertoire for, 464
 sample preparation/practice lesson plan for practicing, 177–79*t*
 teaching strategy for, 265*t*
high ti
 preparation/practice lessons for, 513–20*t*
 in teaching strategy for major scale, 286*t*
history, in curriculum based on Kodály Method and national content standards, 39
Honegger, Arthur, "March," from *King David*, 371
Houlahan and Tacka model of learning and instruction. *See* learning theory model
Hughes, Robert, 406, 415

Subject Index

"Hundred Year Plan, A" [100 Dves terv] (Kodály), 17–18

improvisation
   activities for developing, 362–65
   in curriculum based on Kodály Method and national content standards, 37–38
   and curriculum for upper grades, 545–46
   developing creative, 131–32
   and gifted students, 536–37
   in grade one sample curriculum, 34
   in grade four musicianship skills sample curriculum, 336
   in Kodály's philosophy of music education, 26
   of melodies, 366–72
   as musical skill to be developed in classroom, 330–31
   practicing, using SMART Board, 428–31
   practicing known elements through, 501–5
   in preparation/practice lessons, 491–92
   as primary musical skill area, 395–96
   references for, 373
   rhythmic, 34, 545–46
   sample assessment rubric for, 596–97*t*
   in teaching strategy for eighth note followed by dotted quarter note, 297–98, 299–300
   in teaching strategy for eighth note followed by two sixteenth notes, 252, 254
   in teaching strategy for half notes, 242, 243–44
   in teaching strategy for *la* pentatonic scale, 278, 279–80
   in teaching strategy for *low la*, 260, 262
   in teaching strategy for major scale, 290–91, 292–93
   in teaching strategy for quarter and eighth notes, 221, 222
   in teaching strategy for syncopation, 271, 272
   in teaching strategy for tonic note of major pentatonic scale, 235, 237
   in teaching strategy for two-note child's chant, 226, 228
incomplete pentatonic scales, 66–67
individual singing, 109–10, 111
inner hearing. *See also* aural awareness
   in cognitive phase of learning, 197
   and curriculum for upper grades, 545
   in grade one sample curriculum, 33
   in grade four musicianship skills sample curriculum, 334
   in Kodály's philosophy of music education, 25
   as musical skill to be developed in classroom, 330
   sequential development of, 206
   significance of, for practicing musical skills, 347–48
   in teaching strategy for eighth note followed by dotted quarter note, 297, 299
   in teaching strategy for eighth note followed by two sixteenth notes, 252, 253
   in teaching strategy for half notes, 242, 243
   in teaching strategy for *la* pentatonic scale, 277, 279
   in teaching strategy for *low la*, 259, 261
   in teaching strategy for major scale, 290, 291
   in teaching strategy for quarter and eighth notes, 221, 222
   in teaching strategy for syncopation, 270, 272
   in teaching strategy for tonic note of major pentatonic scale, 235, 236–37
   in teaching strategy for two-note child's chant, 226, 227
inner smile, 104, 552
instruments
   connection to grade handbooks, 145–46
   in curriculum based on Kodály Method and national content standards, 37
   and curriculum for upper grades, 544
   digital, 413
   and evaluation of instructor's musicianship, 582*t*
   and gifted students, 537
   in grade one sample curriculum, 30, 31
   in grade four musicianship skills sample curriculum, 334
   harmonic, 137–38
   improvisation on, 368–69
   incorporating, into curriculum, 136–37
   in Kodály's philosophy of music education, 23–24, 134–35
   as musical skill to be developed in classroom, 332
   sequence for introducing, 135*t*
   singing and playing, 135–36
   songs for playing on, 57–58
   and special needs students, 533–34
   using, in classroom, 136
interactive whiteboards
   and developing aural awareness, 419–22
   and developing kinesthetic awareness, 417–19
   and developing visual awareness, 422–24

Subject Index

interactive whiteboards (*Cont.*)
    Kodály-based lessons for, 414–17
    labeling sound using, 424
    as learning resource, 413
    practicing music concepts using, 426–31
    presenting name of music elements with, 424
    presenting notation using, 425–26
    as teaching resource, 410
internal upbeats
    focus song for, 266*fig.*
    sample preparation/practice lesson plan for practicing, 177–79*t*
    teaching strategy for, 264*t*
intervals
    in teaching strategy for *la* pentatonic scale, 277, 280
    in teaching strategy for *low la*, 259, 262–63
    in teaching strategy for major scale, 289, 290, 294
    in teaching strategy for tonic note of major pentatonic scale, 235
Ionian Mode, 69
iPods, 409, 412–13
iRetrieval, 410
Iskolai Dnekgyüjtemény I-II [Collected Songs for Schools] (Kodály & Kerényi), 17
Ives, Charles, *Three Places in New England*, movement 2, 371

Jazzy Day, 414
Joio, Norman Dello, Piano Sonata No. 3, 370
JoyTunes Recorder Master, 414

Kabalevsky, Dmitry, "Short Story," Op. 27, Book 1, No. 13, 245
kinesthetic activities. *See also* movement
    for improvising melodies, 366–67
    for improvising rhythm, 363–64
    internalization of music through, in cognitive phase, 195–97, 200
    in teaching strategy for eighth note followed by dotted quarter note, 294–95
    in teaching strategy for eighth note followed by two sixteenth notes, 249–50
    in teaching strategy for half notes, 239
    in teaching strategy for *la* pentatonic scale, 274
    in teaching strategy for *low la*, 256–57
    in teaching strategy for major scale, 286–87
    in teaching strategy for quarter and eighth notes, 218–19, 223–24
    in teaching strategy for syncopation, 267–68
    in teaching strategy for tonic note of major pentatonic scale, 231–32
kinesthetic awareness
    in preparation/practice lessons, 492–93
    using SMART Board to develop, 417–19
Klinger, R., 158, 202, 205, 207
Klonoski, Edward, 217
Kodály, Sarolta, 3
Kodály, Zoltár. *See also* Kodály Method; Kodály's philosophy of music education
    on association between folk and classical music, 55
    on authenticity in folk songs and music, 55–56
    biographical outline, 15–18
    on *a capella* singing, 100
    on characteristics of good musician, 25
    on composing for children, 58
    on composition and improvisation, 26
    on development of science, 4
    on folk music, 21, 54–55
    "Hungarian Rondo," 300
    on instruments, 134–35
    on lesson planning, 485
    Let Us Sing Correctly, 445
    on listening, 26–27, 375
    on musicianship, 540
    on music literacy, 153, 154
    on music suitable for teaching, 21–22
    Peacock Variations, 370
    on roots of science and art, 25
    on singing, 22–24
    on teaching technique, 486
Kodály Method
    adaptation of, 4
    and Common Core Standards, 39–40
    concerns in teaching according to, 2–3
    curriculum based on national content standards and, 37–39
    development of, 25
    hallmarks of, 27–28
    renewed interest in, 2
    teaching according to, 3–4
Kodály's philosophy of music education, 19–27
    designing curriculum based on, 28–35
    instruments in, 134–35
    repertoire development in, 54–55
Kokas, Klára, 4
Kontra, Zsuzsanna, *Let Us Try to Sing Correctly*, 111

Subject Index

labeling sounds
   in associative phase of learning, 201
   example presentation lesson for, 179–81*t*
   presentation lesson for, 506
   in teaching strategy for eighth note followed by dotted quarter note, 296
   in teaching strategy for eighth note followed by two sixteenth notes, 251
   in teaching strategy for half notes, 240
   in teaching strategy for *low la*, 258
   in teaching strategy for major scale, 288
   in teaching strategy for quarter and eighth notes, 220
   in teaching strategy for tonic note of major pentatonic scale, 233
   in teaching strategy for two-note child's chant, 224–25
   using SMART Board in, 424
la pentatonic scale
   grade four focus song for, 284*fig*.
   grade four teaching strategy for, 273–81
   lesson plan incorporating technology, 431–37
   repertoire for, 464
la pentatonic tetrachord, 66
learning theory model, 191–95
   assimilative phase in, 195, 202–4
   associative phase in, 195, 201–2
   cognitive phase in, 195–201
   compared to Choksy model of learning, 204–8
   connecting lesson plans to, 308–24
   connection to grade handbooks, 208–9
   incorporating interactive whiteboard into, 417
   phases of learning in, 306–8
lesson plan(s). *See also* preparation/practice lessons; presentation lessons
   adaptation of, 532–38, 584*t*
   for assimilative phase, 512–20
   for associative phase, 506–12
   choral rehearsal, 447–52*t*
   for cognitive phase, 491–505
   connection to grade handbooks, 538
   designing, that include music skills, 138–45
   developing, 40–41, 306–24
   for developing musicianship skills, 396–401
   evaluation of, 530–31, 578, 579–81*t*, 582–85*t*
   general considerations for, 529–31
   incorporating technology, 431–37
   for interactive whiteboard, 414–17
   key components of, 42–47

   learning phases and, 489*t*
   music literacy and, 176–84
   for older beginners, 564–68
   outcomes and, 489–91
   for progression of rhythmic and melodic elements, 170–75
   and repertoire development, 74–86
   sequencing and, 485–89
   transitions in, 520–29
letter names, 155
Let Us Sing Correctly (Kodály), 445
Let Us Try to Sing Correctly (Kontra), 111
line games, 128
listening
   assessment of, 589, 590
   in curriculum based on Kodály Method and national content standards, 38
   folk and art music and, 380
   in grade one sample curriculum, 34–35
   in grade four musicianship skills sample curriculum, 336–37
   integrating, into music lesson, 375–79
   introducing excerpts based on musical elements, 380–83
   in Kodály-based curriculum, 29
   in Kodály's philosophy of music education, 26–27
   maps, 388–90
   as musical skill to be developed in classroom, 331
   as part of comprehensive music education, 21
   references for, 394–95
   sample activity, 385–93
   songs for, 58–59
   teaching strategy for, 384–85
   in teaching strategy for eighth note followed by dotted quarter note, 300
   in teaching strategy for eighth note followed by two sixteenth notes, 255–56
   in teaching strategy for half notes, 244–45
   in teaching strategy for *la* pentatonic scale, 280
   in teaching strategy for *low la*, 262–63
   in teaching strategy for major scale, 294
   in teaching strategy for quarter and eighth notes, 222–23
   in teaching strategy for syncopation, 273
   in teaching strategy for tonic note of major pentatonic scale, 238
   in teaching strategy for two-note child's chant, 228
   in upper grades, 542, 546
literacy. *See* music literacy

633

Subject Index

LiveBinders, 410
Louhivuori, Jukka, 611n22
low la
   focus song for, 266*fig.*
   grade three teaching strategy for, 256–63
   preparation/practice lesson for cognitive phase, 310–14*t*
   repertoire for, 463
low so
   focus song for, 266*fig.*
   repertoire for, 464
   teaching strategy for, 264*t*
low ti
   grade four focus song for, 285*fig.*
   repertoire for, 465
   teaching strategy for, 283*t*
Lydian modal scale, 69, 70*fig.*

Mahler, Gustav, "Funeral March," Feierlich und gemessen, Symphony No. 1 in D, 393
major modal scale, 69
major pentatonic scale
   in canon, 475–76
   focus song for introducing, 248*fig.*
   focus song for introducing second degree of, 247*fig.*
   focus song for introducing tonic note of, 247*fig.*
   grade two teaching strategy for tonic note of, 231–38
   repertoire for, 463
   repertoire for subsets of, 462–63
   teaching strategy for, 246*t*
major scale
   grade five focus song for, 304*fig.*
   intervals in, 112, 289
   repertoire for, 465
   solfège syllables for, 155*fig.*
major seconds, 371
manipulatives, 116
melodic concepts and elements
   aural awareness of, 197
   and curriculum for upper grades, 544
   in grade one sample curriculum, 32, 33
   in grade four musicianship skills sample curriculum, 335
   introducing songs focusing on, 119
   lesson plan design for notating, 83–84*t*
   in lesson plans, 76
   outcomes for developing aural awareness of, 497–98

   in presentation lesson plan, 80*t*, 81*t*, 144*t*
   presentation of, 308n19
   presenting, to older beginners, 564
   in sample lesson plan for preparing *high do*, 178*t*
   sequence for teaching music literacy, 162–64
   and teaching music literacy, 154
   teaching strategies for, 216–18
   teaching strategies for grade one, 218–31
   teaching strategies for grade two, 231–46
   teaching strategies for grade three, 248–65
   teaching strategies for grade four, 267–83
   teaching strategies for grade five, 286–303
   tools and visual aids for, 535
melodic connections, 522–23
melodic contour
   in teaching strategy for major scale, 286–87
   visual representation of, 206
melodic ostinati
   in choir rehearsal part work, 456
   and incorporating instruments into curriculum, 136
melody
   accompanying, with tonic and dominant chord roots, 469, 470
   activities for developing writing, 352–54
   with chord inversions, 474
   common characteristics of folk songs and melodic pattern, 175–76
   descending melodic patterns, 108
   dictation in older students, 570*t*
   examples of aural awareness questions for, 198
   examples of kinesthetic activities for, 197
   improvising, 366–72
   Kodály on, 19
   pentatonic, 609n5
   practicing, 337–42
   in sequence for older beginners, 553
   teaching, to older students, 566*t*, 568, 569*t*
   teaching complex ideas with simple, 611n25
   visual awareness activities for, 200
Melody Street series, 414
memory. *See also* music memory
   performing from, 197–98
   rhythmic, 442
Mendelssohn, Felix, Symphony No. 4 in A, "Italian," Movement 1, Allegro vivace, 494*t*
mentors, 537
microphones, recording, 409–10

Subject Index

MimioStudio, 411, 413
MimioTeach, 410, 413
minitablets, 409, 412–13
minor pentatonic scale, in canon, 475–76
minor scale, intervals in, 112
minor thirds, 371
Mixolydian modal scale, 69, 70, 465
modal scales, 69–73, 164, 475–76
Morton Subotnick series, 414
moveable *do*, 25, 155
movement. *See also* kinesthetic activities
   body warm-ups and creative, 132–34
   in combination with singing, 109
   connection to grade handbooks, 145–46
   and curriculum for upper grades, 543
   developing, sequence, 123–31
   developing creative, 131–32
   in grade one sample curriculum, 30
   in grade four musicianship skills sample curriculum, 333
   improvisation, 363
   introducing songs with, 118
   in Kodály's philosophy of music education, 24
   lesson outcomes for, 493, 498, 502, 506, 509–10
   in lesson plan for notating rhythmic or melodic elements, 84*t*
   as musical skill to be developed in classroom, 330
   in preparation/practice lesson plan, 76*t*
   singing games and, 120–31
   songs for, 57–58
   teaching songs by rote through, 114–15
Mozart, Leopold, "Toy" Symphony, Allegro, 228
Mozart, Wolfgang Amadeus
   "Fugue" from the Toccata, 362
   Fugue in D minor for Organ, 362
   Piano Concerto No. 21, "Andante," 507*t*
   Rondo alla Turca, 78*t*, 81*t*
   Symphony No. 1, "Allegro," 238
   "That Music Enchanting," from *The Magic Flute*, 293
Music Ace series, 413
musicality
   and auditioning for elementary choir, 442
   and evaluation of instructor's musicianship, 581–82*t*
musical taste, 21–22, 35
music education, comprehensive, 20–27
musicians
   Kodály on characteristics of good, 25
   teachers as excellent, 19–20
musicianship skills
   connection to grade handbooks, 401
   curriculum for upper grades, 541–46
   developing, in music lesson plan, 396–401
   developing form, 358–62
   developing improvisation and composition, 362–72
   developing older students' singing skills, 549–53
   development of, 329
   evaluation of teacher's, 578, 581–82*t*
   expanding students', 337–58
   inner hearing and, 347–48
   integrating listening into music lesson, 375–79
   lesson design for older beginners, 564–68
   and lesson evaluation, 583*t*
   multiple dimensions of, in Kodály's philosophy, 20–27
   practiced in classroom, 329–32
   sample curriculum for, 332–37
   selecting repertoire for older beginners, 547–49
   three primary areas of, 395–96
   in upper grades, 540–41, 546, 562–64, 568–72
music literacy. *See also* learning theory model; notation; reading; writing
   applying sound-to-symbol orientation to, 204
   assessment of, 589, 590
   in choral rehearsal, 445–46
   connection to grade handbooks, 184–85
   and curriculum for upper grades, 542, 544–45
   Elliott on, 153
   in grade one sample curriculum, 31–33
   in grade four musicianship skills sample curriculum, 335–36
   Kodály on, 153
   in Kodály's philosophy of music education, 24–25
   lesson planning and, 176–84
   and melodic patterns and common characteristics of folk songs, 175–76
   as part of comprehensive music education, 21
   preparation, presentation, and practice of musical elements, 170–75
   relationship between musical concepts and elements, 164–70
   repertoire for, 459–65
   rhythmic and melodic sequence for developing, 162–64
   teaching tools for developing, 154–62

Subject Index

music memory
    activities for developing, 355–57
    developing, in older beginners, 571
    in grade one sample curriculum, 33–34
    in grade four musicianship skills sample curriculum, 334
    as musical skill to be developed in classroom, 331
    practicing rhythm and melody through, 337–42
    in teaching strategy for eighth note followed by dotted quarter note, 299
    in teaching strategy for eighth note followed by two sixteenth notes, 253
    in teaching strategy for half notes, 243
    in teaching strategy for *la* pentatonic scale, 279
    in teaching strategy for *low la*, 261
    in teaching strategy for major scale, 292
    in teaching strategy for syncopation, 272
    in teaching strategy for tonic note of major pentatonic scale, 237
    in teaching strategy for two-note child's chant, 227
music teaching, assessing effectiveness of, 577–86
Mussorgsky, Modest, "Great Gate of Kiev," from *Pictures at an Exhibition*, 245

national content standards for music education, 37–39
natural minor scale
    grade five focus song for, 304*fig.*
    grade five teaching strategy for, 301*t*
    repertoire for, 465
Nemesszeghy, Márta, 18
Nettl, Bruno, 53
notation. *See also* music literacy; writing
    in associative phase of learning, 201–2
    and developing sight reading skills, 343, 344–47
    of folk songs, 73–74
    lesson plan for, of rhythmic or melodic elements, 83–84*t*
    memorization from, 356
    presentation lesson for, 509–10
    presenting, using SMART Board, 425–26
    in repertoire analysis, 61
    sample presentation lesson for, 182–84*t*
    and "sound before symbol" principle, 193
    and teaching music literacy, 162, 164
    in teaching strategy for eighth note followed by dotted quarter note, 296–97, 299
    in teaching strategy for eighth note followed by two sixteenth notes, 251

    in teaching strategy for half notes, 240–41
    in teaching strategy for *la* pentatonic scale, 276
    in teaching strategy for *low la*, 258
    in teaching strategy for major scale, 288–90
    in teaching strategy for quarter and eighth notes, 220
    in teaching strategy for syncopation, 269–70
    in teaching strategy for tonic note of major pentatonic scale, 233–34
    in teaching strategy for two-note child's chant, 225–26
note
    part music taught by, 478
    teaching difficult two-part song arrangement by, 481
    teaching second part by, 466–67
    teaching simple two-part song by, 468
    teaching songs by, 116–18, 563–64
Note Squish, 414

octave displacement, 369–70
older beginners. *See* upper grades
ostinati, in choir rehearsal part work, 454, 456, 457. *See also* melodic ostinati; rhythmic ostinati
outcomes
    lesson plans and, 489–91
    in preparation/practice lessons, 492–93, 497–98, 501–2
    in presentation lesson, 506, 509–10

pacing
    and lesson evaluation, 584*t*
    for special needs students, 534
partner games and songs, 122, 128, 457–58
part work
    activities for developing memory, 357
    in children's choir repertoire, 477–78
    in choral rehearsal, 446–59
    and curriculum for upper grades, 543
    developing, in older beginners, 572, 573*t*
    in grade one sample curriculum, 31
    in grade four musicianship skills sample curriculum, 333
    as musical skill to be developed in classroom, 331
    repertoire for, 459–65
    and score preparation, 480, 481
    in teaching strategy for eighth note followed by dotted quarter note, 297, 300

Subject Index

in teaching strategy for eighth note followed by two sixteenth notes, 252, 254–55
in teaching strategy for half notes, 241, 244
in teaching strategy for *la* pentatonic scale, 277–78, 280
in teaching strategy for *low la*, 259–60, 262
in teaching strategy for major scale, 290, 293
in teaching strategy for quarter and eighth notes, 221
in teaching strategy for syncopation, 270, 272–73
in teaching strategy for tonic note of major pentatonic scale, 235, 238
in teaching strategy for two-note child's chant, 226
teaching two-part song arrangements, 466–76
peer helpers, 534
pentatonic music, 56–57
pentatonic scales, 62–67
in canon, 458, 475–76
in sequence for teaching melodic elements, 163–64
singing, from same starting pitch, 370
teaching strategy for second degree of, 245t
pentatonic tone clusters, 370
Peretz, I., 196
perfect fourths, 371
performance
assessment of, 588–89, 590
in curriculum based on Kodály Method and national content standards, 37
and curriculum for upper grades, 541, 543–44
of folk songs, 73–74
and gifted students, 536–37
in grade one sample curriculum, 30–31
in Kodály-based curriculum, 29
in Kodály's philosophy of music education, 22–24
lesson outcomes for, 492–93, 497, 501–2, 506, 509
as part of comprehensive music education, 21
and special needs students, 534–36
Perkins, David, 199
personal philosophy of music education, 15
Pestalozzi, Heinrich, 192
Petzold, R. G., 197
philosophy of music education, 15
phonation exercises, 444
phrase-by-phrase song presentation, 114
Phrygian mode, 71
Pink, Daniel H., 29
pitch class. *See* tone set
pitch exploration exercises, 107

podcasts, 409–10
polytonality, 371
Poorman, A., 197
portfolio, teaching, 600, 602–4
posture
breathing, 102
in choral rehearsal, 444
for singing, 100–101
and singing skills in older beginners, 549–50
Potter, D., 406, 415
predictability, for special needs students, 533
preparation/practice lessons
for cognitive phase, 491–505
designing, 138–42
for developing musicianship skills, 397–99t
for dotted eighth and sixteenth note, 494–97t, 498–501t, 502–5t
explanation of segments of, 42–44t
for *high ti*, 513–20t
incorporating music literacy activities into, 176–77
key components of, 42t
planning, 42
for practicing improvisation, 323–24t
for practicing reading, 321–22t
for practicing writing, 322–23t
for progression of rhythmic and melodic elements, 170–75
and repertoire development, 75–80
sample for preparing *high do* and internal upbeat, 177–79t
template for associative phase, 314–17t
template for cognitive phase, 309–16t
with and without transitions, 524–29t
presentation lessons
in associative phase, 506–12
designing, 142–45
for developing musicianship skills, 399–401
example, for labeling sounds, 179–81t
example, for notation, 182–84t
explanation of, 45t, 46–47t
key components of, 44t, 46t
for listening, 384–85
planning, 42
and repertoire development, 80–86
template for associative phase, 317–20t
Prezi, 412
Promethean ActivBoard, 410, 413
puppets, 534

Subject Index

quarter notes. *See also* dotted quarter note
    grade one focus song for, 230*fig.*
    grade one teaching strategy for, 218–23
    repertoire for, 462
    in sequence for teaching rhythmic elements, 163
questioning techniques
    and lesson evaluation, 584*t*
    in teaching songs by rote, 112–14

rationale, in repertoire analysis, 72–73
reading. *See also* music literacy; sight-reading and -singing
    assessment of, 591*t*
    in curriculum based on Kodály Method and national content standards, 38
    and curriculum for upper grades, 544, 545
    developing, in older beginners, 568
    in grade one sample curriculum, 31–33
    in grade four musicianship skills sample curriculum, 335–36
    in Kodály Method, 28
    lesson segment for practicing, 321–22*t*
    as musical skill to be developed in classroom, 330
    practicing, using SMART Board, 426–27
    practicing rhythm and melody through, 337–42
    in preparation/practice lessons, 491–92
    as primary musical skill area, 395–96
    procedures for developing, 342–47
    sample assessment rubric for, 595*t*
    in teaching strategy for eighth note followed by dotted quarter note, 298
    in teaching strategy for eighth note followed by two sixteenth notes, 252–53
    in teaching strategy for half notes, 242
    in teaching strategy for *la* pentatonic scale, 278–79
    in teaching strategy for *low la*, 260, 262–63
    in teaching strategy for major scale, 291
    in teaching strategy for quarter and eighth notes, 221–22
    in teaching strategy for syncopation, 271
    in teaching strategy for tonic note of major pentatonic scale, 236
    in teaching strategy for two-note child's chant, 227
recorder, 136–37
recording microphones, 409–10
relative solmization, 110–12, 154–55
repertoire
    analysis of, 59–73, 162
    assessment of, 589, 590
    in assimilative phase, 202–3
    and authenticity in folk music, 55–56
    and children as stewards of cultural heritage, 21–22
    for children's choir, 476–78
    connection to grade handbooks, 87
    creating alphabetized list for each grade, 59
    in curriculum based on Kodály Method and Common Core Standards, 40
    in curriculum based on Kodály Method and national content standards, 37
    and curriculum for upper grades, 542
    developing, 53–54, 57–59, 162
    and evaluation of lesson plan format, 580*t*
    in grade one sample curriculum, 30
    in grade four musicianship skills sample curriculum, 332
    in Kodály Method, 27–28
    lesson outcomes for learning new, 493, 497, 502, 506, 509
    in lesson plan for notating rhythmic or melodic elements, 83*t*
    lesson planning and development of, 74–86
    listening, 376–77
    for older beginners, 547–49
    for part work and music literacy, 459–65
    pentatonic music, 56–57
    and performance and notation of folk songs, 73–74
    in preparation/practice lesson plan, 43*t*, 76*t*
    in presentation lesson plan, 80*t*, 142*t*
    rhythmic and melodic patterns and common characteristics of folk songs, 175–76
    and tailoring curriculum, 36
    in teaching portfolio, 603
    in unit plan, 487*t*
resonance, 102, 551
rest. *See also* eighth note rest
    grade one focus song for, 230*fig.*
    grade one teaching strategy for, 229*t*
rhythm
    activities for developing writing, 351–52
    in choir rehearsal part work, 453
    clapping motives as accompaniment, 458
    common characteristics of folk songs and rhythmic patterns, 175–76
    dictation in older students, 570*t*

Subject Index

examples of aural awareness questions for, 198
examples of kinesthetic activities for, 196–97
and incorporating instruments into curriculum, 136
introducing songs focusing on, 119
kinesthetic activities for improvising, 363–64
Kodály on, 19
in Kodály's philosophy of music education, 25
and lesson plan development, 41
practicing, 337–42
reading and sight-reading, in older beginners, 568, 569t
in repertoire analysis, 72
and score preparation, 478–79
in sequence for older beginners, 552–59
and teaching songs by note, 117
visual awareness activities for, 199–200
rhythmic concepts and elements
   aural awareness of, 197
   and curriculum for upper grades, 544
   in grade one sample curriculum, 32–33
   in grade four musicianship skills sample curriculum, 335
   lesson plan design for notating, 83–84t
   in lesson plans, 76
   linking rhythm syllables to common, 160–61
   outcomes for developing aural awareness of, 497–98
   in preparation/practice lesson plan, 78t
   in presentation lesson for labeling four sounds on beat with rhythm syllables, 82t
   in presentation lesson plan, 80t, 81t
   presentation of, 308n19
   presenting, to older beginners, 563–64
   in sample presentation lesson for labeling sounds, 180t
   in sample presentation lesson for notation, 182t
   and teaching music literacy, 154, 162–64
   teaching sequence for beginning, 165–68t
   teaching strategies for, 216–18
   teaching strategies for grade one, 218–31
   teaching strategies for grade two, 231–46
   teaching strategies for grade three, 248–65
   teaching strategies for grade four, 267–83
   teaching strategies for grade five, 286–303
   tools and visual aids for, 535
rhythmic ostinati
   in choir rehearsal part work, 454
   improvising, 369

and incorporating instruments into curriculum, 136
rhythm syllables
   example of, 161
   linking common rhythmic elements to, 160–61
   performing rhythm canons with, 455
   presentation lesson plan template for, 80–83t
   and teaching music literacy, 158–59, 164
rondo, 362
rote
   folk songs taught by, 477
   part music taught by, 477
   teaching second part by, 466
   teaching simple two-part song by, 467–68
   teaching songs by, 112–15, 562–63

"safe space," for special needs students, 536
"scaffolding" theory, 192
scale. *See* tone set
Scarlatti, Domenico, Sonata in D minor, K. 64, 256
Schoenberg, Arnold, String Quartet No. 4, movement 3, 371
Schubert, Franz, *Rosamunde*, 255
science, Kodály on development of, 4
score preparation, 478–82
Scott-Kassner, Carol, 192
Scripp, Larry, 192–93, 217
seating arrangements
   for elementary choir, 443–44
   for special needs students, 532–33
second grade. *See* grade two
Seeger, Ruth Crawford, 21
sequencing
   and evaluation of lesson plan format, 580t
   in Kodály Method, 28
   in learning theory model, 205–6
   lesson planning and, 485–89
   sample, for older beginners, 553–62
Shehan-Campbell, Patricia, 192
si
   grade five focus song for, 305*fig.*
   grade five teaching strategy for, 302t
sight-reading and -singing
   and auditioning for elementary choir, 443
   changing reading activity into, activity, 347
   and clapping in cannon, 458
   considerations for unknown melodies, 349–51
   developing, in older beginners, 568, 569t
   hand signs and, 611n39
   versus reading, 337

Subject Index

singing. *See also* tuneful singing
  assessment of, 591*t*
  in curriculum based on Kodály Method and national content standards, 37
  and curriculum for upper grades, 543
  in grade one sample curriculum, 30
  in grade four musicianship skills sample curriculum, 333
  individual, 109–10, 111
  in Kodály Method, 27
  Kodály on, 18, 19
  in Kodály's philosophy of music education, 22–24
  modeling, 109
  as musical skill to be developed in classroom, 330
  in older beginners, 549–53
  and playing instruments, 135–36
  posture for, 100–101
  rehearsal exercises for, 445
  simplified score for, 390–92
  songs for, 57–58
  teaching, 100–110
  in teaching strategy for eighth note followed by dotted quarter note, 297
  in teaching strategy for eighth note followed by two sixteenth notes, 251–52
  in teaching strategy for half notes, 241
  in teaching strategy for *la* pentatonic scale, 277
  in teaching strategy for *low la*, 259
  in teaching strategy for quarter and eighth notes, 220–21
  in teaching strategy for syncopation, 270
  in teaching strategy for tonic note of major pentatonic scale, 234–35
  in teaching strategy for two-note child's chant, 226
  in tune with relative solmization, 110–12
singing games
  chain improvisation, 363–64
  in developing movement sequence, 125–30
  and development of creative movement and improvisation, 131–32
  guidelines for teaching advanced, 130–31
  Kodály on, 54
  in repertoire analysis, 72
  sequential progression for teaching, 120–23
  and teaching songs by rote, 116
singing voice, finding, 106–10
single-line games, 122
sixteenth note combinations
  elementary choir pieces with, 463
  in sequence for teaching rhythmic elements, 163–64
sixteenth notes
  focus song for, 247*fig.*
  focus song for eighth note followed by two, 265*fig.*
  focus song for two, followed by eighth note, 266*fig.*
  grade three teaching strategy for eighth note followed by two, 249–56
  grade four focus song for dotted eighth note followed by, 285*fig.*
  preparation lesson plan for, 78*t*
  preparation/practice lesson for dotted eighth note and, 494–97*t*, 498–501*t*, 502–5*t*
  presentation lesson for dotted eighth note and, 507–9*t*, 510–12*t*
  repertoire for, 463
  repertoire for combinations with eighth notes, 463
  in sequence for teaching rhythmic elements, 163
  teaching strategy for, 246*t*
  teaching strategy for dotted eighth note followed by, 283*t*
  teaching strategy for two, followed by eighth notes, 264*t*
SMART Board
  and developing aural awareness, 419–22
  and developing kinesthetic awareness, 417–19
  and developing visual awareness, 422–24
  Kodály-based lessons for, 414–17
  labeling sound using, 424
  as learning resource, 413
  practicing music concepts using, 426–31
  presenting name of music elements with, 424
  presenting notation using, 425–26
  as teaching resource, 410
SMART Notebook, 411, 413
smart phones, 409, 412–13
social media, 411–12, 414
software and apps, 410–11, 413–14
solfège syllables
  activities for developing writing, 352–54
  and developing sight reading skills, 344–45
  and incorporating instruments into curriculum, 136–37
  and introducing songs focusing on melody, 119
  and labeling sounds in teaching strategy for two-note child's chant, 224–25

Subject Index

presentation lesson plan template for, 80–81*t*
in rehearsal warm-ups, 445
singing pentatonic melodies as canons with, 458
singing with, 110–12
and teaching music literacy, 154–55, 164
in teaching strategy for *la* pentatonic scale, 275–76, 277, 278–80
in teaching strategy for *low la*, 258, 260, 262
in teaching strategy for major scale, 288, 289, 290, 291, 292, 293
in teaching strategy for tonic note of major pentatonic scale, 233–34, 236–37
solmization, relative, 110–12, 154–55
solo singing, 109–10, 111
songs
    assessing presentation of, 117–18
    focus, 80
    focus, for grade one, 230–31
    focus, for grade two, 246–48
    focus, for grade three, 265–67
    focus, for grade four, 283–85
    focus, for grade five, 304–6
    introducing, within lesson, 118–19
    for older beginners, 547–49, 562–64
    partner, 457–58
    repeating, 118
    teaching, by note, 116–17
    teaching, by rote, 112–16
so pentatonic scale, repertoire for, 464
"sound before symbol" principle, 192–93, 197
sounds, labeling. *See* labeling sounds
sound-to-symbol orientation, 192–94, 204, 206–7, 610n5
Sousa, John Philip, *New Mexico March*, 177*t*
special needs students, 532–36
square dances, 123, 130
square games, 122, 130
starting pitch, comfortable
    and lesson evaluation, 582–83*t*
    in repertoire analysis, 61
Stravinsky, Igor
    "Finale," from *Firebird Suite*, 370
    "Greeting Prelude," 370
structural reductions, 523
student learning, assessment of, 585–86*t*
student profiles, 588–97
subdominant chord roots, accompanying melodies with, 470
summative assessment, 589–90

symbol-to-sound orientation, 610n5
symmetrical scales, 370–71
syncopation
    grade four focus song for, 283*fig.*
    grade four teaching strategy for, 267–73
    repertoire for, 464
Szabò, Helga, 157–58

ta
    grade five focus song for, 306*fig.*
    grade five teaching strategy for, 303*t*
tablets, 409, 412
Tacka, Philip, "Dear Companion," from *Sourwood Mountain*, 293
takadimi syllables, 158–60, 161
target phrase, 80
taste, musical, 21–22, 35
Tavener, John, "The Lamb," 371
Taylor-Howell, Susan
    "Dear Companion," from *Sourwood Mountain*, 293
    "I Will Give My Love an Apple," from *The Owl Sings*, 293
    "Oro, My Bodeen," from *The Owl Sings*, 293
Tchaikovsky, Peter
    "Finale" (Allegro con fuoco), Symphony No. 4, 387
    "Little Russian," Symphony No. 2, 385–87
teachers
    in Kodály Method, 27
    in Kodály's philosophy of music education, 19–20
teaching, assessing effectiveness of, 577–86
teaching philosophy, 602–3
teaching portfolio, 600, 602–4
teaching resource folder, 600, 601–4
teaching resources, organization of, 600–604
teaching strategies
    for compound meter in grade five, 301*t*, 302*t*, 303*t*
    connection to grade handbooks, 324–25
    developing lesson plan design based on, 306–24
    for dotted eighth note followed by sixteenth note in grade four, 283*t*
    for dotted quarter note followed by eighth note in grade four, 281*t*
    for eighth note followed by dotted quarter note in grade five, 294–301
    for eighth note followed by two sixteenth notes in grade three, 249–56

Subject Index

teaching strategies (*Cont.*)
   and evaluation of lesson plan format, 580*t*
   for external upbeats in grade three, 265*t*
   for *fa* in grade four, 282*t*
   for *fi* in grade five, 302*t*
   for four-beat meter in grade two, 246*t*
   for grade three, 248–49
   for half note in grade two, 239–46
   for *high do* in grade three, 265*t*
   for internal upbeats in grade three, 264*t*
   for introducing tonic in grade two, 231–38
   for *la* pentatonic scale in grade four, 273–81
   for listening, 384–85
   for *low la* in grade three, 256–63
   for *low so* in grade three, 264*t*
   for *low ti* in grade four, 283*t*
   for major pentatonic scale in grade two, 246*t*
   for major scale in grade five, 286–94
   for natural minor scale in grade five, 301*t*
   for quarter and eighth notes in grade one, 218–23
   for rhythmic and melodic elements, 216–18
   for second degree of pentatonic scale in grade two, 245*t*
   for *si* in grade five, 302*t*
   for sixteenth notes in grade two, 246*t*
   for syncopation in grade four, 267–73
   for *ta* in grade five, 303*t*
   for triple meter in grade four, 282*t*
   for two-note child's chant in grade one, 223–30
   for two sixteenth notes followed by eighth note in grade three, 264*t*
teaching technique, 486
technology, 405–6
   best practices, 431
   choosing and assessing, 406–8
   developing aural awareness with SMART Board, 419–22
   developing kinesthetic awareness with SMART Board, 417–19
   developing visual awareness with SMART Board, 422–24
   labeling sound using SMART Board, 424
   and lesson evaluation, 585*t*
   lessons for interactive whiteboards, 414–17
   practicing music concepts using SMART Board, 426–31
   presenting name of music elements with SMART Board, 424
   presenting notation using SMART Board, 425–26
   resources for students, 412–14
   resources for teachers, 408–12
   sample lesson plan incorporating, 431–37
tempo markings
   and score preparation, 479
   and singing skills in older beginners, 553
   and teaching tuneful singing, 105
ternary form, 362
third grade. *See* grade three
three-beat meter
   focus song for, 285*fig.*
   repertoire for, 465
three-note child's chant
   grade one focus song for, 230–31
   grade one teaching strategy for, 229*t*
   repertoire for, 462
three-part singing, 456
tone production, 102–4, 551–52
tone set, 61–62, 71
tone steps, 157
tongue twisters, 104, 552
tonic chord roots, accompanying melodies with, 469, 470
tonic note of major pentatonic scale
   in choir rehearsal part work, 454
   grade two teaching strategy for, 231–38
tonic-solfa system, 25, 155
transitions, 520
   connecting several lessons, 520–21
   connecting several segments in a lesson, 521–22
   and evaluation of lesson plan format, 581*t*
   between lesson segments, 522–24
   preparation/practice lessons with and without, 524–29*t*
triad inversions, 473–74
triads, 471–74
trichords, 68
Trinka, Jill, 74
trio form, 362
triple meter
   grade four focus song for, 285*fig.*
   teaching strategy for, 282*t*
tuneful singing
   and correcting students, 106–7
   in grade one sample curriculum, 30
   and lesson evaluation, 583*t*
   sample assessment rubric for, 594*t*
   and singing skills in older beginners, 552–53
   teaching, 105–6

Subject Index

Twitter, 411–12
two-note child's chant
    grade one focus song for, 230*fig.*
    grade one teaching strategy for, 223–30
two-part song arrangements, 466–76

unconscious melodic connections, 522–23
unconscious rhythmic connections, 522
unit plan(s). *See also* lesson plan(s)
    sequencing and, 486–89
    in teaching portfolio, 604
upbeats
    focus song for external, 267*fig.*
    focus song for internal, 266*fig.*
    repertoire for external, 464
    sample preparation/practice lesson plan for practicing internal, 177–79*t*
    teaching strategy for external, 265*t*
    teaching strategy for internal, 264*t*
upper grades
    considerations for teaching, 572–74
    curriculum for, 541–46
    developing musicianship skills in, 568–72
    lesson design for, 564–68
    repertoire for, 547–49
    teaching musicianship skills in, 540–41
    teaching songs to, 562–64

variation form, 362, 370
visual awareness
    preparation/practice lesson for developing, 501–5
    using SMART Board to develop, 422–24
visual practice
    in teaching strategy for eighth note followed by dotted quarter note, 298–301
    in teaching strategy for eighth note followed by two sixteenth notes, 252–56
    in teaching strategy for half notes, 242–45
    in teaching strategy for *la* pentatonic scale, 278–81
    in teaching strategy for *low la*, 260–63
    in teaching strategy for major scale, 291–94
    in teaching strategy for quarter and eighth notes, 221–23
    in teaching strategy for syncopation, 271–73
    in teaching strategy for tonic note of major pentatonic scale, 235–36
    in teaching strategy for two-note child's chant, 227–30
visual representation
    in cognitive phase of learning, 199–201
    of melodic contour, 206
    in teaching strategy for eighth note followed by dotted quarter note, 296
    in teaching strategy for eighth note followed by two sixteenth notes, 250–51
    in teaching strategy for half notes, 240
    in teaching strategy for *la* pentatonic scale, 275
    in teaching strategy for *low la*, 257
    in teaching strategy for major scale, 288
    in teaching strategy for quarter and eighth notes, 219
    in teaching strategy for syncopation, 269
    in teaching strategy for tonic note of major pentatonic scale, 233
    in teaching strategy for two-note child's chant, 224
visuals
    introducing songs with, 118
    for special needs students, 533, 535
    and teaching songs by rote, 116
vocalizations, in choral rehearsal, 444–45
vocal ranges, 104–6, 441–42, 551
voice, head and chest, 106–10
voice modulation, 107
vowel scales, 103, 551, 552
vowel sounds
    correct pronunciation of, 110
    and singing skills in older beginners, 551, 552
    and tone production, 103–4

warm-up exercises
    in choral rehearsal, 444
    and creative movement, 101, 132–34
    and score preparation, 480
    and singing skills in older beginners, 550
Webern, Anton, Symphony, Op. 21, movement 2, 371
websites, 411–12
Welsh, Patricia, 192–93, 217
whiteboards, interactive. *See* interactive whiteboards
Williams, Ralph Vaughan, *Variations of Greensleeves*, 362
wind up games, 120, 125
Wordpress, 411, 414
writing. *See also* music literacy; notation
    activities for developing, 351–55
    assessment of, 592*t*
    in curriculum based on Kodály Method and national content standards, 38

Subject Index

writing (*Cont.*)
    and curriculum for upper grades, 544, 545
    developing, in older beginners, 568–70
    in grade one sample curriculum, 31–33
    in grade four musicianship skills sample curriculum, 335–36
    in Kodály Method, 28
    lesson segment for practicing, 322–23*t*
    as musical skill to be developed in classroom, 330
    practicing, using SMART Board, 427–28
    practicing rhythm and melody through, 337–42
    in preparation/practice lessons, 491–92
    as primary musical skill area, 395–96
    sample assessment rubric for, 596*t*
    in teaching strategy for eighth note followed by dotted quarter note, 299
    in teaching strategy for half notes, 243
    in teaching strategy for *la* pentatonic scale, 279
    in teaching strategy for *low la*, 261
    in teaching strategy for major scale, 292
    in teaching strategy for quarter and eighth notes, 222
    in teaching strategy for syncopation, 272
    in teaching strategy for tonic note of major pentatonic scale, 237
    in teaching strategy for two-note child's chant, 228

Youth Choral Movement, 16–17